THE LIVING TRADITION

SECOND EDITION

*Art, Music,
and Ideas
in the
Western
World*

Henry Vyverberg

*Southern Illinois University
at Carbondale*

HBJ

HARCOURT BRACE JOVANOVICH, PUBLISHERS

*San Diego   New York   Chicago   Austin   Washington, D.C.
London   Sydney   Tokyo   Toronto*

Preface

This Second Edition of *The Living Tradition* offers a comprehensive introduction to the role and achievements of the humanities in the Western world. The humanities stressed in this book are the visual arts, music, literature, and thought. All of these are essential parts of civilized living.

There are many problems in teaching and studying the humanities, particularly in survey courses. First, there is the sheer wealth of available information. So much must be covered in so little time; the work and ideas of so many people must be presented. How do we sift the most important information from the vast richness of past cultures? Second, the information must be organized. How can we bring all these creative minds, currents, and movements into a helpful but unforced order? Third—and perhaps most important of all—is the problem of effective presentation. How can material be enlivened in a way that will sustain the interest of today's college students?

The Living Tradition deals with these problems by focusing initially on the historical period. After a brief overview of the major events of the times, each chapter begins with a large section devoted to establishing the setting and the atmosphere of the age. The idea is to give the reader a feeling for each time and place before introducing the major figures and works. Through references to the social, political, and economic events that shaped the period, to books and ideas, and above all to human interests and preoccupations, the cultural achievements of the period come to life. Diary excerpts that record the threats of wolves and thieves outside the walls of Paris remind us of the physical insecurity that helped give rise to the devotional art of the late Middle Ages, while a description of the splendid Feast of the Pheasant in 1454 reveals the fantastic medieval imagination that underlay nearly all art of that time. After all, the humanities spring from human experiences; that is what they are all about.

NEW TO THIS EDITION

The Second Edition of *The Living Tradition* has been expanded significantly. Discussions of all areas of the humanities have been enhanced and updated by new material, and important topics have been added. A general introduction to the arts is now presented at the beginning of Chapter 1. These early pages provide some basic insights into what we mean by *the arts* and *the humanities*. The historical conditioning of the humanities is also explained; students will come to understand that creative works arise not only as spontaneous expressions but also as responses to their particular historical period. This introductory discussion is followed by new sections on prehistoric art and the art, literature, and life of ancient Egypt and Homeric Greece.

The two chapters of the first edition of *The Living Tradition* on the ancient and medieval worlds have been expanded to six. These six new chapters not only present a much wider panorama of art and life in those times—classical Greece, ancient Rome, and the medieval periods known as Early Christian, Romanesque, and High Gothic—but they also present two additional periods, the Hellenistic and Byzantine worlds. Finally, coverage of the modern period in Europe and America has been expanded by the addition of new material on the late twentieth century.

Many new pages on literature and thought appear in the Second Edition. These include the realms of prose fiction, poetry, drama, philosophy, political thought, and the writing of history. Substantial excerpts from these types of writing have been added.

In addition to the greatly expanded coverage of literature and thought, there is much new discussion of people's daily lives in each of the periods discussed. Students will see the development of the humanities in their social, everyday contexts. The lives of individuals and families are discussed, and the important roles of women in the social and economic life of their time are conscientiously included.

Consistent acknowledgment is given in this edition to women's contributions throughout history, not only as participants in everyday life but also as creators in the humanities. Among the notable women highlighted in this new edition are Gentileschi, Vigée-Lebrun, Nevelson, and Bartlett in art; Bessie Smith, Laurie Anderson, and Ellen Taaffe Zwilich in music; and Wollstonecraft, Dickinson, de Beauvoir, and Henley in literature. All of these women have contributed richly to the cultural development of Western civilization.

Several features new to this edition enhance the book's usefulness and appeal. *Maps* have been added to most chapters, and a *chronological table* is now provided with each chapter. At the end of each chapter appears an up-to-date list of *recommended readings,* each with a notation of its main features. Within the text, italicization of important terms as they are introduced alerts students to their importance. Again in this edition, an extensive *glossary* is included to help students assimilate the vocabulary of the humanities. The *index* has been expanded, and more *color illustrations* and more *musical examples* are provided. Finally, an Instructor's Manual is available that will help instructors to enrich their student's classroom experience.

ACKNOWLEDGMENTS

I am very grateful to friends and colleagues for their support and help in producing this book. Special thanks go to Edward A. Krupa, Patricia Krupa, Julia A. Hull, and Robert N. Mory for their encouragement. Specific advice has come from many knowledgeable sources, to all of whom I offer my heartfelt thanks. The advice of William Dyckes on visual art was invaluable in the preparation of the first edition. The suggestions of my Southern Illinois University colleague,

Steven Barwick, have greatly improved the discussions of music in both editions.

Stimulating advice for the revision has come from David C. Riede (University of Akron), Robert Platzner (California State University at Sacramento), Diane Hudson (Wilbur College), Harold Sunshine (Broome Community College), Larry McHolland (Pima College), Larry Brock (Brevard Community College), and Janet Florick (University of Nebraska at Omaha). The editorial and production staff at Harcourt Brace Jovanovich has been extraordinarily helpful and efficient. I thank particularly Carole Hallenbeck, manuscript editor; Julia G. Berrisford, acquisitions editor; Rebecca Lytle and Robin Risque, art editors; Martha Berlin, production editor; Jane Carey, designer; and Sharon Weldy, production manager.

Above all, I wish to express my deep appreciation for the work and example of four distinguished teacher-scholars, all now deceased, who influenced the course of my personal and scholarly development in areas with which this volume deals: Arthur J. May, of the University of Rochester, in history; and, from Harvard University, Crane Brinton in intellectual history, Chandler Post in art, and G. Wallace Woodworth in music. To all of them I owe more than I can possibly express, and to their memory I dedicate this book.

HENRY VYVERBERG

Contents

List of Color Plates

THE LIVING TRADITION

SECOND EDITION

Art, Music,
and Ideas
in the
Western
World

1

Beginnings of the Arts: From the Cave People to Homer

umans have responded creatively to social and personal needs for many thousands of years, and among those responses have been pictures, sculpture, architecture, dance, music, imaginative literature, and ideas. We often refer to these types of expressions as the arts. The arts have engaged a multitude of creators and art consumers since the days of human prehistory and have involved a multitude of materials, forms, and styles. This book will show how the varying circumstances of the past have strongly influenced the direction and expression of these creative responses to human needs as well as the ways in which the various works have been interpreted by their audiences.

We cannot see the art of prehistoric times as the men and women of those times saw it, of course, but it can still be stimulating to our sensibilities. Civilization—which for the Western world began in the eastern Mediterranean area about five thousand years ago—brought the first writing, and the existing artistic and written records give us valuable insights about the people who produced them. One of the most striking examples of older civilizations is ancient Egypt. For roughly three thousand years Egypt had an independent and brilliant culture that amazes and fascinates the modern eye and mind.

3

Ancient Egypt developed its own written language, great cities, and powerful governmental and religious institutions some three thousand years before the Christian era. The quest for individual immortality is especially evident in the Egyptian worldview. We see this in the mummification of important persons, the painstaking provisioning of burial sites for the afterlife, and the building of immense monuments commemorating their power and achievement. Egyptian literature and visual arts reflect the same overriding concern for the afterlife.

Ancient Egyptian history is conventionally divided into three kingdoms—the Old Kingdom (2685–2160 B.C.), the Middle Kingdom (2040–1785 B.C.), and the New Kingdom (1600–1085 B.C.)—with two intermediary periods, an archaic prologue, and at the end, a period of slow decline. Overlapping the brilliant Egyptian civilization chronologically were a succession of kingdoms in western Asia, a substantial civilization on the island of Crete (2000–1400 B.C.), and a more modest Mycenaean civilization on the mainland of Greece (1600–1100 B.C. or earlier). The Mycenaean period was followed in Greece by a Dark Age (1100–750 B.C.), which, though illiterate, saw the gradual formation of an oral tradition of folksinging. The words of the songs portrayed a fabled Mycenaean age. An important tale concerned the fall of Troy in Asia Minor to the besieging Greeks and then the adventures of the Greek leader Odysseus on his leisurely way home to the island of Ithaca. The Greeks credited a poet named Homer (late eighth century B.C.) for giving this epic tale its largely finalized form.

The world described by Homer consisted of Mycenaean kingdoms ruled by an upper class of aristocrats with the help of bureaucratic administrators. Records of this time still survive in "Linear B," a written language from which modern Greek is descended. The society was warlike, with the territories of southern Greece often fighting each other and occasionally cooperating—as in the joint venture referred to as the Trojan War.

Homer's epic also reflected the age in which the verses originated—the Dark Age that followed the Mycenaean period. This newer Greek world, which included islands in the Aegean Sea and settlements of "Ionians" in Asia Minor, was even more fragmented than its Mycenaean predecessor. Hundreds of small tribal units now existed in lands that often were separated by sea and mountains. Life was difficult in this age, but slowly the heroic spirit, the religion, and the epic poetry of the Greeks were taking forms that would shape the Greek achievement for centuries to come.

CREATIVITY AND CREATIVE RESPONSE

What are the arts, and why are they important and exciting components of human life? Clearly the arts include more than the traditional visual arts of painting, sculpture, and architecture, for they include such other endeavors as drawing, printmaking, and design. The arts certainly also include those organized sounds that we call music, whether or not the sounds are combined with words as in songs and in works for the stage. Also among the arts we must include the many kinds of verbal expression that go beyond exclamation, explanation, and simple narrative. Among these arts are such "pure" literature as poetry and fiction and also the speculative and inspirational realms exemplified most obviously in philosophic and religious thought.

All of these arts—visual, musical, literary, and speculative—comprise the area of study called the humanities. Like such other areas of human activity as daily life, work, emotion, and aspiration, and like such other disciplines and pursuits as the sciences and the social studies, the *humanities* deal with an immense range of making and doing and of thinking and feeling by artists and their audiences. After all, the arts involve both the artists' creativity and the creative responses of those who are confronted by the art works. Sometimes the arts may seem a bit irrelevant in a life of practical needs and challenges. After all, what can a painting, a poem, a song, or a speculative idea mean to those who are faced with the daily necessities of surviving, making a satisfactory living, and relating well with others? However, both daily experience and the evidence of history demonstrate the vigorous continuing roles of painting, poetry, music, and ideas to human life. It is obvious that the humanities can fulfill enduring needs of mind and spirit for persons of all ages and conditions, and in the most varied situations. This book will examine creative expressions and responses within the tradition most immediate to the majority of its readers—the Western world and spirit that arose in

CHRONOLOGY

HISTORY		THE ARTS	
		30,000 B.C.	earliest prehistoric art
		16,000–13,000	cave art
8000/7000	end of last Ice Age and of Old Stone (Paleolithic) Age; beginning of New Stone (Neolithic) Age		
3000	beginning of Bronze Age		
3100–2300	Sumerian civilization		
Egypt			
3100–2685	Archaic Period		
2685–2160	Old Kingdom	2530–2470	the Great Pyramids
		2450	Ptah Hotep's *Instruction*
2160–2040	First Intermediary Period		
2040–1785	Middle Kingdom	2000	*Hymn to the Nile*
1785–1600	Second Intermediary Period		
1600–1085	New Kingdom		
early 15th century	reign of Hatshepsut		
mid 14th century	reign of Tutankhamen		
		1300 and later	*Book of the Dead*
1085–332	decline of ancient Egypt		
332	conquest by Alexander the Great		
The Early Greek World			
2000–1400	high Cretan (Minoan) civilization		
1600–1200	high Mycenaean civilization		
		16th century	grave-shaft burials, Mycenae (discovered by Schliemann)
		early 15th century	Vapheio cups
		early 13th century	Lion Gate, Mycenae
13th century	Trojan War		
1200–1100	decay of Mycenaean civilization		
1100–750	Greek Dark Age		
		9th and 8th centuries	geometric style in pottery
		late 8th century	*Iliad* and *Odyssey* written down

All dates are B.C. (Before Christ) and are approximate.

the Near East and Europe and that has now spread to the Americas and much of the rest of the world.

Functions of the Humanities

The humanities have existed throughout history and—except for the arts that require a written language—throughout prehistory as well. The need of artists to create and the need of viewers, hearers, and readers to respond to the artists' creations appear to be ingrained

expressions of the human spirit. What functions have the arts come to serve among artists and those who respond to the arts? Roughly we can group these functions under three headings: the physical or utilitarian, the social or communicative, and the personal or emotional. In practice, of course, these functions are seldom distinct from one another but intersect and overlap in ways that can be challenging and pleasurable. As a point of departure let us use the visual arts of painting, sculpture, and architecture as examples.

THE NEAR EAST ABOUT 1200 B.C.

Among the visual arts it is architecture whose origins and functions may seem most directly physical and utilitarian. Architecture arose to meet the human need for shelter and has seldom departed from that basic requirement. Also, it has come to serve a variety of industrial and spiritual needs. Painting and sculpture, too, seem to have been similarly utilitarian in prehistoric times, serving such purposes as increasing agricultural and human fertility and providing supernatural support for human existence and success. These arts have continued to serve useful functions, as when they have been used to impress contemporaries or in some way influence divine forces.

Social and communicative needs also have been served by the visual arts. Humans are social beings and need to relate to other humans. Hence, the arts have been used to celebrate and communicate social requirements and goals, whether playfully or solemnly and purposefully. Temples and churches have arisen to serve the spiritual needs of groups and whole societies, while smaller-scale arts have expressed political and social views, and even attempts to disrupt these social groups. Humanitarian concerns, the urge to arouse sympathy for the unfortunate and to aid them have often been the focus of the arts. Belligerent and destructive urges have also been expressed and served by the arts, in arousing, for example, enmity or disgust toward particular groups or societies.

The personal functions of the arts may at first be less evident, but the reality and urgency of these functions have been displayed again and again across the centuries. Personal needs, urges, and aspirations have frequently supplemented or supplanted more general practical, physical, or social requirements. Love and hatred, fear and courage, the thirst for understanding and control of the environment—all of these are most often viewed in a highly personal context, and they are served by all of the arts. Artists have created because of urges such as these, and other human beings have responded appreciatively to these creations because of their own similar or different urges.

Human creativity and expression remain the keys to the power of art—of course to the literary, speculative, and musical arts as well as the visual. A poem, a novel, an inquiry into divine forces or human ethical standards, an attempt to speculate on the nature of reality or the meaning of history—all these, too, have called for a creative spirit and a corresponding response. Perhaps the correspondence will be only at a general level of human sympathy—for it is by no means inevitable or even necessary that the response should match exactly the expressive thrust of the artist. Often, in fact, we cannot be sure of the artist's expressive intent: what, for example, did Vincent van Gogh seek to convey in his *Starry Night* (fig. 1-1)? Is it important that the viewer respond to this very evocative work with the same terror, spiritual ecstasy, or visual hypertension van Gogh felt when he painted the work? Perhaps when confronting *Starry Night* we need speak only in terms of a sort of explosive intensity— and not every viewer would agree on even this generality. Nor, to consider other realms of the humanities, would every listener agree that the spirit of Beethoven's Fifth Symphony is strenuous and heroic, or that the philosophical teaching of Plato is disembodied and inspirational.

Perhaps the crucial point, in all of these areas, is that a work of music, painting, or philosophy must awaken a genuine response of one sort or another, ideally a response that is sensitive and informed. The best that can be offered the newcomer to a serious study of the humanities is some helpful tools for approaching the study and for making creative personal responses. Essentially the sensitivity and the reaction must be the student's own—but some basic information and guidance can aid the process of interpretation and appreci-

1-1 Vincent van Gogh, *Starry Night*, 1889. Oil on canvas, 28¾″ × 36¼″. Collection, The Museum of Modern Art, New York [acquired through the Lillie P. Bliss Bequest].

ation. Ultimately the question must be this: has the song, the painting, or the writing given us insight into a world that goes beyond our daily experience and enriches our lives in some way?

Material, Form, Style—and History

Each creative realm within the humanities has its own set of materials—its own building blocks. This is quite literally true in the domain of architecture, of course, but in other humane disciplines the building materials vary substantially. Sculpture employs materials like wood, stone, bronze, or plastic, together with a varied collection of tools. Painting uses canvas and brushes, and pigments dissolved in an assortment of liquids such as oil. Literature employs words grouped meaningfully— words that are often written down but many times directly transmitted orally or indirectly through media such as radio, television, and recordings. Literature can hardly avoid employing ideas, often of the most primitive sort but sometimes of great complexity. In actuality, ideas can be significant components of the nonverbal arts, too—even of the type of unsung music whose most obvious materials are musical tones grouped for effect by using such devices as melody, harmony, and rhythm.

In all of these arts, form goes beyond the basic materials and their most elementary groupings or

1-2 Edouard Manet, *The Fifer*, 1866. Oil on canvas, 63″ × 38¼″. Louvre, Paris.

combinations. Form is a matter of the structure of a whole work or its components; form goes beyond single words and sentences, beyond basic material elements of any sort, to construct large patterns. Form differentiates brief lyric poetry from lengthy epic verse and an unpretentious composition for piano or guitar from a weighty, highly organized symphony played by a hundred-piece orchestra.

In a painting, form involves the application, for example, of color or line, and usually the predominance of one over the other. Although van Gogh's *Starry Night* does involve line—indeed, heavily accented outlines for its buildings and hilltops—the

work comes alive primarily through its brilliant, shocking contrasts in color. Outside of wholly abstract art, which represents nothing in nature or everyday life, color must be color of *something*—and often these things are defined by line. When color predominates as the most effective component, we speak of a *coloristic* work; when line predominates, as in the nearly flat figure of *The Fifer* by Edouard Manet (fig. 1-2), we speak of *linear* art.

Style, in turn, goes beyond form, whether this form expresses itself in overall structure (or *composition*) in a single work or in differentiating between broad types of works. In effect, style expresses the spirit of a work and its creator. The works of van Gogh and Manet shown here exemplify great differences in form as well as two very different styles—an extraordinarily expressive style in the van Gogh, and considerable formal restraint and orderliness in the Manet. Despite a certain cuteness-appeal in the Manet, its style is primarily one of formal control and pattern; in the van Gogh painting we have an emotional, highly expressive work that can arouse similarly intense reactions in the viewer. The shifting contrasts between formalism and expressionism have been a touchstone of style in all of the arts as well as a predictable feature in the history of Western culture.

Quite clearly we are dealing here with stylistic issues much deeper than passing fads in the visual, literary, and musical arts. Broad change in style has been slow at times, indeed it has been almost imperceptible—especially in the thousands of years of late prehistory and the dawn of civilization. From the days of the historic Greeks, several hundred years before the Christian era, the pace of many kinds of changes has gradually quickened, finally to explode in the exciting confusion of recent times. But more than change has been involved, at whatever pace: the Western world has also seen a deep-rooted coordination and struggle among styles in the various arts and remarkably consistent relationships between styles and the historical eras in which they have flourished.

History has often determined the direction and the voice of the various arts, quite as strongly as have any formal and stylistic currents within the arts. The attitudes of each age in Western history have influenced the arts of the age. Because of this, only by understanding the history can the art of a particular period be fully explained and appreciated. We must consider the arts in the context of their time. Each

1-3 Tintoretto, *St. Mark Freeing a Christian Slave*, 1548. Oil on canvas, 13′8″ × 11′7″. Galleria dell'Accademia, Venice.

period of history has its own concerns and preoccupations, and its own views of life and death. For example, Christians—as well as other groups of believers—have regarded the supernatural differently at different periods of time. The distance between the dramatic human bustle of Tintoretto's *St. Mark Freeing a Christian Slave* (fig. 1-3), painted in the late Renaissance, is a spiritual world away from the consoling, heavily symbolic calm of the early Christian wall mosaic of Jesus separating the saved from the damned (fig. 1-4) produced a thousand years before.

Not only do different ages have different worldviews; they also have different needs. We can see readily enough how changing needs have brought new purposes to the arts across the centuries, especially relevant to the first two functions noted earlier—the physical-utilitarian and the social-communicative. Many of this book's illustrations, and most of the literature and music it discusses, are evidence of the changes in people's needs from one age to another. Moreover, the visual arts, music, literature, and thought of the Western world have been produced under different conditions. Artistic creations may well be products of human genius, but they also reflect the conditions under which the artists have worked, the requirements of the age in general, and the needs, ideals, and foibles of patrons and purchasers—that is, of a kaleidoscopic procession of art consumers through centuries of history.

Further, even the spirits of individual creators in the arts have been influenced by the attitudes of the times. Artists, like other men and women, are products of their time, and each age has its distinctive problems and achievements, its own worldview, ideas, and faith. If even Michelangelo—that mighty and sturdily independent artist of the Renaissance—could embody in his art the particular piety and civic pride prevalent at his time, and a deep gloom with regard to the special

1-4 *The Good Shepherd Separating the Sheep from the Goats*, c. 520. Mosaic. Sant'Apollinare Nuovo, Ravenna, Italy.

political woes of Italy as he knew it, should we expect lesser artistic creators to be more untouched by the conditions and demands of their own worlds? Continuing themes in our exploration of the humanities will be how creative spirits throughout Western history have portrayed in their art the world in which they lived and how they met the expectations of their audiences.

PREHISTORIC ART: THE OLD STONE AGE

Archaeology—the scientific study of the material remains of human life—informs us that the earliest evidences of visual arts date from the later Old Stone (Paleolithic) Age, many thousands of years back into prehistory. Indeed, archaeology is the only direct source of our knowledge of prehistory, since by definition no written records exist for that long period. In our day several methods of dating prehistoric remains are available. The method that measures the rate of decay of radiocarbon (carbon-14) in organic materials such as charcoal, wood, and hair is the most useful to archaeologists. Since carbon-14 atoms disintegrate at a known rate, approximate measurement of time for tens of thousands of years is possible if organic remains exist.

Prehistory not only knew no writing, it also knew no cities. Human settlements sometimes existed, but they were small and usually left no large-scale remains. The principal means of human subsistence in the later Old Stone Age were hunting and the gathering of food from the environment. Simple tools of stone were used, some of them having been chipped into more useful shapes. In addition to tools, some artistic remains of that time also exist today; these artifacts include sculpture and the extraordinary paintings on cave walls that have been found in Europe. In France, for example, was found a tiny, carved-ivory woman's head that dates from some twenty thousand years B.C. (fig. 1-5). The bust, featuring braided hair, is apparently a fragment of a larger carving, possibly a fertility figure. More remarkable still are later cave paintings, mainly of animals but sometimes including hunters—for it was still an age of the hunt. Most of this cave art has been found deep in the earth, in barely accessible caves. An example of painted bison and arrows (fig. 1-6) dates from 15,000 B.C. or later and is a startlingly vivid representation of the wild beasts.

What was the function—or more likely, what were the functions—of prehistoric art, especially the art on cave walls? Nobody can answer this question definitively, but speculation has centered on those ritual or magical uses that would involve both the physical-utilitarian and social-communicative functions of art. Hunted bison were sources of food, clothing, and lighting (from the burning of animal fat), and the cave paintings have been thought to aid in the hunt. Other modern speculation has involved the celebration of myth or the honoring of totems (animals thought to be related to specific human groups). It is tempting to imagine also that some purer aesthetic pleasure—a joy

1-5 Woman's head from the Grotte du Pape, Brassempouy, France, c. 22,000 B.C. Ivory, 1⅓" high. Musée des Antiquités Nationales, Saint-Germain-en-Laye, France.

in the beautiful—may have been derived from these works by our distant ancestors. Fantasy, illusion, and a sense of awe may well have been entwined in some way with this amazing pictorial naturalism as cave dwellers viewed these striking images deep in the caverns of the earth.

HISTORIC ANCESTORS OF WESTERN STYLES

In the New Stone (Neolithic) Age—from seven or eight thousand years B.C. in the Near East—subsistence was much less precarious than before. Farming, the domestication of animals, and human settlement in villages became the norm. The making of pottery, polished stone tools, and cloth became common, and remains of pottery and tools from this age are abundant today, many of them very well preserved. Then out of this prehistoric age there eventually came historic times, or what we may call, perhaps too smugly, "civilization." For the Near East—that is, the areas of Africa, Asia, and Europe around the eastern Mediterranean Sea—the rise of civilization may be dated from some three thousand years B.C.

Scholars have defined the rise of civilization rather variously, but most would agree on roughly five characteristics—the rise of cities, the growth of powerful governments and powerful religious establishments, the development of warfare, and the appearance of writing. Of these five criteria, the first—the rise of cities—does have its exceptions. For example, the Mycenaean civilization, which we will examine briefly later in this chapter, had fortress complexes but few if any true cities. Where early cities did exist, they went far beyond clusters of villagers: they became units for producing goods and trading over a sizable territory.

The early cities of the eastern Mediterranean area were dominated by governmental and religious institutions of some complexity and with awesome authority. Labor forces were organized by the governments, and in many cases this labor was specialized according to occupation, not merely differentiated in the predominant prehistoric fashion according to sex and age. The undertaking and supervising of great irrigation works involved tight governmental control—a crucial function in partly arid areas such as Mesopotamia that depended upon irrigation for survival. Religions arose to

1-6   Painted bison, after 15,000 B.C. Paint on cave wall, approximately 3'3" long. Niaux, France.

provide explanations for many phenomena that would later be seen scientifically as natural forces. Religious control by a priestly organization was rigorous and closely allied with a strong government. Armies were organized, and large-scale warfare became one of history's greatest scourges. To serve the needs of a sternly organized state and religion, a written language became necessary. The people wrote on such materials as stone, baked clay, and papyrus (a plant product) that could withstand the passage of time—thousands of years in some instances.

The Sumerian civilization, the earliest of these civilizations that stand directly in the ancestry of the Western world, arose in Asia. Sumer was a state in Mesopotamia—the later Greek name meaning "land between the rivers," the Tigris and the Euphrates, which empty into the Persian Gulf. Beginning in the late fourth millennium B.C. and retaining powerful offshoots through the third millennium, Sumerian civilization eventually merged with other Mesopotamian cultures centered farther to the north. These states would remain, shifting in boundaries but often powerful, until the Greek conquest of the fourth century B.C. From the Tigris and Euphrates valleys, and even from the Persian state to the east, an immense area was ripe for cultural diffusion and military conquest. It extended to the west as far as the Mediterranean and ultimately to the Aegean Sea, and south along the

Mediterranean to that other great Near Eastern civilization in early times, Egypt.

Of the many artistic remains from Sumerian times, one of the most attractive to modern eyes is the sculpture and inlay work on the soundbox of a harp from around 2685 B.C. (fig. 1-7). The music once performed on stringed instruments such as this is as much a mystery to us as is the music of prehistoric times, but the artwork is still vivid and delightful. Modeled gold forms most of a realistic bull's head, and stone of a naturally intense blue color (lapis lazuli) was used for the hair, horn tips, and false beard of the animal. Four scenes in skillfully inlaid pieces of shell survive on a panel beneath the head; the original harp with its strings has long since disappeared. Animals appear in the inlay as humans, perhaps as illustrations of Sumerian myths. This handsome work far surpasses merely utilitarian art; it was surely intended to enchant the human eye.

Egypt—Religion and Civilization

Ancient Egypt was a land made possible by the Nile. This great river begins in the heart of Africa and flows northward to the marshy delta of Lower Egypt. Although the delta possessed good pasture land, most of the Egyptian civilization was in Upper Egypt, stretched out along the Nile from the area of the Great Pyramids and modern Cairo to the blockage of the river's First Cataract, some six hundred miles away. The bulk of Egypt was, all together, approximately seven hundred fifty miles long and, except for the delta area, it was seven to ten miles wide at the most, including both banks of the Nile. Desert land lay beyond the river valley, and steep cliffs to the east yielded most of the stone that was used in Egyptian building—in contrast to the brick structures of Mesopotamia.

"Hail to thee, O Nile, that issues from the earth and comes to keep Egypt alive!" So begins the famous *Hymn to the Nile,* which may have taken its original form two thousand years B.C. "When the Nile floods," the hymn continues, "offering is made to thee, lions are hunted for thee in the desert, fire is provided for thee. An offering is made to every other god, as is done for the Nile, with prime incense, oxen, cattle, birds, and flame." This passage not only introduces us to Egyptian polytheism (belief in many gods) and religious sacrifice, but reflects the great miracle of ancient Egyptian life—the annual flooding of the Nile valley. After the summer flooding had receded, depositing rich soil as well as water in this virtually rainless land, the irrigation system would be repaired, seeds would be planted, and eventually a harvest (or two) would be gathered. In addition to food, flax also was grown in the valley for linen clothing and cords, and papyrus for its reedy pith on which much of Egyptian writing was inscribed. The river itself served for transportation and communication and provided an abundant stock of fish.

Egyptian writing existed in several forms, the earliest of which was hieroglyphs. The hieroglyphic system used many obvious pictorial elements and remained the favored system for use on public buildings and tombs. The symbols were cut into or painted on

1-7 Soundbox of a harp from Ur, c. 2685 B.C. Gold with lapis lazuli and inlaid shells, 17″ high. The University Museum, University of Pennsylvania.

1-8 Pyramids of Mycerinus (c. 2470 B.C.), Chefren (c. 2500 B.C.), and Cheops (c. 2530 B.C.). Giza.

walls and columns of stone throughout Egypt's independent existence and into the Roman period (see figs. 1-9, 1-11, and 1-15). Some hieroglyphic characters represented recognizable things, while others were phonetic elements; together they formed one of the most aesthetically appealing writing systems the world has known. Other writing systems were also developed, and all were finally deciphered in the nineteenth century of our era, after ages of oblivion and mystery.

Ancient Egypt offers a prime example of the tremendous power of Near-Eastern kingship and religion—two things that were characteristically intermingled. The king was considered a god, both in this world and in the afterlife—not a mere mediator between humans and gods as in Mesopotamia. The majesty of the kings, or pharaohs, is most memorably recalled in the Great Pyramids at Giza, near Cairo (fig. 1-8). Each of these immense structures, constructed presumably by highly organized, forced labor during the Nile floodings when there was little agriculture to attend to, not only celebrated the power of its builder, the god-king, but offered his spirit and his mummified body a safe refuge after death. Tomb chambers, often protected by decep-

tive false passages, were in the heart of the pyramid or even below ground level. (As it turned out, nearly all of the royal burial places, in pyramids and elsewhere, were successfully looted in ancient times during ages when there was a breakdown of central government and law and order.)

Although pyramids went out of style rather abruptly in the mid third millennium B.C., the quest for spiritual security would persist throughout Egyptian history. Egyptian religion in the early historic period at first stressed animal gods, perhaps because of the Egyptians' closeness to the beasts and fowl of the Nile delta and the more southerly river valley. Eventually the animal deities were humanized, and often they were depicted as part-human and part-animal. (Note that the deities in figure 1-11 have bird or animal heads and human bodies.) Supreme among all of these gods was the sun-god Re. Re was a universal deity with functions beyond those of the specialized functions of the animal-human gods. All of the deities served a cult of immortality, helping their believers—at least the kings and their more substantial subjects—to achieve an afterlife that greatly resembled mortal life at its best.

1-9 Painted limestone relief sculpture from the tomb of Ptah Hotep at Saqqara, Egypt, c. 2450 B.C. 33″ high.

Early Egyptian Art and Literature

The earthly life was not scorned by the Egyptians, and it was portrayed in much of their art. A painted limestone relief sculpture (a type of carving in which figures do not stand free but project somewhat from a background) of around 2450 B.C. (fig. 1-9) shows servants leading or prodding cattle, geese, and cranes. Despite a total disregard for naturalistic scale, and despite the hieroglyphs at top and side, the scene is a pleasant slice of real Egyptian life.

This relief sculpture comes from the tomb of Ptah Hotep, a high governmental official in the Old Kingdom. Ptah Hotep is remembered, though, less for his tomb than for a writing of his that remained popular in Egypt for many centuries. The *Instruction* (or *Teaching*) *of Ptah Hotep* was one of many collections of wise sayings treasured in ancient Egypt; it deals very much with concerns of this life. Two excerpts concern the management and discipline of sons and wives by the male

head of the family—in terms that have become unfashionable only in very recent history:

> If thou art a man of standing and foundest a household and producest a son who is pleasing to god, if he is correct and inclines toward thy ways and listens to thy instruction, while his manners in thy house are fitting, . . . seek out for him every useful action. . . . But a son often creates enmity. If he goes astray and . . . does not carry out thy instruction, so that his manners in thy household are wretched, and he rebels against all that thou sayest, while his mouth runs on in the most wretched talk . . . , thou shouldst cast him off: he is not thy son at all. . . .
>
> If thou art a man of standing, thou shouldst . . . love thy wife at home as is fitting. Feed her belly; clothe her back. . . . Make her heart glad as long as thou livest. . . . Thou shouldst not contend with her at law, and keep her far from gaining control.

It should be noted that Ptah Hotep's *Instruction* says not a word about daughters. According to the thinking of that time, a female became useful only when she became a wife and mother.

A typical, though idealized, portrayal of an Egyptian ruler and his wife is the freestanding statue of *King*

1-10 *King Mycerinus and Queen Kamerernebty,* c. 2470 B.C. Stone (schist), 4′9″ high. Harvard University/Museum of Fine Arts Expedition. Courtesy Museum of Fine Arts, Boston.

1-11 *Last Judgment before Osiris* from *The Book of the Dead*, c. 1300 B.C. Papyrus, 2¾" high. Reproduced by Courtesy of the Trustees of the British Museum, London.

Mycerinus and His Queen (fig. 1-10). Statues such as this were intended to be viewed only from the front. Typically, the figures stand erect; the fists are clenched; the left leg is advanced stiffly before the right without suggesting a walking movement. The wife in this case grasps the husband's waist and formally touches his arm, perhaps signifying both affection and submission. Presumably the statue was originally painted, for that was the custom for both freestanding and relief sculpture.

The New Kingdom in Egypt— Art and Literature

The history of ancient Egypt between the archaic period and the conquest by Alexander the Great in 332 B.C. is traditionally divided into three kingdoms—the Old, the Middle, and the New—with two intermediary periods of trouble and confusion, and a final slow decline. Egypt saw many significant changes across these twenty-three centuries, most obviously in governmental institutions, religion, the visual arts, and literature, but the changes were incredibly slow by modern standards.

By the time of the New Kingdom (1600–1085 B.C.), the religion of the Egyptians had undergone a number of changes, all of which are reflected in the visual arts and literature. A new sun-god, Amon, had emerged, eventually to be combined by the priests with the old as Amon-Re, a god of warfare and conquest. But the most important and pervasive development in religion was the increasing formalization and complexity of beliefs about the afterlife. New ways were developed for assuring a safe and pleasant immortality for individuals of high standing. (As we see so often in history, the poor could not expect to share the privileges of the well-to-do, even in the next life.) The *Book of the Dead,* which was placed near corpses in the tombs, was conscientiously and slowly compiled. It contained prayers, formulas, and incantations that would speed the deceased past the traps laid by certain deities and beasts and into a glorious life after death.

This whole process is portrayed clearly in the visual arts as in a scene of the last judgment from a papyrus scroll of about 1300 B.C. (fig. 1-11). Here, at the right, the god Osiris presides, by virtue of his earlier happy reassembling of his own dismembered body. He had thus become a symbol and a medium of resurrection and immortality for others. Successive scenes are also portrayed, from the introduction of the soul by a jackal-headed deity and the weighing of the soul, to the presentation before Osiris on his throne. As usual in Egyptian painting and relief sculpture, figures of humans and deities are portrayed in a combination of frontal and side views; that is, the torso and shoulders are pictured frontally, whereas the head and feet are seen from the side.

The New Kingdom also saw new emphases in literature, although the writing system used was sometimes the same that was used in earlier days. Occasionally we can sense a tone of disillusionment with the predominant emphasis on the afterlife. In a banquet song current in the New Kingdom it is suggested that people look to the present life for their pleasure and happiness:

> Bodies pass away and others remain
> Since the time of them that were before.
> The gods that were aforetime rest in their
>   pyramids. . . .
> None cometh from thence
> That he may tell us how they fare. . . .
> Spend the day happily and weary not thereof!
> Lo, none can take his goods with him.
> Lo, none that hath departed can come again.

On the other hand, in contrast both to this call for earthly happiness and to the formalistic, supernatural ritualism that it seemed to disavow, New Kingdom literature could also reveal a note of personal piety:

> Do not raise your voice in the house of god,
> He abhors shouting;
> Pray by yourself with a loving heart,
> To him whose every word is hidden.
> He will grant your needs,
> He will hear your words,
> He will accept your offerings.

The intimate tone of this verse reminds us that Egyptians, like modern Americans, functioned on a private level as well as the public and the ceremonial. Their homes, of varying size and spaciousness according to the owners' resources, were usually of sun-dried brick, since large trees and wood were in short supply and stone was used mainly for public structures. The more lavish homes were colorfully painted with pictures of birds, fish, and flowers. Though the furnishings may have been elegant, they were rather sparse by our standards. Woven mats might cover floors and hang on walls when painted scenes were beyond the owners' means. Beds were wooden-framed, with cord or leather strips instead of springs; the bedding was of linen, and wooden headrests were used instead of pillows. At mealtime the Egyptians ate with their fingers from metal or pottery vessels, and at banquets a good

deal of beer and wine was consumed, generally to the musical accompaniment of harps, small drums or tambourines, and occasional woodwind instruments. Dancing, acrobatics, and wrestling were primarily spectator sports. Few Egyptians could read, and storytelling was a popular amusement. Travel for pleasure was common, sometimes in order to visit Egypt's own antiquities—as evidenced by New Kingdom visitors' graffiti on Old Kingdom temples and pyramids. By the late New Kingdom many of the older Egyptian monuments were as ancient as the great monuments of "ancient" Rome are to us today.

The place of women in Egyptian society, as suggested previously, was not wholly enviable. Women could not be priests, and few professions were open to them. They did have the right to own property, however, and to a few women across the centuries there came the special dignity of marriage to kings. One queen of the New Kingdom, in fact, was ruler in her own right. This was the celebrated Hatshepsut, who

1-12 *Hatshepsut* (detail of stone statue of a seated figure 6′5″ high), c. 1485 B.C. The Metropolitan Museum of Art, Rogers Fund and Edward S. Harkness Gift, 1929.

1-13 Funerary temple of Hatshepsut, c. 1485 B.C. Deir el Bahari, Egypt.

prize for the grave robbers who swarmed over Egypt in ancient times. Even more impressive is its skilled workmanship, its handsome inlays contrasting richly with the polished gold that pervades the work. A modern viewer may be less impressed by the lavish coffin symbols of Tutankhamen's political and spiritual power than by the serene idealized features of the youthful king. The work invokes not only ceremonial majesty but also a real human presence.

These royal tomb chambers contained a multitude of other objects, some of which may have been adapted from works of an earlier period since Tutankhamen's reign was brief. Some of the craftsmanship was perfunctory, but the larger pieces were carefully made, all very much in traditional styles. Aside from the mummified royal viscera in their own container, there was a variety of furnishings that had surrounded the young king in life such as jewelry and ceremonial chairs, and also a vast number of painted and sculpted images of protective deities, royal officials, and servants, all of

usurped the throne from her nephew and ruled for more than twenty years. Her portrait in stone (fig. 1-12) is not only ceremonial but sensitive and delicate. This monarch (who alternately referred to herself as king and queen) left as her greatest monument a splendid funerary temple (fig. 1-13). Its columns and ramps stand in striking, memorable contrast to the rough cliffs that tower above its three terraces. Huge statuary was part of this complex originally but has disappeared.

A century and more after Hatshepsut there came the seven- or eight-year reign of the boy-king Tutankhamen, whose importance, if only modest in the annals of political history, is unique in the modern record of Egyptian art. Tutankhamen succeeded to the throne near the midpoint of the fourteenth century B.C. His burial chambers, in a rock-cut tomb, were discovered almost intact in 1922, and their beautifully preserved furnishings are of extraordinary magnificence and elegance. The king's principal coffin, in stylized human shape (fig. 1-14), is gold, inlaid with precious stones. Weighing 250 pounds, it would have made a valuable

1-14 Coffin of Tutankhamen (detail), mid 14th century B.C. Gold with precious stones; coffin is 6′11″ long. Egyptian Museum, Cairo.

1-15 *Tutankhamen Hunting*, mid 14th century B.C.
Painted wood; scene is approximately 20″ long.
Egyptian Museum, Cairo.

whom would serve the king in the afterlife. From a
fleet of model boats to handmills for grain and strainers
for filtering beer, the tomb provided all the necessities
of royal immortality.

Among the many fine objects found in
Tutankhamen's burial chambers was a painted chest
showing the king engaged in the royal diversions of
battle and hunting. (It is unlikely that the boy-king,
always sickly, had actually engaged in such strenuous
activity.) In one hunting scene (fig. 1-15) hieroglyphs
fill much of the space near the chariot, but to the right
is an unusual depiction of wounded and fleeing animals
in a complex if rather indefinite landscape. Such portrayals of landscape are not common in an art so thoroughly devoted to human beings, animals, and deities.
It is a reminder that there can be freshness of subject
matter and style even in an age so wedded to tradition
as that of ancient Egypt.

Emergence of the Greek World

Against the sophistication and splendor of ancient
Egypt, the tombs and fortresses of early Greece, though
certainly impressive, may at first seem modest. Otherwise the visual art of very early Greece lacked the ripe
richness of Egyptian art, and we may presume the same
for its music. This period in Greece is distinguished for
a very different medium of expression—the poetry of
Homer. Despite the obscurity of Homeric origins, despite questions even on the historical reality of a single

poet named Homer, the poetry itself is part of the legacy of Western civilization. The Homeric worldview
became the foundation of Greek religious and ethical
thought, and Homeric tales and images have inspired
Western visual art, literature, and music again and
again for thousands of years.

Epic poetry deals with heroic themes in a noble,
elevated style. Later Greeks would agree that the two
great Homeric epics, the *Iliad* and the *Odyssey*, had
been composed by a blind bard—a singer of tales—
named Homer, of whom little was otherwise known.
Modern scholarly opinion has reached a rough consensus on a bardic, preliterate genesis of these imposing
verses. They seem to have been transmitted and elaborated orally for generations and to have been written
down in the late eighth century B.C. Regardless of
whether or not an actual, single poet named Homer
existed, or whether he was a mere compiler of folk
poetry or a great creative genius, the poetry itself is a
monument of Western culture.

The focus of the *Iliad* and the *Odyssey* was the
Trojan War—that is, the siege of a fortress in Asia
Minor named Troy, or Ilios. Recent scholars have generally agreed that something like this siege may well
have taken place, and that certain ancient remains at
Hissarlik, Turkey, near the Aegean Sea are probably
the site that Homer immortalized. The historical siege,
most agree, took place in the mid or later thirteenth
century B.C. It was presumably an incident in the restless movement of Greeks and island peoples that would
usher in the end of Mycenaean civilization.

Mycenae was the most important palace-fortress
of southern mainland Greece, the large peninsula
known as the Peloponnesus. In the thirteenth century
it may well have had a king named Agamemnon—the
king Homer portrayed as the official leader of the
Greeks besieging Troy for ten years. Agamemnon and
several other Mycenaean rulers were not heads of an
integrated empire; more likely they were only first
among equals, and with domains that at best were
loosely federated. In any case, Mycenae's claim to preeminence was well established and was symbolized
throughout antiquity by the monumental Lion Gate
(fig. 1-16) that led into the fortress-palace. (The heads
of the upright lions disappeared long ago.) In the late
nineteenth century of our era the amateur German ar-
chaeologist Heinrich Schliemann crudely excavated
Troy and found fabulous gold objects in a burial site
within the Mycenaean walls. Schliemann believed he

1-16 Lion Gate at Mycenae, before 1250 B.C. Stone; opening is approximately 9′9″ high and wide.

had discovered Agamemnon's tomb, but later investigations revealed that the grave objects dated from centuries earlier.

Modern archaeological finds have shown that the Mycenaean administrators were literate and that they used a writing system also used in the even more splendid civilization on Crete, a large island south of the Aegean. This "Linear B" script, now deciphered, is believed to have been an early form of the Greek language, an ancestor of Homer's tongue. The Cretan culture, in turn, had been strongly influenced by Egypt, especially in its art forms. (Examples of Cretan, "Minoan," art have been found also in the Peloponnesus.) The best-known remains are two cups of beaten gold that were found at Vapheio, within the Mycenaean sphere of influence. If one of them is of Mycenaean workmanship, as has been argued, the work of both is distinctly in the Cretan manner. A herdsman roping a bull is depicted on one of these cups (fig. 1-17). The human figure has a Cretan, even Egyptian, slenderness and adheres to the ancient combination of frontal and profile views, but it also reveals a sense of tense exertion. The art is of uncommon subtlety and elegance.

Mycenaean civilization began to decline around 1200 B.C. and was quite thoroughly extinguished within a hundred years. In the so-called Dark Age that followed, the written language seems to have been forgotten in Greece—a situation in which singing bards could be expected to flourish. During this period the Homeric stories were gradually amplified, altered, and embellished over centuries of oral tradition. In the eighth century literacy reappeared in Greece; the new Greek writing system was composed of characters adapted from the alphabet developed by the traders of Phoenicia in the eastern Mediterranean area of Asia. This alphabet has been handed down to modern Greeks, although the language of Homeric and later classical times has become almost unrecognizable to most modern Greeks.

The Homeric epics as they were first written down reflect three periods of Greek development. There are at least dim reminiscences of the Mycenaean age that furnished the ostensible setting of the poetry, and surely there are reflections of the time of Homer himself, the eighth century when Greece was gradually climbing back into a literate culture and on into an age that would later be labeled *archaic* Greece—that is, "old" Greece, as contrasted with the still-later classical or Golden Age of the Greeks. Most of all, though, the Homeric poems reflect the centuries-long Dark Age in which the legend and the poetry took shape.

After the Mycenaean culture died out, due mainly to attack and infiltration by outsiders, the peoples of

1-17 "Vapheio cup," after 1500 B.C. Gold; approximately 3¼″ high. National Museum, Athens.

Greece led a tribal, fragmented existence. A people known as the Dorians occupied the Peloponnesus. The Ionians, among others, were established farther north before many of them emigrated across the Aegean to settle on islands and the part of the Turkish coast that came to be known as Ionia. According to the later Greeks, Ionia was the homeland of Homer. On the islands in the Aegean and on both coasts of that sea, villages were established and fertile river valleys were claimed for cultivation and control; thus hundreds of little states were formed. The economy was agricultural and, to some extent, commercial. Language and a number of religious beliefs were the principal ties among the Greeks. Religious worship usually took place outdoors around a sacrificial altar, but sometimes also in caves and other dark spots. There were no free-standing temple structures until the eighth century, when modest shrines were first constructed.

Life was crude and hard in the Dark Age, and all the more so for the segment of the population that were slaves. Decorated pottery, which we will discuss in the context of Homer's poetry (see fig. 1-19), did exist, and some of it was very pleasing in form and decorative design. Sculpture produced at this time included small bronzes, such as handles and decoration on metal vessels. Probably it was a decorative urge of this sort that inspired the tiny bronze of a deer nursing her fawn illustrated in figure 1-18. Far from representational naturalism, the figures are nonetheless evocative and delightful—note the penguinlike bird perched on the deer's back.

Despite the visual art of the time, the greatest monuments of the Dark Age and the late eighth century B.C. are the two long Homeric poems. The *Iliad*, almost certainly the earlier of the two, tells of several weeks in the siege of Troy by Agamemnon with his Achaean allies and companions—"Achaean" being the name Homer used most often for the Greeks. The leading hero of the *Iliad*, however, is the redoubtable warrior Achilles. The *Odyssey* tells of the vividly adventurous homeward voyage from Troy of another Achaean hero, Odysseus, and his reestablishment as husband and ruler on the island of Ithaca, off the western coast of Greece. Eventually Homer's successors would fill in the details of the Trojan War and its aftermath by composing six other epics; thus the *Iliad* and the *Odyssey* became the second and seventh parts of an eight-epic story.

Both the *Iliad* and the *Odyssey* depict an aristocratic society in which each tribe was headed by a chief

1-18 *Deer Nursing Fawn*, 8th century B.C. Bronze, 2½" high. H. L. Pierce Fund. Courtesy, Museum of Fine Arts, Boston.

or king who also led his troops into battle when required to do so—which was often. Commoners as well as aristocrats had the privilege of fighting and dying for their king. Although the *Odyssey* includes few battle scenes, the *Iliad*'s most crucial type of scene is that of organized (and sometimes disorganized) battle. Battles, in fact, comprise more than a third of the *Iliad*. Many of the men and women in both epics are heroic, but they are also of ordinary flesh, blood, and emotion—and so seem also the gods and goddesses, as they counsel and struggle among themselves and intervene in human affairs.

The *Iliad*, opening in the Greek camp of Troy's besiegers, concerns a central theme announced at the outset—the wrath of Achilles:

> Sing, goddess, of Achilles' ruinous anger
> Which brought ten thousand pains to the Achaeans,
> And cast the souls of many stalwart heroes
> To Hades, and their bodies to the dogs
> And birds of prey.

The god Apollo, it soon appears, has demanded the return of a daughter of one of his priests. However, such is the distress of Chryseis's master Agamemnon that he in turn seizes a captive of Achilles, the fair Bryseis. Achilles is furious at this affront to his honor and withdraws from fighting the Trojans. At this point Achilles' mother, the minor goddess Thetis, intervenes on Mount Olympus, home of the gods, with Zeus, head of the whole divine Olympian family. Zeus promises her that he will see to it that the Greeks remain unsuccessful against the Trojans until the wrong done to Achilles is righted.

Two-thirds of the *Iliad* ensues before Achilles is finally moved to return to battle—and then not for the purpose of settling old accounts but because of the battlefield death of his dear companion Patroclus in combat against the mightiest Trojan warrior Hector. Agamemnon, for his part, offers reparations for past behavior, and Achilles enters the fight in a magnificent suit of armor newly made for the occasion by the god-craftsman Hephaestus. Achilles fights gloriously and finally kills Hector. The next-to-the-last of the *Iliad*'s twenty-four books concerns the funeral of Patroclus and the funeral games held by the Greeks in his honor. In the final book the anguished old king of Troy, Priam, approaches Achilles and successfully pleads for the return of his son Hector's body. The epic concludes as the Trojans, in turn, mourn the death of a hero.

In this poem, as well as the *Odyssey*, the most obvious reminiscence of the bardic, orally recited verse is the use of verbal formulas—repeated word-groups. These may apply to natural phenomena—"rosy-fingered dawn" being the most celebrated—or more often to deities and human beings. Thus again and again we encounter "cloud-gathering Zeus," his brother Poseidon "the earth shaker," "white-armed" or "ox-eyed" Hera (sister and wife of Zeus), "bright-eyed" Athena (his daughter), "lord-of-men" Agamemnon, and "swift-footed" Achilles.

By no means, however, are all descriptions curt and formulaic. Achilles, for example, is described both in vivid simile and as bursting in a primitive expression of grief. First let us look at the *simile*—a figure of speech in which one person or thing is explicitly compared with another. Achilles goes forth as the furious warrior:

> As raging fire sweeps through a mountain valley
> Of dry wood, setting ablaze depth of timber,
> And blasts of wind lash on the flames, Achilles
> Swept with his spear like some immortal creature,
> Harrying men who died, and earth ran blood. . . .

Then Achilles' primitive ritual grief when told of the death of Patroclus is described:

> A cloud of sorrow closed upon Achilles.
> He took up dust and poured it on his head

> With both hands, and befouled his handsome face,
> And scattered black ash on his lovely tunic.
> Then stretched his mighty self out on the dirt,
> And took his hair, and tore it with his hands.

Of course the *Iliad* involves much more than literary technique. Also crucial are the ways in which the poet reflects attitudes of his time when he portrays gods, men, and the human condition. Women are rather peripheral in most of Homer's work, especially in the *Iliad*. But even before men, for Homer, there were the gods, who looked very much like human beings but were immortal and ageless, and powerful far beyond human possibilities. The gods, male and female, were among themselves a family that lived on Mount Olympus; they were, however, an exceedingly jealous and quarrelsome lot. Often they altered the course of human events by personal intervention, at times by inhabiting the shapes of specific mortal individuals. Often the deities' influence operated, so to speak, at a distance, as when, early in the *Iliad*, Apollo sends a plague and Zeus is described by Achilles as a sender of dreams. All in all, the Homeric gods seem to have acted upon human beings and natural events in a willful and quite unpredictable way.

Yet men, and on rare occasions women, could be seen by Homer as living heroic lives and as deserving some of the credit for their own heroism; the deities could not take all the glory for human actions. Human heroism was expressed most obviously on the battlefield, sometimes with cruel barbarism, but the heroic ideal also appeared in the many rituals that encompassed the battlefield experience, including death. An entire book of the *Iliad* was devoted to the mourning for Patroclus and the sad festivities surrounding his funeral.

The visual arts of Homer's time, as embodied in the painting of pottery, also often embodied the ritual solemnity of heroic death. A large vessel created and decorated around 750 B.C. (fig. 1-19) reflects the Homeric spirit—in its geometric patterns (perhaps a parallel with Homer's verbal formulas) and two bands showing solemn funeral rites. At the top is the body of the deceased on its processional bier, and at the bottom is the continuing procession with warriors on horse-drawn chariots. The painting portrays figures schematically rather than realistically: the dead body and the mourners are stylized silhouettes, the chariots' wheels are suggested by two detached circles, the warriors' shields have indented forms that greatly exaggerate the reality, and each pair of horses is represented by

1-19 Geometric krater from Athens, c. 750 B.C. Pottery, 4½″ high. National Museum, Athens.

a single head, neck, and trunk to which eight legs are attached.

In the Homeric epics the interaction of gods and men is a crucial means of defining the human condition on earth. The *Iliad* often stresses the total dependence of human beings on the will of the gods—a concept memorably expressed by Achilles when confronting Priam, as both men lament their cruel losses in battle:

> The gods have woven life for mortals so
> We live in grief, while they are free from care.
> There are two jars that sit upon Zeus' threshold,
> With gifts, some of them evil, but some good.
> Cloud-loving Zeus may give one man a mixture;
> Sometimes he hits on evil, sometimes good;
> But to another ruin and abuse,
> And grinds him to the earth. . . .

Still, despite man's impotence before the will of the gods—or even because of this dependence—Homer's heroes do not typically brood over their fate; they love life, and life for them can indeed be beautiful. All of the heroes are strong and handsome, their arms and armor gleam, their lands and palaces (as in Odysseus's Ithaca) are rich and goodly. When, in the *Odyssey*,

Odysseus encounters even the lower classes in the persons of his old nurse and his swineherd, their lives and characters, too, possess true dignity.

In the *Odyssey* the reader turns from the heroic field of battle to a mythic realm of adventure much in the spirit of folktales of all ages. The ten-year trek of Odysseus back to his palace and his wife Penelope is full of escapes from the magical wiles of enchanting women and from monsters like the one-eyed cyclops. Its ending is as happy and decisive as in most (but not all) folktales: Odysseus displays great endurance and guile in rejoining his wife and son, and in slaying Penelope's unpleasant suitors. Odysseus had been a conventional Greek hero on the battleground of Troy. In his homecoming he is a survivor as well as a conquering hero; he lives less by muscle than by wit. The Homeric ideal is, after all, somewhat flexible, coming into play whenever leaders of men courageously carry out any challenging mission whatsoever. Yet all the heroes, from the brave Hector and Achilles to the resourceful Odysseus, are men of action. All of them can decisively and firmly seize the moment and do what has to be done.

Of course the gods do intervene in the *Odyssey*, though less freely than in the *Iliad*. Zeus, for example, causes a storm and shipwreck in which Odysseus is spared but his companions are drowned, for they have committed sacrilege by devouring the cattle of the gods. A contemporary vase painting (fig. 1-20) conveys, however crudely, the excitement of this or a similar scene, in which men flounder confusedly in the sea as one self-possessed figure sits astride the capsized boat. It is in the mouth of Zeus, however, that Homer puts words placing at least partial responsibility for men's misfortunes upon themselves:

> Well now, how indeed mortal men do blame the gods!
> They say it is from us evils come, yet they themselves
> By their own recklessness have pains beyond their lot.

Even so, the Olympian deities still played an important role in Homer's world, not as pervasive a role as in ancient Egypt, but still decisive many a time in the lives of human beings. A clearer contrast existed between Egyptian and Homeric religions when they viewed the afterlife. The key passage in the *Odyssey* concerns the visit that Odysseus made to Hades, the underworld, to consult a deceased well-known seer. This world of the dead was by no means the ideal after-

1-20 *Shipwreck (of Odysseus?),* c. 725 B.C. Detail of geometric oinochoe. Staatliche Antikensammlungen und Glyptothek, Munich.

life fondly expected by the Egyptians. Many of the dead, Odysseus discovered, were undergoing excruciating punishments—such as Tantalus striding into a lake to quench his thirst but finding the water always receding beyond his reach when he leaned over to drink. Whereas the Egyptian underworld could bring its punishments to those not fortified by the proper formulas, in Homer's Hades even the fortunate and heroic dead

could not find an enjoyable afterlife there, but were insubstantial ghosts having, bluntly, no fun at all. When Odysseus greeted the great hero Achilles, who had perished in the final phase of the Trojan War, Achilles lamented that in Hades "the dead dwell senseless, the phantoms of mortals who are worn out." Even ruling over the dead was, for Achilles, no joy; he would, he declared,

> . . . rather serve on the land of another man
> Who had no portion and not a great livelihood
> Than to rule over all the shades of those who are dead.

Homer's Greece, it is clear, was very different from the land of the pharaohs. Though much more modest in physical monuments and in many of the arts, it was developing a worldview more akin to the modern Western spirit than the Egyptian outlook. A search for earthly pleasure and for heroic achievement was common to both civilizations, and both set up ideals of earthly behavior that were by no means wholly dissimilar. Egypt, however, found its most glittering goals in the life after death, whereas Homer's Greece looked to this world for its satisfactions. In the centuries after Homer, Greece would turn to this world not only for its pleasures, but also for scientific and philosophical explanations of the world itself and for interpretations and justifications of human life on earth.

Recommended Reading

Aldred, Cyril. *Egyptian Art in the Days of the Pharaohs 3100–320 B.C.* (1980). Handy survey.

Beye, Charles Rowan. *The Iliad, the Odyssey, and the Epic Tradition* (1966). Background and analysis.

Clarke, Howard W., ed. *Twentieth-Century Interpretations of The Odyssey* (1983). Essays by various authors.

Desroches-Noblecourt, Christiane. *Tutankhamen: Life and Death of a Pharaoh* (1963). Fascinating picture book on the discovery and contents of the boy-king's tomb.

Fagan, Brian M. *People of the Earth* (1980). Prehistory around the world.

Gowlett, John. *Ascent to Civilization* (1984). Well-illustrated archaeological survey.

Groenewegen-Frankfort, H.A., and Bernard Ashmole. *Art of the Ancient World* (1971). Comprehensive and well-illustrated.

Hallo, W. W., and W. K. Simpson. *The Ancient Near East: A History* (1977). Up-to-date text.

Higgins, Reynold. *Minoan and Mycenean Art* (1981). Good survey.

Homer. *The Iliad,* trans. by Denison Bingham Hull (1982). Readable translation.

Homer. *The Odyssey,* ed. and trans. by Albert Cook (1974). Straightforward translation with comments and criticism.

Lichtheim, Miriam, ed. and trans. *Ancient Egyptian Literature: A Book of Readings* (2 vols.) (1973). Authoritative translations of primary sources.

Lloyd, Seton, et al. *Ancient Architecture: Egypt, Mesopotamia, Crete, Greece* (1974). Text with unusually handsome photographs.

Matz, Friedrich. *The Art of Crete and Early Greece* (1962). Another good survey.

Mertz, Barbara. *Red Land, Black Land: The World of the Ancient Egyptians* (1978). Daily life and death in ancient Egypt.

Pfeiffer, John E. *The Creative Explosion: An Inquiry into the Origins of Art and Religion* (1982). Enlightening discussion of the cave dwellers.

2

Ancient Greece: 560–323 B.C.

he high level of civilization in ancient Greece evolved over many centuries. From the end of the Mycenaean period about 1100 B.C., through the Dark Age, and well into the eighth century B.C., Greece was the scene of tribal migrations and conquests. At last, in the eighth century B.C., came a great revival of cultural, political, and economic life. This revival brought the consolidation of city-states, widespread colonization throughout the central and eastern Mediterranean area from Italy to Asia Minor, and a striking growth of commerce and urban society. The seventh and sixth centuries B.C., known today (together with the early fifth century) as the *archaic*, or old, period in Greek (Hellenic) history, continued these trends and gave rise to a magnificent flowering of the visual and literary arts.

The most striking event in the political and economic life of the archaic Greek world was the rise of the city-state of Athens. This city-state was one of the many territorially small, political units that were either independent or at least self-governing. The Greek world was divided this way throughout the ancient period until the Macedonian conquest of 338 B.C. Each city-state included a dominant city, by whose name it was generally known; thus all of Attica was referred to as Athens, and the whole of Laconia (southwest of Athens in the Peloponnesus) was called Sparta.

In the sixth century B.C. Athens, as an important exporter of pottery and olive oil, replaced nearby Corinth as the leading commercial city of mainland Greece. Its government at that time alternated between aristocratic control and "tyranny," but a trend toward democracy was emerging. The regime of the tyrant Peisistratus (560–527 B.C.) reversed that trend for awhile. Although he, like Greek tyrants elsewhere, had seized control illegally, he did solicit and generally obtained popular support; he represented his goal as the good of the whole state, not of any faction. Peisistratus's rule was firm but benevolent, and the Athenians of his day enjoyed unprecedented security, wealth, and prestige.

Beginning with the Athenian statesman Cleisthenes, the effective leader for several years after 510 B.C., the city-state saw a renewed growth of democratic institutions. Democracy, or "rule by the people," was in fact carried to greater lengths in Athens than has been usual in Western history: eventually most Athenian citizens were, at some time in their lives, not merely represented in the government but were selected by lot to serve as governmental officials. In the meantime Athens and all of mainland Greece had turned back their most alarming threat, when the mighty Asian kingdom of Persia, which had already seized the Greek city-states of Asia Minor, invaded and unsuccessfully attempted to subjugate the mainland west of the Aegean Sea (490–479 B.C.). The Persian sacking of Athens in 480 B.C. is commonly regarded as the symbolic transition point from archaic to *classical* Greek civilization.

The period after the Persian Wars marked the culmination of Athenian democracy and the rise of Athenian domination in the Greek world, under the leadership (461–429 B.C.) of Pericles. Resisting this expansionism, the authoritarian state of Sparta and its allies at last decisively defeated Athens in the Peloponnesian War (431–404 B.C.). The next half-century witnessed several shifts in the internal Athenian regime and in the relative prestige of the Greek city-states. Philip, ruler (359–336 B.C.) of Macedon, commenced his conquest of Greece, effectively completing the process in 338 B.C. The brilliant rule (336–323 B.C.) of his son Alexander the Great would usher in a new period in history, the Hellenistic age.

THE GREEK VIEW OF LIFE

The imposing theater at Epidaurus (fig. 2-1) was constructed during the fourth century B.C. Already the greatest days of Greek culture had largely passed; most modern historians regard the art and literature of the fifth century or even earlier as being the best of ancient Greece. Yet if the fifth century saw the culmination of Greek creative genius, and was thus the truly "classical" age, or venerated high point, of Greek civilization, the fourth century had its own distinctions, notably as a period of cultural consolidation and extension. The Epidaurus theater, built to accommodate some thirteen thousand spectators, reminds us that Europe's first highly advanced civilization was enjoyed by far more than a handful of its citizens. Epidaurus was, to be sure, a special city; its celebrated shrine to the god of healing, Asclepius, brought throngs from the entire Greek world—from the eastern reaches of the Mediterranean westward to Italy and beyond. Despite petty political divisions, the Greeks shared a proud cultural heritage that set them apart from those other Mediterranean peoples that they called barbarians. The Greeks tended to underestimate their predecessors and contemporaries.

Nonetheless, the Greek world had much cause for pride. In particular, the city-state of Athens had justification for satisfaction and confidence in the fifth century B.C. In its golden age, Athens was the supreme symbolic embodiment of the Greek genius. By the fourth century its art and its literature, dramatic and otherwise, had become the standard by which Greek culture was measured.

The Greek Tragic Theater

The theater at Epidaurus was hardly unique in its time: it was simply one of the larger outdoor theaters built of stone against the natural hillside slopes of the eastern and central Mediterranean. The inhospitable ruggedness of the Greek terrain, as seen beyond the tiers of seats at Epidaurus, was only one of the many harsh facts of Greek life that may well have contributed to the "tragic view" so often embodied in Greek theatrical drama. Plague, drought, shipwreck, recurring warfare, too, were constants of the Greek experience, and life was precarious indeed. For most Greeks life was an unremitting struggle for survival against brutal forces

2-1 Theater at Epidaurus, c. 350 B.C.

that were commonly thought to be supernatural and certainly beyond human understanding.

Greek theater began as tragic drama, and the Greeks' preoccupation with tragedy was related to the worship of the god Dionysus. In the early fifth century B.C. Dionysus was a relatively new intruder into the circle of deities on Mount Olympus headed by Zeus. Being a god of fertility and wine, Dionysus was a symbol of emotional as well as physical exaltation and intoxication. To ordinary men and women, Dionysus may have seemed closer, in fact, to the many obscure, local earth-deities the Greeks had honored for centuries than to the splendid divine family on Mount Olympus. In Athens, the tyrant Peisistratus encouraged and patronized the cult of Dionysus, and soon many educated Greeks joined their humbler neighbors in finding satisfaction in worshipping him.

For most Greeks the Olympian deities seemed far removed from daily life. These brilliant gods and goddesses, moreover, brought no sense of mystery: they seemed all too human in Homer and in current legend. Certainly the bickering and conniving on Mount Olympus offered no exemplary patterns of high moral behavior to encourage and inspire men and women.

Above all, as Odysseus had learned from the ghost of Achilles, the Olympians offered no promise of an enjoyable afterlife. The worship of Dionysus, on the other hand, brought with it some basis for morality and the promise of a happier life after death. Still better, many Greeks found Dionysian worship exciting.

It had long seemed appropriate to the Greeks to worship the god of wine and fertility with lively rites. In early archaic times Dionysian worship seems to have been taken up most typically by groups of cultists, usually female (the "maenads"), who at their most excited ran in packs in the countryside and up wooded mountains, inspired by an unrestrained exaltation that they took to be possession by the god himself. The painting on the vase in figure 2-2 shows maenads dancing with abandon, ladling wine, and playing the tambourine to honor the image of Dionysus (the crowned mask on a dummy in the center). Grapevines or ivy frame the image of this god of wine, and a wreath is attached to its belt. Several ritual offerings lie on the table beside two large vases of the same type as the vase on which the scene is painted. Two round ritual cakes—further offerings to the god—are balanced on each side of the god's mask. Although some of the wine will be offered

2-2 Dinos Painter, *A Festival of Dionysus*, c. 420 B.C. Red-figure stamnos vase, 19¼″ high. Museo Nazionale Archeologico, Naples.

to the god, it is likely that most of it will go, sooner or later, into the drinking cup held in the ladler's hand—for the maenads themselves.

As time passed, Dionysus was viewed more often as moderating or purging the emotions than as arousing them. Later worship downgraded the robust jollity and the physical lusts and often invoked a gentle, spiritual calm. Neither of these modes of Dionysian worship, however, was fully absorbed into the other. A fruitful tension between reason and emotion always characterized Dionysian worship and indeed the overall spirit of ancient Greece. This tension was incorporated into that offshoot of Dionysian worship, the Greek tragic theater.

Today it is impossible to know by exactly what steps Greek tragedy evolved from the early Dionysian festivities and the more dignified singing and dancing that later honored the god. It was, however, from such beginnings that eventually emerged the mature tragic theater of the fifth century B.C., especially in Athens. Even in the full bloom of Athenian tragic drama, the performances still took place only once each year, at

the spring festival known as the City Dionysia, over which the leading priest of Dionysus presided. Many thousands of Athenians attended—more, even, than could later be accommodated at Epidaurus. Visitors to Athens today can still see some remains of the stone-built theater that eventually arose on the slope below the acropolis fortress on which Athenian religious life centered.

By the time of the three great Athenian dramatists Aeschylus, Sophocles, and Euripides, playwrights competed with each other at the annual City Dionysia, and a prize was awarded to the author-producer whose three tragedies were judged the best. (A fourth, livelier play was added by each writer.) Of the many hundreds of fifth-century Athenian plays that were written, just over thirty complete tragedies exist today. These include only one full trilogy—three tragedies by the same author designed to be presented as a unit. These, however, are enough to display the skill and dramatic sense of the playwrights. The plays, to be sure, were not the realistic "slices of life" that theater audiences tend to expect today. The Greek subjects were mainly taken from ancient legend and featured group singing and dancing by a "chorus," which commented and often passed judgment on the actions of individual characters. With only a few exceptions, no more than three actors participated, but each might take several parts, aided by the backstage changing of masks. Since the ancient legends portrayed were known to the viewers, there was little if any suspense as to the outcome of the action. Audiences looked, rather, for the skill and sophistication with which the stories were developed, and for the aptness and beauty of the language that expressed the dramatic action.

In 458 B.C. Aeschylus (died 455 B.C.) won the prize for the one Greek trilogy that still exists today, the *Oresteia*. All three plays concern the legendary house of Atreus and are set in Argos (near Mycenae) after king Agamemnon's victorious return from the Trojan War. The royal house lies under a divine curse that arose after Atreus got revenge over his feuding brother Thyestes by serving him the flesh of his own slain sons at a banquet. Agamemnon, son of Atreus, in turn had killed a family member, his own daughter Iphigenia, in order to appease the wrath of the goddess Artemis, who was sending contrary winds that were preventing Agamemnon's fleet from sailing to Troy. In the *Agamemnon* tragedy, the king's wife Clytemnestra

CHRONOLOGY

HISTORY		THE ARTS	
c. 1000	Greek migrations to the east (Aegean islands and Ionia)		
c. 776	first Olympic games		
c. 750	beginning of Greek colonization to the west (Sicily and southern Italy)		
		late 8th century	Iliad and Odyssey written down
		630–480	archaic Kouroi
		c. 600	poetry of Sappho and Alcaeus of Lesbos
560–546	Croesus, king of Lydia	560–480	archaic Korai
560–527	Peisistratus, tyrant of Athens		
		6th century	Milesian philosophers and Pythagoras
		534	first tragedy performed, Athens
		c. 520	funerary statue of Kroisos
510–?	Cleisthenes promulgates Athenian laws tending toward more democracy		
500	Ionian Greeks revolt in response to subjugation by Persia; beginning of the Persian Wars		
490–479	Persian Wars; invasions of mainland Greece west of Aegean	c. 490/480– second half of 5th century	Herodotus
480	Persian devastation of Athenian acropolis	c. 480	Critias Boy
479	battle of Plataea; end of Persian invasions		
		472	earliest surviving Greek tragedy, The Persians by Aeschylus
		c. 471–400	Thucydides
		c. 470–399	Socrates
461–429	Pericles' leadership in Athens	458	the Oresteia by Aeschylus
		456	completion of Temple of Zeus, Olympia
		455	death of Aeschylus
		c. 450	Poseidon(?) from Cape Artemisium
		447–433	construction of the Parthenon
431–404	Peloponnesian War: Athens defeated by Sparta	429–347	Plato
		c. 421–406	construction of the Erechtheum
		406	deaths of Sophocles and Euripides
404–338	shifting supremacies of states in mainland Greece (Sparta, Thebes, etc.)		
		384–322	Aristotle
		c. 350–340	original "Hermes of Praxiteles"
338	Philip of Macedon defeats the Greeks at Chaeronea		
336	Alexander the Great becomes king of Macedon		

All dates are B.C.

and her lover Aegisthus (son of Thyestes) plot to kill Agamemnon for sacrificing Clytemnestra's daughter, and this fresh murder is accomplished by the play's end. Along the way there are repeated appeals by the chorus to Zeus, as embodying the Unknown God, highest of all deities, who tracks down and punishes the sinner, whoever he or she may be. Zeus also may bestow wisdom upon human beings through suffering.

'Tis Zeus who shows the perfect way
Of knowledge. He hath ruled that
Men shall learn wisdom, by affliction.

Sometimes in the same tragedy it is Fate that casts down those of high estate or those upon whom fortune has seemed to smile—here in an Aeschylean metaphor of shipwreck at sea:

. . . Too fair they blow,
The gales that waft our bark on Fortune's tide!
Swiftly we sail, the sooner all to drive
Upon the hidden rock, the reef of woe.

The second tragedy in the *Oresteia* trilogy is *The Choephori*, or *The Libation Bearers*—the "choephori" being the female suppliants who come to the tomb of Agamemnon some years after his murder. Agamemnon's daughter Electra prays that her long-exiled brother Orestes may return to carry out their joint vengeance against Clytemnestra and Aegisthus, who now together rule over Argos. Orestes does return, at first in disguise, and does indeed strike down the murderers. Now two new murders—including the especially reprehensible crime of matricide—remain to be avenged. The grisly self-perpetuating cycle of homicidal vengeance is finally ended in the last play of the trilogy, *The Eumenides,* in which the divine furies are finally appeased and become goddesses of mercy (the Eumenides). This supernatural transformation occurs through the intervention of Athena, divine patroness of Athens, presumably near the very spot where the Aeschylean trilogy was produced.

The supernatural also plays a role in such plays of Sophocles (died 406 B.C.) as *Oedipus the King,* one of several works concerning the legendary royal house of Thebes, again roughly in the Trojan War period. Long before the action of the play begins, King Oedipus had rescued the city of Thebes from the monstrous Sphinx, a creature part woman, bird, and lion. The scene on the vase in figure 2-3 would seem to portray the moment when the Sphinx propounds her famous riddle:

2-3   *Oedipus and the Sphinx.* Red-figure vase painting. Vatican Museums.

what creature walks on four legs in the morning, two at midday, and three in the evening? Oedipus proposes the correct answer—man, who crawls as an infant, walks erect in his prime, and uses a cane in old age—at which the furious beast destroys herself, lifting the curse from Thebes. In *Oedipus the King* a new crisis has arisen: after many prosperous years under Oedipus as king, Thebes has been struck by a terrifying plague. The god Apollo has proclaimed that only banishment of the criminal whose deeds have occasioned the plague will end the affliction. Oedipus vows to discover the offender who, he discovers through a series of revelations well devised by Sophocles, is himself. Unwittingly, in the Sphinx's day, he killed his father Laius, then king of Thebes, and later married the widowed queen Jocasta, his own mother, who then bore him four children.

By usual human standards the parricide and incest into which Oedipus has blindly fallen might not seem blameworthy, since he was totally ignorant of what he had done. However, he has violated the natural, divinely ordained order of things and recognizes his guilt; he blinds himself bloodily and has his brother-in-law Creon, as the new king, send him into exile. Oedipus is doomed by his discovery of the truth, and by his offenses against the moral order. No mortal, the chorus concludes in the tragedy's final lines, can be called happy "until he hath crossed life's border, free from pain."

Like most Greek legends adapted by fifth-century dramatists, the Oedipus story is rich in possible interpretations. These range from an emphasis on the jealousy of the gods confronted by excessive human pride and fortune, to an insistence that evil in the universe is unpredictable and irrational. In any case, Sophocles' hero exemplifies the nobility with which a strong personality can meet the total collapse of a comfortable world. When Oedipus at last confronts the truth, he faces its consequences with courage, accepting without whimpering the limitations of his humanity. A Greek audience could not have been wholly unsympathetic to the plight of Oedipus or indifferent to the tragic dignity with which he transcends his fall.

In addition to old concerns, there were new ones in the plays of Euripides, who like Sophocles died in 406 B.C. but at a somewhat younger age. Aeschylus had been the celebrant of divine order and justice as upheld by Zeus. Sophocles had struggled with problems of moral order and human fate and in so doing discovered the nobility of which human beings are capable. Euripides came to focus on the personalities and characters of human beings themselves, and not necessarily noble ones—which is one reason he is usually considered today the most modern of the three great Athenian dramatists. His tragedy *Medea,* produced in 431, exemplifies his new emphasis.

Medea's setting is a legendary age impossible to pinpoint but clearly enough visualized by Greeks of the fifth century. Well before the play's action begins there had come the great adventures of Jason and his Argonauts, the companions with whom he sailed in the ship *Argo* to the far-off land of Colchis in pursuit of the Golden Fleece. The fleece was magically protected, but finally Jason was able to seize it through the countermagic of a sorceress, the barbarian princess Medea. Medea had fallen desperately in love with Jason, and their union produced two sons. Eventually they found themselves in exile in Corinth, near the isthmus that connected the Peloponnesus to the rest of mainland Greece. This city is the site of the play's action.

Medea has learned that Jason has in effect abandoned her and the two children they both love in order to marry a Corinthian princess. Jason explains the move in his typically rational and patient but maddeningly self-satisfied way: he says he is consolidating not only his own position in Corinth but that of Medea and their sons as well. Medea, however, is no cool rationalist but a woman of intense emotion, and she is enraged by what she considers Jason's heartless betrayal after her long and vital service to him. In plotting her revenge she momentarily fakes a reconciliation and sends to the bride a gown and headdress she has powerfully poisoned through her magic arts. The bride and her horrified father, who tries to tear the burning gown from her body, are consumed by flames. In order to deny Jason even the consolation of keeping his two small sons, she stabs them to death. The end of the play deviates from the previous focus on the conflict between emotion and calm, deceitful rationality: Medea disappears with the children's bodies in a dragon-drawn chariot that she has conjured up by her magical spells.

Euripides' *Medea* has often been regarded as feminist: the sorceress is, after all, a woman—a woman driven to extremes by the injustice done to her by a plausible but cruel male egotist. She is not, to be sure, a pleasant woman, but pleasantness is seldom an issue in desperate circumstances. Aside from the rather melodramatic difficulties that develop, the play also succinctly presents the condition of women in general, as do others of Euripides' tragedies at greater length. It is Medea who utters the often-repeated words on childbirth: "I would gladly take my stand in battle array three times o'er, than once give birth." These words would remain remarkable in a civilization that dignified the role of man far more than that of woman.

The Greek Historians

The exaltation of the male is characteristic of Greek historical writing as well as of the tragedies and the visual arts; there are very few heroines in any of these arts. For the Western world, history, like tragedy, is essentially a Greek invention that reached maturity in the fifth century B.C. By that time certain elements of historical writing were already known in Greece; legendary tales, for example, had already been recorded, as in the Homeric epics. In the early fifth century these dubious tales were being supplemented by narrative "human geographies" that described different peoples on the three known continents and by local chronologies, year-by-year accounts of particular city-states, usually based on the specific evidence of state and

ANCIENT GREECE

priestly records. With Herodotus, the "father of history," true history came into being. His *Histories* combined legendary tales and local chronologies with sympathetic research concerning foreign peoples and were serious attempts to accurately record all past events, great and small, in the known world. His work was one of the Western world's most spectacular debuts of a whole new type of creative expression. Inaccuracies and inadequacies abound in Herodotus—but his celebrated *Histories* were at least as successful and epoch-making as were, in a different genre, the tragic dramas of Aeschylus.

Not much is known of the life of Herodotus. He was born in Asia Minor, probably between 490 and 480 B.C. He traveled extensively, not only to mainland Greece west of the Aegean but also through much of Egypt and Mesopotamia, always making inquiries into the past and the old and new customs of the lands he

visited. His curiosity was insatiable. He consulted whatever written records he could find and attempted to sift the likely from the unlikely from those records and the tales that he was told. Frequently, when confronted by two versions of a story, he would cite both versions in his writing. Sometimes his writing was slyly or even openly skeptical: "My business," he once noted, "is to record what people say, but I am by no means bound to believe it." Generally, he applied common sense to his reading of events—but not to the extent that he omitted supernatural omens, sometimes derived from dreams, or the pronouncements on the future provided by oracles, the mouthpieces of the gods. He believed, at least to some extent, in the Greek deities of his day, and one of the leading themes of his writing was his belief that specific deities, or divine power in general, become "envious of human prosperity."

This belief, in fact, pervades the first set of narratives in his history—those concerning the Lydians, the first foreigners to conquer the Ionian Greek city-states of Asia Minor. King Croesus of Lydia is the subject of many stories, including one concerning a very close escape from a spectacular burning on a flaming pyre after his capture by the Persians. The fire beneath him was already lighted when he was heard to pronounce several times the name of Solon, a great Athenian lawgiver of the early sixth century; the Persian king was curious and ordered his servants to put out the flames. Solon, it appeared, had told Croesus that "no man could be called happy until his death" (an anticipation of Sophocles). King Cyrus was so impressed by both Croesus and Solon—and especially by the fact that the heavens had answered Croesus's prayer to extinguish the still persistent flames—that he retained the captive Croesus as his friend. As for Croesus's capture in the first place, Herodotus notes that he had only himself to blame. When he had asked Apollo's oracle at Delphi whether he should march against the Persians, the god had said that if he did, he would "destroy a mighty empire," and so he did—his own.

After conquering Lydia and the Ionian states, the Persians proceeded to attack the centers of Greek power, including Sparta and Athens. Their lack of success was the main theme of Herodotus. As he wrote at the outset, he hoped to "do two things: to preserve the past by putting on record the astonishing achievements both of our own and of the Asian peoples, and secondly . . . to show how the two races came into conflict." This he did with a remarkable degree of impartiality, even though at the end he obviously rejoiced in the triumph of Greek freedom, as against the Persian autocracy that might have stifled it. Herodotus called the final Persian defeat at Plataea (479 B.C.) "the most splendid victory that history records"—and at that or any other point he may well have been right. Thereafter, Western peoples were not crushed in slavery but were free to develop the open society that, despite all its abuses and setbacks, has come to characterize the Western world.

Herodotus exemplified the spirit of free inquiry, and he exercised his freedom in strange and wonderful ways, as in his very lengthy digression and speculations concerning Egypt. The second great historian of the fifth century, Thucydides, had a narrower, though still extremely important, theme—the Peloponnesian War in which Athens was humbled by Sparta and its allies between 431 and 404 B.C. Thucydides' tale of the war breaks off abruptly, in mid-sentence, in 411 B.C., but by that time the Athenians had already met their most devastating defeat, outside the walls of Syracuse in Sicily.

Thucydides' history of the war and its background lacks some of the spontaneity and charm of the histories of Herodotus, but it is in general a more careful and accurate narrative of past events. Thucydides was more soberly sure of his facts than the genial Herodotus was, yet in a sense he also invented more than the earlier writer did, in the lengthy speeches and dialogues he inserted into the narrative. Although the speeches and dialogues may be fanciful in detail, they serve to reveal two sides of issues and to develop the personal characters of the speakers and the spirit of their time. In the first category is the famous "Melian dialogue," which records one of the saddest blights on the memory of the Athenians. In the dialogue the representatives of Athens, at the peak of Athenian military muscle, argue their case for taking over the much weaker island of Melos. They will do so, they admit, on no better grounds than that they are the stronger of the two, for "the strong do what they can and the weak suffer what they must."

The "Melian dialogue" marks a depressing descent from the glowing Athenian idealism near the beginning of the war, as represented by Thucydides in the great funeral speech he puts into the mouth of the Athenian leader Pericles. The speech may be as accurately reported as are any by Thucydides: it was delivered at an important public event in Athens to some of the same Athenians Thucydides addressed in his history—and many of those people could have remembered at least the speech's spirit and main substance twenty years later. Any total fabrication by Thucydides would have been quickly noted.

In his speech Pericles praises not only the bravery of the fallen Athenian soldiers, but also the free Athenian institutions under which they had been nourished. Deaths of Athenian youths in battle, Pericles acknowledges, lie heavy upon the hearts of their survivors. (Today we are reminded of all wistful military leave-takings by those that were painted on many Greek vases, as shown in figure 2-4.) The many Athenian institutions of which, Pericles believed, all Athenians should be proud included its democratic government, the availability of "equal justice to all," the opportunity to advance one's station in life by merit,

2-4 Kleophon Painter, *Warrior's Departure from Home,* c. 430 B.C. Red-figure stamnos vase, 17⅓" high. Museum Antiker Kleinkunst, Munich.

and freedom of the individual. Happily, despite the many failings and ultimate collapse of ancient Athens, it is still possible, by and large, to remember the Athenians as Pericles rather hopefully portrayed them 2400 years ago.

Education, Music, and Lyric Poetry

The ideal Athenian values emphasized by Pericles were seemingly well established by his time; most of them, despite the Melian episode, would outlive even Athens' shattering defeat by Sparta in 404 B.C. Pericles saw his Athenians as capable of self-control and discipline—and certainly self-control was among the qualities most highly valued by the Greeks. Essentially a young, lusty, immoderate people, they advocated and often truly embraced moderation as a safeguard against the potential excesses to which they were admittedly subject. The Greeks were neither cold nor dull, but more typically in a state of controlled tension that guarded against the potential one-sidedness of passing impulse and undirected emotionalism and made possible rich and full personal development. Greek tragic drama, for

example, channeled emotion into a highly stylized dramatic form that nevertheless could deal with the most intense of human crises, the most challenging of human problems.

The conscious molding of man was, in fact, a frequent goal of classical Greek tragedy and the primary concern of all Greek education. Man, it was believed, could be deliberately formed in accordance with an ideal—the ideal of a perfected wholeness, not of a fragmented, specialized knowledge or a random confusion of ends or an internal struggle between flesh and spirit. Very significantly, the Greeks tried to view most areas of human activity as interrelated. Art and politics, architecture and religion, ethics and athletics, all were routes toward the harmoniously integrated and nearly equivalent goals of the good, the true, and the beautiful. Music, for the Greeks, was still another way toward this integrated ideal and toward the truly whole human being.

Music was as important in the Greek educative process and, indeed, in Greek life as the literary and artistic evidence emphatically indicates. Approximate reconstruction of the bits of Greek vocal music that have been rediscovered (almost all of it originating well after the fifth century B.C.) indicates a wholly monophonic art (that is, with a single melodic line)—at least for strictly vocal music. In it we are sometimes aware of a rather primitive charm, but our ears are not Greek, and we find it hard today to credit this music with the influence assigned it by ancient writers and artists.

Yet we are wrong on both counts: the music of the Greeks, far from being primitive, was highly sophisticated, especially at the theoretical level, and it was indeed a vital ingredient of Greek life. Music, both vocal and instrumental, adorned performances of Greek tragedy, thus joining with dance, brilliant costumes, and masks to make a dramatic tragedy a "complete art work" of stylized splendor. Other poetry as well, wherever performed, seems most typically to have been sung, not recited, and often to the accompaniment of instrument and dance. Among the most common instruments were the aulos, a wind instrument with reed mouthpiece, and such stringed instruments as the lyre and the kithara (fig. 2-5). The aulos provided rhythm for athletics, military marching, and religious rituals. Stringed instruments, on the other hand, were favored in schooling, partly because they

2-5 Achilles Painter, *Muse Playing the Kithara,*
c. 445 B.C. White-figure vase. Private collection,
Lugano, Switzerland.

permitted the student to accompany his own singing of
poetry.

Then, too, the sound of strings was often considered more wholesome than that of the shrill aulos.
Wholesomeness was very much on the minds of Greek
teachers and musical theorists, most of whom were
convinced that varying types of musical expression,
notably the different modes or scales, had definitely
assignable effects on the emotions and moral development. We are reminded that throughout Western history, society's elders have often denounced the potential wickedness lurking within certain musical forms
that entice the young. The doctrine of art for art's sake
alone, with ethical consequences irrelevant, has found
only rare acceptance in the Western world and never
less acceptance than in classical Greece.

Fortunately, Greek musical theory went well beyond dire prophecy and dubious negative. Although
the sensuous beauty of musical sound was seldom
stressed, much thought was given to the mathematical
basis of music and its rational structure. Music was believed to reflect the underlying harmony of the universe, and its purpose was the achievement of a harmonious, rational order within the human soul. If the
theory of music, together with its ethical implications,

was thought more worthy of elevated discussion than
actual musical practice, this is only one of many illustrations of the common preference among advanced
Greek thinkers for theory over practice, for rationalism
over the more mundane aspects of *empiricism*, or factual investigation.

Not all Greek writing dealt with rational abstractions. Lyric poetry, particularly, very often dealt with
events of the real world and especially with human
emotions. If the spirit of much Greek literature may
seem to float on a stylized, noble, elevated plane rather
distant from daily life, such was not the case with the
verse of Sappho of Lesbos, the famous sixth-century
poet pictured in a fifth-century vase painting with her
poet-friend Alcaeus (fig. 2-6). Each poet holds a lyre,
since their verses were sung to its accompaniment,
thus giving *lyric* poetry its name.

2-6 *Alcaeus and Sappho,* c. 475 B.C. Red-figure
vase. Glyptothek und Museum Antiker Kleinkunst,
Munich.

Sappho's poetry reflected both her life and that of the society in which she lived. In the early sixth century the island of Lesbos, as well as much of Ionian Asia Minor, was home to some of the strongest commercial development, most refined civilization, and liveliest intellectual life of the entire Greek world. The landowning aristocracy, to which both Alcaeus and Sappho belonged, lived very well for their day, and their poetry reflects the pleasure-loving Lesbian existence. For Alcaeus this could mean delight in an ample armory of weapons, or the joyous banishing of winter's stormy chill from a snug home with a great hearth-fire and a good quantity of wine.

For Sappho it was all a bit more complicated, although not necessarily just because of the stresses of being a woman in a male-dominated society. The upper-class women of Lesbos seem to have been remarkably emancipated, and Sappho herself was a complex personality of many moods and many loves. The few remnants of Sappho's works that survive offer vivid insights into the delight and tumult of a soul aroused by nostalgia, passion, and desire. One of her most celebrated portrayals of love involves a quiet moment when speech fails her:

> . . . My tongue is palsied;
> Thrilling fire through all my flesh hath run;
> Mine eyes cannot see, mine ears make dinning
> Noises that stun;
> The sweat floweth down,—my whole frame seized with
> Shivering, —and wan paleness o'er me spread
> Greener than the grass; I seem with faintness
> Almost as dead.

Moreover, Sappho wrote often of nature and used natural images to help express her feelings. Such a preoccupation was rare among Greek poets of the archaic and classical periods. Perhaps, after all, the most striking feature of Sappho's writing is that she was an exceptional figure in the poetic world of her day: she did not follow the usual pattern. Among the Greeks there was room for strong individuality, and deviations from the cultural norm were not only accepted but frequently even encouraged.

CITY-STATES AND DAILY LIFE

For two centuries or so before Greece was conquered by the Macedonians in 338 B.C., and to a lesser degree thereafter, the central fact of Greek political and social organization was the city-state. The most surprising feature of these city-states was their very small territorial and economic scale and their small populations. Athens, one of the largest and most prosperous of these independent political units, is thought to have had a population of fewer than two hundred thousand free adults in the fifth century. Moreover, even such a bustling trading city as Athens fell short of our modern standards of affluence, despite the existence of a number of wealthy individuals who were obliged to contribute heavily to public projects such as dramatic productions and naval armament. Large-scale industry was virtually unknown, and scientific and technological development in most areas was primitive. No large middle class separated the few aristocrats from the many working citizens and slaves, and private life was simple and spare for nearly all.

With homes that were small, and favored with a year-round mild climate, Greek town dwellers spent much of their time outdoors and in public places. The *agora* was one of these. Literally a "gathering place," the agora combined the functions of market and civic center. The great comic dramatist Aristophanes regarded the Athenian agora with scorn, as a noisy gossip mart, and counseled more time in the gymnasia. There, if young, one might exercise or, if older, simply observe and chat in pleasant surroundings.

In the democratic state of Athens, civic activities also could occupy much of the citizens' time. Military service was compulsory for two years after a young man's eighteenth birthday, and after that there was the continuing possibility of civic duties—for, as noted before, Athens was a direct rather than a representative democracy. Citizenship was the privilege of freeborn, adult Athenian males; foreigners residing in Athens had neither the privileges nor the duties of citizens. Some foreigners were slaves, but others, the metics, could lead very respectable and prosperous lives as industrious craftsmen and merchants. The Greek citizen class often spoke well of work, or manual labor—especially when it was done by others. Working for one's daily bread did not appeal to the free Athenian male; for most citizens such work seemed an almost unbearable servitude. Avoidance of daily labor was the most obvious prerequisite for the Athenian devotion to public service and for the leisured existence that permitted extended relaxation and participation in sports and intellectual life.

2-7 Onesimos, *Girl Preparing to Wash*, c. 480 B.C. Red-figure painting inside a cup. Musées Royaux d'Art et d'Histoire, Brussels.

Slaves and Women

Certain types of work did remain honorable for Athenian citizens. Working the agricultural land of one's ancestors was considered admirable—the work that produced grains, grapes (for wine), figs, and olives. Horse and cattle breeding also was acceptable, although tending sheep, goats, and swine held less prestige and was usually left to servants or slaves. Artisan labor was respected, and the craftsmanship and true art that went into creating sculptures and making and decorating pottery were in fact very highly valued. Blacksmithing and stonecutting were lower on the prestige scale, and mining was lower yet and generally left to slaves.

Indeed part of the work in all occupations was done by slaves. Like other ancient peoples, and some modern ones, the Greek world of that time required a slave caste and had few qualms about the institution of slavery. The more fortunate slaves lived and worked alongside their masters and were barely distinguishable from them; this was especially true in the workshops of Athens. Even so, slaves enjoyed no basic rights. They had only a few safeguards against gross abuse even in the relatively enlightened and humane city of Athens, and the best-situated slaves, like the worst, could legally be whipped or beaten in the streets at a citizen's whim.

A rather similar situation was that of women, even women of the citizen class. With occasional exceptions, women were to stay at home, laboring at many chores barely imaginable in a modern world of labor-saving devices. A scene painted inside a cup (fig. 2-7) shows a girl on her way to wash; she carries her clothes and a heavy bronze bucket, presumably filled with water. Above all, women were to be wives and mothers: they were a necessity and a diversion for men. A good number of young women and girls were gainfully employed, though pitifully ill-paid, as musicians and entertainers—for the enjoyment of men. Such was the role, presumably, of the girls in a late archaic vase painting of *Men and Girls Reveling* (fig. 2-8). The men, and perhaps the girl at the right, are enjoying themselves in a lively fashion; the girl to the left requires some persuasion. The painting technique for both vases is red-figure, which had largely replaced black-figure work in the later sixth century; the red in each case was the color of the clay used to make the pottery. Lines indicating details of anatomy and clothing were more strikingly drawn, it was decided, against a lighter color—and often were drawn very skillfully indeed.

It was definitely the men and boys, not the women and girls, who led the more enviable existence in ancient Greece. Vase paintings and smaller sculpture, as well as literature, confirm this historical fact. Glimpses of males at leisure or play are a great deal

2-8 Brygos Painter, *Men and Girls Reveling*, c. 490 B.C. Red-figure vase. 7¾″ high. Louvre, Paris.

2-9 *Youths with Dog and Cat,* late 6th century B.C. Stone relief sculpture from a statue base found in Athens, 13″ × 32″. National Museum, Athens.

more common than are scenes of females enjoying themselves, and the scenes portrayed are often revealing and intimate. In a relief sculpture that formed one side of a statue base (fig. 2-9) we see four Athenian youths at leisure, all with the staffs that were in vogue in the late sixth century. The two seated figures hold a dog and a cat on leashes, either holding them back from fighting or, more likely, egging them on. Both animals are in very lifelike postures of alarm and defense. For the young men, at least, the fun is relatively harmless.

Greek Athletics

The most favored of all public modes of male relaxation and pleasure was athletics, as both participant and spectator sports. The ideal of a sound mind in a sound body was peculiarly Greek—and as is usual in all civilizations, prowess of the body was probably more accessible to most than the subtler exercise of the intellect. In any case, the pictorial record of athletic activities is far fuller and more vivid than that of the mind—and immensely fuller for males than for females. At least for boys and younger men, the conditioning of the body seems to have been a daily concern. The most usual locale for exercise and sport was the *palestra,* or gymnasium.

A number of Greek sporting events, most notably chariot racing and foot racing in armor, required substantial equipment. Most sorts of athletics, however, required no equipment and indeed no clothing. The complete male nudity seen in Greek paintings and sculpture was not just an artistic convention; it was a fact of daily life in the sports world. For the typical Greek male there was no problem of embarrassment over male nudity, even in public, and no need to apologize for ascribing beauty to unclothed male youthfulness or for frankly admiring it when portrayed in stone, bronze, or paint. Even, it appears, quite apart from any sensual implications, Greeks early came to consider the youthful, handsomely developed male body as one of the most fitting and natural subjects for pictorial representation.

The various sports, of course, furnished ideal opportunities for studying and admiring the body in action as well as in repose. Wrestling was the most popular of all sports, but boxing, running, javelin throwing, and discus throwing also drew countless athletes and spectators. Two other sides of the same statue base from which the cat-and-dog relief was taken depict athletes engaged in various sports; one side (fig. 2-10) shows a runner in starting position, two wrestlers, and a javelin thrower. In each case the athletic moment is portrayed in convincing, vivid fashion.

Religious Festivals and the Games

The various Greek sports were not always local affairs, or occasions for mere exercise and diversion. They also were taken up with spirited, competitive fervor at four great series of religious festivals for Greeks from all of the eastern and central Mediterranean area. Of these festivals, that at Olympia, in honor of Zeus, was probably the most famous, rivaling the festival of Apollo at Delphi. Priests presided at all the festivals, much as they presided over the year-round maintenance of holy sanctuaries and sacrificial rituals. Priestly association with the games becomes more understandable when we look at the functions of Greek priests. Usually they were elected civic officials, certainly not theologians, preachers, or moral advisers. They were not part of any complex clerical organization or repositories of authoritative religious teaching—for such teaching did not exist in Greek religion. Ancient Greek religion was extraordinarily free and tolerant.

Religion was also extremely pervasive in Greek culture. Perhaps the very absence of religious compulsion contributed to the cheerful willingness of the Greeks to entwine religion so generously with their daily life, sports, and art. Quite certainly most Greeks would have rejected such later frequent concomitants of religion as ponderous spiritual gloom or intricate theological subtlety. The religion of the Greeks, for good or for ill, was largely popular and nonthreatening, and an essential part of their whole enthusiastic civic enterprise.

Nowhere was this popular exuberance more evident than at the great pan-Hellenic (all-Greek) festivals in the Peloponnesus at Olympia—not to be confused, incidentally, with Mount Olympus far to the north, with its "Olympian" deities. Although the Olympic games took place within a sacred context and were preceded and concluded by religious ritual, there can be little doubt that the sheer joy and excitement of sport must have been uppermost in the minds of participants and spectators during the competitions themselves. For the Greek, energetic competition was of surpassing importance in individual and civic life; a winning contestant brought honor to himself, his state, and his gods. Even in 480 B.C., when Greece was threatened most desperately by the invading Persians, the Olympic festivities were held as usual.

SCULPTURE, GODS, AND HEROES

The stadium at Olympia can still be seen by visitors, but the most striking remains from the site are the sculptures honoring the Greek gods and heroes. Most of these works once adorned the great Temple of Zeus.

2-10 *Runner, Wrestlers, Javelin Thrower*, late 6th century B.C. Marble relief sculpture from a statue base found in Athens, 13″ × 32″. National Museum, Athens.

2-11 Temple of Zeus, Olympia, second quarter of 5th century B.C. Reconstruction drawing of the east facade.

The Sculpture of the Temple of Zeus, Olympia

Greek temple pediment sculpture was traditionally of marble or other stone and fully freestanding. At Olympia the east pediment statues, rather poorly preserved, depict the legendary origins of the foundation of the Olympic festival and its games. In the reconstruction we can make out the tallest figure beneath the pediment's peak: this, once more, is Zeus himself. To either side the figures tell the story, rather stiffly, of the legendary chariot races that were a precedent of the Olympic games.

The west pediment sculpture (fig. 2-12) is of a livelier scene. Its figures are fitted more ingeniously into the sloping triangular space and are more vigorously sculpted and better preserved today. Here the central figure (fig. 2-13) is not Zeus but Apollo, one of the most popular of the Olympian deities. Across the centuries Apollo acquired many attributes and functions; from literature we know he was regarded as an interpretor of law and religion and as a proponent of moderation in all things. It is in this latter function that he appears in the Olympia pediment.

Sculpted somewhat before the completion of the temple in 456 B.C., the Apollo figure survived only in part the earthquakes that destroyed the structure a

Today the temple itself is thoroughly ruined; only the foundations and parts of the fallen columns remain on the site. In figure 2-11 we see a reconstruction of the east end, or east facade, of the temple, just beneath the gabled roof. The west front of the temple once afforded a view of the interior, in which stood an immense statue of Zeus. That statue has long since vanished, but much of the sculpture in areas above the columns has been preserved, mainly in the Olympia Museum.

2-12 *Battle of Lapiths and Centaurs,* second quarter of 5th century B.C. Sculpture from the west pediment of the Temple of Zeus, Olympia; pediment is 10′10″ high. Museum, Olympia.

2-13 *Apollo*, c. 460 B.C. Detail from the marble sculpture on the west pediment of the Temple of Zeus, Olympia; detail is 10′8″ high. Museum, Olympia.

thousand years later. It remains, however, even in mutilation, a magnificent example of the heroic, severe manner of earlier fifth-century sculptural classicism. Majestically and authoritatively, but with impassive features, Apollo extends one arm to end the strange struggle being waged around him: centaurs (half-horse, half-man), excited by wine at a royal wedding feast, have tried to abduct the women of the Lapiths but now are about to be vanquished, at Apollo's direction, by the Lapith heroes. The moral was clear to all Greek worshippers at Olympia: the animal in man must be subdued by the human, and thus must brutish excess be conquered by law and moderation, as symbolized by Apollo himself. Similarly, the unity and symmetry of the whole scene represent the triumph of early classical Greek artistic restraint and proportion over a violent episode from ancient mythology.

The relief sculpture at the two ends of the Temple of Zeus taught a similar lesson. This sculpture appeared in the *metopes*—the marble slabs (left blank in the figure 2-11 reconstruction drawing) between the *triglyphs*, or plain grooved panels; triglyphs and metopes together constituted the temple *frieze*, or horizontal band of sculpted panels, beneath each pediment. At Olympia the pictorial frieze panels depicted episodes in the life of the legendary hero Herakles, better-known today as Hercules.

The Herakles relief sculpture, like the freestanding pediment statues, are in the "severe" style of early classicism (480–450 B.C.) that followed archaic and preceded high classical Greek art. This style is severely simple, or monumental—a term that may not refer at all to size, but rather to directness and breadth of style. The severe style is more naturalistic than that of most archaic art, but it indulges in neither softness nor minute detail. The Greek severe style parallels the heroic struggle embodied in the great Persian Wars.

The severe manner seems particularly appropriate to the theme of the Olympia metopes, the twelve labors of Herakles. This great hero of legendary strength was reputedly a son of Zeus and founder of the Olympic games. He was, in fact, a prototype of the later Olympic athlete—strong, single-minded, and brave. The labors were seemingly impossible feats that he performed on the instruction of a Mycenaean-age king, as originally commanded by Apollo's oracle at Delphi. In the metope pictured in figure 2-14 Herakles is fulfilling the king's order to bring to him the Golden Apples of the Hesperides. Herakles has persuaded the giant Atlas to get the apples for him, and Atlas has been able to do this only because Herakles momentarily took over Atlas's crucial job, the unenviable one of holding up the vault of the heavens. In the metope, Herakles, with the aid of the goddess Athena, is still supporting the heavens as Atlas returns with the apples. Atlas will soon resume his job, as Herakles hastens to the king with his golden prizes.

The figures portrayed in the metope, then, are only three—apparently all that the sculptor felt could be clearly visible from ground level. Except for the outstretched hands of Atlas and the bent arm of Athena, the composition is all verticality. There is little detail, even in the handsomely stylized flowing garments of the goddess. The sculpture is totally appropriate to the simple, powerful structure of the temple it helps to adorn.

Other Greek Sculpture, Sixth and Fifth Centuries

"Man," said the philosopher Protagoras, "is the measure of all things." Man, he might have added more explicitly, was the measure of even the gods. Compared to the high civilizations of the Near East that preceded the Greek flowering, the Greek world was indeed *secular*—that is, earthly oriented. Death brought few, if any, supernatural terrors; the funerary monuments that are among the most appealing of classical Greek sculpture typically depict only the most domestic scenes and objects. On the attractive *stele*, or funerary monument, in figure 2-15, the dead youth is shown very much alive, with birdcage and with bird in hand, accompanied by his pensive servant boy and an animal, possibly a cat, which may be either a pet or a part of another monument.

This stele is from the high classical period of the second half of the fifth century B.C. The figures are more supple in posture than those created in the preceding severe style, and more detail is included—note the complex folds of the young man's robe. Shortly we

2-15 *Funerary stele from Aegina, c. 420 B.C. Marble, 43″ high. National Museum, Athens.*

2-14 *Athena, Herakles, and Atlas,* second quarter of 5th century B.C. Metope from the Temple of Zeus, Olympia; original metope 5′3″ high. Museum, Olympia.

will return to the high classical style, in the sculpture of the Athenian acropolis—but first, for contrast, we must see several more examples of earlier art.

In the fifth century B.C., many archaic *kouroi* (statues of young men) must still have been on view with their later, more realistic sculptural descendants. Some kouroi were funerary statues, like the sixth-century work shown in figure 2-16; the inscription on its base reads, in part, "Stop and grieve at the tomb of the dead Kroisos, slain in the front rank of battle." Many other kouroi were dedicated to the gods in gratitude for athletic victories. The pose was standard—the body standing rigidly, with arms stiffly at the sides and one foot somewhat advanced—and exemplifies particularly well the willingness of most Greek artists before the fourth century B.C. to work within the traditional

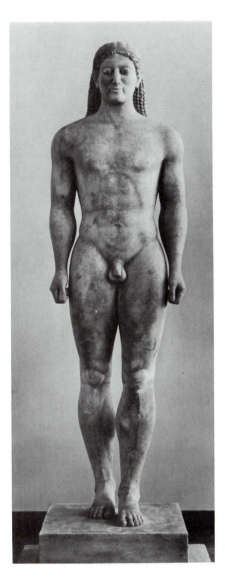

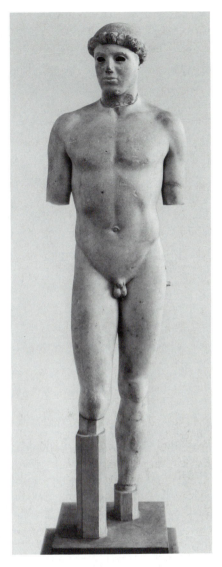

2-16 (left) Kroisos, c. 520
B.C. Marble, 6′ high. National
Museum, Athens.

2-17 (right) Critias Boy,
c. 480 B.C. Marble, 33″ high.
Acropolis Museum, Athens.

bounds of relatively few themes. Neither originality
nor plagiarism was a concern of the Greek sculptor,
and changes in technique, vision, and subject matter
came only gradually through the sixth and fifth centuries. Realism did advance, however, and by the time of
the Persian sack of the Athenian acropolis in 480 B.C.,
the kouros had become infinitely more supple and indeed sensuous, as we note in the so-called Critias Boy
(fig. 2-17), once thought to have been by a sculptor of
that name.

The ethical content and the sculptural forms of
the Temple of Zeus sculptures are still more closely
paralleled by a splendid bronze figure, better preserved

than the Olympia marbles, which was left by shipwreck in the sea until its discovery in the 1920s (fig. 2-
18). The subject would seem to be Poseidon, god of
the sea, who is presumably about to throw his trident,
or three-pronged spear. The statue was created perhaps
a bit later than the Apollo, and the sturdy body is somewhat more flexible, although no less majestic. In earliest legend Poseidon had been horselike in shape, but
later he became a tamer of horses and also the giver of
spring water to the Greeks. A blow from his trident on
the rocky ground of the Athenian acropolis had caused
a spring to flow there—an occasion later cited to explain his veneration as one of the city's patron deities.

2-18 *Poseidon*(?), c. 450 B.C. Bronze sculpture found in the sea off Cape Artemisium, 6'10" high. National Museum, Athens.

2-19 Votive relief dedicated to Athena, c. 470–450 B.C. Marble, 21" high. Acropolis Museum, Athens.

Even more revered by Athenians was their own Athena, seen also as patroness of knowledge and wisdom. The originals of several massive statues of the goddess in Athens have long since disappeared, but a small marble relief found on the acropolis may well possess greater charm (fig. 2-19). (The relief is an example of *votive* sculpture—a devotional work dedicated or offered to a deity, usually in fulfillment of a promise.) In this delicate work Athena is pictured as a thoughtful young woman, apparently reading an inscription. This relief sculpture is contemporary with the *Apollo* and the *Poseidon;* sculptural female nudity was not common until the following century and was hardly considered appropriate to the chaste modesty of this virgin goddess.

We do not know the name of the sculptor of any of these handsome works, or of most other surviving pieces of original Greek sculpture. However, we do know many Greek sculptors' names, and sometimes a good deal about their work, from copies and from literary evidence. In the fifth century B.C. and later, the best Greek sculpture was far from anonymous. In the greater cultural centers such as Athens, sculptors were often held in much esteem and some of them moved in the highest civic circles. Their eminence must have been due in part to the Greek love of beauty and a willingness to value the dignity of individual personality and achievement. Still more, it seems to have come from recognition of the notable public contribution made by artists to the ennoblement and glorification of the state. For it was, above all, the architects and the sculptors who made visible the collective pride and common ideals of the Greek community. Large-scale art in classical Greece seldom if ever existed strictly for its own sake—as a luxury object to be collected by private citizens; few could have afforded it anyway. Art was for all, and it was valued and honored accordingly.

The Athenian Acropolis

The most magnificent of such grand community projects, which called upon the talents of the best of contemporary Greek artists, was no doubt the reconstruction of the Athenian acropolis during and immediately after the rule of Pericles. During the Persian Wars the invaders had destroyed and desecrated the temples and other monuments on the acropolis. Thus it was only natural that the revived, self-confident state of Athens would institute an ambitious program of rebuilding and embellishing its most sacred ancient precinct. This great project was largely completed at the high point of Athenian grandeur and at the full maturity of that artistic style that has become known as "classical."

Many a Greek city had its *acropolis* (high city), which commanded a view of the town and became its principal fortified area. Fortification was the original function of the Athenian acropolis, a rocky plateau roughly 1,000 by 500 feet that rose some 350 feet above the plain of the city. Here, according to legend, once dwelt the king Erechtheus, near where Poseidon and Athena had contested the possession of the city

and the honor of its patronage. (Both, as it turned out, were honored—Poseidon for producing the spring of water and Athena for an olive tree.) Here, amid the squalor of mud-brick huts, arose shrines to these and other deities and eventually several large temples. Innumerable votive statues crowded the area, all of which were painted brightly, like much of the temple structure itself. The Persian burning of the acropolis in 480 B.C. had meant not only destruction but desecration, and much of this statuary was piously buried by the Athenians on the acropolis itself, to be unearthed only in modern times. From these circumstances comes our possession of a significant number of Greek statues with their original painting, however fragmentary and faded. Among the most attractive of these are several archaic maidens (*korai*) from the sixth century B.C., one of which is illustrated in figure 2-20. The outstretched hand, now missing, once held a votive offering, possibly to the great Athena herself.

Later came the Periclean reconstruction, of which several shattered but monumental remnants can still be seen. Much of the archaic clutter on the hill was eliminated then, although there was little attempt at overall symmetry, as shown by the ground plan (fig. 2-21). Dominated by the massive Parthenon, even the columned entranceway and the sacred Erechtheum were relatively dwarfed. The whole, including buildings now irrevocably lost, was a magnificent tribute by the Athenians to their own proud past—from their legendary beginnings to their humiliation by the Persians, and down to their glorious, if short-lived, dominance in the Greek world.

Although the Parthenon (fig. 2-22) is not the largest (it is some 237 feet long) or the best-preserved of classical Greek temples, it has remained the most famous of all and the symbol of perfection in the Doric architectural style. It was the culmination of centuries of development and cautious experimentation in temple building in Greece, southern Italy, and Asia Minor. By the time the plans of the architects Ictinus and Callicrates were realized in stone (447–433 B.C.), the basically straightforward Doric manner had become highly refined and sophisticated—as we know not only from careful study of the Parthenon's remains but from ancient theoretical treatises as well.

Classical Doric temples—named for the early Greeks known as Dorians—are distinguished from temples in the Ionic and Corinthian styles by their

2-20 *Kore,* c. 525 B.C. Marble, 22" high.
Acropolis Museum, Athens.

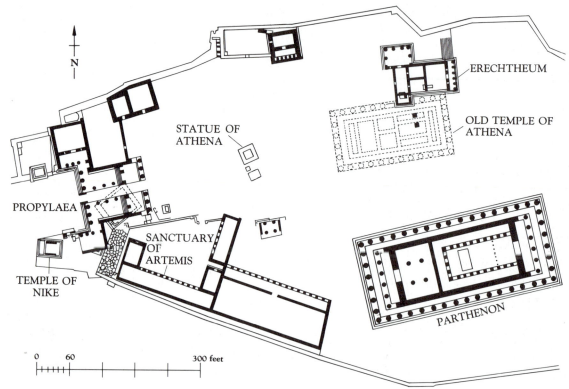

2-21   Plan of the Athens acropolis, c. 400 B.C.

general sturdiness, the unadorned square tops of the column capitals, and usually by a sculptured frieze in high relief, with panels alternately geometrical and pictorial, under the triangular pediments. (See figure 2-25.) The pictorial panels (*metopes*) of the Parthenon, just like the sculpture of the west pediment at Olympia, feature the legendary combat of Lapiths and centaurs. The iconography, or representational scheme, of the pedimental sculpture concerns the birth of Athena and her contest with Poseidon. Set within the recessed space at east and west ends of the temple, this pedimental sculpture (now largely removed to London) is monumental, although hardly as massive as the enormous cult statue of Athena by Phidias, which disappeared long ago but once faced the rising sun from the easternmost inner chamber. (The west end of the Parthenon, favored by photographers because of its better state of preservation, is actually the back of the temple.) The *cella*, or enclosed area surrounded by open rows of columns on four sides, was surmounted by

a continuous sculptured pictorial frieze in low relief. Some panels of this frieze long remained in place, but all now are in museums in Athens, London, and elsewhere.

Without mortar and, of course, without a steel skeleton, the Parthenon stood essentially intact until the seventeenth century, when a wartime explosion of gunpowder stored there ruined a large part of it. Basically the temple took a rather unadventurous form—a rectangular box with gabled roof. Its structural subtleties, however, were impressive. Based on mathematical calculations and carried out with refined workmanship, these subtleties included such features as the tapering of columns at the top (to accentuate the impression of height) and the outward bulging of columns somewhat above the base (to increase the appearance of sturdiness and vitality). Corner columns were thicker than the others, since otherwise they might have appeared a bit unsubstantial against the sky, and were spaced relatively closer to the next columns. The

2-22   Ictinus and Callicrates, the Parthenon, acropolis of Athens, 447–433 B.C.

floor was slightly mounded, sloping downward to the corners; and all columns inclined somewhat inward so that extensions of their axes tend to meet high in the sky. Although some practical considerations might have been involved, such as the drainage of rainwater from the sloping floor, it seems clear that the aim of much of this subtlety, especially the repeated substitution of curved for straight lines, must have been aesthetic. The Parthenon builders often deviated quite deliberately from the rigid correctness of the mathematical norm in order to achieve a more living, resilient structure.

Forms that were basically geometrical appealed to the Greek love of clarity, regularity, and pattern; and it is with these qualities that *classicism*, a stylistic rather than a historical term, has usually been associated. But the Greek variations upon these forms, balancing the coldness of mathematics with human warmth and liveliness, are even more significant. When we define stylistic classicism as the embodiment of formal pattern and proportion, we should always add that classicism at its best also implies the tempering of formalism by human considerations. In short, classicism is formalism humanized.

For the sculptural embellishment and completion of the Parthenon, Pericles commissioned the prestigious Phidias to create the massive statue of Athena and to supervise the whole sculptural program of the temple. In the second half of the fifth century B.C., as in earlier decades, sculpture sought to portray men and women and deities that looked like men and women. As before, it usually portrayed them as generalized and idealized, not as distinct and unique personalities; representation of fleeting changes in facial expression was almost as uncommon in sculpture as was the portrayal of physical idiosyncrasies. Various formal rules of bodily proportions were being proposed and applied, all of them straining toward the ideal rather than imitating the individually real. However, the trends toward humanization and flexibility continued, just as they

2-23 *Horsemen*, c. 442–438 B.C. Detail from the west frieze of the Parthenon, marble, 42″ high. Reproduced by Courtesy of the Trustees of the British Museum, London.

did in the architecture with which sculpture collaborated. All of these characteristics were exemplified in the sculptures of the Parthenon.

The frieze of the cella wall may be taken as typical. Here, in adjoining panels stretching to about 530 feet, was a lively, continuous scene of deities and mortals, idealized but with genuine human appeal. In modern times it has been commonly accepted that these panels were intended to represent the Athenians themselves, assembled in the Panathenaic procession that every four years would proceed from the lower city to the shrine of Athena Parthenos (the Virgin Athena) in order to present her with a new ceremonial gown. Another theory is that these panels might have commemorated the first Panathenaic festival, centuries earlier. Even if the second theory is correct, it remains likely that the Athenians of the late fifth century did see themselves, and their contemporary Panathenaic festivals, mirrored in this multitude of sculptured figures. Here, for example, were seen horsemen

curbing their spirited mounts to maintain the dignified processional pace (fig. 2-23). The marble panels were carved with uneven skill, but the best, including those with superimposed planes of horses and riders, have not been surpassed in the long history of pictorial relief sculpture.

A similar gracefulness is seen in the whole structure of the most sacred of other fifth-century monuments on the Athenian acropolis, the Erechtheum (fig. 2-24). This smaller building, housing an agglomeration of shrines, is not in the Doric style but the Ionic. The Ionic manner, of Near-Eastern origin, is distinguishable from the Doric primarily by its somewhat more decorative quality, its greater delicacy, and its relatively slender columns topped by scroll-like capitals (fig. 2-25). Construction of the Erechtheum, begun after Pericles' death and finished shortly before the fall of Athens at the hands of Sparta, had to incorporate several sacred spots, including the mark of Poseidon's trident in the rock and an ancient wooden

2-24   The Erechtheum, acropolis of Athens, c. 421–406 B.C.

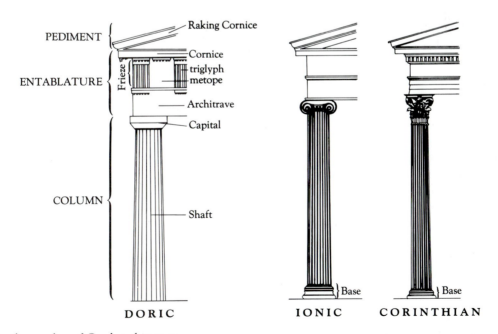

2-25   The three orders of Greek architecture.

2-26   Caryatid Porch, the Erechtheum.

statue of Athena that had escaped Persian destruction. The several rooms were at different levels and the four porches of different designs. As restored in the early twentieth century, the Erechtheum possesses for us the pleasant charm, unusual in individual Greek buildings, of a disorderly whole of orderly parts.

The most celebrated part of the Erechtheum is the Caryatid Porch (or Porch of the Maidens) at the southwest corner (fig. 2-26). Six sculpted figures of young women serve here as columns (all now are replicas) for supporting the porch's superstructure. We do not know the precise meaning of these gracefully draped figures, and perhaps we need go no further than the reference a Greco-Roman traveler made many centuries after their creation to "the maidens who bear on their heads what

the priestess of Athena gives them to carry." In any case, they are among the most popular and most ineptly imitated of Greek statues in the later Western world.

GREEK PHILOSOPHY, THROUGH SOCRATES

It was the ancient Greeks who invented philosophy for the European world. *Philosophy* is a sustained, persistent inquiry into the basic nature of human beings and the world around us. Primarily an intellectual pursuit, it does not involve the ritual and worship that usually characterize religion. Across the centuries philosophy has tended to emphasize the use of human reason, whereas religion has tended (with some notable exceptions) to emphasize faith, whether through following one's inner voice or the authority of others, or both. For many people in the Western world, philosophy has been a risky and exciting adventure, since it requires setting forth on one's own, equipped only with intellect and observation, to discover the basic principles of the universe and human life.

Philosophy may well offer, and usually does, a worldview that incorporates some sort of divine power. It is not necessarily opposed to religion; its approach to the great problems of life and death, of the natural and sometimes the supernatural, is simply different from that of religion. By and large, religion teaches principles authoritatively, while philosophy engages in intellectual discussion and persuasion.

The Earliest Greek Philosophers

Some of the earliest Greek philosophy did, almost of necessity, take on at least an implicit antireligious tinge. The early philosophers sought a more naturalistic explanation of how the world operates than offered by the traditional Greek religions. Instead of explaining natural events by spirits within them, or as the whims of deities Olympian or otherwise, such sixth-century philosophers as the Milesians (from the Greek city of Miletus in Asia Minor) tried to observe and reason in order to discover the most basic principle of the universe. One of them (Thales) decided that it was water, another (Anaximenes) that it was air, and still another (Anaximander) that it was "the boundless," which was nothing-in-particular. Others, a bit later, tackled the problem of whether it was change or permanence that most fundamentally characterizes the universe; Heraclitus, around the beginning of the fifth century B.C., thought it was change, whereas others thought it was permanence. (The latter view has been more prevalent in Western history; permanence and fixity are perhaps more satisfying to the human spirit than is a slippery change or flux.)

Some Greek thinkers of the archaic and classical periods addressed such basic questions as whether rational, abstract logic should prevail over common sense when their results were incompatible and whether it is mind and spirit or an unthinking material substance that forms the universe. Do people have free will, or is their whole being controlled by deterministic forces of some sort? Does the universe serve some divine or supernatural purpose, or is it something of a mess? Except to those whose answers are illumined by religious faith, most of these questions have remained arguable down to our own time.

Philosophy has not, however, been confined to questions of such great cosmic importance as these, and this was true already with the Greek thinkers. One of the most important and practical of philosophic concerns has always been *ethics*—speculation about how people as individuals or groups should relate to others and what standards of behavior are valid. The sixth-century Pythagoreans, for example, were interested in more than mathematical theory (they made many contributions to the understanding of the mathematical bases of musical sound); they also were a sort of exclusive brotherhood that followed specific rules of behavior. In Athens the Sophists of the later fifth century were greatly concerned with matters of *rhetoric*—expressive or persuasive speech—as well as with human behavior in the community. Protagoras, cited earlier for his belief in man as the measure of all things, was a Sophist. He believed that humans are variable and thus come to different conclusions on what is proper behavior and thought. To him, the best rule seemed to be to adapt and conform to the higher notions and practices of one's own time. In religion Protagoras was an agnostic: "As for the gods," he said, "I have no means of knowing whether they exist or not or what they are like. There are many obstacles to such knowledge—the obscurity of the subject and the shortness of human life."

Socrates

It was against this cheerful Sophist incertitude and the *relativism* that held that values are not fixed and absolute but related to different circumstances, that two of the most celebrated Greek philosophers reacted with special indignation. Neither Socrates (c. 470–399 B.C.) nor Plato always arrived at definite final answers to big questions, but both insisted that such answers do exist. Socrates (fig. 2-27), who left no written works to later ages, was a brilliant conversationalist and informal teacher. His views are known to us mainly through his pupil Plato's extensive writings, but they are seldom neatly disentangled from Plato's own opinions. Certain broad principles of the Socrates seen in Plato's works, however, have generally been agreed upon as authentic reflections of the older thinker's philosophy.

Above all, Socrates was a determined rationalist; he enjoyed rigorous thinking and debate, and initiated many eager young Athenian men into the pleasures of the mind. The pursuit of truth, he believed, was usually best served by a *dialectical* approach—a logical question-and-answer method in which inadequate notions would be exposed and replaced by deeper insight. Human potentialities, he believed, would reach their highest fulfillment through exercise of the intellect. Above all, the mind should concern itself with rational analysis and self-examination. "The unexamined life," he asserted, "is not worth living." At the same time that he emphasized self-development in this earthly life, however, he insisted that the mind, or soul, should struggle against the body that imprisons it. Absolute truth, he continued, can be attained only in an afterlife when the soul is free of the body and its selfish urges and desires.

For decades Socrates talked and taught in Athens, and made enemies. In his own words, as reported by Plato, he became a "gadfly" to the Athenians, questioning their opinions and beliefs, "arousing and persuading and reproaching" them. Although he gained many enthusiastic followers, his way was no route to popularity with the Athenian majority. Finally, in the bitter years after Athens' defeat at the hands of Sparta, Socrates was accused and brought to trial for subversion of the good old Athenian ways of life and belief—a very rare exception to the usual Athenian tolerance of diversity. He was judged guilty—in a memorable trial reported, probably accurately, by Plato in *The Apology*—and condemned to die by taking poison.

2-27 *Socrates;* 2nd century A.D. Roman copy of an original probably by Lysippus, 4th century B.C. Marble, 10¾″ high. Reproduced by Courtesy of the Trustees of the British Museum, London.

During his final days in prison, as recorded especially in Plato's *Crito* and *Phaedo,* he continued his philosophical discussions with visiting friends and disciples and firmly refused to permit them to bribe the authorities into letting him escape: he would die, he said, as he had lived, by Athenian law. And so at last, as Plato has Socrates' disciple Phaedo say, died the man "that of all men of his time whom I have known, . . . was the wisest and justest and best."

THE FOURTH CENTURY

Many historians include most of the fourth century within the period of classical Greece. For our purposes in this book, we consider the death of Alexander the Great in 323 B.C. as the symbolic division between late classical Greece and the Hellenistic, or late Greek, age. The years from 400 to 323 were a time of transition, but they were also a period with its own brilliance. The visual arts of the century produced some of classicism's most famous sculpture, and philosophy saw the mature thought of Plato and Aristotle, the two writers who contributed perhaps the most imposing philosophical achievements of Western civilization.

Plato (fig. 2-28), who lived from 429 to 347 B.C., followed Socrates in emphasizing the opposition of body and soul and the search for the ideal models on which all desirable earthly things and qualities are based. These models, existing in a realm beyond the human senses, Plato said, are unchanging and eternal; they are absolutes that all earthly phenomena should attempt to approximate. Human beings, for example, should strive to rise as near as possible to the absolute ideal of humanity, and earthly wisdom and beauty should seek to achieve the perfection of ultimate wisdom and beauty.

Plato admitted that the realm of absolute ideals was extraordinarily difficult both to define and to imitate. He demonstrated this difficulty through a vivid *allegory* (an extended narrative analogy), his famous Allegory of the Cave. We must imagine, he wrote, a cave in which human beings have been chained as prisoners since childhood so that they cannot move or turn their heads. "Above and behind them a fire is blazing at a distance, and between the fire and the prisoners there is a raised way," along which men pass and statues stand. The prisoners see on the wall facing them only shadows of these moving or stationary be-

2-28 *Plato.* Roman copy (?) of a Hellenistic original. Marble, head is 13½″ high. Vatican Museums, Rome.

ings. They have given names to these shadows, which they have taken as real, never realizing their origin.

But, Plato continued, we should then visualize the release of these prisoners after many years, and their reactions as they turn backward toward the real objects that cast the shadows. Although now they see a brighter reality, they find this reality blinding, and they resist recognizing that all they have seen before—the shadows—were illusions. If the prisoners are dragged out of the cave into the sunlight, their eyes will be dazzled and they will not be able at first to see any of the real world now stretched out before them. Only after a difficult time of adjustment will the former prisoners fully realize that illusion has been replaced by reality.

This real world, said Plato, corresponds to the realm of absolutes, which are the truest realities of all.

Not all men are released from their chains of illusion—or, once released, they may even flee back to the easier, familiar illusions of their upbringing. In fact, however, only the world of broad daylight is the world of true reality. Only those who can see the true realities, and above all the highest reality of the Good, should teach and rule mankind. Plato, in fact, made his ideal of a benevolent dictatorship of the truly enlightened the focus of his political theory.

Plato was not always lost in a transcendent world of ideal models or, as he called them, "ideas"—that is, not concepts in human minds but the truest, firmest, most absolute realities of all. He realized that one must also cope with the everyday world of human life. Even here, even for ordinary people, he insisted on the need to have some glimmer of knowledge of ideal truth, beauty, and wisdom—or at the very least a willingness to follow the guidance of those who truly "know." Only knowledge can lead to virtue; if one truly, not casually or partially, knows what is virtuous, he or she cannot do wrong. With this basic principle firmly in mind, the Socrates of Plato's dialogues (for Socrates is Plato's usual spokesman, conversing and arguing with others) goes on to discuss a broad range of human life, including such predominantly earthly concerns as love and friendship, temperance and justice, humaneness and virtue, and the nature of the ideal state, or republic. In all of this, Plato does not usually develop his thought as part of a whole system, but throws out a multitude of suggestions, almost at random. Later in the fourth century B.C. Aristotle would come forth with a more comprehensive, integrated philosophical system.

Fourth-Century Art

Sculpture, the most distinctive art form of the fourth century B.C., saw a continuation of high classical trends—more suppleness of human figures, more detail, and in general more naturalism. The human body was still idealized to some extent, but more and more individualized realism was introduced. The art of portrait sculpture became increasingly popular, as witnessed in the sculpted faces of Socrates and Plato shown in figures 2-27 and 2-28. Unlike Plato, Socrates was notoriously not a handsome man, and his early portraitists, and later copiers, seem to have delighted in his unconventional looks.

Large sculptures of gods and goddesses had the same idealized features and bodies of an earlier age but incorporated new details and sometimes more adventurous bodily postures. Among the finest examples of such work are the large bronze statue of Athena recently discovered at Piraeus and the long-familiar *Hermes of Praxiteles*. The *Piraeus Athena* (fig. 2-29) does not have the rather formal stance of early and high classical statues and is much more graceful and reassuring. Although this Athena wears the traditional helmet, she is less a warrior than an agreeable maternal figure. This effect, to be sure, is unfairly exaggerated by the loss of the shield and balanced spear for which a lead attachment exists in her left hand. The extended right hand once held some small object, perhaps the owl sacred to Athena. Her sash is a rather prettified, domesticated reminiscence of the Medusa story—the

2-30   *Hermes of Praxiteles,* c. 350–340 B.C., or a Hellenistic copy, perhaps 1st century B.C. Marble, 7′1″ high. Museum, Olympia.

2-29   *Piraeus Athena,* c. 350 B.C. Bronze, 7′8½″ high. Museum, Piraeus, Greece.

slaying by the hero Perseus of the monstrous Gorgon with hair of writhing snakes. The drapery falls easily and naturalistically. Unfortunately, the sculptor of this masterful work is unknown.

The *Hermes of Praxiteles* (fig. 2-30) is a justly renowned marble work found in 1877 in the ruins of the

Temple of Hera at Olympia. It depicts Hermes, god of travelers, supporting the baby Dionysus on his arm, which he is resting on a tree trunk. The elder god's missing right hand once held a bunch of grapes, toward which the small Dionysus, the god of wine, is reaching. Some recent scholars have argued that the statue is not an original by the famous sculptor Praxiteles, but a copy from three centuries later. If so, it is an excellent, subtle copy. The figure of Hermes is fully relaxed and graceful, although the god does not concentrate upon the infant's gesture but seems lost in thought. The work represents Greek humanized idealism at its best.

As an example of Greek painting of the fourth century, we use a work that is definitely a copy, and it may not be a precise copy. We know that much large-scale painting was done by classical Greek artists and that many paintings were well known in their day, but no first-rate examples exist except for some sketchy

though charming tomb paintings in Greek-settled Italy. Most historians accept several well-preserved Roman wall paintings of the first century A.D. as the best available evidence of what large fourth-century Greek wall paintings looked like. In the painting illustrated in figure 2-31, Perseus, still carrying the severed head of Medusa, is rescuing the princess Andromeda from the dragon that guarded her. Following the style of the time, the faces are impassive and the male's body is markedly darker than the female's, but the bodies suggest real solidity. The style of *Perseus Freeing Andromeda* is far removed from the almost exclusively linear art of traditional Greek vase painting.

Aristotle and the Greek Ideal

A final peak in the record of fourth-century Greek intellectual achievement was the imposing system of thought developed by Aristotle (384–322 B.C., fig. 2-32), whose school in Athens, the Lyceum, came to rival Plato's Academy. In many ways Aristotle's thought contrasts with Plato's: Aristotle was much more systematic than Plato, and his works lack the spontaneity and charm of the on-going play of ideas that enliven the Platonic dialogues. Yet Aristotle never repudiated the whole body of Platonic thought; in fact, he retained many of its elements. Above all, both thinkers were seeking a viable way of human life and a sound theoretical justification for that way. In the process, both repudiated Sophism, which had upheld the importance of the technical knowledge related to a particular society. In the view of both philosophers, extreme relativism would undermine all individual and social values.

Much of Plato's philosophy had stemmed from, and been supported by, his doctrine of "ideas"— transcendent, absolute ideals. Aristotle hesitated to break completely with this doctrine, but usually found it simply irrelevant, given the extreme difficulty (as Plato himself had admitted) of contacting such "ideas" as absolute beauty, justice, and virtue. Inevitably Aristotle's ignoring of Platonic "ideas" affected nearly all branches of his thought. Ethics, for example, could not be based upon the quest for the "idea" of virtue or goodness. Aristotle thought it much more to the point to turn to the experience of the senses and indeed to common sense. Thereafter moral excellence would be the result of habit or custom inculcated in the young by

2-31 *Perseus Freeing Andromeda;* 1st century A.D. Roman copy of a 4th-century Greek original, possibly by Nycias. Wall painting, 47¼″ × 38½″.

2-32 *Aristotle.* Roman copy of a late-4th-century original. Marble, 11½″ high. Kunsthistorisches Museum, Vienna.

substantially developed the science of logic as well as virtually every other science known to his day. He contributed (not always correctly in the light of today's knowledge, of course) to physics and especially to botany and zoology. When writing on political theory he was much less absolutist and authoritarian than Plato: Aristotle proposed a middle-class regime within the framework of the traditional city-states of the Greek world that he knew. Aristotle also contributed significantly to aesthetic theory, mainly in his analysis of the Greek tragic theater.

In effect, for Aristotle the universe and all of human life formed a cosmos, an orderly whole of interrelated parts. His philosophical system is one of the most ambitious syntheses of human knowledge and aspirations that Western civilization has developed. While not repudiating the existence of divine purpose, his system regarded the world and human life as comprehensible and human goals as achievable. Aristotelian thought contained such a richness of fertile suggestions that future ages would turn to it again and again for guidance as well as justification for their own concepts and beliefs.

The classical Greeks have been among the most admired of Western peoples, although sometimes idealized and idolized to the point of caricature. One of the greatest glories of ancient Greece is that so much of its record has seemed pertinent to its heirs. However limited their range, Greek achievements have been recognized remarkably often as the best of their kind—the very symbol of high aims and preeminent achievement.

To be sure, much in the cultural ideal of the Greeks seems confiningly static and finite to a restless modern world. Even in their arts, so glowingly praised over the centuries, the Greek expressive range can seem startlingly limited. Still, the Greeks gave us not only a goodly number of brilliant monuments to human greatness but many of our most provocative seminal ideas and goals. However inadequate or perverse these goals have sometimes been judged, it is scarcely possible to overrate their significance to the developing Western civilization. Humanism and secularism; rationalism and idealism; peculiar sensitivities to beauty, the wholeness of things, and human and social responsibility—with such qualities and goals as these, ancient Greece earned its grip on the Western imagination.

patient training. In most respects a moral life for Aristotle was thus an exercise in moderation, the avoidance of extremes. Human reason, too, entered Aristotle's picture of the mature, confident, humane individual—the standard being the reasoning ability of "the prudent man."

Aristotelian philosophy would appear in many respects to be more earthbound, more secular, than Plato's; it seemed closer to everyday life. This does not mean, however, that Aristotle was a materialist—one who sees only matter, not mind or spirit, in the world. On the contrary, he saw a sort of overriding divine purpose pervading all that happened in the universe. Nor did Aristotle's emphasis on common sense make him reject rationalism—pure thought—for either himself or others. He thought long and hard, and he

Recommended Reading

Andrewes, Antony. *The Greeks* (1967). Good social, economic, and governmental analysis.

Baldry, H. C. *The Greek Tragic Theatre* (1971). Historical overview, especially of theaters and performances.

Boardman, John. *Greek Art* (1985). Fine introduction, good illustrations.

Boardman, John, et al. *Greek Art and Architecture* (1967). Massive, authoritative, lavishly illustrated.

Boardman, John. *The Parthenon and Its Sculptures* (1985). Short, readable text with fine photographic record.

Bonnard, André. *Greek Civilization*, vols. 1 and 2 (1957, 1959). Fine introduction to literary and social history.

Charbonneaux, Jean, et al. *Classical Greek Art, 480–330 B.C.* (1973). Handsome, comprehensive study.

Drees, Ludwig. *Olympia: Gods, Artists, and Athletes* (1968). Fascinating description of the site and the Olympic games.

Fine, John V. A. *The Ancient Greeks: A Critical History* (1983). Solid, up-to-date text, largely political.

Guthrie, W. K. C. *The Greek Philosophers from Thales to Aristotle* (1960). Brief survey of Greek thought.

Hale, William H., ed. *The Horizon Book of Ancient Greece* (1965). Beautifully illustrated survey of history, visual art, and literature.

Herodotus. *The Histories*, trans. by Aubrey de Sélincourt (1954). The fascinating work complete.

Hooper, Finley. *Greek Realities: Life and Thought in Ancient Greece* (1967). Readable political-cultural history; well illustrated.

Lefkowitz, Mary R., and Maureen B. Fant. *Women's Life in Greece and Rome* (1982). Collection of primary sources.

Liberman, Alexander. *Greece, Gods and Art* (1968). Description of principal deities and art sites with handsome photographs.

Melchinger, Siegfried. *Euripides* (1973). Introduction to the playwright and the plays.

Thucydides. *The Peloponnesian War*, trans. by Crawley, rev. by T. E. Wick (1982). The most important accurate Greek history.

Webster, T. B. L. *Athenian Culture and Society* (1973). Comprehensive social history.

Webster, T. B. L. *Life in Classical Athens* (1978). Good introduction.

3

The Hellenistic World: 323–31 B.C.

Although the peoples of Macedonia, a country to the north of the old mainland-Greek city-states, were related to the Greeks, the civilized Greeks regarded the Macedonians as barbarous. Under the leadership of two vigorous kings, Philip II and Alexander III (Alexander the Great, ruled 336–323 B.C.), Macedonia's military strength made it the dominant power of the entire eastern Mediterranean area from Greece to Egypt and eastward as far as India. This realm, with many fluctuations in its borders over three centuries, was the Hellenistic, or late Greek, world—a Greek civilization superimposed on diverse native cultures. Partly because of the teaching of his tutor Aristotle, Alexander had absorbed many Greek attitudes and remained an admirer of the classical Greek ideals. The effective spearhead of Hellenization was Alexander's establishment of thirty or more new cities, largely Greek in language and culture. Egypt's Alexandria, a new port-city in the delta area, was the largest and most splendid of these cities.

By the early third century B.C. the Hellenistic world was fairly well stabilized into three kingdoms, each allowing its major cities some autonomy and even certain Greek-inspired democratic forms, but firmly controlled by dynastic monarchs descended from Alexander's most successful generals. In Egypt the Ptolemies ruled, beginning with Ptolemy I, until the defeat of the famous queen Cleopatra and her Roman patron Mark Antony by the Romans in 31 B.C. Antigonus I founded the Antigonid dynasty in Macedonia, which overshadowed the whole of mainland Greece but permitted a substantial degree of self-government to such city-states as Athens; many of these city-states were federated in several leagues, or alliances. In the second century B.C. this area was gradually absorbed by Rome.

The vast, partially Hellenized areas in Asia were controlled for a time by Seleucus I, becoming the variegated Seleucid kingdom. By 280 B.C. Antiochus I, with a new capital at Antioch, was the sole monarch. Thereafter the kingdom had mixed fortunes, but the general tendency was toward disintegration. In Asia Minor, near the site of ancient Troy, Pergamum became the brilliant capital of a prosperous independent state under Eumenes I. The Pergamene king Attalus I (ruled 241–197 B.C.) gave his name to the Attalid kingdom, pushed back encroachments by the barbarian Gauls, and allied himself with Rome. His son, Eumenes II (197–159 B.C.), made the kingdom the strongest in Asia Minor. When the dynasty died out in 133 B.C., the Pergamene kingdom was willed to Rome.

Hellenistic culture was almost wholly a Greek phenomenon. Some of the dominated peoples gained access to the ruling and cultured elite, but only by first transforming themselves into Greeks through education, language, and custom. Within the Greek ruling class and the network of largely Greek cities there existed a common Greek language, the *koinē*, which replaced the dialects of earlier Greece. This allowed Greek and Hellenized individuals to travel and be accepted readily, even in distant Hellenistic lands. Cosmopolitanism—the sense of being a citizen of the world—was strong, but only within the magic circle of a privileged social and cultural class.

The Hellenistic master-class was created and perpetuated not only by military power, a common culture, and the traditional Greek attitude of condescension toward barbarians, but also by the economic prosperity of the Hellenistic world. Manual labor, to be sure, was still looked down upon, and slave labor continued to be considered essential by most of the ruling class. Mass markets and mass production of useful goods for the expanding upper and middle classes exceeded anything seen in the old Greek city-states. Large bureaucracies—bodies of specialized governmental officials—arose at royal and other administrative centers, with the more important ranks being occupied exclusively by men of wealth. Although the privilege of holding high office was effectively limited to the wealthy, the wealthy were also expected to contribute heavily to such public causes as education, sports, and the embellishment of cities. Public and private affluence greatly surpassed the modest scale of private living known in the city-states of classical Greece.

THE OLD AND THE NEW

Alexander the Great (fig. 3-1) was a leader of vast ambition and grandiose vision. Some evidence exists that his vision was not only military and territorial but also broadly cultural and humanitarian; it is quite possible that Alexander did dream of a true equality and unification of peoples

3-1 *Alexander in Battle Mounted on Bucephalus,* 2nd or 1st century B.C. (probably from a 4th-century original by Lysippus). Bronze statuette. Museo Nazionale, Naples.

CHRONOLOGY

HISTORY		THE ARTS	
336–323	Alexander the Great		
331	founding of Alexandria		
323–283	Ptolemy I controls Egypt		
		c. 322 or later	Zeno inaugurates the Stoic school in Athens
		321–292	comedies of Menander, Athens
313	beginnings of Seleucid realm		
306–304	Ptolemy, Antigonus, and Seleucus adopt title of king	c. 306	Epicurus founds school, Athens
		c. 300	Ptolemy I founds museum and library, Alexandria; *Elements* of Euclid; Tanagra statuettes; *Stag Hunt* mosaic, Pella
283–261	Ptolemy II, Egypt		
281	Seleucus assassinated		
280–261	Antiochus I, Seleucid kingdom		
263–241	Eumenes I of Pergamum, beginning of the building program	c. 270	poems of Theocritus
		246	Eratosthenes becomes head of the library at Alexandria
241–197	Attalus I, Pergamum		
238–227	wars of Attalus I against the Gauls (Galatians)		
		c. 220	victory monuments of Attalus I
		c. 210–200	*Marsyas* and *Scythian Slave* statues
209	Attalus I allied with Rome	c. 200–c. 118	Polybius, historian
197–159	Eumenes II, Pergamum		
183	Gauls crushed by Eumenes II	180–160	Altar of Zeus, Pergamum
		174	Construction begun on Temple of Olympian Zeus, Athens
167	Macedon conquered by Rome		
159–138	Attalus II, Pergamum		
		c. 150	stoa of Attalus II, Athens
148	Macedonia made a Roman province		
146	Carthage destroyed by Rome; end of Greek independence		
142	independence of the Jews		
133	Pergamum passes to Rome by the will of Attalus III		
129	Pergamum becomes the Roman province of Asia		
		c. 100	hollow-cast bronze portrait head from Delos
50–30	Cleopatra VII, Egypt		
43	Octavian in control, Rome		
31	Mark Antony and Cleopatra defeated by Octavian at Actium		
30	suicide of Antony and Cleopatra; Egypt incorporated into Rome		

All dates are B.C.

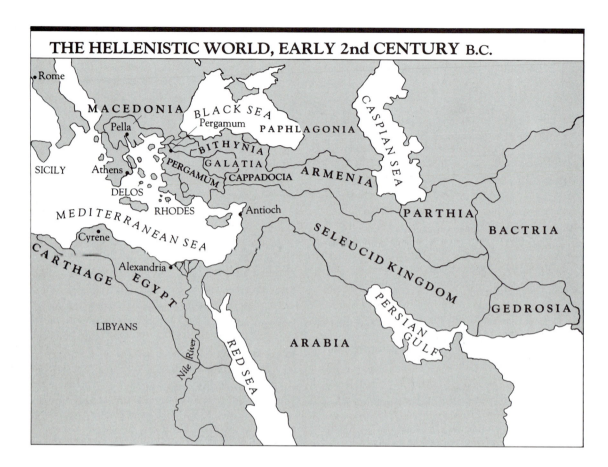

THE HELLENISTIC WORLD, EARLY 2nd CENTURY B.C.

throughout the known world. If so, any such hopes were quickly watered down in the "successor kingdoms" by the more restricted goal of superimposing a wholly Greek ruling-class culture upon varied native populations. In other respects Alexander foreshadowed more accurately the Hellenistic reality; for example, he was determined to be an unquestioned autocratic ruler, but he quietly permitted certain old political forms to exist and power to be judiciously delegated. He wished to be honored as a god by his subjects and he inaugurated policies of colonization and commercial expansion. Although the territorial integrity of his realm was not maintained after his death, the independent successor kingdoms followed the same patterns of autocracy, ruler-worship, and economic growth.

Great cultural differences remained within the Hellenistic world, however, and not only among the native peoples with their traditional institutions and customs that often were wisely left undisturbed. Further differences arose from the psychological and spiritual distance that separated such new cities as Alexan-

dria and Pergamum from the old Greek city-states of the mainland and the Aegean islands. To a large extent all the cities shared in the Hellenistic prosperity, but the newer centers were generally much more dynamic and adventurous than the older states, which tended toward cultural conservatism. Athens above all remained a proud conservator of the old Greek traditions in arts and letters, and it was always accorded full cultural honors by those Greeks in Asia and Africa who were pioneering in new modes of expression. Athens and the other old cultural centers did not, however, stagnate or become fossilized in creative expression. Artistic, philosophical, and literary creativity continued to bloom there, but within more or less traditional forms.

Hellenistic Athens

In Athens the glories of the classical age were scarcely dimmed by the city's political submission to the Antigonid kingdom of Macedonia. The acropolis temples and statues still glittered as they had in the all-too-brief days of late-fifth-century Athenian independence and political prestige, and the Panathenaic festivals were still celebrated regularly in honor of Athena. Travelers streamed into the city from the Hellenistic East and even from Rome to the west—and all of them, we are told, were stirred by the Athenian past and impressed by the city's continuing cultural activity. At the same time the city was undergoing some major physical changes: Hellenistic cities abroad, such as Pergamum, were sending samples of their progressive sculpture and were sponsoring such new construction as an extensive new *stoa* (portico or open porch) in the Athenian marketplace. Attalus II of Pergamum (159–138 B.C.) had studied in Athens as a youth and was eager to leave his mark on the city he had learned to venerate.

Work also was beginning on what was expected to be the grandest Athenian temple of all, the Temple of the Olympian Zeus; the Roman emperor Hadrian would finally complete it in the second century A.D. Today only fragments of the temple remain, but they are imposing, majestic remnants indeed (fig. 3-2). Around the temple was a double row of Corinthian columns—that is, columns in the third great style or "order" of classical Greek architecture. This newer order, which had evolved in the fifth century, is contrasted with the earlier Doric and Ionic orders in figure 2-25. The Corinthian order is more similar to the Ionic than to the Doric but is more slender and somewhat more decorative. The column capital offers a stylized, elegant version of leaves from the acanthus plant, as against the square-and-round Doric capital and the scroll-like Ionic. The Corinthian style became especially popular in the fourth-century and Hellenistic periods and, just as with the Doric and Ionic orders, its appeal has continued into the modern Western world.

Athens, however, was less renowned in the Hellenistic age for its visual art and architecture than for its philosophical activity. As far as philosophy was concerned, Athens was still—as Pericles had asserted—the school of Greece, even though many of the philosophers active in the city had come there from other Greek lands to gain recognition and set up schools. We will discuss several of the newer schools later in the chapter. For the moment, only the continuance of the

schools of Plato and Aristotle need be mentioned. Plato's Academy still existed, carrying on the tradition of Socrates and Plato rather timidly and unadventurously. Aristotle's Lyceum flourished, enjoying the opportunity to specialize in any of the many interests of the master, from biology and physics to logic and poetry. Aristotle's followers were called the *Peripatetics* ("walkers"), reflecting the traditional walking in the Lyceum, which was in fact a covered walkway. As they walked, of course, they talked and discussed. The life of the mind was still alive and well.

Also alive and well was the theater in Athens. Professional actors, all male, were the norm, and they often presented classic tragedies like those of Sophocles and Euripides. Many other actors traveled widely throughout the Hellenistic kingdoms, for all Hellenized cities had their hillside theaters similar to those of Athens and Epidaurus.

If classical Greek tragedy was familiar to all educated persons in the Hellenistic orbit, the classical comedy of Aristophanes had fared less well. This "Old Comedy" from around 400 B.C. was too specifically topical and political to have much popular appeal a hundred years later. So it was that Hellenistic Athens saw the rise of the "New Comedy." In an age when

3-2 Temple of the Olympian Zeus, Athens. Construction begun 174 B.C.

political power was virtually monopolized by men of wealth in Athens and elsewhere, political satire was not as enjoyable, or perhaps as relevant, as it had been in a more open, democratic age. The Athenian New Comedy turned instead to family problems and domestic misadventures such as those in the plays of Menander (c. 342–292 B.C.).

Menander became the amused and amusing chronicler of the weaknesses, follies, pleasures, and misunderstandings of families and individuals. Marital infidelity was a staple of his comedy, as were disguises, unidentified or misidentified children, and happy reconciliations. To a very considerable extent, Menander realistically portrayed everyday life—ordinary middle-class people in all their ordinary confusions and problems. He retained, however, the use of performers' masks and choruses, although his choruses were confined to interludes between acts. Many of his characters were types—the sly, ingenious servant or slave, the greedy businessman, the wayward husband, but the types were often treated with much subtlety. Menander's characters show both the individuality of specific personalities and circumstances and—reflecting the urban Hellenistic cosmopolitanism of the day—the universality of the human condition. "We live," Menander concluded, "not as we will, but as we can."

Alexandria and the New Spirit

Located near one of the mouths of the Nile, Alexandria was founded by Alexander himself in 331 B.C. and rapidly became the most populous city in the Mediterranean world. Almost nothing of the physical city remains today, since most of it has subsided into the sea and other sections have been destroyed to make way for new construction in more recent times. In the third century B.C. it was a very busy port-city, for it had two superb harbors. A most extraordinary lighthouse on Pharos island just north of Alexandria harbor came to be regarded as one of the wonders of the ancient world—it stood from 279 B.C. until the fourteenth century A.D. The light, fueled by wood fires, could be seen from thirty miles out to sea, and the structure had a steam-powered siren or foghorn for warnings during bad weather.

Alexandria was laid out and built according to comprehensive, all-new plans. Such town planning had been all but impossible in archaic and classical times. Unencumbered by pre-existing structures, the streets of the new city were laid out in a grid network, with perhaps ten of them as very broad boulevards. Five separate quarters provided housing for different segments of the population—for example, a royal palace for the ruler and the countless officials, a native Egyptian quarter, and a Jewish quarter. Half-a-million people—perhaps even a million—lived in the city and its luxurious suburbs.

The population of Alexandria was notoriously pleasure-loving, and the affluent element (mainly Greeks) was well known for high living. A fitting reflection of Alexandrian hedonism (the philosophy and life of seeking pleasure) was the Greek goddess Aphrodite—the symbol, together with the winged boy Eros, of love and enjoyment. All classical Greek hesitancies concerning sensuous female nudity in sculpture were discarded, as seen in the celebrated Aphrodite (fig. 3-3) that originated in another north-African Greek city, Cyrene.

Alexandria was a lively place not only because it was a capital with a vast bureaucracy, but even more because of the bustling commercial life of the city. As Egypt's one great port, its export and import business was extensive. As a transit port, it reshipped goods from the distant African interior (gold, ivory, wild animals, black slaves) and from India (silks, spices, and perfumes). It must be remembered, however, that, although many different peoples rubbed elbows in this cosmopolitan trading center, only Greeks were citizens.

The great public structures of the city were mainly Greek-inspired. They included the magnificent funerary monument for the embalmed body of Alexander, the royal palace, and the temple precinct of the recently adopted god Sarapis. The heart of the city was the immense gymnasium and playing fields where Greek education and ideals were perpetuated until the definitive triumph of Christianity in the late fourth century A.D. Even more important to later ages were Alexandria's museum and library. The library housed many hundreds of thousands of manuscripts in scroll form, since bound books were not as yet known. Under the patronage of the Ptolemies, scholarship and antiquarianism—the study of past arts and letters for their antiquity's sake—flourished at both of these institutions. Aristotle, with his immense range of interests, had founded Western scholarship and had encouraged scientific and poetic analysis and criticism. The schol-

3-3 *Aphrodite of Cyrene,* late Hellenistic period. Marble, 4′8¼″ high. Terme Museum, Rome.

ars of Alexandria applied the Aristotelian critical ideals, producing lengthy studies and catalogues not only of ancient Greek poetry beginning with Homer, but also of science, visual art, and history.

It would by no means be fair to Alexandrian culture to view it as simply a critic and preserver of the past. In any case, its great scholarly collections have long since disappeared—a profound loss to modern historical and literary scholarship. Alexandria's more original contributions to culture also were impressive: they fall mainly within the three categories of historical writing, science, and poetry.

Polybius (c. 200–c. 118 B.C.), the greatest historian of the Hellenistic age, visited Alexandria only briefly. He spent most of his life in mainland Greece, but he also served time as a prisoner of war in Rome and later in his life traveled throughout the Mediterra-

nean area. Although he wrote in Greek, Polybius found his main inspiration in the history of Rome, the military giant that was overrunning the Hellenistic world of his day. Polybius, like Herodotus, praised personal investigation as "the very cornerstone of history," and more historical documents were available to him than had been available to Herodotus. He was particularly interested in governmental forms and historical causation, and he discussed these subjects repeatedly in his histories of Rome from the third century B.C. through the Roman victory over the strong north-African state of Carthage in 146 B.C. Generally he dismissed causation by supernatural intervention and wrote of the very natural, this-worldly progression and decay of governments, their wars, and their political fortunes. Although his focus was Rome, Polybius tried to write a universal history, since he believed causes and effects to be broadly interrelated over the whole known world.

Science was even more significantly developed than historical writing in the Hellenistic age and was more closely associated with Alexandria. Scientific studies no longer fell within the general province of philosophy and most often were connected with the practice of engineering and medicine. Much of the scientific research was sponsored by kings such as the Ptolemies and the Pergamene Attalids. The astronomical relationships of the sun, the fixed stars, and the earth were investigated. Aristarchus of Samos, for example, declared that the sun, not the earth, is the center of the universe. He also measured the sun and its distance from the earth. Another astronomer, Hipparchus, calculated with remarkable accuracy the circumference of the earth. Geometry was advanced in Euclid's systematic *Elements.* Great advances were also made in geography, medicine, and human anatomy during this age. Dissection of bodies was practiced in Alexandria, and simple surgeries were performed (often using opium as an anesthetic). There even existed a public physician in that city and others, and apparently some sort of state medical care was available, at least in Alexandria.

Sometimes Hellenistic science was allied with technology. Technological invention, however, was limited, and it was never applied in industry. (A true industrial revolution, with machines powered mechanically, would not be seen until the eighteenth and nineteenth centuries A.D.) The widespread availability of cheap labor, including slaves, is probably the princi-

3-4 *The Attack of the Laestrygonians.* Roman wall painting from a Hellenistic original of c. 150 B.C. 4′11″ high. Vatican Museums.

pal reason. Hellenistic conservatism in financial investment may also have contributed, not to mention the absence of effective experimental and testing devices. In the Hellenistic age, technology advanced almost exclusively in military engineering, where the kings, with their large-scale military operations, saw possible practical benefits.

In the much less practical area of poetry, the Hellenistic rulers sponsored efforts that presumably would have arisen from individual creativity anyway. The poet Theocritus (c. 315–c. 250 B.C.), born in Sicily, came to Alexandria to seek the patronage of the Ptolemies and became one of the brightest lights in a luminous age of Alexandrian verse. He is best remembered for his idylls. An *idyll*, or "little picture" is a simple descriptive work of poetry (or prose), theoretically on any subject but usually describing a scene of nature or love. It was probably no coincidence that the Hellenistic age, with its large, noisy cities, welcomed so eagerly these idyllic poems that took the reader into a bucolic countryside or the private recesses of the heart.

Theocritus's eleventh idyll is loosely based on the Homeric story of the cyclops Polyphemus, the one-eyed monster; he gracefully turned this rough, quite alarming Homeric story into a tale of love. His seventh idyll concerns a harvest festival with mythological references. Spring poplars and elm trees in a green "shadowy glade" form the setting—a reminder that people of the Hellenistic age, unlike the classical Greeks, were much attracted to nature and the landscape. A Roman wall painting copied from a Hellenistic original of the second century B.C. (fig. 3-4) gives an impression of the imagined late-Greek landscape, in which human figures are dwarfed by trees, rocks, and mountains. A battle from Homer's story of Odysseus is portrayed at the right, while at the left are a shepherd and a nymph, and sheep that are sleeping or drinking from a pond. In the background we glimpse a goatherd with his flock.

Still another Theocritan idyll, the first, invokes a confusion of natural processes in a cry of anguish over the death of Daphnis. All of nature has been turned upside down by the death of this handsome Sicilian shepherd of Greek legend:

> Now violets bear, ye brambles,
> Ye thorns bear violets;
> And let fair narcissus bloom
> On the boughs of juniper!
> Let all things with all be confounded:
> From pines let men gather pears,
> For Daphnis is dying!
> Let the stag drag down the hound,
> Let owls from the hills
> Contend in song with the nightingales.

These deliberately contorted images of nature reveal a poetic sensitivity to both the reality of nature and poetic fantasy.

HELLENISTIC SOCIETY

Religion was one of the few areas of Hellenistic life in which cultural exchange did take place between Greek and indigenous civilizations. Very often, but not always, this was a melding of Greek rationalism and oriental *mysticism*—the emotional expansion that comes from presumed direct contact with the divine. One obvious problem with any neat contrast between rationalism and mysticism was noted in chapter 2—the existence of the Dionysian cult at the very heart of classical Greek culture. Despite this, it is true that the religious tolerance of classical and Hellenistic Greeks facilitated the absorption of Oriental cults.

Other cults, like the cult of Sarapis in Egypt, a majestic yet healing god, were deliberately manufactured to bring together deities and supernatural functions from two or more cultures. In the case of Sarapis a Zeus-like figure was combined with emblems and attributes of both Greek and Egyptian deities. The new god did not catch on with the Egyptians but was immensely successful among the Greeks and Romans. For the Greeks, the new god's receptivity to individual emotional needs partly compensated for the sense of rootlessness that many Hellenistic men and women must have felt when surrounded by alien cultures. The customary deification of Hellenistic kings did not serve the individual, personal needs of ordinary Greeks, but it did serve the political necessities of the kings themselves, who were striving to establish unquestionable authority over mixed peoples.

Education and Music

Education was a vital tool for instituting and maintaining Greek culture in the Hellenistic world. The educational process for boys and young men was normally comprised in three stages. Boys from seven to fourteen attended private schools (their parents paid the tuition), where they were taught reading, writing, athletics, music, and sometimes painting. In secondary schools, which were publicly supported, youths of fourteen to seventeen or eighteen received a predominantly literary education, with books surpassing physical culture in importance. Elements of mathematics and science were occasionally taught, and Greek civic and ethical ideals were always inculcated at this stage. As in classical Greece, the gymnasium was the usual setting of general secondary schooling. At least for the elite among the young men, education might continue at the gymnasium for another two years, mainly in athletics, civic concerns, and sometimes military training and philosophy.

The physical sports that pervaded all of the schooling continued to be played in the nude, as they had been in earlier Greek times. This practice applied to running, jumping, gymnastics, javelin-throwing, wrestling, boxing, and ball games—the whole gamut of physical education—and again it had obvious consequences in the visual arts, especially in sculpture. Since nudity was offensive to most non-Greek peoples in the Hellenistic world, this Greek custom became, whether intentionally or inadvertently, a device of cultural exclusion that must have kept many a non-Greek youth from realistically aspiring to become part of the ruling-class culture. It is hardly an exaggeration to say that only by shedding one's clothes among his peers and elders could a youth in the Hellenistic era become truly Greek. Those who would not would remain "barbarians."

Another distinctive emphasis of Hellenistic schooling was music, again following classical precedent. A bit of this music has been written down and preserved so that we can hear it today. As in classical times the primary purpose of creating music was not to make a beautiful sound, however; music was primarily an organized, systematic art for influencing human emotion and conduct. Music was still characterized, with some rare or dubious exceptions, by *monophony*, or single-line melody. It was nearly always linked with either words or dance, or both.

Music took various forms, of which the most prestigious apparently were choral hymns to the gods and choral singing in dramatic productions, and only boys and men were permitted to sing in these. Such stringed instruments as the lyre and such woodwind instruments as the double flute, or aulos, were still played, often by females. An instrument that first evolved in the Hellenistic period was the organ. This early organ employed water to generate air pressure that was directed by the performer through pipes of different lengths deployed in two or three rows. Various other wind instruments, as well as percussion instruments, also existed.

Hellenistic music was performed by both amateurs and professionals. Figure 3-5 shows the Roman mosaic copy of a Hellenistic picture of a troupe of strolling professional musicians—or more likely stage musicians, since three of them wear masks. (*Mosaics* are pictures or designs constructed of tiny pieces of differently colored, hard materials, in most cases stone.) One masked, wreathed man strikes a large tambourine, another plays small cymbals, and a masked woman plays the aulos. From the pictorial viewpoint, the

3-5 Dioscourides of Samos, *Musicians*, Roman copy of a Hellenistic original of the 3rd century B.C. Mosaic, 1′5½″ high. Museo Nazionale, Naples.

shadows cast and the shading of the figures are notable; these features are not always encountered in the art of this period.

A notational system of music did exist in the Hellenistic period; it employed Greek letters, not the notes and staff lines of modern times. The system was complex but modern scholars have at least a tentative understanding of it and can thus reconstitute approximations of the original sounds. Fragments of actual notation and a few brief hymns exist today. The best-known, most substantial piece of Hellenistic music is the epitaph that a man named Seikilos had engraved on the stone of his wife Euterpe's funerary monument in Asia Minor. The dating of this "Epitaph of Seikilos" is uncertain, although it must come from the second or first century B.C. or a bit later. Both the notation and the words exist; in modern notation and English words they are as follows:

Oh, laugh while you— may,

Keep— toil and— trou-ble at bay,

For life is short and— in its day—

The night of death—soon takes you a-way.

The attractive melody employs a *diatonic scale*, a sequence of whole and half-tones of the sort used in most music today.

The Hellenistic Woman

Woman's place was still in the home in the Hellenistic era. For the fortunate minority of women, those of the middle and aristocratic classes, the typical home was more comfortable than for the same classes in classical Greece. For these classes, as from the beginning of historical time, comfort was largely made possible by large contingents of servants and slaves. House design followed the traditional Mediterranean pattern of an enclosure around a private courtyard, but houses had become larger and they were more lavishly furnished and decorated than before. Hellenistic homes were well on the way toward the spacious, luxurious houses that we will find later, better preserved, in Roman Italy.

Hellenistic women were by no means confined strictly to the home, however. More and more they appeared in social life, dressed tastefully and elegantly. A woman of sophistication is portrayed in the Tanagra statuette illustrated in figure 3-6. (Of painted terracotta, Tanagra statuettes are named for the town near Athens where they were first found, but they apparently followed Athenian models.) The woman is gowned mostly in pink (the colors of the statuette are well preserved). She carries a fan and boasts a somewhat eccentric but no doubt fashionable hairdo incorporating an ivy wreath that may have been appropriate for a drinking party. From this hint it is possible to conclude that the woman is, after all, an entertainer in the classical Greek tradition—but other statuettes give no such indication and may simply portray relatively emancipated women.

Greek women of classical times—with such exceptions as Sappho and the women of Euripides—were generally farther from emancipation than those of the Hellenistic world. Hellenistic women, for one thing, had before them many convincing examples of powerful and otherwise prominent contemporary women, not just the goddesses and faithful wives of earlier legend. Arsinoe II, daughter of Ptolemy I and wife of her brother Ptolemy II, was obviously the dominant figure in her marriage—royal sister-brother marriages became common in Ptolemaic Egypt. She was ambitious, hardworking, shrewd, and skilled in warfare. Like her husband and her female successors, Arsinoe was deified. One of her successors was the well-known and able Cleopatra VII, with whom the Ptolemaic kingdom would come to its end.

At a less exalted level, the ordinary Hellenistic middle- or upper-class woman was situated somewhat better legally than before. Some marital agreements, for example, included the minimal requirement that the wife must approve of any other woman with whom her husband set up housekeeping. Much more important, women's property rights were extended so that they almost equaled those of men. Formal education

3-6 *Woman with Fan,* Tanagra statuette, c. 300 B.C. Painted terracotta, 9¼″ high. Reproduced by Courtesy of the Trustees of the British Museum, London.

became more accessible to girls, and even a few gymnasia were opened to girls. Female poets, artists, and philosophers became more common. The outcome was still far from equality of the sexes, but the status of women was improving.

THE ART OF PERGAMUM

The famed Hellenistic city of Pergamum in Asia Minor was not a port-city; the Caicus (now Bakir) River, above which it rose, was a rather insignificant stream. Although the city dominated a fertile plain, it never became a commercial metropolis. However, its hilltop location was eminently defensible, the land was rich, and above all, it had an able, energetic royal dynasty. The modern Turkish town of Bergama now lies below the once-gleaming hill and citadel of the Hellenistic city, whose splendor and magnitude are convincingly

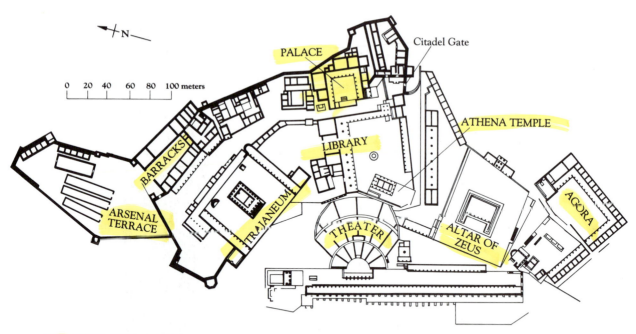

3-7 Ground plan reconstruction of the upper citadel of the acropolis of Pergamum in the 1st century A.D. (Adapted with permission from Elisabeth Rohde, *Pergamum, Burgberg, und Altar,* Henschelverlag, Berlin, 1961.)

evoked today only by the substantial remains of a great theater. The surviving monuments reflecting Pergamene glory were mostly set up elsewhere or copied in the Hellenistic or Roman age, or moved to Europe in the modern period.

The royal Attalid dynasty was established in the early third century by Eumenes I—although we refer to it by a name derived from that of Attalus I, who declared himself king in 240 B.C. Prestigious victories over the Gauls and an alliance with Rome firmly established the kingdom, which in its lifetime of little more than one hundred years, became one of only a handful of cultural leaders in the Hellenistic world. Attalus and his son Eumenes II not only won military victories, but sponsored a brilliant explosion of art and scholarship through 159 B.C., the date of Eumenes' death. Both rulers taxed their small population heavily in order to erect fine gymnasia, a superlative library, and a vast public complex including temples and a royal palace on the citadel. Figure 3-7 shows the ground plan of a reconstruction of the upper acropolis. The theater appears at the bottom center, and the library is above it; the Altar of Zeus is at the lower right, below the entrance to the citadel proper. Still lower stood the upper

marketplace (*agora*) and three gymnasia, not shown in the ground plan. Most inhabitants lived in the lower town, near the gymnasia, a lower marketplace, and the main road to the city. In typical Hellenistic fashion, the lower town was aligned more geometrically than the irregular contours of the hill permitted on the acropolis.

The Pergamene library, second in size to Alexandria's, contained two hundred thousand scrolls when it was finally moved to Alexandria as Mark Antony's gift to Cleopatra, to replace the fire-destroyed Alexandrian library. Presumably the Pergamene library collection in its prime under the Attalids was about the same size. Its scrolls were largely of parchment, animal skins that have been prepared for writing—the word for it is derived from *Pergamene.* Parchment largely replaced the more fragile Egyptian papyrus in the ancient world as a writing material. Its use in modern times has been mainly in the form of true "sheepskin" university diplomas.

Pergamum's library, like that at Alexandria, was a center of scholarly research and writing. It was here that Antigonus wrote biographies of the great Attalids and a mass of art criticism, some of which would be pointedly questioned, in true scholarly combative fashion, by other, jealous Pergamene critics. Grammarians, poets, scientists, and historians all converged on Pergamum for its renowned scholarly resources.

In the library precincts stood an imposing statue of Athena (fig. 3-8) as goddess of wisdom; it was a smaller adaptation of the colossal Pheidian statue of Athena that stood in the Parthenon of Athens. The substantial marble fragment that remains of the Pergamene copy is truly majestic—possibly as much so as the more detailed and ornate gold-and-ivory original. If Eumenes II, in erecting the statue, hoped that it would awe his scholars into less belligerent scholarly combat, he was not successful. However, his Athena did fulfill his ultimate objective—to symbolize wisdom and scholarship and to validate Pergamum as the New Athens.

The Victory Monuments of Attalus I

The classical Greeks had created new art as it was required for their time. So, too, did the Hellenistic world, and so have all ages as long as the creative spirit has flourished. It was in the Hellenistic age, though, that people began to collect old art works, even in styles that had been superseded in current work. This is a clear parallel with the Hellenistic world of literary scholarship, which collected, classified, and criticized the literary works of past ages. Attalus I was the earliest collector of memorable art works from other locations, and Eumenes II set up the growing collection in the precinct of Athena on the Pergamene acropolis for all to see.

It was Pergamene artists, moreover, who made some of the first copies of art works. This was not a surprising development in a situation where originals could not necessarily be seized or purchased, and when artistic beauty, even in outmoded styles, was coming to be appreciated as such. Some copies of three-dimensional work were in part produced mechanically, but others, like the *Athena of Pergamum,* were copied more freely, as seems also to have been the practice in the case of painting. The vogue of copying in Pergamum would soon spread to Rome and thus be responsible for our acquaintance with several splendid works from Pergamum itself, in cases where the originals have been lost.

These works included several victory monuments that Attalus commissioned to commemorate his vic-

3-8 *Athena of Pergamum,* 180–160 B.C. Marble, 10'2¼" high. Staatliche Museen zu Berlin DDR.

tories over the Gauls (Galatians) early in his reign. This warrior tribe had long raided Pergamene territory—or been bought off by Pergamene tribute money. Attalus declined to continue this policy of appeasement and defeated the Gauls when they entered his lands to enforce the payment. Later Gallic incursions led to their further defeat. Copies of many of the individual or group figures from these commemorative monuments have survived, including a monument on the Athenian acropolis that involved not only defeated Gauls but also defeated Persians and Amazons (legendary female barbarian warriors). The parallel between Athens' defeat of the barbarians and Pergamum's victory over the Gauls was surely intentional—a boastful gesture that also paid respect to Athens' honorable place in Greek history.

A victory monument also stood, of course, on the Pergamene acropolis, in the precinct of Athena that also served as a courtyard of the library. It has generally been believed that the two best-known statues of the victory series (see figs. 3-9 and 3-10) are copies from the bronze originals of this monument, although the two show stylistic differences. In any case, all the statue copies known to us are of figures depicting dead or dying barbarians, not their Greek conquerors—an approach that can only be explained by the Pergamene attraction (and soon that of the entire Hellenistic and Roman worlds as well) to emotional pathos. The whole sculptural series is a tribute to the defiance, suffering, and death of the barbarians who perished while fighting the Greeks as well as to the victories of Pergamum (and Athens). The nobility of the conquered foe raises their defeat and death to a truly epic, tragic plane.

In two quite different moods and artistic styles, the celebrated marble copies of the *Dying Gaul* (fig. 3-9) and the *Gaul Killing Himself* (fig. 3-10) exemplify this tragic nobility. The *Dying Gaul* represents indubitably a barbarian figure; there is hardly a suggestion of the clean-cut beauty of body that Greek sculptors had been perfecting for centuries. The barbarian nature is suggested rather by a somewhat coarse but strong phy-sique, a plaited necklace, and heavily greased, matted hair. A sword, horn, and other equipment lie beside him. The wound in his side oozes blood as he props himself up feebly, not yet surrendering to death.

The *Gaul Killing Himself* is a more vigorous and complex work, again bringing surprising sympathy to its subject. Rather than be taken prisoner, the Gaul has first killed his wife and now, glancing over his shoulder at the advancing Greeks, he plunges a dagger into his own breast. It is a moment of melodramatic action. In a forthright appeal to emotionalism, no detail is omitted, from the fierce gaze of the defiant Gaul, to the limp body of his wife, and even to the blood flowing from his own wound. The drooping body about to slip from his grasp contrasts dramatically with his own vigorous action, reflecting not despair but violent courage. The two bodies seem to rotate, and to invite viewing from several angles. The man's form is idealized and almost extravagantly muscled; it looks forward artistically to the magnificently powerful male bodies on the Altar of Zeus of the next century.

3-9 *Dying Gaul,* copy of a bronze original of c. 220 B.C. Marble, 3'7¾" high including base. Capitoline Museum, Rome.

3-10 *Gaul Killing Himself,* copy of a bronze original of c. 220 B.C. or later. Marble, 6′11″ high. Museo Nazionale Romano, Rome.

The Altar of Zeus

With the great Altar of Zeus we have access to original work, not simply to copies. In the late nineteenth century archaeologists excavated the site in Pergamum, recovering fragments of much of the sculpture, and in 1930 the west front (fig. 3-11), with wings, was finally reconstructed in the Pergamum Museum in Berlin (now East Berlin). Sculpture from the unreconstructed sides and interior was placed around the walls of the museum's great hall and in an adjacent room.

Eumenes II, described by his contemporary Polybius as possessing "intelligence, industry, and political skill," was also a military conqueror. After decisively crushing the Gauls in 184–183 B.C. he was given his father's title of "Savior" and ordered the construc-

tion of a thank-offering to Zeus and Athena—one of the most impressive votive offerings in Western history. The architectural plan (see fig. 3-7) was that of a rectangle with courtyard plus two wings. Access was by a high flight of stairs leading the viewer's eye upward to the altar proper. Around the sides of the wings and the three exterior walls ran the sculpted Great Frieze for which the structure was most famous in antiquity, in fact as another of the wonders of the world. In contrast with classical Greek temples such as the Parthenon, the altar has several notable characteristics—an expansion of the earlier rectangular form, an emphasis on visual movement toward interior space as well as on the exterior, and an inversion of the positioning of columns and sculpture.

The sculpture of the Great Frieze, too, differs strikingly from that of the Parthenon or the Temple of Zeus at Olympia. There the prevailing impression was of calm, commanding Olympian majesty; in this Hellenistic work there is restless, surging activity—dynamic, almost ruthless tension. At times, even, the sculpture bursts its frame and flows into exterior space, as we see in figure 3-12, where figures spill out onto the steps of the altar itself. Here, also, we see the extremely high relief of the figures and the feeling of violent movement.

The subject of the whole Great Frieze, some four hundred feet long and seven-and-a-half feet high (except as it tapers up the entrance stairway) is a *gigantomachy,* or battle of giants and gods. A vast number of deities appear and they are labeled by name; presumably they had been authenticated and catalogued for mythological accuracy by the scholars of the library, as were the hordes of giants as well. Zeus, hurling his thunderbolts, leads the deities against the giants and Titans who vainly yet valiantly support his father Cronus in the decisive struggle for rule over gods and human beings.

Although the outcome of the struggle is never seriously in doubt, the tension of battle is seldom relaxed. Nor are the viewer's sympathies constantly engaged on behalf of the victorious gods. It is true that some of their adversaries approach the vile monster category with uncouth shapes and often with serpentlike extremities that writhe through the sculpted design, uniting and invigorating its parts. Others, though, are merely winged and have superbly developed, quite human bodies. The panels depicting Athena battling with the giant Alcyoneus (fig. 3-13)

3-11   Reconstruction of the Altar of Zeus (Pergamum, c. 180–160 B.C.), with original marble sculpture. Reconstruction 1930. Staatliche Museen zu Berlin DDR, Antikensammlung.

3-12   Reconstruction of northwest wing and stairway of the Altar of Zeus at Pergamum. Staatliche Museen zu Berlin DDR, Antikensammlung.

3-13   *Athena Battling with Alcyoneus*, detail of the Great Frieze of the Altar of Zeus at Pergamum. Marble; frieze is 7′6″ high. Staatliche Museen zu Berlin DDR, Antikensammlung.

reveal a handsome winged giant whose hair is seized by Athena as his mother, the earth goddess Gaia, rises at the right to beg mercy of the great goddess for him and her other sons, giants and Titans alike. The myth stated that Alcyoneus could not be conquered while touching the earth: thus his foot barely touches his mother's breast as the invincible Athena prepares to drag him away. The face of Alcyoneus is anguished—a vivid example of Hellenistic emotion and pathos in art.

A lesser sculpted frieze also embellished the Altar of Zeus: the Telephus Frieze of the inner courtyard. Less well preserved than the Great Frieze, something of its spirit and style may still be seen in a skillful Roman wall painting of two centuries later (fig. 3-14); this is believed to be a copy of a Pergamene painting inspired by the Altar's relief sculpture. Here we see the infant

3-14   *Herakles and Telephus in Arcadia*. Wall painting from Herculaneum copied from a Pergamene original of c. 150–133 B.C. 6′7½″ high. Museo Nazionale, Naples.

Telephus, grandson of Zeus and son of Herakles, being suckled by a doe as his father looks on. The painting provides another example of heroic male nudity, but tension and drama are replaced by idyllic calm. Presiding over the scene is a personification of Arcadia, the mainland-Greek territory where Herakles found the infant abandoned by its mother. Behind Arcadia is a jolly, impish boy with panpipes—an example of individualistic facial realism. The scene was wholly appropriate to Pergamum, since Telephus would become the legendary founder of the Attalid dynasty.

OTHER HELLENISTIC ART

Most of the art we have discussed thus far served the purposes not of the whole community as in classical Athens, but rather of individual dynasties. A great deal of Hellenistic art followed the same pattern, most obviously of all in the countless remarkably realistic and individualized royal portraits that graced the coinage of the era. Even when earthly rulers were not portrayed or glorified in art, the Hellenistic artist tended to celebrate the individuality of the persons portrayed, not only in physical features but in the emotions of the particular moment. The days of generalized, idealized human beings in art had largely passed; no longer was life serene and all its handsome people at ease in the world. Certainly, even in classical times there were exceptions to this picture of human existence, but in the Hellenistic age the exception seems to have become the rule.

Stress and Emotion in Art

On occasion the human bodies created in Hellenistic sculpture were handsome but portrayed in situations in which the emotional factor could be highlighted. Such was the case with the Attalid sculpture in Pergamum, and also in the celebrated sculpture known as the *Laocoön* group (fig. 3-15). The subject matter of this work was ready-made for the anguished emotionalism so often favored by Hellenistic artists and art clients: the death struggle of the legendary Trojan priest and his sons. The Greeks besieging Troy had constructed a great wooden horse, had filled its interior with soldiers and rolled it up to the gates of Troy, counting on the Trojans' curiosity. Only Laocoön begged, in vain, for the Trojans not to bring it inside. Their failure to heed

his warning of course led to the city's fall. In the meantime, two great serpents had risen from the sea to strangle the priest and one or both of his sons. The single-son version of the legend seems to be portrayed here, with the son at the right, however great his alarm and horror, appearing to stand some chance of escaping. His anguished father and his brother, on the other hand, are obviously doomed.

Ancient Roman sources asserted that the *Laocoön* group was sculpted by artists from the island of Rhodes, and out of a single block of stone. Even if so, the Roman copy illustrated here is constructed of several blocks. There are striking similarities to the struggling figures of the Altar of Zeus, even to the unifying element of serpent coils. Again there is mortal agony portrayed, especially in the father's features, for the younger son, to the left, seems to be beyond anguish as he gasps his last breath. Even though the elder,

3-15 *Laocoön and His Sons,* 1st century A.D. Roman copy of a Hellenistic original of 150–100 B.C. Marble; figures are 6′½″ high. Vatican Museums.

stronger son to the right may escape, he is horrified by the cries of his doomed father. Thus the emotions expressed by the three figures are different but interrelated, and the figures are skillfully united in a compositional whole.

Still another representation of a most dire human predicament can be studied in the statues of Marsyas and the Scythian slave that today are housed in separate museums (fig. 3-16). Their legend, also, is rather complex and markedly melodramatic. The satyr Marsyas is portrayed strung up on a tree; momentarily he will be skinned alive by the knife a slave is grimly sharpening. Marsyas had been possessed by the fatal boldness of competing in a music contest with the god Apollo and had been defeated—hence this drastic punishment. Still earlier, Athena had experimentally played the aulos (double flute), but had been disgusted when she saw her facial contortions in a mirror and had cast away the instrument in anger. Marsyas repaired the damaged instrument and mastered its playing. When he challenged the lyre-playing Apollo to a contest, the Muses (sponsors of the various arts) had declared the god the clear winner, and Apollo decreed the skinning as punishment. The horror of the forthcoming torture is apparent in the helpless despair on the face of the old satyr and the anticipatory grimness of the slave.

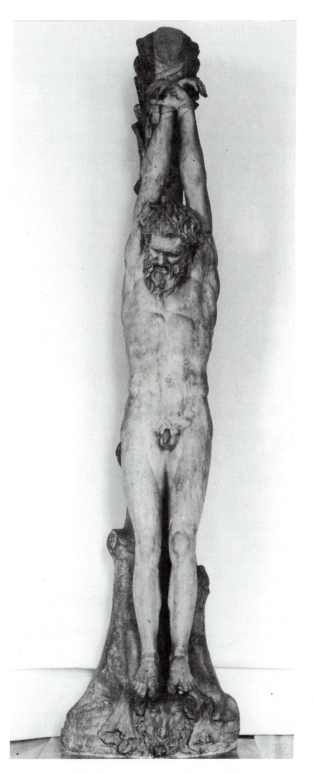

3-16 *Scythian Slave* and *Marsyas*. Roman copies of Hellenistic works of c. 210–200 B.C. *Scythian Slave:* Marble, 3′5″ high. Uffizi, Florence. *Marsyas:* Marble, 8′5″ high. Louvre, Paris.

Portraiture and Genre

It might at first appear that Hellenistic visual art was devoted almost exclusively to the depiction of passionate and dramatic moments in life—for example, to the excitement and pathos of warfare or to extraordinary human fear and suffering. Inevitably, though, art of that time could not sustain such peaks of drama in all its creative efforts. Reaction did not necessarily mean a return to the calm serenity and beauty of the classical age, however. The subject matter of art had been broadened: the male athletes and dignified maidens, the deities, statesmen, and heroes were sharing their place in art with shepherds and servants. All age groups, too, were being portrayed. The pudginess of half-formed childish bodies and the slackened flesh of old age were sharing the artistic limelight with hard-muscled youths and soft, sensuous women. Moreover, the Hellenistic world effectively invented portraiture—the depiction of individualized, personalized human features.

Behind this attention to individual human beings was a genuine interest in people, people of all classes and conditions. The Hellenistic Greeks had a word for it: *philanthropia, the love of mankind.* The word had been used earlier for the gods' care and concern for human beings. By the fourth century, the term was being applied to the assiduous care of rulers for their subjects. In the Hellenistic age the earlier meanings were not forgotten, but "philanthropy" was being praised as a feeling that all human beings could extend to others. It seems to have been a Hellenistic Greek, perhaps Menander, who first formulated the sentiment usually assigned to the Roman playwright Terence: "I am a man, and nothing human is alien to me."

These feelings of humane sympathy and a new taste for gritty realism, together, contributed to the Hellenistic interest in biography. A series of Hellenistic authors produced short biographies of real people—usually well-known personalities of the time. There were biographies of rulers and public men, of course, but also of poets and philosophers. Most formal portrait art—that is, heads or full-length figures—drew on the same categories of subjects. Other closely observed depictions of real individuals commonly fall more properly into the category of *genre art*—the realistic treatment of anonymous subjects from the modest everyday world.

Hellenistic portraiture was primarily a sculptural art. Most often the portraits were in the form of full-length figures. (Individually sculpted heads were often attached to presculpted bodies, and the modern age possesses many heads whose bodies have been lost.) Portraits were generally made not for people's homes but for public viewing on tombs and religious structures or in libraries. Sometimes they were imaginary, as when Homer or other long-dead worthies were honored, but more and more portraits were of real persons, alive or recently deceased.

The identity of the subject of the fine portrait head from Delos shown in figure 3-17 is unknown today; we see only a real man in early middle age. The head is *hollow-cast* in bronze—that is, made from a mold, not hammered out—and eyes were inserted into spaces left for them in the bronze. The whites of the eyes are of an ivory-colored, now somewhat darkened

3-17 Agasias of Ephesus?, c. 100 B.C. Bronze portrait head from Delos, 12¾" high. National Museum, Athens.

3-18 *Drunken Old Woman,* Roman copy of a late-3rd-century-B.C. original by Myron of Pergamum. Marble, 3′3″ high. Staatliche Antikensammlung und Glypothek, Munich.

paste, and the irises are of black marble. After casting, the sculptor used a cutting tool to strengthen certain details in the hair and eyebrows. The sculpture-portrait shows a person of great strength (note the thick, powerful neck) but of perhaps less than decisive personality. The lips are parted, and the man's expression is one of troubled uncertainty or melancholy. The sculptor must have had remarkable qualities of observation and skill. The pathetic feeling achieved in the head of Alcyoneus for the Pergamene Altar frieze (see fig. 3-13) has become still more refined and subtle in this striking head from Delos.

The realism in Hellenistic genre sculpture might be as thorough-going as it is in portraiture. The *Drunken Old Woman* (fig. 3-18) is a Roman marble copy of a Greek original dating to the late third century B.C. The woman is shown in advanced old age, with face deeply wrinkled, neck flesh deeply sagging, and most teeth rotted away. The woman clasps tightly to her body a large jug from which she has apparently

drunk very deeply. Her head is thrown back in stupefied abandon, and her gown has slipped completely off one shoulder and partly from the other. In lonely, miserable old age she has become not so much an object of amusement as of pity.

From the uncertainties or pathos of middle and old age, Hellenistic artists frequently turned also to childhood, and they portrayed it much more convincingly than did the classical Greeks. The bronze statuette in figure 3-19 sympathetically depicts a *Young Black Musician,* possibly an Ethiopian. An instrument, perhaps a small harp, is presumably balanced on the boy's right shoulder, and his hip is sharply thrust out to help bear the weight. His arms and especially his legs are unusually thin; his life, it would seem, has not been easy. The facial expression, as he sings, is sad and wistful—an emotional effect beloved by the Hellenistic art public as well as one that seems wholly appropriate to this particular subject. This little work evokes not only an age but an intense humanity.

3-19 Two views of *Young Black Musician,* 2nd or 1st century B.C. Bronze statuette, 7¾″ high. Bibliothèque Nationale, Paris.

3-20 Gnosis, *Stag Hunt*, c. 300 B.C. Pebble mosaic. Museum, Pella.

An example of mosaic work may round out this survey of Hellenistic art and demonstrate that not all art of the period sought either emotional or wholly realistic effects. A large pebble mosaic of a *Stag Hunt* found at the Macedonian capital of Pella (fig. 3-20) is primarily decorative, although it communicates a real sense of immediacy. Two men are about to slay a small stag that also is being attacked by a hunting dog. The scene is dramatic, in proper Hellenistic vein, but little specific feeling is conveyed despite the intense action that is shown. Mild shading marks the treatment of the billowing cloaks, but otherwise light and dark are not emphasized. The mosaic was probably copied from a painting; if so, we are not likely to get closer in time, place, and skill to large-scale Hellenistic painting than in this work.

NEW STYLES IN THOUGHT

Among those of Greek language and culture, philosophy remained one of the most honored pursuits in the Hellenistic age. All important cities had their resident philosophers, often partly supported by kings or city governments—a remarkable state of affairs that has not often been seen in Western history. The most significant thinkers still tended to gravitate to Athens, the traditional home of philosophy. There and elsewhere they formed societies, "schools," or sects. These were not schools in the ordinary institutional sense, nor were they simply "schools of thought." Rather they were associations of persons, mainly men, who were in frequent contact (some even lived communally) and who participated in discussions and at least occasionally attended lectures together. Generally each group had its prestigious local leader, and looked back to a venerated founder, most often a person of the early Hellenistic period. Greek freedom of thought still flourished (short of subversive political thought, at least) and many Hellenistic Greeks drifted from school to school. Lively arguments were known to occur within individual schools, since there were no requirements of rigid conformity.

Although there was no enforceable uniformity within the schools, each group embodied certain fairly specific emphases. The educated Greeks to whom philosophy appealed would have some idea before joining a school of what they could expect. Some of the general emphases of the three major schools will be outlined shortly, but always with the warning that deviations did occur from these norms. But first, did the several major sects have any characteristics in common?

Not surprisingly, they did. Even the Cynics, whose name suggests to moderns some disillusionment with humankind, usually professed to love humanity, as did the Hellenistic age in general. All philosophic schools were primarily secular, humanistic, and humanitarian, and none of them regularly raised their eyes to the heavens or even to such a transcendent realm as that of the Platonic "ideas." All of the philosophic sects, even when engaging in lively and fairly subtle discussion within their own ranks, cultivated a public image of embodying understandable, relatively simple doctrines. Few of the Hellenistic philosophers stressed the sort of complex subtleties often encountered in Plato and Aristotle; the strengths of the schools often lay in their ability to popularize their ideas, make them seem reasonable to the rest of society. All sects downplayed or even omitted the more abstract, metaphysical concerns of philosophy, and stressed instead the ethical and social needs of ordinary people of intelligence. Despite or because of the Hellenistic artistic preoccupations with emotion and pathos, all schools stressed freedom from emotional troubles and tensions. Finally, the major schools all tended toward *eclecticism,* or the bringing together of teachings from several sources, not necessarily with wholly coherent results.

Stoics, Epicureans, and Cynics

The most widespread philosophical school was Stoicism. The Stoics were literally "men of the porch," so-named for the Painted Porch (stoa) in Athens where they often congregated. Their founder was Zeno of Citium, who opened his Athens school in the late fourth century. The Stoics preferred no single approach to gaining knowledge but advocated a cautious use of rationalism and empiricism. Although they tended to see divine purpose as pervading the universe, they avoided reliance upon any personal god and denied the efficacy of prayer, except when appealing for strength to follow divine providence willingly. Divinity, they believed, was expressed in all things in the universe; the Stoics tended to be *pantheists,* seeing God everywhere. As for ethical guidelines, the Stoics rejected the pursuit of pleasure and saw virtue as the greatest good—virtue pursued in a spirit of moderation. Man, said Zeno, must "live consistently," not following fleeting impulse. It was man's duty to himself, to his family, and to the community to conduct himself with benevolent dignity and self-control.

The philosophic school that most nearly rivaled Stoicism in popularity was founded in Athens about 306 B.C. by Epicurus (fig. 3-21). The Epicurean school was the more daring of the two schools, and its membership included a substantial number of women. Very much aware of the uncertainties and insecurities of his world, Epicurus counseled strength through intellect and science rather than through the emotional mystery religions, which he regarded as unworthy of thinking people. His goal was not to reform the world, or even to rationalize it into a neat system, but rather to make it possible for his followers to lead wise, meaningful, and tranquil lives. He believed that, above all, people should conquer the fear of death. Death, he insisted,

is nothing to us. For all good and evil consists in sensation, but death is deprivation of sensation. And therefore a right understanding that death is nothing to us makes the mortality of life enjoyable, not because it adds to it an infinite span of time, but because it takes away the craving for immortality. . . . That which gives no trouble when it comes, is but an empty pain in anticipation. So death, the most terrifying of ills, is nothing to us, since so long as we exist, death is not with us; but when death comes, then we do not exist. It does not concern either the living or the dead, since for the former it is not, and the latter are no more.

The aim of human life, Epicurus continued, is "to enjoy not the longest period of time, but the most pleasant." A pleasant life involves, most basically, "the health of the body and the soul's freedom from disturbance"—that is, the avoidance of pain and fear. Pleasure is "the beginning and the end" of the good life—not all pleasures, to be sure, since the sensual pleasures often end in distress and pain. "Not continuous drinkings and revellings, nor the satisfaction of lusts," nor luxurious dining will bring true satisfaction and pleasure. Only the life of the mind, and the peace of mind that comes from banishing superstitious fears, can make one's existence truly pleasant. "It is better for you," Epicurus concluded, "to be free from fear lying on straw, than to have a golden couch and a rich table and be full of trouble."

3-21 *Epicurus,* ancient copy of the head of a portrait statue from an early-3rd-century-B.C. original. Marble, 1′4″ high. The Metropolitan Museum of Art, New York. Rogers Fund, 1911.

Neither Epicureans nor Stoics were atheists, but the Epicureans did reject the all-pervading pantheism of their rivals. The gods exist, said Epicurus and his followers, but they are far from life in this world. Gods cannot be angry with human beings or show favor to some of them; they do not punish or reward men and women, for this would violate their own happiness and peace of mind. Surely, moreover, gods cannot have made the world: if so, the world would not be so full of imperfection and evil. Human beings, said Epicurus, are on their own, and this is as it should be. His message, after all, is not so far from that of Hellenistic Stoicism, even though the two philosophies took different routes to a similar goal.

If Hellenistic Epicureanism and Stoicism both stressed individual solutions to human problems, so too did the more radical Cynicism. The Cynics, or "dogmen," revered Diogenes of Sinope ("the dog") as their founder (actually a pre-Hellenistic figure since he died in the time of Alexander), whereas non-Cynics were likely to regard Diogenes as either amusing or extraordinarily crude. The statuette in figure 3-22 shows him as an old man, with his dog and a begging bowl. It was he who declared himself a "citizen of the world" and a devotee of the "life according to nature." With less theoretical substructure to their thought than the Stoics and Epicureans, the Cynics were oriented strictly to the concerns of individuals. They attacked all human institutions (marriage, government, property holding, and so on), for these, they said, created dependency. Detachment from all worldly things was their means of achieving the goal of peace of mind. Cynics could be fanatically ascetic, denying themselves many of the simple pleasures permitted by the Epicureans. Their critics charged them with trying to reduce human beings to the level of animals.

The Hellenistic Way

Stoicism, Epicureanism, and Cynicism were by no means the only philosophical schools in the Hellenistic world. Another group, the Cyrenaics, exalted *hedonism* as a way of life—the unabashed quest for pleasure, even of the most bodily and earthy sort. Still another school, Skepticism, was based on the startling though not completely new proposition that reason and the senses yield no absolute ideas, standards, or values whatsoever. The Skeptics insisted that lasting knowledge is not necessarily derived from either rationalism

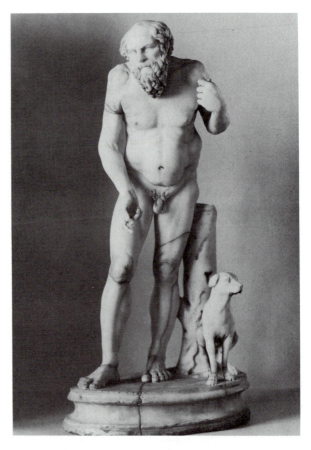

3-22 *Diogenes*, ancient copy of a 3rd(?)-century-B.C. statuette, extensively restored. Marble, 19" high. The Metropolitan Museum of Art, New York. Rogers Fund, 1922.

or the senses, or from authority or intuition. Even all ethical standards, they said, are relative to the culture in which the person lives.

Obviously, the Hellenistic world held no single view of life. Similar evidence comes from the historical writing, science, religion, poetry, and visual art of the period. It was an age of striking contrasts—sensuous beauty against passionate emotionalism, and rational scientific and historical inquiry against the raptures of religious mystery. The politics of the time were characterized by intense power struggles as well as benevolent civic sponsorship of education and the arts. It was an age not of small, self-absorbed city-states but of large nations tied to each other by language and culture. Against these immense states and remote bureaucracies, individuals must have felt small and alone, yet also challenged by their remoteness from others toward new personal outlets. Never had individualism and freedom of mind flourished so proudly on a truly international scale.

In all these respects the Hellenistic age seems remarkably similar to our own. To be sure, no past age can or should appear wholly alien to ours, especially one that provides admirable ideals and inspirations for a new world. Classical Greece was such an age; it has been a gleaming beacon for the humanistic, secular side of more recent Western civilization. Hellenistic civilization is not as well known as the classical Greek world in our day. However, it seems to have shared some of the complexities of modern times and such ugly modern realities as theories of racial superiority. Hellenistic culture fell short of being modern mainly in its failure to advance technologically. In the end it collapsed when faced by the armies of a country only slightly further advanced, the great military power of Rome.

Recommended Reading

Bamm, Peter. *Alexander the Great* (1968). Readable, handsomely illustrated.

Bonnard, André. *Greek Civilization*, vol. 3: *From Euripides to Alexandria* (1961). Good introduction to cultural life.

Charbonneaux, Jean, et al. *Hellenistic Art: 330–50 B.C.* (1973). Scholarly; brilliantly illustrated.

Farrington, Benjamin. *The Faith of Epicurus* (1967). Epicurean thought in the context of its time.

Ferguson, John. *The Heritage of Hellenism* (1973). Fine guide to art and culture.

Grant, Michael. *From Alexander to Cleopatra: The Hellenistic World* (1982). Political, social, literary, and art history.

Havelock, Christine M. *Hellenistic Art* (1971). A general survey, but concentrates on individual works.

Lane-Fox, Robin. *The Search for Alexander* (1980). Excellent illustrations.

Onions, John. *Art and Thought in the Hellenistic Age* (1979). Stimulating, impressionistic study.

Polybius. *The Histories*, 2 vols. (1889). The original text in translation.

Rist, Anna. *The Poems of Theocritus* (1978). Modern translation with explanatory essays.

Schmidt, Evamaria. *The Great Altar of Pergamon* (1962). A nearly complete pictorial account.

Walbank, Frank W. *The Hellenistic World* (1981). Good overview of history, ideas, and science.

Webster, T. B. L. *Hellenistic Art* (1967). Good survey.

4

Imperial Rome: 27 B.C.–A.D. 180

he legendary founding date of the city of Rome is 753 B.C. The monarchy that developed was replaced near the year 500 B.C. by a republic, which endured until 27 B.C. In the meantime Rome had progressed from a community in central Italy, to the predominant power in the Italian peninsula, and finally to the master of the whole Mediterranean area and much of northwestern Europe. Throughout the republican (nonmonarchical) period, the Roman government was dominated by an upper-class senate and remained basically authoritarian and aristocratic, although the people retained certain safeguards and powers. Rule by the "Senate and People of Rome" continued through much of that part of the imperial period known as the Principate or Early Empire (27 B.C.–A.D. 285). Central government weakened after A.D. 180, however, and the third century was largely an age of military rebellions and anarchy. A period of centralized despotism was inaugurated in 285, and despotic power permitted the empire to flourish for several more decades. In the later fourth and early fifth centuries the western Roman empire went into its final decline.

Thus the greatest days of early imperial Rome came during the two centuries after 27 B.C. The last century of republican rule was turbulent; power was alternately seized and lost by such military leaders as Pompey and Julius Caesar (died 44 B.C.). At last Caesar's heir, Octavian, established his own primacy as *Princeps* ("first man") of Rome and in 27 B.C. was given the title of *Augustus.* Augustus ruled firmly and, by and large, justly as the first "emperor" until his death in A.D. 14. His successors were an extraordinarily varied lot—the harsh Tiberius (A.D. 14–37), the depraved Caligula (37–41), the scholarly Claudius (41–54), and the vain and cruel Nero (54–68). Among the brief reigns that followed was that of Titus, which is best remembered for the great eruption of Mount Vesuvius that buried Pompeii and Herculaneum in A.D. 79. The eight decades before A.D. 180 were distinguished by several lengthy reigns: the soldier-emperor Trajan, 98–117; Hadrian, 117–138; Antoninus Pius, 138–161; the philosopher-emperor Marcus Aurelius, 161–180. External as well as internal peace characterized much of this period when "eternal Rome" seemed at its most stable and glorious.

Military might was the foundation of Roman power, and the empire retained its air of invincibility as its boundaries expanded through Trajan's time. Hadrian withdrew somewhat from the ambitious boundaries established by his predecessor, and Marcus Aurelius had to fight to maintain the European frontiers against barbarians to the north. In Europe, Asia, and Africa there were six thousand miles of frontiers to be watched by an army of almost a half-million men. Also vital to Roman power was the empire's initial success in governing large areas efficiently and the sense of community that unified the vast empire under Roman law.

The barbarians who ringed the Roman empire, and who infiltrated it heavily in its last centuries, especially from the north, were often more interested in enjoying the benefits of the empire than in destroying it, and many of them fought in its armies. The potential for friction grew, however, as Roman weaknesses became more apparent. The armed forces deteriorated, inadequate capital investment left trade and industry underdeveloped, taxation policy was unenlightened and brutal, and the masses, with little hope of ever improving their lot, eventually felt little commitment to the empire. These dangers, and others, are already evident to us as we look back to the early imperial period. In later years, barbarian attacks would increase in strength and ultimately overwhelm the whole western empire.

FROM THE GREEKS TO HADRIAN

The ancient Roman experience overlapped in time with the Greek, but Rome reached its cultural summit several centuries after the Athenian Golden Age. Moreover, the gap between the two high points was a matter not simply of chronology, but of underlying outlook and ideals. The "ancient world," even in Europe alone, was far from being a single, undifferentiated cultural unit. Nor were Greece and Rome individually uniform. Just as classical Greece would have been unrecognizable to Greeks of the earlier Homeric age or the later Hellenistic civilization, so would have been early imperial Rome to its more austere republican precursor or the decadent, orientalized late empire. Early imperial Rome did, however, continue many features of its republican predecessor and forecast several significant trends of ancient Rome's final phase. Rome in its middle period, from Augustus through Marcus Aurelius (27 B.C.– A.D. 180), is thus a logical focus for our attention here.

The Greek Model

In no realm is the distance between Greece and Rome more clearly defined than in the visual arts. First of all we may note the rather remarkable change in the status of the artists themselves, notably sculptors and painters. The more distinguished Greek artist, although not entirely free of the "craftsman" categorization, was often much honored and by no means anonymous. In contrast, the Roman artistic record is one of virtual creative anonymity, and not simply because the number of signed works that have survived is small. Art in Rome, although produced in vast quantity, never achieved the dignity of its Greek prototype, and recognition of its creators lagged accordingly.

The function of art changed significantly from the age of Pericles through the Hellenistic period to the Hadrianic highpoint of early imperial Rome; art was moving gradually from a civic to a predominantly private function. From its position as an auxiliary to community pride and piety, it became more and more a luxury item for the individual connoisseur or seeker of cultural prestige. The shift toward art as decoration and embellishment, moreover, was strongly underlined by the preponderance in Rome of mere copying—

CHRONOLOGY

HISTORY		THE ARTS	
		70–19 B.C.	Vergil
		68–65 B.C.	Horace
		59 B.C.–	
		A.D. 17	Livy
46–44 B.C.	Julius Caesar dictator		
43–31 B.C.	civil wars: Mark Antony, Octavian, etc.	43 B.C.–	
		A.D. 18	Ovid
		c. 30 B.C.	amphitheater at Nîmes
27 B.C.	Octavian receives the title of "Augustus"		
27 B.C.–			
A.D. 14	Augustus "first emperor"		
27 B.C.–		13–9 B.C.	Altar of Augustan Peace, Rome
A.D. 285	early imperial period of Rome	c. A.D. 14–19	*Augustus of Prima Porta*
A.D. 14–37	Tiberius emperor		
37–41	Caligula emperor		
41–54	Claudius emperor		
44	Britain a Roman province		
54–68	Nero emperor		
		c. 55–c. 120	Tacitus
		c. 60–117	Epictetus
79–81	Titus emperor		
79	eruption of Mt. Vesuvius buries Pompeii and Herculaneum		
		80	Colosseum inaugurated, Rome
		81	Arch of Titus
98–117	Trajan emperor	98	Tacitus publishes *Germany*
101–2, 105–7	Trajan's Dacian Wars		
		113	consecration of Trajan's Forum and Column
117–38	Hadrian emperor		
		125–35	Hadrian's villa at Tivoli
		126–27	Hadrianic baths at Leptis Magna
		126 and later	reconstruction of the Pantheon
138–61	Antoninus Pius emperor		
161–80	Marcus Aurelius emperor		
167–75	Marcus Aurelius campaigns in the north		
		170/174	Marcus Aurelius begins his *Meditations*
		c. 173	equestrian statue of Marcus Aurelius

usually from Hellenic and Hellenistic art—by artists who themselves were Greeks, not native Latin-speaking Romans. In this way the most admired works of earlier times became widely known through their replicas in Rome, as often in the homes and gardens of private individuals as in civic temples and shrines.

However we regard this changing role of art, we must at least credit Rome for its immense contribution to the Western heritage in preserving some idea of innumerable Greek art works otherwise irretrievably lost. The copies could seldom have been wholly faithful to the original, and many were poor indeed; others were genuinely skillful. Among the latter were numerous marble evocations of Myron's *Discus Thrower* (fig.

THE ROMAN EMPIRE

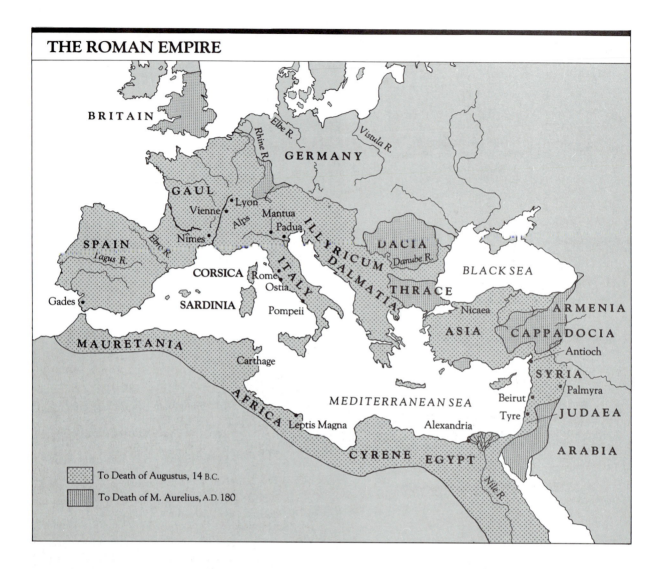

To Death of Augustus, 14 B.C.

To Death of M. Aurelius, A.D. 180

4-1), originally a bronze of the mid fifth century before Christ. Here, in a pose of exceptional sculptural originality for that age (we should remember the stiff kouroi of not many decades before in Greece), the naked athlete has drawn himself back to the point just before the leaping, forward thrust of body and discus. The pose is balanced and indeed almost restful in sculptural, if not athletic, terms. Despite the masculine vigor of its subject, the statue is all curves and graceful balance, as we may expect from the best of classical Greek sculpture.

Although a nostalgia for classical calm frequently haunted the Romans as they sought suitable subjects for sculptural copy and imitation, at other times they followed their own more natural bent for the dramatic and the violent. Here the Hellenistic Greeks offered

the main opportunities. We have already seen Roman copies of dramatic sculpture from Pergamene monuments commemorating Attalid victories over the barbarian Gauls. For Romans of early imperial times these works not only reflected emotions to which they, too, responded; the works also echoed an urgent military necessity of their own world—the expansion and vigilant protection of their own frontiers. Warfare with barbarians was as much a constant of the Roman experience as it had been in the Hellenistic age.

The Romans, in fact, had seen even more than the late Greeks had seen of barbarians, both as peaceful settlers within the empire and as enslaved captives of war. It was primarily by force of arms that Rome had become a vast empire extending from north Britain to denced by the remains of his sprawling, luxurious villa near Tivoli, outside the city of Rome. Here Greek influence can be seen everywhere. In the columns and statuary of the Canopus Canal (fig.4-2) one notes particularly the sculptured maidens (in the left foreground in figure 4-2). These were obviously adapted from the caryatids of the Athenian Erechtheum and are quite as sturdy as their originals, even though they are out of the Greek architectural context and were intended to support nothing more substantial than the top of an arcade.

The vast collection of Greek statuary, largely in copies, at Hadrian's villa made it a virtual museum—an institution and a concept unknown to the classical Greeks, whose accumulations of art works always served a civic or religious cause. Hadrian, like many of his contemporaries, favored the calm spirit of classical works over later Hellenistic sculptural showmanship

4-1 Myron, *Discus Thrower,* Roman copy of a c. 450 B.C. original. Marble, 5′ high. Museo Nazionale Romano, Rome.

4-2 Canopus Canal, Hadrian's villa, Tivoli, c. A.D. 130.

the Persian Gulf. Yet if its roots were military, by Hadrian's time the empire rested at least as much upon cooperation as upon force and exploitation; for a brief century or so Rome almost achieved its ideal of becoming a true commonwealth of peoples. Certainly its impressive success in achieving internal harmony would not have been possible without some acceptance by Italian Rome of foreign cultures on their own terms. Cultural internationalism, or cosmopolitanism, was one of the most striking characteristics of imperial Rome at its best, and perhaps most fully of Hadrianic Rome.

Hadrian set the tone for his reign by being an ardent admirer of Egyptian and especially of Greek civilization. He traveled widely, as did many other cultivated Romans. His passion for things Greek is still evi-

and imported many Eastern craftsmen to work specifically in the classical manner. In the year 130 came an event of major consequence to their work—the death by drowning of Hadrian's young friend Antinous. Not only did Hadrian thereafter found cities in the boy's honor, he fostered a veritable cult in memory of the young Asian Greek and ordered innumerable sculptured likenesses to be made. The Naples *Antinous* (fig. 4-3), from Hadrian's villa, represents the general type in its classical restraint, although the figure has a sensuous softness more typical of fourth-century Greek sculpture than of earlier work.

Also found at Hadrian's villa were many mosaics, some excellently preserved. Mosaics—pictures made by fitting together bits of colored materials, usually stone, against a flat or nearly flat backing—were among many Roman art forms borrowed from the Hellenistic Greeks. In the floor of a hall at Hadrian's villa,

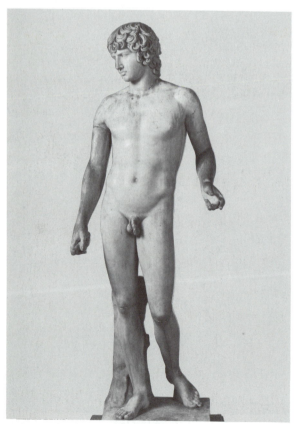

4-3 *Antinous* from Hadrian's villa, c. A.D. 130. Marble, 6'7" high. Museo Nazionale, Naples.

eighteenth-century excavators found the mosaic *Centaur and Centauress Attacked by Lion and Tigers* (fig. 4-4). The animal-human forms are from Greek mythology, and the scene is atypically violent and bloody for a Hadrianic art work.

Nature and Romanticism

The Roman mosaic in figure 4-4 is sometimes thought to be a copy of a Hellenistic work, but in any case a new emphasis had appeared since the classical Greek period—the prominent depiction of natural landscape in art. In Rome this became common in both mosaics and paintings and was encountered in sculpture as well. The classical Greeks had centered their whole vision on human beings, who they felt could personify all things; the Romans were more aware of nature and its power, whether brutal or soothing, over humanity. Elemental forces could be seen in external nature and did not need to be embodied in men or women, as had been the case in the great Greek tragedies and classical sculpture. It is arguable that in this new approach mankind was the loser. Still it is also arguable that the Roman view was more like our own, in an age tending toward romanticism, with its emphasis on feeling and emotion and often on the violent and the exotic in nature.

ROMAN ENGINEERING AND ARCHITECTURE

In one other important area the Romans were very much concerned with nature—in their highly successful attempts to conquer and utilize it in architecture and engineering. To achieve these ends they employed stone construction as well as two new building materials, concrete and brick. For the Romans, brick was a small block of clay that had been molded and baked; concrete was a plastic mass formed of binding material (such as lime and water) together with gravel and rubble. Both brick and concrete were cheaper than high-quality stone and they were much more easily handled; concrete particularly was extremely malleable as well as strong. The Romans used concrete especially as foundation and filler material, over which they would place smooth plaster or a facing of marble, other stone, or brick. Since the plaster they applied has deteriorated and most of the facing has been removed for

4-4 *Centaur and Centauress Attacked by Lion and Tigers* from Hadrian's villa, early 2nd century A.D. Mosaic, 23″ × 36″. Staatliche Museen zu Berlin DDR.

other uses across the centuries, Roman ruins today tend to be less elegant in appearance than the marble monuments of the classical Greek and Hellenistic worlds.

It was in large part the use of brick and concrete that made possible the expanded scale and complexity of Roman building. Brick was used especially for domestic architecture, storage buildings, and public baths. Concrete was used for palaces and other large-scale projects as well as in the baths. Concrete was the basic material, for example, of the Arch of Titus (fig. 4-5), which then was faced with plain and sculpted marble. This arch was one of many Roman triumphal arches commemorating military conquests—in this case the suppression of a Jewish revolt and the looting of the temple in Jerusalem in A.D. 71. The future emperor Titus shared the military glory or ignominy of this event with his father, the emperor Vespasian.

Arches and Vaults

Triumphal arches were so far extended in depth as to become virtual vaults, not mere arches. The arch and the vault, together with the dome, are the most characteristic structural devices of Roman architecture.

4-5 *Arch of Titus*, Rome, A.D. 81. Concrete faced with marble.

Arches, of course, are employed to span space, whether for decoration or utility, for enclosure or support. (Roman arches were rounded at the top, not pointed.) For illustration here, we will consider monuments from Hadrian's reign and just before, if only to stress the fact that neither he nor his contemporaries

were by any means solely absorbed in romantic aestheticism and Greek antiquarianism.

To facilitate travel, and above all to make possible the military and administrative control of even the most distant outposts of empire, the Romans became great builders of roads. Along these roads were a great number of triumphal arches. More practically, the roads themselves made use of arches in the form of bridges. (So, too, did aqueducts, which sometimes were combined with bridges.) Under Hadrian's predecessor, Trajan, a handsome structure arose in distant Spain—the bridge at Alcántara (fig. 4-6). An arch in honor of the emperor arose near its center, but far more impressive were the ninety-foot spans of the supporting central arches. Although somewhat reconstructed, this Roman bridge, like many others, has proved quite capable of sustaining heavy modern traffic.

Vaulting is generally used less for support than for enclosing and covering space. A simple rounded vault is known as a *barrel vault;* when a long barrel vault is crossed by another vault, or successively by several vaults, the result is known as *cross vaulting* or *groin vaulting* (fig. 4-7). The most spectacular Roman applications of cross vaulting were often in the large bathhouses of Rome and the provincial cities. Since these

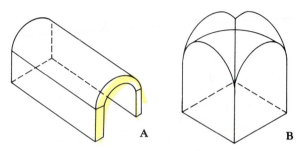

4-7   (A) Barrel vault. (B) Cross (groin) vault.

baths are now in a ruinous state, the illustration here is an artist's reconstruction drawing of the splendid Hadrianic Baths at Leptis Magna in the North African province of Tripolitania (fig. 4-8). The cross vaulting is ornamented with painted stucco reliefs, and the whole interior, with its multicolored marble, is extraordinarily grand and sumptuous. The *frigidarium* (cold room) is in the foreground in figure 4-8, and other units are visible beyond. The late Roman bathhouse, such as this one at Leptis Magna, had come far from the casual asymmetry typical of classical Greek planning and was a severely organized, almost totally symmetrical complex of rooms and open-air areas that catered to the numerous hygienic and recreational desires of its patrons.

4-6   Bridge over the Tagus River, Alcántara, Spain, A.D. 106.

4-8 Reconstruction drawing of the frigidarium of the Hadrianic Baths at Leptis Magna (North Africa), A.D. 126–127.

Lucian, an author of the second century, left a description of a typical bathhouse of his time and its clientele:

> On entering, one is received into a public hall of good size, with ample accommodations for servants and attendants. On the left are the lounging rooms. . . . Then, besides them, a hall, larger than need be for the purposes of a bath, but necessary for the reception of richer persons. Next, capacious locker rooms to undress in, on each side, with a very high and brilliantly lighted hall between them, in which are three swimming pools of cold water. . . . On leaving this hall, you come into another which is slightly warmed instead of meeting you at once with fierce heat. . . . Next to it, on the right, is a very bright hall, nicely fitted up for massage. . . . Then near this is another hall, the most beautiful in the world, in which one can sit or stand with comfort, linger without danger, and stroll about with profit. . . . Next comes the hot corridor. . . . When you have bathed, you need not go back through the same rooms, but can go directly to the cold room through a slightly warmed chamber. Every-

where there is copious illumination and full indoor daylight. . . . Moreover, it [the bath] is beautified with all other marks of thoughtfulness—with two toilets, many exits, and two devices for telling time, a water clock that makes a bellowing sound and a sundial.

Until Hadrian's day the relaxations of bathhouses were generally shared by men and women together. After numerous scandals, however, the sexes were kept separate, often by assigning them different hours. Romans of both sexes remained the most hygienically clean people in Western history until the nineteenth century.

The Pantheon

The third great Roman architectural device, the dome, is a concave covering for space that can be thought of as a continuous revolving succession of arches with the same center. Our example of a dome is a religious structure for which no reconstruction is required—the great Pantheon that still stands in the city of Rome (fig. 4-9). The facade was built in 27 B.C. by order of Agrippa, minister of Augustus, as the bold lettering above the columns indicates. The main construction, including the domed rotunda, was accomplished under Hadrian. The decoration and facing of the Pantheon's exterior have disappeared, but the interior remains substantially as it was in ancient times. The dome, with its central opening to the sky (twenty-nine feet across), is most effectively seen in an eighteenth-century painting (fig. 4-10). Scholars still debate the precise materials and the building technique of the dome, but much of it, like the thick vertical walls of the rotunda, is concrete, which in this case must have been laid in coffered molds probably supported by massive temporary scaffolding. The resultant coffers, or successively indented squares, once were ornamented in bronze; the bronze and the pagan statuary disappeared long ago.

GODS AND PHILOSOPHERS

Now a Christian church, the Pantheon originally was dedicated, as its name implies, to the service of "all the gods"—another indication of Hadrian's wide-ranging cultural ideals. Presumably he and his successors truly meant all the gods, not just the Roman equivalents of the Greek Olympians. Jupiter, the Roman Zeus, was

4-9 The Pantheon, Rome, largely after A.D. 126.

4-10 Giovanni Panini, *Interior of the Pantheon,* c. 1750. Oil on canvas, 50½″ × 39″. National Gallery of Art, Washington, D.C. (Samuel H. Kress Collection).

one of these. Figure 4-11 shows a bronze statuette of Jupiter with his traditional thunderbolts in hand.

Innumerable deities had been brought into Rome from the Orient, and Rome made room for almost all of them. The worship of the newer gods sometimes involved a measure of spiritual elevation and ethical aspiration, as in the mystery cult of the Egyptian goddess Isis. Truly pious devotion is reflected in a prayer of Isis recorded or imagined by the novelist Apuleius:

> Holy goddess, everlasting savior of mankind, ever generous in your help to mortals, you show a mother's warm love for the misfortunes of those in distress. No day passes, no night, no moment however fleeting without a gracious act of yours. You protect human beings by sea and land. You lull the storms of life and stretch out your hand to rescue them. . . . Your majestic presence overawes the birds flocking in the sky, the wild animals roaming over the mountains, . . . the monsters swimming in the sea. My ability is too scanty to praise you properly, my resources too scanty to honor you with sacrifice. . . . But poor as I am I have taken a vow of devotion and will be dutiful in doing all that I can. I shall always guard the picture of your divine features and your holy godhead in the secret places of my heart.

Despite the lofty spirit sometimes seen in the worship of Isis, or such other oriental deities as Cybele (the Great Mother) and Mithras (a Persian god of light), Roman religion tended to be ceremonial, un-

4-11 *Jupiter,* 1st–2nd century A.D. Bronze, 23½″ high including base. Musées Royaux d'Art et d'Histoire, Brussels.

imaginative, and legalistic. In public prayers, Pliny the Elder noted that the "chief magistrates use set prayers. No word must be omitted or out of turn" lest the sacrifice being performed be hopelessly botched. Public religion, and much private religion also, was predominantly a matter of formulas and rigid ceremonialism containing scarcely any intellectual content or value.

Roman Philosophy

It was in part this empty, mechanical ceremonialism that turned a few educated Romans from religion to science. Here the Romans (typically, Greek-speaking Romans) displayed some talent for synthesis—the weaving together of many strands—in given areas of science; for example, Pliny the Elder in biology, Galen in medicine, and Ptolemy in a subtle but mistaken astronomical system that saw the earth as the center of the universe.

Fewer Romans, though, turned to science than to philosophy—notably to two outstanding philosophies

of the Hellenistic world, Epicureanism and Stoicism. In Rome, both flourished brilliantly in the late republican period before Augustus—in the work of Lucretius among the Epicureans and of Cicero among the Stoics. Subsequently Epicureanism lost favor: it was simply too much of a challenge to Roman civic and ethical ideals to gain lasting popularity. Roman Epicureans and Stoics alike emphasized peace of mind, with the Epicureans finding it in detached contemplation and the Stoics turning more toward civic accomplishment and fulfillment. Both schools were eclectic, in the sense of mingling incompatible principles. In fact, in philosophy and in science alike, the Romans were remarkably unadventurous: they considered compilations of ancient, untested ideas quite adequate.

Roman Epicureanism had stressed the remote impersonality of the gods and had slighted family ties and public service in favor of individual self-sufficiency. Stoicism, on the other hand, could accommodate the traditional gods and the traditional pieties; it also accepted the Roman ideals of the close-knit family, social duty, and political responsibility that had developed in Rome across many centuries. In short, Stoicism fitted much more neatly into conventional Roman patterns of thought and life than did Epicureanism.

The two most interesting proponents of Roman Stoicism were, rather startlingly, a former slave and a ruling emperor—Epictetus and Marcus Aurelius, respectively. Epictetus (c. A.D. 60–117), fittingly enough for a man once in bondage, emphasized the distinction between things that are in our power and those that are not. Our "body, property, reputation, and office" and "everything which is not our own doing" are beyond our control, and we must, he wrote, acquiesce in such circumstances. On the other hand, our minds can and should be free; at least they must rise above the fortune imposed upon us from outside. "Ask not," he admonished his readers, "that events should happen as you will, but let your will be that events should happen as they do, and you shall have peace."

Divine power, Epictetus was convinced, establishes each man's lot and the span of his life:

> Remember that you are an actor in a play, and the Playwright chooses the manner of it: if he wants it short, it is short; if long, it is long. If he wants you to act a poor man you must act the part with all your powers; and so it must be if your part be a cripple or a magistrate or a private

4-25 Altar of Augustan Peace (Ara Pacis Augustae), Rome, 13–9 B.C.

Disposing peace and war by thy own majestic way;
To tame the proud, the fetter'd slave to free:
These are imperial arts, and worthy thee.

Paternal authority, not individual freedoms, would be the keynote of Roman government. As Plutarch would cautiously observe a century later: "Of liberty the people enjoy as much as our rulers allot them, and perhaps more would not be better." This spirit of patriarchal authoritarianism is still more vividly seen in the Altar of Augustan Peace.

Nearly square, the altar is only thirty feet or so along each side and is very delicately carved. Aeneas appears in the upper relief panel to the right of the entrance; in keeping with the purpose of the altar, he is portrayed making a sacrifice to the gods of his household, who were to be the ancestral gods also of the family of Augustus. And when in another panel the emperor himself appears, it is with the heroic solemnity of his distant ancestor. The great processional frieze (fig. 4-26) is reminiscent of the classical Parthe-

4-26 *Procession*, detail from the frieze of the Altar of Augustan Peace showing the family of Augustus.

non frieze, but its figures portray a people grown older, more solemn, less spontaneous than the Greeks of Pericles' time.

The Augustan age was not only more solemn than the Periclean but far more regulatory. Democratic Athens had had its strong civic and social pressures but never the formal censorship of Rome or the flock of petty governmental informers who insinuated themselves everywhere into imperial Roman life. Political and civic freedom were the most obvious casualties in Rome, but literature, thought, and visual arts suffered too. No Western artistic outlook has changed less, or been permitted to change less, over a lengthy period than that of Rome. The empire in its long decline may offer some small encouragement to those who counsel strict adherence to traditional ways, but it demonstrates more clearly the stultification that can result from unadventurous—and humorless—traditionalism. A civilization that has lost its confident good spirits and its trust in natural spontaneity is in serious trouble indeed.

Recommended Reading

Bianchi Bandinelli, Rannuccio. *Rome: The Center of Power* (1970). Art to A.D. 200, magnificently illustrated.

Clark, M. L. *The Roman Mind* (1956). Good introduction to Roman thought.

Davenport, Basil, ed. *The Portable Roman Reader* (1951). Fine selection of original sources.

Davis, J. J. *Herculaneum: Italy's Buried Treasure* (1966). Fascinating, well-illustrated.

Dudley, Donald. *The Romans: 850 B.C–A.D. 337* (1970). Fine, brief general history.

Earl, Donald. *The Age of Augustus* (1968). Good survey, handsomely illustrated.

Grant, Michael. *History of Rome* (1978). Good general history.

Hadas, Moses. *A History of Latin Literature* (1952). Standard survey with excerpts in translation.

Hooper, Finley. *Roman Realities* (1979). Very readable narrative history; discusses literature.

Livy. *The Early History of Rome*, trans. by Aubrey de Sélincourt (1960). Good modern translation.

Oates, Whitney J., ed. *The Stoic and Epicurean Philosophers* (1940). Includes writings of Epictetus and Marcus Aurelius.

Ogilvie, R. M. *Roman Literature and Society* (1980). Handy introduction.

Tacitus. *The Complete Works of Tacitus*, trans. by A. J. Church and W. J. Brodribb (1942). The writings, in English.

Usher, Stephen. *The Historians of Greece and Rome* (1969). Good coverage of Livy and Tacitus.

Ward-Perkins, John B. *Roman Architecture* (1976). Splendid illustrations.

Wheeler, R. E. Mortimer. *Roman Art and Architecture* (1964). Good survey, well-illustrated.

5

The Early Christian and Byzantine Worlds: A.D. 200–600

esus of Nazareth lived and taught during the reigns of Augustus and Tiberius. His message of human love and compassion and of the benevolent fatherhood of a single, universal God had a widespread appeal. The first converts to his teachings were from among the humbler classes of his own people, the Palestinian Jews, and some of them accepted Jesus as the Christ or Messiah (derived from the Greek and Hebrew words, respectively, for "anointed one")—the savior the Jewish people had long expected. From its beginnings in the eastern Mediterranean, Christianity spread throughout the Roman empire and to people of various classes and backgrounds.

For nearly three centuries the growing religion remained in part an underground movement. Scorned and feared by the government, Christianity was subjected to periodic outbursts of repression. A particularly violent wave of persecution at the beginning of the Late Empire (A.D. 285–476) was by no means thorough enough to wipe out the faith, and the large number of martyrs it produced strengthened the zeal of the Christian masses. At last, toleration of Christianity was firmly established by the emperor Constantine in A.D. 313. Through

111

most of the fourth century, Christianity was the religion favored by the state, and at the end of the century it became the exclusive, official religion.

By that time the government and institutions of the vast European segment of imperial Rome were in an advanced state of decay. Constantine had contributed to a great territorial schism by founding a new capital at Byzantium (later renamed Constantinople) on the eastern fringe of Europe; this Eastern Roman, or Byzantine, empire flourished for centuries and endured on a smaller scale until 1453. The traditional date for the end of the Western Roman empire, 476, is largely symbolic. It commemorates the deposition of the last Latin Roman emperor and his replacement by a Germanic king—simply one step in the gradual transformation from antique to medieval institutions.

The basic institutional organization of the Christian churches had been established long before the end of the Western empire. The early centuries of Christianity saw the growth of a movement that offered an organization and a set of loyalties that were alternatives to those supplied by the Roman state. Priests presided over local groups of Christians and in turn accepted guidance and supervision from bishops. One of the most eminent of the bishops was the bishop of Rome, whose office would eventually evolve into the papacy, which laid claim to the ultimate earthly allegiance of all Christendom.

Christian belief and authority spread throughout the empire, and most of the northern "barbarians" who in the fifth century took control in the heart of the old Western empire were also Christians. Thus the German Odoacer, who overthrew the last Latin emperor in 476, was Christian, as was his non-German barbarian successor Theodoric, who controlled much of Italy. The Frankish peoples who overwhelmed Roman rule in Gaul (roughly modern France) soon followed the lead of their king Clovis, who became a Christian in 496. The conversion process took longer in Britain, since the "Anglo-Saxons" from the Continent who had overrun the land in the fifth century were thoroughly pagan. At the end of the sixth century only the Celtic outskirts of England—in Ireland, Wales, and Scotland—retained Christianity from the Roman period. In 597 Roman missionaries led by Augustine of Canterbury began the task of conversion.

In the meantime, parallel and rival governments and faiths evolved in the eastern Mediterranean area. For a time, under the emperor Justinian (ruled 527–565), the Byzantine empire extended its control into Italy and across most of the African coast and into southern Spain. When his western capital Ravenna finally succumbed to the Germanic Lombards in 751, the other Byzantine possessions in the West had already been overrun by Muslims professing the faith of Islam, founded earlier in Arabia by Muhammed (c. 570–632).

EARLY CHRISTIANITY

Behind Jesus of Nazareth lay the long tradition of Judaism. The Jewish Holy Scriptures would become the Old Testament—the longer part of the authoritative sacred writings, or *Bible,* of Christianity. The Jewish (or Hebrew) people had always been small in number and they had sometimes been confronted by eastern Mediterranean powers that threatened their extinction or their absorption by other states. On occasion the Hebrews had risen to a degree of earthly glory, as they had under their tenth-century B.C. kings David and Solomon, but more often they had had to rely upon their own God and their own inner strength and proud traditions for survival. Inspired by eloquent prophets, spokesmen for God's will, the Jewish people developed ideas of a sole, sovereign, transcendent God who sternly judges those who stray from his commands, and who requires that men and women go beyond religious ritual to lead lives of ethical purity and social concern.

These matters also were central in the teachings of Jesus. He, too, taught with authority—not through the sort of subtle reasoning that was favored by thinkers of ancient Greece and Rome. His followers, the first Christians, not only responded to the earlier Hebrew messages of justice and righteousness, but found additional hope and assurance in the Christian message of compassionate human solidarity under God's rule. Jesus, moreover, had forecast a glorious life after death for his followers, especially for those who had been oppressed and persecuted in their earthly lives. The New Testament—the Christian addition to the Hebrew sacred writings—memorably presents the

CHRONOLOGY

HISTORY		THE ARTS	
193–211	Septimius Severus emperor	from 200	Tertullian and Origen writing
		early 3rd century	sarcophagus of the Via Salaria
249	persecution of Christians by emperor Decius		
284–305	Diocletian emperor		
303–304	anti-Christian edicts; major persecution of Christians begins		
306–37	Constantine emperor (sole emperor from 324)		
313	Edict of Milan: toleration of Christianity		
		c. 350	Santa Costanza, Rome
360–63	pagan reaction under Julian, emperor		
374–97	Saint Ambrose, bishop of Milan		
379–95	Theodosius I emperor	late 4th century	Abrosian hymns
390s	edicts against paganism; Christianity the official Roman religion		
		early 5th century	Saint Jerome's Latin Bible; Saint Augustine's *City of God*
		430	death of Saint Augustine
		431	Church council at Ephesus: the Virgin declared Mother of God
476	Romulus Augustulus, last Latin emperor, replaced by Odoacer		
476–93	Odoacer king in Italy	490–c. 527	Sant' Apollinare Nuovo, Ravenna
493–526	Theodoric king in Italy	early 6th century	*Virgin and Child Enthroned* icon, and *Archangel Michael*
527–65	Justinian I, Byzantine emperor		
528–34	Justinian's codification of the Civil Law	532–37	Hagia Sophia, Constantinople
		533–49	Sant' Apollinare in Classe
535–54	Justinian's wars for the recovery of Sicily and Italy		
540	Justinian's commander Belisarius captures Ravenna	547–48	consecration of San Vitale, Ravenna
548	death of empress Theodora	second half of 6th century	mosaic additions to Sant' Apollinare Nuovo
		558–62	new dome of Hagia Sophia
636	beginnings of Islamic conquests in Asia and Africa		
751	Ravenna, Byzantine capital in Italy, overthrown by the Lombards		
1453	Byzantine empire overthrown by the Muslim Turks		

All dates are A.D.

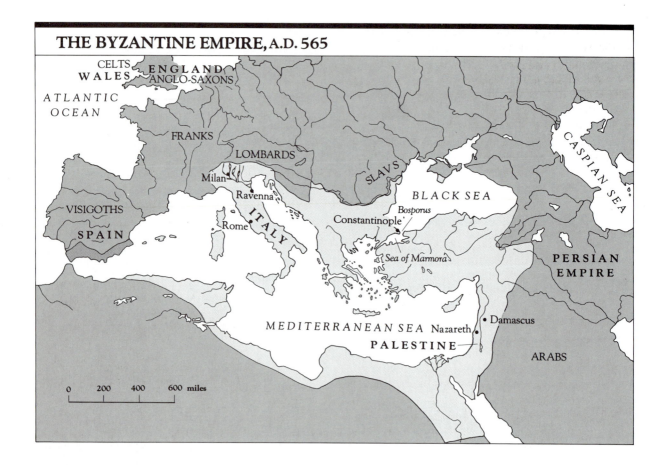

THE BYZANTINE EMPIRE, A.D. 565

words of Jesus on this subject, in the "Sermon on the Mount":

> Blessed are the meek:
>   For they shall inherit the earth. . . .
> Blessed are the pure in heart:
>   For they shall see God.
> Blessed are the peacemakers:
>   For they shall be called the children of God.
> Blessed are they which are persecuted for righteousness' sake:
>   For theirs is the kingdom of heaven.

Many early Christians found more than comfort in the message of Jesus: they also found conviction in the stories of miracles reported in the Christian writings. Jesus' reputation as a miracle worker was one of the great strengths of the faith. His reported ability to raise the dead to life (see fig. 5-1) and perform other miracles provided the evidence the humble Christians sought for Jesus' divinity. Moreover, according to the

teachings of such missionaries and organizers of the faith as Saints Peter and Paul, Jesus' sacrificial death on the cross and subsequent resurrection assured eternal salvation for the faithful.

The daily life of the early Christians differed little outwardly from that of other Romans. The Christians, like others, worked for a living, often (especially those who were slaves) under very harsh conditions. "We Christians," as the writer Tertullian asserted, "do not live apart from the rest of the world. We visit the forum, the baths, the workshops, the stores, the markets, and all the public places." However, in the days of actual and potential persecution, before A.D. 313, the Christians also visited catacombs cut into soft rock near Rome. Primarily burial places for the dead, these underground mazes served in times of greatest danger as places of worship and refuge.

Women as well as men shared in Christian faith and worship, although they did not assume leadership roles. The lives of Christian women were limited to

Plate 1 Vincent van Gogh, *Starry Night,* 1889. Oil on canvas, 28¾″ × 36¼″. The Museum of Modern Art, New York (acquired through the Lillie P. Bliss Bequest).

Plate 2 Edouard Manet, *The Fifer,* 1866. Oil on canvas, 63″ × 38¼″. Louvre, Paris.

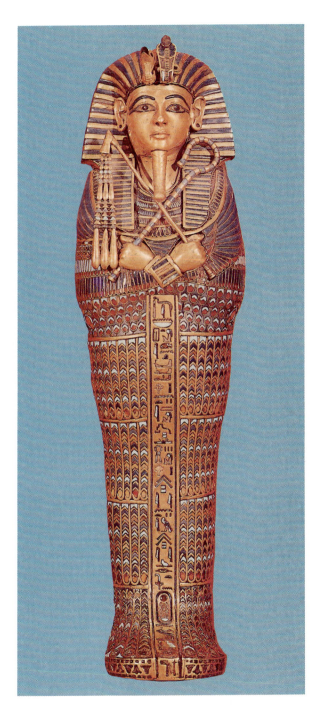

Plate 3 Coffin of Tutankhamen, mid fourteenth century B.C. Gold with precious stones; coffin is 6′11″ long. Egyptian Museum, Cairo.

Plate 4 Sound box of a harp from Ur, c. 2685 B.C. Gold with lapis lazuli and inlaid shells, 17″ high. The University Museum, University of Pennsylvania.

Plate 5 *Kore,* c. 525 B.C. Marble, 22″ high. Acropolis Museum, Athens.

Plate 6 *Woman with Fan,* Tanagra statuette, c. 300 B.C. Painted terracotta, 9¼″ high. Reproduced by Courtesy of the Trustees of the British Museum, London.

Plate 7 Agasias of Ephesus?, c. 100 B.C. Bronze portrait head from Delos, 12¾″ high. National Museum, Athens.

Plate 8 So-called *Lost Ram*, detail of a wall painting transferred to a panel, from Pompeii, first century A.D. Approximately 17″ high. Museo Nazionale, Naples.

Plate 9 *Perseus Freeing Andromeda,* first century A.D. Roman copy of a fourth-century Greek original, possibly by Nycias. Wall painting, 47¼″ × 38½″. Museo Nazionale, Naples.

Plate 10 Column of Trajan, Rome, A.D. 113.

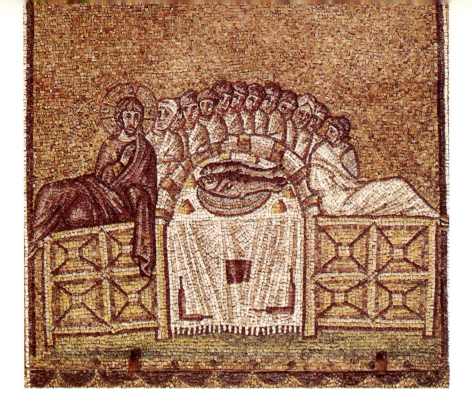

Plate 11 *The Last Supper*, c. 520. Mosaic. Sant' Apollinare Nuovo, Ravenna.

Plate 12 *Empress Theodora and Her Retinue*, c. 547–548. San Vitale, Ravenna.

5-1 *Jesus Bringing a Corpse to Life*, c. 450–460. Panel of an Italian diptych, ivory. By courtesy of the Board of Trustees of the Victoria & Albert Museum, London.

home responsibilities and religious observances, and when it was necessary for them to go out in public they usually wore veils. A good number of men and women took up an ascetic, celibate community life in monasteries and convents. For husbands and wives in the everyday world Saint Paul condoned marital relations. This sort of adjustment to human nature helped make Christianity a faith not just of extreme ascetics—of saints and martyrs alone—but a faith that could serve general social and personal needs as well.

In Paul's letters to the early churches, he greatly advanced the development of Christian *theology*—those theoretical considerations concerning divinity and God's relationship with human beings. Paul stressed not only the basic teachings but also the divinity of Jesus, as the Christ or Savior promised in the Hebrew holy writings. Within two centuries the relatively simple religion of the first Christians gave way to increasingly complex speculations and ideological clashes among followers of the new faith.

Among the greatest challenges facing the early Church was the need to define and standardize Christian belief. Much argumentation was involved, and

final decisions on *orthodoxy*—that is, correct belief—were often painful. Many crucial definitions of belief that were accepted in the later Church were not formulated until the fourth and fifth centuries after Christ. One of the most central formulations was a statement of the nature of the *Trinity*—a single God within whom there exist the three "persons" or manifestations of Father, Son (the Christ), and Holy Spirit. It was never maintained that the dogma of the Trinity, or other dogmas, followed human, rational logic or common sense; statements of dogma were, rather, mysteries that Christians must accept on faith. Early Christianity, by and large, rejected the clear-eyed rationalism and freedom of thought idealized in classical Greece and turned to the mysterious, the miraculous, and the authoritative.

Among the thinkers who helped establish new Christian directions were Tertullian, Jerome, Ambrose, and Augustine. Tertullian, in the early third century, proclaimed the irrelevance and spiritual peril of pagan philosophy and demanded the acceptance of Christian authority stemming from a stern and awesome deity. Christianity, for Tertullian, deserved special authority precisely because it required the deliberate renunciation of those powers of human reason that were available even to non-Christians. He also was one of early Christianity's most outspoken opponents of women, whom he viewed as "the devil's gateway" through whose sexual appeal men are lured to eternal damnation. Saint Jerome, who died in 420, was somewhat more moderate than Tertullian in his support of *asceticism*—the denial of bodily desires—but retained the typical Christian distrust of the senses and of all earthly goals. He produced the *Vulgate,* the Latin translation of the Bible that became the authoritative version for the Roman Catholic Church.

Saint Ambrose (fig. 5-2), the eminent bishop of Milan who died in 397, was known in his day as an eloquent orator. He was a defender of the Christian mysteries, of the absolute supremacy of bishops over emperors on religious matters, and of the spiritual merits of virginity. Ambrose is best remembered, however, as the reputed author of nearly a hundred church hymns, of which he may actually have written as many as twenty. One of these, *Aeterne rerum conditor,* was authenticated by his protégé, Saint Augustine. Like the other Ambrosian hymns, it served a utilitarian purpose in the early Christian community, that of expounding Christian teaching—in this case the doc-

5-2 *Saint Ambrose*, fifth century. Mosaic. San Vittore in Ciel d'Oro (adjoining Sant' Ambrogio), Milan.

trines of God's benevolent rule, God's grace, and the mysterious Trinity:

Framer of the earth and sky,
    Ruler of the day and night,
With a glad variety
    Tempering all, and making light;

Gleams upon our dark path flinging,
    Cutting short each night begun.
Hark! for chanticleer is singing,
    Hark! he chides the lingering sun. . . .

Jesu, Master! when we sin
    Turn on us Thy healing face;
It will melt the offense within
    Into penitential grace. . . .

To the Father and the Son
    And the Spirit, who in heaven
Ever witness, Three in One,
    Praise on earth be ever given.

The most influential of early Christian theologians was Saint Augustine of Hippo (in North Africa), who died in 430. After successive allegiances to several pagan philosophies, including that of Plato, he had turned to Christianity, not out of intellectual assent, but as a spiritual awakening through God's miraculous intervention to assure eternal salvation. Although a subtle thinker, Augustine thereafter defended vigorously the priority of Christian faith over reason. One accepts the crucial Christian teachings, said Augustine, because they come ultimately from God, and only after this wholehearted acceptance should one's faith be buttressed by reason or the evidence of the senses.

The City of God, as Augustine wrote in his massive book of that name, is not a collection of rationally convinced Christians but the mysterious congregation of all true believers on earth and the saints in heaven. It is distinguished from the very different "city," or earthly community, of "those who wish to live after the flesh," as against the spirit. The two cities must, however, "live in peace, each after their own kind." The earthly city has its uses in pursuing earthly peace; "the heavenly city, or rather the part of it which sojourns on earth and lives by faith, makes use of this peace only because it must, until this mortal condition which necessitates it shall pass away. Consequently, so long as it lives like a captive and a stranger in the earthly city . . . , it makes no scruple to obey the laws of the earthly city, whereby the things necessary for the maintenance of this mortal life are administered."

Despite this hoped-for earthly partnership between Church and state, the ultimate goal of Christians, according to Augustine, must remain the "eternal felicity of the city of God"—that is, in the heavenly life beyond the grave. Those dwelling in heaven will be filled, he wrote, "with all good, enjoying the inalienable delights of eternal joys, oblivious of sins, oblivious of sufferings, and yet not so oblivious of its deliverance as to be ungrateful of its Deliverer." Augustine's vision of heavenly blessedness as the goal of human life would be shared by countless people for many centuries to come; it would be a predominant force in artistic, musical, literary, and ideological expression through a thousand years of Western history.

EARLY CHRISTIAN SCULPTURE

It was inevitable that the art of the early Christian era would offer a sharp contrast to the civic and idealized humanistic expression of the classical Greeks, the dynastic and individualistic motivations of the Hellenistic peoples, and the alternate utilitarianism and aestheticism of the pagan Romans. On occasion, the very survival of the visual arts seemed endangered: secular art, certainly, had little point in the context of the Christian vision, and some thinkers questioned the merit of even religious art. Many early Christian writers, like Augustine, were mistrustful of religious imagery in the visual arts. Not only was their own imagination more verbal and spiritual than pictorial, but they often feared the literalness and the lack of spirituality in precise artistic images. Moreover, not only the thinkers but ordinary Christian believers were aware of Old Testament warnings against "graven images." This may have encouraged avoidance of large statues in early Christian times, although it did not stop production of sculptural art on a more modest scale or nonsculptural pictorial representations. For example, elaborately sculpted *sarcophagi,* stone coffins intended for display, were common among the well-to-do families who could afford them.

The Sarcophagus of the Via Salaria (fig. 5-3), dating from the early third century, typifies the sculptural art of the period and reflects the preoccupations of the Christian community in Rome. The rams at the corners derive from pagan Roman decorative tradition, as do many other features of early Christian art: the artists, after all, were Romans and not necessarily Christians themselves. On the left and the right are groups of three figures: men forming a teaching scene, and a group of holy women. The sculpted man and woman representing the deceased couple hold scrolls (still the books of the day) and may be giving or receiving instruction in the Christian faith. Men and women were spiritually equal in the Church, but Church offices and teaching roles were becoming increasingly male prerogatives at that time.

At the center of the Via Salaria sarcophagus relief is the figure of a shepherd carrying a sheep. The symbolic reference is to Christ, the Good Shepherd who cared lovingly for his flock and who, according to both Old and New Testaments, would sacrifice himself for them. The Good Shepherd theme appeared again and again in early Christian art—on sculpted sarcophagi, as statuettes, in paintings on underground tomb walls, and in pictures on church walls.

Also popular was the theme of Jonah, the Hebrew prophet whom a sea monster had swallowed but then spit forth on dry land. A sculpture like *Jonah Cast Up* (fig. 5-4) would symbolize for early Christians the resurrection of Christ from the dead and the rising of the Christian soul from the night of death to the light of eternal life. In the marble statuette illustrated here, Jonah resembles a pagan Roman sea god, and the fanciful monster combines the snout of a boar and the paws of a lion with a fishlike body. The whimsy and visual appeal of this little work should not, however, obscure its original symbolic significance.

Symbolism—the use of visible signs or forms to suggest intangible concepts—characterized a large part of early Christian and medieval art. These centuries saw the unquestioned triumph of the Christian faith in Europe—a faith whose spiritual and artistic vision was directed not toward outward, earthly things but inward toward the soul. For Christians, the secularism, humanism, and realism of classical Greece and imperial

5-3 *Good Shepherd between a Teaching Scene and a Group of Holy Women,* detail from the sarcophagus of the Via Salaria, early third century. Marble. Musei del Laterano, Rome.

5-4 *Jonah Cast Up*, second half of the third century. Marble, 16" high. Cleveland Museum of Art (John L. Severance Fund).

Rome were replaced, for more than a thousand years, by spirituality and supernaturalism and by the symbolism that often alone seemed appropriate to express them.

THE SETTING FOR CHRISTIAN WORSHIP IN THE WEST

Early Christianity could not subsist by otherworldly vision alone. Above all, Christians required specially constructed places to congregate for worship and for veneration of the remains and other relics of their saints and martyrs. To be sure, in the early Christian period, at least in the Latin West, few of these structures exceeded modest dimensions aside from old Saint Peter's in Rome, now destroyed. It should be noted that, from the fourth century on, nearly all of these church buildings were literally "oriented"; that is, the altar and choir areas, toward which worshippers faced, were at the east end of the church.

Churches in Centralized Form

In general, early Christian churches were built on either the centralized plan or the basilican plan, although combinations of the two were not unknown. The centralized plan was particularly popular in the West in the fourth century and is exemplified in a small church in the city of Rome, Santa Costanza (fig. 5-5). Like other centralized churches, it is structurally organized around a central point. Santa Costanza is essentially round, although centralized churches can take somewhat different shapes, such as an octagon. Paired classical columns help form an arcade around the inner room and largely support the weight of the dome above it. At the base of the dome are sixteen large windows that directly light the central area but not the vaulted *ambulatory*, the covered passage that encircles the central area. Even with the elaborate capitals and entablatures of the columns, the overall impression is one of rather severe elegance.

The centralized church plan is exemplified on a larger and more complex scale in the church of San Vitale in Ravenna. Ravenna, in northeastern Italy, was near the Adriatic Sea yet defensible on its land side because of swamps and marshes; several last attempts to defend the old Western empire had been based there, and in the sixth century it again became a city of critical importance. From 493 to 526 it flourished brilliantly as capital of the enlightened "barbarian" king Theodoric and, from 544, as western capital of the Byzantine emperor Justinian, who had added Italy to his other domains. It was especially under Theodoric and Justinian that major building programs were initiated in Ravenna—most notably the construction of a palace and numerous churches. Ravenna was therefore an extraordinary exception to the general cultural decay of the age and today is a city of handsome architectural mementos of its brief period of glory. This architecture is early Christian in style.

San Vitale was one of the most distinguished of the Ravenna churches. Financed by a prosperous banker, its construction was begun in the 520s and 530s, and the church was dedicated in 547 or 548 by Archbishop Maximian. Much of the interior was lavishly adorned with mosaics—an art form popular not only in ancient Rome but also in sixth-century Constantinople. The plan of San Vitale (fig. 5-6) had both Roman and Byzantine precedents. The basically round—actually octagonal—design is clear. Its other features include the narthex, or hall, to the west, a colonnaded central section for the congregation, circular stairways leading to the upper level, and a rectangular sanctuary to the east (for the performance of the Christian ritual), completed by a semicircular apse. As a view of the exterior (fig. 5-7) shows, the main portal today is to one side. The basic construction is of brick. Window space, on three levels, is rather generous for the period, but the original windows were presumably of translucent stone, not glass. Thus the interior lighting was less intense than it is today. A slanting, pyramidal roof covers the *cupola,* or small dome, which can be seen from inside the church.

Churches in Basilica Form

The alternative plan of early Christian churches, increasingly popular during the fourth, fifth, and sixth

centuries, was the basilican plan, so named from the large public buildings of pagan Rome such as the Basilica Ulpia, whose general outlines they followed. The typical form of a Christian basilica can be observed in an aerial view of Sant' Apollinare in Classe (fig. 5-8), a sixth-century church of brick construction, in the port-city of Classe some two miles from Ravenna.

The aerial view of the structure shows its simple organization. As in most pagan Roman basilicas, a long, narrow central hall, called the *nave* in churches, is flanked by lower side aisles. Windows line the *clerestory*—the upper zone of the nave that stands clear of the slanted aisle roofs. The entrance is at one end of the nave, preceded by a low vestibule, or *narthex;* at the other end is a projecting, semicircular construction known as the *apse.* The original courtyard (*atrium*) in front of the church has been destroyed, and a bell tower was added in the Middle Ages. The plan, figure 5-9, shows not only nave, aisles, and narthex but also the atrium and other sections that have been destroyed.

The plain brick or stone exterior of early Chris-

5-5   Interior of Santa Costanza, Rome, c. A.D. 350.

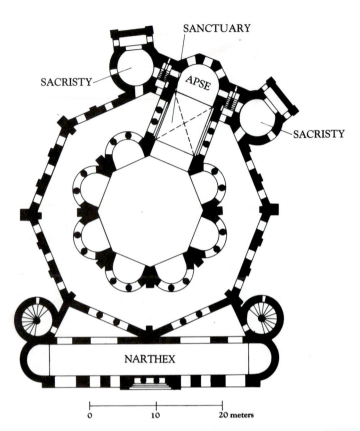

SANCTUARY

SACRISTY

APSE

SACRISTY

NARTHEX

0   10   20 meters

5-6 Plan of San Vitale, Ravenna.

5-7 San Vitale, Ravenna, second quarter of the sixth century.

5-8 Sant' Apollinare in Classe (near Ravenna), c. 533–549.

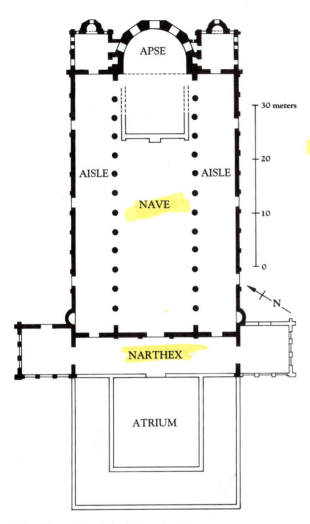

5-9 Plan of Sant' Apollinare in Classe.

Mosaics for the Faithful

As explained in our earlier discussions of the Hellenistic and imperial Roman periods, mosaics are made by placing bits of hard, colored material such as stone or glass on a surface that has been covered with gum or cement. In the earlier periods the mosaic pieces (*tesserae*) were most often pieces of stone, and mosaics were floor decoration. By the sixth century the pieces generally were of glass, and the designs were sacred scenes for decorating walls. In early Christian churches the smooth, shiny bits are ordinarily positioned at somewhat different angles, thus producing an ever-varying visual effect as sunlight from the windows shifts in direction. Mosaics were the preferred pictorial medium for decorating the expanses of flat walls typical of Ravenna's churches.

At the top right in the photograph of Sant' Apollinare Nuovo is a mosaic of the front of Theodoric's palace. The original figures within the arches were replaced in Justinian's time by mosaic curtains. Along each nave wall, above the processional of saints and martyrs and between the clerestory windows, the mosaics portray figures from the Old and New Testaments, and in the top-most zone they portray scenes from the life of Christ. Among these is *The Last Supper* (fig. 5-11). Jesus and his twelve Apostles recline in ancient Roman style around a semicircular table; Judas, who is about to betray his master to the Roman authorities, is opposite him. Following Christian tradition, the fish on the table symbolize Christ, since the Greek initials for "Jesus Christ, Son of God, Savior" form the Greek word for fish. In the Last Supper scene, more specifically, the two fish may symbolically represent the body and the blood of Jesus Christ, which the disciples ate as bread and wine, thus foreshadowing the Communion ceremony of the Christian Church. Another mosaic scene from the same series in Sant' Apollinare Nuovo, *The Good Shepherd Separating the Sheep from the Goats*, was discussed in chapter 1 (see fig. 1-4).

The complexities of mosaic symbolism are suggested by the apse decoration of Sant' Apollinare in Classe (fig. 5-12). In the horizontal band at the summit of the arch is the figure of Christ flanked by symbolic representations (derived from the New Testament Book of Revelation) of the four Evangelists. Just below them twelve sheep ascend from the gates of Jerusalem and Bethlehem; these are the saved souls of

tian basilican structures was in strong contrast to the colorful interior, as seen in the church of Sant' Apollinare Nuovo in Ravenna (fig. 5-10). The church, dedicated to Christ, was essentially complete by the time of Theodoric's death. Later it was rededicated to the French Saint Martin, and then again (in the ninth century) to Ravenna's first bishop and patron saint, Apollinaris. The richly coffered ceiling is a seventeenth-century embellishment, and the apse a twentieth-century reconstruction, but the original longitudinal orientation, with the altar as the focal point, remains clear. This orientation is reinforced by the figures of saints and martyrs in procession toward the apse, in the lowest tier of mosaics above the columns and arches that form the nave arcades.

5-10 Interior of Sant' Apollinare Nuovo, Ravenna, 490–c. 504. The mosaics were added in the second half of the sixth century.

Christians rising to heaven. In the vaulting, or half-dome of the apse, stands Saint Apollinaris surrounded by the sheep of his faithful Christian flock. Above him is a cross with a small head of Christ at the intersection. Above the cross and the circle around it is the hand of God the Father, with a Hebrew prophet to each side. In an attractive, stylized garden below are three sheep gazing upward. The whole scene symbolizes the Transfiguration of Christ, as it appeared to the apostles Peter, James, and John.

The early Christians did not think of their architecture and its decoration in terms of beauty; their churches, rather, were functional and inspirational. A church, unlike a classical temple, was a gathering place for worshippers and celebrants of religious rites. A sense of almost total enclosure or isolation from the outside world was encouraged by the usual high placement of most of the windows. This sense of shelter and of Christian community through pictorial symbols of the faith would persist in churches into the Romanesque period, which succeeded the early Christian era.

THE BYZANTINE WORLD

The early Christian world of the West was not the only heir of the ancient Roman empire, nor the most brilliant. To the east, on the shores of the Bosporus—part of the water link between the Mediterranean and the Black Sea—lay the great city of Constantinople. Today known as Istanbul, this city was the imposing and highly civilized capital of the Byzantine empire and the direct heir to the Eastern Roman empire founded by Constantine. At least until the end of the early Middle Ages, around the year 1000, Byzantine civilization displayed an economic prosperity and a highly developed cultural life that was well in advance of most Western achievements of the time.

In A.D. 323 the emperor Constantine determined to establish a new capital in the East. Already the Western empire was plagued by barbarian threats as well as internal dissension. Having restored order in the West, Constantine ordered the building of a new

5-11 *The Last Supper*, c. 520. Mosaic. Sant' Apollinare Nuovo, Ravenna.

fortified city on the site of the ancient Greek town of Byzantium located on a peninsula just across the Bosporus from Asia. To the north was the inlet known as the Golden Horn, and to the south was the Sea of Marmora; now to the west he built strong walls against any attack from the European side. A tenth-century Byzantine mosaic (fig. 5-13), over the south doorway to Justinian's great sixth-century church of Hagia Sophia, portrays Constantine (on the right) presenting a model of the walled city of Constantinople to the enthroned Virgin and Justinian presenting her with a model of Hagia Sophia itself. The scene reflects the splendid, ceremonial formality characteristic of a great deal of Byzantine mosaic art.

In 325 the site of the greatly enlarged Byzantium was consecrated, and a great building program initiated, for the purpose of bringing to fruition Constantine's vision of grandeur—a New Rome for the Eastern empire. A new street plan was superimposed on the old, and a multitude of new forums, palaces, churches, gardens, and gates came into being. For embellishing

5-12   Apse of Sant' Apollinare in Classe.

5-13 *Constantine and Justinian Offer Homage to the Virgin*, c. 1000. Mosaic, 16′2½″ × 7′5½″. South entrance, Hagia Sophia, Istanbul.

the new structures, the entire Greco-Roman world was looted for art treasures and such Christian relics as the cross on which Jesus was said to have died. The building program proceeded rapidly, and the gleaming new city was dedicated in May 330. More public buildings, especially churches, were added in subsequent centuries and a new wall farther west was constructed, but the basic features of Constantine's city endured for more than a thousand years.

By the reign of Justinian (527–565) the population of Constantinople had surpassed a half-million and may have reached a million. It was an extraordinary mixture of peoples, with a babel of languages. Greek, however, was the common linguistic currency as well as the language of court and church. At the symbolic center of the bustling city was a square, the Augusteum, near which were located the new church of the Holy Wisdom (Hagia Sophia), the ancient Greek public baths, the imperial palace, and the Hippodrome, an arena for chariot racing. Chariot races were the main focus of excitement and passion among sports fans, factions of whom engaged in political battles and rioting on occasion. The Mese, a great boulevard lined with porticoes and punctuated by grand squares adorned with monuments, extended from the Augusteum to the Golden Gate of the Theodosian

Wall five miles away. There were other broad avenues, also, and behind all of them lay mazes of narrow streets and alleys laid out irregularly on the hilly contours of the city land. There were hundreds of churches and many monasteries, the latter for monks who had retired from the world, presumably to live lives of ascetic self-denial.

Wharves succeeded wharves on Constantinople's Golden Horn; here foodstuffs and handmade goods were loaded or unloaded to support the city's life and promote economic prosperity. Only the state armament factories and workshops were exceptions to the predominant rule of small private shops. Many skilled craftsmen labored in the city, producing handsome works in precious metals, ivory, enamel, stone, mosaic, paint, and cloth. Some less skilled work was done by slaves, but much more by free labor. For the protection of both producers and consumers, trade guilds controlled prices, although not always effectively. In such cases, or because of other pressures, riots might break out, sometimes accompanied by arson. Deliberately set or not, fires periodically devastated whole sections of the city, whose humbler buildings were of wood. Stone and brick were used for public, more noble construction.

Byzantine government was highly authoritarian, and society, too, was highly structured if not fossilized. Rank was important but did not determine all political and social relations; many Byzantines rose from humble poverty to positions of great wealth and influence. For example, there was Justinian's wife, Theodora. The daughter of a bear-keeper (for bear fights in the arena), she led an early life that was scandalous to many Byzantines. However, her wit, cleverness, and beauty gained her, it was said, a vast number of male companions and admirers, including Justinian, the heir to the throne. They were married in 525, and shortly thereafter Theodora was at Justinian's side as empress of the Mediterranean world. The Byzantine mosaic in figure 5-14 portrays her and a group of attendants in full courtly splendor as if at the ceremonial dedication of Ravenna's San Vitale, where the mosaic is found. The lower part of Theodora's garment emphasizes the Biblical parallel to her gift-bringing: the Three Wise Men are portrayed bearing gifts for the infant Jesus. Few Byzantine women were as fortunate as Theodora, but their legal rights were well recognized and they were not confined to their homes, as their predecessors had been in the ancient Greek world.

5-14 *Empress Theodora and Her Retinue*, c. 547–548. San Vitale, Ravenna.

Byzantine Learning and Literature

The Byzantine empire, essentially an agrarian land, knew not only extremes of wealth and poverty but also extremes of literacy and illiteracy and of civilized polish and uncivilized crudeness. Of course, the historical record has preserved primarily the happier of these extremes. For example, we know a great deal about Byzantine Christianity; with its distinctive forms and attitudes, this religion was the empire's principal social cement. Usually church and state cooperated fully, more in the tradition of the ancient Asian kingdoms than of the tolerant societies of ancient Greece and Rome. The Byzantine church would not split completely and definitively from Roman Christianity until 1054, but throughout the preceding seven centuries it was developing its own distinctive rituals, holy days, and ideas on Christian authority (the preeminence of the pope in Rome was seldom admitted). Eventually the Byzantine church—the Eastern Orthodox Church—would give its spiritual form and tone to all of eastern Europe, including Russia.

The Byzantine world placed much importance on education and scholarship. To some extent education followed the Hellenistic and Roman pattern of private tutoring or private schools for young children, and state schools for older children, mainly boys. The education provided by state schools was supplemented by religious teaching, usually in schools connected with monasteries. It is noteworthy that in spite of the great political and social influence of the Byzantine church, a young male Byzantine could still receive a fine secular education. As for scholarship on a higher level, the Byzantine record is less impressive than the Hellenistic; philosophy, science, and medicine were still studied and expounded, but few original insights were generated. Much more effort was expended upon theology, following the lead of the Greek scholar Origen (died 254). His thought was distinguished by both a subtle rationalism and an intense mysticism that sought union with transcendent divinity. Fine theological points attracted great interest and discussion in the Byzantine empire, and many Byzantine authors would later be read and admired in the medieval Western world. The last Byzantine church father of importance was John of Damascus (died 754), who preceded the Western theologians of the High Middle Ages (after 1000) in making substantial use of Aristotle.

Of Byzantine historians we note only one, the celebrated Procopius of Caesarea (in Palestine). His two official works are the *History of the Wars* of Justinian and *The Buildings,* which describes that emperor's great public works and other achievements. In *The Buildings,* for example, Procopius sums up Justinian's subduing of barbarian threats, his territorial expansionism and religious authoritarianism, his economic policies, and (most importantly) his codification of the imperial laws. On the other hand, Procopius presents a quite different picture of the emperor in his *Secret History,* a subversive blast that portrays Justinian both as a demon and as a puppet of his domineering wife. Are we, for example, to believe his picture elsewhere of Justinian's illustrious, far-seeing, commanding statesmanship, or his view of the emperor in the *Secret History* as "extremely simple, with no more sense than a donkey, ready to follow anyone who pulls the rein, waving its ears all the time" and "making a mess of everything"? There is simply no way to reconcile the many contradictions in the writings of Procopius; the opposing extremes that we find there inspire little confidence in his judgment or objectivity.

Justinian and Hagia Sophia

The Byzantine rulers, Justinian included, touted themselves as God's representatives on earth, and certainly their control over the Eastern church was very real, especially since they controlled the election of its patriarch. Each new ruler was crowned by the patriarch—which gave visible evidence of his standing as an emperor anointed by God. Inspired by his presumed closeness to divinity, Justinian expended vast resources on religious donations, which cast glory upon himself and the God he considered his partner. Thus it was that Justinian built or rebuilt more than thirty churches in Constantinople, including his new Hagia Sophia, or Church of the Holy Wisdom (fig. 5-15). This immense monument remains one of the world's wonders even today.

The planning and construction of Hagia Sophia was entrusted to Anthemius of Tralles, a distinguished geometrician and engineer, who was assisted by Isidore of Miletus. At the time their architectural masterpiece

5-15   Hagia Sophia, Istanbul, 532–537. Dome was rebuilt 558–562, and Muslim minarets were added later.

was described not only as "marvelous and terrifying" but as "the application of geometry to solid matter." The appropriateness of the latter can be sensed from the plan of the structure (fig. 5-16). The most essential construction was completed in late 537, when Justinian presided at the church's consecration. Considering the challenges faced in the work, the less-than-six-year building period was remarkably brief. When the daring shallow dome of the structure collapsed during an earthquake in 558, Isidore's nephew, Isidore the Younger, constructed the steeper dome that crowns the church today. Further earthquakes in the area have caused no real damage to this most solid structure.

Procopius can be trusted on the subject of Hagia Sophia at least, for visitors to Istanbul can see visual evidence to support his remarks. Procopius praised especially the "enormous spherical dome" (see fig. 5-17 for the interior of the church), "which makes the building exceptionally beautiful. It seems not to be founded on solid masonry, but to be suspended from heaven by a golden chain." The whole domed ceiling, well over a hundred feet in diameter, is overlaid with gold, as are the ceilings of the aisles on each side of the structure. Women worshipped on one side, and men on the other—and Procopius was careful to point out

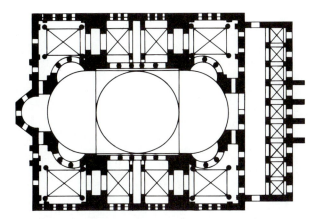

5-16   Plan of Hagia Sophia.

5-17   Interior of Hagia Sophia.

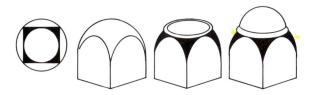

5-18   Construction of a dome resting on pendentives.

that the two areas were equally brilliant. The basic structure of the church is of stone, especially the four immense piers that support the dome, all with massive buttresses pushing in against them. The vaults and arches are of brick, and all interior surfaces are covered by brightly colored marble, gold, and mosaics. The dome rests on *pendentives*—an architectural device for supporting a round dome on a square base. (The pendentives are the spherical triangular areas seen schematically in solid black in figure 5-18; two of them are fully visible in fig. 5-17.)

The exterior of Hagia Sophia is not pleasing to the eye in its utilitarian huddled massiveness, but the interior, as noted, is quite a different matter. The basic design is a compromise between the basilican and centralized forms—the nave and aisles implying something of a basilican plan, but the dome and the chunky exterior outline even more insistently suggesting centralization. In any case, no structure better exemplifies the vast pretensions of Justinian's reign than the great bulk and grandeur of Hagia Sophia.

Byzantine Pictorial Art

The Byzantines were very conscious of their predecessors, the classical Greeks, the Hellenistic peoples, and then the Romans who had taken over the lands of the eastern Mediterranean. The Greek classics such as Homer remained the basis of cultural indoctrination in the Byzantine educational system. However, this nostalgia for the past was balanced by a new emphasis upon formalism. In the visual arts, for example, any evolution toward humanistic realism was held back by formal conventions of bodily proportions. Unnaturally elongated forms, like those of the Virgin in the mosaic of *Constantine and Justinian* (see fig. 5-13), would persist in Byzantine art for a thousand years. Another pervasive characteristic of this art is its almost complete anonymity. In this respect, the Byzantines were more in the Roman than the Greek tradition; there was little conscious experimentation in art and virtually no concept of the creative individuality of the artist.

Anonymity of the artist characterizes the long tradition of the Byzantine *icon,* a religious image typically painted on a small wooden panel. In the Eastern Orthodox tradition an icon is to be venerated—not as an idol or an image to be worshipped, but for the holy prototype of the image made manifest through the picture. Most icons are painted on rectangular wooden panels, either single, double (*diptychs*), or triple (*triptychs*). Others are carved in ivory or other materials. Each attests to some religious teaching or *dogma*—that is, a belief officially established as authoritative and immutable that the faithful must believe.

The Virgin and Child Enthroned, Flanked by Saints Theodore and George (fig. 5-19) is a sixth-century *encaustic* icon on a single panel. (In encaustic painting the pigments are mixed with wax, which then is driven into the backing by applying heat.) An important characteristic of icons with multiple figures is exemplified here: the figures are completely isolated from each other. Saints Theodore and George appear to be oblivious not only of each other but of the Mother of God and her Child as well. This isolation or aloofness of icon figures contributes to the air of contemplative mysticism that pervades much of Byzantine pictorial art. Most Byzantine painted figures face forward unambiguously, although in the *Virgin and Child Enthroned* the Virgin shows some indication of *contrapposto*—that is, part of her body is turned in a direction opposite that of another; her knees are turned to the left and her eyes are turned to the right.

Like early Christian art in the West, Byzantine sculpture was seldom freestanding or large-scale; small-scale relief sculpture predominated. An attractive example is an early-sixth-century ivory panel, once a part of a diptych, portraying the Archangel Michael (fig. 5-20). Michael holds a staff in one hand and an orb (symbolizing imperial power) surmounted by a cross in his other hand. A cross within a wreath is sculpted above his head. More classical or Hellenistic influence is evident here than is usual in Byzantine art, especially in the lavish sweep of the drapery. At the same time, and despite the realistic face and the careful delineation of human contours beneath the robe, the figure is already passing to another, more spiritual plane. The feet bear no real relationship to the stairs on which they might seem to rest; if they are in any contact at all with the stairway they seem to slide down it. Moreover, although the angel is positioned toward the top of the stairs receding from the archway, his right wing and both arms advance in front of the archway. With its delicate carving and partial realism, this panel looks toward the mystical, spiritual realm most often preferred by the Byzantine world in its religious art. This supernatural otherworldliness would also be seen in the art of the subsequent Romanesque age.

5-19   *The Virgin and Child Enthroned, Flanked by Saints Theodore and George*, sixth century. Encaustic icon on panel, 27½″ × 17¾″. Monastery of Saint Catherine, Mount Sinai.

THE BEGINNINGS OF CHRISTIAN SONG

The growth of Christian vocal music in the Eastern empire, as in the West, accompanied the growth of Christianity itself. In both areas the precedent of ancient Greek and Roman *monophony* was followed; that is, music continued to consist of a single melodic line. The languages in which the songs were sung were of course the languages of the respective churches—Greek in the East and Latin in the West. Influenced primarily by Jewish sacred music, early Christian music soon expanded from Old Testament psalms to hymns and prayers and then to complex liturgical services. Among these services was the *Mass*—a collection of prayers and ceremonies focusing on the *Eucharist*, the reenactment of the miraculous transformation of bread and wine into the body and blood of Jesus Christ. The words were sung or chanted by the *priest*—the religious

5-20 *Archangel Michael*, early sixth century. Panel of a diptych, ivory, 17″ × 5½″. Reproduced by Courtesy of the Trustees of the British Museum, London.

chant (often called plainchant or *plainsong*), with its repeated approximation of the opening melody. Characteristics of the Ambrosian *Pater Noster* are its very restricted range of tones and its forthright syllabic setting of the words—one note for each syllable. This chant is easily sung, even though it lacks harmony and regularly recurring accents, or *rhythm*. It seems to have been sung often not only by priests and their assistants but by their congregations as well.

In the East, with typical Byzantine formality, there was less congregational singing. The music of the Eastern church, sung largely by those trained in the liturgy, was more difficult to sing than that of the Latin West. Much, though not all, Byzantine church music was *melismatic*. That is, first of all, it was composed of long melodies, not sturdy brief melodies like those in the Ambrosian manner. Secondly, individual syllables often had to be sung to whole sequences of notes rather than to individual notes. These sequences, or *melismas*, are an ornamental feature that is unnatural and difficult for untrained singers. This is yet another example of the sophistication of the remarkable Byzantine empire at its height.

Recommended Reading

Bovini, Giuseppe. *Ravenna* (1972). Extraordinary photographs of art with short essays.

Brown, Peter. *The World of Late Antiquity*, A.D. *150–750* (1971). On "social and cultural change"; many illustrations.

Browning, Robert. *Justinian and Theodora* (1971). Good narrative history; handsomely illustrated.

Davies, J. G. *The Early Christian Church* (1965). A systematic narrative.

Grabar, André. *The Golden Age of Justinian: From the Death of Theodosius to the Rise of Islam* (1967). Fine text on art with magnificent illustrations.

Gough, Michael. *The Origins of Christian Art* (1974). Good, illustrated survey.

Kähler, Heinz, and Cyril Mango. *Hagia Sophia* (1967). Evocative text with fine black-and-white illustrations.

Markus, Robert A. *Christianity in the Roman World* (1974). Stimulating survey; illustrated.

Randers-Pehrson, Justine Davis. *Barbarians and Romans: The Birth Struggle of Europe*, A.D. *400–700* (1983). Scholarly, interesting narrative; well-illustrated.

Rice, David Talbot. *The Art of Byzantium* (1959). A survey with handsome illustrations and comments.

Saint Augustine of Hippo. *The Confessions*, trans. by Edward B. Pusey (1951). Good translation.

Tierney, Brian, ed. *The Middle Ages*, vol. 1: *Sources of Medieval History* (1983). Handy collection of original sources.

leader who was becoming a mediator between God and Christian laymen—and his assistants.

These practices were well established by the time of Saint Ambrose in the late fourth century. Ambrose's name was given to a group of sacred chants that developed after his death, some of which use verses he wrote. Chant here refers to the repetitive singing of a melody—a succession of single musical tones—adapted to the words of a text by repeating and varying the sequence of tones without regular rhythm. An Ambrosian version of the *Pater Noster* (the "Our Father" or "The Lord's Prayer") exemplifies one type of

6

The Romanesque Age:

A.D. 600–1200

Early Christian and Byzantine civilization was centered in the northern and eastern Mediterranean areas. After A.D. 600, despite continued cultural vigor in Italy and the Byzantine empire, the focus shifted toward more northern regions in Europe. Earlier these regions had been characterized by shifting "barbarian" populations, Christianization, political fragmentation, isolated rural economies, and a decline in many aspects of civilized living. There were notable exceptions to this decline, however, such as revivals of art and learning in Ireland and Northumbria (an area of northern England and southern Scotland) in the seventh and early eighth centuries. Cultural revivals followed in northwestern Continental Europe during the reign (A.D. 768–814) of the Frankish emperor Charlemagne and in the Germanies under Otto the Great (936–973). The prospects of centralized political authority seemed brightest under Charlemagne, but his empire became fragmented during the ninth century.

Economic vigor and strong central governments gained momentum only after the year 1000, the traditional symbolic dividing line between the early and the High Middle Ages. The latter period encompassed three centuries—the eleventh through the thirteenth. Although customs and traditions remained very strong in the High Middle Ages, changes in all realms were more rapid than before,

131

and the spirit of the age was one of confidence and spontaneity. This spirit characterized especially the visual, literary, and musical arts, both in the maturity of the Romanesque style (to about A.D. 1150 in France and to around 1200 elsewhere in Europe) and in the Gothic style that grew out of it.

Although secular concerns occupied a growing, lively segment of western European life after A.D. 1000, the influence of the Christian Church remained strong in the mature Romanesque age, not only in people's spiritual lives but also in general political and cultural life. By the year 1000 Christianity had effectively split into two sections, the Greek Orthodox Church and the Roman Catholic Church; the final, definitive break came in 1054. Several years later Pope Nicholas II solidified the independence of the papacy by inaugurating a system under which designated churchmen, the cardinals, would select new popes, thus repudiating the secular pressures that had sometimes dominated papal selection. From the end of the eleventh century, Church vigor also was manifested in the Crusades against the Muslim occupiers of the Christian Holy Land (Palestine), typically under papal inspiration, and in the gradual ejection of Islam from Spain under Spanish Christian leadership. In the meantime, cloistered Christian monks and nuns had moved to the forefront of cultural life throughout western Europe.

In the secular Western world, however, unity was conspicuously lacking even after 1000. Further barbarian invasions before that date, from the north and the east, encouraged localized defense—usually the only kind possible in an age of wretched transportation and communication. A feudal system, involving localization of administration, became institutionalized well before 1000 and continued as a characteristic feature of the High Middle Ages. Feudalism involved a vast hierarchy, or graded ranking, of persons and functions in political, social, and economic life; its officials ranged from kings and great nobles to minor landlords and knights. The most striking aspect of the system was its decentralization of government and economy. Only rarely would a king arise to exert strong leadership over a substantial geographic area: William the Conqueror of England (reigned 1066–1087) was an exception to the general dominance of feudal lords in Romanesque Europe. Moreover, when clashes occurred be-

tween royal and ecclesiastical authorities, the Christian Church more than held its own, as it did when the Holy Roman (Germanic) Emperor Henry IV was forced to humiliate himself before Pope Gregory VII in 1077, and when the murder of Thomas Becket, archbishop of Canterbury, in 1171 led to a backlash against Henry II of England.

EARLY ROMANESQUE PROLOGUE

The terms *medieval* and *Middle Ages* were coined in the early modern period to cover nearly a thousand years of European civilization, from the decay of Roman institutions until the fifteenth-century revival of antique ideals in literature and visual arts. By those terms and the scorn associated with them, centuries of post-Roman culture were summarily dismissed as an essentially pointless interruption in the classical tradition of culture and good taste. In recent scholarship the tendency has been to retain the "medieval" terminology while acknowledging the creative vigor and achievement of the whole era—and to draw a line between early and High Middle Ages around the year 1000.

The "early Romanesque" label has often been applied to the art of the four centuries before 1000. It is important that we consider the cultural achievements of these centuries that historians once misleadingly called the "Dark Ages." Although this early medieval period did not achieve the highest distinction in art or scholarship, it saw the rise of significant institutions that would flourish later in the Middle Ages. Moreover, the 600–1000 period had its own independent cultural dignity: it was by no means culturally "dark" in such fields as imaginative literature, the visual arts, and architecture. A structure such as Charlemagne's palace chapel in Aachen (fig. 6-1) is a reminder that imposing churches could still be built around A.D. 800. To be sure, exceptional efforts are represented in the Aachen chapel: this west German city was the favorite residence of the emperor Charlemagne, who commanded the building of a princely church fully suitable to his "second Rome." The centralized structure (its exterior is sixteen-sided, its interior central space eight-sided) also benefited from the importation of columns, marbles, and mosaics from Rome and Ravenna. The handsome chandelier of bronze dates from the

CHRONOLOGY

HISTORY		THE ARTS	
c. A.D. 480–			
543	Saint Benedict of Nursia		
596	Pope Gregory the Great sends Augustine (of Canterbury) to Christianize England.	600–1000	early Romanesque
early 7th century	Christianity accepted in Northumbria		
663	official triumph of Roman over Celtic Christianity in England	672–735	the Venerable Bede
681	founding of Benedictine monastery at Jarrow	c. 698	*Lindisfarne Gospels*
		731	Bede's *History* finished
768–814	Charlemagne emperor of the Franks	792–805	palace chapel, Aachen
800	Charlemagne crowned Holy Roman Emperor		
9th century	dominance of kingdom of Wessex in England; Northmen invade England and France	**1000– 1150/1200**	mature (high) Romanesque
		11th century	*The Song of Roland*
1054	final break between Roman Catholic and Eastern Orthodox Churches	1063–1118	main construction of cathedral of Pisa
1066	Battle of Hastings: Normans conquer England		
1066–87	William I king of England		
1073–85	Pope Gregory VII		
1077	Emperor Henry IV humiliated by Gregory VII at Canossa	1079–1142	Peter Abelard
		c. 1080	Saint Sernin, Toulouse, begun
		late 11th century	Bayeux Tapestry; Sant' Ambrogio begun
1095–99	First Crusade	1090–1153	Saint Bernard of Clairvaux
		1093	Durham Cathedral begun
1108–37	Louis VI king of France	1099–1179	Hildegard of Bingen
		12th century	student lyrics
		c. 1115	west end of Saint Pierre, Moissac
		c. 1123	frescoes at Santa María de Tahull
		c. 1130–35	Gislebertus sculpting *The Last Judgment* for Autun Cathedral
1137–80	Louis VII king of France	c. 1146	*Gospel Book of Liessies*
1147–48	Second Crusade	**second half of 12th century**	Royal Pantheon, León
1154–89	Henry II king of England	**late 12th century**	*The Play of Daniel*
1189–98	Third Crusade		

ROMANESQUE AND GOTHIC EUROPE, 1000–1300

twelfth century, the height of the Romanesque period in Germany.

Northumbrian Art and Historical Writing

Two creative realms that, in addition to architecture, demonstrate the considerable accomplishment of the early Romanesque era are manuscript illumination and historical writing. Both of these arts flourished memorably in the monasteries of Northumbria and Ireland. Monasticism will be discussed at greater length when we come to the mature Romanesque period after 1000, when its most imposing monuments were built; for the moment we need note only that Christian monastic

6-1 The palace chapel, Aachen, Germany, A.D. 792–c. 805.

communities very early had become centers of art and scholarship as well as of spiritual striving and achievement. In the monasteries prayer and meditation at a literate level utilized forms of artistic and literary expression that still retain their appeal today.

Irish monasteries had become cultural seedbeds in the sixth century, and they exerted great influence on seventh-century monasteries in northern England such as those at Lindisfarne and Jarrow. Both in Ireland and Britain a Celtic version of Christianity had arisen (the Celts were in the British Isles before the Romans) that was distinguished from the Roman version in several ways—including the method of calculating the date of Easter and the monks' distinctive style of tonsure (head-shaving). In the fifth century, Roman Britain had been invaded by such Continental Europeans as the Angles (who gave their name "Angle-land" to England) and the Saxons, and these relative newcomers were particularly drawn to the Roman Church after Pope Gregory the Great sent missionaries there in A.D. 596.

The seventh-century English transition from Celtic to Roman Christianity brought England within the

catholic (that is, universal) orbit of Rome but did not remove the Celtic influence from English art. (Celtic religious customs would survive even longer in Ireland.) Although artworks, especially illuminated manuscripts (those with hand-painted pictures), were imported from Rome and were influential notably in creating images of human figures, the Celtic manner is evident in the style of the lettering and in a pervasive linearity of pictorial or geometric design.

One of the most memorable products of this English art is the Lindisfarne Gospels created about A.D. 700 by Eadfrith at the Lindisfarne monastery. The initial page of the Lindisfarne Gospel according to Saint Matthew (fig. 6-2) is a handsome example of the formal linear, interlacing type of decorative lettering. A great X in complex monogram form, followed by a smaller R and I (for "Christ"), occupies half of the page. These elaborate curved letters are followed by others in display script, with lines becoming successively smaller in size. The aesthetically satisfying design of the page is the feature most appealing to moderns, but in the late

6-2 Eadfrith, Incarnation initial page for *The Gospel according to Saint Matthew, Lindisfarne Gospels,* c. 698. Manuscript, 13½″ × 9¾″. Reproduced by Courtesy of the Trustees of the British Museum, London.

seventh century much spiritual weight was doubtless given to the sheer care and devotion that went into this complex work created for the glorification of God.

The Roman–Byzantine influence, on the other hand, is obvious in the Lindisfarne portrait of Saint Matthew (fig. 6-3). The angular script for *Matthew*, preceded by *The Holy* in Greek, remains, but the figure drawing is traceable to Eastern origins. Seated on a decorated bench, the saint is writing his Gospel in book form; books had replaced the scrolls of classical antiquity by then. The small angel above his head is the traditional symbol of Matthew, and the angelic trumpet symbolizes the Evangelist's powerful Gospel voice. To the right, peering from behind a curtain, is a holy figure, possibly Jesus Christ himself, who is the mysterious witness of the scene. The three faces are cut with sharp linear emphasis, and the robes do not drape naturally. Linearity, decorative design, and religious symbolism dominate this work, as they do most Northumbrian art of the age.

As the *Lindisfarne Gospels* were being painstakingly created, a monk at nearby Jarrow was engaging in

6-3 Portrait of Saint Matthew, *Lindisfarne Gospels*, c. 698. Manuscript, 13½″ × 9¾″. Reproduced by Courtesy of the Trustees of the British Museum, London.

scholarship that would culminate in a seminal work of Christian historical writing, *A History of the English Church and People.* The Venerable Bede (c. 672–735), as he would be known to later generations, possessed wide learning and wrote (always in Latin) voluminous biographies of saints, commentaries on biblical writings, and other theological studies. His *History of the English Church and People,* however, is his most lasting monument.

In this wide-ranging history of England, from the coming of the Angles to his own day, Bede never allows the reader to forget that this is indeed a Christian, not a secular, history. Its theme is the God-led growth of the Church through its saints, missionaries, and inspired political leaders. Visions and other miracles abound in the narrative, for Bede believed they confirmed the divine role of the Christian God; however, he exercised more historical caution in his reports of miracles than did other monks writing at that time. Bede recorded God's intervention in English affairs in a vast variety of circumstances—visions, satisfactory responses to prayer, miraculous cures and conversions, intact preservation of saintly bodies after death, and the fulfillment of omens and prophecies. It was in such purported miracles, after all, that Bede saw the hand of God and confirmation of the Christian faith; Bede said he recorded these evidences "for the instruction of posterity."

With all this unabashed slanting of the historical narrative, Bede often maintained a substantial level of objectivity. Although a Roman Christian, he recognized the saintliness of certain Celtic Christians as well, and some of his psychological portraits of church leaders, such as Pope Gregory the Great, are penetrating. On occasion Bede wrote of other things; his descriptive writing on the geography, climate, resources, and people of Britain and Ireland is famous. Most important of all in the eyes of modern historical scholarship is his frequent use of, and long quotations from, actual historical documents, especially documents from church archives in Rome. Often he quoted papal letters in their entirety, and these letters have become important primary sources for the earlier Christian centuries. Among them are Pope Gregory's extensive clarifications of doctrinal points, his instructions to the clergy and to all the faithful, and many miscellaneous letters from Gregory's successors on the papal throne. Bede is also notable for his use of "A.D." dating; he was the first major historian to use the *annus Domini* ("year of the Lord") system, which counts years from the presumed birth year of Jesus.

URBAN ROMANESQUE ARCHITECTURE

Bede's preoccupation with Christianity typified his age. Indeed, the concern with Christianity was far from negligible in those centuries after A.D. 1000 when Romanesque culture was in full flower. Even with the rise of powerful urges toward earthly goals that, as we will see, increasingly attracted Romanesque Christian men and women, the otherworldly purpose and framework of life was never seriously challenged in the Christian community—nor in the European Jewish or Islamic communities either. For nearly all of Europe, though, it was the Christian vision that predominated, as did Christian institutions and Christian creative art. Lest this sacred context of the Romanesque world be forgotten, we must now examine the physical setting of general Christian worship—the cathedrals and other urban churches of the age. (Romanesque styles in the more closed monastic world are reserved until later in the chapter.) It is to church architecture that the *Romanesque* terminology most clearly applies, and it was church architecture that set the tone for other types of construction in the eleventh and twelfth centuries and became the most imposing manifestation of the Romanesque spirit. Church architecture was the great architectural expression of the age.

Romanesque is a fairly recent addition to the tangled terminology of medieval art history. Although no final consensus has been reached on when the term can earliest be applied, agreement is general that a mature Romanesque style existed by the year 1000. The Romanesque style, with all its regional variations, reigned triumphant in European visual art, especially in architecture, through the eleventh century and the first half of the twelfth—and still longer outside of France, where the new Gothic style gradually developed out of it after 1150.

If Romanesque architecture was sometimes "Roman-like," as its name implies, it was most so in Italy, the former heart of the Roman Empire. Even there it derived not directly from pagan Rome but from the early Christian style of church building—which usually meant the basilican style. The great cathedral of Pisa, shown in figure 6-4 with its famous leaning bell tower, illustrates several modifications introduced into the relatively simple basilican design by the eleventh century. The exterior walls of the Pisan church are covered (like the bell tower) with tiers of arcades and arcadelike decoration. Between the rectangular nave (at the left) and the semicircular apse (at the right), are a choir (just to the left of the far-right apse, thus continuing the long axis of the nave), two transept arms (extending outward at right angles between nave and choir), and a modest tower (over the nave–transept crossing). The transept arms as well as the choir have a high central hall flanked by lower aisles and terminate in semicircular apses; the transept arms and choir have themselves each taken on the plan of a basilica.

The Romanesque church of Sant' Ambrogio (Saint Ambrose) in Milan, a more modest brick structure, also illustrates the massive expansion of the early Christian basilican church design. The exterior (fig. 6-5) is less innovative than the Pisan cathedral; in fact, it is reminiscent of the straightforward basilican structures of Ravenna, even to the extent of having a courtyard in front of the entrance as early Christian churches did. Two bell towers barely impinge upon the church itself. The one remarkable addition to the exterior profile of Sant' Ambrogio is the small "lantern" tower that seems to mediate between nave and choir, its windows providing light for the otherwise gloomy interior (fig. 6-6).

From the inside, Sant' Ambrogio invokes impressions of sturdiness and breadth but certainly not of great height. Several low arches cross the nave at right angles to the nave arcade. It is in the ceiling of each bay—the roughly square area between two parallel transverse arches—that Sant' Ambrogio displays its most unusual feature; the new structural device is quite unlike the flat, coffered, or timbered ceilings prevalent in early Christian churches. What is seen in each Sant' Ambrogian bay (except the lantern-topped bay) is, rather, a ribbed groin vault. As we saw in ancient Roman architecture, groin vaults are formed by the crossing of two barrel vaults; the diagonal junctures of the Sant' Ambrogian vaults are outlined and partially supported by sturdy stone ribs. At their most structurally successful in Romanesque and Gothic architecture, the ribs help transfer the weight of the vaulting to the piers beneath them. As ways were found to support more weight, vaults could theoretically become

6-4 Cathedral of Pisa with its bell tower, 1063–1118, completed in the fourteenth century.

higher, at least when combined with other supportive devices (see chapter 7). In Sant' Ambrogio the height gained by the ribbed groin vaulting is effectively canceled out by the ribs of the considerably lower transverse arches.

Striking Romanesque churches arose across western Europe. We can note two further examples of urban churches in order to underline the great national and regional variety of Romanesque building. The first is the cathedral of Saint Pierre (Saint Peter) in Angoulême in west-central France (fig. 6-7). Here the most striking features are the arcades and the addition of numerous sculpted figures on the facade. Not visible here is a sturdy bell tower over the north transept arm; it is an integral part of the church structure, as contrasted with detached Italian bell towers. Although the interior of each transept arm is covered by barrel vault-

6-5 Sant' Ambrogio, Milan. Late eleventh and twelfth centuries.

6-6   Interior, Sant' Ambrogio, Milan.

6-7   Saint Pierre, Angoulême, France. Begun c. 1105.

ing, the nave has three low-domed bays, and there is a high lantern dome at the transept crossing. The church construction is of stone, rather than the brick seen in Italy. The domed construction is typical of this regional school of French Romanesque, and the support of the domes on pendentives suggests Byzantine influence.

Durham Cathedral, in northern England, exemplifies another variation of the Romanesque style. One of the most massive and imposing cathedrals of northern Europe, it is also one of the most complete cathedral complexes of the age. The plan of the complex (fig. 6-8) shows the cathedral proper including transept arms and a low chapel called a "Galilee" extending forward from the facade. The chapter house, cloister, library, and *refectory* (dining hall) were all constructed for the use of the many clergymen attached to this regional church center. Many of these clergy were canons—priests living communally, without monastic regulations, rather than in individual parishes scattered about the countryside.

Our view of the interior of Durham Cathedral (fig. 6-9) shows carved columns of the nave and a portion of the nave seen from the south aisle. (At the top, clerestory level of the nave, several vaulting ribs spring from the piers below. These ribs are of nearly equal height, since the transverse ribs are pointed and the diagonal ribs somewhat flattened. This was a great structural and aesthetic advance over the vaulting system at Sant' Ambrogio, and it would come to characterize Gothic building even more than Romanesque, as we will see.) The system of constructing high nave walls at Durham illustrates the evolution of the full three-tiered system typical of large, late Romanesque (and Gothic) churches: a nave arcade with rounded arches above complex piers and truly massive columns, a second or *triforium* level or dark passageway, and at the top a *clerestory* with rounded arches framing small windows that admit light directly from the outside. (This system became the norm in the Gothic period; see the drawing in figure 7-9.) Durham thus exemplifies on a grand, majestic scale the most general characteristics of Romanesque church building—rounded arches, heavy and sturdy construction, and quite limited window space.

All these churches, and hundreds more in England and on the Continent, were constructed in the late eleventh or early twelfth centuries, continuing an ecclesiastical building boom that had followed the pas-

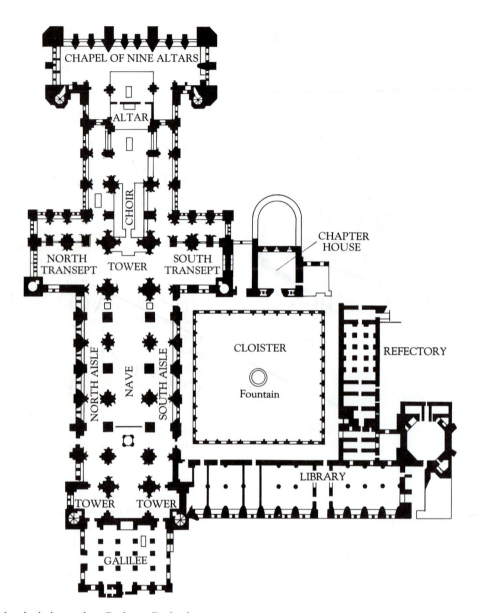

6-8 Plan of cathedral complex, Durham, England.

sage into Christianity's second thousand years. The French monk Raoul Glaber marveled at the great proliferation of building projects then, even when existing structures were sound and functionally adequate. "Every nation of Christendom," he wrote, "rivalled with the other, which should worship in the seemliest buildings. So it was as though the very world had shaken herself and cast off her old age, and were cloth-

ing herself everywhere in a white garment of churches." Fortunately many of these churches survive today, unlike the secular buildings of that time. The sturdy construction of ecclesiastical buildings, as well as the veneration later given them, contributed to their preservation, while secular buildings, generally much more lightly constructed, were frequently destroyed as needs changed across the ages.

6-9 Nave and south aisle of Durham Cathedral. Begun 1093.

6-10 Illustrations of a griffin and boars from an illuminated English bestiary, before 1187. 8½″ × 6¼″ (whole leaf). The Pierpont Morgan Library, New York.

SECULAR LIFE, ART, AND LITERATURE

Certainly the great preponderance of ecclesiastical Romanesque buildings over secular structures in modern Europe is misleading; a vigorous secular life existed alongside the world of religion. Attractive works of art, generally small, still attest to the secular interests of the Romanesque age. The little pictures of a griffin and boars (fig. 6-10) that illustrated an English bestiary in the twelfth century are an example. *Bestiaries,* which enjoyed great popularity at the time, were compilations of information and misinformation concerning the animal world, both real and (as in the case of the griffin) fabulous. Belief in fabulous creatures (dragons being a better-known example) was obviously not confined to the poor and uneducated during the Romanesque age.

The vast majority of poor people were peasants— that is, laborers on the land. No survey of the Romanesque scene can overlook these agricultural workers. We must note at the outset, though, that the European population at that time was small compared with today's hundreds of millions. England in the year 1000, for example, may have been home to fewer than a million souls, and France to fewer than six or seven million. The land, as then cultivated, could simply support no more people than that. For one thing, farming techniques involved hard and extremely inefficient manual labor. Furthermore, most of the land was not cultivated at all but was covered with impenetrable forests or marshes. Only toward the end of the Romanesque period would much of this land, inhabited by wolf and wild boar, be claimed for cultivation.

A poverty nearly incredible to our modern age in the West was the norm for the European peasantry. Most peasants lived in thatched hovels of mud and twigs; their homes were rarely of wood and almost never of stone. Famine was a constant threat, and death from malnutrition and hunger a frequent reality. For its day, Romanesque Europe was in fact overpopulated, and life for most persons was an unremitting struggle simply to stay alive. The survivors, mainly huddled in small villages, lived usually at a bare subsistence level, doing agricultural work in the warm season and making and repairing by hand all of life's material necessities, including tools and clothing, in the cold months. Most domesticated animals were slaughtered in the fall, since there was enough feed for only a few of them during the winter. The autumn slaughter was almost the only time peasants ate meat.

Much of the agricultural labor of peasants was not for themselves at all, but for their lords and the local church. Most typically, a large part of the land in western Europe belonged strictly to the lord of the manor, and this land was cultivated, according to traditional obligations of servitude, by the peasants (fig. 6-11).

Most peasants were *serfs* of one sort or another. Serfdom was a notch above slavery (which largely died out soon after 1000), but it still involved heavy-labor duties and a fixed hereditary attachment to a particular lord's land. Rising out of servitude was seldom possible and was not a normal expectation; children of serfs would also be serfs. The only education of this illiterate class was practical training in agriculture and elementary home handicrafts. In all of this, female children and adults shared with males; they, too, worked in the fields, although many of them did spinning and weaving in the cold season instead of "male" handicraft work.

The economic framework of peasant life, and indeed of most medieval secular life, was commonly the manor, presided over by a nobleman (in some cases a noblewoman) at a manor house ranging from the very modest to the ostentatious. The manor most typically included this house, a church, certain common facilities such as mills, some common land where peasants

6-11   Illustration of farm labor by peasants from an eleventh-century almanac.

might gather wood and berries and pasture their animals, the village or peasant settlement, and the agricultural land. These peasant villages should not be confused with the towns (cities) that were gradually expanding in the later Romanesque age. Towns were corporate entities, not merely physical settlements, and they became centers of the commercial and small industrial activities of merchants and professional artisans. These towns, the seedbed of the middle class, will come under our special scrutiny in the Gothic period, when they reached their medieval peak of wealth and prestige.

In secular Romanesque life outside the towns, organization above the manorial level (and including at its own lowest level the manorial lords themselves) took the form of *feudalism.* Feudalism accepted the economic underpinning of peasant, artisan, and merchant, but officially it recognized the existence of the nobility alone. The cement of feudalism was a complex network of personal ties of obligation and dependence among nobles, and its ethical and behavioral code was *chivalry,* which required honor, generosity, and courtesy. Nobility was inherited, but knighthood, with its chivalric trappings, was conferred upon young nobles only after arduous training. This training was primarily for warfare, which was considered the particular province of the noble class. Warfare was most commonly presumed to be waged in loyal defense of the feudal lord or the Christian religion.

Until sometime in the twelfth century this warlike political and social institution of feudalism, with its chivalric code of behavior, gave only a peripheral formal role to women. Families did of course exist, although a vast number of children died in infancy—perhaps in almost the same proportions among the nobility as among the peasantry, for both classes lacked modern hygiene. The prospect of a woman's dying in or after childbirth was also an enduring and justified fear. Women of the aristocracy exerted much real control over the household, but otherwise they were expected to remain unobtrusive and obedient to their husband-lords. Aristocratic marriages were not for love or marital compatibility but for the maximum economic benefit of the groom and his family, since the bride ideally brought with her a large dowry and useful family alliances.

Once married, a noblewoman who survived frequent childbearing would usually lead a life of predictable routine—raising children, supervising the household, spinning, weaving, and sewing. If she outlived her husband she might enter a convent; many women did, and it was by no means the worst fate for a medieval woman. On occasion medieval women efficiently took full military and economic control of castles and estates when their husbands were absent or incompetent, and sometimes women inherited these properties outright.

To be sure, castles in the Romanesque period were far from idyllic spots. Nearly all of them before 1000, and many thereafter, were indiscriminate clusters of wooden buildings surrounded by wooden defenses. Even as castle building moved more and more to stone construction, castles still were built for defense, not comfort. (Figure 6-12 shows a large stone castle built for crusaders in the Holy Land.) Except for occasional festive banquets, medieval castles must have seemed cold and inhospitable indeed.

Noblemen in the Romanesque age did at least escape the castle more often than did women—for hunting, perhaps, and to engage in battles against other noblemen. Not surprisingly, battles among feudal knights were the subject of much secular art and literature. The most famous Romanesque art work depicting battle scenes is the *Bayeux Tapestry,* woven late in the eleventh century by skilled craftswomen. (Actually it is not a tapestry but a work of embroidery on linen cloth; the designs of tapestries are woven into the cloth

6-12 Krak des Chevaliers, Palestine. After 1142.

itself.) The small section illustrated in figure 6-13 is identified by a Latin caption translatable as "Here English and French Fell Together in Battle." The reference is to the Battle of Hastings, in 1066, when William, duke of Normandy, invaded England and defeated the Anglo-Saxon king, Harold. The story of the Norman Conquest occupies over half of the 231-foot-long work commissioned by Bishop Odo of Bayeux, William's half-brother. The embroiderers seem to have followed the design of a master illustrator who brought a vivid liveliness to nearly all the episodes. Although some of the scenes embody startling effects, such as somersaulting horses, narrative power is far more evident than realism. Many of the figures are distorted, and some of the colors of the design seem to have been chosen quite arbitrarily: one horse has two green legs and two red legs. Victims of battle lie slain and sometimes dismembered in the lower strip, while the upper strip is devoted to decorative birds, animals, and fabulous creatures.

Medieval warfare was, of course, men's business. Since, however, only a small portion of the *Bayeux Tapestry* represents battle scenes, it is noteworthy that only one woman appears prominently in its whole great length. Almost as little attention is given to women in the literary parallel to the tapestry, the *Song*

of Roland. Roland's fiancée, the lady Aude, is mentioned several times, but no vital emotions of either Roland or the narrator toward Aude are portrayed. The bonds between Roland and his companion in arms, Oliver, and between Roland and his feudal lord, Charlemagne, are immensely stronger than any bond between the sexes in this poem.

The *Song of Roland* somewhat antedates the *Bayeux Tapestry* and may indeed have been sung, as tradition has it, to William's troops before Hastings to arouse their martial fervor. Doubtless the words were of far greater significance than the music, which probably followed a very simple, repetitive pattern—and the words, in old French, told a story of feudal loyalties and heroism in battle. The most memorable part of the *Song* concerns Roland's unsuccessful, but glorious, rearguard action against Muslim forces in the Pyrenees. Although the story is set in Charlemagne's reign, that period had already become legendary three hundred years later, and the institutions and ideas reflected in the poem are of the eleventh, not the eighth, century. Such chivalric elements as a forthright, sometimes foolhardy battle-hunger are supplemented by a robust religious zeal that some modern readers would regard as misguided fanaticism.

Several translated excerpts will convey the tone

6-13 *Here English and French Fell Together in Battle,* detail from the *Bayeux Tapestry,* late eleventh century. Wool embroidery on linen, 19½″ high. Musée de la Reine Mathilde, Bayeux, France.

of the *Song of Roland*. First there is the warlike brotherhood of feudal knights:

> Roland is valiant, Oliver is wise,
> And both are matchless in their chivalry.
> When they are armed and mounted on their steeds
> For fear of death neither will shun the fray.

On the eve of battle archbishop Turpin exhorts Roland's forces to fight the Muslims: "Lend aid now to maintain the Christian faith!" The knights kneel, are absolved, and "as penance he commands that they strike hard."

As the battle begins, Roland makes effective and bloody use of his good sword Durandal:

> Count Roland rides about the battlefield
> With Durandal cutting and cleaving well:
> He wreaks great slaughter on the Saracens.
> Would you had seen him piling corpse on corpse,
> And all the bright blood flowing in that place!
> His hauberk and both arms are red with gore,
> Bloody his good steed's withers and its neck.

Further slaughter ensues, and when Oliver and Turpin at last are slain,

> Now Roland fears that his own death is near,
> For from his ears his brains are running forth.

Turning toward the enemy, he comes to rest beneath a tree:

> Upon a steep hilltop he faces Spain,
> And with his hand he beats upon his breast:
> 'God, I confess my sins before your might.
> Forgive me for the faults both great and small
> That I've committed since I first drew breath
> Until this day, when I am stricken down!'
> Then his right glove he held aloft to God.
> Angels descend from Heaven to his side.

And the archangel Gabriel received the glove from Roland's hand—the glove he had offered much as a knight would give a glove to his feudal lord in fealty.

There is more, of course, than chivalric heroism, battlefield gore, and religious dedication in the *Song of Roland*. The heroic, measured majesty of the verse moves at times with almost sledgehammer force and at others with an appeal to sentiment—as when Roland mourns the death of Oliver. There is even some portrayal of individual character; Roland, for example, is courageous and proud to the point of extraordinary rashness.

However, it is less in the heroic verse of *Roland* than in the lyric verse of the Romanesque period that we get some feeling of vibrant human life in an everyday world. Two student lyrics, in Latin, from the twelfth century reveal youthful joys and longings quite infectiously—above all, the joys of carefree wandering, love, wine, and freedom.

> Let's away with study,
>   Folly's sweet.
> Treasure all the pleasure
>   Of our youth;
> Time enough for age
>   To think on Truth.
> So short the day,
> And life so quickly hasting,
> And in study wasting
>   Youth that would be gay!

The poet opts to dance rather than study:

> Down into the street!
> Down among the maidens,
>   And the dancing feet!

The same theme continues in the *Confession of Golias*, a legendary patron saint of wandering students:

> Down the broad road do I run,
>   As the way of youth is;
> Snare myself in sin, and ne'er
>   Think where faith and truth is.

Subsequent verses become specific in their bold confessions to the pursuit of sensual love (even invoking the pagan goddess Venus), the vice of gambling, and the boisterous life of the tavern:

> In the public-house to die
>   Is my resolution;
> Let wine to my lips be nigh
>   At life's dissolution:
> That will make the angels cry,
>   With glad elocution,
> 'Grant this toper, God on high,
>   Grace and absolution!'

Such expressions of vivacious earthiness demonstrate that the Romanesque age could not direct all of human nature into religious, otherworldly paths. Student verse, moreover, was only one of several types of secular Romanesque literature; there were also, for example, earthy stories in prose and some significant writing in history and political theory. What is still more characteristic of the Romanesque spirit, however, is that even in this ostensibly secular literature there was usually a strong component of Christian piety and a Christian worldview. The Middle Ages, and the Romanesque era in particular, simply cannot be described as truly secular.

In short, religion entered virtually all realms of eleventh- and twelfth-century creative art, even when produced at secular courts. However, the religious element in courtly art and literature, such as in the *Bayeux Tapestry* and *Song of Roland,* is minor compared with that in the productions of churches and monasteries of the time. There the surviving evidence indicates an almost exclusive preoccupation with spiritual, rather than secular, concerns.

RELIGIOUS THOUGHT AND ART

The Christian faith provided the framework for nearly all serious intellectual creativity in the Romanesque era. Although Latin was the language of scholarship, and although the twelfth century saw a measurable recovery of classical Latin literature, the classical influence on medieval writing before 1200 was very minor. Most Christian devotional and instructional literature was drawn from strictly Christian sources that were subjected to only sporadic challenge. Peter Abelard (1079–1142) attempted to deal rationally and logically with Christian authorities. He cheerfully noted that the authorities sometimes seemed to be in conflict among themselves. However, Abelard saw this conflict as a challenge to be met, a problem to be solved, rather than as an invitation to wholesale skepticism toward Christian teachings. Abelard's sort of rational analysis might appear to later, more secular ages as corrosive to the Christian worldview, but rational analysis in the twelfth century was far from the dominant interest it had been in classical times.

Several contemporaries of Abelard were, in fact, both aware of the potential dangers of his approach and temperamentally disinclined to follow his rational method. Especially distrustful of Abelard's approach, and also of potential subversion of faith by classical Latin literature, were the twelfth-century writers classifiable as *mystics.* Mystics renounced the subtleties of reason, sought to surrender their whole beings to divine power, and believed that they were in personal contact with God—an ultimate achievement that made rational investigations seem petty and irrelevant.

The French Saint Bernard of Clairvaux (1090–1153) was such a mystic. He typified the mystics' fear of pagan literature and much of the natural, physical world and he campaigned vigorously and effectively against Abelard's rationalism. One must, he wrote, renounce the world and aspire to a vision of the divine before one's soul can be truly purified. Yet Bernard, like many other mystics, combined his spiritual aspirations with religious and political activism here on earth: he was a major inspiration to monastic reform and a respected and feared adviser to kings and popes.

Mural Paintings and Reliquaries

The churches of Europe sought to place the divine image and purpose within the sight and understanding of all Christian believers. For religious images, mural paintings replaced mosaics as the dominant large-scale pictorial medium. These murals were ordinarily *frescoes*—paintings made on fresh plaster, which maximizes permanency. The half-dome of the apse, above a church's focal altar, was reserved for the most solemn subjects. An example is the majestic *Virgin and Child Enthroned* from the church of Santa María de Tahull in Spain (fig. 6-14). The figures are awesome rather than intimate, and highly stylized rather than realistic. The garments fall in folds that are not natural but decorative, and heavy outlines and the lack of fine detail give an impression of *monumentality*—that is, of directness, simplicity, and power. These qualities characterize many of the religious murals painted in the Romanesque period.

Not all Romanesque mural painting, even in Spain, was as formal and monumental as the Tahull painting. *The Annunciation to the Shepherds* (fig. 6-15) in the Royal Pantheon in León is an example. An angel is announcing to the shepherds in the fields the miraculous birth of Jesus. Though the winged angel is a supernatural creature, it is not awe inspiring to the viewer or the shepherds portrayed in the painting. The shepherds appear in informal posture, one playing a shepherd's pipe, another feeding a beast. The animals outnumber the angelic and human forms and are thoroughly charming. The embellished border exemplifies the popularity of decorative settings in Romanesque art, whether painting or sculpture.

The Christian faithful were inspired and instructed not only by large-scale murals but by sculpture and items made of gold. The goldsmith, in fact, was among the most honored of medieval craftsmen. His

6-14 *Virgin and Child Enthroned,* from Santa María de Tahull, Spain, c. 1123. Fresco. Museo de Arte de Cataluña, Barcelona.

most obviously precious and sumptuous product, and the one with the holiest of purposes, was the *reliquary*— a container for sacred relics. Godefroy of Huy's *Reliquary of Saint Alexander* (fig. 6-16) was created in the Meuse River region near the present Belgian–German border and was the proud possession of a monastery there. Like many other celebrated reliquaries at monasteries, it was venerated not only by the local monks but by countless pilgrims who traveled to visit the sacred shrines of Europe. Pilgrimages were a prime aid in the quest for individual salvation. Monasteries were the usual shelter for pilgrims on their travels to Rome, Jerusalem, Santiago de Compostela (the Spanish shrine of the Apostle James), and many less prestigious holy sites.

Monasteries and Manuscripts

The main purpose of monasteries (often known as abbeys) was not, however, the care of pilgrims; rather it was the salvation of souls—primarily the souls of the men or women who lived there under vows of poverty, chastity, and obedience to the monastic superior, or abbot. Monasteries were subject to written rules of daily life and organization, the most commonly accepted rule being that of Saint Benedict of Nursia (c. 480–543). The *Rule of Saint Benedict* prescribed a highly organized, disciplined life of work and prayer,

6-15 *The Annunciation to the Shepherds,* second half of twelfth century. Fresco, Panteón de los Reyes, San Isidoro, León, Spain.

6-16 Godefroy of Huy, *Reliquary of Saint Alexander*, 1145. Silver, gilt, wood, bronze, brass, enamel, crystal, and precious stones; 17½″ high. Musées Royaux d'Art et d'Histoire, Brussels.

with an emphasis on silence, humility, and communal sharing. As the *Rule* instructed, "The first degree of humility is prompt obedience. This is necessary for all who think of Christ above all else. These souls, because of the holy servitude to which they have sworn themselves, whether through fear of hell or expectation of eternity, hasten to obey any command of a superior as if it were a command of God." Other parts of the *Rule* dealt with such mundane but vital matters as weekly kitchen duty, daily manual labor, and the monks' democratic election of an abbot for his virtue and wisdom rather than his monastic rank.

Benedict's *Rule* continued as the basic guide for Romanesque monasticism for many centuries. In this monastic world the sexes were segregated, usually in separate communities. Although the communities for men substantially outnumbered those for women, many nuns achieved high levels of learning and scholarship and produced creative works of genuine distinction. As early as the tenth century a remarkable Ger-

man nun, Hrotswitha of Gandersheim, was writing Latin prose plays that may or may not have been produced at her convent. Following pagan Latin models, many of her plays celebrated the chastity and martyrdom of legendary and historical Christian women. Her *Paphnutius* dealt with the miraculous conversion of Thaïs, a woman who "abandoned lust and ease and idle luxury" for a nun's room in a convent to contemplate her sins and live chastely—and finally to be welcomed among God's saints in Heaven.

A later German nun, the mystical Hildegard of Bingen (1099–1179), achieved fame for the detailed and vivid prose records of her extraordinary supernatural visions. She was careful to specify that these visions arose not from dreams or delirium but in a fully alert mind receptive to God. As she recorded them, her visions ranged from splendid pictures of dazzling heavenly bliss to terrifying revelations of hellfire, and on to visions of Christ and the mysterious Trinity of Father, Son, and Holy Spirit.

Both male monasteries and female convents provided education for prospective members and some young people who would remain in secular life. Monasteries had contributed far more than any other agency to the survival of literacy and scholarship during the earlier medieval period, but their virtual monopoly on education was being strongly challenged by cathedral schools toward the end of the Romanesque age. In the twelfth century a two-tier educational system was generally recognized—primary schools at the parish level, and secondary schools at monasteries and cathedrals. Instruction at monastic schools was free of charge, and at cathedral schools generally only the wealthy paid tuition. Female education was separate and generally inferior. In all cases, the studies were primarily literary and theoretical.

As in the early Christian period, there was much debate in monastic circles as to the spiritual merit of the arts. Saint Bernard raised his influential voice in opposing lavish artistic display, and his viewpoint prevailed in many monastic establishments. Fortunately for the Western world's artistic heritage, it did not prevail universally. Through the Romanesque age monasteries remained the principal centers of artistic creativity in Europe. Secular craftsmen seem to have predominated in architectural construction and large-scale stone sculpture, and they infiltrated other fields as well—but monks were the prime creators in the writing, copying, and illustrating of books, and shared the fields of painting and metal sculpture with secular workmen.

Hand-produced, hand-illustrated books are among the most enduring and attractive art works of the Romanesque period. Bound books with leaves of parchment had superseded antique scrolls. Some books were simple and strictly utilitarian without any decorative display, but others possessed embellished margins, elaborate capital letters (fig. 6-17), and even full-page paintings. Such hand-decorated books are often called *illuminated manuscripts,* and the small illustrations themselves, *manuscript miniatures.* Many are done with extraordinary skill and delicacy, such as the painting of Saint John the Evangelist from the *Gospel Book of Liessies* (fig. 6-18). The anonymous artist of this painting was far more concerned with linear pattern than with anatomical correctness or naturalistic representation of the saint's robes. The Evangelist—whose sym-

6-18 *Saint John the Evangelist,* c. 1146. Manuscript miniature from the *Gospel Book of Liessies,* 13½" high. Société Archéologique, Avesnes, France.

6-17 Initial letter of the Book of Exodus in the *Winchester Bible,* c. 1160. Cathedral Library, Winchester, England.

bol, the eagle, is seen at the left—dips his pen in the inkwell offered by Abbot Wedric of Liessies as God the Father sends the dove of the Holy Spirit to dictate the Gospel to him. Nearby are scenes from John's life and rich geometric and floral designs. The page is a masterpiece of sacred imagery and decorative fantasy.

Monastic Churches and Sculpture

Few manuscript miniatures were available for the admiration and edification of ordinary Christians in the Romanesque age. Most typically the books were for scholarly study or (like the *Gospel Book of Liessies*) the liturgical use of the clergy. Much more accessible to the faithful were the new Romanesque churches and the large architectural sculpture that adorned them.

National and regional traditions and preferences gave birth to an almost infinite variety of Romanesque styles across Europe. Some of the most fully developed Romanesque architecture and most interesting sculpture can be seen in south-central France, where monastic (abbey) churches arose in great profusion in the late eleventh and twelfth centuries.

One of the most imposing of Romanesque buildings in France was the abbey church of Saint Sernin at Toulouse (figs. 6-19 and 6-20). Built on one of several pilgrimage routes across France to the shrine of Santiago de Compostela, Saint Sernin is related to the basilican style of early Christian years, although less obviously so than its Italian contemporary, the cathedral of Pisa (see fig. 6-4). Double aisles, as at Pisa, line each side of Saint Sernin's nave, but the inner aisles are almost as high as the nave itself, and the outer ones much lower. Small chapels radiate from the ambulatory of the semicircular apse and, in fact, continue along the apsidal side of the transept arms. The tower at the crossing rises far higher than it does at Pisa and it

functions as a bell tower. The nave and the *choir* (the central area reserved for the clergy, beyond the transept crossing) have been covered by a stone vault rather than a coffered ceiling as at Pisa; it is a long *barrel* (or tunnel) *vault*, with ribs crossing it at right angles. These ribs rise above the columns of the nave arcade—one of several medieval means of concentrating the pressure of heavy vaulting on the strongest support available. No exterior light enters the nave directly, since the clerestory is in the walls of the high inner aisles. Light-colored brick and stone bands in the arcade columns give a rosy tan glow to the nave—a less gloomy impression than in many of the most massively constructed Romanesque churches. And rounded arches—perhaps the most obvious feature of Romanesque architecture—are everywhere, in the windows and arcades as well as the vaulting ribs.

In contrast to its early Christian, basilican predecessor (see fig. 5-10), the Romanesque style embodies not only the complexities already mentioned but a new approach to interior walls. Early Christian nave walls,

6-19 Saint Sernin, Toulouse, France, c. 1080–1120.

6-20   Nave and choir of Saint Sernin.

above the columns, had been flat—a zone essentially unintegrated with the nave arcade below. In the Romanesque style, arcades typically are linked with upper nave (and transept and choir) walls by the continuation of vertical piers from floor to vaulting ribs, as at Saint Sernin. This integration of interior structure established the impression of an immense architectural whole, and must have suggested to medieval worshippers the divine order of the universe and the relative insignificance of individual human beings.

Romanesque Sculpture

In the early Christian period, large architectural sculpture (except in column capitals) was virtually unknown in church interiors, and this persisted during the Romanesque period. However, the exterior of Romanesque churches, especially the entranceways, became the site of extensive, large-scale sculptural decoration. This sculpture was generally in relief, not in freestanding form, and was closely adapted to the architecture of the church.

Such was the sculpture at the pilgrimage church of Saint Pierre at Moissac, France. At the main entrance of this abbey church one sees *Christ amid Symbols of the Evangelists and the Twenty-four Elders of the Apocalypse* (fig. 6-21) portrayed on the *tympanum*—a large, roughly semicircular, sculpted panel above a doorway. The theme is a standard one in Christian iconography: Christ enthroned in glory, accompanied by the four spiritual "beasts" of the Apocalypse. From very early Christian times these creatures (out of Saint John's prophetic vision described in the Book of Revelation) had symbolized the four Evangelists—the angel for Matthew, the lion for Mark, the ox for Luke, and the eagle for John. Stylized, patterned, and symbolic, this tympanum unabashedly celebrates the life and aspirations of the Christian soul.

The stylized elongation of the figures at Moissac is also seen in a single sculpted figure in nearby Souillac. The life-size relief of the Hebrew prophet Isaiah (fig. 6-22) once decorated the portal of the abbey church of Sainte Marie but is now set up inside the church. The verticality of the doorjamb is echoed in the elongation of the prophet's figure, which appears as if in an ecstatic, ceremonial dance. The figure is almost convulsively expressive—expressive not of everyday life but of supernatural vision.

Still more extreme elongation is seen outside the monastic sphere, in a sculptural relief at the entrance of the cathedral at Autun, France (fig. 6-23). The awe-inspiring Christian theme of the *Last Judgment* is portrayed. Souls are being weighed in the center of this detail, and in the bottom tier we see the hesitant, fearful rising of souls from the dead. Notice the immense hands pulling the soul in the middle up to judgment. To the sides of the weighing scale stand an angel and a fierce, hairy demon, the latter trying to pull down his side of the scale so as to claim yet another soul—a soul already howling in terror. Saved souls, on the other hand, cling apprehensively to the angel's robe; they will nonetheless be safely taken to heaven, whereas the damned will be cast into hell by grinning devils. Of the many imaginative portrayals of the Last Judgment in Western art, this is surely one of the most frightening and powerful.

Sculpture has survived the centuries far better than such other large-scale arts as the frescoes and colorful glass windows that once adorned Romanesque

6-21 *Christ amid Symbols of the Evangelists and the Twenty-Four Elders of the Apocalypse,* c. 1115. Relief sculpture. Tympanum of Saint Pierre, Moissac, France.

6-22 *Isaiah,* c. 1120. Relief sculpture, stone, 5′9″ high. Sainte Marie, Souillac, France.

churches. But even today's impression of the sculpture is inadequate, since most medieval sculpture seems to have been colored originally. Occasionally, as in the tympanum sculpture at Moissac (fig. 6-21), we can visualize with some confidence the original appearance. The Book of Revelation states that the twenty-four elders wore white robes and crowns of gold; almost certainly that is how they appeared, painted and gilded, at Moissac. Aside from sculpture, even the inside walls of churches were often covered with paints or washes (whitewash was by no means the only possibility). Virtually all of this has disappeared in the course of time, together with the decorative and pictorial frescoes that must have made the typical church interior a feast of color.

An early-twelfth-century artist, Theophilus, not only hinted at the rich adornment of the churches he knew but told us what impression it might have made, ideally, upon worshippers of his day:

> The human eye is not able to consider on what work first to fix its gaze; if it beholds the ceilings they glow like brocades; if it considers the walls they are a kind of paradise. But if, perchance, the faithful soul observes the representation of the Lord's Passion expressed in art, it is stung with compassion. If it sees how many torments the

6-23   Gislebertus(?), detail of *The Last Judgment*, c. 1130–35. Relief sculpture. West tympanum, Autun (France) Cathedral.

saints endured in their bodies and what rewards of eternal life they have received, it eagerly embraces the observance of a better life. If it beholds how great are the joys of heaven and how great the torments in the infernal flames, it is animated by the hope of its good deeds and is shaken with fear by reflection on its sins.

Of all this decorative wealth, one sees little indeed in the bare, but majestic, remains of Romanesque churches today.

MUSIC OF THE ROMANESQUE AGE

Our knowledge of the music of the Romanesque era is limited because we do not know much about its actual performance. We do, however, have a fairly clear view of the musical theory of the early and mature Romanesque periods. We also have at least the bare notes of much of the music, and we can visualize and indeed reconstruct many musical instruments of the age. Some instruments were used within the church as well as in secular music: they had gained ecclesiastical respectability—that is, acceptance in church practice—for various historical reasons. The Old Testament, it was noted, states that King David played the harp; thus the harp was the most prestigious of plucked-string instruments. Our illustration (fig. 6-24) of King David playing the harp dates from the late Romanesque period and shows one of his attendants playing a stringed instrument with a bow and two other attendants playing wind instruments.

In the preceding chapter we noted the beginning of Christian music in our discussion of Ambrosian and Byzantine chant. Pope Gregory the Great, who reigned around A.D. 600, was long given the credit, incorrectly, for the further formulation of Christian chant, especially from the standpoint of modal organization.

A *mode* is a particular sequence of tones, ascending or descending, within the range of an octave. The many church modes of the Middle Ages may be thought of as sequences of notes that can be played on the piano's white keys, but starting on different tones and hence incorporating different orderings of whole

6-24 *King David Playing the Harp under the Inspiration of the Holy Spirit, while One Attendant Juggles and Others Play the Rebec, Trumpet, and Horn,* eleventh century. English manuscript miniature. Reproduced by Courtesy of the Trustees of the British Library, London.

from the ninth century. Its music is in the eighth of eight church modes accepted in Gregorian chant—the mode beginning on the tone G and emphasizing C. The hymn, though still monophonic and with no regular rhythm, is far more complex than the Ambrosian *Pater Noster*: its range is wider and its melody more inventive, and the musical repetition is of whole verse settings rather than brief phrases. Here is the first verse, translated from the Latin.

Come, O Creator Spirit, come,
And make within our heart thy home:
To us thy Grace celestial give,
Who of thy breathing move and live.

In *monophony* (music with a single melodic line) a fixed rhythm became popular earlier in secular music than in sacred music. An example is *O admirabile Veneris ydolum*, a Latin love song invoking the Christian God but more concerned with pagan imagery. ("O lovely image of Venus, in whom there is no blemish, may the Lord who made the stars and the heavens and fashioned the seas and the earth protect thee.") It may have been sung by young wandering scholars of the Romanesque age.

Long before the end of the Romanesque era, monophonic music was being supplemented by *harmony*—different tones sounding at the same time. The simplest, least flexible type of harmony is illustrated by the ninth-century sacred song *Sit gloria Domini* ("May the glory of the Lord abide forever"). This is a type of *organum* (a harmonic adaptation of a plainsong melody) in which the musical lines begin simultaneously on different tones of the scale and proceed in exactly *parallel* sequences—that is, always separated by the same interval of the scale. Parallel organum is the most mechanical type of harmonic writing imaginable. By the Gothic period harmonies had gradually become much freer and more interesting, as we will see in the next chapter.

Harmonic compositions, however, did not monopolize the Romanesque music scene. Monophony persisted as a valid form of music (as it does today in many people's showers), and also in a new dramatic context. This innovation in music arose quite early in the Romanesque era with the addition to the church liturgy of short dialogues sung responsively by different persons (always male). Whether or not this primitive dramatic musical dialogue was the direct ancestor of later medieval music-drama, full-fledged dramatic musical productions on religious themes were being of-

and half steps. Modal composition dominated sacred music from earliest Christian times and would flourish through the sixteenth century. Since then, at least until the self-conscious musical antiquarianism and experimentalism of the twentieth century, only two modes have been in common use, the major and minor scales. Thus the scale system of most present-day music represents a narrowing, not an extension, of modal possibilities.

Many "Gregorian" chants, known collectively as *plainsong*, actually date from well after Gregory's time. The celebrated hymn *Veni Creator Spiritus* may date

6-25 *Daniel in the Lions' Den, with Habakkuk and the Angel.* Detail of a manuscript illustration for *De Danielem*, from Santo Domingo de Silos, 1109. Reproduced by Courtesy of the Trustees of the British Museum, London.

fered by the eleventh and twelfth centuries. These music-dramas became routine at many large churches, most commonly in conjunction with the observances of Christmas and Easter but sometimes also for dramatizing Bible stories, such as the raising of Lazarus from the dead by Jesus, the adventures of Joseph and his brothers, or the story of Daniel. These were produced as plays, with costumes and sometimes scenery, within the church building or outdoors in front of the sculpted church portals.

The text of *The Play of Daniel* is a medieval-Latin-verse adaptation of the biblical story of the Hebrew prophet Daniel. As the play relates, Daniel predicted doom for Belshazzar, the king of Babylon. Later Daniel was miraculously saved from the punishment ordered by Belshazzar's successor Darius, who had been tricked by evil counselors: God transformed the hungry lions into whose den Daniel had been thrown from blood-thirsty beasts into unexpectedly placid friends. (The scene was a familiar one in medieval imagery, as in the small manuscript illustration shown in figure 6-25.) The evil counselors would benefit from no such benevolent intervention when they in turn were thrown to the lions.

The music of *The Play of Daniel* is derived from plainsong but generally has a regular rhythmic beat. Musical instruments were used in medieval music-

dramas, but the surviving manuscripts do not indicate which instruments or how they were used. Their main use was probably in formal processions or during interludes in the storytelling. Modern reenactments have generally utilized viols, wind instruments, and small drums, and when they have been used with the vocal monophony their function has been accentual, not chordal or independently melodic. The frequent insertion in *Daniel* of the acclamation *Rex, in aeternum vive!* ("King, live forever!"), always with the same melody, gives a certain thematic unity to the work. When colorfully staged in such French cathedrals as the one at Beauvais, *The Play of Daniel* must have been a striking production for Christians of the Middle Ages. For us today, it is a memorable musical, visual, and literary demonstration of the abundant creativity of the Romanesque era.

Recommended Reading

Beckwith, John. *Early Medieval Art* (1964). Very compact text with fine photographs.

Brooke, Christopher. *The Monastic World 1000–1300* (1974). Beautifully illustrated overview.

Cahn, Walter. *Romanesque Bible Illumination* (1982). Splendid, well-illustrated introduction.

Daniel-Rops, Henri. *Cathedral and Crusade* (1957). Detailed narrative.

Gibbs-Smith, Charles H. *The Bayeux Tapestry* (1973). Excellent summary, fully illustrated.

Grabar, André and Carl Nordenfalk. *Romanesque Painting from the Eleventh to the Thirteenth Century* (1958). Good introduction with colorplates.

Henderson, George. *Early Medieval* (Style and Civilization series; 1972). Brief, scholarly introduction to Romanesque art.

Jones, Charles W., ed. *Medieval Literature in Translation* (1950). Poetry and other medieval literature.

Kunstler, Gustav. *Romanesque Art in Europe* (1969). Primarily a picture book.

Shahar, Shulamith. *The Fourth Estate: A History of Women in the Middle Ages* (1983). Scholarly and interesting.

The Song of Roland, trans. by D. D. R. Owen (1972). Modern, readable translation.

Souchal, François, *Art of the Early Middle Ages* (1968). Handsome picture book.

Tierney, Brian, ed. *The Middle Ages,* vol. 1: *Sources of Medieval History* (1983). Sources for history through the twelfth century.

Zacour, Norman. *An Introduction to Medieval Institutions* (1976). Good summary of medieval institutions and society.

Zarnecki, George. *The Monastic Achievement* (1972). Good survey with good illustrations.

7

Gothic France: 1150–1300

othic art styles were emerging out of Romanesque styles by the middle of the twelfth century in France and around the end of that century in the rest of Europe. Romanesque high culture, in the eleventh and early twelfth centuries, had arisen primarily in monasteries and feudal castles and had expressed the ideals of those centers of civilization. Gothic culture had different origins—the secular and religious life of newly vigorous towns and the royal courts of several large, increasingly unified kingdoms in western Europe. Of these kingdoms, France was the richest, the most powerful, and in many respects the most creative.

Although change occurred much more slowly and deliberately in the Middle Ages than in our fast-moving modern world, change was no less real in those days. Cultural, political, and social change in Gothic France and the rest of Europe was based primarily upon far-reaching economic changes after 1000—seen first of all in significant increases in the productivity of the land. Much land was converted from marsh and forest into cultivated fields. Technologies were developed for plowing fields and harnessing draft animals. Windmills greatly speeded the grinding of grain, and a rotation system of land-use further increased productivity. Commerce expanded on an international scale, and towns and cities grew greatly—that is, incorporated communities dominated by a middle class of merchants, bankers, skilled craftsmen, and professionals in law and medicine.

Much of Europe—most notably Italy and the Germanic lands to the north—remained divided among small principalities or city-states. Over most of Italy and the Germanies a "Holy Roman Empire" maintained only a shadowy, nominal rule. In France, England, and Spain, however, unified kingdoms emerged. By the late thirteenth century the kingdom of Castile controlled most of Spain, with only the smaller kingdoms of Portugal and Aragon as significant Christian rivals, and with the Moorish (Muslim) kingdom of Granada still resisting Christian advances in the south. England in the thirteenth century was a centrally administered kingdom; English kings could concentrate their efforts at home, having lost most of their Norman and other French territories early in the century.

Philip Augustus (reigned 1180–1223) was the French monarch who expelled the English king John from northern and central France, thereby tripling the land he controlled directly in France. Further areas of France fell securely under French monarchical rule during the time of Louis IX, or Saint Louis (1226–1270), and his immediate successors. By the early fourteenth century this French "royal domain," combined with the lands of feudal lords who owed obedience to the king, covered most of what would become modern France.

Over all of western and central Europe, except of course Granada, the papacy in Rome claimed spiritual lordship. Indeed Pope Innocent III (1198–1216) assumed a degree of secular lordship as well. Innocent claimed moral authority over kings and on occasion also successfully asserted feudal lordship. (The English king John actually granted England to Innocent as a feudal possession.) At the same time that Christian power and pretensions were at their peak in Europe, dissenting spiritual movements were disrupting the Church's unity and being sternly repressed by the Dominican friars, an order of noncloistered monks, and by the papal *Inquisition,* a harsh investigation of deviations from Church teaching. Also perpetually segregated and looked down upon, and periodically plundered by Christian rulers, were the small Jewish populations in Europe, who doggedly maintained a rich cultural tradition of their own.

GOTHIC ART IN FRANCE

A Frenchman of the year 1250 would have been greatly puzzled to hear that his world was Gothic—puzzled and, if he was learned enough to have heard of the barbarian Alaric the Goth

and his sack of Rome in A.D. 410, highly indignant. Although in modern times *Gothic* did at first mean barbaric, the term is now used noncommittally for the post-Romanesque culture of the Middle Ages. It is generally agreed that France saw the birth of the Gothic style out of the Romanesque in the middle of the twelfth century, and that in France the style flourished most bountifully in the High Gothic age of the thirteenth century.

Towns and Cathedrals

The French High Gothic period was an age of cathedrals as well as of towns. Cathedrals were the churches of bishops, the key administrators among the "secular" clergy whose Christian duties lay with the ordinary population, not with monks. Gothic towns, sometimes referred to as cities, were generally enclosed within defensive walls. A medieval town (city) of five thousand people was considered large, and few towns had populations of over twenty thousand. (Paris, as we will see, was the great French exception.) Towns became the most flourishing and typical centers of the impressive cultural resurgence of the period, continuing the trend that had begun in the late Romanesque age.

While the outlook and the routine life of monks, as of country-dwelling peasants and nobles, moved only slowly into new paths, the prosperous middle class (the *bourgeoisie*) of city merchants and skilled craftsmen became the focus of change. Their rise was aided by the increasing authority of government, which more and more successfully kept order in towns and suppressed plundering on land and sea, thus making commercial activity a safer, more attractive enterprise. Several elements of a modern money economy were introduced—more efficient bookkeeping, for example, and credit and banking services. Certainly the daily routine of these medieval traders and small industrialists was very different from that of monks. Thousands of them prospered and built substantial homes (fig. 7-1) with the same pointed arches and gables seen in the great churches that towered over the town.

The house in figure 7-1 was a modest, middle-class dwelling; larger stone houses in the thriving cities of western Europe often had five or six stories. As in ancient Rome, members of all except the very lowest classes might, if fortunate enough, live in such sturdy houses. Ordinarily the ground floor housed the shop of a substantial craftsman or the showroom of a merchant as well as rooms for cooking and storage. On the floor

CHRONOLOGY

HISTORY		THE ARTS	
early and mid 12th century	flowering of cathedral school of Chartres	1134	Chartres Cathedral begun
1137–80	Louis VII king of France	1163–1325	Notre Dame Cathedral, Paris
mid 12th century	beginnings of University of Paris	**late 12th century**	Chrétien de Troyes writing *Lancelot* and other Arthurian romances; Léonin and Pérotin composing polyphonic music for Notre Dame Cathedral
1180–1223	Philip Augustus king of France	**12th–13th centuries**	troubadour and trouvère songs
1189-99	Richard I (the Lion-Hearted) king of England	1194	destruction of most of older part of Chartres Cathedral by fire
1198–1216	Innocent III pope	1194–1240	Chartres Cathedral largely built
1199–1216	John king of England	1214–1300	Reims Cathedral largely built
1214	defeat of John by Philip Augustus at Bouvines		
1216–72	Henry III king of England	1220–69	Amiens Cathedral
		c. 1225	*Roman de la Rose*, first part
		1225–74	Saint Thomas Aquinas
1226–70	Louis IX (Saint Louis) king of France	1228	death of Walther von der Vogelweide
1239	Louis IX receives the reputed relic of the Crown of Thorns	1243–48	the Sainte Chapelle, Paris
		1247–72	cathedral of Beauvais
1248–54	Louis IX on crusade, and briefly (1250) prisoner of the Saracens	**13th century**	motet *Ave gloriosa Mater; Orientis partibus* ("Song of the Ass")
1252	death of Blanche of Castile, mother of Louis IX	1267–73	*Summa Theologica* of Thomas Aquinas
1270	Louis IX again on crusade; his death	c. 1275	*Roman de la Rose*, second part
1270–85	Philip III king of France	**after 1290**	Dante's *La Vita Nuova,* including earlier sonnets on Beatrice
1285–1314	Philip IV (the Fair) king of France		

above lived the craftsman or merchant and his family, and perhaps a senior associate or workman and his family. The upper stories were for helpers and younger craftsmen, plus live-in servants. Less fortunate workers and unskilled laborers lived in tenement structures, generally of wood, in a crowded, filthy slum section of the town. At the bottom of the socioeconomic scale, a good number of unfortunates lived (and died) in the streets. We should note, however, that the towns included charitable groups, usually church-connected,

that cared for some of the oldest, sickest, and most destitute members of society. Convents or monasteries in the towns were only the largest of such groups.

Among nonreligious groups that furnished care for the elderly in the Gothic era were the guilds. These guilds, whether of merchants or of craftsmen, were primarily commercial or industrial organizations of employers, but they also helped support widows and families of deceased members. It was the full-fledged members of the merchant guilds, and in some cases the

7-1 Hôtel de Vaubuissant, a Gothic merchant's house in Provins, France; second half of the thirteenth century.

as wives and mothers. Often they learned and practiced trades, of which a few were reserved for women but most were shared with men. Although many women were maid-servants or did such other lowly work as washing clothes and selling fish and poultry in the marketplace, some women participated in highly skilled crafts, including the illuminating of manuscripts.

In relationship to the part of the male world that was artistically active, women sometimes provided romantic inspiration but they were often the objects of crude jokes, especially in the literary genre known as *fabliaux*, earthy tales in verse of urban life. The image of woman as the prime propagator of sin would die hard across the centuries—and certainly the Gothic world that honored Mary, the Blessed Mother of Jesus, never forgot Eve, the sinning mother of all subsequent human life. A statue on the Cathedral of Reims (fig. 7-2) depicts Eve caressing the serpent that, due to

more prestigious craft guilds, who governed the towns. Occasionally the guilds had seized this power violently, but more often they had bought their governmental privileges from the king, nobleman, or important clergyman who had earlier held the town as his personal property. Usually (although not in Paris, which was administered by royal officials) the privileges of a local government were embodied in a charter, with the town becoming an *incorporated* entity; that is, it was recognized as a body legally acting as one person. Guilds—and universities, too—would be given similar corporate recognition. None of these groups, however, exemplified a democracy of "the people." All of them were organizations for the politically and socially privileged segments of Gothic society, who were also at least modestly well-to-do.

A far more numerous group, women, shared only marginally in the privileges of Gothic times. Although town office and university study were closed to women, they could join guilds and they could own property. In fact, those were the only ways they could become town citizens. Of course, townswomen were primarily valued

7-2 *Eve Caressing the Serpent,* thirteenth century. Stone. Cathedral of Reims, France.

Eve's weakness, brought the spiritual downfall of the human race.

The Cathedral at Chartres

It is, of course, such churches as the great cathedral in Reims that today symbolize with greatest impact the spirit and the achievement of the Gothic era. Their surpassing significance is neither an invention of modern commentators nor an accident of physical preservation. Like the temples and shrines of classical Greece, medieval cathedrals were the prime focal points of civic pride as well as the people's faith. Those *episcopal* cities—cities with bishops—whose older cathedrals had become inadequate or had recently burned down undertook new building programs with immense civic and religious zeal. Since the bishop's own available resources were inadequate, major fundraising campaigns were launched; rich and poor paid heavily, often with enthusiasm, for the honor and the spiritual merit of having a part in the great enterprise. The king of France himself, Saint Louis, contributed magnificently to the great cathedral at Chartres, but so too did the clergy, the aristocracy, and the many local guilds of merchants and craftsmen, from money-changers to pastry cooks. Donations are most easily identifiable today in the handsome stained-glass windows, which customarily contain emblems or pictorial "signatures" of the donors. For example, a colorful medallion at Chartres (fig. 7-3) depicts a wine merchant on his way to market. The vintners dedicated the whole window, of which this is a small part, to Saint Lubius, a shepherd boy who later became bishop of Chartres—and here, amid scenes of the saint's career, is a reminder of the window's donors.

Sometimes the townspeople's contributions to cathedral building were in the form of direct physical labor, again from all classes of society. As an observer wrote in 1144 concerning the rise of the remarkable cathedral at Chartres:

> In that year were to be seen for the first time at Chartres the faithful harnessed to carts, laden with stones, timbers, grain, and whatever might be needed for the work of building the cathedral, the towers of which rose like magic into the heavens. And this was happening not only here, but almost everywhere in France. . . . Everywhere men humbled themselves, did penance, and forgave their enemies. Men and women could be seen dragging heavy loads through mire and marsh, praising in song the miracle which God was performing before their eyes.

7-3 *Wine Merchant*, detail from the *Window of Saint Lubius*, c. 1200–1220. Stained glass, 32" across. Northern nave wall, Chartres Cathedral.

Clearly, though, the skilled planning and workmanship evidenced in these cathedrals were the achievement of experienced professionals, not of pious volunteers or contemplative monkish amateurs. Especially in the Île-de-France region around Paris in the thirteenth century, cathedral building became one of the biggest businesses of the day—and by no means was it a wholly anonymous business, since many master architects and some of the sculptors are known to us by name. Like classical Greek art, medieval art was prestigious not as an object of private luxury but as an expression of the high aspirations of the community. The medieval artist was the channel of divine expression; he was seer and skilled technician in one. Although heir to a long tradition and bound to certain general, established forms, he could often stretch form and tradition to allow for individuality of expression. Still, extremes of individualism are seldom encountered in art of the High Gothic period—and the comparative rarity of forthright portrait sculpture is witness to the age's generalized idealism.

The skill, the traditionalism, and the idealism of Gothic artists, and also the growing humanism and naturalism of their work, are reflected in the long evolution of Chartres Cathedral. Actually the cathedral's facade, or west front (fig. 7-4), is partly pre-Gothic: the two towers, the south spire, and the two lower

7-4   West front of Chartres Cathedral, 1134–1513.

levels of the central facade are reminiscent of Romanesque. All of these date from the mid twelfth century when the Gothic style with its pointed arches was barely emerging from the traditional round-arched style. A great fire in 1194, however, destroyed the older portions of the structure, and most of the present church dates from the first half of the thirteenth century, under fully Gothic inspiration. From this period come the choir to the east (for the clergy), with its ambulatory and the chapels radiating from it (for individual or small-group worship), and the nave to the west (for large-scale, public worship). The nave's gabled roof rises above the round "rose" window of the facade. The transept—the rectangular area that crosses the nave–choir axis at right angles and separates the nave from the choir—is also from the thirteenth century. The south transept arm and porch are barely visible in the photograph, but are clear in the ground plan (fig. 7-5). The ornate north spire was added in the early sixteenth century. Even without this late spire,

the west front of Chartres represents a century of evolution. In French Gothic architecture we must not expect total unity of historical style. Only in the recent past, an era far more historically conscious than the Middle Ages, has stylistic consistency been regarded as desirable in itself.

Among the most admired features of the Chartres facade is the Royal Portal with its three sculpted doorways. Dating from about 1150, the portal's form is typical of transitional Romanesque-Gothic, while its sculptural content embodies a long tradition of religious art. Here, for example, is a familiar subject for a medieval tympanum: Christ in glory with the symbols of the Evangelists (see fig. 6-21).

It cannot be overemphasized that symbolism pervaded the medieval period, both in literature and in the pictorial arts. Symbolism was regarded as essential for helping people to visualize and verbalize spiritual concepts. However, with themes characteristically thought of in human terms, such as the life of the Blessed Virgin Mary, the Chartres sculpture required little symbolism. Certainly a great deal of Chartres, like the southernmost facade portal, did deal with the Virgin—for this was her church, Notre Dame de Chartres ("Our Lady of Chartres"), which was honored above all for housing the tunic she wore at Christ's birth. The Gothic preoccupation with the theme of the Blessed Virgin was echoed in the imaginative literature of the time, as in the famous story of *Our Lady's Tumbler* concerning the illiterate young acrobat (tumbler) who, on becoming a monk, could honor the Virgin only by his tumbling. The acrobat's efforts were miraculously rewarded when the Virgin came down from her pedestal to wipe the perspiration from his forehead.

To discuss all of the symbolism of the Chartres Cathedral sculpture would go beyond the scope of this book; it is a vast and complex subject. For now we will simply observe several typical sculptural qualities of the early and High Gothic styles. The first age is represented by the large columnar figures on each side of the three west doorways (fig. 7-6). The subjects are uncertain: they may be patriarchs, rulers, or ancestors of Christ. In any case their most notable characteristics are their stylization and the harmony of the sculpture with its architectural setting. Although the figures were carved in sculptors' workshops and later put into place, they match very well the slender vertical columns and patterned panels behind them. They reveal little interest in human anatomy, and the drapery is as

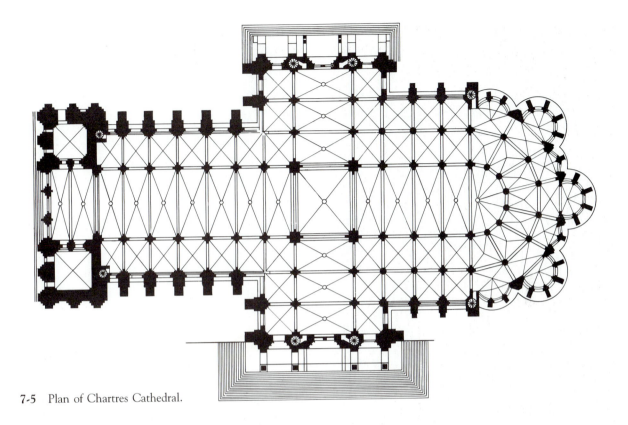

7-5 Plan of Chartres Cathedral.

7-6 Figures on the west portal of Chartres Cathedral, c. 1150.

stylized as the bodily forms. The faces possess real human charm, but there is little indication of individual personality. Abstract form predominates over realism, and idealism over individualism.

The sculpture of the thirteenth-century transept portals at Chartres shows a marked shift away from stylization. A set of column figures on the north transept (fig. 7-7) depicts Old Testament Hebrew leaders—note Abraham about to sacrifice his son Isaac—with more realistic bodies and more natural draperies than in the figures of a half-century before. Still, this was only a small step in a long transition. *Naturalism*—that is, realism in representing any forms from nature—was the obvious direction for sculpture to take in an age that was becoming more and more secular, but it was introduced in minor carving long before it reached the central figures. While the major figures representing the history and ideals of Christianity were generally treated in a traditional way, such elements as the capitals of columns were decorated with realistic foliage

7-7 Figures on the north transept portal of Chartres Cathedral, c. 1200–1210.

7-8 *Dragons Entwined with Foliage,* capital of column in Reims Cathedral, thirteenth century.

that contrasted strongly with the stylized acanthus leaves of antique Corinthian columns—even when, as in our illustration from Reims Cathedral (fig. 7-8), fanciful dragons are inserted amid the greenery.

Gothic architecture represents the combined and harmonious application of three devices first used, but only tentatively, in the Romanesque period: the flying buttress, the pointed arch, and the ribbed vault. Since pointed arches were particularly uncommon in Romanesque architecture, they are usually regarded as the single most reliable recognition feature in the Gothic style. In fully realized combination, these three devices made possible the extensive window space and awesome height of the great cathedrals (fig. 7-9). Buttressing of high walls had always been necessary in medieval church architecture unless the walls were of truly massive thickness—at least when the outward thrust of heavy vaulting had to be countered. At first, care was taken to enclose the buttressing within the church structure, and the low aisles outside the nave and choir were particularly useful for that purpose. However, by the time the main body of Chartres was built, exterior

buttressing structures called "flying" buttresses were being used as both support and decoration (fig. 7-10).

Impressively grand Gothic interiors, such as that at Chartres (fig. 7-11), vindicate the formidable exterior masonry. Although the distant ancestry of pagan Roman basilicas is apparent in the long hall with columned side aisles (see fig. 4-18), the Gothic whole is of a different scope and spirit. The main vaulting of Chartres Cathedral spans 54 feet and rises 122 feet from the floor. The walls of the nave and choir, and of

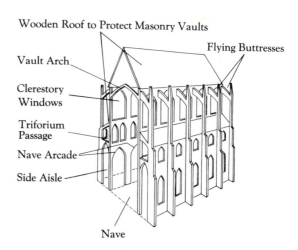

7-9 Section of a Gothic cathedral.

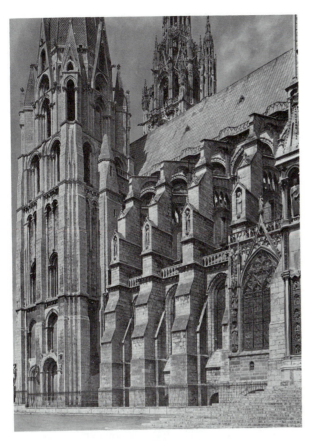

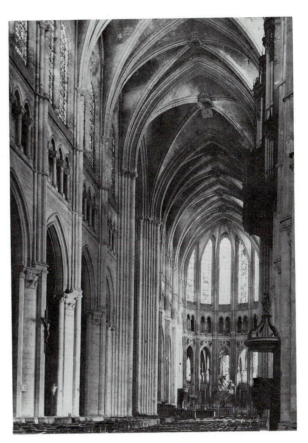

7-10 South side of nave and aisle of Chartres Cathedral, late twelfth and early thirteenth centuries.

7-11 Nave and choir of Chartres Cathedral, late twelfth and early thirteenth centuries.

the transept extending to either side between the enormous piers of the crossing, are divided into three zones containing pointed arches. These are the nave arcade, the gallery (*triforium*) passage above, and the clerestory, with its 44-foot-high window areas. The interior is crowned by ribbed *groin vaulting*—a development of cross vaulting (see fig. 4-7) by which the slightly uneven juncture of the vaults is hidden by ribs that often (but not always) carry much of the thrust down to the piers and outward through the buttresses to the ground. The whole represents an engineering achievement of impressive magnitude.

The Spirit of Gothic

In the architecture and sculpture of Chartres Cathedral we see the evolution of the Gothic style from the Romanesque. The Romanesque style is apparent, for example, in its sturdy west front, where the recessed portals barely point at the top and the sculpture is imposing but stiff. In the cathedral nave, transept, and choir, on the other hand, we see a fully Gothic style in architectural structure, and the transept portal sculpture is significantly more relaxed than the sculpture at the west portal. To find an example of consistent, fully developed High French Gothic we must turn from Chartres to such cathedrals as those of Amiens and Reims. After looking at the mature French Gothic style there, we will be able to venture an assessment of the spirit of cathedral Gothic in France.

Well to the north of Chartres and Paris, Amiens was a center for cloth and dye making in the thirteenth century. It was noted for the production of blue dye from the leaves of the woad plant. In 1218 the Romanesque Cathedral of Saint Firmin—a local saint, the first bishop of Amiens—was largely destroyed by fire, and in 1220 the foundation was laid for a new cathedral dedicated to the same saint. The cathedral at

7-12   West front of Amiens Cathedral, 1220–69 and later.

Amiens (fig. 7-12) is a relative rarity among the greatest French cathedrals in that it is not dedicated exclusively to the Blessed Virgin Mary. The nave and west front were constructed first (except for the upper towers, which were added much later), and then the transept arms and choir. The overall plan was by an architect named Robert de Luzarches, and the main structure was completed in 1269.

The west front of Amiens Cathedral is organized less on the model of Chartres than on that of Notre Dame in Paris, since the *Gallery of Kings* (representing kings of France) is below the rose window rather than above it (see figs. 7-4, 7-12, and 7-l9). The facade of Amiens, however, differs immensely from those of both Chartres and Paris in its luxuriant statuary and other sculpture. Because of the height of the whole, up through the rose window, the effect is much less of fussiness than of remarkable grandeur. The three portals extend outward from the facade wall, as do the

transept portals at Chartres, with the central portal recessed more deeply than the others. The subject of the central tympanum relief is the Last Judgment, and the others depict scenes from the lives of Firmin and the Blessed Virgin.

On the pier separating the two sides of the central doorway stands one of the most attractive representations of Christ in French Gothic, the figure of *Christ Teaching* (fig. 7-13). The robes of the majestic statue fall naturally around a realistically proportioned body. The face is impassive but compassionate—a nebulous combination of the divine and the human.

Other French sculpture of the High Gothic period may be even more naturalistic and yet inspirational. The sculpted figures of *Melchizedek and Abraham* on the inside west wall of Reims Cathedral (fig. 7-14) are noteworthy. The scene represents Abraham, at the right, in the armor of a medieval knight and in a submissive pose, as he is being offered the bread and wine

7-13   *Christ Teaching (or Blessing) (Le Beau Dieu d'Amiens)*, c. 1230. Stone. Pier of the central doorway, west front, Amiens Cathedral.

7-14 *Melchizedek and Abraham,* after 1251. Stone. Interior west wall, Reims Cathedral.

of the Catholic Communion ceremony (the focal point of the Mass) by Melchizedek before Abraham departs for battle. Melchizedek is a rather obscure figure in the Hebrew Scriptures, the Christian Old Testament. His life as a king and high priest was taken by medieval Christians to foreshadow the role of Jesus Christ. That this obscure person was portrayed in this way exemplifies not only High Gothic realism but also the extremely broad range of subject matter, both narrative and symbolic, in cathedral sculpture. Church leaders of that period sought to summarize nearly the whole Judeo-Christian tradition of narrative and doctrine in their cathedrals.

But let us return to Amiens. From our view of the cathedral's west front we may correctly guess, by the height of the rose window, that the height of the nave exceeds that at Chartres or at Paris: the Amiens vaulting is 139 feet high. (Only the 157-foot transept and choir vaulting at the cathedral at Beauvais exceeds Amiens Cathedral in height—but Beauvais lacks a nave.) The Amiens nave and choir (fig. 7-15) convey an impression of perfect balance and discipline without negating the splendid majesty of the whole. Nave arcade, triforium, and clerestory levels are separated by clear but not overpowering horizontals (including an

unusual strip of carved foliage just below the triforium), but the overwhelmingly predominant impression is of almost infinite verticality.

By general consent, both medieval and modern, the French Gothic cathedral is not only a true highpoint in the history of Western architecture, but also a grandiose manifestation of the spirit of Christian aspiration. With whatever theological or astronomical justification, the Gothic world generally looked literally upward to its God—an orientation clearly strengthened by the height and the verticality of its churches. Gothic cathedrals lifted Christians from their earthly concerns into the realm of the spirit, and the outstanding symbolic gateway to that higher realm was felt to be the radiance of the many stained-glass windows that adorned all major churches.

The windows at Chartres Cathedral are better preserved than those at Amiens or Reims, and they remain among the most important and fascinating art works of the Gothic age. From a distance, the great windows high along the walls display a jewellike richness. A riot of strong primary colors is set off by dark lead tracery similar to that in the medallion depicting a wine merchant in figure 7-3.

7-15 Nave and choir of Amiens Cathedral, 1220–36 and later.

Most of the imagery in the windows, aside from the pictures that identify their donors, is biblical. An attractive example is a double *quatrefoil* (four-leafed) medallion in the south aisle of the nave—a low location that permits the viewer to see more detail than is possible with higher windows. This south-aisle window (fig. 7-16) depicts the parable of the Good Samaritan as interpreted in a commentary by the Venerable Bede, who was well-known in the Chartres cathedral school. The lowest leaf of the quatrefoil shows the Samaritan tending the battered victim of highway robbery that he had found by the wayside. (Bede wrote that Christ, in the same spirit, tended and saved the human race, the victims of sin.) The four other sections of the medallion depict God's creation of Adam (at the left), Adam seated in the Garden of Eden (in the center), the creation of Eve out of Adam's rib (at the right), and God forbidding the two to eat of the tree of knowledge (at the top). The anatomy of the unclothed First Couple is eccentric—very far indeed from either the realism or the idealism of ancient Greek pictorial art.

In all Gothic stained glass, however, overall pattern and manipulation of light are much more evident and important than precise, realistic detail. Despite the many beauties discoverable in the windows under careful scrutiny, their main power derives from the way they enliven the interior of the cathedral. Inside the cathedral light glows mysteriously everywhere, highlighted by richly colored shafts that pierce the darkness.

Gothic cathedrals, then, were designed not only for the practical purpose of accommodating Christian worship but also to work upon the hearts of the worshippers. This was not simply a subjective function. Cathedrals possess symbolism that was presumed to be inherent and objective, and as writings of that time make clear, this symbolism was of the kingdom of God itself. Chartres, like the other great cathedrals, was to be the very image of heaven.

IDEAS AND LITERATURE IN THEIR SETTING

The ultimate kingdom of God has many mansions, according to the words of Jesus, and much rebuilding and redecorating have been done by prospective tenants of those mansions across the centuries. As it turned out, the master builder among masters in the Gothic age was not an architect at all, but a writer, the Scholastic theologian Saint Thomas Aquinas (1225–74). *Scholasticism*, the philosophical movement behind all formal Gothic thought, sought to adjust and harmonize Christian teaching by accommodating both reason and faith. Scholasticism further sought to synthesize Christian teaching with the best of pagan Greek philosophy, especially Aristotelianism. Aristotle not only seemed a reliable guide to logical reasoning, but his emphasis on the role of purpose in the universe bolstered the medieval Christian view of purposive divine guidance throughout human affairs. The Scholastics sharpened their wits on all problems of earth and heaven that bore even remotely on God's plan and human salvation—and this excluded only the crudest of daily concerns. In this "Age of Faith" virtually everything was relevant to God's scheme and had to be made to fit the Christian framework—hence the Scholastic concern with such business practices as pricing commodities and charging interest on loans. If freedom of thought sometimes suffered grievously in this comprehensive religious vision, most persons were not

7-16 *Genesis Story,* detail from the *Window of the Good Samaritan,* late twelfth century. Stained glass. South aisle of the nave, Chartres Cathedral.

aware of the limitations on their freedom, for they conceived of no alternative system.

Thought and Education

Let us look a bit more closely at the most eminent Scholastic, Saint Thomas Aquinas. One of Aquinas's most basic propositions is that knowledge of God, and of God's creation, is the ultimate goal of enlightened religion. According to him, knowledge derives from divinely aided faith and natural human reason, and these two approaches, properly conceived, never truly conflict with each other; faith and reason are simply different approaches to different aspects of human knowledge. Yet Aquinas's whole "Thomist" theological synthesis—especially his massive theological summation, the *Summa Theologica*—is characterized by constant collaboration and entwining of faith (based on authority) with logical, rational argument. It soon becomes clear, however, that this seeming contradiction was not a contradiction to Aquinas, since the reason he applied is not, ordinarily, natural human reason independent of Christian teaching, but rather a process of deduction from what he accepted as inspired authority. This authority is primarily divine revelation as found in the Bible and other revered Christian teaching. Frequently, also, the authority is "the Philosopher," Aristotle—but only in those instances when Aristotle seems to support, rather than undermine, Christian doctrine and revelation. The outcome of the Thomist approach is a laboriously constructed, carefully argued, massive synthesis of nearly all matters a Christian theologian would believe essential for explaining the divine and human order of the universe. Most commentators have found the Thomist synthesis virtually unassailable on its own terms. The real problem, its critics say, is that its terms may be dubious. Above all, not all thinkers would grant infallibility to Christian authority and to particular segments of Aristotle's work. Aquinas, as a man of the Gothic age, willingly granted infallibility to both of these.

The sheer bulk and magisterial presence of Aquinas's work can hardly be conveyed by a handful of topics and snippets from the Thomist writings, but some specifics can serve to demonstrate his method. A celebrated case is his demonstration of the existence of God in the *Summa Theologica.* The third *article* of his *question* on God's existence exemplifies the sequence of demonstration he followed throughout his entire synthesis. First come two *objections* to what Aquinas's an-

swer to the question will be. These objections are specifically answered only at the end of the *article*. *Objection 1* for the question "Whether God exists" is

It seems that God does not exist; because if one of two categories be infinite, the other would be altogether destroyed. But the name *God* means that He is infinite goodness. If, therefore, God existed, there would be no evil discoverable; but there is evil in the world. Therefore God does not exist.

The *Reply to Objection 1* that eventually follows is

As Augustine says: *Since God is the highest good, He would not allow any evil to exist in His works, unless His omnipotence and goodness were such as to bring good even out of evil.* This is part of the infinite goodness of God, that He should allow evil to exist, and out of it produce good.

Although Aquinas's reply is intended as a full refutation of the initial *objection,* and although it illustrates the author's reliance upon Augustinian authority and pointedly pronounces on the cosmic question of evil in the world, these two paragraphs are almost peripheral to the Thomist conception of the question of God's existence. Immediately following his two initial *objections* comes the decisive, succinct statement of his definitive answer to the question:

"*On the contrary,* it is said in the person of God: *I am Who am* (Exodus 3:14)."

In this case the statement is from Scripture; in other cases he cites other unimpeachable authority.

Actually the great bulk of this *article* and most other *articles* is the succeeding section that begins "*I answer that . . .*", in which Aquinas argues from logic or reason for the truth of the authoritative statement. In the *article* "Whether God exists" Aquinas states that "the existence of God can be proved in five ways," the first being the argument from motion: that movement evident to our senses must be traced to a First Mover, which is God. We should note that this argument, and at least two of the other four, would seem to demonstrate only the existence of an impersonal divine force in the universe, not of a specifically personal Christian deity responding to individual human situations. Many scores of further *articles* were devised by Aquinas to fill out this large question of how God acts in the universe.

At first sight the scope of Saint Thomas's elucidation of Christian knowledge seems immense. The *Summa Theologica* covers not only the immense issues of God Himself but also of God's creation of the world, human beings, and angels. On God's "production of woman" he insists that woman is an occasion of male sin, and that "If God had deprived the world of all those things which proved an occasion of sin, the universe would have been imperfect." The expanding financial world of the Gothic era is similarly reflected in Thomist demonstrations of the sinfulness of charging interest on money lent, but the lawfulness of paying interest to sinful Christians (or of course, by implication, to Jews) who would sin anyway by charging interest to others. Thus it is permissible to make use of the sin of others while not consenting to their sin. Such seemingly earthbound matters, in the Thomist view, relate to the divine moral order, and thus they call for the same painstaking authoritative demonstration as the large questions of theology.

It is certainly arguable today that Saint Thomas, and Scholasticism in general, did not in fact cover the whole realm of knowledge. Aquinas did, though, cover much of the knowledge thought to be important in the thirteenth century. Other writers of the age concentrated more exclusively than he did on questions of political thought. The feudal realities of the age and the concept of divine governance usually led those writers to espouse limitations upon royal power. In the realm of science, authority rather than new investigation dominated, despite occasional calls for empirical study and many practical technological advances. In all of these areas—theology, ethics, politics, and science—it was recognized that only God could know all. Men and women would, however, at least try to make sense of their own world and to strive to know God's creation as far as their earthbound understanding could reach; full knowledge would come to them only in heaven. Scholastic thought could only sketch final answers and thereby offer some substantial basis for Christian life and thought—and for Christian education.

Scholasticism arose in the cathedral schools, many of which had been established in the Romanesque age. Later it flourished in the schools of the great Gothic cathedrals, which had been built with the intent of mirroring the image of God's kingdom. Certainly the French cathedral schools of the twelfth century supplied the best educational training then available. This education comprised both sacred and secular subjects, of course, for all of God's universe was the object of human knowledge. Thus had arisen the

Seven Liberal Arts, a structured program of general education in Latin at all levels. Grammar, rhetoric, and logic were the literary studies and the most basic of all. Also included were four areas of "science"—arithmetic, geometry, astronomy, and music. Since it was Chartres that, through much of the twelfth century, was reputed to have the most distinguished cathedral school in western Europe, it seems only natural to find amid its cathedral sculpture a representation of the Liberal Arts and their presumed founders. Illustrated in figure 7-17 are reliefs relating to music and grammar. Pythagoras, the musical theoretician, appears below music's personification, the latter with lute, bells, and other instruments. Donatus, the grammarian, is portrayed beneath a teacher brandishing a switch, as one playful pupil pulls another's hair.

Paris under Saint Louis

By the thirteenth century educational leadership had passed to Paris with the rise of the University of Paris, the most prestigious of European universities and especially supreme in theological studies. Law, medicine,

7-17 *The Liberal Arts,* detail, c. 1150. West portal of Chartres Cathedral.

and theology were the accepted advanced studies in medieval universities, and all involved arduous mastery of a great body of authoritative knowledge, not usually any original or empirical study. It was the university students at the lower (bachelors and masters of arts) levels, and the renegades from student ranks, who seem to have been most involved in the tavern brawls and bloody confrontations with townspeople that enliven chronicles of medieval university life. The fact that all university students by definition were *clerics*— supposedly all of them had taken at least minor orders in the Church—was hardly an inhibiting influence upon their activities—but it justified portrayal of even the most secular side of student life in the sculpture of the cathedral of Notre Dame in Paris. Shown in figure 7-18 are four small relief panels depicting (from the lower left, counterclockwise) the student's departure from home, his appearance before a judge in a case involving a young townswoman, the taking of further information, and the punishment of the young woman—hoisted upon the "bishop's ladder" outside

7-18 *Life of the Students,* after 1227. South portal of Notre Dame Cathedral, Paris.

Notre Dame; she is being pelted with refuse by vengeful students.

Student liveliness was only one aspect of the spirited Parisian scene in the thirteenth century. Nowhere better than in Paris could the emerging urban worldliness of the High Gothic era be seen. A walled city of over one hundred thousand people, it already had largely assumed its modern division into an administrative and cathedral zone (the large island called the Cité), the wealthy quarter of merchants and craftsmen (the right bank of the Seine), and the students' quarter (the left bank). Noisy, crowded, and dirty, the city housed an immense variety of traders and craftsmen. Secular preoccupations and ambitions must have been strong and often in conflict with spiritual goals.

For several decades King Louis IX, Saint Louis, presided over Paris. His canonization liturgy proudly described him as "peaceful, pious, and virtuous." The years 1226 to 1270 were a period of consolidation for the French monarchy, which only recently had come to exert some real control over the unruly feudal lords of France. The symbol of the royal city's new prestige was its great cathedral, Notre Dame de Paris, which alone among the Virgin's cathedrals in France has become known to history simply as "Notre Dame." The nave and choir were completed by the beginning of the thirteenth century, and by mid-century the west front (fig. 7-19) looked much as it does today. Magnificent both in solidity and grace, it is among the most imposing and best balanced of Gothic facades. By the time of the saintly king's death in 1270, the transept arms had been built. The slim and soaring buttresses of the choir were added during the late-thirteenth- and early-fourteenth-century reconstruction of the east end (fig. 7-20).

A contemporary Parisian monument, equally striking on a much smaller scale, is the Sainte Chapelle ("Holy Chapel") of the royal palace on the Cité. Constructed by order of Saint Louis, it resembles in design and decoration an enormous reliquary. The relics in the Sainte Chapelle included the Crown of Thorns of Christ's passion, which was brought to Paris from the Near East in 1239. The upper chapel (fig. 7-21) is sumptuously painted and gilded, and it is especially notable for the high, slender windows that occupy nearly all of the wall space. Although much of the painting and brilliant glass has been reconstructed, the jewellike ensemble is among the most splendid of all Gothic remains.

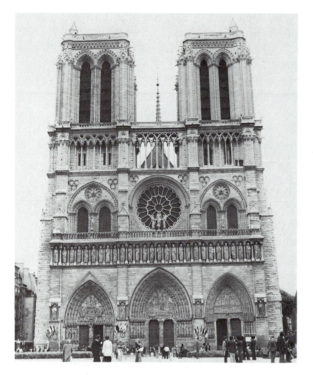

7-19   West front of Notre Dame Cathedral, c. 1200–1250.

The Gothic appreciation for color is displayed in still another art of the age, the painting of manuscript miniatures. Miniatures are, in fact, our main evidence for Gothic skill in painting, since few large-scale paintings were produced during that time. Both of the two miniatures illustrated in this chapter, figures 7-22 and 7-23, are from *psalters,* books of psalms for private devotions, and both are lavish in the use of gold.

From the so-called *Psalter of Blanche of Castile* comes the handsomely regal *Crucifixion and Descent from the Cross* (fig. 7-22). (We say *so-called* because it is uncertain whether or not the mother of Saint Louis owned the volume.) The tiny painting displays the medieval lack of concern for realistic anatomy. In *Joshua Bidding the Sun Stand Still* (fig. 7-23) from the *Psalter of Saint Louis* we are struck by the quaint disproportion of human figures and the walled city and also by the use of Gothic architectural elements—gables, lancets, and rose windows. In typical medieval fashion, the artist saw biblical times in contemporary terms, in costume as well as architecture. Joshua and his companions in this miniature are hardly Old Testament figures, but gallant knights of the age of chivalry.

7-20   Notre Dame Cathedral from the southeast, 1163–1325.

7-21 Upper chapel of La Sainte Chapelle, Paris, 1243–48.

7-22 *Crucifixion and Descent from the Cross* from the *Psalter of Blanche of Castile*, c. 1230. Manuscript miniature, 8″ × 6″. Bibliothèque de l'Arsenal, Paris.

Courtly Love and Literature

Just as the earlier, Romanesque age, the thirteenth century in France was an age of knighthood and chivalry—for the nobility, not for commoners. Whereas nobility was an inherited social and legal status, *knighthood* was an honor conferred upon young nobles, and *chivalry* was the nobles' code of honor and duty. Against these concerns of the aristocratic class, we must consider the significant growth of medieval towns and the urban middle class. However, an emphasis on the prosperity of urban life in the thirteenth century can distort the realities of Gothic France. The emerging urban culture must not blind us to the fact that Europe still remained, and would remain for centuries to come, essentially rural. Of course the nobility continued to preside over rural Europe as well as at the innumerable courts, both large and small, and they

still vigorously resisted monarchical and princely pressures toward political and cultural centralization.

Europe in the late twelfth and the thirteenth centuries was still essentially feudal, and feudal chivalry was adding a zealous devotion to aristocratic womanhood to its earlier preoccupation with bravery in warfare. The new rules of courtesy and love applied only within noble circles; behavior toward women of lower social classes certainly knew no such rules. "Courtly love" was indeed for courts alone—and it was almost never, according to chivalric prescription, for a man's own wife. Although it formalized with incredible complexity the ritual of a pure love from afar, its fundamental outlook was masculine and its practical consequences were often adulterous.

Chivalry and courtly love were not simply matters of social behavior; frequently they were embodied in literature. Generally in verse, the literature of courtly love ranged from brief lyrics to such lengthy narratives as the *Lancelot* of Chrétien de Troyes, written in the

7-23 *Joshua Bidding the Sun Stand Still* from the *Psalter of Saint Louis,* c. 1256. Manuscript miniature, 5″ × 4″. Bibliothèque Nationale, Paris.

late twelfth century. Chrétien celebrated the entourage of a legendary British king, Arthur, whose crude military court, if it ever existed, had been transformed into Camelot—a scene of chivalric pageantry, eroticism, and perilous knightly quests in the name of love, honor, and religion.

The world portrayed in *Lancelot* is a world of knightly courage and honor—a powerful relic from the Romanesque age. Again and again the tale celebrates valor in man-to-man combat, whether in tourneys (mock battles) or in individual encounters. Honor, however, is displayed in the scrupulous keeping of one's word or sworn oath as well as in heroic fighting; even the villainous knight in *Lancelot* fights bravely and honors his oath. This latter sort of honor is related to the general medieval preoccupation with forms and

symbols. For example, mounting a horse-drawn cart was held to symbolize dishonor and shame. Lancelot's momentary hesitation in mounting such a cart when it seemed to be his only mode of transport in quest of his beloved was so grave an offense to the lady that she nearly disowned him—chivalric love having an even stronger claim on a knight than the avoidance of personal dishonor. Oaths in *Lancelot* are always religious more than personal vows, and indeed the Christian religion is a pervasive element in the story.

However, courtly love, more than honor and religion, is the focus of *Lancelot.* Lancelot loves queen Guinevere, wife of his feudal lord king Arthur, and will do almost anything to prove his love, even disgrace himself in a tourney when she so commands. Although Lancelot acts honorably toward all aristocratic maidens in distress (and damsels in distress appear with frequency in the environs of Camelot), he remains loyal to his true love. "The knight," Chrétien explains, "has only one heart, and this one is really no longer his, but has been entrusted to someone else, so that he cannot bestow it elsewhere. Love, which holds all hearts beneath its sway, requires that it be lodged in a single place." In *Lancelot* as in many other poetic narratives, chivalric love develops into a physically consummated passion. Significantly, as Lancelot leaves Guinevere and the scene of their lovemaking, "he bows and acts precisely as if he were before a shrine"; for him the secular and the sacred have become one.

In the thirteenth century, well after Chrétien's time, courtly love became far more complex, and a lengthy French poem, the astonishingly popular *Roman de la Rose* ("Romance of the Rose"), codified the many rules of love. The same century saw the full flowering of brief secular lyric poetry, much of it dealing with love. In order to forestall any impression that all literary creativity in Gothic Europe was confined to France, we will glance at some verses written in Germany and Italy that reflect the courtly rather than the popular tradition.

Early in the thirteenth century the lyrics of the German *minnesinger* (or knightly singing poet) were in their fullest flower. One of these poets, Walther von der Vogelweide (died 1228), is remembered for poems on a great array of subjects as well as his love lyrics. In *Träumerei* ("Dreaming") the subject is the poet's revery in a natural setting that evokes heavenly bliss:

> 'Twas summer,—through the opening grass
>   The joyous flowers upsprang,
> The birds in all their diff'rent tribes
>   Loud in the woodlands sang:
> Then forth I went, and wander'd far
>   The wide green meadow o'er;
>
> Where cool and clear the fountain play'd,
>   There stray'd I in that hour.
>
> Roaming on, the nightingale
>   Sang sweetly in my ear;
> And by the greenwood's shady side,
>   A dream came to me there;
> Fast by the fountain, where bright flowers
>   Of sparkling hue we see,
> Close shelter'd from the summer heat,
>   That vision came to me.
>
> All care was banish'd, and repose
>   Came o'er my wearied breast;

> And kingdoms seem'd to wait on me,
>   For I was with the blest.

From the last decades of the thirteenth century there come several memorable love lyrics of the great Italian poet Dante. Although Dante composed them in an urban rather than a courtly environment, they celebrate a love truly from afar; they portray Dante's absorption in the ideal beauty of Beatrice, to whom he may never have spoken directly the three times she crossed his path. Here is one of his *sonnets*—a fourteen-line poetic form Dante helped to establish, which has survived as a viable poetic medium to our own day:

> My lady looks so gentle and so pure
>   When yielding salutation by the way,
>   That the tongue trembles and has naught to say,
> And the eyes, which fain would see, may not endure.
> And still, amid the praise she hears secure,
>   She walks with humbleness for her array;
>   Seeming a creature sent from Heaven to stay
> On earth, and show a miracle made sure.
> She is so pleasant in the eyes of men
> That through the sight the inmost heart doth gain
>   A sweetness which needs proof to know it by:
> And from between her lips there seems to move
> A soothing spirit that is full of love,
>   Saying for ever to the soul, "O sigh!"

The verse of the Gothic period was usually intended for oral presentation rather than for reading. Thus French chivalric tales and courtly verse in general were recited or sung at aristocratic courts, and German and Italian lyrics were presented for genteel society, courtly and urban. In France, much poetry was composed by *troubadours* and *trouvères*—the former writing in the southern dialect, the latter in the northern, which was to become modern French.

Very often, especially in the earlier period, the troubadours and trouvères were themselves nobles. It appears that they did not recite their verses—they sang them or had them sung—and that in many cases they had written the music as well as the words. As the troubadour Folquet of Marseilles (early thirteenth century) expressed it, "A verse without music is a mill without water." By Folquet's time the complex, affected phrases of many earlier troubadour and trouvère lyrics had largely been replaced by more natural expression, and there was a greater emphasis on musical subtleties. Troubadour and trouvère songs had become entertainment for the bourgeois public as well as the aristocratic. It is worth noting that some twenty troubadours are now known to have been women.

MUSIC IN THE GOTHIC AGE

The songs of troubadours and trouvères were of course largely secular, and they were monophonic (with a single musical line) but often quite complex. One of the most celebrated trouvères was Thibaut IV, count of Champagne from birth and later king of Navarre. The words of Thibaut's *Tuit mi desir* rise well above conventional platitudes:

> All my desire and all my bitter grief come from that source where all my thoughts are fixed. I fear greatly, since all who have seen her, who is fair and beautiful, are overcome by good will toward her. God himself loves her, I know it truly: it is a marvel when he suffers so much.

The ascription of such earthly emotions to deity was not uncommon in Gothic France, where the divine was so familiar and where sacred and secular were so often entwined.

Troubadour and trouvère songs, together with some dance music, were among the last examples of wholly monophonic composition in the Middle Ages and among the first to slip away, on occasion, from the framework of traditional church modes (scales). *Tuit mi desir* employs a modern *major scale*—the sequence of half and whole steps typified by the key of C, in which all tones of the scale can be played on the white keys of the piano.

In Gothic musical performance, the melodic line of troubadour and trouvère songs may have been reinforced at times by an instrument such as the lute. Other instruments continued their evolution in Gothic times, especially encouraged by the development of harmonic music. String, wind, and percussion instruments proliferated. By the thirteenth century, organs were the most useful of all wind instruments. Hand-operated bellows supplied the pipes with air, and a keyboard was developed to replace the less agile slider devices of earlier years.

From the Romanesque period on into the Gothic period, composers experimented by increasing the independence of the musical lines. The music that resulted was polyphonic. *Polyphony* is a type of harmony in which the musical lines are independent of each other melodically and often rhythmically. Each line, in effect, makes independent musical sense in itself rather than being a random succession of notes that fill in a sequence of chords. Monophonic plainsong, with its many modal possibilities, had become a subtle and complex art of great melodic inventiveness; by the mid thirteenth century experimentation with polyphony, notably in Paris, had produced a still more remarkable and elaborate art.

In addition, musical notation was becoming more exact. Composers were beginning to use a notation system by which they specified *note values,* the duration of each tone, as well as pitch—a necessity in guiding polyphonic performances not under the composer's direct supervision. With the less precise notation of the preceding centuries, performance had usually been guided by tradition, guesswork, and improvisation, which made for considerable variation in the performances of a given work. Now the composers could guide the performances of their compositions. Some improvisation in performing the new music doubtless still took place, but the largest area still escaping the composer's control was instrumentation, which, in fact, would not be consistently indicated in musical scores until centuries later.

To the ear unaccustomed to medieval music, the harmonic combinations in thirteenth-century compositions may seem dissonant and haphazard and the harmonies themselves spare and "primitive," especially on final or other accented chords. The reason for this is that most of the harmonies consist of intervals of *octaves* and *fifths*—that is, notes that are eight scale tones and five scale tones apart, respectively. After our ears have adjusted to this as well as modern ears can (for each age has its own notions of suitable harmonies), we become better able to appreciate the structural complexities of this music and its charm.

A new form of sacred composition in the thirteenth century was the *motet.* In this polyphonic form, the highest voice part sang clearly distinguishable words (in French, *mots*) rather than long, drawn-out syllables. Three parts, or melodic lines, were usual. One part, commonly the lowest, was called the *tenor,* for its notes were held for a long time. This slowly moving line was generally borrowed from earlier music, such as plainsong, and it seems less often to have been sung than played on an instrument such as the viol, ancestor of the violin family. The sung parts often were *polytextual*—that is, with completely different texts; both might be in Latin or in the vernacular, or just one might be in Latin. On occasion, one text might be secular—another juxtaposition of the divine and the human, as in the cathedrals and the theological summations of the day. As an example of the thirteenth-century motet we use *Ave gloriosa Mater* ("Hail, glorious mother of the Savior"). This poem and another, *Ave Virgo regia* ("Hail royal Virgin, mother of mercy"), are set above the tenor on the notes of the word *Domino* in the plainchant *Benedicamus Domino*. The parts are clearly differentiated melodically, and each has a fixed rhythmic pattern of its own. Here is the beginning of this motet in modern notation, with the *Domino* of the earlier *Benedicamus Domino* plainsong melody beneath it:

Certainly with two or more sets of words sung simultaneously it must have been difficult for listeners to understand the sacred texts—as in fact the pope was to declare early in the next century. However, for centuries to come, verbal comprehension by the congregation was seen as less important in sacred music than the mood of worship and the liturgical necessities. Both of these emphases, it may be noted, were "functional": sacred music was to glorify God and raise men and women closer to Him. As in classical Greece, music was not regarded as an isolated aesthetic experience but as a meaningful, instructive element of everyday life.

Of course, some sacred and secular music of the thirteenth century was more popular than the generally solemn and complex music being devised for regular church services. Dance forms were among the most popular, and the *estampie* was the favored dance of the century. Many estampie compositions have survived to this day. The writing, often in two parts, is characterized not surprisingly by a strong beat; a forthright rhythmic appeal has marked much of the most popular music of all ages.

This has been true, it should be noted, of even much popular church music—such as, in Gothic France, the famous *Song of the Ass, Orientis partibus* (see fig. 7-24). The most celebrated version comes from the cathedral town of Beauvais, where it was sung each January during the Feast of the Ass. Other French towns also celebrated this parody of church rites, which was sometimes known as the Feast of Fools. Local versions differed, but all of them prominently featured a high-spirited reenactment of Jesus' ride into Jerusalem on a donkey. Much jollity and buffoonery were involved, even inside the churches themselves—with occasional lapses, we are told, into ribald indecency. At one point *Orientis partibus* would be sung: "Out from the lands of the Orient was the ass divinely sent. Strong and fair was he, bearing burdens gallantly. Hee haw hee, sir Ass." Frightful sacrilege, later ages were to say—and even medieval French churchmen had passing qualms over the festival's propriety. Its popularity nevertheless continued through the Middle Ages, attesting once more to the Gothic French lack of distinction between things sacred and secular, and to the easy terms on which, at carefree moments, the people could live with their God.

The rich diversity of Gothic music, and of the whole medieval experience, has only been hinted at in

7-24 Manuscript of *Orientis partibus* (showing the second verse and parts of the first and third), thirteenth century. Reproduced by permission of the British Library (Egerton 2615, 43v).

these pages. Although musical forms, like other cultural expressions, may seem to have differed rather widely, there is a further point to be made: each form, whether in the sacred or secular realm, had its parallels in the other realm. By the thirteenth century, France was, in fact, experiencing a remarkable unity of basic cultural style despite its underlying tensions.

Recommended Reading

Artz, Frederick B. *The Mind of the Middle Ages* A.D. *200–1500* (1965). Good introduction to medieval thought.

Bony, Jean. *French Gothic Architecture of the 12th and 13th Centuries* (1983). Massive, well-illustrated survey.

Brooke, Christopher. *The Structure of Early Medieval Society* (1971). Short, illustrated survey.

Chrétien de Troyes. *Arthurian Romances* (1914). *Lancelot* and other twelfth-century stories.

Delort, Robert. *Life in the Middle Ages* (1974). Handsome picture book with thoughtful text.

Gies, Frances and Joseph. *Life in a Medieval City* (1969). Fascinating description of life in a small French city.

Gies, Frances and Joseph. *Women in the Middle Ages* (1978). A survey, with sketches of individuals.

Jones, Charles W. *Medieval Literature in Translation* (1950). Splendid compilation.

Kraus, Henry. *The Living Theatre of Medieval Art* (1967). The social setting and significance of medieval art.

Labarge, Margaret Wade. *A Small Sound of the Trumpet: Women in Medieval Life* (1986). Attributes occasional high status to medieval women.

Leff, Gordon. *Medieval Thought: St. Augustine to Ockham* (1958). General survey.

Lindsay, Jack. *The Troubadours and Their World of the Twelfth and Thirteenth Centuries* (1976). Detailed and interesting on the poetry, with excerpts.

Martindale, Andrew. *Gothic Art from the Twelfth to the Fifteenth Century* (1967). Fine introduction.

Mundy, John H. *Europe in the High Middle Ages, 1150–1309* (1973). Good general history.

Ross, James Bruce, and Mary Martin McLaughlin. *The Portable Medieval Reader* (1950). Many excellent primary sources.

Swaan, Wim. *The Gothic Cathedral* (1969). Magnificent photographs, good text.

Wieruszowski, Helene. *The Medieval University* (1966). Solid overview, with primary sources.

Zacour, Norman. *An Introduction to Medieval Institutions* (1969). Good summary of medieval institutions and society.

8

The End of the Middle Ages: Northern Europe, 1300–1470

he period from 1300 to 1470 saw striking developments in European culture. However, in France and its northern neighbors—the Low Countries, Germany, and England—the pace of political and social change was slow, as befitted the general medieval respect for tradition. Indeed the basic institutions of these lands remained those of the preceding centuries—the Church, the Holy Roman Empire, the feudal system, and the towns. In France and England there came a progressive encroachment of royal control over the feudal lords. National monarchies that originated in the earlier Middle Ages were solidly established by 1470 both in France and across the English Channel. The Roman Church was still a key spiritual and economic factor, although it was much humbled in its pretensions to European leadership. For nearly seventy years (1309–76) the popes were obliged to reside at Avignon, a papal possession within France. Then, after the return to Rome, there came the still more distressing Great Schism within the Church (1378–1417), when two and ultimately three popes claimed at the same time to be the authentic head of Christendom. Simultaneously, the Holy Roman Empire was weakened by the increasing power of the states within its boundaries. Towns, on the other hand, flourished everywhere in Europe. No effective international political authority existed, and wars were frequent. The most memorable international struggle

was the Hundred Years' War waged by France and England intermittently between 1337 and 1453, with the powerful Burgundian dukes often aiding the English.

Burgundy is mainly a term of convenience in the history of the late Middle Ages: it is a misnomer for the conglomerate realm of certain great dukes of the French royal (Valois) family. There was, however, a true duchy of Burgundy, in east central France, and it was from this base that the Valois dukes gradually accumulated extensive further territories, mainly by marriage and inheritance. In 1363 the French king John the Good had granted Burgundy to his son Philip the Bold as an autonomous duchy. The acquisition of Flanders midway in Philip's reign, and then of other territories in the northern French and Netherlandish regions, slowly drew the realm's center of gravity northward. This shift, in addition to deepening Franco-Burgundian enmity and longstanding Flemish-English ties, eventually brought about a Burgundian alliance with England and the capture of the French heroine Joan of Arc in 1430. A formal reconciliation between Philip the Good (ruled 1419–67) and the French monarchy in 1435 left Burgundy with more autonomy than ever. The last Valois duke, Charles the Bold, was killed in battle in 1477 and his lands were divided, with the French king and the Hapsburg ruler of the Holy Roman Empire as the chief beneficiaries. Thus ended the century-long career of the "Burgundian" state, one of Europe's most brilliant powers, although it had never had an official name.

Today this state is best remembered for its extraordinary wealth and its patronage of the arts. The wealth was concentrated in the cities, and much of it was generated there, especially in the woolen goods industry, commerce, and finance. This economic prosperity—notably in the northern Franco-Flemish provinces—was firmly in the hands of a commercial-financial-industrial complex of substantial townspeople intermarried with the nobility. It appears that they were a hard-headed, realistic lot, except for certain aristocratic pretensions—and they had a great deal of money. Many of their faces are known to us, fixed forever with sometimes unflattering realism by the distinguished artists from whom they could well afford to commission altarpieces and portraits.

THE TRANSFORMATION OF MEDIEVAL LIFE

By the middle of the fourteenth century the glorious days of French chivalry were numbered. In 1346 at Crécy and again in 1356 at Poitiers, the flower of French knighthood charged gallantly and recklessly toward the opposing mass of English foot soldiers and was cut down relentlessly by the efficient and deadly longbow. For a time, however, the warning of those battlefields went unheeded, despite the continuation of the war with England. Fortunately the Hundred Years' War saw only fitful fighting, and under the capable Charles V, king from 1364 to 1380, France seemed to have largely recovered from its humiliation at English hands. After Charles's death France not only knew relative peace and stability for three or four decades, but witnessed the most splendid outward display of chivalric pomp and circumstance that the Middle Ages had yet seen. John, duke of Berry (died 1416), and Philip the Bold, duke of Burgundy, brothers of Charles V and lavish patrons of the arts, presided over courts whose magnificence was duly commemorated by their own painters and sculptors. Just as a Frenchman of Saint Louis's time might have been startled to be called Gothic, the courts of dukes John and Philip might have resounded with laughter if told they were in the midst of the waning of the Middle Ages.

Their laughter would not have been unjustified, for theirs was a lively and productive culture. Yet the times had changed, far more than they knew: the High Gothic age of Saint Louis, with its relatively stable, balanced culture, had already undergone a major transformation. Northern Europe, however, took a path differing from that of contemporary Italy, which was entering the period commonly known today as the *Renaissance*. Both northern Europe and Italy would contribute to the transition to modern times, but northern Europe—or more accurately, non-Italian Western Christendom—was less conscious of its innovations and maintained more scrupulously its traditional outward cultural forms.

Within these traditional forms, the most readily discernible change in the arts and thinking of the period was a shift of emphasis from theory to practice. Investigation and manipulation of materials often received more attention than did abstract theory. To be sure, theologians continued to wrestle with questions of the most elusively abstract nature, even outdoing

CHRONOLOGY

HISTORY		THE ARTS	
1285–1314	Philip IV king of France	13th–15th centuries	York Cathedral
1309–77	the papacy at Avignon ("Babylonian Captivity" of the Roman Church)	late 13th–mid 15th centuries c. 1300–	Strasbourg Cathedral
1337–1453	Hundred Years' War between France and England	c. 1377 c. 1340–1400	Guillaume de Machaut Geoffrey Chaucer
1346	Battle of Crécy: English victory over the French	14th–15th centuries	Winchester Cathedral
1348–49	the Black Death kills about a third of European population		
1356	Battle of Poitiers: English victory over the French	c. 1350–1406	Claus Sluter
1363–1404	Philip the Bold, first Valois duke of Burgundy		
1364–80	Charles V king of France		
1378–1417	Great Schism in the Roman Church		
		c. 1387–1400	Chaucer's *Canterbury Tales*
		late 14th–15th centuries	Saint Martin's Church, Landshut
		c. 1395–1403	Claus Sluter's Fountain of Champmol, Dijon
1404–19	John the Fearless, second Valois duke of Burgundy	c. 1400–74 c. 1400–64 c. 1411–16	Guillaume Dufay Rogier van der Weyden Limbourg Brothers court painters to John, duke of Berry
1415	Battle of Agincourt: English victory over the French		
1416	death of John, duke of Berry	c. 1420–81	Jean Fouquet
1419–67	Philip the Good, third Valois duke of Burgundy		
1422–61	Charles VII king of France	c. 1425–32	Jan and Hubert van Eyck's *Ghent Altarpiece*
1429–31	Joan of Arc inspires French fighting against the English	c. 1435–38	Rogier van der Weyden's *Descent from the Cross*
1438	beginning of Hapsburg dynasty as Holy Roman Emperors		
1438–50	invention of printing by movable type	1443–51	house of Jacques Coeur in Bourges
1453	end of Hundred Years' War: England expelled from France, except for Calais	c. 1450 c. 1460	*Imitation of Christ* *Pietà of Avignon*
1461–89	Louis XI king of France		
1467–77	Charles the Bold, last Valois duke of Burgundy		

Saint Thomas Aquinas on occasion. However, many of the newer thinkers denied the validity of a strictly rational approach to the great mysteries of the Christian faith. For example, those theologians felt it was unnecessary to prove the existence of God, thus pushing aside one traditional preoccupation of theology.

Fourteenth-century theology encouraged approaches to life and thought that were less strictly theoretical and, in fact, considerably closer to the practical realities of everyday life than the speculations of the thirteenth century.

One new direction, although it was pursued only

FRANCE, ENGLAND, AND THE BURGUNDIAN REALM BEFORE THE DEATH OF CHARLES THE BOLD (1477)

NORTH SEA

IRELAND

IRISH SEA

York

HOLY ROMAN EMPIRE

WALES

ENGLAND

Oxford

London

Thames R.

Canterbury

Winchester

Bruges

Ghent

FLANDERS

Calais

Lille

Scheldt R.

Tournai

Brussels

HAINAUT

Meuse R.

LIMBURG

Cologne

LUX.

Moselle R.

ALSACE

Rhine R.

Agincourt

Crécy

ENGLISH CHANNEL

Rouen

NORMANDY

Seine R.

CHAMPAGNE

Reims

Marne R.

Strasbourg

Paris

Troyes

LORRAINE

BRITANNY

Orléans

Loire R.

NEVERS

Dijon

DUCHY OF BURGUNDY

FRANCHE COMTÉ

Bourges

BERRY

Saône River

SWISS CONFEDERATION

Poitiers

FRANCE

Rhône R.

DAUPHINY

Garonne R.

Avignon

Toulouse

——— Boundary of France, 1453

Burgundian Realm

MEDITERRANEAN SEA

hesitantly in the late medieval period, was science—which would later have great practical importance in Western civilization. A second new direction was *mysticism*—the attempt to attain spiritual truth not through rational thought, ancient authority, or scientific study of earthly facts, but rather through direct communication with God. Some medieval mystics saw, or believed they saw, visions; others, like the author of *The Imitation of Christ*, more modestly sought to imitate the spirit of Jesus. Thomas à Kempis (1380–1471), the probable author of this celebrated devotional guide in Latin, proposed that Christians meditate on the life of their Savior and follow a humble path of pious meditation and good deeds.

The *Imitation* was particularly eloquent on inner spiritual comfort and receptivity to God's voice:

> Blessed is the soul which heareth the Lord speaking within it, and receiveth the word of consolation from his mouth. Blessed are the ears which receive the echoes of the soft whisper of God, and turn not aside to the whisperings of this world. Blessed truly are the ears which listen not to the voice that soundeth without, but to that which teacheth truth inwardly. Blessed are the eyes which are closed to things without, but are fixed upon things within. Blessed are they who search inward things and study to prepare themselves more and more by daily exercises for the receiving of heavenly mysteries. Blessed are they who long to have leisure for God, and free themselves from every hindrance of the world. Think on these things, O my soul, and shut the doors of thy carnal desires, so mayest thou hear what the Lord God will say within thee.

The practical ethical orientation of much late medieval piety is shown in another popular work of the period, the drama *Everyman*. Best known in English versions of the fifteenth century, this was one of countless morality plays that were performed in the open air on festive occasions in Europe's towns and cities. The cast of *Everyman* includes God himself and characters representing death, the average Christian ("Everyman"), and a host of personified qualities that help or hinder Everyman's eventual salvation. The most important of these is "Good Deeds." In emphasizing the central role of good deeds on earth as a way of achieving eternal life, *Everyman* shows the practical orientation of much religious thought in the Middle Ages.

Further manifestations of a practical approach in the late medieval spirit are to be found in other arts. In these cases "practicality" refers not to everyday usefulness but to the solving of practical, technical problems in the respective arts. Music, for example, tended away

from the relatively direct and deceptively simple manner of the thirteenth century toward a style of extraordinary complexity. Painting achieved hitherto unimagined heights of detailed realism. And above all in the daily conscious experience of northern Europeans, there were the showpieces of structural and decorative skill newly created in Gothic architecture.

Late Gothic Architecture

Northern European Gothic architecture offers perhaps the most visible example today of late medieval innovation within a clearly traditional framework. The Gothic style, of course, had originated in France, where by the end of the thirteenth century it had passed the peak of its first and most perfect bloom. In the meantime it had spread to other countries. Its diffusion and development continued after 1300 and was hardly a simple case of inept copying of the French manner. Each large area, from Spain and Portugal to parts of central eastern Europe such as Bohemia, soon achieved its own forms, its own "national" style, usually with some variation from region to region within the large area. In contrast to the relative homogeneity of early Gothic culture throughout western Europe, the period from 1300 to 1470 saw a remarkable flourishing of national architectural styles—an instance of breakdown within the Gothic synthesis. It would seem not coincidental that the fourteenth century in western Europe also saw a parallel linguistic phenomenon—the literary acceptance and standardization of national languages.

Despite national and regional variations, most of late Gothic architecture has been categorized under one generic label—*flamboyant*. The term suggests a style of exuberant elaboration and a flamelike, restless movement—which are precisely the most distinctive qualities of flamboyant Gothic. The lower west front of Strasbourg Cathedral (fig. 8-1), begun in 1277 but completed in the following centuries, displays the style very handsomely. The basic design of the facade is much like that of Notre Dame in Paris. However, in front of the facade wall is a shimmering stone screen whose purpose is solely decorative. The screenlike arches and pinnacles of the central portal's steep gable add still more thrust to earlier Gothic aspiration and a feeling of structural depth as well.

The fireplace wall of the great hall of the Palace of the Counts in Poitiers, France (fig. 8-2), achieves a similar effect on a much more modest scale. Here in

8-1   Lower west front of Strasbourg Cathedral, late
thirteenth century to mid fifteenth century.

the late fourteenth century, John, duke of Berry, had a
whole new wall constructed—with tracery above the
fireplace and a balustrade with pierced screen standing
in front of the earlier Gothic window wall. The added
decorative, delicate flamboyance is all the more effective for its contrast with the windows and the stolid
plainness of the thirteenth-century arches of the side
walls. Architecture has been set in motion in this fireplace wall; it has become fantasy.

On occasion, flamboyant Gothic became rather
disorganized and even tormented through undulating
decoration or the unsettling use of immense, tortured
spiral columns. More typical, however, is the imposing, more restrained tradition of English cathedral architecture. Two examples will give some notion of
English architectural trends in the late Gothic period.

York Cathedral (fig. 8-3) is a full 524 feet in
length; though English churches were not as high as
the great French cathedrals, they tended to be longer.
The main construction at York was begun in the thirteenth century, but the most admired sections, the facade and the three towers, were built in the fourteenth
and fifteenth centuries, respectively. In the tracery of
the large west window, the particularly flamelike
curves and counter-curves above the two major lower
divisions are notable. These decorative *ogee arches* are
among the most characteristic of flamboyant architectural devices.

8-2   Fireplace wall, great
hall of the Palace of the
Counts, Poitiers, France,
1384–86.

8-3   York Cathedral, England, thirteenth to fifteenth centuries.

The nave of Winchester Cathedral (fig. 8-4) is the longest in Europe, though only seventy-eight feet high. Almost totally reconstructed in the fourteenth and fifteenth centuries from the original Romanesque, it is notable for its west window, spreading the whole width of the nave, and for its complex vaulting. As is usual in English building, a long ridge rib extends down the nave—and the vaulting is complicated by many *liernes*, or subsidiary ribs, which neither spring from the corner columns nor reach the ridge rib directly.

In the Germanies, the church of Saint Martin at Landshut (fig. 8-5) exemplifies the *hall church*—a form popular in central Europe and England but rarely seen in Gothic France. The interior of hall churches is treated as a single large hall, with aisle vaulting rising as high (or nearly so) as the central vaulting, thus contrasting with the low aisles and the high choirs and naves of French basilica-type churches. And outside, a

single high roof covers the whole width of the hall church's main body. Saint Martin is also of interest for its architect, the celebrated Hans von Burghausen (died 1432). Each of the many churches he designed is distinctly different—and his experimental architectural individualism is echoed in the portrait bust on his memorial monument (fig. 8-6). Such strong individuality would have been unthinkable in the thirteenth century; it is a symptom of the individualism that marked much of the art of the following centuries throughout Europe.

Late Medieval Life and Arts

Individualism is likely to flourish in an age when life is bleak, whether in a bitter struggle for physical survival or in a withdrawal into oneself. Certainly the world was often cheerless and bleak in the fourteenth and fifteenth centuries. Famine and pestilence were rampant, and the people of war-torn France were frequently assaulted by military and civilian thugs and looters. During the last decades of the Hundred Years' War, a Parisian burgher vividly described the sufferings of Parisians and country folk. "It was the longest winter," he wrote early in 1421, "that one had seen for forty years. The wolves were so ravenous that they unearthed with their claws the bodies of people buried in the villages and fields; for everywhere one went, one found people dead in the fields and towns, from the great poverty, the high prices, and the famine which they suffered, through the cursed war which always grew worse from day to day." In 1439 he reported that in one week the wolves "ate fourteen persons, both large and small," just outside the gates of Paris. In the summer of 1444 Parisian tribulations rose from another quarter:

> At the beginning of July there came a great company of thieves and murderers who lodged in the villages around Paris, and it was such that, up to six or eight leagues from Paris, no man dared go out to the fields or come to Paris, nor dared to pick in the fields anything at all. Nor could a man of any estate, whether monk, priest, or nun, or musician, or herald, or woman, or child of any age go outside Paris that he was not in great peril of his life.

In addition to the famine and warfare, there was the routine occurrence, again and again in the fourteenth and fifteenth centuries, of devastating plagues that swept the land. The infamous Black Death (1348–49), which killed perhaps a third of Europe's popula-

8-4   Nave of Winchester Cathedral, England, fourteenth to fifteenth centuries.

8-5   Saint Martin's Church, Landshut, Germany, late fourteenth and fifteenth centuries.

8-6   Hans Stetheimer(?), *Hans von Burghausen,* after 1432. Detail of life-size, stone funerary monument, Saint Martin's Church.

tion, was only the worst of many waves of pestilence. Even the noble and wealthy were not wholly exempt from the cruel insecurities of the age—and possibly those insecurities caused many of them to turn to the diversions of courtly splendor. Others turned to religion or debauchery—and a goodly number turned to all three of these things at once. As noted by the historian Johan Huizinga, piety was often spasmodic indeed. At the peak of excitement during a hunting party, Charles V would suddenly feel impelled to hear Mass. Philip the Good of Burgundy, well-known for his pride and his sumptuous feasts, would fast on bread and water four days a week—at least until late afternoon. Even as respect for the Church and the papacy declined (these were the centuries of the Avignonese papacy and the subsequent Great Schism), the pious forms and rigid mental habits of an overripe religion saturated the air. If symbolism had been prevalent in the thirteenth century, it now ran riot, often demolishing a more everyday type of thought that proceeds from natural cause and effect. *Mysticism*—the attempt to get into direct touch with divinity without external formal or priestly intervention—and extravagant religious expression flourished. Amid examples of this extravagance of expression were the copious and pious tears and a frequent melancholic absorption in suffering, death, and decay. Even that most original and emancipated of fifteenth-century French poets, François Villon, frequently dwelt upon the inexorable passing of youth and his horror of old age and death. The artists went further, depicting with grisly detail the disemboweling of Saint Erasmus or the quartering of Saint Hippolytus, not to mention innumerable beheadings. Portrayals of a more commonplace death and decay were still more usual—not surprisingly in a time that saw the repeated ravages of famine and pestilence and the routine burial-ground exhumation and exposure of decomposed bodies to make room for the newly dead. Sculptured tombs of even the powerful of the earth did not shrink from portraying the most unpleasant postmortem decay. The Tomb of Cardinal Jean de La Grange (fig. 8-7) is actually among the less ghoulish of

the lot. Everywhere art and literature proclaimed the physical equality of all people after death.

The many religious dramas so popular in these centuries—*Everyman* among them—conveyed this same stern message and inspired further artistic endeavor. The passion and death of Jesus Christ was a common theme of paintings and sculpture as well as of the religious dramas (see the *Pietà of Avignon*, fig. 8-19). Perhaps most congenial of all to the morbid religious sensibility of the day was the overwhelming vision of the Last Judgment, in which the themes of mercy and salvation came through far less vividly than did damnation and eternal suffering. Even the German painter Stephan Lochner (died 1451), best known for the gentleness and sweetness of his images, attacked the subject with zeal (fig. 8-8), contriving grotesque details of demonic entrapment and human torture.

The religious dramas, as well as the art inspired by them and by pious sentiment in general, appealed to all classes. Other literature of the age often was addressed more exclusively to a single social group—for example, courtly romances to the nobility and earthy prose tales to bourgeois readers or lowly commoners who heard them recited at markets and fairs. One suspects, however, that the aristocracy took a good deal of interest in the earthier, more naturalistic popular literature. And it is well known that wealthy burghers were fascinated by the courtly literature of their social betters, whom they flattered by jealousy and imitation. Then, too, occasional works appealed to all social classes, such as the *Canterbury Tales* of Geoffrey Chaucer (c. 1340–1400), with their memorable panoramas of nearly all social strata.

The *Canterbury Tales* are set within the framework of a pilgrimage from London to the shrine of Saint Thomas Becket at Canterbury in southeastern England. Let us look for a moment at the London of the day. (The tavern where the pilgrims assembled before setting forth on their journey was across the Thames River from the city, in a quarter later absorbed by the metropolis, but even in the fourteenth century it was a recognized extension of the city.) This London, home to about fifty or sixty thousand people, was already in Chaucer's day the dominating focus of most aspects of English life.

8-7 Detail of the tomb of Cardinal Jean de La Grange, early fifteenth century. Stone, life-size. Calvet Museum, Avignon.

Chaucer's London comprised handsome mansions, town houses, and crowded, squalid tenement dwellings. Some one hundred churches and nearly two hundred taverns occupied much of the remaining urban area. The streets were narrow and filthy, and particularly odorous in sections dominated by butchers and tanners. Street crime was rampant, though probably no more so than in modern cities. Market areas were especially lively, but crowds also congregated around the stocks where male and female offenders were on display for public amusement and insult. Colorful religious processions were common.

Fourteenth-century Londoners were keenly conscious of social hierarchy and class status. However, this sense of group affiliation and rank could not completely destroy personal and family sensibilities, even in crowded neighborhoods where almost no individual or family had much privacy. Families were generally small—not because of deliberate family planning but because many children died in infancy. Men were thought to be the stronger of the sexes, possibly with some reason at that time; many men spent much of their lives outdoors, while women were confined to homes ill-heated in winter and always (given the English climate) damp and drafty. Wives were kept firmly subordinate to husbands, and wife-beating was common and expected, especially at the lower levels of society. Children, too, were often beaten; the people of that time did not recognize gradual moral development, and misbehavior was thought to be willful and deliberate. Children typically hated school and were happiest at games and sports. (Many children enjoyed skating on ice-covered swamps north of London in wintertime, on skates improvised from animal bones.) Schooling was available in numerous forms, and elementary literacy in English is thought to have extended to about half of London's adult male population. The education of girls was much more haphazard than that of boys.

The language of Chaucer was a richly developed Middle English—a language recognizable today as English but requiring modern adaptation for all except scholars. Let us look briefly at the *Canterbury Tales* in updated English, and especially at the "General Prologue" and the Pardoner's "Prologue and Tale." The whole great poem was begun around 1387 and was still unfinished at the time of the author's death in 1400. The Canterbury pilgrimage it purports to record was one of many medieval pilgrimages, all of them occasions, it would seem, not only for spiritual benefit but for such touristic jollity as storytelling. In the Prologue, Chaucer introduces us to the twenty-nine pilgrims and their innkeeper-host, who will accompany them on their journey. The pilgrims range from Christian knight to sturdy plowman, from daintily pretentious nun to earnest but impoverished student. (See fig. 8-9 for a fifteenth-century manuscript painting of several of the Canterbury pilgrims.)

Chaucer introduces the Oxford student, or "clerk" (cleric), as follows in the "General Prologue":

A clerk from Oxford was with us also,
Who'd turned to getting knowledge, long ago.
As meagre was his horse as a rake,
Nor he himself too fat, I'll undertake,
But he looked hollow and went soberly.
Right threadbare was his overcoat; for he
Had got him yet no churchly benefice,
Nor was so worldly as to gain office.
For he would rather have at his bed's head
Some twenty books, all bound in black and red,
Of Aristotle and his philosophy
Than rich robes, fiddle, or gay psaltery.
Yet, and for all he was a philosopher,
He had but little gold within his coffer;
But all that he might borrow from a friend
On books and learning he would swiftly spend,
And then he'd pray right busily for the souls
Of those who gave him wherewithal for schools.
Of study took he utmost care and heed.
Not one word spoke he more than was his need;
And that was said in fullest reverence
And short and quick and full of high good sense.
Pregnant of moral virtue was his speech;
And gladly would he learn and gladly teach.

Others among Chaucer's characterizations are far less sympathetic, far more biting, than his characterization of the student. The most evil pilgrim, and one

of the most prosperous, is a pardoner, whose cynical ecclesiastical business is threefold—to sell *indulgences* or pardons (which in the late Middle Ages were sometimes seen as remissions of punishment for sin and, hence, as passports to heaven), to sell holy relics (largely or entirely fraudulent), and to preach sermons that would encourage both types of sale. As the pardoner admits quite freely to his fellow pilgrims:

For my intent is only pence to win,
And not at all for punishment of sin.

The tale told by the pardoner involves the dregs of society—blasphemous tavern-ruffians without fear or conscience, whose murderous greed brings them all to death at each other's hands.

Chaucer's breadth of social vision affords us invaluable insight into his age. This vision, however, was not shared by his more elegantly established contemporaries. Today we can see what the courts of France, Berry, and Burgundy could seldom if ever see—that the strength of European states and courts lay more in the wealth, initiative, and labor of the despised commoners than in the magnificence of the ruling aristocracy. Still, if chivalric aristocracy did not note its own decadence, it did at least perceive the social threat of the wealthy bourgeoisie. Quite possibly this uneasy perception enhanced an already formidable urge toward the conspicuous wastefulness of the courtly life style.

Further, the shadow of the bourgeoisie may have contributed to the higher walls that the aristocracy erected around itself through elaborate artificial distinctions, formality, and ceremonies. Although the conventions of courtly love had become numerous before the end of the thirteenth century, they now proliferated still more, culminating in the "courts of love" in which the fine points of aristocratic love were debated interminably. These ceremonies had their parallel in the realm of warlike activities, the other prime preserve of chivalry, in the increasing splendor of tournaments.

Several wartime defeats of French knights by efficient English foot soldiers highlight the decadence and the futility of late medieval French chivalry. The diffi-

8-9 *The Canterbury Pilgrims,* fifteenth century. Manuscript miniature from *Canterbury Tales.* Reproduced by Courtesy of the Trustees of the British Museum, London.

culty was not simply a matter of battlefield technique; outdated attitudes were probably still more significant. French knighthood was not only reckless in battle but deliberately blind when utilitarian strategic considerations might better have won battles and saved lives. However, the knight first of all had to embody the heroic ideal, whatever the practical consequences. The chivalric world of the late Middle Ages had become one of unreality and fantasy, a dream world smacking of the fairy tale.

Thus chivalry became ever more decorative, artificial, and ritualistic, especially through the making of elaborate ceremonial vows and the institution of new and solemn knightly orders. Of all recorded tournaments, wedding festivities, and civic and pious celebrations in the Burgundian realm, the best remembered is the Feast of the Pheasant, which took place in 1454 in the city of Lille. The banquet hall had been decked out with the most elegant silks and canopies, and the tables groaned with immense "dishes" that were actually either mechanical marvels or elaborate, gigantic pastries from which people or animals emerged. The table of Philip the Good, reported a chronicle of the time, held "a church with vault and windows made most beautifully, wherein a bell sounded and four singers sang and played on organs when their turn came." The table of Philip's heir, the future Charles the Bold, held "a pastry within which twenty-eight live persons played various instruments, each one when his turn came." A smaller table displayed curious animals "which moved by themselves, almost as if they were alive." After various musical, allegorical, and mythological diversions, a dignitary of the Order of the Golden Fleece introduced a richly decorated live pheasant. The duke and the principal lords then pronounced a mighty vow to God, the Blessed Virgin, the ladies present, and the pheasant to go on a crusade against the Turks, who had recently captured Constantinople. The crusade was never undertaken, not surprisingly.

Obviously great numbers of skilled artists and craftsmen contributed to the amazing décor of this and other magnificent festivities, and some of the greatest painters of the age assisted in the work. We cannot know how truly stunning these colossal creations were, since they have long since disappeared. Fortunately, we have other examples of aristocratic taste on a smaller scale. In fact, some of them are on a miniature scale. Among the most precious artistic relics of the

age are many colorful devotional books, such as "books of hours," illustrated with tiny paintings of great charm. *Books of hours* had developed from the *psalters* (psalm books) of an earlier time and included prayers, a church calendar, and various other items required for private devotions. Everybody of wealth or noble blood was expected to own a book of hours, but few could commission or buy such handsome ones as those owned by John, duke of Berry.

A miniature painting of the duke and his elaborately attired retinue starting on a journey (fig. 8-10) is

8-10 Limbourg Brothers, *The Duke Starting on a Journey*, c. 1415. Manuscript miniature from the *Petites Heures of John, Duke of Berry*, 7″ × 5″. Bibliothèque Nationale, Paris.

typical; it is from one, and not the most splendid, of his books of hours. To the great distress of his subjects, John imposed notoriously excessive taxes—and to the enrichment of our artistic inheritance, much of the tax money he collected financed artistic projects. He was a lavish patron of architects and miniaturists and an enthusiastic collector of tapestries and all sorts of precious and exotic objects. In all this he was rivaled in his day only by his brother, Philip the Bold of Burgundy.

Berry was in central France, with Bourges its leading town. The northern parts of the Burgundian realm were much more distinctly urban than was Berry; Brussels and Antwerp in Brabant and the Flemish towns (that is, towns in Flanders) of Ghent and Bruges were bustling focuses of economic life and the arts. Shortly the harbor of Bruges would become silted up, leaving the city to the picturesque decadence of succeeding centuries. However, a great building program continued there through much of the fifteenth century, leaving us with a striking bell tower and a fine town hall

(fig. 8-11). Under the supervision of the rulers of Burgundy and the guidance of prosperous leading citizens, the great northern cities enjoyed a considerable degree of autonomy.

The governmental alliance between ruler and burgher was not peculiar to the Burgundian realm. It played a sizable role, for example, in the remarkably swift recovery of France toward the end of the Hundred Years' War and after the peace of 1453, which at last expelled England from all its major Continental holdings. The territorial and administrative consolidation of centralized states was the wave of the European future, and in this trend France helped to lead the way. Even Charles VII, who had needed Joan of Arc to arouse him from his lethargy, eventually became a strong monarch, wise enough to rely heavily on the administrative and financial skills of bourgeois advisers such as Étienne Chevalier and Jacques Coeur.

The arts had languished in France during the last decades of war and misery and since the deaths of the

8-11 Town Hall, Bruges, 1376–1420.

8-12 House of
Jacques Coeur,
Bourges, France,
1443–51.

brilliant brothers of Berry and Burgundy—but from the 1440s their comeback was strong. The very capable painter Jean Fouquet was a native of Tours, and in Bourges there was the patronage not only of the French court but of the famous financier Jacques Coeur. One of the finest examples of late medieval architecture is Coeur's house (fig. 8-12), in which nearly all the devices of more imposing ecclesiastical Gothic appear in miniature.

NEW STYLES IN THE ARTS

Jacques Coeur participated in the tradition exemplified two and three centuries earlier at Chartres—the patronage accorded religious art by the wealthy and by guildsmen rich and poor. Bourgeois patronage increased very significantly in the late medieval period, although it was not necessarily this increasing influence that inspired the detailed realism of late medieval

art. Rather, realism seems to have been the product of a gradual growth in technical skill, transmitted through the guilds, and of general late medieval thinking. People of that time seem to have tried to visualize everything, to put everything into precise images.

Bourgeois interest in art was undeniably on the increase, and a good many art works went into bourgeois homes. With the status of painters and sculptors now regulated and protected by the guilds to which they were required to belong, many of the artists moved into the ranks of the bourgeoisie. A few favored ones, such as Jan van Eyck, moved upward still farther, receiving positions at court and living more like courtiers than craft workers. Some even took to signing their works. A fortunate artist of recognized skill now was far more than a simple artisan, and never since Greek antiquity had the general prestige of art risen higher.

Then, too, art in northern Europe retained its importance in religious and civic life. To be sure, the first major inroads upon this traditional public role of

8-13 *The Virgin* and *Christ,* c. 1322. The choir of Cologne Cathedral.

the arts were being made; patrons such as John, duke of Berry, sometimes must have commissioned or bought an art work simply as an object of luxury for private contemplation and satisfaction. Still, the visual arts, like the music of the time, remained overwhelmingly functional in orientation. Art and music served the Church, they contributed to courtly grandeur and diversion, and they enhanced the proud dignity of bourgeois ceremonial occasions, whether in town hall or guild hall. Art and music, in short, were still very much parts of daily life.

Sculpture

Sculpture was primarily an expression of religious feeling and an accessory to Christian piety in late medieval northern Europe. On occasion, especially in the fourteenth century, sculpture remained an integral part of its particular architectural setting. Increasingly, how-

ever, it became emancipated, at least in spirit, from the walls and columns of the churches and began to be treated as a separate entity. In the process, works of sculpture ceased to function as part of a general panorama and began to receive more detailed treatment. Altarpieces and altar figures now attracted more attention than the works that formed the background, and individual pieces were more in demand, especially for private chapels and homes.

Even when firmly, physically attached to architecture, late Gothic sculpture typically maintains its formal independence. The two column figures from Cologne Cathedral shown in figure 8-13, *The Virgin* and *Christ*, are columnar only in location, for their stylized curves counteract their verticality. Their elegance echoes the rather precious mannerism of the countless carved Madonnas of this era that were destined for churches and homes, and contrasts emphatically with the solemnity of High Gothic monumental sculpture.

We should note that the Cologne statues are richly painted, like nearly all northern stone and wooden sculpture of that and earlier times. The painting of sculpture was, in fact, a highly esteemed art. This practice, at least, was solidly traditional, although the uses and spirit of sculpture were changing markedly.

Perhaps the most striking change of all was the revival of the sort of forthright, individualized portraiture seldom seen since the days of pagan Rome. It has been suggested that the use of funerary images (molded or carved from masks made on the body of the deceased) at funeral ceremonies accounted for the new trend, but historical chronology indicates that the funerary image custom encouraged the individualization already well under way. Claus Sluter's portrait statue of a kneeling Philip the Bold at the doorway of the Chartreuse de Champmol (fig. 8-14) is an instance of individualized portraiture antedating most funerary images and certainly antedating Philip's own.

But the remarkable Sluter (c. 1350–1406), a Dutchman who came to serve Philip in his Burgundian duchy, is distinguished for more than his portraiture, or for divorcing his figures from their architectural context. (Note in the Champmol portal that the kneeling duke and duchess, and the saints commending them to the Virgin, hardly fit into the columnar background at all but establish an almost theatrical scene inviting entrance to the building.) More personal to Sluter's

8-14 Claus Sluter, portal of the Ducal Chapel of the Chartreuse of Champmol, Dijon, c. 1390–97. (Philip the Bold is the second figure from the left.)

work are the swelling, swirling garments and the grand majesty of the total artistic conception.

These features are also seen in his famous Fountain of Champmol, or "Well of Moses" (fig. 8-15). Philip the Bold had initiated the building of the Carthusian monastery outside his capital of Dijon in 1385. The portal of the projected ducal chapel and mausoleum had been built in the 1390s, and the symbolic Fountain was begun by Sluter later in the decade. Only fragments and the largely intact base of the Fountain remain. At one time this base, surmounted by other figures and an immense crucifix, stood in a pool of water, into which flowed, symbolically, the blood of Christ from the fountain of his wounds. On the base, Moses, David, and four prophets seem to debate the mysterious divine sacrifice. Traces of color and gilt remain—but Jeremiah's spectacles, ordered from a Dijon goldsmith, have been lost. Each figure, if scarcely portrayed from life, is strongly individualized— Moses, for example, as an imposing visionary, David as

a somewhat languid psalmist-king, and Jeremiah as an earnest, contemplative scholar.

The many figures of mourners from the Tomb of Philip the Bold (fig. 8-16), planned and partially executed by Sluter before his death in 1406, are usually individualized less in face than in posture, if only because many of the faces are covered by enveloping hoods. The figures represent the hundreds of actual mourners who took part in Philip's funeral rites; the ducal account books record the cost of the somber hoods and gowns. Sluter's command of broad drapery lines lends the small sculptured mourners a monumentality far exceeding their size.

Monumentality in pictorial art has usually suited modern tastes better than minute, descriptive detail, and undoubtedly Sluter's work has received attention because of this preference. At the same time, the intricate detail of innumerable late medieval altarpieces and statuettes is sometimes overlooked.

Before turning to painting, we may note in passing a very detailed and handsome, if somewhat amusing, sample of the Flemish goldsmith's art from the very end of the period—the gold and enamel *Reliquary of Charles the Bold* (fig. 8-17). Charles, kneeling, presents the relic of a saintly finger as Saint George, patron of Burgundy, doffs his helmet. Judging from other portraits, Charles's likeness is careful and accurate, even to the violent intensity of expression that may well have typified this last, unfortunate Valois duke of Burgundy.

Painting

The customary subject matter of late medieval painting ranged farther than the routine iconography of sculpture and well beyond the ordinary inspiration of earlier Gothic painting. Secular themes were very common in painting, especially with the rise of manuscript illustration, for the whole realm of literature provided subject matter for miniaturists. Scenes from legends were common, all in modern dress; even classical antiquity contributed legendary subjects with Hercules and Caesar and Alexander appearing as medieval courtiers. Minstrel and troubadour scenes were common, and the earthy and the bawdy were portrayed in collections of popular tales. Tournaments, battles, and hunts were favorites of aristocratic patrons, and exotic travel scenes accompanied up-to-date travel literature on the mysterious Orient. Individualized portraits were still

8-15   Claus Sluter, detail of the Fountain of Champmol, c. 1395–1403. Stone; figures are approximately 6′ high.

8-16   Claus Sluter and Claus van der Werve, *Mourners*, c. 1384–1411. Detail of the Tomb of Philip the Bold. Musée des Beaux-Arts, Dijon.

most commonly encountered in the figures of pious donors of religious art. As to religion itself, such standard themes as Madonnas and crucifixions remained popular. But these were supplemented now by more complex scenes of Christ's suffering and death (the *Pietà* was a favorite—the dead Christ held in his mother's lap) and by joyous themes similarly suitable for quiet devotional contemplation, such as the journey and the adoration of the Magi after Christ's birth.

Of the various nonsculptural pictorial mediums, large-scale work was generally in the form of tapestries or other wall hangings; these replaced in popularity the wall paintings and mosaics of the classical world and the stained glass of the High Gothic era. For smaller-scale work, panel painting was gaining greater and greater acceptance, paralleling the rise of independent, portable sculpture. However, at least until the advent of the great Flemish panel painters of the fifteenth century, it is manuscript miniatures that are best known to

us, since they are the best-preserved of all pictorial forms from late medieval times.

A great many miniaturists are known to us by name, even though they did not sign their works. Most famous of all were the three Limbourg brothers, who executed several major commissions for John, duke of Berry. The Limbourgs represent the "international" style that, in the years around 1400, brought a degree of stylistic uniformity to all Western painting. Among the leading characteristics of this style were its delicately swirling outlines and its air of courtly luxury and elegance.

We have already noted the little picture of the duke of Berry starting on a journey (see fig. 8-10); this may be the Limbourgs' one contribution to the duke's "Small Book of Hours." The elegance and stylization of the international manner are seen in the brilliant, flowing costumes, the golden arabesques in the otherworldly sky, and the tiny hovering angel and surrounding buildings. The buildings are not only disproportionate in size to the persons portrayed but are in rather haphazard perspective.

The Meeting of the Three Magi at the Crossroads (fig. 8-18), from the most celebrated book painted by the Limbourgs for the duke, the *Très Riches Heures*, is still more complex and magnificent. In the far distance are the readily recognizable shapes of Paris's Notre Dame and the Sainte Chapelle—recognizable indeed but anachronistic in this supposedly ancient, Oriental context. Despite the pervasive stylization, there are many highly naturalistic details.

As the years passed, painting on wooden panels became increasingly popular. One of the largest of fifteenth-century French panel paintings is the majestic *Pietà of Avignon* (fig. 8-19) by an unknown artist. This monumental work virtually ignores space, landscape,

8-18 Limbourg Brothers, *The Meeting of the Three Magi at the Crossroads*, c. 1416. Manuscript miniature from the *Très Riches Heures of John, Duke of Berry*, 9″ × 6″. Musée Condé, Chantilly, France.

8-17 Gerard Loyet(?), *Reliquary of Charles the Bold*, 1467–71. 21″ high. Cathedral of Saint Paul, Liège.

and perspective by employing an austere background in tooled gold, with only the slightest hint of landscape. An exotic city, presumably ancient Jerusalem but more closely reflecting Muslim construction, is discernible in the distance. In the foreground the figures of mourners—Saint John, the Virgin, and Mary Magdalene—are stark and strong, while the dead body of Christ is greenish, emaciated, and contorted. Aside from the realistic, matter-of-fact portrayal of a kneeling donor at the left, the work exemplifies above all the anguished devotional piety of the late Middle Ages.

However, devotional piety was generally quite alien to the work of Jean Fouquet, artist at the courts of

8-19 *Pietà of Avignon,* c. 1460. Panel painting, 64″ × 86″. Louvre, Paris.

Charles VII of France and his successor Louis XI. Primarily a miniaturist, Fouquet also produced a number of handsome panel paintings in which fine detail, never obtrusive, combines with broad conception and psychological insight. In *Étienne Chevalier and Saint Stephen* (fig. 8-20) we see the advances made in painted portraiture by the middle of the fifteenth century in France. Half of the *Melun Diptych* (a two-paneled altarpiece), the work is primarily a portrait of Charles VII's famous "treasurer of France." Chevalier is a tight-lipped, unassuming commoner, and the more patrician features of his patron saint, Stephen, the first Christian martyr, are no less individualized.

Portraits at this time, it appears, were not painted directly from life but from careful preliminary sketches; sketches of this sort by Fouquet and Jan van Eyck are still preserved. The execution of all paintings, not just portraits, employed a variety of mediums, with egg still the most usual binder for the pigments. Oil painting— that is, with oil as the pigment binder—was more and more common during the fifteenth century, but it only gradually displaced the older mediums.

The most celebrated of Flemish panel paintings— Flemish, that is, in its commissioning and its intended site, although its creators were Dutch—is the large

8-20 Jean Fouquet, *Étienne Chevalier and Saint Stephen,* from the *Melun Diptych,* c. 1450. Panel painting, 36½″ × 33½″. Gemäldegalerie Staatliche Museen Preussischer Kulturbesitz, West Berlin.

8-21   Hubert and Jan van Eyck, *The Ghent Altarpiece* (open), c. 1425–32. Tempera and oil on 24 panels, 11′6″ × 15′2″. Cathedral of Saint Bavon, Ghent.

Ghent Altarpiece (fig. 8-21), by Hubert and Jan van Eyck. An inscription, of slightly dubious authenticity, on the frame states that Hubert, "than whom none greater was to be found," undertook the work and that Jan, "second in art," completed it on May 6, 1432, as commissioned by one Jodocus Vyd. Hubert remains a dim figure in art history; his status has not been fully clarified. Some historians consider him responsible for virtually all of the *Ghent Altarpiece,* whereas others suspect that he may never have existed. Recent compromise positions find Hubert real enough, and responsible for the basic conception of all or much of the altarpiece, which after his death was modified and completed by his younger brother Jan.

The *Ghent Altarpiece* is a *polyptych,* a hinged piece of more than three panels; with its wings open, it measures over fifteen feet in width. Twenty-four panels, including those that are back to back on the folding wings, depict scenes and figures from Christian iconography and, typically, the kneeling donor and his wife. The lower central inside panel, "Adoration of the Lamb," is the largest of all and the key to the whole conceptual scheme. On an altar the living "Lamb of God, which taketh away the sin of the world" bleeds into a chalice; the metaphor, of course, was John the Baptist's, referring to human redemption through Jesus Christ. Around the Lamb are angels, and groups of male and female martyrs approach from left and right. In the foreground is the Fountain of the Water of Life, symbol of sanctifying grace, with Old Testament patriarchs and prophets at the left and Christian apostles and richly attired confessors to the faith at the right. The lower wing panels depict the approach of just judges and knights of Christ on horseback, and of holy hermits and pilgrims on foot, to contemplate and participate in the miracle of divine redemption. Flanked by the Virgin and John the Baptist, a majestic God towers over the central panel, and angels make music to glorify Him (see fig. 8-27). In the outermost panels, unidealized figures of Adam and Eve shrink from the shame of their original sin against God's will.

The *Ghent Altarpiece* summarizes the whole mysterious heart of Christian theology and faith, and further ennobles the mystery through art. Figures, clothing, landscape—all is painted in meticulous, loving detail and splendidly glowing color. To be sure, in the Adoration panel, with the two focuses of Lamb and Fountain, perspective is spiritually symbolic rather than mathematically correct. Otherwise the naturalism is scrupulous; indeed, every type of plant and tree can be identified.

The *Madonna with Chancellor Rolin* (fig. 8-22) is an attractive but more modest work and is assigned to Jan van Eyck alone. Nicolas Rolin, the bourgeois donor, was chancellor for Philip the Good for four decades and virtual prime minister. Still more powerful than Étienne Chevalier of the French court, in Van Eyck's painting he requires no saintly patron for his presentation to the Virgin and Child. The Virgin, apparently about to receive a crown from the hands of a tiny hovering angel, supports rather precariously the infant Jesus. Both sacred and secular themes are represented in the sculptured column capitals of the hall, and also in the lower garden outside that is seen through the three open arches symbolizing the Trinity. In the landscape that stretches out beyond, the artist captured the most minute detail in bridge and city, even the microscopic inhabitants. The distant mountains, however, are enveloped in light bluish haze, as they were in the Lamb panel; Van Eyck applied the principle of *atmospheric perspective*—that far-away objects have a filmy, lighter appearance. The city is seen symbolically through God (the arches of the Trinity), and everywhere the sacred and the secular are mingled. For Van Eyck everything had meaning and beauty—if not always in precise symbolism, at least in its dignity as part of God's realm.

Much of the same transcendental symbolism exists in Van Eyck's painting of *Giovanni Arnolfini and His Wife* (fig. 8-23). The little dog, for example, probably symbolizes fidelity, and the single candle in the chandelier points to the presence of God. A carving of Saint Margaret, patroness of childbirth, is seen on a chair. Traditionally the whole has been identified as a wedding scene, but more recently as a betrothal. In either case Van Eyck might have acted as witness, for above the mirror are the words "Jan van Eyck was here."

Certainly the painting is memorable, both in psychological and artistic terms. The shrewd, sharp features of the Italian merchant seem overcast with a pensive humility matching the shyness of his wife. In the discreetly sumptuous bedroom setting, all is painted with Van Eyck's meticulous respect for individual materials, from the fur cloak of Arnolfini and the ermine trim of his wife's gown to the glow of the chandelier and the tiny curved reflections of the mirror. Even if Jan van Eyck may not have been witness in any legal sense to the scene portrayed, the panel itself bears witness to a keen artistic vision of unprecedented intensity and subtlety. Indeed Jan van Eyck was here—and, so it seems, not really very long ago.

Even in his own day Van Eyck's fame was extraor-

8-22 Jan van Eyck, *Madonna with Chancellor Rolin*, c. 1433. Oil on panel, 26″ × 24½″. Louvre, Paris.

8-23   Jan van Eyck, *Giovanni Arnolfini and His Wife*, 1434. Oil on panel, 33″ × 24″. Reproduced by Courtesy of the Trustees, The National Gallery, London.

dinary—and not just in Ghent or Bruges, where he settled in his last years. In the decades immediately after Jan's death in 1441, only Rogier van der Weyden (c. 1400–64) could compete with Van Eyck's achievement and reputation. Born in Tournai, a royal French enclave surrounded by Burgundian possessions, he long lived in French territory as Roger de la Pasture. By 1435 he had moved to Brussels and was made official painter to that city; there, presumably, he acquired the Flemish name by which he is generally known today. Unlike Van Eyck, he neither signed nor dated any pictures.

Van der Weyden's art is of the highest quality. It differs from Van Eyck's work in its direct, unintellectual Christian piety and emotional fervor. Whereas the older artist often dealt in symbols—for example, a bleeding lamb to represent Christ—Van der Weyden usually treated his subjects as living people. The monu-

mental *Descent from the Cross* (fig. 8-24) is notable less for minute naturalism or involved symbolism than for emotional and dramatic intensity. This power is supported by a strong composition; the two outer foreground figures (of Saint John and Mary Magdalene) bend forward, uniting the group, and the Virgin loses consciousness in a position almost identical to that of her crucified son's body. The largely static and impassive mood of Van Eyck has given way to action and pathos; in this painting Van der Weyden may well seem the more "late medieval" of the two. In fact, the formal gold background and the consequent restricted spatial enclosure are reminiscent of still-earlier centuries as well. Yet the naturalism of the figures and the rich colors of their robes, sometimes in light shadow, place the work squarely in the later period.

The *Adoration of the Magi* (fig. 8-25), from the *Saint Columba Altarpiece*, dates from the last years of Van der Weyden's life and shows him in a much more genial mood. The ruinous Romanesque structure with partially thatched roof, before which the Virgin receives the Magi, is in marked contrast to the quasi-Oriental splendor of the three visiting dignitaries. The most splendid of all three, raising his hat, resembles Charles the Bold. The Gothic background is intricate, and the scene preserves an air of simultaneous nobility and stability, of humbleness and grandeur, of solemnity and almost festive good humor. However, this is the late Middle Ages—and on the pier behind the Virgin hangs a crucifix, a premonition of Christ's suffering and death.

Music

In music, as in the visual arts, there was much vigor and vitality in the late Middle Ages and a line of development similarly revolutionary. In fact, as early as 1324 Pope John XXII felt that various developments in ecclesiastical music were carrying revolution much too far, and in that year a decree from Avignon demanded a return to the simpler style of the past. The Pope did not condemn either harmony or polyphony in itself, but rather those recent elaborations that, he felt, had come to obscure the sacred texts and hamper Christian devotion. Certain composers, he noted, had distorted the traditional melodies and buried them among unnecessary additions, even to the insertion of secular tunes. There were too many rapid passages; the voices were "incessantly running to and fro, intoxicating the

8-24 Rogier van der Weyden, *The Descent from the Cross*, c. 1435–38. Tempera on panel, 7'3" × 8'7". Prado, Madrid.

ear, not soothing it." Further, he implied, the harmonic intervals of octave, fourth, and fifth were really the only appropriate ones for Christian use. Curiously, the decree seems to have had virtually no effect on those who continued the practice of sacred music, for the complexities of northern church music continued to increase during the subsequent years of the fourteenth century. Possibly, though, the decree was a factor in the rather sharp rise in production of secular music, where papal views could be disregarded.

Just what was the *ars nova*, the "new art" of the fourteenth century that the Pope condemned? Briefly, it was polyphonic music, sacred or secular, that concerned itself far less with mathematical and modal theory than with performance and that seemed to delight in structural subtleties and complexities for their own sake, most notably in rhythmic construction. One basic device, *isorhythm*, imposed a rhythmic pattern with a certain number of pulses upon a melody with a different number of notes. When repeated, the rhythmic pattern would begin at a different point in the melody, and several repetitions of both would be needed for the melody and the rhythmic pattern to end

together. The device would seem extremely artificial—a technical plaything matched only by the *hocket*, which divided a melody between two voices by alternating the notes contributed by each, usually in rapid succession. The music that embodied these and other complex devices was so difficult that only trained musicians could perform it. At least amid these complexities there was a growing use of intervals that seem harmonious to us: thirds and sixths, for example, became somewhat more common.

Among the practitioners of the ars nova the most famous is Guillaume de Machaut (c. 1300–c. 1377), the poet and composer whom we see in the manuscript miniature *Nature Presents to Guillaume de Machaut Her Children: Sense, Rhetoric, and Music* (fig. 8-26). Born in the French province of Champagne, Machaut was a cleric but led a remarkably secular life. He traveled widely, serving a king of Bohemia as well as John the Good of France, and wrote great quantities of love poetry that, in the manner of the trouvères, he set to music himself.

In addition to his literary excursions into the artificial thickets of courtly love, much of his music, too,

8-25 Rogier van der
Weyden, *Adoration of
the Magi,* c. 1460–62.
Panel from the *Saint
Columba Altarpiece,*
54″ × 60″. Alte
Pinakotek, Munich.

8-26 *Nature Presents to Guillaume de
Machaut Her Children: Sense, Rhetoric, and
Music,* c. 1370. Manuscript miniature.
Bibliothèque Nationale, Paris.

was of great artificial complexity. An extreme example is his *Ma fin est mon commencement et mon commencement ma fin* ("My end is my beginning, and my beginning my end"). In this three-part song the notes of the middle voice part are imitated in exactly reverse order by the high voice, while the notes of the low voice part are exactly reversed in the middle of the song. The end of the song is indeed its beginning—and except for a transposition of two voices, when sung backward the notes are precisely the same.

Machaut's one mass, sometimes called the *Notre Dame Mass*, employs all the more conventional musical devices of the time, including isorhythm and the hocket. Considered to be the first complete setting in polyphonic form of the main part (the *Ordinary*) of the Roman Catholic Mass by a single composer, it also employs the unifying device of repeating a particular short melodic sequence in each section of the mass. In the opening of the Agnus Dei ("Lamb of God"), for example, the sequence is heard in the highest voice with the first quick run of six notes. The use of the hocket is especially recognizable to the ear in the Benedictus by its rather jerky effect. The Machaut mass is a summation of French ars nova, and as such, it strikes most moderns as more interesting on paper than pleasant to the ear.

No less complex was the music of the several decades after Machaut's death, although musical predominance was passing from France to Italy. Then for some time after the English victory over the French in the Battle of Agincourt (1415), in the bleakest days of the Hundred Years' War, French music followed the visual arts into near eclipse. For a while English music became the most influential of all in Europe, especially through the genius of John Dunstable (died 1453), who soon was universally admired for his euphonious (sweet-sounding) style. *Dissonance*—the use of clashing harmonies—was now more sternly regulated than before, and the *triad*—the three-tone chord consisting of the root, the third, and the fifth—became acceptable. The trend away from "paper music"—music less interesting to the ear than to the eye—picked up momentum throughout western Europe as music gradually became more "natural." The simultaneous use of more than one text (as in much thirteenth-century music and carried over into the fourteenth) was usually dropped: all musical lines came to use the same words.

With this return to simplicity and "naturalness," music once again could often be performed by ama-

teurs. As early as the reign of Philip the Good, lords and ladies of the Burgundian court were beginning the genteel tradition that we have come to associate particularly with the High Renaissance; they were expected to have at least modest musical performing ability, whether vocal or instrumental. The courts also employed professional musicians for their chapels and their many social events. However, these musical resources were not grandiose in scale; a group of even twenty singers and instrumentalists was considered luxuriously massive.

The fifteenth century saw the continuing development and increasing use of various musical instruments. Three of the most common are shown among the angel musicians of the *Ghent Altarpiece* (fig. 8-27)—the organ, the harp, and the viol. Just as with High Gothic music, however, we do not know a lot about where, when, and how these instruments were employed. Certain music, such as most dance music, was clearly intended for instruments alone, but notation for other music seldom indicates even which parts are to be sung and which played. (Sometimes, for example, lines with no words inserted in the manuscript may have been vocalized without words rather than played on instruments.) Moreover, music was not specifically composed for any particular instrument, since instrumental color was apparently never a consideration except in ceremonies where penetrating sounds were required. It was only around the middle of the fifteenth century that a group of pieces might be designed even for the same general family of instruments, such as bowed or keyboard instruments.

By this time, also, the most common types of composition had become relatively standardized. There was, of course, the mass with its five sections—Kyrie, Gloria, Credo, Sanctus, and Agnus Dei. There was the *motet*—a vocal form, fairly short, with Latin text. Although motets can be either sacred or secular, we limit them here to the sacred and call secular vocal works *songs*, or *chansons*.

All these forms were available to the most celebrated composer of the mid fifteenth century, Guillaume Dufay (c. 1400–1474). Originally from the Franco–Flemish borderland, Dufay eventually returned there, his fame already insured in Italy, to direct the music program at the cathedral of Cambrai. During a long career he served the pope as well as the duke of Burgundy and developed a new stylistic reconciliation of the French, English, and Italian manners of

8-27   Hubert and Jan van Eyck, *Angel Musicians*,
c. 1425–32. Portion of the *Ghent Altarpiece* (fig. 8-
21), 65″ × 29″. Cathedral of Saint Bavon, Ghent.

composition, thus making possible the international musical style of the High Renaissance. To the pleasing sonorities of the English school he added the unifying influence of French and Italian imitative devices, especially the canon. The *canon* is a type of polyphony in

which a musical line is imitated strictly by one or more other lines that often proceed from different initial pitches. Moreover, Dufay embraced a far-reaching recent innovation—moving the main melody of a work from a middle or lower part to the top to give it greater effect and expressive power.

An example of his manner might be the first part of the Kyrie ("Lord have mercy") from the mass *Se la face ay pale*. The mass's subtitle derives from Dufay's repeated use of the tenor from his own secular song of that name: "If my face is pale, know the cause is love." A very secular song indeed—but in the mass it is not only buried in the tenor but sung so slowly as to be unrecognizable except to the attentive ear.

The Kyrie from the mass *Se la face ay pale* is quite different in sonority from the Machaut mass of the previous century; the Dufay is far smoother and richer, and it avoids all obtrusive dissonance. Partly because it is in four parts it may seem more advanced than his own three-part chanson *Pour l'amour de ma doulce amye* (which begins with the line "For the love of my sweet friend I want to sing this roundelay, and give it to her with all my heart that she may be the happier for it"). The musical style here is sprightly and elegant despite the conventionality of the words. Love and pain engendered by love are perennial themes of fifteenth-century songs, as they had been for centuries; however, the admixture of bitter melancholy and resignation is stronger in music of the late medieval period than it had been before.

But the age knew all extremes of emotion, and Dufay's songs range from the tender and the melancholy to the exuberant. *He, compaignons!* is high-spirited enough to be a drinking song—which it may well have been. ("Hey, good fellows, up and revel! Away with care! Fine times are coming soon, and then all well-being will be ours.") But its bluff energy is tempered by courtly refinement, especially in its delicately brilliant instrumental parts. All in all, this is the way that, perhaps twisting history a bit, we may wish to remember the astonishing Burgundian court of Philip the Good.

Recommended Reading

Brewer, Derek. *Chaucer and His World* (1978). Well-illustrated evocation of Chaucer's world.

Cali, François. *Bruges, The Cradle of Flemish Painting* (1964). Background for the painting.

Chaucer, Geoffrey. *Canterbury Tales*, translated by J. V. Nicolson (1934). Good modern rendition of the Middle English.

Cuttler, Charles D. *Northern Painting: From Pucelle to Bruegel* (1968). Comprehensive study.

Dupont, Jacques, and Cesare Gnudi. *Gothic Painting* (1954). Good introduction, with colorplates.

Ferguson, Wallace K. *Europe in Transition, 1300–1520* (1962). Good general survey.

Herlihy, David, ed. *Medieval Culture and Society* (1968). Includes late medieval sources.

Martindale, Andrew. *Gothic Art from the Twelfth to the Fifteenth Century* (1967). Good survey.

Myers, A. R. *London in the Age of Chaucer* (1972). Good impression of London and social institutions.

van Puyvelde, Leo. *Flemish Painting from the Van Eycks to Metsys* (1970). Good introduction, well-illustrated.

Ross, James Bruce, and Mary Martin McLaughlin, eds. *The Portable Medieval Reader* (1950). Many excellent primary sources.

Thomas, Marcel. *The Golden Age: Manuscript Painting at the Time of Jean, Duke of Berry* (1979). Picture book with text.

Tyler, William R. *Dijon and the Valois Dukes of Burgundy* (1970). Good view of society.

Wescher, Paul R. *Jean Fouquet and His Time* (1947). Fine introduction.

9

Transition to the Modern: Italy, 1300–1470

hysical remains of the ancient Roman Empire—especially its architecture and sculpture—were everywhere in the Italy of the Middle Ages. Literary remains from ancient Rome also were treasured by educated and patriotic Italians as reminders of their heritage. These cultural remains helped insure that the cultural forms that emerged in late medieval and early modern times followed ancient precedents more faithfully in Italy than they did elsewhere.

Despite this closeness of Italy to its ancient history, it possessed most of the typical European institutions of the High Middle Ages: the Church (whose very center, except during the Avignonese period, was in Rome), the Holy Roman Empire (which claimed overlordship throughout Italy), the feudal system, and the towns. However, feudal institutions had not secured as firm a grip in Italy as they had in northern Europe, and they collapsed more quickly in the path of the "urban revolution" of rapidly growing towns. In the fourteenth and fifteenth centuries, commerce, finance, and crafts were as flourishing in Italy as in Flanders, and Italy was the scene of lively business competition. Notably absent was any national monarchy to oversee this competition: Italy remained politically fragmented. The leading states of Italy were commonly known by the names of their principal cities—Milan, Venice, Florence, and Naples—with the Church controlling central Italy.

Among these and other rival states, the most culturally fascinating in the period from 1300 to

1470, and one of the wealthiest, was Florence. The city of Florence was not even a port, but an inland town on the Arno River, ringed by jealous neighbors. Not until its greatest prosperity and creative heyday were past, in the sixteenth century, did it completely dominate even the whole of the area known as Tuscany. At first possessing scarcely more fertile land than had surrounded classical Athens, Florence straddled the great north-south trade route that became the basis of its prosperity as early as the eleventh and twelfth centuries. As its wealth grew, so too did its independence from the far-away Holy Roman Emperor and the local ecclesiastical and feudal lords. By the thirteenth century, Florence was truly self-governing. By the fourteenth, civil strife brought only occasional aristocratic dominance, and by the fifteenth, Florence was a demonstrably independent republic firmly controlled by its middle-class citizenry (the *bourgeoisie*).

After 1434, effective rule in Florence became concentrated in the hands of the Medici, one of many important merchant-banker families in the city. The head of the family, Cosimo de' Medici, respected the republican forms of the state, while rigging the political process to insure his own dominance as political boss. With the power of money, the cooperation of other wealthy families, and the popular support of the lower classes whom he flattered and aided, Cosimo was undisputed master of the state for three decades before his death in 1464. An amiable and effective ruler, he permitted the citizens much freedom of expression and personal life, and much participation in civic affairs. The rule of Cosimo, and of his son Piero who succeeded him, saw a happy collaboration of political stability with civic pride and confidence—a striking parallel with that other small but brilliant state nearly two thousand years before, Periclean Athens.

THE EARLY RENAISSANCE

Few terms in the vocabulary of historical writing have been so evocative, so fruitful, and so questionable as the single word *renaissance*. The Italian equivalent for this French word meaning "rebirth" had been introduced in the Renaissance itself, in reference to the presumed revival of arts and letters after an age of "Gothic" bleakness. But as a term for a whole historical age, *renaissance* came to be used internationally only after the middle of the nineteenth century. However, by the beginning of the twentieth century the *renaissance* terminology was scorned in many scholarly quarters—and some historians down to the present have fervently wished to ban both the word and the concept forever. Others, certainly the vast majority, have continued to write of a "renaissance," although their definitions and interpretations vary. Bothersome and fascinating, the "renaissance problem" remains unresolved.

As a matter of convenience, most historians now accept the Renaissance in Italy as a time period from the late fifteenth century through at least the sixteenth. For the preceding age in Italy—the century or so before 1470—there is much disagreement on terminology. Renaissance traits appear often enough, however, to justify a tentative "early Renaissance" label for the art and literature of the period from 1300 to 1470.

The Italian transition to modernity was uneven and complex. At the forefront of the transition was the city of Florence, whose Renaissance characteristics gradually came into prominence before 1420 and flourished most brilliantly after that date. Although many Florentine institutions remained medieval, the city's cultural and intellectual life did indeed come to embody an early Renaissance.

FLORENCE: THE CITY AND ITS ART, 1300–1420

"What city," asked an enthusiastic author in 1403, "not merely in Italy, but in all the world, is more securely placed within its circle of walls, more proud in its palaces, more beautiful in its architecture, more imposing in its gates, richer in public squares, happier in its wide streets, greater in its people, more glorious in its citizenry, more inexhaustible in wealth, more fertile in its fields?" The rhetoric evokes an impressive vision of civic glory, and it is with some difficulty that we visualize the reality behind the words—a troubled little city of perhaps fifty thousand people. Yet essentially this author was right. Already in 1403 Florence was among the most prestigious, though not the largest, of European cities, and justifiably proud of its prosperity, its freedom, and its scattered monuments of

CHRONOLOGY

HISTORY		THE ARTS	
c. 1200	Emergence of a strong, republican Florentine state		
		1265–1321	Dante
		c. 1267–1337	Giotto
		1299–1310	Palazzo Vecchio, Florence
1303–77	papacy at Avignon ("Babylonian Captivity" of the Roman Church)	1304–74	Petrarch, the "first humanist"
		1305	consecration of Arena Chapel, Padua; Giotto's frescoes begun
14th century	continuation of Florentine republic; factional dissension through the century	1313–75	Boccaccio
		1321	Dante's *Divine Comedy* finished
		1325–97	Francesco Landini
1347–54	attempts by Cola di Rienzi to set up an Italian state based on Rome	1333	*Annunciation* by Simone Martini
		1370–1444	Leonardo Bruni
1378–1417	Great Schism in the Roman Church	1377–1446	Brunelleschi
		c. 1381–1455	Ghiberti
1396–1400	Chrysoloras, from Constantinople, lecturing on Greek	1386–1466	Donatello
		c. 1400–55	Fra Angelico
		1400–74	Guillaume Dufay
1406	absorption of Pisa by Florence; emergence of Medici family	1400–82	Luca della Robbia
		1401–28	Masaccio
1414–17	Council of Florence reforming the Church and ending the Schism	1404–72	Leon Battista Alberti
		c. 1420–92	Piero della Francesca
		1421	Brunelleschi's rebuilding of San Lorenzo, Florence, begun
		c. 1425–27	Masaccio's frescoes in Santa Maria del Carmine
		1425–38	Jacopo della Quercia's portal of San Petronio, Bologna
		c. 1425–52	Ghiberti's "Gates of Paradise"
		1431–38	Luca della Robbia's *Cantoria*
		1431–1506	Mantegna
1434–64	Cosimo de' Medici ruler in Florence	early 1430s	Donatello's *David*
		1436	cathedral of Florence, with Brunelleschi's dome, dedicated
1439	agreement on reunion of Western and Eastern Churches, which was soon repudiated in Constantinople	c. 1440–61	Pazzi Chapel, Florence
		1444–59	Michelozzo's Medici–Riccardi Palace
1447–55	Nicholas V pope (former humanist-scholar)	1445–50	Donatello's *Gattamelata*
1453	fall of Constantinople to the Turks: end of Byzantine Empire	1453	beginning of Piero della Francesca's frescoes of the True Cross in San Francesco, Arezzo
1458–64	Pius II pope (former humanist-scholar)		
1464–69	Piero de' Medici (the Gouty) ruler in Florence		

ITALY IN THE FIFTEENTH CENTURY

noble beauty. And it was, as nobody in 1403 could have known, the very eve of one of the Western world's great cultural phenomena—the formidable artistic age of Donatello and Masaccio, and then of Botticelli, Leonardo, and Michelangelo.

Daily Life in Florence

Florence was the dominant town in a city-state of half-a-million or so inhabitants. As such, Florence controlled the foreign affairs of the city-state and granted domestic autonomy to the other, smaller cities. The great artistic flowering in Florence would arise out of material conditions similar to those that existed in London, Dijon, and Bruges. There were flourishing trade routes and manufacturers; there were guilds of merchants and craftsmen, and only guild members enjoyed full civic rights or citizenship. (In Florence the proud old local nobility were obliged to earn guild membership before they could hold civic office—a requirement their northern European counterparts would have thought excessively demeaning.) As elsewhere in these centuries, male dominance was a fact of life. All Florentine male citizens were equal in theory, if not always in practice: bankers and merchants of woollen goods tended to be "more equal than the others." There was much strife among Florentine families, with their respective supporters, until governmental control fell definitively to the Medici banking family in 1434.

Like all European cities of the day, Florence was laid out on a highly irregular plan of very narrow streets and was abominably congested. There were, however, about fifty small squares (*piazzas*), and many of them, as well as many of the streets, were paved with stone and had sewers; for its day, Florence was a clean city. Its houses, even those of the poorest classes, were of stone. There were over one hundred churches, some of them faced with stone in bold patterns of contrasting colors. But the main visible focus and symbol of Florentine civic pride as the fifteenth century began was the hundred-year-old town hall, the Palazzo Vecchio (Old Palace) with its spacious public square (fig. 9-1). If cathedrals dominated the landscape of Gothic Europe, the towers of sturdy civic buildings became typical of Italy in the thirteenth and fourteenth centuries. They were, of course, built by the towns themselves—but so, too, were many churches, which today we might assume to have been financed by ecclesiastical revenues. The parallel with classical Greek building

9-1 Town Hall (*Palazzo Vecchio*), Florence, 1299–1310.

and with High Gothic construction in northern Europe is evident: in all three cases art served primarily as an embodiment of community aspiration and pride. It continued to do so, by and large, well into the fifteenth century, with the completion of the Florentine cathedral its most spectacular achievement.

But before then, what were the great structures that rose above the bustle of Florentine daily life at the dawn of the Renaissance and that facilitated Florence's artistic leadership in the new era? Aside from another great public palace that later became the celebrated Bargello Museum, there were the many private palaces of the wealthy and an array of imposing ecclesiastical structures that shortly would be further adorned by much of the greatest of Renaissance art. Most impressive were the two largest monasteries, Santa Maria Novella and Santa Croce, but most revered by Florentines was the octagonal baptistery (fig. 9-2) that faced the uncompleted cathedral.

If the rounded arches of the baptistery and its

9-2   Cathedral baptistery, Florence, c. 1060–1150. On the right are the east doors (the *Gates of Paradise*) by Lorenzo Ghiberti, 1425–52.

the French cathedrals. The interior of the great cathedral of Florence seems remarkably subdued, and on the outside the contrast with French Gothic is even more striking (fig. 9-4). French Gothic building had reveled in the extraordinary and daring complexity required for the support of immense window areas. But whereas northern builders strove to bring as much light and warmth as possible into dark and often chilly interiors, Italian architects sought to provide physical and spiritual refuge from the sun's heat and brilliance. The Florentine cathedral amply demonstrates this concern; its nave wall has only small and sparse window areas and is quite lacking in spectacular buttressing.

Giotto and His Successors

Italian architecture, of all periods, afforded unusual opportunities for the decorative arts. Many Italian churches of Gothic and Renaissance design were faced

9-3   Coppo di Marcovaldo(?), *Christ in Judgment,* detail from the *Last Judgment,* second half of the thirteenth century. Mosaic. Cathedral baptistery, Florence.

twelfth-century completion date may categorize the exterior as Romanesque, the mosaic decoration of the interior is Byzantine in style. Byzantium (Constantinople) was to maintain the tradition of an eastern Roman empire until its fall to the Turks in 1453, but its last great surge of artistic influence on Italy had begun several centuries earlier. The great mosaic vision of the *Last Judgment* on the baptistery vaulting is dominated by a huge and majestic Christ (fig. 9-3) that embodies the most characteristic qualities of Italo-Byzantine pictorial representation—stylization, flat pattern, and a suggestion of unapproachable, transcendent divinity. In Byzantine art the image of Christ in judgment was not, and was never intended to be, an earthly, human image.

Florentine architecture of the period derives more from Western tradition than from Byzantine influence. The city was dotted with Gothic buildings of great interest, although on a far less adventurous scale than

9-4 Cathedral of Florence; exterior was completed in the second half of the fifteenth century. On the left, the bell tower, 1334–1350s.

handsomely in colored stone and marble patterns, and their abundant interior wall space served to foster a magnificent national tradition of mural painting.

In Gothic Italy the supreme muralist, and one of the West's greatest painters in any medium, was Giotto di Bondone (c.1267–1337). Giotto, who had been born near Florence, contributed most impressively to that city's art—as a painter of murals and panels and as an architect. In 1334 the famous artist was given charge of the continuing building program of the cathedral and of all public works in the city. Already he had executed two notable series of murals in the church of Santa Croce, but much of his renown had been gained outside his native region.

The greatest of Giotto's new projects in Florence would be a splendid *campanile* (bell tower) just to the south of the cathedral (see fig. 9-4). Almost immediately the foundations were laid, though only the lowest level of the tower was completed before his death two-and-a-half years later. As far as we know, Giotto's architectural imagination had previously been exercised only in the backgrounds of his paintings. Yet nobody seems to have thought of protesting his apparent lack of practical architectural experience when he was suddenly elevated to professional architectural leadership in Florence. Giotto's appointment seems to have set a precedent for the whole Italian Renaissance; the best

architects were very rarely architects by training. This is only one facet of the versatility of many artists of the Gothic and Renaissance eras. Artistic versatility in several mediums fits in with the Renaissance ideal of the well-rounded person, but it was also the heritage of medieval craftsman-oriented practice, such as we noted in Netherlandish painting.

As a painter, Giotto subscribed to the naturalistic, and sometimes monumental, trends of late and High Gothic in northern Europe. He was, nonetheless, a revolutionary figure in art history, as we sense immediately when we compare the baptistery's mosaic figure of *Christ in Judgment* with the *Madonna Enthroned* (fig. 9-5), which Giotto painted for the high altar of the Ognissanti (All Saints' Church) in Florence. Although both works display an imposing monumental tranquillity, Byzantine formality and patterned flatness have yielded in the Madonna to naturalness and a feeling of solid three-dimensionality; supernatural aloofness has had a substantial infusion of approachable humanity.

Persuasive parallels can be drawn between the new humanity of Giotto's art and the life of his time. There was, for example, the humanizing trend begun by Saint Francis of Assisi less than a century before. It is certain that Giotto knew well the Franciscan spirit and legend, for he painted scenes from the saint's life

9-5 Giotto, *Madonna Enthroned* (Ognissanti Madonna), c. 1310. Tempera on panel, 10'8" × 6'8". Uffizi, Florence.

in Santa Croce and in Assisi itself. Unfortunately the Santa Croce frescoes are poorly preserved, and controversy surrounds Giotto's contribution to the Assisi paintings. For a brief glance at those characteristic qualities of Giotto's mural painting that were familiar to Florentines of the early fifteenth century, we may turn to the great frescoes of the Arena Chapel in Padua.

Like all frescoes, these works were primarily painted on fresh plaster, which easily absorbs powdered pigments dissolved in water. Unlike panel painting, for which wood surfaces are glossed with a glue and plaster mixture, fresco mural painting involves the quick drying of fresh plaster and the obscuring of preliminary

drawings by the coat of fresh plaster for a given work area. These circumstances, and the considerable distance of the frescoes from the viewer, required that the artist work fast and avoid details. (Perforated "cartoons," through which the design could be dusted directly onto fresh plaster, were a development of the fifteenth century.) Giotto seems to have accepted cheerfully these conditions of the fresco art.

Padua's Arena, or Scrovegni, Chapel (fig. 9-6) had been built at the beginning of the fourteenth century at the site of a pagan Roman arena. The chapel seems to have been built by Enrico Scrovegni to make amends for his father's sinful interest charges on loaned money. Less than seventy feet long, the chapel was dedicated to the Virgin of the Annunciation, and the general theme of its frescoes is divine judgment and human salvation. The best-known scenes derive from biblical and apocryphal stories of the life of the Virgin and of the life and death of Jesus Christ.

The *Meeting at the Golden Gate* (fig. 9-7) represents the solemn yet tender moment when Anna and Joachim, after long years of childless marriage, meet at

9-6 Arena Chapel (Scrovegni Chapel), Padua, consecrated 1305.

9-7 Giotto, *Meeting at the Golden Gate,* early fourteenth century. Fresco. Arena Chapel, Padua.

the Golden Gate of Jerusalem, both aglow with the recent revelation that Anna will give birth to Mary, future mother of the Savior. In the background are several delighted young women, in the finery of Giotto's day, and a more reticent veiled woman; at the left a friendly young peasant approaches, perhaps carrying Joachim's belongings. Although the scene has immense and devout significance, it is presented in the most everyday, unspectacular human terms. Despite the subdued drama, the story is told with masterful simplicity—clearly, economically, and expressively. The physical background, too, is simplified and straightforward. The whole is marked by a sense of solidity and three-dimensional volume.

In the *Flight into Egypt* (fig. 9-8) the same qualities are evident, this time in a natural outdoor setting. Mountains and trees are stylized. Foreground figures (including the donkey) are genial and appealing, even with the heavy, pyramidlike mass of Virgin and Child. No significant shadows are cast by the figures; shadows

9-8 Giotto, *Flight into Egypt,* early fourteenth century. Fresco. Arena Chapel, Padua.

were almost never given importance in Italian painting until the fifteenth century, nor was perspective.

Similar qualities characterize the famous *Lamentation* (fig. 9-9). However, a new element predominates—the almost frenzied grief of most of those gathered about the dead Christ and, indeed, the angels in heaven. Drama is no longer subdued; it is intense and passionate.

Giotto, of course, had his assistants, who acquired at least the superficial qualities of his style, and his followers and imitators. But his revolutionary ideas were too startling to be fully absorbed in his own century, and for decades much Italian painting followed quite different paths. In Siena, another prominent city of the region around Florence, Byzantine reminiscences lingered especially long, sometimes with superbly decorative effect. In the celebrated *Annunciation* (fig. 9-10), the central figures by Simone Martini (died 1344) are set off crisply against a background of tooled gold. They are far more stylized and ethereal than the solid, earthly creations of Giotto. Moreover, in both Florence and Siena an unusually violent plague of the mid fourteenth century encouraged a turn to sterner, more formal religious subjects than the life of the Virgin or Saint Francis. Toward the end of the

century, as physical and spiritual anguish faded before the forces of partial recovery and normalization, Italy joined the widespread European current known as the International style.

Art historians best remember the early fifteenth century for its revival of Giotto's ideals under new classical inspiration—that is, for the first flowering of a fully conscious artistic renaissance in Italy. However, this new art was far less typical of contemporary taste than were the International-style painters of elegance such as Gentile da Fabriano (c. 1385–1427). His handsome, if cluttered, *Adoration of the Magi* (fig. 9-11) has a colorful appeal that was to be echoed in the decorative arts of that century and beyond.

Music in Italy

The visual arts of Italy in the century after Giotto will probably never be regarded as high points of the Western artistic imagination. A similar judgment seems appropriate to Italian music of that period. Despite a momentary flowering of Italian music in the late fourteenth century, it is difficult to rank it among the Western world's best.

For those few decades Italian music became the

9-9 Giotto, *Lamentation,* early fourteenth century. Fresco, 91″ × 93″. Arena Chapel, Padua.

9-10 Simone Martini and Lippo Memmi (?), *Annunciation*, 1333. Tempera on panel, 10′ × 8′9″. Uffizi, Florence.

most vigorous and original in Europe. It used many of the forms and conventions of the ars nova in France but had a different emphasis. As against the vast structural complexities of Machaut's style, Italian works preceded English and Netherlandish music in turning toward melodiousness. The convoluted rhythms of the French were simplified; polytextual and polylingual writing almost disappeared, and music came to appeal more to the senses than to the intellect. Parallels have been drawn to developments in Italian art and literature of that time. Southern architecture, for example, rejected northern complexity, as did the direct, naturalistic art of Giotto and the lyrical verse of the Italian poets who flourished in his day.

The compositions of Francesco Landini (1325–97), the blind organist at the Florentine church of San Lorenzo, rate high in later fourteenth-century Italian music. Landini's musical versatility was praised by one writer of the time: "Francesco, blind of body but enlightened of spirit . . . understood both the theory and practice of every instrument, and especially of the organ, by means of which he delighted the weary with

pleasing sweetness." Landini's *ballate* (ballads, usually polyphonic) embody Italian as well as northern European trends toward secularism and private entertainment as well as public performance. Among pleasant examples are the two-part *Chi più le vuol sapere* ("Who wishes to know them more") and the three-part *Amar si li alti tuo gentil costumi* ("Love so holds and constrains me"). Both are melodious, graceful, and without undue complexity—and both, well in advance of Guillaume Dufay, have the melody in the upper part.

Far more substantial, in the following century, are the works by Dufay (1400–74) with Italian texts, such as the splendid three-part sacred song *Vergine bella* ("Beautiful Virgin"). During his many years in Italy Dufay absorbed a great deal—not only canonic technique but also a taste for Italian melody. Already, though, Italy knew who was the master. In 1467 the Florentine ruler, Piero de' Medici, chose to specify not an Italian composer but Dufay as "the greatest ornament of our age." And long before this it was Dufay who had been called upon to write a new motet for one of Florentine history's grandest occasions—the papal

9-11 Gentile da Fabriano, *Adoration of the Magi,* 1423. Tempera on panel, 9′10″ × 9′3″. Uffizi, Florence.

consecration in 1436 of the newly completed cathedral. A sad fact was evident: native Italian music was being submerged amid the stronger creations of Franco-Netherlandish visitors. In the early Renaissance, Italy excelled primarily in the visual arts and in literature.

HUMANISM AND THE REVIVAL OF ANTIQUITY, 1300–1470

Renaissance can mean many things or, according to a few historians, nothing at all. For the moment we will confine our attention within a somewhat restricted area to which the word seems fully applicable—the new approach among Italians, from 1300 to 1470, to classical antiquity.

Classical antiquity had not been unknown during the Middle Ages. In the early fourteenth century, the great poet Dante Alighieri (1265–1321) was making no startling innovation when he featured prominently a pagan Roman, Vergil, in his monumental poem the *Divine Comedy.* Dante's *Comedy* stands at the frontier between Middle Ages and Renaissance—but it is less impressive as a forerunner of the later period than as a grand summation of the earlier. The element in the work that most clearly forecasts the Renaissance is the importance of the role given to the writers of classical antiquity. Many of these are listed reverently in Dante's description of Limbo in the afterlife—a place not of punishment but simply of hopelessness, since its inhabitants in their lifetime knew nothing of the saving grace of Christianity. Moreover, Vergil—Dante's guide through hell and much of purgatory, and hence a constant presence through more than half of the *Comedy*—was hailed by Dante as his honored master in the art of poetry, the "glory and light of all the poets' throng."

Although it is true that the people of the Middle Ages knew a good deal about pre-Christian antiquity, and that people of the Renaissance seldom understood ancient Greece and Rome as well as they thought they did, Renaissance understanding of the classical world, in fact, went far beyond medieval understanding. Renaissance classicism attempted to be comprehensive and achieved remarkable success in doing so. The new approach, moreover, did not often seek to force classical scholarship into the service of Christian thought, as most medieval scholars and poets, including Dante, had done. Relevant here is the status of the scholars themselves: in the Middle Ages virtually all scholars were clerics, whereas virtually all were laymen in the Italian Renaissance.

Medieval learning, in short, generally took from the classics only what it found could illuminate its own view of the world. It chose its antique examples with almost total disregard for their context in a quite different society and, in fact, was quite uninterested in those differences. The Renaissance mentality, on the other hand, recognized historical change—or at least the changes that had come in the Middle Ages, nearly all of which it judged deplorable. Its understanding of history was flawed, however, since in admiring and trying to imitate the classical past it did great injustice to historical continuity and to its own medieval ancestors.

Above all, the Renaissance believed in itself—that is, in the possibility and reality of reviving, imitating, and perhaps equaling the supremely admirable civilization of ancient Greece and Rome. Although a comprehensive philosophy of earthly progress would only evolve centuries later, there is no denying the buoyant optimism with which the Renaissance frequently regarded its own image, even in the massive shadow of antiquity.

The clearest reproduction of this image, at least until its eventual embodiment in the visual arts, is to be sought in the writing and other activities of the

Renaissance *humanists.* Most strictly speaking, the humanists were students of the classics—of such "humane" disciplines as literature and rhetoric. This meant mainly Latin literature and rhetoric; the revival of interest in Greek literature did not occur until the end of the fourteenth century.

Francesco Petrarch (1304–74) is generally cited as the first important Italian humanist. "I dwelt especially upon antiquity," he wrote in old age as he reviewed his career, "for our own age has always repelled me." His humanist studies, his Latin verse, and his passionate and sometimes successful search for forgotten Latin manuscripts now are less remembered than his lovely Italian sonnets in honor of Laura. Like Dante's Beatrice, this shadowy woman inspired great poetry, very much in the tradition of medieval courtly love. Petrarch's devotion to her in poetry was much more exclusive than it was in real life. The historical Laura perished of the plague in 1348, and Petrarch died a quarter-century later; today only the poetry is real. In this sonnet, the poet envisions his beloved in paradise:

> In thought I raised me to the place where she
> Whom still on earth I seek and find not, shines;
> There mid the souls whom the third sphere confines,
> More fair I found her and less proud to me.
> She took my hand and said: Here shalt thou be
> With me ensnared, unless desires mislead;
> Lo! I am she who made thy bosom bleed,
> Whose day ere eve was ended utterly:
> My bliss no mortal heart can understand;
> Thee only do I lack, and that which thou
> So loved, now left on earth, my beauteous veil.
> Ah! wherefore did she cease and loose my hand?
> For at the sound of that celestial tale
> I all but stayed in paradise till now.

In the Renaissance itself, Petrarch and his humanist successors were most highly honored as restorers of the ancient tongues of Latin and Greek. One of the finest humanist scholars was Leonardo Bruni (c. 1370–1444), who in 1436 saluted Petrarch as the first writer in Latin "who had such grace of talent, and who recognized and restored to light the ancient elegance of style which was lost and dead." Bruni also wrote of his youthful enthusiasm for the study of Greek, hitherto almost unknown in the West, when a Byzantine scholar, Chrysoloras, took up residence in Florence in 1396. Bruni later recalled the irresistible enticement of Greek literature, from which he would extract "great

9-12 Bernardo Rosselino, Tomb of Leonardo Bruni, detail, late fifteenth century. Stone. Santa Croce, Florence.

advancement of knowledge, enlargement of fame, and increase of pleasure."

Bruni—whose calm features can be seen in his tomb effigy (fig. 9-12)—is best known today for a history of Florence that praised its republican traditions. Some humanists were high-level secretaries for their governments, while others were teachers who developed educational programs in which classical training was not only a goal in itself but an encouragement to ethical thought and civic participation. Few Italian humanists advocated or practiced mere ivory-tower scholarship.

The Florentine humanists, though, had their limitations. They were not profound thinkers and they were not much interested in science. Despite their occasional enthusiastic republicanism—support for public-spirited, middle-class government—the humanists certainly were not *democrats* advocating an active political role for the lower classes. In their intellectual and educational goals, the humanists were *elitists*: humanistic scholarship was for the privileged. Similarly distressing to many moderns is the sad fact that the humanists' admiration for classical antiquity usually led to results more imitative than creative. The Florentine humanists, like medieval scholars, turned

to earlier authority for their basic ideals—a fact that, however, should not blind us to the very considerable differences between the two authorities. Medieval religious tradition and the secular heritage of the ancient past, after all, are hardly the same thing.

Here, precisely, is a link between the narrower humanism of the Renaissance scholars and humanism in its modern broader sense. For the broader humanism doubtless existed in the Renaissance, as it has existed in all great civilizations, including the medieval. The context of the broader humanism—humanism, that is, as an emphasis on human beings on earth and their potentialities—has varied in different ages; in the Italian Renaissance the context, in part, was the humane secularism of so much of the literature studied and translated by the humanist scholars. However, in all likelihood, the classics did not bring the broader humanism to Italy; the classics were appreciated because Italy was ready for them. Although religious life was not forgotten—nearly all of the greatest art of the age was religious in subject matter—and although complete skepticism was almost unknown, the fundamental tone of the Italian Renaissance was secular.

This is the tone of the sometimes bawdy *Decameron* of Giovanni Boccaccio (1313–75). This collection of stories reflects the author's evident joy in the sensual nature and powers of womanhood and the delights of love. The young men and women who serve as Boccaccio's narrators, whiling away the days of isolation in the country as they seek to escape the dreaded plague (the Black Death of the mid fourteenth century), seem free of any sense of sin or its punishment. In Chaucer's *Canterbury Tales* the pardoner had a comparable view of the world, but he was an evil exception among his fellow pilgrims. Boccaccio's people and his stories reflect the simpler, more amiable sensuality of a natural, secular world.

Life on this earth and human potentialities—that was the emphasis of much of Italian Renaissance culture. Individualism played a large part in this emphasis, and it is often the first characteristic one associates with the period. But if there are examples enough of colorful, passionate individualism in the Renaissance— among women as well as men—we should nonetheless remember that the ideal was never anarchic self-will, but a harmonious life for both the individual and society. Even the passion for fame, encouraged by ancient ideals, was countered precariously by the urge for harmony—and the two drives were often combined in the striving for outstanding versatility of achievement. The well-rounded, or universal, person was not a self-effacing image. Leonbattista Alberti's memorable description of himself—as athlete, mathematician, artist in all mediums, author in every literary form—bursts with pride but is reasonably accurate. "Men," wrote Alberti, "can do anything with themselves if they will." The context of his remark is well forgotten (it concerns getting accustomed to disagreeable objects), but the words do evoke for us a vivid aspect of the Renaissance in Italy.

THE REVOLUTION IN ITALIAN ART, 1420–1470

Our earlier brief survey of Italian visual art after 1300 brought us only to the third decade of the fifteenth century and to the brilliant International style, with its detailed but unsystematic realism. Yet already in 1423, when Gentile da Fabriano was finishing his *Adoration of the Magi*, a striking new manner in art was being born: the Renaissance manner that, in varying degrees and with shifting emphasis, is characterized by monumentality, scientific naturalism, and the inspiration of antiquity. Shortly we will consider several of the greatest individual practitioners of early Renaissance art. First, however, we must glance at an important transitional artist, then at the position and nature of early Renaissance art in Florentine society, and finally at several exemplars of Renaissance artistic ideals in Italy as a whole.

Not all distinguished Italian art of the age was produced in Florence. Jacopo della Quercia (c. 1374–1438), one of history's great sculptors, was a native of Siena. His major projects were executed there and in Bologna, where from 1425 until his death he created his masterwork, the main portal of the church of San Petronio. Here, both in freestanding figures and in relief panels, all in stone, he revealed a powerful concentration of vision focused almost wholly on the human form. During the Renaissance only Michelangelo, who admired Jacopo's work, was to surpass him in the powerful portrayal of monumental human form.

Monumentality is not necessarily a matter of size; it also derives from simplicity and breadth of style. Each of Jacopo's ten Genesis panels flanking the main entrance of San Petronio is less than three feet high. In

the *Creation of Eve* (fig. 9-13) God blesses Eve with one hand while he extends the other to support her as she gracefully emerges from the body of a sleeping Adam. Clothed in powerfully sweeping drapery, God is majesty personified, contrasting strikingly with the soft nakedness of Eve. Eve's lovely sensuousness in this panel, and in the *Temptation* (fig. 9-14), had not been seen in sculpture since classical antiquity and must certainly have been influenced by the antique example. In the glowering Adam of the *Temptation* we find another magnificent conception—again a physically idealized nude, but decisive in gesture and starkly virile in form. Although Jacopo's stylized landscape settings are medieval, his bold glorification of the human body was matched since antiquity only in the work of his Florentine contemporaries Ghiberti and Donatello.

Italy and Artistic Creativity

In Florence itself, the continuing rivalry for prestige and the increasing sophistication of the leading fami-

9-13 Jacopo della Quercia, *Creation of Eve*, 1425–38. Stone, 34″ × 27″. Main portal, San Petronio, Bologna.

9-14 Jacopo della Quercia, *Temptation of Adam and Eve,* 1425–38. Stone, 34″ × 27″. Main entrance, San Petronio, Bologna.

lies led in the fifteenth century to more and more private patronage of the arts in contrast to the predominantly communal, civic patronage of earlier ages. Fortunately, the wealth and taste of the patrons were matched by the genius of the artists. Fortunately, too, the leading citizen of Florence after 1434 had more money and taste than most. Thus the Florence of Cosimo de' Medici came to rival, in the arts though not in literature, the Athens of Pericles. The backroom politics of the day, the social injustice, the pretentious ostentation and snobbery—all, or almost all, of this can be forgotten today. Cosimo remains one of history's most discriminating patrons of the arts.

The new art was produced under conditions not much different from the old or from northern European practice. The training of artists was as thoroughly practical as before, in the guild-regulated workshops of masters in painting, sculpture, and the minor arts. Art works in Italy, as in France and the Netherlands, were still commissioned for specific purposes, whether by church, secular ruler, or wealthy burgher. Moreover,

even major artists were still expected to execute, or at any rate to supervise, the most lowly of craftsman-type projects.

Yet differences from the northern European situation were slowly but unmistakably appearing, all symbolized by the decreasing anonymity and increasing individuality of Italian Renaissance artists. Controversy may still rage about the proper attribution of many important Netherlandish, French, or German art works of the fifteenth century, since (within national styles) their stylistic differences are frequently slight and their authorship carelessly documented, if at all. In Italy, on the other hand, not only was individual achievement considered important enough to deserve extensive written comment, but individual artistic styles were both tolerated and applauded in their day and (with only a few exceptions) readily identifiable in ours.

It is possible—though the point is much disputed—that the early Italian Renaissance may simply have been more receptive to individualism than was contemporary northern Europe. Reinforcing Italian individualism, in any case, was the new conception of the artist that Leonbattista Alberti was advocating as early as 1435. Artists, he wrote, should transcend their old role as artisans and assume a dignified position among practitioners of the liberal arts. Not only should each painter "make himself familiar with poets, rhetoricians, and others equally learned in letters" for scholarly aid in treating subject matter, but all artists should become naturalists and geometers. Traditional, uneducated craftsmanship was to be replaced by an informed, scientific approach to nature. In fact, art was a supreme instance of science in action.

Art then, in the view of Alberti, was closely linked to the humane and scientific studies and hence, admittedly, not fully autonomous. Yet artists in his day were, in fact, gaining immensely in professional stature and prestige; the finest among them were no longer humble artisans but creators seeking lasting fame. When, later on, Alberti looked back on his own artistic achievements in Florence, mainly in architecture, he wrote: "All these things have given me, and are giving me, the greatest satisfaction and the sweetest feelings. For they do honor to the Lord, to Florence, and to my own memory." The quest for artistic fame had officially joined the civic and religious purposes of art.

Fame, of course, was a secular ideal. Although the

desire of artists for recognition seldom conflicted with Christian spirituality, this goal implied a new focus on earthly rather than heavenly rewards. Moreover, fame had been one of the most prominent goals of the ancient Greeks and Romans, for whom enthusiasm had already become great among literary humanists. Now, in the early fifteenth century, a similar enthusiasm struck the world of art and architecture.

A New Way of Seeing

We have noted the significant, though still somewhat tentative, moves toward classicism that were made in sculpture by Jacopo della Quercia. With the passing decades, the rejection of Gothic medievalism became still more self-conscious—and for a few artists it became virtually complete. We may look, for example, at the Medici–Riccardi Palace courtyard (fig. 9-15) designed for Cosimo de' Medici by Michelozzo (1396–1472); it is hard to imagine a much more thorough break with the aspirational Gothic of Chartres or the Sainte-Chapelle. Horizontality has replaced verticality; simplicity has overcome complexity; clarity has routed mystery. The courtyard represents an honest attempt to incorporate a whole impression of antiquity, not just to borrow (as the Middle Ages had done) isolated devices and subjects of ancient art for fragmentary application. The parallel with literary humanism is evident; the new theme was a rejection of all compromise with the "Gothic" manner, which was now seen as a barbarous corruption of the true, or antique, style.

Still more comprehensive in its attempt to resuscitate Roman antiquity is the panel painting of an ideal city once attributed to Luciano Laurana (fig. 9-16). This is only one of many Renaissance architectural visions of whole urban complexes rigorously patterned after classical models. In the 1460s Filarete, a Florentine, produced a treatise on town planning. In his new city, disorderly and disease-laden medieval congestion would give way to airy, orderly geometric design. Although ambitious projects of this sort were never executed, the new dream of symmetry and spaciousness would be embodied in numerous individual structures and small complexes of buildings.

Typically, the *Ideal City* painting is also a study in perspective. Flemish painters had achieved considerable skill in pictorial *perspective*—the art of reproducing our visual recognition of spatial depth when look-

ing around us—but their skill was unsystematic and intuitive. Italian artists, inspired by the writings of Alberti and others, and doubtless by their own desire to embrace visual reality, now experimented with more precisely geometrical schemes of linear perspective. In the *Ideal City*, the columns, pavement designs, and foreground rooftops all indicate, for example, a central vanishing point on the distant horizon. And when perspective was applied to individual objects, startling effects of *foreshortening* could be achieved, as in Andrea Mantegna's painting, the *Dead Christ* (fig. 9-17).

Mantegna (1431–1506) was an artist of real stature, not simply an experimenter; the chill, pathetic majesty of the *Dead Christ* is more important than its geometry. Moreover, another trait he shared with the architect-painter of *An Ideal City* was also put to creative use—his zeal for the antique. After directly studying Roman art and archaeology, Mantegna contrived to invoke the spirit of antiquity as well as to reproduce antique costumes and settings with historical accuracy. For Mantegna, as for many literary humanists, the classical past was not just a dim memory to be studied but a vigorous stimulant to creative activity. Its frequent alliance with perspective and other phases of the new scientific naturalism in the visual arts was by no means incongruous.

Thus once more we are reminded of the growing alliance, noted by Alberti, between literary humanism and the visual arts. Until the earlier fifteenth century, the two had tended to go their separate ways, with

9-15 Michelozzo di Bartolommeo, courtyard of the Medici–Riccardi Palace, Florence, begun 1444.

9-16 Formerly attributed to Luciana Laurana, *An Ideal City,* third quarter of the fifteenth century. Architectural perspective, 33″ × 87″. Walters Art Gallery, Baltimore.

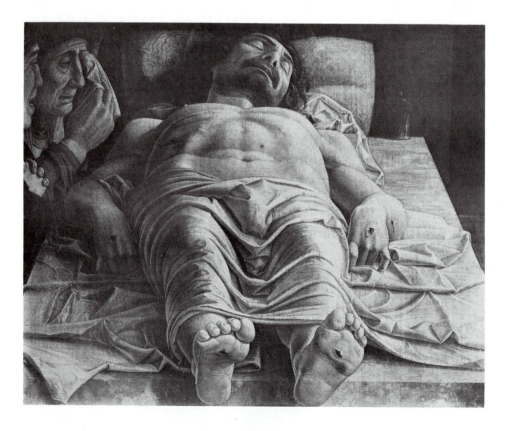

9-17 *Dead Christ,* after 1466. Oil on canvas. 27″ × 32″. Pinoteca di Brera, Milan.

each finding the other's work irrelevant, or at best a peripheral distraction. Now, at least from the third decade of the new century, social and intellectual contacts between the artists and humanists began to flourish, solidified by shared enthusiasms. When humanists could become zealots for antique art, when artists like Mantegna could become seriously interested in ancient literature, and when at last real competence in both visual art and literary humanism could come together in the single person of Alberti—*then* the Renaissance in its full cultural sense had truly begun.

Masters of Florentine Architecture

The early architectural studies of Filippo Brunelleschi (1377–1446) were varied. Not only did he acquire some archaeological knowledge of ancient Roman structures, he also examined medieval Florentine building styles and techniques. In 1420 his self-confident belief that he could surpass his architectural predecessors, of all ages, was put to the test when he was given the responsibility of capping the unfinished cathedral of Florence with an immense dome (see fig. 9-4). The outcome of this was a very complex octagonal ribbed vault, really quite Gothic in concept. Its steepness and the use of two mutually supportive shells

minimized the lateral thrust, which in any case was countered by great belts of wooden beams linked by iron, inside the masonry of the dome's base. The outward simplicity of the dome structure reflects a generalized classical spirit, and the lantern (completed by Michelozzo after Brunelleschi's death) and the four semicircular protuberances outside at clerestory level are unmistakably classical.

While the great dome was slowly rising, Brunelleschi was busy with other major Florentine building projects. In 1421 he began the thorough rebuilding of the church of San Lorenzo, whose nave and choir are seen in figure 9-18. In addition to the inspiration of early Christian basilicas, various elements of ancient Roman design are obvious: flat coffered ceiling, rounded windows and arches, Corinthian columns, and (on the side walls) flattened attached columns, or *pilasters*. Yet horizontals predominate, as in much antique building.

Brunelleschi was a student of perspective and an almost compulsive geometer. In this he was encouraged by the architectural theory and practice of ancient Rome, especially by the newly reexamined writings of Vitruvius. Obedience to symmetry and proportion was a Vitruvian imperative in temple construction, and Brunelleschi carefully applied these

9-18 Filippo Brunelleschi, San Lorenzo, Florence, 1421–69.

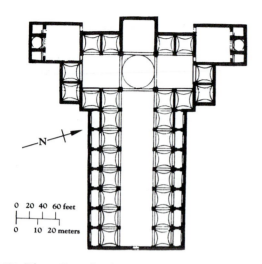

9-19 Filippo Brunelleschi, plan of San Lorenzo.

succession of clearly defined units, Brunelleschi achieved an admirably harmonious, unified interior space enhanced by the simple contrast of grey stone and white stuccoed walls.

Yet the lucid simplicity, decorative and formal, of San Lorenzo and Brunelleschi's other buildings may well put us somewhat on our guard, since few major Roman buildings were quite so clearly simple. Brunelleschi's creative spirit obviously had much to do with his work—and so, too, it appears, did early medieval Italian Romanesque building. The quiet simplicity of the Pazzi Chapel facade (fig. 9-20) also goes well beyond Roman precedent in its calm rationality and the restraint of its unobtrusive relief patterns. This chapel, inside and out, embodies a balanced geometricism that represents Renaissance harmony at its best.

qualities in San Lorenzo, thereby revolutionizing church architecture in Italy and eventually throughout western Europe. The main body of San Lorenzo is a consistent system of squares and of multiples of two and three, as suggested by the plan (fig. 9-19). Out of a

Florentine Sculptors

Among the rarest of all rarities in art history have been those comprehensive judgments of a person's own time that have not been revised in later centuries. Sin-

9-20 Filippo Brunelleschi and others, Pazzi Chapel, Florence, c. 1440–61.

9-21 Lorenzo Ghiberti, east doors (*Gates of Paradise*) of the baptistery of Florence Cathedral, c. 1425–52. Gilt bronze, 15′ × 8′3″ without outer frame.

gling out greatness in one's contemporaries is among the most difficult of all types of criticism. Not the least of the accomplishments of Leonbattista Alberti, then, was his list of Florentine artists whose genius, in his opinion, exceeded that of all other artists of the early fifteenth century. As early as the mid 1430s Alberti elected to supreme distinction five pathfinders among his contemporaries—Brunelleschi, Masaccio, Ghiberti, Donatello, and Luca della Robbia. We could hardly improve upon this list today. And of special interest to us at this point is the fact that, along with

one architect and one painter, Alberti listed three sculptors.

The career of the eldest of these sculptors, Lorenzo Ghiberti (c. 1381–1455), began most illustriously when at an early age, in a 1401 competition, he defeated Jacopo della Quercia and Brunelleschi, among others, for the privilege of creating a set of bronze doors for the Florentine cathedral's baptistery—a major project that required more than two decades to complete. Then, in 1425, after considerable experience in larger-scale sculpture, Ghiberti was entrusted by the greatest Florentine merchant guild (which had also commissioned his earlier doors) with the project of a new pair of baptistery doors. "The commission," he wrote later, "gave me permission to execute it in whatever way I believed would result in the greatest perfection, the most ornamentation, and the greatest richness." The ten panels of this set of doors were cast in the mid 1430s, but the laborious work of finishing them, and of completing the frame, went on (with the help of a small factory of assistants) until all was put into place in 1452. They face the east, toward the cathedral—and since the space between an Italian cathedral's baptistery and the cathedral entrance was called the *paradiso*, and since the new doors were marvelous indeed, Ghiberti's east doors (fig. 9-21) came to be called the *Gates of Paradise*.

The design of the doors differed markedly from that of the earlier ones; instead of twenty-eight small panels, each with an individual scene or figure, these doors had only ten, each almost three feet square, depicting two or more individual but related events. Thus the *Genesis Panel* (fig. 9-22) narrates four separate stories—the creation of Adam, the creation of Eve, the Temptation or Fall, and the expulsion of Adam and Eve from paradise. The events in a panel retain their compositional separateness and sometimes are further differentiated by size and by degree of relief, both suggesting distance. Ghiberti himself was particularly proud of his avoidance of muddle amid all this complexity, and of the pictorial unity he had achieved—a unity enhanced by the uniform gilding of each panel, which cast a golden haze over the whole.

The largely pictorial quality of the *Paradise* panels is obvious—an orientation little admired in our own age. Another quality of Ghiberti's work is the combining of classicism and naturalism that is typical of the Renaissance. The naturalism here, of both setting and figures, has advanced well beyond Jacopo's, and per-

9-22 Lorenzo Ghiberti, *Genesis*, detail from the *Gates of Paradise* (fig. 9-21). Approximately 31″ × 31″.

spective is consciously applied. As to classicism, scholars have pointed out numerous specific borrowings from antiquity. Moreover, Jacopo's typically classical joy in the human body is shown still more consistently in Ghiberti; note, for example, Eve's sensuousness at the moment of creation. Despite occasional Gothicisms, the *Gates of Paradise* stand open to the Renaissance.

Donatello (1386–1466), too, is of the Renaissance, although with fewer direct classical allusions. This extraordinary sculptor is notable above all for the powerful individuality of his work; few artists have been more independent of contemporary fashion or more intensely personal. Celebrated and honored in his day, he contrived, unlike the sociable Ghiberti, to live his daily life quite apart from public view, and few great artists are less well known to us as private personalities. His individuality is wholly in his sculpture, where a thirst to explore all creative possibilities drove him to cover a range from classicism and Gothicism to an almost modern expressionism. Although he chose to work only in the area of sculpture, Donatello embodied Renaissance versatility quite as passionately as did the multitalented Alberti.

Donatello's marble *Prophet with Scroll* (fig. 9-23) was one of several statues commissioned for Florence's

campanile in 1415 and completed within a few years; thus it is one of the early large works of the century. Its destined placement in a niche high above street level possibly influenced the lack of detail in the powerful, deep-cut drapery—but some of Donatello's other works show comparable treatment. The visible bodily extremities—head, foot, and most noticeably the right hand—are exaggerated in size, and the facial expression is brooding and grim. It is a deeply impressive image, even today in its museum setting.

In sharp contrast to the majestic maturity depicted in the sculptured *Prophet* is the unformed boyishness, or even the femininity, of Donatello's famous *David* (fig. 9-24). The *David* may have been intended for a fountain, and we know that by 1469 it was set on a pedestal in the Medici Palace courtyard; in any

9-23   Donatello, *Prophet with Scroll*, c. 1416–18 or later. Marble, 6′4″ high. Cathedral Museum, Florence.

9-24 Donatello, *David*, early 1430s? Bronze, 5'2" high. Museo Nazionale, Florence.

not the first equestrian monument of its time, but it was the first in bronze, the most imposing, and the most classical.

After working a decade in Padua, Donatello returned to Florence, where in old age his vision ranged as widely as in his youth and middle age. In his pair of fine bronze pulpits for San Lorenzo, the aged master was helped by assistants, and after his death much work remained to be done. Almost certainly, however, Donatello had left the general design, and probably sketches and fragmentary models, of the *Lamentation* (fig. 9-26). The scene by Christ's body at the foot of the cross is almost frantically expressionistic. Not only are the faces contorted with grief, as in Giotto's fresco, but the whole scene explodes with frenzied movement.

The work of Luca della Robbia (1400–1482) is stylistically varied but not as far-ranging as Donatello's. One of Luca's earlier creations is the best known of all—the striking *Cantoria* ("singing gallery") of the cathedral of Florence (fig. 9-27). To contain the *Cantoria's* sculpture, a distinctly contemporary architectural ensemble was designed—the essence of it inspired by the very ancient style of pagan Rome. The reconstruction illustrated here is conjectural and apparently not wholly accurate, but its general style and decoration seem to reflect Luca's intentions. The Latin

9-25 Donatello, *Gattamelata*, 1445–50. Bronze, 12'2" high. Piazza del Santo, Padua.

case it appears to have been the first large, freestanding nude statue since antiquity. The pose is supple and nonchalant, though thoughtful, as the boy-conqueror of Goliath idly stands with one foot on the severed head of the Philistine giant. Certainly Donatello's approach in this case is better suited to garden statuary in a self-indulgent age than to pious biblical imagery in a church.

The psychological ambivalence of the *David* is countered by the equally thoughtful, but far more fixed, character revealed in the face of Gattamelata in Donatello's great equestrian statue of that name (fig. 9-25). Here all is masculine determination and gravity without brutality—an ideal portrait of a strong-minded but reflective military leader. The horse, moreover, is as noble as the rider. This work was commissioned by the Venetian captain's heirs for display in Padua. It was

9-26 Donatello and others, *Lamentation*, c. 1460–70. Bronze; pulpit is 54" high. San Lorenzo, Florence.

inscription, in three tiers, is the text of Psalm 150, which urges humanity to praise God in song and dance and with musical instruments. Luca's marble panels illustrate the words quite literally, in a joyous depiction of youthful high spirits. The two side panels, not visible in the reconstruction illustration, show the unaccompanied singing of young boys and youths. Note the realistic touch in the right foreground of one panel (fig. 9-28): a boy beats time, tapping with his left foot.

It is such pictorial details of human interest that we are sometimes taught to scorn, but that reflect the very human orientation of the Italian Renaissance.

Despite the vigor of much of Luca's subject matter, and of his sculptural technique, he remains an artist of dignified gesture and human gentleness and warmth. This warmth is again illustrated in his *Visitation* figures (fig. 9-29) in Pistoia. The aged Elizabeth, who miraculously will give birth to Saint John the Baptist, humbly and respectfully acknowledges the promise of a still-greater miracle, the birth of Jesus from the virginal womb of Mary. Like the *Cantoria* panels and so much other Italian Renaissance art, the *Visitation* is a religious scene humanized.

The *Visitation* is a work of enameled *terracotta*—that is, baked clay with a hard, glossy enamel surface. The technique, which became extremely popular for decorative schemes as well as religious figures, was a Renaissance innovation. In later generations the colors of enamel sometimes were gaudy, but Luca himself often kept, wholly or largely, to the simplest contrast of white and blue. The *Visitation* figures are monochromatic white, set off against a rich background of red marble.

We should note that the Italian Renaissance still used color in its statuary, as had the medieval and ancient worlds. Richly colored stone was frequently used for decorative detail; figures of wood were painted or gilded, and bronze reliefs, too, were often gilded. Yet a change was slowly occurring before 1470 and would later accelerate: the more serious sculptors were seldom applying color for strictly naturalistic effect. Color,

9-27 Luca della Robbia, *Cantoria* (reconstruction, with panels in replica), original 1431–38. Marble, 17' long. Cathedral Museum, Florence.

9-28 Luca della Robbia, *Singing Boys,* detail from the *Cantoria* (fig. 9-27), approximately 38″ × 24″.

when used, became a formal element, not an attempt at realism. Moreover, works in stone and freestanding bronzes were seldom colored or gilded. An appreciation for the basic nature and appeal of materials was entering sculpture—encouraged no doubt by the fact that any original coloring on the much-admired antique statuary now being rediscovered had generally disappeared. Centuries of chastely unadorned stone and metal statuary were to follow—a practice that would not be challenged significantly until the late twentieth century.

Masaccio and the Revolution in Painting

Sculptural innovation in the third, fourth, and fifth decades of the fifteenth century was more widespread and generally less hesitant than the parallel revolution

in painting. Still, Florentine painting of that period produced one extraordinary and revolutionary genius: the painter known to history as "Big Tom," or Masaccio (1401–28). In his short lifetime he made a revolution of which most Florentines were quite unaware but that later would be gratefully acknowledged. Such masters as Piero della Francesca and Michelangelo credited Masaccio as a prime source of their vision.

Masaccio's historical role, as it turned out, was to revive, broaden, and transcend the revolution in painting initiated by Giotto a century before—the revolution toward naturalism, humanism, and monumentality. However, Masaccio not only bridged the century after Giotto's Santa Croce frescoes, which he studied, he also was moved by the most advanced of his contemporaries who were inaugurating the artistic Renaissance. He responded quickly to Brunelleschi's feeling for harmonious spatial integration, and apparently learned perspective and even the new architecture from him. Then in Donatello he found the monumental naturalism and magnificent creative energy that he himself possessed. Never has the spiritual unity within a whole art movement been more strikingly

9-29 Luca della Robbia, *Visitation,* c. 1445. Enameled terracotta, San Giovanni Fuorcivitas, Pistoia.

embodied than in this remarkable innovative trio of the 1420s.

Masaccio had very little time for his own revolution, and its greatest immediate impact was felt in a rather obscure church on the less prestigious side of Florence's Arno River—the Carmelite Church, or Carmine. Here, in the cloister, he did a major fresco, long ago destroyed, depicting the church's consecration. Its majestic figures, all (we are told) with recognizable features of Florentine worthies, are known to us only in several sketches, including Michelangelo's. Here also, above all, he did a series of frescoes in the Brancacci Chapel—the frescoes on the life of Saint Peter that have made this small chapel as famous in art history as Giotto's larger chapel in Padua. Masaccio's co-worker in the Brancacci Chapel was his friend Masolino, whose personal and artistic temperament was far more gentle and conservative than Masaccio's. The portions by Filippino Lippi, who completed the work later in the century, are in a third style, also more subdued than Masaccio's but not clashing with it.

The largest of the scenes by Masaccio himself is *The Tribute Money* (fig. 9-30), one of the most influential paintings in Western art history, and still one of the most imposing. The three events depicted are from Matthew 17:24–27; Peter has been confronted with the secular Roman authority's demand for a tax pay-

ment. Jesus, amid the apostles, questions the validity of the demand but tells Peter nonetheless to go to the shore and catch a fish, in whose mouth he will find a coin that can be given to the tax collector. This seemingly minor Gospel incident was to be used in later centuries to reinforce the injunction to give to the state the state's due. It also had acute significance in Florence in 1425, since a new Florentine tax was being heatedly discussed. Masaccio's setting, then, is recognizably by the Arno, where at the left Peter retrieves the coin from the fish's mouth. In the center is the group of Christ and his companions, with Peter arguing the case and Christ announcing his decision, while to the right Peter delivers the coin to the tax collector.

Narrative painting has usually fared better with modern critics than narrative sculpture, and many who decry the elaborate storytelling of Ghiberti's east doors admire Masaccio's *Tribute Money*. Certainly the simplicity and majesty of the *Tribute Money* speak persuasively for it. Although its technical innovations are perhaps matched by those of Ghiberti, Ghiberti's innovations were not accepted by the main sculptural stream; Masaccio's innovations, on the other hand, were to be the lifeblood of centuries of later painting. Masaccio introduced a realistic but simple, uncluttered representation of nature, and an illusion of spatial depth unseen in earlier painting. Not only are increas-

9-30 Masaccio, *The Tribute Money*, c. 1425. Fresco, 8'4" × 19'7". Brancacci Chapel, Santa Maria del Carmine, Florence.

9-31 Masaccio, *Saint Peter Healing with His Shadow*, 1427. Fresco, 91″ × 64″. Santa Maria del Carmine, Florence.

9-32 Masaccio, *Trinity*, 1428. Fresco, 10′5″ wide. Santa Maria Novella, Florence.

ingly distant objects represented on a progressively smaller scale, the gradual fading of colors and the blurring of outlines in the distance demonstrates an awareness of *atmospheric perspective*. When, in addition to all this, we feel the energy of the massive figures and the expressive human drama of the whole work, we recognize Masaccio's stature among the masters.

Other scenes by Masaccio in the chapel are fragmentary or smaller than the *Tribute Money* fresco. *Peter Healing with His Shadow* (fig. 9-31) seems wholly by Masaccio, except for a botched attempt at restoring a damaged area at the left. The setting is Florentine and again (except for the restorer's ineptitude) in geometrically correct perspective. The shadows cast, by the way, are not very deep, but their very existence was a novelty in European painting of the 1420s. The faces of the two cripples in the left foreground are moving social documents, while the faces of two of Peter's companions are of great historical interest (if recent theories are justified): the powerful bearded man to the

left is Donatello, and the young man in the rear is Masaccio himself.

It was probably in the year of his death that Masaccio painted another great Florentine fresco that survives, the *Trinity* (fig. 9-32) in Santa Maria Novella. It is a work of tremendous solemnity, as befits the overwhelming mystery it portrays. Except for the realistic faces of the kneeling donors (which would have delighted Jan van Eyck), all is raised to a thoroughly transcendent, spiritual plane by the enormous mass and impassivity of the figures—not only of God the Father, the Virgin, and Saint John but of the crucified Christ as well. The ecclesiastical setting invokes the most beautiful architecture Masaccio could conceive—that is, a Renaissance church such as his older friend Brunelleschi was just then devising.

Masaccio's style would be by no means universally imitated. From the host of other talented and diverse painters in Italy in the middle years of the fifteenth century, we can choose only two of the most memora-

9-33 Fra Angelico, *Descent from the Cross*, c. 1430–34. Panel, 69″ × 72″. Museo di San Marco, Florence.

ble for brief mention, Fra Angelico and Piero della Francesca. Piero sympathized with the solemn monumentality of Masaccio's work, while Angelico appeared to be almost unaware of the great revolutionary's existence.

Fra Angelico (c. 1400–1455) was a monk of great piety and eventually the prior of Cosimo de' Medici's favorite Florentine monastery, San Marco. Although he painted solely in the service of his God, he was by no means inattentive to certain forward-looking tendencies in the art of his contemporaries. The altarpiece format of his splendid *Descent from the Cross* (fig. 9-33) is reminiscent of Gentile da Fabriano's *Adoration of the Magi* (see fig. 9-11), but Angelico's manner is very different from Gentile's International style. The figures, for example, are far more sturdy and indepen-

dent, while the landscape is realistically constructed and recedes progressively in very passable perspective. At the same time, Fra Angelico is in quite another world than Masaccio's, even though both share the humane and formal heritage of Giotto. The passion, drama, and power of the Carmine frescoes have given way to a tableau for pious contemplation and adoration, suggestive of the purest and most serene zones of the Christian faith.

Fra Angelico ("angelic brother") was one of the most spontaneous and the least self-conscious of artists. Piero della Francesca (c. 1420–92) was the artist-scholar-philosopher who meditated deeply on the nature and structure of the visible world. In Florence he absorbed the lessons of Masaccio, Brunelleschi, and Donatello and went on to apply and refine them else-

9-34 Piero della Francesca, *The Queen of Sheba's Visit to Solomon,* 1453–55 or later. Fresco, 11′ high. San Francesco, Arezzo.

where. For example, his great fresco cycle, the *Story of the True Cross,* is the pride of the church of San Francesco in Arezzo.

The cycle's literary framework is a fabulous, involved legend tracing the wood of Christ's cross back to the Garden of Eden's famed Tree of Knowledge and onward to the miraculous identification of the cross and its return, in Byzantine times, to Jerusalem. *The Queen of Sheba's Visit to Solomon* (fig. 9-34) depicts the queen as she prophetically recognizes the beam of wood that will be used for the cross and kneels in ado-

ration before it. Meditative calm has become frozen in the virtually expressionless features and columnar drapery of the women. Even the horses and young male attendants look a bit like a taxidermic display—a very skillful one. Everything in the figures, such as the foreshortening of the white horse, is relentlessly and rigorously plotted out for the effect of rigid stability and order. The work is monumental and majestic—and a handsome, fitting symbol of the age's triumphant imposition of order and discipline on the unruly clutter of visual reality.

Recommended Reading

Batterbury, Michael. *Art of the Early Renaissance* (1970). Fine introduction.

Bishop, Morris. *Petrarch and His World* (1964). Good, nontechnical introduction to his life and writings.

Cole, Bruce. *Masaccio and the Art of Early Renaissance Florence* (1980). Good, very thorough study.

Cronin, Vincent. *The Florentine Renaissance* (1967). Introduction to Florentine art and civilization.

Duby, Georges. *Foundations of a New Humanism, 1280–1440* (1966). Stimulating study of the arts in their setting.

Eimerl, Sarel, ed. *The World of Giotto* (1967). Giotto in his time.

Ergang, Robert. *The Renaissance* (1967). Fine textbook overview of all aspects of the Renaissance.

Gadol, Joan. *Leon Battista Alberti: Universal Man of the Early Renaissance* (1969). Specialized but fascinating.

Hartt, Frederick. *History of Italian Renaissance Art* (1979). Fine, comprehensive study.

Hay, Denys. *The Italian Renaissance in Its Historical Background* (1977). Good, brief introduction.

Janson, H. W. *The Sculpture of Donatello* (1963). Comprehensive, detailed study.

Krautheimer, Richard. *Ghiberti's Bronze Doors* (1971). Fine illustrations with text.

Martinelli, Giuseppe. *The World of Renaissance Florence* (1968). Handsome picture book with good text.

Paatz, Walter. *The Arts of the Italian Renaissance* (1974). Well-illustrated survey.

Ross, James Bruce, and Mary Martin McLaughlin. *The Portable Renaissance Reader* (1958). Collection of primary sources.

Seymour, Charles. *Jacopo della Quercia, Sculptor* (1973). Fine study.

10

The Flowering of the Renaissance: 1470–1530

osimo de' Medici, behind-the-scenes ruler of Florence, died in 1464, predeceased by his favorite son, Giovanni. For several years the Medici business and the Florentine state were superintended by Giovanni's brother Piero, who in turn was succeeded, in 1469, by his twenty-year-old son, Lorenzo. Piero and Lorenzo were less interested than Cosimo in business management and were unable or unwilling to exert the leadership that might have mitigated the gradual decline of the network of Medici banks throughout much of Europe. But the almost princely rule of Lorenzo the Magnificent (the title was used both officially and unofficially in his own day) seemed to suffer little; in political as well as cultural prestige these were among the happiest days for the Medici and their city on the Arno.

Shortly after Lorenzo's death in 1492 there began an abrupt decline in Florentine fortunes and a period of political turmoil in Florence and all of Italy. In 1494 the French invaded Italy and expelled the Medici from Florence, where a puritanical regime inspired by the monk Savonarola was established. A few years later Savonarola was overthrown and executed, and Florence became a secular republic, which existed until 1512, when renewed warfare led to the return of the Medici. A final attempt at republicanism in Florence ended in 1530 with the imposition of an autocratic Medicean regime blessed by the Holy Roman Emperor, Charles V.

239

In the meantime, papal Rome had succeeded to much of the political and cultural prestige that had been Florence's before 1494. Since the end of the great Church schism early in the fifteenth century, papal policy had repeatedly neglected spiritual and institutional reform in favor of sheer physical recovery and survival in a violent, often amoral age. The Church achieved success at the price of thorough secularization and even corruption. When the dying Lorenzo warned his seventeen-year-old son Giovanni, a cardinal of the Church since fourteen, of the temptations of "Rome, that sink of all iniquity," his words reflected the common opinion. By the time of Giovanni's accession to the papacy as Leo X, conditions had not improved very much. With such popes as Julius II (1503–13), Leo X (1513–21), and Clement VII (1523–34), the papacy was less a spiritual than a political institution. Under Clement, moreover, it suffered humiliation by the troops of Charles V when Rome was sacked in 1527.

The most significant political and religious trends outside Italy in the period were overseas exploration and conquest, further consolidation of several national monarchies within Europe, and the outbreak of the Protestant Reformation. Spain was largely united under Ferdinand and Isabella and sponsored much of the geographical expansion of European civilization, especially in the Americas. England emerged from civil wars as a solidly established monarchy under the Tudor kings Henry VII (1485–1509) and Henry VIII (1509–47). In France the most notable ruler was Francis I (1515–47), who maintained perhaps the most splendid princely court of the Renaissance. The Germanies remained parceled out among numerous secular and ecclesiastical princes as well as free cities, all presumably owing allegiance to the Holy Roman Emperor. Charles V of the Hapsburg family, emperor from 1519 to 1556, had also become the ruler of Spain (1516–56) and the Netherlands by inheritance. His extended realm, however, was being gravely shaken by the Protestant revolt from Catholicism, begun in 1517 by Martin Luther, with various German rulers becoming Protestant themselves and carrying their states with them into Protestantism in defiance of imperial authority. By 1530, the Europe of 1470 was a dim, almost unrecognizable memory.

THE NORTHERN RENAISSANCE

In the six decades after 1470, innovation and peaks of genius in the visual arts appeared far more often in Italy than in other parts of Europe. Even in the realm of music, long a virtual monopoly of the north, Italy became increasingly prominent by attracting some of the finest northern composers to its towns, courts, and churches. The Renaissance was in full flower in Italy, for this was the splendid age of the composer Josquin des Prez, and the artists Leonardo, Raphael, and Michelangelo.

We see now that this age of cultural advancement was in many ways a twilight period for Italy. We note the increasing political and economic importance of the Atlantic powers resulting from their overseas exploration and trade—and the Italian roots of Columbus and Amerigo Vespucci may no longer seem very relevant. We see the intense religious, economic, and nationalistic ferment in the north that led to the Protestant Reformation—and we may forget this great movement's often catastrophic effect on the arts within its home territory. We deplore the disunity of Italy and approve the national consolidations of France, England, and Spain, for such was the wave of the future. History, however, shows no essential correlation between powerful national states and great cultural flowerings. Despite all its disabilities, Italy not only held its own in the arts until 1530 but was strengthening its cultural leadership in Europe for the next hundred years.

Any history of the visual and musical arts must emphasize the Italian scene in these decades—and, in doing so, the gap between Italian and non-Italian culture in the period shortly before 1530 may be exaggerated. Actually there was a continual interchange of ideas between Italy and the rest of Europe: there was, for example, a sizable influence of Flemish painting on Italian art before 1500 and then a reversal of that flow in the sixteenth century. By the late fifteenth century, humanistic scholarship, too, was entering the north, even though it tended to support traditionally Christian goals there more than it did in Italy. Northern Europe in the early sixteenth century saw not only the dynamic and rebellious zeal of Martin Luther but also the studious Christian scholarship and urbane reformist hopes of Erasmus and Thomas More.

CHRONOLOGY

HISTORY		THE ARTS	
		1445–1510	Botticelli
		c. 1450–1521	Josquin des Prez
		1452–1519	Leonardo da Vinci
		c. 1453–1516	Hieronymus Bosch
		1463–94	Pico della Mirandola
		1465–83	Verrocchio's *Christ and Saint Thomas*
		1466–1536	Desiderius Erasmus
1469–92	Lorenzo de' Medici (the Magnificent) ruler of Florence	1469–1527	Niccolò Machiavelli
		1471–1528	Albrecht Dürer
		1470s and 80s	Botticelli painting in Florence
		1475–1564	Michelangelo
1478	Pazzi Conspiracy in Florence: Lorenzo de' Medici wounded, Giuliano killed	1478–1529	Baldassare Castiglione
		1478–1535	Sir Thomas More
		c. 1478	Botticelli's *Spring*
		c. 1481–96	Verrocchio's *Colleoni* monument
1483–98	Charles VIII king of France	1483	Leonardo begins *Virgin of the Rocks*
1485–1509	Henry VII king of England	1483–1520	Raphael
		1486–92	Josquin des Prez composing in Rome
1492	Columbus first in the Americas		
1492–94	Piero de' Medici ruler of Florence		
1492–1503	Alexander VI (Borgia) pope		
1493–1519	Maximilian I Holy Roman Emperor		
1494	French invasion of Italy		
1494–98	Savonarola ruler of Florence		
1494–1559	the Italian wars (Spain, France, Holy Roman Empire)	1498–1500	Michelangelo's first *Pietà*
1498–1512	Florentine Republic		
1498–1515	Louis XII king of France	1501–04	Michelangelo's *David*
		c. 1502	Bramante's *Tempietto*
1503–13	Julius II pope	1503–06	Leonardo's *Mona Lisa*
		1506	Bramante begins work on new Saint Peter's, Rome
		1508–12	Michelangelo's Sistine Chapel ceiling
1509–47	Henry VIII king of England	1509	Erasmus's *Praise of Folly* written
		1509–11	Raphael painting in the Vatican Palace (*School of Athens*, etc.)
1512–27	Medici control in Florence	1513	Machiavelli's *The Prince* written
1513–21	Leo X (Giovanni de' Medici) pope	1513 and later	Michelangelo working on tomb of Julius II
1516–56	Charles I king of Spain		
1517	Martin Luther begins Protestant Reformation		
1519–56	Charles V (Charles I of Spain) Holy Roman Emperor	1519–34	Michelangelo's Medici Chapel in San Lorenzo, with Medici Tombs
1523–34	Clement VII pope		
1527	sack of Rome by Spanish and Imperial mercenary troops		
1527–30	Florentine Republic	1528	Castiglione's *Book of the Courtier* published
1530	Medici rule in Florence restored		

EUROPE IN 1526

The Dutch scholar and essayist Desiderius Erasmus (1466–1536) was the most celebrated humanist of his day (fig. 10-1)—a clear indication of the northward expansion of Italian humanist concerns. Humanists of all lands from Poland to Spain and from England to Italy comprised an elite brotherhood of gentleman-scholars united by a common absorption in antiquity (whether Hebraic-Christian or Greco-Roman) and by at least one common language, Latin. The Greek and ancient Hebrew languages also were much cultivated, especially in the north, where they were used in religious scholarship.

Erasmus is best remembered for his moderation (he declined to join the great Protestant revolt from

Rome), his cosmopolitanism and humaneness (he rejected all warfare as well as the strong nationalism of the German and English revolts from Rome), and his alternately playful and barbed wit—a quality seldom seen in the earnest Protestant reformers. In his book *Praise of Folly* the main character, Folly, introduces herself as her own best publicist and proceeds to celebrate her triumphs among all classes of society. In this way Erasmus could pointedly satirize the superstition of the masses, the greed of the merchants, the pomposity of the clergy, and the absurdities of the theologians. His younger, English friend Thomas More (1478–1535) went beyond this sort of amusing but effective negativism when he dreamed of a "utopia"—a land of

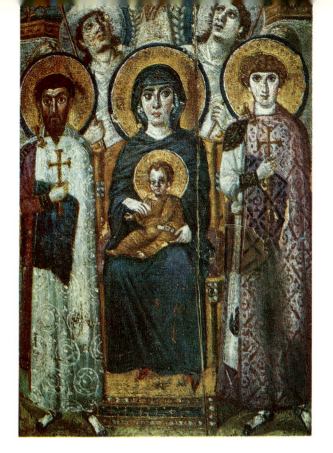

Plate 13   *The Virgin and Child Enthroned, Flanked by Saints Theodore and George,* sixth century. Encaustic icon on panel, 27½″ × 17¼″. Monastery of Saint Catherine, Mount Sinai.

Plate 14   *Virgin and Child Enthroned,* from Santa María de Tahull, Spain, c. 1123. Fresco. Museo de Arte de Cataluña, Barcelona.

Plate 15 *(above left)* Initial letter of the Book of Exodus in the *Winchester Bible*, c. 1160. Cathedral Library, Winchester, England.

Plate 16 *(above right) Joshua Bidding the Sun Stand Still* from the *Psalter of Saint Louis*, c. 1256. Manuscript miniature, 5″ × 4″. Bibliothèque Nationale, Paris.

Plate 17 *(right) Wine Merchant*, detail from the *Window of Saint Lubius*, c. 1200–1220. Stained glass, 32″ across. Northern nave wall, Chartres Cathedral.

Plate 18   Limbourg Brothers, *The Meeting of the Three Magi at the Crossroads*, c. 1416.
Manuscript miniature from the *Très Riches Heures of John, Duke of Berry*, 9″ × 6″. Musée Condé,
Chantilly, France.

Plate 19 Giotto, *Meeting at the Golden Gate,* early fourteenth century. Fresco. Arena Chapel, Padua.

Plate 20 Masaccio, *The Tribute Money,* c. 1425. Fresco, 8'4" × 19'7". Brancacci Chapel, Santa Maria del Carmine, Florence.

Plate 21 Jan van Eyck, *Giovanni Arnolfini and His Wife*, 1434. Oil on panel, 33″ × 24″. Reproduced by courtesy of the Trustees, The National Gallery, London.

Plate 22 Rogier van der Weyden, *The Descent from the Cross*, c. 1435–38. Tempera on panel, 7′3″ × 8′7″. Prado, Madrid.

Plate 23   Sandro Botticelli, *Birth of Venus*, after 1482. Tempera on canvas, 5′9″ × 9′2″. Uffizi, Florence.

Plate 24 Leonardo da Vinci, *Virgin of the Rocks*, begun 1483. Oil on panel, 79″ × 48″. Louvre, Paris.

Plate 25   Jacopo Carucci de Pontormo, *The Descent from the Cross (The Entombment)*, 1525–28. Panel, 10′3″ × 6′4″. Santa Felicità, Florence.

10-1 Hans Holbein the Younger, *Erasmus*. The Metropolitan Museum of Art, New York. (Robert Lehman Collection, 1975.)

harmonious social adjustment and prosperity in which religious toleration would reign, rather than the narrow zealotry of his own age.

In the visual arts, the tone in the north differed fundamentally from that in Italy. Above all, the revival of interest in classical antiquity had made scarcely any inroads on the northern Gothic architectural style, which became, in fact, more complex than ever. It may seem amazing that the fantastic pendant ("stalactite") vaulting of the Henry VII Chapel in Westminster Abbey (fig. 10-2) dates from the early sixteenth century, almost a hundred years after Brunelleschi was developing a simplified, Roman-inspired architecture.

In the meantime most Flemish painting also had been following traditional lines. In all the Netherlands the most original artist of the early sixteenth century was the Dutch painter Hieronymus Bosch (c. 1453–1516), best known for the whimsical creatures that inhabit his surrealist visions of demonism and human folly and sensuality. Modern criticism, however, has de-emphasized Bosch's whimsy and stressed the sternness of his message and his medieval piety. Among his more conventional works is *Christ Carrying the Cross* (fig. 10-3), a moralistic sermon on the evil surrounding the purity of a suffering Savior.

10-2 Detail of the vaulting in the Henry VII Chapel in Westminster Abbey, London, early sixteenth century.

10-3 Hieronymus Bosch, *Christ Carrying the Cross,*
c. 1515. Panel, 30″ × 33″. Museum voor Schone
Kunsten, Ghent.

Moralism does indeed appear as a major theme in
northern European piety on the eve of the Protestant
revolt; Italy, too, took religion seriously, on occasion,
but usually without the intensity and fervor of northern devoutness. The single northern artist of giant stature in the period just before 1530 was one who combined earnest Christian feeling with an Italianate love
of beauty. This was the German Albrecht Dürer
(1471–1528), who not only crossed the Alps stylistically and physically (he visited Italy more than once
and painted there) but truly bridged the worldviews of
the Middle Ages and the Renaissance. Certainly Dürer
was typical of the Renaissance in his posture as a creative artist, not a mere artisan. His ego was Renais-
sance-sized—he once painted himself as Christ—and
he did, in fact, have much for which to congratulate
himself. As a painter he rarely approached Italian
heights, but his many woodcuts and engravings reveal
him as one of history's greatest draftsmen and an artist
of inspired vision.

Printing with movable type is generally considered a German innovation of the mid fifteenth century—and it was Germans, too, who most notably
developed the art print. Succeeding the woodcut in
popularity, *engraving* was the preferred medium by
Dürer's time. (To create an engraving, the design is cut

into a metal plate; to print it, the paper is pressed
against and into the inked grooves.) Among the many
handsome Dürer engravings is the *Fall of Man,* or
Temptation (fig. 10-4). Although Dürer commonly asserted his individuality by initialing his works, he
proudly and prominently signed this one in full. Scholars have pointed out the pervasive symbolism of the
picture, but the casual viewer is likely to be struck
more by the bodies of Adam and Eve. Dürer seems to
have expended no great effort on Eve's beautification,
but his Adam is painstakingly proportioned, following
the conclusions of his study of anatomy and his mathematical speculation. Although Dürer seems never to
have copied antiquity directly, he absorbed much of
the Italian enthusiasm for such presumably ancient
ideals as clarity, humanism, and harmonious proportion.

His famous engraving *Knight, Death, and the Devil*

10-4 Albrecht Dürer, *The Fall of Man*
(Temptation), 1504. Engraving, 10″ × 7½″. The
Metropolitan Museum of Art, New York (Fletcher
Fund, 1919).

10-5 Albrecht Dürer, *Knight, Death, and the Devil,* 1513. Engraving, 10″ × 8″. Reproduced by Courtesy of the Trustees of the British Museum, London.

(fig. 10-5) reveals a thoroughly German imagery. The knight is a stern medieval warrior, a "Christian knight" whom Dürer apparently equated with the "Christian soldier" of a book of Erasmus. This then is the Christian who resolutely does his duty in the world, heedless of danger and temptation. It is a powerful image that reveals a good deal of the supercharged tension and medievalism of the German religious atmosphere on the eve of Luther's revolt.

Dürer would shortly become a supporter of Luther, but his eyes had been trained and his spirit formed well before the Reformation. Luther himself was a hearty soul, a rare German stylist in prose and poetry, and a musician of some accomplishment, but shortly the leaders of the Reformation would come to distrust the sensual allurements of the arts, with their humane suggestions of earthly beauty. The vigorous mainstream of European art was carried on during this time in the Italy of Medicean Florence and the worldly Renaissance papacy.

THE ITALIAN SCENE

Shortly after the death of their father, Lorenzo de' Medici and his teen-aged brother Giuliano commissioned a joint tomb in Florence for their father and their uncle, Piero and Giovanni. The work was unveiled in 1472, and as one chronicle records, the Florentines "flocked to see it as though it were a wonder of the world."

The Tomb of Piero and Giovanni de' Medici (fig. 10-6) was made by Andrea del Verrocchio, whom we will encounter again in this chapter. It was not a wall tomb, in the usual Florentine manner, but stood in an

10-6 Andrea del Verrocchio, Tomb of Piero and Giovanni de' Medici, 1470–72. Porphyry, marble, and bronze; 14′9″ high (internal height of the arch). San Lorenzo, Florence.

archway between the Old Sacristy of San Lorenzo and a transept chapel. Still more surprisingly, it had no sculptured human figures and no Christian symbolism whatsoever: the Medici, one supposes, could be remembered on earth and could get to heaven without such props as these. The deep red porphyry of the sarcophagus, with its green medallions, was complemented by the marble and ungilded bronze that predominated in the monument. Achieving a rare balance between the sumptuous and the restrained, it remains one of Europe's most memorable funerary monuments—and a remarkable witness to the stylistic gulf that separated Italy and the north in the late fifteenth century.

After his commissioning of the tomb, Lorenzo was not a major patron of artistic creativity. His impact on Florence, rather, was in politics and diplomacy, literature and humanism, and his example of an ebullient and civilized life. Lorenzo was shrewd of intellect and physically vigorous; his sheer animal vitality was noted by all. A great sportsman, drinker, practical joker, and composer of bawdy verse, he was also highly sensitive to beauty and an accomplished writer of both fervent religious poetry and lively carnival and pastoral lyrics. Significantly, he wrote in the Tuscan vernacular dialect rather than Latin, which confirmed the trend away from the Latin of the early humanists.

Our knowledge of the catastrophes that overtook Florence shortly after Lorenzo's death in 1492 overcasts the outward joviality and sophisticated hedonism of his day with a degree of poignancy. Perhaps he was aware that the end of this glorious time was near; the words of his well-known carnival song, *Quant' è bella giovinezza* may hint at that:

> Fair is youth and void of sorrow;
>   But it hourly flies away.
>   Youths and maids, enjoy today;
> Nought ye know about tomorrow.

In any case, the worldview of Lorenzo and his privileged Florentine contemporaries had changed from aggressive acquisitiveness to a mood of consolidation and earthly enjoyment. As the merchant Giovanni Rucellai noted in his later years, it was more pleasant spending money than making it. And along with consolidation came conservatism. In politics, anti-Medicean republicanism had gone underground since the suppression of the 1478 Pazzi Conspiracy, in which Giuliano was killed and Lorenzo barely escaped

death. The historian Guicciardini was to write a generation later that although Florence under Lorenzo was not free, "nevertheless it would have been impossible for it to have had a better or more pleasing tyrant." Still, the accusation of tyranny must be qualified: Medicean political manipulation and control did permit, under Lorenzo as well as Cosimo, almost total freedom of speech and opinion, so prized by the vivacious Florentines.

In Lorenzo's Florence the services of artists were in great demand, most often by private patrons. Happily these patrons were a group seldom matched in history for sophistication and taste. Architects, for example, were kept busy designing and renovating country villas for those who could afford to escape the dirt and noise of the city. Lorenzo's villa at Poggio a Caiano (fig. 10-7), by Giuliano da Sangallo (1443–1516), is among the most handsome. Whereas the double staircase is a seventeenth-century addition, the main novelty in Lorenzo's day was the application of an antique temple facade to the entranceway of a private home. Probably no innovation in the history of Western domestic or civic architecture has been more often imitated than this.

Florentine art at the end of the fifteenth century and later was definitely an art for the elite—an art for well-to-do connoisseurs—and it was created by artists who themselves were becoming gentlemen. The increasing stature of the individual artist, however, is more marked in the Roman continuation of the Florentine Renaissance. The greatest artists of this later age not only were handsomely rewarded but were admitted to the highest social circles. Moreover, with Leonardo, Raphael, and Michelangelo, recognition of creative genius was supplemented by a growing awareness of the proper autonomy of the arts. Art was coming to stand on its own, ultimately needful of no external justification, whatever its specific context. For centuries Western art would teeter on the brink of the art-for-art's-sake theory; that it did not go the whole way until the nineteenth century is perhaps more surprising than the theory itself.

The Cultural Shift from Florence to Rome

In the decades after the death of Lorenzo the Magnificent, the focus of Italian art passed from Florence to Rome. The symbolic figure of Florence in that period has come to be not an artist but the historian and polit-

10-7 Giuliano da Sangallo, detail from the facade of Lorenzo de' Medici's villa at Poggio a Caiano, near Florence, 1480s.

ical theorist Niccolò Machiavelli (1469–1527). Machiavelli recorded his speculations on the origins, nature, and maintenance of political power most succinctly in *The Prince,* a short book that would have much influence on later ages. With a cynical outlook atypical of the generally optimistic Renaissance, Machiavelli saw human beings as basically selfish and evil and, hence, malleable by a hard-headed ruler who would take advantage of human weaknesses. In this context, Christian morality was irrelevant, and the end—the power of prince and state—would justify the means.

Along the way, Machiavelli strews miscellaneous memorable admonitions, mostly tough and hardheaded. No prince—that is, ruler of any sort—needs to deal honestly and keep his word with his rivals or to possess the traditional Christian virtues; it is important and useful, however, to maintain appearances. "It is well to seem merciful, faithful, humane, sincere, religious, and also to be so—but you must have the mind so disposed that, when it is needful to be otherwise, you may be able to change to the opposite qualities." In specific instances his advice is to be decisive when taking stern, even cruel measures: "men must either be caressed or else annihilated. They will revenge themselves for small injuries but cannot do so for great ones; the injury therefore that we do to a man must be such that we need not fear his vengeance." Similarly, "injuries should be done all together, so that being less tasted, they will give less offense. Benefits should be granted little by little, so that they may be better enjoyed." Men are self-centered and greedy, even to accommodating themselves to their father's death at the hands of the state: "men forget more easily the death of their father than the loss of their patrimony."

Machiavelli's most celebrated metaphor pictures the ruler as both lion and fox, neither of which is a model of Christian scruples: a prince

> must imitate the fox and the lion, for the lion cannot protect himself from traps, and the fox cannot defend himself from wolves. One must therefore be a fox to recognize traps, and a lion to frighten wolves. . . . Therefore, a prudent ruler ought not to keep faith when by so doing it would be against his interest, and when the reasons which made him bind himself no longer exist. If men were all good, this precept would not be a good one; but as they are bad, and would not observe their faith with you, so you are not bound to keep faith with them.

As a foundation for a prince's successful rule, he must possess not only strength, skill, and few ethical scruples, but must be a student of the past: "the prince ought to read history and study the actions of eminent men" to see, for example, "how they acted in warfare, and examine the causes of their victories and defeats in order to imitate the former and avoid the latter." Many of the historical precedents that Machiavelli cites in *The Prince* are drawn from classical antiquity; others are from more recent history. We should note, though, that he usually cites only one historical example to demonstrate his ideas; political philosophers might well consider this inadequate. Machiavelli's doctrine of historical "imitation" and the rather casual way he applied it in his work may indicate less political or scientific realism than he is often credited with. As in other areas, the Renaissance appeal to ancient authority was not fully persuasive.

A different appeal to antiquity, for a quite different reason, is found in the writing of another Florentine author, Giovanni Pico della Mirandola (1463–94). Pico dabbled in many ancient systems of thought; perhaps the breadth of his interests and his early death excuse him for not doing much more than dabble. He especially admired Plato but had studied other Greek thought, too; he read the ancient Roman authors, the Hebrew scriptures, and later mystical thought, and even knew something of ancient and medieval Middle Eastern speculation. Thus Pico's *Oration on the Dignity of Man* draws on cosmopolitan, if somewhat ill-digested, sources in its pursuit of mystical aspirations and demonstration of human potential.

It is for Pico's defense of human dignity and broad capabilities that his *Oration* is cited today as a treatise on the humanistic optimism of the Renaissance. In marked contrast to Machiavelli's view that man is bad, Pico derived a view of vast human potentialities from a fanciful evocation of a scene occurring just after God created the universe and before the creation of man. Among God's archetypes, wrote Pico, "there was none from which He could form a new offspring. All now was filled out; everything had been apportioned to the highest, the middle, and the lowest orders."

Finally, Pico continued,

the Great Artisan ordained that man, to whom He could give nothing belonging only to himself, should share in common whatever properties had been peculiar to each of the other creatures. He received man, therefore, as a creature of undetermined nature, and . . . said to him: "Neither an established place, nor a form belonging to you alone have We given to you, O Adam, and for this reason, that you may have . . . according to your desire and judgment, whatever place, whatever form, and whatever functions you shall desire. The nature of other creatures . . . is confined within the bounds prescribed by Us. You, who are confined by no limits, shall determine for yourself your own nature, in accordance with your own free will. . . . You may fashion yourself in whatever form you shall prefer. You shall be able to descend among the lower forms of being, which are brute beasts; you shall be able to be reborn out of the judgment of your own soul into the higher beings, which are divine.

Neither Pico's dream of a human being regenerated by using its God-given abilities nor a Machiavellian prince could restore Florentine power and prestige and thus reestablish that city's dynamic political role in Italy. Papal Rome already was rising as a secular and cultural power in Italy, especially under the leadership of Julius II. The overriding goals of the Julian papacy were secular, not spiritual—the consolidation of the papal domains in central Italy, the expulsion of the foreign troops that since 1494 had periodically threatened and oppressed the peninsula, and the revival of the city of Rome. The sprawling, ruinous village to which ancient Rome had been reduced was far from the city envisioned by the new pope; Julius was convinced that Rome could not be Rome without grandeur. Thus not only were routine building projects inaugurated, but the three greatest available artistic talents of the High Renaissance were called upon to ennoble the city—Bramante, Raphael, and Michelangelo. The impact of this extraordinary trio, as masters of architecture, painting, and sculpture, can only be compared to the influence of the previous century's great Florentine innovators—Brunelleschi, Masaccio, and Donatello.

Donato Bramante (1444–1514), the least known today of the three, came from the town of Urbino, as did Raphael. Bramante, too, was a painter until he turned to architecture in the 1480s. Having arrived in Rome several years before the accession of Julius II, he constructed in 1502 one of Europe's most attractive small buildings—the Tempietto ("little temple") of San Pietro in Montorio (fig. 10-8). Erected on the presumed site of Saint Peter's crucifixion, the shrine is only thirty feet in diameter on the outside and fifteen on the inside. It is round—that is, completely centralized—in plan and borrows such motifs from antiquity as the Tuscan version of Doric columns. Like the rest of Bramante's work, it does not imitate the antique but grows out of it and continues its spirit.

The largest of Bramante's projects would be to realize Julius II's grandest dream—the remodeling of the Vatican Palace and the replacement of the ancient Roman basilica of Saint Peter by a completely new, more up-to-date church. Thus began the demolition of the old and the construction of the present Saint Peter's—a project not completed until the height of the post-Renaissance era, in severely modified form. Bramante's church would be sternly centralized in the form of a Greek cross with apses and filled out as a

10-8 Donato Bramante, The Tempietto, c. 1502. San Pietro in Montorio, Rome.

manuscripts and antiquities. Raphael's splendid portrait *Leo X with Two Cardinals* (fig. 10-10)—the cardinal with a vacuous smile is Leo's cousin, Giuliano de' Medici's illegitimate son, who would become Pope Clement VII—shows a puffy-faced Leo, seated with a treasured manuscript and an ornate silver bell in front of him.

Leo was not depraved, and he was even pious in his own rather jovial fashion. But most certainly he was self-indulgent, as was much of high Roman society in his day. This restricted elite (which included merchant-banker families as well as high clergy) often was ostentatious and vulgar in flaunting its wealth. Fortunately, although medieval asceticism was forgotten, new secular ideals of courtly decorum and well-rounded gentility mitigated the ostentation and vulgarity. The most memorable spokesman for aristocratic sophistication would be Baldassare Castiglione (1478–1529), who wrote the *Book of the Courtier*. This work was the product of long observation at a Renaissance court of unusually genteel taste and would be admired for centuries by aristocratic Europe—and Castiglione would be further immortalized by his friend Raphael's masterly portrait (fig. 10-11).

10-9 Donato Bramante, plan of Saint Peter's, Rome, 1506.

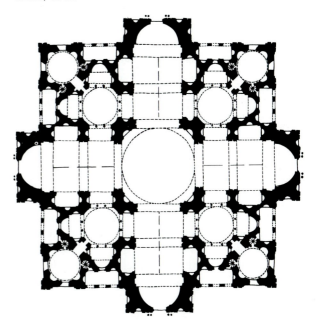

square; the central section would be topped by a great dome (fig. 10-9). During his own lifetime not much more was completed than the piers and the arching of the crossing.

The papacy of Leo X saw a continuation of several Julian projects but exemplified a quite different spirit. Presumably Leo never actually uttered the famous words long ascribed to him upon ascending Peter's throne—"Let us enjoy the papacy, now that God has given it to us"—yet they do characterize much of his reign. Leo's vision was far less grand than his predecessor's, and a cultivated hedonism replaced imperialistic vigor as the papal style. Even the ominous Lutheran revolt aroused Leo's interest far less than did his musical dabbling (he had refined musical tastes and was an amateur composer of some skill), his spectator's love of hunting and clowns, or his collections of precious

10-10   Raphael, *Leo X with Two Cardinals*,
c. 1517. Oil on panel, 61″ × 47″. Uffizi, Florence.

The court celebrated and no doubt idealized in *The Courtier* was that of Urbino, where during most of this period the ducal Montefeltro family ruled undisturbed with the blessing of the papacy. This tiny city-state, with its highly polished court, produced Bramante, Raphael, and Castiglione, whose civilizing influence on Italy and all of Europe was by no means insignificant. Although the ideal courtier envisioned by Castiglione may have remained, by and large, a dream, the dream was typical of the Renaissance in its quest for fame, decorum, pleasure, and the many-sided perfection of mind and body. The Western world has given birth to sterner, more elevated, and more unselfish ideals than this, but seldom to one of more urbane tolerance or greater refinement.

In our modern age the ideal of the civilized, refined person may seem quaint or nostalgic to some; to others it still appeals as a viable and even vital necessity in an age of destructive violence and vulgarity. In either case, Castiglione's ideal helps us to understand his age, the Italian Renaissance of the early sixteenth century. In doing so, for example, he makes countless

respectful references to classical antiquity and almost never mentions the ordinary folk who formed, then as now, the largest proportion of the earth's population.

The *Book of the Courtier* also reveals the ideals and realities of its time in its discussion of the ideal Renaissance woman—that is, the court lady. Since the *Courtier* is cast in dialogue form, with frequent clashes of ideas and ideals, a standard antifeminine view is aired—that woman is a defective, imperfect creature and that, if it had been biologically feasible, all human beings would have been created male. Clearly, though, Castiglione does not himself approve of this denigration of woman, as he puts much longer and more closely reasoned arguments into the mouth of woman's defender Giuliano de' Medici, son of the great Lorenzo.

Even Giuliano, to be sure, still conceives of the women of the court as an adornment of court life, whose existence provides pleasure for gentlemen as love partners and agreeable, affable conversation and feminine gentleness and grace. What is much more surprising than this standard view is its extension by

10-11   Raphael, *Baldassare Castiglione*, c. 1515. Oil on canvas, 32″ × 27″. Louvre, Paris.

Giuliano to envisioning women as fully developed equivalents to men in the arts. He points out that a woman's mind is fully equal to man's: "I say that everything men can understand, women can too; and where a man's intellect can penetrate, so along with it can a woman's." In addition, he regards women's firmness of character as by no means inferior to that of men—and, to demonstrate the point, cites examples of "remarkable women" from both ancient and modern times. Furthermore, Giuliano is completely unimpressed by the use of women's frequently expressed wishes to have been born men as a sign of female inferiority. On the contrary, "The poor creatures do not wish to become men in order to make themselves more perfect but to gain their freedom and shake off the tyranny that men have imposed on them by their one-sided authority." Such strong, uncompromising assertions would seldom be heard again until the day of Mary Wollstonecraft, the late-eighteenth-century feminist.

RENAISSANCE MUSIC

"I am not content with the Courtier," wrote Castiglione, "unless he be also a musician and unless, besides understanding and being able to read notes, he can play upon divers instruments." A rather astonishing requirement, when we think of it—that a gentleman should be versatile in music, even to being able to sing music at sight. Musical ability was a social necessity in Renaissance society as never before, except perhaps in classical Greece, and never since.

It is not surprising that the musical thought of the Renaissance sometimes drew upon the example of classical antiquity. Although the actual tonal art of the ancients was unavailable to the Renaissance, ancient texts were cited on the importance of music in antiquity and on the social role of ancient instruments. A few humanists were genuinely interested in music and themselves became musical performers of skill. Among the artists, too, there was occasional interest: Leonardo da Vinci was praised both for his singing and for his playing of the lyra, a stringed instrument.

Despite his own musical abilities, Leonardo took care to argue that music as an art is inferior to painting. In fact, that was the general Renaissance opinion, at least until the music of Josquin des Prez had impressed itself upon Italy. Traditionally, music had served as an adjunct to piety or pomp or frivolity, not as an autonomous art of independent worth. In humanist and courtly circles, music was most commonly regarded simply as a means of relaxation and diversion, not as an art possessing real spiritual power.

Parallel to the greater prestige of the visual arts over music was the greater prestige of artists over musicians. Composers—even the great Josquin at first—were more likely to be valued and paid for their contribution as choral singers than as composers. The printing of musical scores with movable type proved to be of no financial help, since copyright was unheard of and printers rather than composers benefited from sales. Only a small part of the music composed was printed anyway; larger-scale music, at least, was generally composed for a specific occasion and ordinarily was printed, if at all, mainly to commemorate that event, not for future use. New music could and would be composed for future occasions, and the public performance of old music was considered undesirable. The case of music for amateur use in private homes or palaces, still relatively uncommon, was necessarily rather different—but even here there was no glorification whatsoever of older music, such as has developed in more recent times.

The common musical instruments of the High Renaissance—that is, the end of the fifteenth century and the beginning of the sixteenth—continued to be those of the preceding period. Most popular of all was a plucked-string instrument, the lute, that differed in appearance from the modern guitar in its halved-pear shape with round back. Bowed strings characterized the family of viols, of different sizes and ranges, whereas keyboard instruments included various types of organs and stringed instruments such as the virginal (with plucked strings) and clavichord (with hit strings). Yet the human voice remained the most prestigious medium of musical expression. Its esteem was solemnized in the famous Papal Choir in Rome—a group of roughly two dozen singers recruited from all of Europe that performed with no instrumental accompaniment.

Despite occasional music making in bourgeois homes, it was church and court that remained the most typical sites of musical activity in the High Renaissance. At Italian courts, theatrical events usually required some musical participation. In the churches, regular liturgical forms were supplemented for festive purposes by "sacred representations" that frequently spilled out into nearby squares and streets and gave rise to some of the lively outdoor music for which Florence under Lorenzo the Magnificent was noted.

Music was, of course, not the only ingredient of Florentine outdoor festivities, nor was piety their leading characteristic. The most memorable celebrations came during the carnival season before Lent and again in May and June. Impromptu singing and dancing might occur, but the festive nucleus was a procession with elaborate "cars," or floats, representing mythological or historical subjects—apparently derived far more often from antique pagan legend than from Christian tradition. "It was a very fine sight," recollected one witness, "to see passing through the streets in the evenings, after dinner, twenty-five or thirty pairs of horses richly decked out, with their noble riders disguised and masked according to the nature of the representation, six or eight lackeys for each of them, carrying torches which sometimes numbered more than four hundred, rendering the night as bright as day, and the spectacle beautiful and pleasing and, in truth, superb." The floats followed, whether serious in nature or jovially depicting different aspects of Florentine guilds or popular life. In either case, singers and instrumentalists took part—most memorably in carnival songs of a jolly, satirical, or earthy nature.

Most Renaissance music has remained anonymous, and infinitely more of it has been lost than preserved. Little even remains of the carnival compositions by the distinguished Flemish composer Heinrich Isaac (c. 1450–1517). Chapel master at the cathedral and pride of Lorenzo's musical entourage, Isaac also taught music to Lorenzo's sons and thus helped form the musical taste of the future pope, Leo X.

Isaac's works were extraordinarily varied, and many of them retain great appeal today. A master of polyphony, he was also influenced by Italian melodiousness and by the popular music he encountered in Florence, especially at carnival time. His *Donna di dentro* ("Lady, in your house are roses"), for example, is a *quodlibet*—a combination of two or more well-known tunes—and the tunes here are Florentine folk songs put together with broad humor and much polyphonic inventiveness. Like most music of that time, it could be performed vocally or instrumentally or both, with the possibility of improvised embellishment. Simpler is the setting of Lorenzo's poem *Un dì lieto giamai* ("I have not had one happy day, Love, since from your snares I freed myself"), a straightfor-

ward melody with an accompaniment that is predominantly chordal.

With the passing of Lorenzo came the puritanical influence of Savonarola in Florence, the abolition of Isaac's chapel position, and the exile of the Medici. Despairing of any Medici restoration, Isaac took a position as court composer to the Holy Roman Emperor, Maximilian I. The emperor was a bit eccentric—he even considered obtaining the papacy for himself after Julius II's death—but he was also a discriminating enthusiast for music and the arts. An old woodcut (fig. 10-12) shows him among his musicians, including singers (in the background) and players on harp, organ, and stringed keyboard instrument. Some of Maximilian's musicians doubtless followed the movements of his court, and Isaac seems to have spent some time in the Tyrolian town of Innsbruck, which he commemorated in his best-known song, *Innsbruck, ich muss dich lassen* ("Innsbruck, I must leave you"). The melody may have been original or a folk borrowing; in any case, the nostalgic, largely chordal piece remains an attractive blending of northern and Italian styles in a period when modern musical expressiveness was re-

10-12 Hans Burgkmair, *Maximilian I with His Musicians*, c. 1506–14 (printed 1775). Woodcut, 9″ × 8″. Osterreichische Nationalbibliothek, Vienna.

ceiving even greater impetus from the equally cosmopolitan work of Josquin des Prez.

Josquin des Prez

Born about 1450 (or perhaps a decade earlier) in the Franco-Flemish borderland province of Hainaut, Josquin led a life as international as Isaac's; records indicate he held many different posts in France, Italy, and the Netherlands, including several years as a singer in the Papal Choir. Although he returned to the north well before his death in 1521, he seems to have passed the larger part of three decades in Italy and to have lived briefly in Florence at the time of Lorenzo. His fame surpassed even Isaac's and permitted him a degree of spiritual and financial self-assurance rare among musicians of his day. When Duke Hercules of Ferrara was debating the hiring of either Isaac or Josquin, his secretary noted in a report that Isaac would be better suited to ducal service, since he composed rapidly and had gentlemanly good manners. "Not," he added, "that Josquin is not perhaps the better composer, but he writes only when he feels like it. Besides, he wants two hundred ducats in payment, and Isaac will settle for one hundred and twenty."

Previous chapters have noted many of the forms and devices of Josquin's musical inheritance, most of which he unhesitatingly used when he was so inclined or, we would suspect, when the circumstances of patronage so demanded. His masses especially were conservative, while incorporating the whole gamut of traditional techniques.

Modal feeling generally persisted at that time, although the effect of modern major and minor tonality was becoming more common. Melodies taken from other works appeared frequently, whether in a slow *cantus firmus* (a fixed, borrowed melody) or elaborated in "paraphrased" forms. Sometimes the borrowing was so extensive as to result in a "parody" mass, in which not just one musical line but several were taken from sacred or secular sources. The use of four voices was continued and still further standardized, with a distribution of ranges familiar to us today—soprano, alto, tenor, and bass. *Polyphony* predominated—the simultaneous sounding of two or more independent musical lines, as against a random succession of notes in each voice, which simply build up chords supporting a melody. Often polyphony was subtly combined or alternated with chordal passages.

However, Josquin did not simply continue, perfect, and extend the use of his predecessors' forms and devices. He often brought to them a newly expressive content, and sometimes he transcended them altogether. It is in these two vital senses that we must recognize Josquin's position as one of music's great revolutionaries. Insofar as creative freedom and emotional expression have been part of the mainstream of later Western music, Josquin was truly the first modern composer.

An obvious aspect of musical expression furthered by Josquin was his frequent attempt to match verbal and musical accents. That is, the accented words and syllables of the text of his vocal music (and nearly all his music was vocal) coincide with the emphasized notes of the melody line more often than in medieval or early Renaissance music. More significantly, Josquin reflected to a quite unprecedented degree, especially in his sacred music, the emotional subject matter of the text. Earlier music had occasionally included tonal painting of individual words, such as when the words *descending* and *ascending* were sung to descending and ascending sequences of notes. Secular music had even achieved some correspondence between the mood of the text and musical expression—but in sacred composition just about any music was put with just about any words. Josquin's matching of textual and musical moods, whether in individual phrases, sections, or whole compositions, was a development of immense importance in the history of music.

Opportunities for textual-musical emotional correspondence arose, of course, within the formal structure of the mass, but they are best seen in Josquin's motets. (The motet is a relatively short vocal form, generally religious, with Latin text.) Rather quickly Josquin and his immediate successors saw the expressive possibilities of the motet, and they turned more and more to texts with emotional potential. These were not texts of remote, theological symbolism or mystery but texts with subjective, human feeling—for example, not the Trinity or the Incarnation but the trials of Mary or the sufferings of the crucified Christ. The Old Testament, too, was searched for texts of grief and despair. It was in the Old Testament that Josquin found inspiration for his motet *Absalon fili mi*, David's lament for his son—"Absalom my son, my son Absalom, would that I had died for thee, my son Absalom! Let me live no longer, but go down weeping to my grave." As a pioneer on the frontier of dramatic musical despair, Josquin would be surpassed in effective intensity later in his own century, but the evocative emotional power of *Absalon* is by no means inconsiderable.

Absalon, like many others among Josquin's motets, also illustrates the second aspect of his musical revolution—the transcending, although not the complete abandonment, of medieval formalism. Musical *imitation*—a common medieval device in which a melody is closely followed by successive restatements in other parts—is evident enough in the opening phrases of *Absalon,* but it is then forgotten. Similarly, even the occasional inclusion of medieval devices in the other motets never draws our attention or detracts from the homogeneous musical texture. One of the more remarkable demonstrations of Josquin's genius is his use of polyphonic structure for expressive effect in the brief *Ave vera virginitas* ("Hail, true virginity") section of his motet *Ave Maria virgo serena.* Although the tenor strictly imitates the soprano at a fifth below, and one beat later, this rigid device is unobtrusively absorbed within the total effect of the section:

A-ve ve-ra   vir - gi - ni - tas

Josquin clearly placed the expressive, organic whole far above technical sleight of hand. In the best of music before Josquin, with relatively few exceptions, we find a skillful superimposing of musical elements, including melody, but no great conscious concern for the actual sound of the passing mixture or the expressive significance of the whole. Most likely the *linear* manner of composition—consecutively imposing one musical line upon another—was at the root of this earlier style. However, from the time of Josquin there is more and more evidence of simultaneous harmonic composition, even in polyphonic writing; a deliberately harmonic conception now began to complement inventive polyphonic linearity.

Josquin's secular music often possesses great charm but is less innovative than his motet style. Inspiration for his secular works came from many sources, most notably from Italian popular forms and Franco-Netherlandish chansons. In the first category fell the *frottola*—a simple four-part song in chordal style on an unpretentious, generally light-hearted subject. The melody is sung by the highest voice part and supported by the bass line below, with chords filled in by the other two voices—an eminently familiar approach to popular music making in later ages. Josquin's *El Grillo* ("The Cricket") represents the frottola at its most attractive. "The cricket," run the words, "is a good singer who sings for a long time." In this work we hear a suggestion of chirping and the long hold and the inner-voice repetition on "long time." Josquin's chanson *De tous biens playne* ("My mistress is full of all good things") is far more intricate, since it adds to the two relatively stately top voices (borrowed from an earlier song by Hayne) a lively canon in the lower voices, which jump about quite merrily.

Thus music flourished in the Renaissance and demonstrated distinct affinities with other arts of the age. Above all, the musical thinking and practice of Josquin's time embraced eagerly the concept of change, of a new beginning, of exploratory curiosity. Rejecting past authority as such, but perfectly willing to utilize its example, it implied, however tentatively, the composer's freedom to obey his own laws. Like the visual arts, music was almost ready to justify itself by its own creative urge, responsive to autonomous musical impulse.

SCULPTURE AND PAINTING BEFORE MICHELANGELO

In the realm of sculpture there was less innovation than in musical life—or, for that matter, than in painting. It is tempting to explain this by pointing to sculpture's more literal classical models, then being rediscovered, as opposed to the comparative absence of antique authority in music and painting; in fact, this may account for the classicism of some of the sculpture then being done. But the trend of the age's most memorable monuments seems to have been away from the classical, not toward it. As examples from the period before Michelangelo, we may glance at typical works of the two finest sculptors of the 1470s and 1480s, Verrocchio and Pollaiuolo. The fact that both of these Florentines were distinguished painters as well as sculptors may well have influenced their emancipation from antique models.

The bronze *Christ and Saint Thomas* (fig. 10-13), of Andrea del Verrocchio (c. 1431–88), was put in place in its outdoor niche in 1483, and there it remains on one of Florence's busiest shopping streets. The figure at the left spills out of the confines of the niche, which had been intended for a single figure—note the position and footing of the doubting Thomas, as he tentatively approaches the lance wound of his risen master. The drama of the moment depicted is enhanced by gesture and by the deep-cut, sweeping robes. Dynamic in a different way is Verrocchio's great bronze equestrian monument, cast posthumously from his models, of Bartolommeo Colleoni (fig. 10-14) in Venice. Although the hero-on-horseback theme is Roman, the warrior Colleoni is in Renaissance armor, not antique as in the case of Donatello's *Gattamelata* (see fig. 9-25). Ferocious vigor of expression replaces Gattamelata's introspection, as both horse and rider advance proudly into battle.

Dynamic vigor of still another sort marks the small bronze *Hercules and Antaeus* (fig. 10-15), by Antonio del Pollaiuolo (c. 1431–98). Here an antique subject has become an exercise in scientific naturalism, a study in muscular strain. The compact composition of earlier Renaissance sculpture is flagrantly disregarded, as Pollaiuolo looks forward, even beyond Michelangelo, toward the contortions of late Renaissance Mannerism.

Botticelli

The outstanding Florentine painter of the age of Lorenzo, Sandro Botticelli (1445–1510), is among the Western world's most popular, and most sentimentalized, artists. His *Adoration of the Magi* (fig. 10-16), now in the Uffizi, certainly owes some of its perennial ap-

10-13   Andrea del Verrocchio, *Christ and Saint Thomas*, 1465–83. Bronze; figure of Christ is 7'7" high (to top of raised hand). Exterior of the Or San Michele, Florence.

peal to speculation concerning the identification of its many portraitlike figures, beginning with the elderly first Magus, perhaps posthumously representing Cosimo de' Medici. Most likely of all is the identification of the bright-robed young man to the far right: his appropriate age and the traditional direct gaze of self-portraiture may justify the assumption that this is Bot-

10-14 Andrea del Verrocchio and Alessandro Leopardi, *Bartolommeo Colleoni*, c. 1481–96. Bronze, c. 13′ high. Campo Santi Giovanni e Paolo, Venice.

ticelli himself. If so, in placing himself so prominently in the foreground, the artist can scarcely be accused of excessive humility. Among the work's more unusual characteristics is the very secular sociability of the scene portrayed. The religious theme of the work is not enough to invest it with an air of genuine piety.

An aura of high seriousness is generally less characteristic of Botticelli's religious paintings than of his famous works on subjects drawn from pagan mythology. This is not as unusual as it may seem today, for at the height of the Renaissance religious practice tended to exhibit a kind of worldly cheerfulness, while it was the fashion of the time to invest pagan thought with a living spiritual content. Here the prime philosophical inspiration was the Neoplatonist movement that pervaded Medicean circles in the late fifteenth century and that was led most notably by the scholarship and speculation of Marsilio Ficino (1433–99). Like other *Neoplatonists*, Ficino stressed such doctrines as the contemplative role and the immortality of the human soul, together with the communion of souls and their transcendent ethical yearnings. Ficino, Pico della Miran-

dola, and Neoplatonists in general found truth not only in Platonic thought and Christian teaching but in the essential insights of all philosophies and all religions—many of them, of course, classical. They dreamed of combining and reconciling all systems of thought, imparting a new dignity and significance to all.

Modern writers have sometimes found precise Neoplatonist references in the art of Botticelli and Michelangelo, but their conclusions are speculative and agreement is by no means unanimous. Mainly we should note the general correspondence of mood—the ethical and spiritual striving in both art and thought—and then pass on to less debatable qualities of the art.

In Botticelli's celebrated *Spring* (fig. 10-17) modern interpreters find not only pagan allegory but ethi-

10-15 Antonio del Pollaiuolo, *Hercules and Antaeus*, 1470s. Bronze, 18″ high including base. Museo Nazionale, Florence.

10-16   Sandro Botticelli, *Adoration of the Magi*, early 1470s. Panel, 44″ × 53″. Uffizi, Florence.

cal and even Christian purpose, above all in the central figure of Venus. Although hardly requisite to our enjoyment of the painting, this interpretation is rendered especially plausible by Ficino's words, written to the commissioner of the work, the teen-aged Lorenzo di Pierfrancesco de' Medici. "Venus, that is to say Humanitas, is a nymph of excellent comeliness, born of heaven and more than others beloved by God all highest. Her soul and mind are Love and Charity, her eyes Dignity and Magnanimity, the hands Liberality and Magnificence, the feet Comeliness and Modesty." The metamorphosis from ancient goddess of love and beauty to complex symbol is startling.

More obviously, the theme of *Spring* is simply the seasonal rebirth of nature and a dreamlike celebration of human love. At the right a god of winds pursues a nymph, who is perhaps in the process of transformation into the goddess of spring, Flora, who stands beside her. The three ethereal Graces dance languidly as Mercury points heavenward, perhaps to calm the elements, and as Cupid aims his dart earthward. Flowers

bloom luxuriantly, and oranges dot the grove; it seems that only they will remain when the magical vision has vanished. For it will surely vanish, rarefied and insubstantial as it is. Botticelli's figures are almost without mass; they float unanchored to the world, and the filmy garments obey no earthly laws but those of the painter's gracefully linear inspiration. For a moment we are transported to another world—to a lyrical dream world that has sprung from Lorenzo's Florence.

It was an escapist vision and, one should add, a vision of eternal youth. Renaissance Italy, especially the twilight of Lorenzo's Florence, knew and valued the charm of youth. Portraits, too, were often of the young: an appealing example is Botticelli's *Portrait of a Young Man* (fig. 10-18). Incisive line, not subtle modeling, defines the face and the hair of this boy, who still gazes deep within us, confident and challenging, across the centuries.

For a final glimpse at Botticelli's world we turn to the *Birth of Venus* (fig. 10-19). Again the subject is ostensibly mythological, although various scholars

10-17   Sandro Botticelli, *Spring*, c. 1478. Panel, 6'8" × 10'4". Uffizi, Florence.

10-18   Sandro Botticelli, *Portrait of a Young Man*, c. 1482. Panel, 15" × 11". Reproduced by courtesy of the Trustees, The National Gallery, London.

have interpreted the scene Neoplatonically, as one of spiritual rebirth, and even religiously, with the lovely nude goddess embodying the spirit of the Virgin Mary. Immediately striking is the union of spirit and delicate sensuality in the Venus figure, the thorough unreality of the scene, and Botticelli's graceful, linear conception. The humanized forms exist in solitary isolation, as foreground figures against a stylized stage set without depth. It is a realm not only of lyrical, melancholic grace but of enchanted artificiality. Moreover, it is a world that, by and large, died with Botticelli and the Florentine problems of the century's end. In fact, a new world had already been born, at least in painting: Leonardo's *Virgin of the Rocks* seems to have been almost exactly contemporaneous with Botticelli's *Birth of Venus*.

10-19 Sandro Botticelli, *Birth of Venus*, after 1482. Tempera on canvas, 5'9" × 9'2". Uffizi, Florence.

Leonardo

The achievements of Leonardo da Vinci (1452–1519), and certain aspects of his thought, are among the best-documented and best-known landmarks in the history of human genius. Nearly every Western schoolchild has heard of the *Mona Lisa* or the *Last Supper,* and most educated men and women know of the amazing notebooks that are evidence of Leonardo's wide-ranging interests and profound insights in art, science, technology, and philosophy. Of course, there were gaps in his interests: he left, for example, almost no word on the political, social, or economic problems of his day, or on his impressions of the important people he knew and served. That he was attracted to powerful personalities seems evident simply from the list of his patrons, most notably Duke Ludovico Sforza of Milan, Pope Alexander VI's son Caesar Borgia, and the young French king Francis I—all supremely ambitious and unscrupulous men. However, the realm of Leonardo's private feelings and emotions is almost completely unknown to us. Historians probe for clues but do not agree on the key to the enigma. Quite possibly the keys were many and the mystification at least partly intentional. Leonardo may still, after all, have a right to his privacy.

In any case, his public legacy is our main concern. The diversity of Leonardo's activities is impressive; he worked in such areas as cartography, the design of canals and fortifications, the design and management of courtly pageantry, and the empirical study of anatomy, botany, and geology. In theory and speculation he was at least equally far-reaching, whether in mathematics, aesthetics, or natural philosophy, or in his visionary sketches of mechanical inventions. Throughout, the most atypical features of Leonardo as a Renaissance man were his relative neglect of literary scholarship and his refusal to accept antique authority. His guide was nature, and his main instrument of investigation and discovery the human eye.

Certainly Leonardo was not the first person to observe nature carefully, but to him nature was an awesome, almost religious force and the undisputed center of aesthetics and philosophy. Leonardo's curiosity concerning the mechanisms of nature was obsessive, both in nature's most minute details and in its cosmic power and significance. From the veining of a leaf and the articulation of human bone and muscle to the greatest cataclysms of the sea and mountain storms, nature for Leonardo had to be intellectually comprehended and mastered scientifically as well as artistically.

"The painter," wrote Leonardo, "strives and competes with nature." Leonardo was able to do this—to the delighted popular applause of his own and later ages. Yet his professional frustrations were many. Historical circumstances prevented the execution of his large sculptural projects, and many of his paintings were left uncompleted or were later lost or damaged—but the paintings and drawings that remain attest to the great skill with which he conquered the visual world.

The Louvre's *Virgin of the Rocks* (fig. 10-20) was probably begun in 1483, soon after Leonardo left Florence and his native Tuscany for Milan. Its innovative naturalism consists far less in the splendid details of rocks and plants than in the fully understood human forms, but most realistic of all are the atmospheric effects that envelop the whole scene. Painters earlier in the fifteenth century had developed *chiaroscuro,* the shadow-formed contrast of light and dark color; Leonardo supplemented chiaroscuro with *sfumato,* "smoky" tones that result from subtle color gradations and the defining of areas not by precise outline but by blurring and subtly intermingling the boundaries between objects—as in normal human vision.

Yet all its cunning visual illusions, such as the startling foreshortening seen in the Virgin's extended left hand, and all its physical realism, typified by the chubby bodies of Saint John and the baby Jesus, cannot obscure our feeling that the *Virgin of the Rocks* goes well beyond pictorial realism. Realism may have been Leonardo's greatest historical contribution to painting, but it was combined with a keen awareness of form. We note in this work the solidly pyramidal arrangement of the four figures and the geometrical variety brought by the different hands, which at the same time further unify the group dynamically by their high-

10-20 Leonardo da Vinci, *Virgin of the Rocks,* begun 1483. Oil on panel, 79″ × 48″. Louvre, Paris.

lighted gestures. Also, beyond form, we note the mysterious quality of the deeply shadowed, cavernous setting.

The *Mona Lisa* (fig. 10-21), probably the world's most famous portrait, presumably dates from Leonardo's three-year return to Florence, 1503–1506, and he carried it with him on his travels until his death in France in 1519. Like the *Virgin of the Rocks,* it is discolored by age and varnish. However, laboratory analysis indicates that the traditional description of its original lively coloration was exaggerated and that its cool tones may not be wholly due to the passage of time. Certainly today there is an almost glacial chill about the sterile, rocky landscape in the background, despite

10-21 Leonardo da Vinci, *Mona Lisa*, c. 1503–6. Panel, 38″ × 21″. Louvre, Paris.

Raphael

Of these two artists, Raphael and Michelangelo, the less striking to most modern eyes is Raphael Sanzio (Raffaello Santi), who lived a relatively uneventful life from 1483 to 1520. For more than three centuries Raphael was the most beloved of all Western painters, and even today he often seems to best embody the spirit of the mature Renaissance. The gigantic personalities of Leonardo and Michelangelo were unique; Raphael's genius was wide-ranging and serene, absorbing almost effortlessly the most advanced techniques of his elders and bringing them to a perfection hitherto unimaginable.

Raphael's father was also a painter, and father and son apparently moved in the genteel, idealistic circles at Urbino that later would be celebrated in Castiglione's *Book of the Courtier*. In his early twenties Raphael settled for a time in Florence, where a flood of new influences, including Leonardo's, soon coalesced to help form his first mature style—the style most commonly associated with a famous series of Madonnas. Of these, one of the most charming would later be nicknamed *La Belle Jardinière*, or "the lovely gardener" (fig. 10-22). The modeling and color are subtle, and the pyramidal group of Virgin, Christ Child, and infant Saint John represents the most idealized perfection of human beauty. The countryside, too, is beautiful and recedes smoothly from foreground to remote distance.

In 1508 Raphael moved to Rome, where he was to remain until his death. Bramante had urged Julius II to employ the young painter in the decoration of the Vatican, where Michelangelo was already at work. Soon Raphael was planning, executing, and supervising the mural decoration of a new group of *stanze* (rooms). His increasing popularity in Rome and the urgency of countless other commissions would eventually lead to his turning over more and more of the Vatican painting tasks to his assistants. However, the frescoes he planned for the Stanza della Segnatura (1509–11) seem to be wholly by his own hand. Among these is the large work commonly called the *School of Athens* (fig. 10-23).

Clearly much had changed since *La Belle Jardinière*. Presumably we will never know what contact Raphael had with Michelangelo and how the young painter's work might have been influenced by the work going on in the Sistine Chapel close by. In any case, Raphael, in his fluent adaptability, recognized the

its hazy sfumato—and there is not much warmth in Mona Lisa's impenetrable smile either. We must temper the emphasis on Leonardo's naturalism by the recognition of psychological ambiguity and of a genius that far transcended realistic literalism.

Leonardo was very much aware of his genius, and of his place as a pioneer in what he considered the finest of fine arts. He upheld vigorously the theoretical supremacy of painting among the arts—and his own work only confirmed, for knowledgeable contemporaries, his bold comparison of the painter's creativity with that of God. "The divinity inherent in painting," he wrote, "transmutes the painter's mind into a resemblance of God's spirit, for with free forcefulness it gives itself to the creation of diverse things." Both his theory and his example prepared the way for his brilliant successors, Raphael and Michelangelo.

10-22 Raphael, *Madonna (La Belle Jardinière)*, 1507. Panel, 48″ × 32″. Louvre, Paris.

implications of grandeur in scale and theme and produced a work of unusual strength and majesty. Here, under painted vaults inspired by Bramante, are gathered in solemn debate the great figures of ancient thought. In the center are Plato, pointing heavenward to transcendental vision, and Aristotle, gesturing toward the more mundane realm below. Other figures are sometimes identified as antique sages or sixteenth-century personalities or both. A glance at the original sketch makes it clear that the brooding figure resting against a marble block in the central foreground was an afterthought. Quite certainly the features are Michelangelo's; the addition is a generous tribute from a great artist to a greater one.

As the *School of Athens* implies, Raphael's enthusiasm for classical antiquity was much stronger than Leonardo's. Significantly, Raphael was to receive from Leo X the position of safekeeper of the ancient inscriptions of Rome, and later that of curator of Vatican antiquities. He apparently found time to take these jobs seriously while also distinguishing himself as an architect of classical bent. Commissions for portraits (see figs. 10-10 and 10-11) and larger paintings overwhelmed him, as did general public adulation in Rome. His death at thirty-seven was widely mourned,

10-23 Raphael, *School of Athens*, 1510–11. Fresco, 26′ × 18′. Stanza della Segnatura, Vatican Palace, Rome.

and he was buried in the ancient Roman Pantheon. Although his serenity of temperament perhaps denied him the ultimate heights of artistic inspiration, his work united for a brief historical moment the humane ideals of the pagan and Christian worlds in a brilliant style of universal appeal.

MICHELANGELO: YOUTH AND MATURITY

Raphael's tribute to Michelangelo in the *School of Athens* was not the earliest accorded to that master, nor, of course, the last. During his creative career of seventy-five years Michelangelo Buonarroti (1475–1564) came to be revered as virtually divine, and he retains to this day his title of supremacy among artists.

Born into a poor but genteel Florentine family, Michelangelo began his formal artistic training at thirteen, and at fifteen he was honored by Lorenzo's grant of lodging in the Medici Palace for the duration of his artistic training. There his idols and true masters were not his older contemporaries but such giants of the past as Giotto, Masaccio, and Donatello. Shortly, during the youth's visit to Bologna, Jacopo della Quercia would join the select circle.

Early in Michelangelo's career he showed great skill in portraying the beauty of the human body, a subject that would fascinate him for the rest of his life. Most of his work accepts and celebrates bodily beauty. The structure, posture, and movement of the human body reflected for Michelangelo the complex life and aspirations of the soul; it was, in fact, the only subject of vital pictorial interest to him.

By 1498 the young Michelangelo's abilities had so far matured that the contract for his first Pietà (fig. 10-24) specified that it would be "the most beautiful work in marble which exists today in Rome." The group is of extraordinary triangular compactness and includes only the Virgin and the crucified Son lying on her lap. Her draperies recall but surpass the convoluted complexities of those of Verrocchio's *Saint Thomas* (see fig. 10-13) and offer support and stability to the naked body of Christ. The grief portrayed in the Pietàs of earlier artists is wholly transcended: the Virgin's face and pose convey compassion and resignation. Her face is idealized and suggests not matronly years but the ageless purity that had been the channel of God's mys-

10-24   Michelangelo, *Pietà*, 1498–1500. Marble, 5'9" high. Saint Peter's, Rome.

terious grace. Thus at the very outset of Michelangelo's sculptural maturity we learn to expect from him no literal imitation of nature, but the subtle subservience of nature to soul and symbol. Although the *Pietà* is a superb demonstration of sculptural skill and possesses sensual beauty, it also affirms the sculptor's fervent religious aspirations. Not the least of Michelangelo's qualities would be his ability to communicate at several significant levels in a single work.

However, Christian piety never restrained Michelangelo's veneration for the sculpture of classical antiquity. Indeed, he revered ancient sculptural remains precisely because he thought their primitive setting to be closer to natural and divine inspiration than his own age could ever be. It followed, then, that since precise imitation of the ancients was impossible, he had full authorization to express freely his own creative vigor, building on the classical experience but going well beyond it. He was never to do this more strikingly than in the next of his major projects after the *Pietà*— the marble *David* (fig. 10-25), which he executed in 1501–1504 for the cathedral of Florence.

For this colossal monolith, classical antiquity suggested not only the total nudity but the theme of cou-

10-25   Michelangelo, *David*, 1501–4. Marble, 14′3″ high. Galleria dell' Accademia, Florence.

rageous fortitude. While the body reveals an infinitely greater understanding of anatomy than the classical world had generally shown, there are startling exaggerations of natural proportions, most notably in the enormous, noble head and the magnificently powerful hands. These exaggerations are probably only partially explained by the intended outdoor placement of the work forty feet above street level. Actually it was never so placed; the city of Florence placed it in a more visible and more pointedly symbolic location—in front of the Town Hall.

It was evident to all that this statue represented more than the boy in the biblical Goliath story. Michelangelo must have shared the general Florentine feeling that the *David* was a symbol of the proud young Florentine republic defying its enemies. The tragic personal struggles of Michelangelo's later years and Florence's renewed civic agony are not foreshadowed here; *David* remains a monument to the self-confidence and idealism of youth as well as the vigilant optimism of a passing phase of Florentine history.

Michelangelo's next civic project, this time not in stone but in paint, was a mural for the Town Hall on a Florentine military subject, the Battle of Cascina. Never completed and now destroyed, it is known today only through the artist's sketches and copies by others. Typically it featured prominently the dynamic representation of nude males. The work's popularity among other artists was extraordinary; Michelangelo's success as a painter was even more immediate than his fame as a sculptor. Shortly thereafter, in the Sistine Chapel ceiling, he created one of painting's most imposing monuments.

The Sistine Chapel Ceiling

The Sistine Chapel (fig. 10-26) was over a quarter-century old when Michelangelo was commissioned to supply a more impressive ceiling fresco than the original pattern of yellow stars on a solid blue background. A largely independent structure within the Vatican complex, the chapel owed its internal simplicity to the intention of its founder, Pope Sixtus IV, that much of the interior would be covered with mural painting. Indeed, most of this had been done, by Botticelli and others, before the chapel's consecration in 1483. Along the 130-foot length of the left lateral wall were frescoed scenes from the story of Moses, signifying Hebraic life under the Law. On the right were scenes from the life of Christ. Since the wall space between windows above these panels contained paintings of the popes, suggesting the institutional history of the Christian Church, the most obvious subjects remaining for Michelangelo's work were the beginning of the world and its end at the Last Judgment. He would attack the majestic Last Judgment three decades later on the front altar wall; first of all, for four years (1508–12), he labored at the formidable ceiling project, whose prime concerns were the Creation and the earliest history of humanity.

10-26 The Sistine Chapel, consecrated 1483. Vatican, Rome.

Historians hold determined and contradictory opinions on whether and to what extent Michelangelo received theological advice on the complex iconography of the ceiling paintings. However, the mind of the artist himself is surely evident in the prominence given to the magnificent male nudes (the *ignudi*) and in the honest adaptation of the pictorial scheme to the architectural forms. Random pictures or decorative designs are not crammed willy-nilly into the available space; rather, each structural element is assigned a particular type of subject matter. The *lunettes* (semicircular wall areas around the window tops) and the triangular *spandrels* above them contain the most earthly subjects. Each springing of the vault, extending higher, contains the image of an inspired prophet or sibyl. The uppermost, flattened area of the barrel vault contains the nine narrative panels and the ignudi.

The total expanse rejects not only the concept of mere decorative design but also the illusionism that was becoming popular in Italian ceiling painting, by which figures would be painted so as to recede into a simulated sky. Michelangelo's ceiling possesses thematic unity, but only limited pictorial unity: the figures are on vastly varying scales, and from no one vantage point can all the scenes and figures even appear right side up. Interlocking pictorial and symbolic motifs effectively ward off chaos, but naturalistic illusionism is neither achieved nor intended.

The source and final meaning of Michelangelo's titanic theme remain the subject of scholarly argument. Recent interpretations usually stress either a traditional theological approach or the Neoplatonist doctrine of the soul's divine origin and its reunion with God. Quite possibly elements of both approaches entered Michelangelo's scheme. Ideal forms and idealistic yearnings of Ficino's doctrine may well have reinforced Michelangelo's more personal impulses, while the pictorial organization of the ceiling suggests definite theological linkages among biblical and pagan traditions. The pagan sibyls of ancient Greece and Rome as well as Hebrew prophets were often presumed by theologians to have seen the inherent Christian content of Old Testament history. Thus, next to the large *Drunkenness of Noah* panel, the *Delphic Sibyl* (fig. 10-27) stares with wide-eyed concentration into the future after examining the prophetic scroll. Inner dynamism and abrupt movement are implied in the parted lips and the contrasting directions of bodily thrust, despite

10-27 Michelangelo, *Delphic Sibyl*, detail from the ceiling of the Sistine Chapel (fig. 10-26), 1508–12.

the figure's self-containment. The face is of an idealized femininity, although the muscular arms remind us that Michelangelo used male models for his Sistine sketches.

Although his female forms may seem deliberately to have sought an idealized blending of the sexes, his male nudes almost always are fully masculine. The most prominent of the latter are the twenty ignudi at the corners of the large narrative panels; figure 10-28 shows the four figures surrounding the *Creation of Eve.* On no single feature of the ceiling's iconography has scholarly argument been more inconclusive. All critics agree that the ignudi symbolize something, although few agree on what it is. The common basic assumption appears to be that, in this spiritual center of Christendom, they cannot be simply male nudes. Another common assumption is that the decorative and functional value of the nudes—as supporters of oak leaf and acorn garlands and several large bronze-colored medallions, and as relief to the potential monotony of a row of rectangular panels—cannot justify their prominence in the ceiling's scheme. We may reflect, though, that

throughout Michelangelo's career his sensual imagery was seldom frivolous but was symbolic of spiritual beauty and yearning. In any case, the decorative effectiveness of the ignudi, in their varied poses, is dependent on their size and supreme visibility.

Thus, although there may be validity in such explanations of the ignudi as incarnations of the "rational" prophetic and sibylline souls, we may also emphasize the psychological and decorative aspects of the ignudi and the cosmic energy these expressive figures seem to embody. (Five of the nine large panels deal with God's creative power.) Whatever further symbolic freight the ignudi may bear, they are a veritable gallery of spiritual and emotional reflections of the sublime events that surround them.

The *Creation of Eve* is probably the least effective of the nine panels, quite possibly because Michelangelo remembered too well Jacopo della Quercia's splendid treatment of the theme in Bologna (see fig. 9-13). However, no apologies are required for the neighboring panel, the celebrated *Creation of Adam* (fig. 10-29). Stolid, earthbound figures now have given way to otherworldly dynamism. God the Father majestically appears, the whole heavenly host seemingly contained within His billowing cloak. All power and majesty, He extends his hand toward Adam, who has raised himself slightly from the barren rock. The body of the youthful nude, although still relaxed, already begins to flow with energy, while the face is transfigured by yearning for the divine. Never, before the *Creation of Adam* panel, had sensual languor and spiritual vigor coexisted so harmoniously; here pagan humanism and sacred imagery have been miraculously reconciled.

In three more consecutive panels the history of divine creation is carried chronologically backward, as God summons forth earthly vegetation, separates the earth from the waters, creates the sun and moon, and divides light from darkness. Michelangelo may well have been justified in hinting in one of his sonnets (he wrote some distinguished poetry) that his own creative powers as an artist were akin to those of the Almighty. Such has been the world's judgment ever since the Sistine Chapel was reopened to the public on the eve of All Saints' Day, 1512.

The Two Tomb Projects

With the death of Julius II early in 1513, resumption of work on the pope's tomb, which Michelangelo had begun in 1505, became urgent. Despite Michelangelo's

10-28 Michelangelo, *Creation of Eve*, with ignudi, detail from the ceiling of the Sistine Chapel (fig. 10-26), 1508–12.

strenuous, if intermittent, labors over several decades, many interruptions and crushing discouragements prevented the completion of the tomb on anything like its planned grandiose scale. Isolated figures for it remain scattered today in Florence and Paris. The final monument, placed not in Saint Peter's basilica but in the small church in Rome where Julius had once been cardinal, includes only three figures by the master. The most famous of them is *Moses* (fig. 10-30), a figure of awesome strength. In the grandeur and superhuman distortions of the face and figure, posterity has sensed the terrifying vigor and resolve of Julius as well as of the inspired Hebrew leader. Heroic self-control, under God's commandments, may also be suggested in the *Moses*—and here, not surprisingly, parallels have been drawn to the sculptor's own struggles for self-mastery.

10-29 Michelangelo, *Creation of Adam*, detail from the ceiling of the Sistine Chapel (fig. 10-26), 1508–12.

10-30   Michelangelo, *Moses,* detail from the tomb of Pope Julius II, c. 1515. Marble, 7′9″ high. San Pietro in Vincoli, Rome.

Miscellaneous uncompleted figures for the tomb include several captives, or prisoners, only partially emerging from their marble blocks. As in the two more fully finished figures now in the Louvre, the tortured forms preserved in Florence (for example, fig. 10-31) imply human bondage to sin—all the more so for the stone that still imprisons them. Michelangelo himself may well have been aware of their heightened significance in this rather amorphous state, although it seems clear that he did originally hope and expect to finish them.

In the meantime until 1534, alternating with work on the Julian tomb, Michelangelo was engaged on another herculean project that would remain incomplete—the construction and sculptural elaboration of the Medici Chapel, or New Sacristy of the Florentine church of San Lorenzo. Fortunately, a great deal more of this sculpture was brought to full or near completion by Michelangelo than for the Roman proj-

ect, and nearly all of the work is gathered in one spot—in the setting designed by the artist himself. Despite its various divergencies from his intentions, the ensemble constitutes one of Western sculpture's supreme achievements.

The building was begun for Cardinal Giulio de' Medici in 1519. Michelangelo's architectural design exemplified Renaissance classicism, although its elements were more heavily, less functionally molded than had been customary. The chapel contains tombs for Lorenzo the Magnificent, his brother Giuliano (father of the cardinal), and Lorenzo's son Giuliano (duke of Nemours) and grandson Lorenzo (duke of Urbino). The elder, more famous Medici rest in a double tomb improvised after Michelangelo's abandonment of the project; the younger Medici are honored by individual tombs of extraordinary beauty.

The two finer tombs are against opposite walls. On each sarcophagus rest two nudes, one male and one female. These, as the sculptor himself tells us, represent the times of day. In a niche above each sarcophagus is a figure in Roman armor evoking the memory of the respective duke but with no attempt at portraiture. The ducal figure for the tomb of Giuliano, duke of Nemours (fig. 10-32) is an idealization of superb

10-31   Michelangelo, *Crossed-Leg (Awakening) Captive,* 1527–28 or later. Marble, 8′10″ high. Galleria dell' Accademia, Florence.

10-32 Michelangelo, Tomb of Giuliano de'
Medici, 1519–34. Marble; central figure is c. 5'2"
high. Medici Chapel, Church of San Lorenzo,
Florence.

youthful masculinity, almost incredibly muscled yet
strangely languorous. Beneath him are *Night* as a mature female nude and *Day* as an enormously powerful
male.

The serious mood of the Medici Chapel is intensely somber, which is not wholly surprising or inap-
propriate for a room of tombs, but the intensity is Michelangelo's own; it is the product of personal genius
and his reaction to the historical circumstances of his
time. The role of circumstances in artistic creativity is
often vital, and the final agony of Florentine and Italian independence may well have deepened the expressive power of the Medici Chapel sculpture. Surely Michelangelo's genius was crucial in the Medici tombs—
and genius remains perhaps the supreme human
mystery. In the following chapter we will note the continuing course of Michelangelo's genius in his final
decades.

Recommended Reading

Anzelewski, Fedja. *Dürer, His Art and Life* (1981). Excellent
    text and illustrations.
Busignani, Alberto. *Botticelli* (1968). General survey with
    color plates.
Castiglione, Baldassare. *The Book of the Courtier*, trans. by
    Friench Simpson (1959). Good abridged translation.
Cuzin, Jean-Pierre. *Raphael, His Life and Works* (1985). Fine
    coverage and illustrations.
Erasmus, Desiderius. *The Praise of Folly*, trans. by Clarence
    H. Miller (1979). Modern translation with notes.
Ergang, Robert. *The Renaissance* (1967). Historical overview
    of all aspects of the Renaissance.
Faludy, George. *Erasmus* (1970). Sympathetic survey of life
    and works.
Hale, J. R. *Renaissance Europe: Individual and Society, 1480–
    1520* (1971). General survey with social and economic
    background.
Hartt, Frederick. *History of Italian Renaissance Art: Painting,
    Sculpture, Architecture* (1979). Fine, comprehensive
    study.
Hibbard, Howard. *Michelangelo* (1974). Comprehensive
    study, good black-and-white illustrations.
Machiavelli, Niccolò. *The Prince* (1977). The text in trans-
    lation, with background and interpretive essays.

Martinelli, Giuseppe, ed. *The World of Renaissance Florence*
    (1968). Vivid, comprehensive picture book with good
    text.
Mitchell, Bonner. *Rome in the High Renaissance* (1973). In-
    teresting view of a civilization.
Plumb, J. H., ed. *The Horizon Book of the Renaissance*
    (1961). Picture book with fine essays on individuals.
Ross, James Bruce, and Mary Martin McLaughlin. *The Port-
    able Renaissance Reader* (1958). Collection of primary
    sources.
Venturi, Lionello. *The Sixteenth Century, from Leonardo to El
    Greco* (1956). Overview of painting with good
    color plates.
Wasserman, Jack. *Leonardo* (1984). Fine introduction, well-
    illustrated.

11

The Late Renaissance: 1530–1600

f all ages in Western history, the sixteenth century after 1530 was certainly among the most colorful, though by no means the happiest. Protestant defiance of Roman Catholicism had disrupted the nominal unity of west European Christianity. For more than a century religious wars, domestic and international, convulsed most of the Continent at one time or another. The wars were most vicious in the Germanies of the emperor Charles V (1519–56), the France of Henry II's widow Catherine de Medici (died 1589), and the Netherlands of William the Silent (1572–84), where the Dutch were attempting to establish a republic free of Spanish rule. In Italy the worst was over: Rome had been sacked by Charles V's troops in 1527. After 1530, and still more definitively with the Spanish–French treaty of Cateau-Cambrésis in 1559, Spain was the dominant foreign influence in the Italian peninsula, although such states as Venice, Tuscany (the former Florentine state, finally a hereditary duchy under the Medici family), and Rome retained nominal independence.

In the meantime, several celebrated European rulers enjoyed the good fortune of relative national tranquillity—Francis I of France (1515–47) and his son Henry II (1547–59); Henry VIII of England (1509–47) and his daughter Elizabeth I (1558–1603), and Elizabeth's arch-rival, Philip II of Spain (1556–98), champion of Spanish Catholicism. However, these rulers' marks on history may well be dimmer than that of the Protestant leaders Martin Luther (1483–1546) and John Calvin (1509–64) and such stalwarts of militant Catholicism as Ignatius Loyola (1491–1556). In any case, fervent if misguided religious zeal joined the most unscrupulous political "realism" to give the century a tone of violence and persecution. "There is no hostility so fine as Christian hostility," wrote the French essayist Michel de Montaigne—but his plea for toleration made no vivid impression on his century.

Both the Protestant and Catholic reform movements of the age, despite their intolerance, aimed at a purer, more spiritual religious life. The Protestant reform hoped to achieve this through a return to the simplicities of biblical times and early Christian centuries, and the Catholic movement attempted an enlightened cleansing of traditional institutions. The Catholic reformers made no doctrinal concessions, however, and reasserted such medieval teachings as free will, salvation through faith and good works, and the necessity of the sacraments as channels of God's favor, with priests serving as mediators between God and human beings. Protestants such as Luther and Calvin rejected such early medieval accretions as the doctrine of *purgatory* (a way station to heaven for the dead who require further purging of sins for which they have repented) and the veneration of saints and holy relics. In addition, the Protestant leaders preached the reduction of the sacraments to two (baptism and Holy Communion), the priesthood of all believers, the bondage of the human will to sin, and the predestination of salvation by God's grace for His chosen ones. Calvin glorified a sterner, less merciful God than Luther's and insisted on ecclesiastical control over the state and a strict regulation of people's behavior. Calvin waged an ambitious campaign against sin in Geneva, Switzerland, and reformist Catholics did the same throughout those lands that they had preserved against Protestant encroachment.

THE ARTS IN AN AGE OF CONFLICT

The middle and late sixteenth century was Europe's most notorious age of religious zeal and strife. In this strife the concept of *heresy* was central—that is, deviant and erroneous theological belief, which must be eradicated at all costs. Protestants shared the concept with Catholics, but no campaign against heresy was as comprehensive as that unleashed by Rome. The Catholic Council of Trent hurled curses upon those who rejected official dogma. The Society of Jesus, the Jesuit order, required stern spiritual and institutional discipline within its own ranks and extended its influence to many straying minds outside. An index of prohibited books warned against subversive ideas in print; and the Inquisition (wherever the secular power allowed it to take root—mainly in Spain) tracked down heretics and turned the most incorrigible over to the state for execution. For

11-1 El Greco, *Cardinal Fernando Niño de Guevara*, c.1600. Oil on canvas, 67¼″ × 42½″. The Metropolitan Museum of Art, New York (bequest of Mrs. H. O. Havemeyer, 1929; the H. O. Havemeyer Collection).

11-2   Juan Bautista de Toledo and Juan de Herrera, El Escorial, 1563–82.

moderns, the intense fervor of the Inquisition is memorably embodied in El Greco's penetrating portrait of the Spanish cardinal Guevara (fig. 11-1), who was made Inquisitor General in 1600.

Quite as symbolic is the great palace, El Escorial (fig. 11-2), built for Philip II near Madrid. In outward demeanor and public policy, Philip was the sternest defender of the faith. His new palace, piously serving also as a monastery, austerely resisted contemporary Spanish trends toward architectural exuberance. It was grimly laid out on a roasting-grill pattern to commemorate the painful martyrdom of Saint Lawrence, on whose name day Spanish arms had triumphed against the less zealous French.

The degree to which the Protestant and Catholic reformations affected the art and music of the time is debatable. The Protestants tended to abhor images of medieval Roman piety and to distrust aesthetic sentiments that might divert the faithful from a purer spirituality. Much destruction of statuary and stained glass resulted. The sterner Protestants similarly distrusted all complexity in sacred music. Calvin, for example, granted pious merit only to the simplest and gravest settings of the psalms. Not until the end of the century did Continental Protestantism produce much memorable music.

The new ethical militancy of Catholicism, too,

had repercussions in the arts. Early in the period of reform, the results were largely negative in all creative realms, since the point was to minimize the diversion of believers from spiritual goals. In the pictorial arts human sexual organs now implied immorality—and the age of the fig leaf and artfully disposed drapery descended upon Europe. Pope Pius V denounced the "sins and scandals" occasioned by the attraction of young people to "fancy music" in the churches during Holy Week, and a church council decried the joviality of certain festive church music that distracted the pious from religion and reduced them to "giggling and immoderate laughter." We should remember, though, that control over musical expression was not unprecedented: the Roman Church had attempted in the past to curb musical complexities that buried the sacred texts. Later in the sixteenth century, however, after the first flush of reformist enthusiasm, many Catholic thinkers came to see value in luxuriant art and music, for these might well compete successfully for souls against the more austere Protestant trends. By the end of the century, and even earlier in Venice, Catholic lands were coming to recognize the power of the arts as spiritual propaganda.

Predictably, clerical attempts to control art and music were often ignored or circumvented. The most celebrated confrontation was that of the painter Paolo

CHRONOLOGY

HISTORY		THE ARTS	
		c. 1488–1576	Titian
1491–1556	Ignatius Loyola	c. 1490–1553	Rabelais
1509–47	Henry VIII king of England	1508–80	Palladio
1509–64	John Calvin		
1515–47	Francis I king of France		
1516–56	Charles I king of Spain	1518–94	Tintoretto
1519–56	Charles V (Charles I of Spain)	1519–59	Château de Chambord
	Holy Roman Emperor	1525–69	Pieter Bruegel the Elder
		c. 1525–94	Palestrina
1527	sack of Rome	1520s–40s	
1530	Loyola's *Spiritual Exercises*	and later	Mannerism flourishing in Florence
1530	the Medici become hereditary		
	dukes of Florence	1532	Rabelais begins *Gargantua* and *Pantagruel*
1534	Ignatius Loyola founds Jesuit order	1532–94	Orlandus Lassus
	(approved by pope in 1540)	1533–92	Montaigne
1534	Henry VIII's final break with		
	Roman Church	1535–36	Sansovino begins the Mint and Library of Saint Mark, Venice
		1536–41	Michelangelo's *Last Judgment* in the Sistine Chapel
		1538	Titian's *Venus of Urbino*
1541–64	Calvin effectively ruling in	1541–1614	El Greco
	Geneva, Switzerland	1543	Copernicus publishes heliocentric theory of universe
		1543–1623	William Byrd
1545–63	Council of Trent: Roman Catholic Church defines dogmas and inaugurates reforms		
1546	death of Martin Luther		
1547–53	Edward VI king of England	1547	Michelangelo becomes architect of Saint Peter's
1547–59	Henry II king of France		
1553–58	Mary I (Bloody Mary) queen of England	1550	Palladio's Rotondo begun

Veronese with the Venetian Inquisition in 1573. Veronese had been charged with the indecorous inclusion of "buffoons, drunkards, Germans, dwarfs, and similar vulgarities" in a huge canvas apparently representing the Last Supper. The artist summarized his position succinctly: "I received the commission to decorate the picture as I saw fit. It is large and, it seemed to me, it could hold many figures." The outcome was largely a victory for the painter; the offending figures remained, and Veronese changed the picture's title to *Feast in the House of Levi*. His defiance of ecclesiastical authority is a symbolic landmark in the long historical struggle for artistic autonomy.

New Dignity for the Arts

As the arts were gaining in prestige, so too were the artists, and it was not simply a matter of special fame for a few outstanding individuals. All competent practitioners of the major arts gained in status as the process of emancipation from the guilds continued, often encouraged by acceptance as equals by scholars and poets. Artists more and more were expected not just to toil as mere craftsmen but to gain broad knowledge through study and travel. In the later sixteenth century, especially in Italy, the most acceptable locale of study was coming to be the new public "academies," such as the Florentine Academy of Design. Only in

(continued)

HISTORY			THE ARTS	
1556–98	Philip II king of Spain		1557–	
1558–1603	Elizabeth I queen of England		c. 1603	Thomas Morley
1559	Peace of Cateau-Cambrésis, ending the French-Spanish war			
1562–98	French wars of religion		1563	Veronese's *Marriage at Cana*
			1563–82	building of El Escorial
1564–76	Maximilian II Holy Roman Emperor		1564–93	Christopher Marlowe
			1564–1616	Shakespeare
			1564–1642	Galileo
1566–84 and later	revolt of United Provinces of the Netherlands from Spain		1573	Paolo Veronese's confrontation with the Inquisition over *Feast in the House of Levi*
1575–76	Great Plague in Venice		1576	Titian beginning the *Pietà* and dies of the plague
1577	fire in Ducal Palace, Venice; beginning of reconstruction		1577–92	Palladio's church of Il Redentore, Venice
1581	United Provinces of the Netherlands declares independence from Spain		1580	publication of Montaigne's first book of *Essays*
1582	Gregorian calendar introduced (still used today)			
1588	Spanish Armada defeated by English: end of Philip II's threat to Elizabeth I		1588	publication of Montaigne's second book of *Essays*
1589–1610	Henry I first Bourbon king of France			
1598	Edict of Nantes grants toleration to Protestants in France, ending French religious wars		early 1600s	*Triumphs of Oriana* madrigals
			1602	Shakespeare's *Hamlet* produced
			1603	Cervantes begins writing *Don Quixote*

later ages were the academies to become grossly conservative; in their first decades they offered exciting opportunities for artistic freedom and the exchange of new ideas.

Once possessed of solid training, whether in an academy or a more traditional workshop, the late-sixteenth-century artist was dependent for his livelihood on traditional patronage sources—that is, the Church, the aristocratic courts, and the wealthy townspeople. The greatly increased production of prints, mainly engravings, further disseminated knowledge of the arts. Interest grew also in the various schools, or styles, of art, and—in a burst of historicism

unprecedented since Roman times—in the art of the two preceding centuries and of antiquity. Symptomatic of the new trend, and certainly contributing to it, was the publication in 1550 of Vasari's *Lives of the Most Excellent Italian Architects, Painters, and Sculptors,* which found much to be admired in such old artists as Masaccio, Donatello, and Giotto.

With music as with the visual arts, patronage remained in the hands of aristocracy, Church, and commoners—in descending order of generosity. Recognized composers and skilled performers sometimes were much honored and did not starve; Palestrina and Lassus, for example, lived very comfortably. Few of them, however, were able to assume the elegant life style of the more celebrated court artists. The function of music followed the patterns of earlier decades, from participation in grand theatrical and festive occasions down to the most modest of social, amateur music making. Music printing became more common, although no more financially beneficial to the composer than before, and at last a sheet of music could be produced in a single impression. (Another novelty of the time was the introduction of modern oval noteheads, as opposed to the older diamonds, squares, and rectangles.) And in a development parallel to that in the visual arts, musical "academies" for the training of amateurs and professionals, and for private performance, sprang up in Italy and, later, in the north.

New and Old in Literature

Signs of the century's immense vitality were also seen in literature. The age produced many of the greatest Western classics, including the lively memoirs of the boastful and capable sculptor Benvenuto Cellini, whom we will meet again later in this chapter. Most of the prominent writing of the age had no direct connection with the visual arts, however. For example, the verses of Torquato Tasso (1544–95) celebrated the chivalric ideal in *Jerusalem Delivered,* and the prose of Miguel de Cervantes (1547–1616) chided that ideal in *Don Quixote.* There was exuberant lust for life in the stories *Gargantua* and *Pantagruel* by François Rabelais (c. 1490–1553), the respected medical doctor who combined a broad humanism with the grotesque crudities of popular farce; his visionary Abbey of Thélème (in *Gargantua* and *Pantagruel*) is not only a satire on the unlovely asceticism of traditional monkishness but a proclamation of the rights of youth, beauty, gentility, and freedom. The life of the Thelemites, both men and women,

> was ordered not by law, statute, or rule, but according to their free will and pleasure. They arose when they pleased. They ate, drank, worked and slept when the spirit moved them. No one awoke them, forced food or drink upon them or *made* them do anything else. Gargantua's plan called for perfect liberty. The only rule of the house was:
>
> DO AS THOU WILT
>
> because men that are free, of gentle birth, well bred, and at home in civilized company possess a natural instinct that inclines them to virtue and saves them from vice.

In the Abbey of Thélème we see a typical ambiguity in Renaissance doctrine: human beings are "naturally" good, but only a well-bred elite can be trusted to fully share and express this goodness. The giant Gargantua embodies not only a boundless zest for life, but a thirst for knowledge of all sorts. The letter of advice sent by Gargantua to his young son Pantagruel, then a student in Paris, proposes a daunting course of study that includes all ancient languages, including Arabic, and a comprehensive study of history, the liberal arts, law, and religion. Since Rabelais's period is the late Renaissance, not the early period when admiration for antiquity tended to shove aside new scientific work, we find Gargantua also insisting that Pantagruel carefully investigate and study all of the sciences. Gargantua believed this broad study would make his son a cultivated individual and a public-spirited contributor to the well-being of society.

The French Renaissance also gave birth to the extensive, probing curiosity and humane skepticism of the *Essays* by Michel de Montaigne (1533–92). In these essays Montaigne explored a wide spectrum of subjects, nearly always overlaid with classical learning and fascinating in their descriptions of the diversity of the human condition. Certainly he went well beyond the individualism and subjectivism of his announced subject, the portrayal of himself. His search for reliable knowledge, sparked by his curiosity, led him to a rather unsettling conclusion—a pervasive skepticism concerning the attainability of final truth, except as an infallible religion might teach it. Often, he believed, the schools of philosophy seemed to cancel each other out, and often the institutions and customs of peoples around the world varied so markedly as to make universal human certainties impossible. Montaigne devoured all information he could find on the many exotic and primitive peoples that Europe was discovering in the sixteenth century, in the Americas and elsewhere, and from this information he derived a relativism that would not flourish widely until centuries later. Ideas, institutions, and ways of life had arisen around the globe to respond to particular places, ages, and circumstances, and virtually everything, Montaigne came to believe, was relative to its setting. Right and wrong themselves were relative to circumstances—a message that his own world and most later ages would find confusing and unpalatable.

France was by no means the only place where literature flowered in the late Renaissance; England's contribution also was immense, especially in poetry and theater. Sometimes the poetry was conventional in thought but memorably expressed. "My Mind to Me a Kingdom Is," traditionally and probably wrongly attributed to Sir Edward Dyer (1543–1607), reflects the Epicureanism of the Hellenistic and ancient Roman worlds:

> My mind to me a kingdom is;
>   Such present joys therein I find
> That it excels all other bliss
>   That earth affords or grows by kind.
> Though much I want which most would have
> Yet still my mind forbids to crave.

("By kind" means "in nature"; "want" here signifies "lack.") The theme and mood are also antique in the pastoral verse "Come Live with Me and Be My Love" by Christopher Marlowe (1564–93):

> Come live with me and be my love,
> And we will all the pleasures prove
> That valleys, groves, hills, and fields,
> Woods, or sleepy mountain yields.

11-3 *William Shakespeare* (the "Chandos Portrait"). National Portrait Gallery, London.

Marlowe broke new ground, however, when he created for posterity the tragic drama *Doctor Faustus,* a classic portrayal of the thirst for comprehensive knowledge and experience. But far above Marlowe, for poetry and especially for the theater, stands the legacy of William Shakespeare (1564–1616, fig. 11-3), in whose monumental series of plays a whole psychological and existential cosmos of human life and aspirations is evoked magnificently. Many people—and not just in English-speaking lands—have found in his work the high point of all Western literature.

Shakespeare's theater was quite different from that of Sophocles or Euripides. *Oedipus the King* and *Medea* were performed before immense audiences, most of the viewers far from the dramatic action. Perhaps partly because of this, the ancient Greek plays were deliberately stylized and made larger and more formal than life. Like those ancient dramas, Shakespeare's plays typically did not use specific stage settings, and they, too, probed deeply into character and the human condition and did so in eloquent verse. Otherwise there were significant differences, mainly arising from the different function of drama in Elizabethan England—it was simply for entertainment—and the intimacy of the new theater building. Shakespeare's audiences were relatively close to the stage, so his characters could be, and were, more intimate with the audience. Staged scenes of recognizable daily life were demanded by theatergoers, and characters were expected to be lifelike. They were also expected to turn to the audience now and then to share their innermost thoughts. Occasional comic touches also were expected, even in the most serious and lofty dramas. Shakespeare's *Hamlet,* a play of very serious intent, has some rather ghoulish bantering in the gravediggers' scene, for example.

The Tragedy of Hamlet, Prince of Denmark was probably completed in 1601 and was certainly produced the following year. Its action begins with the young prince's realization that his father, the late king, was murdered by his brother Claudius, who then assumed the Danish throne and married the old king's widow Gertrude. The former king's ghost demands revenge, but without harming the queen. Hamlet toys with his intended victim so ominously that Claudius tries to kill the prince, at first unsuccessfully but finally succeeding in a scene that destroys nearly all of the main characters, himself included. Before the concluding procession, in which the bodies are removed, Hamlet's friend Horatio sums up the story, a story

> Of carnal, bloody, and unnatural acts,
> Of accidental judgments, casual slaughters,
> Of deaths put on by cunning and forc'd cause,
> And, in this upshot, purposes mistook
> Fall'n on th' inventors' heads. . . .

The central drama of *Hamlet*, however, is much less in these outward acts than in Hamlet's mind and heart. Leaving aside plot complications and dramatic sequence, let us look only at several typical expressions of Hamlet's ambivalent thoughts and emotions. Hamlet can be superbly pensive, as in the famous soliloquy "To be or not to be"; here the crucial lines are

> Thus conscience does make cowards of us all
> And thus the native hue of resolution
> Is sicklied o'er with the pale cast of thought. . . .

This admission of indecision is countered elsewhere either by high spirits or by world-weariness:

> How weary, stale, flat, and unprofitable
> Seem to me all the uses of this world!

Or, in a long prose-speech, Hamlet at first revels— with Renaissance optimism—in the splendid potentialities of man and then declares his disgust with the human species:

> What a piece of work is a man! How noble in reason! How infinite in faculties! In form and moving how express and admirable! In action how like an angel! In apprehension how like a god! The beauty of the world! The paragon of animals! And yet, to me, what is this quintessence of dust? Man delights me not. . . .

Hamlet is one of the most complex characters in Shakespeare's works, and in Renaissance literature. He is an idealist and a sardonic dissembler, a generous man and an avenger, a brooder as well as a man of deep emotion. More typically, in the lineage of Castiglione's *Courtier*, he is a cultivated prince, gentleman, and scholar. If he lacks in any of Gargantua's prescribed skills, it would be in the area of science—an area in which Shakespeare had little interest.

Nonetheless, scientific knowledge grew quickly in the late Renaissance, most notably in anatomy and astronomy. A single half-century, for example, opened with the Copernican theory that not the earth but the sun is the center of the universe and ended with the early astronomical observations of Kepler and Galileo. In addition, there was the exhilarating expansion of Europe's horizons brought by overseas exploration, colonization, and commerce. It was a time of wide-ranging cultural vitality—tempered by a very realistic awareness of the evils of the day and the cyclical changes in history.

LATE RENAISSANCE ART AND ARCHITECTURE

This quick overview of the age's achievement outside the visual and musical arts has singled out only two Italians, Tasso and Galileo—an honorable showing for the peninsula but certainly indicating no Italian monopoly on European culture. In music, however, Italy was increasingly preeminent, while Italian dominance in painting, sculpture, and architecture continued strong. Although there were instances of northern influence on Italy, most artistic currents flowed in the opposite direction; Italian artists went north to work, and northern artists went to Italy to study and absorb the Italian manner. A symbolic memento of this process of absorption is Maerten van Heemskerck's self-portrait (fig. 11-4). The Dutch artist exudes vitality as he turns abruptly to the viewer, while behind him are the untended ruins of the Colosseum, as he had sketched them earlier during his youthful sojourn in Rome. Van Heemskerck was only one of countless contributors to the Italianate style of painting outside Italy.

Other non-Italians seem to have resisted the Italian fascination. Among them was the celebrated Lowlander, Pieter Bruegel the Elder (c. 1525–69), now perhaps the most admired of the sixteenth-century northern artists. Born apparently near the present Dutch-Belgian border, he spent his brief maturity in Antwerp and Brussels, where, despite earlier studies in Rome, his painting retained an almost belligerently native flavor. An example is his famous *Peasant Dance* (fig. 11-5)—an extraordinarily vivid picture of peasant life, unprettified and unsentimentalized.

Northern sculpture still showed the influence of both Italianism and native styles, but most architecture followed the forms of Italian-inspired classicism.

Of course local characteristics, medieval or modern, were not wholly smothered. For example, we see reminiscences of the past in the châteaux of the Loire valley—the elegant country mansions of Francis I and his courtiers. The outline of the immense Château de Chambord (fig. 11-6) still recalls the round towers of fortified feudal castles, while the classical motifs of the superstructure only partially obscure the general impression of luxuriant Gothic fantasy. However, by the beginning of Henry II's reign a purer classicism was seen in French architecture.

The Golden Age of Venetian Art

The most splendid center of European art in the period from 1530 to 1600 was the Most Serene Republic of Venice. For here arose the greatest single school of painting and perhaps also the greatest architecture of the sixteenth century.

Although the Republic possessed many far-flung outposts, the island-city of Venice was, of course, the center—an unlikely city indeed, as it was already sinking slowly into the mud and sand of the Adriatic lagoons. However, the sea was the city's fortune, for seaborne commerce was the main foundation of Venetian wealth. Despite strong competition from Atlantic ports, Venice still claimed the eastern Mediterranean

11-4 Maerten van Heemskerck, *Self-Portrait*, 1553. Panel, 17″ × 21″. Reproduced by permission of the syndics of the Fitzwilliam Museum, Cambridge, England.

as its commercial province. Its leading families had arisen from mercantile origins and for centuries had jealously controlled the tightly *oligarchical* government (rule by a small group). The government was widely

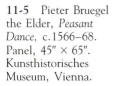

11-5 Pieter Bruegel the Elder, *Peasant Dance*, c.1566–68. Panel, 45″ × 65″. Kunsthistorisches Museum, Vienna.

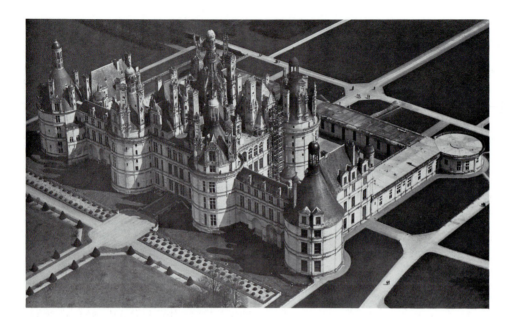

11-6 Château de Chambord, 1519–59.

admired for its stability and businesslike efficiency, but also feared for its autocratic ruthlessness. But the quiet, sinister disappearance of the state's enemies hung not too heavily in the air, for in all but political matters a remarkable tolerance reigned amid the city's luxurious splendor. Even the ferocious Inquisition was kept fairly well leashed. Canals and gondolas, sophisticated grandeur, and festive merriment set the city's style and tone; already it was becoming Europe's carnival and tourist city par excellence.

Long before the sixteenth century the Venetian duke, or *doge*, had been reduced to largely figurehead status. However, his palace, next to the medieval Byzantine basilica of Saint Mark, was the civic focus of the state, since it also housed the Republic's Senate and Council of Ten. The prestige and magnificence of late-sixteenth-century Venice are evident in the colorful grandiosity of the Senate Hall (fig. 11-7), which was rebuilt and redecorated after the fires of 1574 and 1577. Framed within an exuberance of carved and gilded woodwork are some of the most typical and imposing paintings of the period, including Tintoretto's central ceiling canvas, *Venice Enthroned among Gods and Heroes, Receiving the Tribute of the Sea*—a symbolic union of civic pride with fanciful classical allegory.

In Veronese's huge *Marriage at Cana* (fig. 11-8) we get a still more vivid impression of the elaborately festive Venetian spirit. Christ is almost buried among the throng of diners, attendants, onlookers, and musicians; the astonishing biblical miracle of water turned into wine is largely ignored or forgotten. The villagers of Jesus' day have been transformed into comfortable, pleasure-loving Venetians, and dinner music is furnished by a distinguished quartet that includes Veronese, Tintoretto, and (with a large bass viol) the aged Titian. What is visible is not religion but a celebration of Venetian art and hedonism.

The wealthier Venetians loved not only the luxury of their lagoon city but also their hardly less luxurious country estates on the mainland. Venice's greatest architect, Andrea Palladio, prescribed "grandeur and magnificence" for country villas. These qualities are seen most memorably in the famous Rotonda, or Villa Capra (fig. 11-9), in which four severe temple porticoes, colonnaded and pedimented, surround a grand, domed central hall.

The city of Venice had little natural greenery. Perhaps this is the reason that no artistic center contributed more generously to the development of landscape painting. The Venetian nostalgia for country landscapes in the early years of the century is seen in the lyrical canvases of Giorgione (c. 1465–1510) and his colleague Titian (c. 1488–1576). Experts do not agree on the authorship of the Louvre's celebrated *Pas-*

11-7 Senate Hall of the Ducal Palace, Venice, after 1577.

11-8 Paolo Veronese, *Marriage at Cana*, 1563. Oil on canvas, 21′10″ × 32′6″. Louvre, Paris.

11-9   Andrea Palladio, Villa Capra (Rotonda),
near Vicenza, begun 1550.

11-10   Giorgione and/or
Titian, *Pastoral Concert*,
c.1505–10. Oil on
canvas, 43″ × 54″.
Louvre, Paris.

toral Concert (either of the artists might have painted it, or Titian might have finished Giorgione's work), or even on its meaning (it may be an allegory of Poetry)—but the evocation of the sentimental-pastoral ideal is evident, as is the hedonism of subject matter (fig. 11-10). Both of these themes were popular in sixteenth-century Venice, where a relaxed, pleasure-seeking life style could mock the harsh political vicissitudes and moralistic zeal so common in the rest of Europe.

Michelangelo: *The Later Years*

Among the sixteenth-century artists of a sterner breed was the aging Michelangelo. For three decades after the permanent suspension of his work on the Medici Chapel sculpture in 1534, he remained an active artist but turned increasingly to architectural design. He had left Florence, no doubt distressed by the growing Medici despotism, although he never wholly severed his ties with Duke Cosimo I. Establishing himself in Rome on the eve of the Catholic Reformation, Michelangelo has often been taken as the supreme embodiment of that movement—a judgment that must be tempered by recognizing that his profoundly moral orientation

not only antedated the reform but derived from a highly personal spiritual anguish. Michelangelo remained essentially his own man—a free spirit in the individualistic tradition of the Renaissance.

Certainly in his later years he was more and more haunted by the image of death and his consciousness of sin. There is little reason to doubt the sincerity of his poetic plea to the Cross of Christ, in 1532, and his despair that he was "so close to death and yet so far from God." This was the mood in which he created the majestic imagery of the *Last Judgment* on the Sistine Chapel altar wall (see fig. 10-26).

In this grandiose mural painting—with no architecturally prescribed divisions as with the ceiling paintings—Michelangelo evoked an immense, terrifying vision of Christ's final disposition of all humanity. As Matthew's Gospel predicted, heaven and earth here have passed away; except for several graves no specific location of the whirling panorama is suggested. The lack of overall perspective and the unnatural muting of colors further underline the fresco's visionary quality. In most of the fresco, and even in the figure of Christ the Judge (fig. 11-11), most of the prominent male bodies are almost grotesquely bulky; physical beauty is

11-11 Michelangelo, *Christ the Judge,* detail from *The Last Judgment,* altar wall of the Sistine Chapel (fig. 10-26), 1536–41. Vatican, Rome.

not relevant in humanity's final drama. The Virgin averts her eyes as the ultimate scene of Christian history is activated by Christ's decisive gesture. The dead arise, saints as well as sinners, to be consigned to eternal salvation or damnation.

Except for two important works in the Vatican's Pauline Chapel, the *Last Judgment* was Michelangelo's last major painting. Most likely the infirmities of age were more the cause of his abandoning the art than was his disgust with the *Judgment's* first mutilations in the name of modesty. (Keen-eyed clerics were still spotting offenses to modesty as late as the eighteenth century, when the retouching of nude figures finally stopped.) In old age, Michelangelo worked sporadically in sculpture, although he was working on his last Pietà only a few days before his death in 1564. His later years were especially occupied with architecture. Michelangelo's architectural technique reflected his sculptural background, for he seems never to have inaugurated his architectural projects with mathematical calculations but with terracotta (baked clay) models. An emphasis

on sculpturesque form, with the play of light and shadow, was the natural result.

The two greatest architectural projects of Michelangelo's old age were his designs for the square and the three palace facades of the Capitoline Hill in Rome—a distinguished contribution to the developing art of urban planning—and his supervision of the ongoing construction of Saint Peter's Basilica. At Saint Peter's his main impact was on the external unity of the structure (except when seen today from the front, after the later extension of the nave) and the general form of the great dome. Figure 11-12 reveals much of Michelangelo's intent: massive, almost monolithic compactness. Note the colossal Corinthian style, with its traditional, stylized leafy capitals and the large pilasters that unite more than one level of windows. Also notice the ribbed, multiwindowed dome, which seems to press upward to the skies instead of downward on the building mass. These devices were to become common in three centuries of Western architecture.

Venetian Architecture

Sixteenth-century Venice found itself closer to Michelangelo in architecture than in painting or sculpture. Venetian architects, too, were extending the possibilities of an expressive language basically classical in style. Jacopo Sansovino (1486–1570) was an adopted Venetian whose classical conceptions could be even sterner than Michelangelo's. In La Zecca (the Mint), Sansovino superimposed severe classical motifs on earlier Renaissance domestic architecture, while rough horizontal bands make the columns peculiarly sturdy and forbidding (fig. 11-13). In his most famous building, the Library of Saint Mark, adjacent to the Mint (see fig. 11-13), the decoration is much more luxuriant and is based wholly on classical inspiration. Like the Mint, though, it contains heavily molded forms—and the deep-set arcades at street level and the recessed windows above create strong contrasts of light and shadow.

Still more celebrated than Sansovino was Andrea Palladio (1508–80), who through his writings and example vitally influenced European—and American—building for hundreds of years. One of his villas has already demonstrated for us his adaptation of antique elements to sixteenth-century use (see fig. 11-9); one of his churches can serve the same purpose. Il Redentore (the Church of the Redeemer) was built by

11-12 Michelangelo et al., Saint Peter's, Rome.

11-13 Jacopo Sansovino, La Zecca (the Mint), *left,* 1535–45; and the Library of Saint Mark, *right,* begun in 1536 and finished by Scamozzi in 1588; Venice.

the city to commemorate its deliverance from the plague in 1575–76 (fig. 11-14). The doge and the senators made an annual procession on foot from their palace to this church, with the aid of temporary pontoon bridges across two wide canals. The facade owes its impact especially to its graceful, geometrical calm in this city of lavish architectural exuberance. The deliberately incomplete pediment extending sideways beyond the foremost high pediment suggests one temple front behind another—a typical Palladian theme.

Mannerism

To historians the word *Renaissance* has often seemed misleading, and most historians probably would welcome a satisfactory substitute. When it was suggested in recent times that the artistic approach and perhaps even the whole civilization of the middle and late sixteenth century could best be described by a new term, *Mannerism,* many scholars embraced the term enthusiastically. *Mannerism* has indeed entered the useful vocabulary of cultural history. In this book, however, we will refer to the whole period not as the Mannerist age but as the *late Renaissance. Mannerism* will be restricted to one specific movement among several movements in the visual arts.

Mannerism was an all-European phenomenon, although our examples will be largely Florentine. It arose spontaneously out of the Renaissance, whose balance it disturbed by reveling in the technical advances of such masters as Leonardo, Raphael, and Michelan-

11-14 Andrea Palladio, Il Redentore, Venice, 1577–92.

gelo. Traditional classical and naturalistic approaches were not wholly forgotten by Mannerists, but they received much less emphasis than virtuoso performance and refinement of style. Indeed, Mannerism tended to be "the stylish style"—a game of skill in overcoming formal difficulties and a search for visual effect, elegance, and the consciously artificial. In this sense, Mannerism is a characteristic of more than just the sixteenth century. It appears again and again in Western history—as a prominent ingredient of late medieval art, the eighteenth-century Rococo style, and much of the art of the present day. It embodies an urge toward art for art's sake rather than toward art that serves social needs. It is art as virtuosity, as form rather than message. Such art may fulfill a human aesthetic need, but it often fails to touch the heart.

We will now glance at four works of sixteenth-century painting and sculpture that are universally considered Mannerist. An air of utter unreality pervades an early masterpiece of the Mannerist school, *The Descent from the Cross*, or *The Entombment* (fig. 11-15), by Jacopo Pontormo (1494–1557). The title is in doubt since no physical setting for the figures is indicated. This omission, which has been normal enough in the history of sculpture, becomes in the painting of the sixteenth century a startling instance of artificiality. In this work, and often elsewhere in Mannerist painting, the absence of natural setting is reinforced by a superposition of human figures that crowd forward toward the picture plane. Nearly all natural sense of space is lost. Figures are sometimes elongated, and gestures and postures are exaggerated, while stylish serpentine lines twist gracefully through the composition. As an ultimate surprise and affront to the viewer's first impression, the pink torso of the foreground crouching figure turns out to be not flesh but a skintight jacket. Yet, despite virtuosity of execution and poignant facial expression, the work has a rather metallic coldness that scarcely touches the human emotions; its beauty is disembodied and formal.

In the celebrated *Allegory of Venus and Cupid* (fig. 11-16) by Agnolo Bronzino (1503–72), the most prominent feeling is of an explicit eroticism. The title now is thought to be *Exposure of Luxury*, but any moral lesson is clearly subordinate to sensual appeal. Forthright sensuality was one emotional indulgence that many Mannerists were prepared to offer their aristocratic patrons—and all the more blatantly through ef-

fects that shunned sentimental softness and reserve.

Much sixteenth-century sculpture also can be called Mannerist. Certainly many works of Benvenuto Cellini (1500–71) would handily fall within that category—such as his marble *Narcissus* (fig. 11-17). Narcissus was the handsome youth who scorned the love of others and was condemned to love only himself. The statue portrays him twisting his body beside a pool of water to gaze lovingly at his own reflection. This was an inspired choice of subject matter for Mannerist sculpture—not only in its sensuality but as a demonstration of virtuosity in sculptural line that is both tortured and graceful.

11-15 Jacopo Carucci da Pontormo, *The Descent from the Cross (The Entombment)*, 1525–28. Panel, 10′3″ × 6′4″. Santa Felicità, Florence.

11-16 Agnolo Bronzino, *Allegory of Venus and Cupid (Exposure of Luxury)*, c. 1546. Panel, 61″ × 57″. Reproduced by courtesy of the Trustees, The National Gallery, London.

11-17 Benvenuto Cellini, *Narcissus*, 1547. Marble. Museo Nazionale, Florence.

By the middle of the century, Mannerism in the visual arts tended somewhat more toward the academic and the classically imitative than before. The results were mostly mediocre—except perhaps in the sculpture of Giovanni Bologna (1529–1608), a Fleming whose art (and name) had become wholly Italianized. His huge marble group, the *Rape of a Sabine Woman* (fig. 11-18), resembles ancient Roman copies of complex Hellenistic works. Unlike almost all earlier Renaissance sculpture, it was not designed for predominantly frontal view; its melodrama is equally effective from many angles.

Venetian and Spanish Painting

Despite such extraordinary features as its canals and its protective isolation from most mainland dangers, the great port of Venice was very much a part of the real world. Presumably its painters and their patrons found Florentine Mannerism cold and effete; in any case, Venetian painting remained overwhelmingly within the vigorous tradition of the earlier Renaissance. This traditionalism did not mean a lack of originality or subtlety, however. Not only did Venice see the large-scale triumph of oil painting on canvas (the city's damp sea air caused premature deterioration of frescoes and wood panels)—it also perfected a refined treatment of color that for centuries would be the foundation of Western painting. In both developments, the unquestioned leader was the prolific, long-lived Titian (Tiziano Vecellio (c. 1488–1576). By the end of the century Europe was in general agreement with the painter Lomazzo's assessment of Titian as "the sun

11-18   Giovanni Bologna, *Rape of a Sabine Woman*, 1579–83. Marble, 13′5″ high. Loggia dei Lanzi, Florence.

amid small stars not only among the Italians but all the painters of the world."

An adopted Venetian, Titian above all established the supremacy of color in painting—color not as the mere fleshing-out of forms enclosed by lines but as the basic material of which those forms are built. The glossy detail of *tempera* painting (using pigments in a water-miscible medium, usually including egg yolk) was replaced by the richer, more transparent tones and broader brushwork possible with oil-based paint. For Titian and those who came after him, color was virtually the equivalent of light. In fact, as time passed, Titian grew bolder in his use of color and softer and more voluptuous in his forms. His *Venus of Urbino* (fig. 11-19) shows this voluptuousness in both subject and technique.

During a Roman visit in 1545–46, Titian approached a very different subject—Pope Paul III and

his grandsons (fig. 11-20). One of history's keenest portraitists, Titian eloquently revealed the aloof refinement of Cardinal Alessandro Farnese, the suavity of his brother Ottavio, and the alert shrewdness of the aged pontiff who was both the last of the hedonistic Renaissance popes and the sponsor of the Catholic Reformation. Since the painting was not wholly finished, its brushwork is lively and rather sketchy. However, Titian's last work, the splendid *Pietà* (fig. 11-21), affirms a similarly broad but magnificently evocative style. Strong effects are achieved within a small range of colors—in the ghostly statues in the background, the luminosity of the distraught Magdalene's robe, and the supernatural paleness of Christ's body. The *Pietà* is a final, powerful monument to one of art's most comprehensive geniuses.

The greatest among the following generation of Venetian painters was Jacopo Robusti, known as Tintoretto (1518–94). The historian Vasari's description of his work as "swift, resolute, fantastic, and extravagant" seems essentially sound. Starting with tiny, wax-figure models arranged in a boxed stage with a grid across the stage front, he would sketch a projected scene and have his assistants enlarge it and block it in on canvas, using a larger grid, before he began to paint. Trademarks of his style are startling effects with foreshortening and light, as seen in the *Discovery of the Body of Saint Mark* (fig. 11-22). Tintoretto avoided Mannerism by giving his paintings intense human and spiritual drama, and mere formal virtuosity was almost never the outcome. The miracles of Christianity were his favorite subject. In the *Discovery* canvas the patron saint of Venice miraculously appears to the Christians who are opening tombs in Alexandria to locate his remains. When Saint Mark identifies his own body, he orders the ghoulish search ended.

From ghostly Christian melodrama Tintoretto sometimes turned to the lighter realms of classical mythology, although without the voluptuous overtones of Titian. However, Tintoretto always returned to religion—as in the *Last Supper* (fig. 11-23), on which he was working at the time of his death. Appropriate to the zealous dogmatism of the Catholic Reformation and to Tintoretto's personal faith, the scriptural moment chosen is not Jesus' prediction of his betrayal but his distribution of bread and wine as his body and blood—that is, the instituting of the Eucharist. A greater contrast to Veronese's *Marriage at Cana* (see fig. 11-8) could hardly be found than Tintoretto's solemn

11-19 Titian, *Venus of Urbino,* 1538. Oil on canvas, 46″ × 65″. Uffizi, Florence.

canvas, even with its normal Venetian complement of bustling servants. With typical concentration on pictorial depth—Christ is well to the rear, and the hall stretches out into near-darkness—the artist gave the greatest luminosity to the spiritual glow of Christ himself, and then to the flaming lamp and the halos of the Apostles. Heavenly creatures, eerily outlined, flutter through the air to bring a final touch of otherworldliness to the mysterious scene.

Still more otherworldly and mysterious was much of the work of Domenikos Theotokopoulos (1541–1614), known as El Greco ("the Greek"). He had arrived in Venice by 1560—a natural move for the budding painter, since his native Crete was under Venetian rule and Venice was the greatest art center of Italy. After some time in Titian's workshop he settled in Rome, but it was not until he was in his thirties, upon going to Spain, that his extraordinary gifts were fully evident. Scholarly argument about the proportionate influences of his Byzantine background, Venetian training, Spain, and Catholicism on El Greco's art will probably never be fully resolved—and in any case, his own genius was surely still more crucial. We can note, however, that he did nearly all his work in the service of the Roman Church and produced his best

11-20 Titian, *Pope Paul III and His Grandsons,* 1545–46. Oil on canvas, 83″ × 69″. Capodimonte Museum, Naples.

11-21 Titian (finished by Jacopo Palma the Younger), *Pietà*, 1576. Oil on canvas, 11′6″ × 12′9″. Galleria dell' Accademia, Venice.

11-22 Tintoretto, *Discovery of the Body of Saint Mark*, 1562–66. Oil on canvas, 13′2″ × 13′2″. Pinacoteca di Brera, Milan.

11-23 Tintoretto, *Last Supper*, 1592–94. Oil on canvas, 12′ × 18′8″. San Giorgio Maggiore, Venice.

work in the Spain of the Catholic Reformation, where the air was saturated with mystic Christian zeal. Nationally famous in his own day (the principal skeptic was the artistically conservative Philip II, who gave him only two commissions), El Greco was misunderstood and largely forgotten in later centuries. His revived, international fame dates from nineteenth-century romanticism and twentieth-century rejection of pictorial realism.

The subject of Christ on the Mount of Olives, in *The Agony in the Garden* (fig. 11-24), offered splendid opportunities for El Greco's spiritual drama. The betrayal of Christ by Judas is at hand (note the approaching soldiers at the right). Christ has come with three disciples to the mount to pray, and as the disciples sleep he is strengthened in his agony by the appearance of an angel from heaven (Luke 22:39–53). The visionary quality of the scene is enhanced by a mystical play of luminous highlights, cool colors, and the icy gray of much of the background, but especially by the contortion and distortion of forms in space. The rock behind

Christ becomes a billowing cloak; the cave where the disciples sleep becomes a distant cloud on which the angel stands—and yet the angel's garment passes in front of the foreground tree branches. The unreality of space is carried even beyond Mannerism, while other qualities reject the Mannerist style altogether. A slashing brush technique mocks the elegant, enamel-like clarity of the most typical Mannerism, while cool formalism is rejected in favor of emotion and dramatic tension.

In *Christ Driving the Money Changers from the Temple* (fig. 11-25), the agitation is more physical than spiritual. As in the *Agony*, cool but sharply differentiated and highlighted colors prevail, contrasted with deep shadow. Figures are elongated and attenuated. It is interesting to note that the deliberate distortions in El Greco's work coexist with his use of Tintoretto's peculiarly literalistic wax-model technique.

Inner vision conquers outer reality in his famous *View of Toledo* (fig. 11-26). Not only is the topography of the artist's adopted city altered and rearranged, but

11-24 El Greco, *The Agony in the Garden*, c.1590. Oil on canvas, 40¼″ × 44¾″. The Toledo Museum of Art, Toledo, Ohio (gift of Edward Drummond Libbey).

11-25 El Greco, *Christ Driving the Money Changers from the Temple*, c.1584–1604. Oil on canvas, 42″ × 51″. Reproduced by courtesy of the Trustees, The National Gallery, London.

11-26 El Greco, *View of Toledo*, 1595–1614. Oil on canvas, 47¾″ × 42¾″. The Metropolitan Museum of Art, New York (bequest of Mrs. H. O. Havemeyer, 1929; the H. O. Havemeyer Collection).

the scene has a dramatic urgency seldom found even with the more obvious medium of active human figures. Heaven and earth meet in an upward surge of hill and buildings against a cataclysm of threatening clouds. Is it Catholic dynamism or individual genius? The second hypothesis seems quite reasonable, without denying El Greco's overall spiritual symbolism in an age of extraordinary stress and conflict.

MUSIC IN THE AGE OF PALESTRINA AND BYRD

Stress and conflict can also be found in music of the middle and late sixteenth century, most obviously in highly expressive motets. Unfortunately today's casual listener, overwhelmed by the volume, rhythmic excitement, and harmonic freedom of much modern music, may find this music bland. However, with a bit more listening, it is possible to sense its complexity,

subtlety, and internal tension. In developing the implications of Josquin's earlier innovations toward euphony, freedom, and expressiveness, the late sixteenth century was, above all, an age of fulfillment and culmination in music—one of the greatest in musical history. There is a clear parallel with the colorful painting of Venice as an extension of earlier Renaissance achievement. The emotional peaks of El Greco and Lassus are much less typical of their age than is the balanced richness of Titian and Palestrina.

In technique and structure, as well as in general spirit and effect, music after Josquin continued and amplified his methods. Only a handful of musical modes continued to be used, including the modern major scale. *Chromaticism*—the use of half-tone intervals where whole-tones might be expected—was increasingly employed for expressive effect, often making nonsensical any pretense of modality, with its fixed orderings of whole- and half-tones. Polyphonic and chordal music flourished side by side, frequently in the same work, sacred or secular. In sacred music, *polychoral* composition (requiring two or more choirs) was by no means a rarity even outside of Venice, where the two organs of Saint Mark's Basilica encouraged its use.

Instrumental music, too, took on a great variety of forms. Already the principle of the *suite* was becoming common—the loose grouping together of several short pieces, most commonly dances. Here the lute and the stringed keyboard instruments led the way toward the splendid multimovement compositions of later periods. Another innovation of great later significance was the introduction of the violin. The richly sonorous violin family would compete for nearly two centuries with the viol family before the definitive triumph of violin-type instruments in the eighteenth century.

The historical development of musical performance, instrumental and vocal, before 1600 largely continued the trends of the earlier Renaissance, although there is evidence of still greater interpretive freedom and expressiveness. Few precise indications have survived concerning improvisation, embellishment, tempo, and dynamics.

Employment of specific instruments in the post-Josquin period remained fairly haphazard, aside from such contexts as drama and formal dance or out of acoustical necessity. For example, trumpets and percussion were not used for intimate, genteel soirées, nor lutes and virginals for ceremonial processions. But in-

11-27 Philippe Galle, after Johannes Stradanus, *A Religious Service*, 1590s. Engraving, 9″ × 11″. Print Collection of the Bibliothèque Royale Albert I, Brussels.

struments were not yet chosen for strictly musical effects beyond the obvious requirements of range and technical facility. In sacred performance they were still often used to double the vocal parts or to supplement them. An old print (fig. 11-27) depicts musicians at a Roman Catholic religious service. Singers and instrumentalists are gathered into two groups before two lecterns with enormous scores visible to all, apparently for a polychoral performance.

Music on the European Continent

Giovanni Pierluigi (c. 1525–94), named Palestrina after his birthplace, was for centuries the only sixteenth-century composer generally known to the musically literate public. Certainly there are many appealing qualities in his work. In sheer ease and fluency of composition his sacred music has seldom been rivaled. The intelligibility of his texts is outstanding; verbal syllabification in chordal passages is precisely matched in all parts. Palestrina's musical texture is almost never muddy but open and clean—a result of both his own artistic lucidity and the injunctions of the Catholic

reform movement. At the same time, the expressive effect of his work derives far more from the music than the words. In fact, he paid less attention to word-color than did his contemporaries, and his dissonances are promptly resolved.

The best-known of Palestrina's works is his early *Pope Marcellus Mass*, dedicated eventually to the memory of this pontiff who in a three-week reign particularly promoted simplicity and clarity in sacred music. The work is basically modal and is "freely" composed— that is, is not based on preexisting melodies, as most of his other masses were. It has supreme musical and verbal clarity as well as rhythmic, harmonic, and emotive subtleties.

We will consider especially the Benedictus and Hosanna sections from the Sanctus part of the *Pope Marcellus Mass*. The four-part Benedictus ("Blessed is he that cometh in the name of the Lord") is wholly polyphonic in construction: the musical lines move with melodic and rhythmic independence but form a pleasing whole. The Hosanna ("Hosanna in the highest"), in six parts, is largely polyphonic, although its beginning is *chordal*: all parts move together to support the melody. This straightforward chordal solidity on the opening *Hosanna* musically expresses Christian unity in the praising of God.

Palestrina's motet style resembles that of his masses. Free of some of the devices used by his musical contemporaries, his motets possess warmth and human feeling. An example of this warmth is his setting of *Super flumina Babylonis* (from the *Second Book of Motets for Four Voices*), with its nostalgia for the Hebrew homeland ("By the rivers of Babylon, there we sat down, yea, we wept, when we remembered Zion").

Palestrina spent virtually his whole career in Rome, and practically all of his compositions are religious. On the other hand, Orlandus Lassus (Roland de Lattre, or Orlando di Lasso, 1532–94) was a French-speaking Netherlander who composed in all the vocal forms of his day and in such diverse centers as Naples, Rome, Antwerp, Paris, and (for nearly four decades) Munich. The most genial introduction to his work may be his secular part-songs, whose texts are variously in French, Italian, and German. For instance, *Matona mia cara* ("My dear lady") is an Italian song in German accent and Germanized vocabulary—a jolly product of the eighteen-year-old composer's Neapolitan period. Italians found the accent of the German-Swiss mercenary troops amusing and greatly enjoyed this sort of spoofing. Lassus's song is chordal and seems perfectly straightforward except for the variations in the different verses. Lassus also composed hundreds of German songs, French chansons, and Italian madrigals. He is most remembered for his hundreds of motets, some of them unsurpassed in sacred musical literature.

Lassus's motet style is notable for its expressive dependence on the words. Thus his work is in the tradition of Josquin des Prez, toward the minimizing of such formal techniques as imitation and *cantus firmus* except for specific expressive effect. Contrasts of musical mood, following the text, are sometimes sudden and unexpected, and the rhythm is sometimes broken by *syncopations* (off-beat rhythms). Lassus applied these devices most notably to texts of intense emotion, as did Josquin.

Two great motets exemplify the Lassus style. One of them is *Nos qui sumus* ("We who live in this world, in the depths of vice, and have suffered shipwrecks—glorious Saint Nicholas, lead us to the safe port where we will find peace and glory"). The tone is set by the anguished opening cries: the four lines are widely separated, as if in spiritual isolation. The plea to Saint Nicholas reflects a change of mood: the new, bouncier

rhythm suggests the hope of saintly intervention. Our other example is *Tristis est anima mea*. It records, in five vocal lines, Christ's words to his disciples before his betrayal: "My soul is exceeding sorrowful, even unto death: tarry ye here, and watch with me." As Jesus predicts the soldierly tumult that will surround him (*"quae circumdabit me"*), the quick repetitions and chromaticism indicate excitement—and the flight of the Apostles is soon heard in the descending lines of *"vos fugam capietis."* Throughout, contrast between the polyphony of the subjective passages and the chordality of the declarative passages is highly effective. This relatively short motet encompasses a whole spiritual, theatrical drama.

English Music

From intense, Roman Catholic religiosity we now turn to light-hearted Elizabethan England and its music. The different atmosphere can be sensed even in the comparative degree of architectural pretension. Longleat House (fig. 11-28), for example, may seem a paragon of friendly informality next to Philip II's forbidding Escorial (see fig. 11-2), although both are classically inspired buildings of the late Renaissance. English gentlemen competed among themselves in the building of palatial homes fit for housing the queen and her court on their travels through the country.

For the entertainment of royalty and the aristocracy, music ranked high among possible diversions. Queen Elizabeth herself was an accomplished performer on the virginal, and in her youth she had done some composing. Although aristocratic patronage of music often lagged, upper- and middle-class Elizabethans must have had much practical acquaintance with music and an appreciation for the humane value of the art. Through young Lorenzo, in *The Merchant of Venice*, Shakespeare surely spoke for many of his contemporaries:

The man that hath no music in himself,
Nor is not moved with concord of sweet sounds,
Is fit for treason, stratagems, and spoils.
The motions of his spirit are dull as night
And his affections dark as Erebus:
Let no such man be trusted.

Many of the sweetest sounds from the Elizabethan and subsequent Jacobean periods came from the pen of William Byrd (1543–1623). This composer's earthly fame and modest fortune were rather remarkable in an

11-28 Sir John Thynne and Robert Smythson, Longleat House, Warminster, Wiltshire, c.1568–80.

age of religious intolerance, for he contrived to be a successful Catholic musician in a land that had irrevocably broken with Rome. He served the Anglican Church continuously throughout his long career.

In his Latin motets, which enjoyed a flourishing Continental, Catholic market, his techniques are those of his Continental contemporaries. He used the older modes—recognizable in the melodies and their endings, or *cadences*—as well as the modern *diatonic* (major and minor) scales. (The diatonic system ordinarily implies harmonic focal points—"restful" chords—instead of what may seem to us the rather unfocused musical lines of modal writing.) Byrd's favorite texts were deeply devotional, although generally less emotional than those of Lassus. A well-known example is the four-part *Ave verum corpus* ("Hail, true body, born of the Virgin Mary"), which exhibits a rather rarefied but heartfelt piety.

In his writing for the Anglican Church, Byrd composed both choral music and songs to be sung as solos with instrumental accompaniment. *Blessed Is He that Fears the Lord,* for example, could be performed either way; it is particularly effective as a solo accompanied by a quartet of viols. Like Byrd's other Anglican anthems, it is polyphonic, with the voice an integral part of the polyphonic web. In his accompanied secular songs, such as the delicately elegant lullaby *My Sweet Little Darling,* the vocal line has greater melodic independence, and the accompaniment tends more toward *homophony* (the chordal style) than polyphony. Byrd is one of a long line of contributors to the modern art song.

In Byrd's day *My Sweet Little Darling* could have been performed with accompaniment by lute or viols, or by a stringed keyboard instrument—usually the virginal, a predecessor of the harpsichord. Byrd also wrote pieces for these instruments. Among such instrumental works are a number of *fantasias*—a form that can involve "flights of fancy," usually polyphonic, on a number of different themes. Byrd's *Second Fantasia for Six Parts* is rhythmically complex and polyphonically imitative throughout, except for two dancelike sections toward the end, the first of these being a version of the perennially popular *Greensleeves.* Intended for an ensemble of viols, this fantasia is among the distinguished ancestors of later chamber and orchestral music.

Byrd was in the vanguard in all the important forms of late Renaissance English music except the *madrigal;* the English madrigal was essentially an import from Italy. A madrigal is a relatively brief secular composition with words in the language of everyday life, usually for unaccompanied voices. In their heyday, madrigals were never sung by large choruses but rather one voice to a part.

Madrigal texts could be lighthearted or serious; their themes were often pastoral or mythological, and above all they dealt with human love. Some of the best-remembered madrigals today are by Thomas Morley (1557–c. 1603) and are in a decidedly lighthearted vein. Typical are the catchy *Now Is the Month of Maying* and *Sing We and Chant It.* Both have a succession of verses, each rounded off by a lively and florid passage of *Fa la la*'s. The verses are set chordally in five parts and with strong, bouncing rhythm. The *Fa la la*'s are only a bit more complex, with some imitation between melodic lines. It is easy to appreciate the forthright appeal of these lively songs of youth, joy, and love.

Often more serious, and always more complex, are the madrigals in a large collection edited by Morley entitled *The Triumphs of Oriana.* Two of Morley's own compositions are among these, and more than twenty other madrigalists contributed to the project. The pieces have a common refrain: "Then sang the shepherds and nymphs of Diana: Long live fair Oriana." Since Oriana represented the aging Queen Elizabeth, several tardy contributors, after the queen's death in 1603, altered the final line to "In Heav'n lives Oriana" or "Farewell, fair Oriana."

Some of the finest English madrigals were written by Thomas Weelkes (c. 1575–1623); his contribution to the Oriana series may be the best in that collection. His *As Vesta Was from Latmos Hill Descending* is spirited and charming:

> As Vesta was from Latmos hill descending,
> She spied a maiden Queen the same ascending,
> Attended on by all the shepherds swain;
> To whom Diana's darlings came running down amain.
> First two by two, then three by three together.
> Leaving their goddess all alone, hasted thither;
> And mingling with the shepherd of her train,
> With mirthful tunes her presence did entertain.
> Then sang the shepherds and nymphs of Diana:
> Long live fair Oriana.

Beginning in four parts and expanding to six, the madrigal setting precisely reflects the words "two by two," "three by three," and "together"—not to mention the solo soprano on "all alone." "Ascending," "descending," and "running down amain," of course, receive correspondingly appropriate treatment. The polyphonic complexities are greatest in the extended refrain, with its exhilarating interweavings of the phrase "Long live fair Oriana." This madrigal will serve as our cheerful farewell to an age that also was complex—the marvelously rich and varied sixteenth century.

Recommended Reading

Burke, Peter. *Montaigne* (1981). Good coverage of main achievements and ideas.

Ergang, Robert. *The Renaissance* (1967). Historical overview of all aspects of the Renaissance.

Foote, Timothy. *The World of Bruegel* (1968). Fine introduction to life and times of Pieter Bruegel the Elder.

Goldron, Romain. *Music of the Renaissance* (1968). Handy introduction, illustrated.

Hartt, Frederick. *History of Italian Renaissance Art: Painting, Sculpture, Architecture* (1969). Fine, comprehensive study.

Holst, Imogen. *Byrd* (1972). Brief but understandable, with many illustrations.

Koenigsberger, H. G., and George L. Mosse. *Europe in the Sixteenth Century* (1968). Good historical survey.

Montaigne, Michel de. *Selected Essays*, trans. by Charles Cotton and W. C. Hazlitt, rev. and ed. by Blanchard Bates (1949). Standard translation, modernized.

Pignatti, Terisio, and Kenneth Donahue. *The Golden Century of Venetian Painting* (1979). Pictures with notes; good coverage.

Pope-Hennessy, John. *Cellini* (1985). Comprehensive, excellent.

Ross, James Bruce, and Mary Martin McLaughlin, eds. *The Portable Renaissance Reader* (1958). Collection of primary sources.

Rowse, A. L. *Shakespeare the Elizabethan* (1977). His career and historical setting, well-illustrated.

Shakespeare, William. Plays (many editions).

Shearman, John K. G. *Mannerism* (1967). Good introduction.

Tietze, Hans. *Tintoretto: The Paintings and Drawings* (1948). Long essay, many illustrations.

Wangermée, Robert. *Flemish Music and Society in the Fifteenth and Sixteenth Centuries* (1968). A big, handsome art book with good text.

Williams, Jay. *The World of Titian* (1968). Introduction to Titian's life, times, and art.

12

The Flowering of the Baroque: 1600–1660

In politics and international relations the first six decades of the seventeenth century were as unsettled as the late Renaissance period. Italy, badly disunited but overshadowed and partially protected by Spanish Hapsburg connections, knew greater internal peace than most lands and enjoyed creative abundance in the musical and visual arts. Elsewhere in Europe the uncertain shiftings of power were typically accompanied by dissension and strife. The worst was over in the Low Countries, where the southern provinces (modern Belgium) remained under Spanish control, and the northern provinces (the United Netherlands, or "Holland") required only sporadic efforts to maintain their new independence, at last formally recognized in 1648. Germany was the area worst mangled by actual warfare: the Thirty Years' War (1618–48), which involved nearly all the Continental powers, was fought largely on German soil and left the land not only more disunited than ever but cruelly ravaged and depopulated. The German state that was perhaps least unfortunate militarily and territorially was Brandenburg-Prussia, tentatively on its way to becoming a great European power. Far more successful for the moment, however, were the northern Protestant states of Sweden and the United Netherlands. England, although commercially and colonially active, was torn internally by political, religious, and social differences, which finally erupted in civil war; a Puritan republic (1649–60) followed the defeat of the monarchy by Oliver Cromwell.

299

Meantime on the Continent, both branches of the Catholic Hapsburg family—the Holy Roman emperors and the Spanish monarchs—were declining precipitously in power. The reign of Philip IV (1621–65) saw a splendid flowering of Spanish drama and painting, but also a serious decay in Spanish economic and political life and the final breaking away of Holland and Portugal. The Peace of the Pyrenees with France (1659) would be Spain's gravest symbolic humiliation.

By 1659 France was on the eve of its greatest era of military and cultural prestige. French history had already witnessed the rise of the medieval monarchy, the expulsion of the English from French soil, and the growth of *royal absolutism*—the exercise of virtually unlimited monarchial power. Around 1600, after interruption by several decades of domestic religious warfare, the French nation-state resumed its march toward predominance in Europe. Henry IV, the first monarch (1589–1610) of the Bourbon family, was enthusiastically reestablishing French power and prestige, and his work would be continued by Cardinals Richelieu and Mazarin, advisors of Louis XIII (1610–43) and Louis XIV (1643–1715), respectively.

This was, of course, an age of notable European expansion overseas. The Dutch and English were succeeding the Spanish and the Portuguese as the most aggressive empire builders. The Dutch had substantial trade with all continents and often took territorial possession as well; it was only in 1664 that they lost their important North American seaboard holdings to England, with New Amsterdam becoming New York. Throughout the 1600s Holland and the other European countries conducted their commercial and industrial affairs according to the theory of *mercantilism*—a crude sort of protectionism for the presumed good of the state. For better or worse, Europe was starting to take on a modern look in trade and industry.

THE POST-RENAISSANCE WORLD

The seventeenth century and the earlier years of the eighteenth constitute the age generally known to historians of the Western world as *Baroque.* Of obscure derivation (it may be derived from the Portuguese word for an irregular pearl), *Baroque* today commonly describes a number of stylistic trends of the post-Renaissance age.

Those who apply the term to political forms stress the governmental absolutism of the time. Autocratic rule was being supported by new absolutist theories, the most striking being that of the Englishman Thomas Hobbes (1588–1679). Hobbes's *Leviathan* (1651) grounded his political view on a thoroughly materialistic conception of the universe and the need for political stability to promote selfish human needs and wants. He deliberately ignored a traditional religious argument for royal absolutism: the citing of Old Testament paternalism as a precedent—and excuse—for vesting all governing power in one person.

As we noted in chapter 11 in our discussion of the primitivist thought of Montaigne, the early modern period (from the Renaissance through the eighteenth century) knew a bit about "primitive" peoples—and a few authors, like Montaigne, reported descriptions and anecdotes of these peoples that seemed very strange to the Europeans. When Hobbes, in the seventeenth century, was weaving a theory of the origins and foundations of political life, he was less attracted to such empirical studies of primitives than to a rationally constructed political theory based on certain assumptions about the world and its inhabitants. In Hobbes's system, the key assumption is that the world is made solely of matter, specifically of matter that moves. According to Hobbes, humans, as a part of nature, are also material, and their impelling motive is self-preservation.

To construct a political theory from these assumptions Hobbes described a "state of nature" out of which society and government emerged by making some sort of agreement or contract. In the state of nature every man, he wrote, was pitted against every other man: it was a chaotic, fearful, dangerous time in which each man had to improvise his own self-preservation, and man's life was "solitary, poor, nasty, brutish, and short." Finally, society and government arose when men agreed to surrender their self-defense to an autocratic ruler. This ruler would receive absolute obedience from all in return for the legal and military machinery he established to protect their lives and property. However, seventeenth-century monarchs who might be pleased by almost any defense of absolutism were disconcerted by Hobbes's failure to stress he-

CHRONOLOGY

HISTORY		THE ARTS	
		1561–1626	Sir Francis Bacon
		1564–1642	Galileo
		1567–1643	Monteverdi
		1573–1610	Caravaggio
		1577–1640	Rubens
		c. 1580–1666	Frans Hals
1589–1610	Henry IV king of France	1588–1679	Hobbes
		1593–1652	Georges de la Tour
		1594–1665	Poussin
		1596–1650	Descartes
1598–1621	Philip III king of Spain	1598–1666	François Mansart
		1598–1680	Bernini
		1599–1660	Velázquez
		1599–1667	Borromini
		1600–01	Caravaggio's *Conversion of Saint Paul*
1603–25	James I king of England		
		1606–69	Rembrandt
1607	Virginia founded by English	1607	Monteverdi's *Orfeo*
1610–43	Louis XIII king of France	1610	Monteverdi's *Vespers of 1610*
		1610–11	Rubens's *Raising of the Cross*
1612	New Amsterdam founded by Dutch		
1618–48	Thirty Years' War	c. 1618	Ruben's *Rape of the Daughters of Leucippus*
1621–65	Philip IV king of Spain		
1625–49	Charles I king of England		
		1626	Saint Peter's Basilica, Rome, formally opened
		1632	Barberini opera house opened in Rome
1635	France enters Thirty Years' War	1636–37	Poussin's *Rape of the Sabine Women*
		1637	Descartes' *Discourse on Method*
		1638–40	Borromini's *San Carlo alle Quattro Fontane*
1642–48	Civil War in England	1642–50	Borromini's *Sant' Ivo della Sapienza*
1643–1715	Louis XIV king of France	1645–52	Bernini's *Saint Teresa in Ecstasy*
1648	Treaty of Westphalia, ending Thirty Years' War	1648	Rembrandt's *Supper at Emmaus*
1649–60	Puritan republic in England (Commonwealth and Protectorate)	1651	Hobbes's *Leviathan*
		1656	Velázquez's *Maids of Honor*
		1656	Bernini's Saint Peter's Square begun
1659	Peace of the Pyrenees between France and Spain	1658	Bernini's *Sant' Andrea al Quirinale*

reditary monarchy by *divine right*—that is, God's authorization for their right to rule.

In France, the most prominent new absolutist nation, autocracy was celebrated most visibly and symbolically by many building projects in and out of Paris,

the royal capital. Henry IV, for example, ordered two imposing monuments of urban planning that are still seen in Paris—the large public squares known as the Place Dauphine and the Place Royale (now the Place des Vosges). The Valois kings of the French Renais-

EUROPE IN 1648

Austrian Hapsburg Lands
Spanish Hapsburg Lands
German States
Boundary of Holy Roman Empire

sance had built extensively for gratifying their personal tastes; the Bourbons, on the other hand, like rulers of the Baroque age throughout Europe, would build great projects as public symbols of their authority and magnificence.

Yet in France itself the architectural style was so restrained, so "classical," that many experts deny it the Baroque label since architectural Baroque customarily implies decorative and structural exuberance. Indeed, classical restraint characterized all French arts of the century, including literature. Rough edges were polished from the language, and literature (notably poetry and drama) was formalized according to antique rules and models in a manner that pleased the most courtly,

aristocratic taste. This is because it was in aristocratic circles, and the bourgeois circles that copied them, that the details of the revived aesthetics of classicism were worked out.

Aristocratic taste in early and mid seventeenth-century France was also evident in the homes of the wealthy—and never more gracefully than in the *château* (country mansion) built between 1642 and 1650 at Maisons, near Paris. The proud owner of the Château of Maisons-Lafitte (as it is now called) was a wealthy governmental administrator, and the architect was the highly talented François Mansart (1598–1666). A view of the courtyard facade (fig. 12-1) reveals an architectural spirit more graceful, more purely

12-1 François Mansart, courtyard of the Château of Maisons-Lafitte, 1642–50.

classical than that of the Chambord Château a century before.

An Age of Science and Reason

Many valiant attempts have been made to link the spirit and methodology of seventeenth-century science with the art of the day, or even with a "spirit of the Baroque." Scientific *empiricism* (the reliance on experience, experimentation, and the observation of facts) is often credited with inspiring Baroque naturalism. The truth of the matter is that *two* approaches to scientific investigation are clearly distinguishable in seventeenth-century thought—the empirical and the rational. All first-class minds admitted that the two approaches must collaborate somewhat—although any given thinker would temperamentally or philosophically prefer one or the other. Let us look at the prime exemplar of each approach, Bacon the empiricist and Descartes the rationalist.

Sir Francis Bacon (1561–1626) was anxious, first of all, to eradicate the centuries-old habit of accepting past authority in the sciences, and thus bring to an end the consequent "endless repetitions of the same thing" in scholarly books. In contrast to the enthusiasm for

antiquity among the early Renaissance humanist-scholars, Bacon denigrated the wisdom of the Greeks as the mere "boyhood of knowledge," which must be replaced in the new age by mature scientific and philosophical work. In his day, Bacon asserted, "Philosophy and the intellectual sciences . . . stand like statues, worshipped and celebrated, but not moved or advanced." The much-to-be-desired alternative is a move toward "experience and the facts of nature"—not simply, though, toward a mass of random observations, but into a systematic, thoughtful examination of the world, guided by intelligence and the collaborative endeavors of many scientific investigators. This new scientific approach, he asserted, will not simply satisfy intellectual curiosity (whose role Bacon perhaps underestimated) but will have practical results "for the benefit and use of life." "I am laboring," he continued, "to lay the foundation, not of any sect or doctrine, but of human utility and power."

In the same vein the Italian astronomer and physicist Galileo Galilei (1564–1642) stressed the need for an accumulation of empirical data ("all human reasoning," he wrote, "must be placed second to direct experience"). But we must not forget Galileo's own masterful reconciliation of empiricism with a more abstract rationalism and the relative neglect of empiricism by the French philosopher René Descartes (1596–1650) in favor of a deductive type of reasoning inspired by mathematical method.

Descartes (fig. 12-2), in his *Discourse on Method,* offered his own intellectual autobiography as an example of how a scientist might proceed in the quest for knowledge. Like Bacon he professed to be working for "the general good of mankind," and, to this end, said that scientists must fashion themselves as "the lords and possessors of nature." While not denying the utility of scientific experiments, he believed that empirical study must be built on a foundation of "principles or first causes." These principles are best derived, he insisted, on "certain germs of truths naturally existing in our minds." From such inborn "germs of truths" (such as the absolute certainty of one's own existence) and from the consequent "principles or first causes" one could then deduce further scientific truths. Many critics of the Cartesian (Descartes's) system considered this process of deduction too abstract and rational— and it is true that Descartes expended more enthusiasm

12-2   Frans Hals, *René Descartes.* Statens Museum for Kunst, Copenhagen.

on deduction than on any experimental verification of the truths arrived at deductively.

We must remember, though, that, whatever its defects, the Cartesian method marked as much of a break from traditional, ancient authority as did the more experimental Baconian approach. Indeed all seventeenth-century scientists united in rejecting past authority, especially the authority of Aristotle, so revered in the Middle Ages and Renaissance. This firm rejection of authority was the heart of the seventeenth century's great "scientific revolution" and the key to modern liberal thought. It is interesting that this antiauthoritarianism in science was in striking contrast to the classicist respect for ancient rules and models that simultaneously typified the century.

Christianity's distrust of the new science was by no means as total as historians sometimes represent it. Nonetheless, religious leaders were seriously troubled by the implications of the theories of Galileo and others. The Roman Church had the monk Giordano Bruno burned for preaching an unorthodox view of astronomy, and Galileo was forced to recant his idea that the earth was not the center of the universe.

Holland and the Bourgeois Influence

Seventeenth-century Holland—the popular name for those northern provinces of the Low Countries (Netherlands) that had broken away effectively from Spanish dominion—was an area of remarkable toleration for many sorts of religious and intellectual deviance persecuted by most secular rulers of the century. If not always in theory, at least in practice, Dutch toleration was unprecedented. Descartes found refuge there, as did Europe's most liberated Jewish community and a cross section of Protestant dissidents, including America's future Pilgrim Fathers. The Dutch Calvinist religious establishment was not wholly pleased with the strange peoples and unorthodox ideas that flourished in their cities. The solid burghers, however, usually found toleration a sensible prop and even a necessity for their own commercial prosperity.

Although the tastes of some of these prosperous burghers were classical and aristocratic, they were generally characterized by sober, middle-class realism. The commercial and financial center of their astonishing little country was the port-city of Amsterdam. The sugar of Brazil rested in Amsterdam warehouses together with the silk and spices of India and the East

12-3 Frans Hals, *Officers of the Haarlem Militia Company of Saint Hadrian*, c. 1627. Oil on canvas, 6′ × 8′9″. Frans Halsmuseum, Haarlem.

Indies and such less exotic European products as coal, iron, timber, grain, and salted herring. Moreover, Amsterdam embodied a cosmopolitanism not only of merchandise but also of peoples and intellectual and scientific movements.

Bourgeois rule in the United Netherlands did not always enjoy undisturbed dominance, for an aristocratic, quasi monarchist faction frequently held official control of the state and was always significant. Yet the burgher families, with their fortunes in trade, industry, and banking, were the dominant urban social element and commonly the governing class. Thus they tended to become bureaucrats—and they took on some aristocratic airs as well. Their position between the aristocracy and the bourgeoisie is sensed in such group paintings as *Officers of the Haarlem Militia Company of Saint Hadrian* (fig. 12-3) by Frans Hals. Here, decked out in their most elegant finery, these leaders of the local guard are presumably at the beginning, not the end, of one of the banquets and drinking bouts, sponsored by the municipality, that were restricted by law to "three, or at most four days" in duration.

Quite possibly, though, the unimaginative bourgeois materialism of seventeenth-century Holland has been exaggerated. In the greatest money-making city of all, Amsterdam, there arose an extraordinarily lively traffic in books and ideas, and much of the finest litera-

ture, music, and art of the age. Out of this bourgeois culture, after all, rose Hals himself and such other memorable painters as Vermeer and the great Rembrandt.

By 1660 Amsterdam had probably reached a population of two hundred thousand. It had recently completed one of Europe's most concentrated and difficult efforts in urban development—a vast reclamation of muddy land adjacent to the old city (the town hall was built on more than thirteen thousand wooden piles about forty feet long), now newly laid out around three concentric semicircular canals. Some of the handsome homes that still line these canals had been built; more modest structures continued to characterize the smaller connecting canals and narrow streets. Houses, even many of the finest, were quite narrow and were built high in stone or brick—some of them with stepped gables and others with square, classical facade designs. The interiors astounded foreign visitors because of their tidiness and they were frequently portrayed in Dutch painting.

This sort of *genre* painting—that is, realistic painting of everyday scenes—was immensely popular in Holland. So, too, were the paintings of countryside genre, exemplified by *The Ferry* (fig. 12-4) by Salomon van Ruysdael. No classical or biblical motif intrudes; we see only the flat expanse of land and water, the lazy

12-4 Salomon van Ruysdael, *The Ferry*, 1653. Oil on panel, 21″ × 32″. Property of the State-Owned Art Collections Department, The Hague.

clouds and distant church steeple, the cattle, boats, and farmhouses of a commonplace Dutch scene. This was clearly how the Dutch townspeople who bought the paintings wanted to visualize their land—simple, peaceful, and contented.

Essentially, Dutch patronage of painting was bourgeois patronage. However, humble city workers, too, wanted to own paintings. "Butchers and bakers, yea, many times blacksmiths, cobblers, etc" were noted by a startled English visitor to have paintings in their shops. Seldom, if ever, in European history has a similar demand existed for original art in modest as well as wealthy homes. Of course, the supply rose to meet the demand and eventually exceeded it. In the meantime, the painting market had become largely impersonal; most paintings were bought from dealers, who had ordered from artists the types of works that would sell. Individual artists—always excepting Rembrandt—came to specialize more and more in a specific subject matter, such as canal or domestic scenes, cattle pictures, or still lifes. Artists seldom knew the ultimate buyers—and the buyers were hard to identify anyway, since the Dutch often bought paintings as investments, for resale. By mid century overproduction was rampant, and even Rembrandt could make only a precarious living, by selling etchings.

In their patronage of music the Dutch were con-

siderably less enthusiastic than in the realm of painting. Music in Holland was overwhelmingly an amateur, domestic amusement. The situation was similar in the German states, but generous princely and ecclesiastical patronage was far more common than in bourgeois, Calvinist-oriented Holland. By and large, Baroque music was courtly music, most often part of an imposing, festive ceremony. Thus the two greatest musicians of the age, Monteverdi and Schütz, would write mainly for courtly occasions, sacred and secular—and thus would arise in Italy the courtly musical form par excellence, the opera.

Rome in the Early Baroque Age

Among the most sumptuous of Italian cultural centers, of course, was Rome, the "Eternal City." Here the Barberini princes opened their own theater in 1632 for operatic productions—a lavish structure for an audience of three thousand. From the late sixteenth century on, a multitude of new churches, large and small, were built, and they contributed to the Baroque Rome that still survives. Here, too, old churches were redecorated in the new exuberant manner, often to the irreparable loss of historic artistic treasures. Although private patronage was exercised on occasion by connoisseurs of modest pretensions or by resident foreign

12-5 Gianlorenzo Bernini, *Cardinal Scipione Borghese*, 1632. Marble, 31″ high. Galleria Borghese, Rome.

such spiritual warriors as Ignatius Loyola (founder of the Jesuits), Francis Xavier (missionary to the East), and Teresa of Avila (mystic and spiritual activist) were solemnized to the sound of silver trumpets in the gleaming new Basilica of Saint Peter.

Saint Peter's (fig. 12-6), which at last was consecrated and opened to the public in 1626, became the symbol of the Roman Church Victorious. Carlo Maderna had completed the majestic nave and facade in 1614; his work altered measurably the centralized church envisioned by Bramante and Michelangelo and, sadly, obscured the great dome. By the 1660s the last of the celebrated "architects to Saint Peter's," Bernini, had added the imposing curved colonnades that now frame this most famous of European "squares," reaching out (as Bernini himself said) to welcome the faithful. Already he had designed and installed the huge altar canopy, or *baldachin* (fig. 12-7), inside the basilica; its stupendous corkscrew columns were made partly of bronze taken from the ancient Pantheon. Far behind the baldachin is Bernini's later *Cathedra* (episcopal chair) *of Saint Peter*, surmounted by a gloriously

12-6 Saint Peter's Basilica, Rome, consecrated 1626. In the foreground is Saint Peter's Square, by Gianlorenzo Bernini, begun in 1656.

dignitaries, the most generous Roman patrons typically were princes of the Church and those aristocratic families who supplied so many of Rome's ecclesiastics, popes included. Especially notable in this group was the genial Cardinal Scipione Borghese (fig. 12-5), vividly commemorated by his protégé, the sculptor Gianlorenzo Bernini. The keen gaze and parted lips suggest not a formal pose but a lively conversational moment.

The wealth, self-assurance, and worldliness of this Church leader are evidence that much had happened to the papal court since the Catholic Reformation of the previous century. With European Protestantism now on the defensive, Catholic Rome resumed its earlier self-confidence and occasional moral and devotional laxity. The popes ruled in their small secular state as absolutely as any monarch of the day, but they emphasized their spiritual sovereignty over all Roman Christendom. Although few European rulers seriously heeded papal politics any more, festivals and ceremonies in Rome were often as magnificent as at any royal or ducal court. The work of the sixteenth-century Catholic reformers was finished, but their triumphs were still proudly celebrated. The ultimate symbolic moment of the Roman Baroque era was the splendid ceremony of May 22, 1622, when the canonizations of

12-7   Gianlorenzo Bernini, baldaquin over high altar, Saint Peter's Basilica, Rome, 1624–33. Bronze.

12-8   Pietro da Cortona, *Glorification of the Reign of Urban VIII*, 1633–39. Fresco. Barberini Palace, Rome.

gaudy sunburst around a window on which is painted a dove representing the Holy Spirit. Everywhere there are staggering quantities of bronze and gilt, sometimes deceptively simulating other materials, as in the metal draperies of the canopy. It is all a grandiose exercise in theatrical illusionism, an overwhelming visual and even spiritual experience.

The Barberini bees, emblem of the proud Roman family to which the pope of that time, Urban VIII, belonged, not only support the orb at the baldachin's summit in Saint Peter's; they are also the focus of a famous fresco that closely parallels in paint Bernini's baldachin and cathedra. The fresco is the vast ceiling painting in Rome's Barberini Palace, the *Glorification of the Reign of Urban VIII* (fig. 12-8) by Pietro da Cortona (1596–1669). Here a complex allegory becomes courtly and spiritual propaganda of a thoroughly theatrical sort. Figures float weightlessly amid clouds and

false, garlanded moldings, all depicted with the most refined tricks of foreshortening and architectural simulation. It is an extraordinarily virtuosic work—and indisputably Baroque, if any work of art deserves that designation.

THE ROMAN BAROQUE STYLE

The customary definitions of the *Baroque* in visual art apply best to Roman Baroque—and perhaps the term should be limited to the qualities exemplified by that art alone. Recent scholarship has cleared away a few earlier misconceptions concerning the style—that, for example, it marked an abrupt about-face from the Renaissance or a total rejection of classicism. More full-bodied, less artificial than the Mannerist phase of the late Renaissance, Baroque art is usually balanced and classically inspired in form and content.

Above all, Baroque was an art of controlled exuberance, like much of history's greatest art. Most typically, though, it used a special vocabulary of its own—a language leaning toward rhetoric and persuasion, toward theatricality and *trompe l'oeil* (deliberate visual deception), toward enchantment and sumptuousness. It often reached out for infinity, yet attempted to unify its impressions and involve the viewer as directly as possible in the artistic experience. At least, these were some of the trends in Roman Baroque.

Francesco Borromini (1599–1667) is often considered the greatest of Roman Baroque architects—and certainly he was among the most original. In San Carlo alle Quattro Fontane, for example, he resoundingly met the challenge of supporting and enlivening an unusual oval dome (fig. 12-9). The striking honeycomb coffering is an effective visual inspiration, as is

12-10   Francesco Borromini, Sant' Ivo della Sapienza, Rome, 1642–50.

12-9   Francesco Borromini, San Carlo alle Quattro Fontane, Rome, 1638–40.

the illusion of height achieved by reducing the size of the coffers as they approach the distant light of the hidden lantern windows. This church, like many Roman Baroque churches, is quite small. The monumental impression derives from its clarity of modeling and its illusionism.

Borromini was a careful student of ancient Roman architecture and was well acquainted with Italian Renaissance structures, but he was far indeed from slavish acceptance of past authority. Although he used many classical motifs, Borromini contrived repeatedly to furnish new contexts for traditional ideas. In the little church of Sant' Ivo della Sapienza, probably his masterwork, he employed the novel floor plan of a star-hexagon (two superimposed equilateral triangles, in this case with blunted points, alternately convex and concave), covered completely by a dome rising from the walls with no major transitional adjustments (fig. 12-10). Thus the dome interior continues the star-hexagonal shape up to the lantern base. The outer lantern shell, or *cupola*, incorporates the additional novelty of an exterior spiral staircase.

As an architect, Gianlorenzo Bernini (1598–1680) was considerably less daring than Borromini. He was, however, far more prominently in the public eye as both architect and sculptor. In fact, his prestige in the arts equaled that of Michelangelo a century before. Although less personally troubled, less anguished in his faith, and less heaven-shaking in his art than the older master, Bernini was a creator of comprehensive genius who embodied much of the best in his period. Fortunately, the papacy and other ecclesiastical and aristocratic patrons for half a century recognized his worth and commissioned a series of remarkable works.

We have already noted several of Bernini's contributions to Saint Peter's. All of them combined sculpture with architecture; even the colonnades of the square are topped by massive statues. In a much smaller-scale work, Rome's Sant' Andrea al Quirinale (fig. 12-11), sculpture and architecture again are fused in a total aesthetic experience. The oval shape of the interior, with the altar placed on the short axis opposite the door, emphasizes a spreading in width that makes the tiny area seem larger yet also brings the viewer close to the altar and the dramatic figure above it (sculpted by a follower, after Bernini's design)—Saint Andrew ascending to heaven on a cloud. From either side angels descend, against a richly stuccoed and gilt dome, to meet the saintly martyr.

A more celebrated and still more forceful example of Bernini's theatrical union of the arts is the Cornaro Chapel in Santa Maria della Vittoria, as seen here in

12-12 *Cornaro Chapel,* eighteenth-century painting. Staatliche Museum, Schwerin.

12-11 Gianlorenzo Bernini, Sant' Andrea al Quirinale, Rome, 1658.

an eighteenth-century painting (fig. 12-12). The famous altar group, focal point of the chapel, depicts Saint Teresa of Avila in ecstasy (fig. 12-13)—a moment of mystical intensity recorded by Saint Teresa (1515–77) herself.

> Beside me appeared an angel in bodily form, such as I am not in the habit of seeing except very rarely. In his hands I saw a great golden spear, and at the iron tip there appeared to be a point of fire. This he plunged into my heart several times so that it penetrated to my entrails. When he pulled it out, I felt that he took them with it, and left me utterly consumed by the great love of God. The pain was so severe that it made me utter several moans. This is not a physical but a spiritual pain, though the body has some share in it—even a considerable share.

Bernini took care to record this scene almost as literally as the saint described it. The passive receptivity of the saintly form, the ecstatic moan, the repeated plunge of the spear (an arrow in Bernini's interpretation)—all is detailed. Gilded rays descend brilliantly

12-13 Gianlorenzo Bernini, *Saint Teresa in Ecstasy*, 1645–52. Marble and gilt bronze, lifesize. Cornaro Chapel, Santa Maria della Vittoria, Rome.

from the hidden window above and behind the group, while far above, painted on stucco clouds erupting into the chapel, swirl the heavenly host from whom the angel has descended but who constitute a still higher, more ethereal realm. At each side of the chapel is a realistic sculptured group of four kneeling members of the Cornaro family; they pray, converse, and gesticulate, apparently in reaction to the miraculous central event. Behind them, architecture simulated in stucco relief expands the chapel sideways, implying a frontal extension also, which would literally include the viewer. Art has seldom known such unabashed, illusionistic, and intimate theatricality, or such a unity of architecture, sculpture, painting, richly decorated accessories, and natural lighting.

The predominantly sculptural drama of Bernini had had its most distinguished parallel in painting at the turn of the century in the remarkable work of Michelangelo Merisi, known as Caravaggio (1573–1610). Born in a northern Italian village of that name,

Caravaggio settled in Rome as early as 1588 and remained there for most of his creative life. Dead at thirty-six, he had lived with a passionate, sometimes violent intensity that, judging from police records, considerably exceeded the legal limits at times. In his painting as in his life, he was vigorously independent; he was, after all, one of the most daring pathfinders into the Baroque.

But Caravaggio was appreciated by the forward-looking Roman connoisseurs. An early example of the style that delighted them and that would earn him followers throughout Europe was his *Supper at Emmaus* (fig. 12-14) now in London's National Gallery. In this painting the resurrected Christ makes himself known to two disciples as he blesses bread at an inn. It is a moment of high drama for the disciples: the man at the left grasps his chair, while the other flings wide his arms in amazement. Both wear ragged garments, and both, like the puzzled innkeeper, are clearly of the lower classes. Even the unidealized, beardless Christ is a bit disheveled. Such was the naturalism that pleased or distressed Caravaggio's contemporaries as he put the supernatural into realistic, everyday terms.

As to painting technique, the salient feature of the *Supper at Emmaus*, after its thorough mastery of foreshortening, is the predominance of deep shadow out of which rise, with enamellike clarity, several striking highlights. This *tenebroso* effect is seen again in the melodramatic *Conversion of Saint Paul* (fig. 12-15). Again the figures are pushed close to the picture surface and the viewer—almost oppressively so by the enormous horse and the outflung arms of Saul, who lies on the ground stunned by his vision. Never has the fateful episode on the road to Damascus been made so pressingly immediate to the viewer, both physically and emotionally. But by no means does the pictorial and dramatic immediacy of the work imply loss of formal grip. Like Bernini's sculpture decades later, the picture is tightly unified, with all its elements closely interrelated. In its simultaneous tension and control it is a prime exhibit of Roman Baroque art.

One of the finest Italian painters of the generation after Caravaggio, and possibly the best of all, was a woman, Artemisia Gentileschi (c. 1593–c. 1652). A follower of Caravaggio, she painted many historical and legendary scenes of heroic womanhood. A woman of firm resolve and an artist of great personal drive and talent, she is known today also for her striking self-portraits. In figure 12-16 we see her self-portrayed as *La*

12-14   Caravaggio, *Supper at Emmaus*, late 1590s. Oil on canvas, 55″ × 77″. Reproduced by courtesy of the Trustees, The National Gallery, London.

12-15   Caravaggio, *Conversion of Saint Paul*, 1600–1601. Oil on canvas, 50″ × 69″. Santa Maria del Popolo, Rome.

Pittura—that is, as a female allegorical figure of "Painting" itself. Such personifications of painting as a female figure had become common in the previous century; in Gentileschi the personification and the self-portrait were at last merged.

PAINTING OUTSIDE ITALY

Early- and mid-seventeenth-century painting also flowered north and west of the Alps. Non-Italian lands in this period produced several of history's most famous painters—and one, Rembrandt, who is often regarded as the greatest of all. Amid the wealth of important painting in this period, we will glance at the comprehensive achievements of Poussin, Velázquez, and Rubens and the more restricted talents of De la Tour and Hals, before turning to Rembrandt.

12-16 Artemisia Gentileschi, *Self-Portrait as "La Pittura."* London: Kensington Palace. Copyright Reserved to Her Majesty Queen Elizabeth II.

French and Spanish Painters

The reputation of Georges de la Tour (1593–1652) in his own time was largely provincial; he worked and was known mainly in Lorraine, now in eastern France. His *Joseph the Carpenter* (fig. 12-17), like many of his works, is almost Caravaggesque in its realistic figures deeply shadowed and highlighted. But De la Tour was addicted in his painting to artificial lighting, which Caravaggio was not; moreover, De la Tour's scenes commonly were not outwardly dramatic but tranquil, contemplative, or tender. In the *Joseph* painting, the boy Jesus is an image of purity and radiance as he holds a candle to aid the elderly Joseph's labors.

De la Tour may well have visited Italy, but Nicolas Poussin (1594–1665), a Frenchman, lived and worked in Rome during most of his artistic maturity.

By about 1630 he had largely abandoned his earlier thoughts of painting massive decorative compositions, leaving them to such native Italians as Pietro da Cortona, and had turned to the modest-sized canvases for which he remains best known. In his painting as in his personal life, he became the model of high-mindedness, self-control, orderliness, and scholarship for two more centuries of classicists in European painting.

Classical motifs and a rational, geometrical balance characterized Poussin's religious painting and such evocations of pagan antiquity as his *Rape of the Sabine Women* (fig. 12-18). The old Roman legend was considered a sufficiently noble theme to be worthy of artistic attention. In the severe classicist view, personal idiosyncrasies were not to be portrayed; thus bodies and facial expressions in the *Rape* are standardized according to the most admired models. Left of center a Roman soldier abducting a Sabine woman is reminiscent of Giovanni Bologna's sculptured group (see fig.

12-17 Georges de la Tour, *Joseph the Carpenter*, c. 1645. Oil on canvas, 39″ × 26″. Louvre, Paris.

12-18 Nicolas Poussin, *Rape of the Sabine Women*, 1636–37. Oil on canvas, 61″ ×83″. The Metropolitan Museum of Art, New York (Harris Brisbane Dick Fund, 1946).

11-18); the muscular Sabine to the right is clearly derived from the Hellenistic-Roman *Gaul Killing Himself* (see fig. 3-10). Such copying or adaptation of earlier models was by no means a makeshift on Poussin's part. We can feel sure that he and his patrons were proud of the classical references and were gratified to find long-established artistic precedents for presumably universal types of figures and poses. Happily Poussin's vigor and artistic sensitivity saved his best work from utter coldness. In lesser hands, the classicist imperatives of imitation, universality, and rational discipline often suppressed all spontaneity.

Spain in the seventeenth century escaped most of the classicist literalism that would retain its advocates in France and Italy for centuries to come. This may explain Poussin's continued prestige over the centuries and the Western world's long neglect of Diego Velázquez (1599–1660), who would be rediscovered only by Goya and then by the freer spirits of the later nineteenth century. Velázquez surely was not ignorant of antique themes, for he made two trips to Italy—but the Spanish art market offered little demand for classical subject matter. On the rare occasions when he did

attempt a subject from antique legend, he set it amid the commonplace and the undignified, as Caravaggio had often done with sacred themes.

By inclination and by virtue of his position as court painter to the king of Spain, Velázquez was above all a portraitist. His late work *Maids of Honor* (fig. 12-19) is one of history's most admired group portraits and a summation of the Baroque ideal of conceptual unity. To the left, before a huge canvas, stands the painter himself, while in the center is the little Princess Margarita with her attendants, including two of the dwarfs so prized in Spain as court curiosities. The king and the queen are mirrored at the rear of the room. It is a strangely haunting glimpse, elegantly composed and lighted, into an artist's world and the decaying Spanish court.

Painters in the Netherlands

If art still could flourish in Spain, it was also very much alive in the Spanish dependency of the southern Netherlands. Here, roughly the area of modern Belgium, there existed much cultural if not political freedom,

12-19   Diego Velázquez, *Maids of Honor*, 1656. Oil on canvas, 10′5″ × 9′. Prado, Madrid.

and a school of painting that for sheer spontaneity and healthy sensuality was virtually unique in Europe. Not the burghers, as in Holland, but the aristocratic court and its hangers-on were the outstanding patrons, especially of painting. In the court city of Brussels and in a still-prosperous Antwerp (which was not definitively cut off from the sea by treaty until 1648), the art of Flemish painting saw a final burst of vigor that is most memorably associated with Peter Paul Rubens (1577–1640).

In all respects except spiritual depth, Rubens was extraordinarily many-sided. He successfully met every challenge of diverse subject matter, from the most ostentatious to the most intimate. His wide talent and immense fluency, and the aid of many assistants, made him one of history's most prolific and wealthy artists. He was at home in high society and international decision making, serving as diplomat and confidant to the Italian court of Mantua, then to the Hapsburg regent in the southern Netherlands and even to Philip IV himself. The official artistic and diplomatic obligations of his maturity, to the Flemish court in Brussels, gave him permanent residence and special privileges in nearby Antwerp and time to accept the varied commissions that streamed in from all of Europe.

Much of his exuberant, elegant art served the Roman Catholic Church. Shortly after his youthful years in Italy and his settling in Antwerp, Rubens was charged with creating a huge altarpiece for that city's church of Saint Walburga. Now in the Antwerp Cathedral, the *Raising of the Cross* (fig. 12-20), with its attached altar wings, is one of the most imposing monuments of the Catholic Baroque style. The muscular bodies are full of energy and fury; the enormous, taut figures and the diagonal, strongly highlighted body of Jesus seem to push forward from the panel toward the viewer. It is a scene of rare pathos and melodrama.

Similarly, Rubens flung himself with enthusiasm into classical subjects. "I am infatuated with antiquity," he declared. However, there is nothing of mere antiquarianism in his vigorous interpretations of classi-

12-20   Peter Paul Rubens, *Raising of the Cross*, 1610–11. Oil on panel, 15′2″ × 11′2″. Antwerp Cathedral.

12-21   Peter Paul Rubens, *Rape of the Daughters of Leucippus*, c. 1618. Oil on canvas, 88″ × 82″. Alte Pinakothek, Munich.

cal paganism. His *Rape of the Daughters of Leucippus* (fig. 12-21) contrasts strikingly with that other famous abduction scene, Poussin's *Rape of the Sabine Women* (see fig. 12-18); stony, sculpturesque precision has given way to airy color, vital energy, and voluptuous abandon. Ruben's diversified creative inventiveness, splendid technique, and dramatic rhetoric would inspire two more centuries of Western art. Certainly his cosmopolitan taste and manner would prove far more amenable to widespread understanding and imitation than would Rembrandt's more individual and somber insights.

We have already noted the predominantly bourgeois inspiration and considerable variety of Netherlandish art north of the Spanish-controlled provinces. Of course, with specialization in the air, it took many Dutch painters to equal in scope one Rembrandt, or one Rubens. Yet among the many "little Dutch masters" there was much talent (such as that shown by the celebrated woman painter of genre scenes, Judith Leyster) and even—if Hals and Vermeer are included —much true genius. Discussion of Vermeer, as a younger artist, will be deferred until the next chapter; Hals has already been noted for his group portrait of

Haarlem militia officers. Frans Hals (c. 1580–1666) was, in fact, almost exclusively a portraitist. Born in the southern Netherlands of Flemish parents, he painted in the bustling Dutch town of Haarlem. *The Merry Drinker* (fig. 12-22) portrays one of the less inhibited of the Haarlem townsmen in a spontaneous pose. The painting technique is as vivacious as the subject: the colors are cheerful and are applied with broad and daring brushstrokes such as would not be fully appreciated until the nineteenth century. As in so much of Baroque art, the figure depicted reaches out toward the viewer, as if to establish human contact. Few artists have touched modern sympathies more directly and heartily than Hals.

The appeal of Rembrandt van Rijn (1606–69) has been more complex, if only because he generally disregarded such aids to popularity as flamboyant or physically attractive human subjects, dramatic action, or any Baroque play for spectator involvement. His art demonstrates wide versatility, great formal strength,

12-22   Frans Hals, *The Merry Drinker*, c. 1627–30. Oil on canvas, 32″ × 26″. Rijksmuseum, Amsterdam.

his later works—the reds, the greenish golds, the browns, all discreetly highlighted by white or cream. Already the shadows of *chiaroscuro* and the haziness of *sfumato* are an essential part of his vision—elements that were sometimes exaggerated to the point of disfiguration by subsequent varnishings.

By 1640 Rembrandt had long since moved from his native Leiden to Amsterdam. He had become famous, had married both profitably and happily, and had just bought the handsome house that still stands as Amsterdam's Rembrandt museum. The pose of the London self-portrait (fig. 12-24) of that year is the same as that of Raphael's elegant *Castiglione* (see fig. 10-11), which Rembrandt had recently seen and sketched. The artist of 1640 is an eminently substantial citizen, keen-eyed but dignified and genteel.

Rembrandt's next two decades were a period of personal tragedy and seriously declining prosperity and fortunes. After his wife's early death had come other domestic and professional trials and eventual financial

12-23 Rembrandt, *Self-portrait,* c. 1629. Oil on canvas, 15″ × 11″. Mauritshuis, The Hague.

12-24 Rembrandt, *Self-portrait,* 1640. Oil on canvas, 40″ × 32″. Reproduced by courtesy of the Trustees, The National Gallery, London.

and superb psychological insight. Historically he is significant also because he stoutly insisted on the autonomy of the artist. Although he sometimes accepted specific commissions, Rembrandt preferred to choose, and often did choose, his own subject matter—and he consistently demanded the right to treat it according to his own judgment and to complete the painting as he, not his patron or the current fad, wished. In the face of objections that his work frequently seemed ragged and unfinished, his alleged reply was proud and succinct: "A picture is completed when the master has achieved his intention by it." Rembrandt's career truly marks a declaration of independence in the history of art.

Three of the more than fifty surviving painted self-portraits may offer some preliminary insight into Rembrandt as man and artist. The Mauritshuis self-portrait (fig. 12-23) shows him as a self-assertive, stubbornly confident young man on the threshold of a great career. Already the colors are those he would favor in

12-25 Rembrandt, *Self-portrait,* 1659. Oil on canvas, 33¼" × 26". National Gallery of Art, Washington, D.C. (Andrew W. Mellon Collection, 1937).

insolvency. The Rembrandt of the 1659 self-portrait in Washington (fig. 12-25) is a man prematurely aged, vulnerable but unbroken. Clearly, Rembrandt had learned to live with suffering and disillusionment.

Rembrandt's self-portraits and numerous pictures of his family are of an intimacy hitherto unprecedented in painting. More surprising is his familiar insight into the mood and personality of scores of other sitters, many of whom must have been strangers to him. His subjects often were middle-aged or elderly; there is certainly no cult of youth or physical beauty in Rembrandt—an indication of his distance from the classicism of his own and previous ages.

When Rembrandt turned to the past, it was usually the biblical past. His occasional early depiction of dramatic episodes from the Old Testament had given way to quieter, more inward scenes by the late 1640s—exemplified by the Louvre's *Supper at Emmaus* (fig. 12-26). Against a dim, starkly monumental background appear the subdued figures of Christ, servant, and dis-

ciples. Caravaggio's narrative melodrama, contrasting colors, and startling foreshortening are nowhere evident. The resurrected Christ is radiant but gentle, and the mood is hushed, not intense. The solemnity and humanity of Christ's portrayal reflects Rembrandt's own religious faith, which rejected the austerity of dogmatic Calvinism for a humbler, more liberal humanitarianism.

The Old Testament supplies inspiration for *Jacob Blessing the Sons of Joseph* (fig. 12-27), with Hebrew legend perhaps accounting for the nonbiblical presence of Joseph's wife. (Rembrandt lived near Amsterdam's Jewish community, and Jews were among his friends, patrons, and favorite pictorial subjects.) Again the inherent drama is calm and restrained: the turbaned Joseph gently but vainly tries to guide his dying father's hand from the younger to the older boy's head as their mother benignly ponders the unexpected event. Golden light and the deep red of the bed covering provide a rich outward glow for a scene of basically inward, human significance.

Rembrandt gave the world not only many of its most moving paintings but many of its most memorable prints as well. By his time, engraving was the preferred technique for wholesale reproduction of works originally in other mediums. Many of the paintings of Rubens, for example, had been popularized by engravings, sometimes made under his own supervision and other times by independent craftsmen. But for original printed work, etching was now preferred—and it was Rembrandt who best revealed the subtle and diverse potentialities of that medium. The basic process in etching is not the direct gouging of the metal plate but rather the scratching of lines through a coating of resin on the plate. The plate is then bathed in acid, which attacks the uncovered areas. Innumerable variations are possible through successive sketchings and acid baths, through additional direct incision into the metal plate itself, and by varying methods of inking the finished plate. Rembrandt frequently reworked his plates several times, thus achieving different effects and making available to connoisseurs several versions, or states, of a given etching.

The inspirations for his etchings are as diverse as those for his paintings, with a similar predominance of religious subjects. The celebrated *"Hundred-Guilder Print"* (fig. 12-28) depicts simultaneously several episodes from the Gospel according to Matthew, Chapter 19—most prominently Christ preaching, receiving lit-

12-26 Rembrandt, *Supper at Emmaus*, 1648. Oil on panel, 27″ × 26″. Louvre, Paris.

12-27 Rembrandt, *Jacob Blessing the Sons of Joseph*, 1656. Oil on canvas, 69″ × 84″. Gemäldegalerie, Kassel.

12-28
Rembrandt, *Christ Healing the Sick* ("Hundred-Guilder Print"), c. 1648–50. Etching, 11" × 16". Rijksmuseum, Amsterdam.

tle children, and healing the sick. The work is a magnificent study in lighting and composition, quite aside from its variegated human and narrative interest.

Even in such scenes as these, Rembrandt transcends mere sentimentality, whether through his profound humanity or through his vigorous formal gifts. Rejecting the classicism of his contemporaries and sharing only incidentally some of their Baroque trademarks, he may seem to have belonged primarily to the romantic-realistic undercurrent in Western art that would surface most obviously in the nineteenth century. Above all, though, he was simply Rembrandt—an artist of genius and a unique and powerful witness to the diverse ambiguities of human life.

EARLY BAROQUE MUSIC

In the form and technique of his art, if not always in its content and spirit, Rembrandt was the beneficiary of a long and well-developed artistic tradition. His role was primarily to fulfill a long-standing historical promise. European music in the early and mid seventeenth century could show no strictly parallel phenomenon, for here a revolution was challenging the basic forms themselves. In this unsettled, revolutionary situation, with its groping musical experimentalism, it is astonishing that at least one great composer, Monteverdi, could create so quickly a rich and mature art of far more than historical interest.

In the realm of strictly instrumental music, however, changes in seventeenth-century Europe were evolutionary rather than revolutionary. Instruments obsolete today, such as the *cornett* (a long and straight, or somewhat curved, woodwind with a cup-shaped mouthpiece), flourished alongside the increasingly popular violin family. The greatest changes came in keyboard instruments. The harpsichord had evolved from its several smaller-scale plucked-string ancestors; at last several strings, in variable combinations, could be plucked by striking a single key. Still greater coloristic effects could be achieved at the organ keyboard, not to mention the organ pedalboard that now was common at least in northern Continental Europe. Some early seventeenth-century organs had three separate keyboards *(manuals)* and scores of stops to activate pipes of diverse ranges and timbres. It is not surprising that composers more and more were writing not indiscriminately "keyboard" music but music exploiting the multitude of special new organ and harpsichord sonorities. Obviously the period was maintaining its predecessor's recognition of a legitimate instrumental music fully independent of vocal forms.

The Rise of Opera

It was in the larger forms of vocal music, however, in the opera and the oratorio, that the most spectacular developments were occurring—music in which instruments were used in a predominantly vocal context. The rise of opera, like the sculptural effusions of Bernini, was probably inevitable in an age so dedicated to theatricality. In Italy, the birthplace of opera, the "sacred representations" and carnival skits of the fifteenth century not only had their popular equivalents in the following centuries but their courtly descendants and relatives, the pastoral plays and the *intermezzi* (interludes). Spectacle was the main function and characteristic of these courtly productions; music was only an intermittent embellishment. An etching of the period (fig. 12-29) gives some idea of the elaborate stagecraft that lay behind the spectacle. This *Forge of Vulcan*

scene was the fifth intermezzo in a mediocre pastoral play, *The Judgment of Paris,* produced originally in Florence in 1608 to celebrate the wedding of a Medici prince. The set depicts a cavernous labyrinth seething with smoke and flame, as Mars appears in a chariot on a cloud to select armor for the future grand duke of Tuscany—all this being the occasion for the singing of two madrigals.

By that time, though, full-fledged opera also existed. As courtly diversion, it was a spectacle quite as lavish as its theatrical predecessors. But opera also served to embody serious scholarly theory, since it was presumed to re-create classical Greek drama. Florentine academicians of the late sixteenth century evolved the theory that the all-important words of a drama should be effectively underlined by music. Music, still, should not dominate; independently conceived melodies were regarded with suspicion by composers in the new "monodic" manner.

Monody, which became the crucial musical vehicle for advancing the early operatic plots, was a type of singing whose notes rose out of the chordal harmonies; the "melody" often became as jagged and dramatic as

12-29 Remigio Cantagallina, *The Forge of Vulcan.* Etching of a stage set designed by Giulio Parigi for *The Judgment of Paris,* 1608. Bibliothèque Nationale, Paris.

rhetorical speech itself. The dramatic and musical appeal would be heightened, ideally, by vocal ornamentation, commonly improvised by the singers. And the whole would be founded on a bass line, the lowest instrumental part, which in the Baroque period would help reinforce a complex harmonic fabric known as the *continuo*—which continued throughout the work. Although early monody was far more simple and mechanical than later Baroque writing, and often dull, it did make early *opera*—the complete musical setting of a stage drama—possible by freeing individual stage characters from the interwoven dependencies of polyphonic imitation.

The very earliest operas are not much more than historical curiosities. To make monody interesting, and to combine it with other vocal and instrumental techniques so as to achieve dramatic and musical unity, a composer of genius was required. Such a composer was indeed at hand—one whose musical talent had already matured in the polyphonic school of the sixteenth century. Claudio Monteverdi (1567–1643) would write the first great opera and an imposing body of sacred and secular music in most of the vocal forms and styles then popular.

For more than twenty years Monteverdi served Vincenzo, duke of Mantua, in various musical capacities, finally (after 1602) as his "master of music." (During his last three decades he would have the still more prestigious position of chapel master at Saint Mark's, Venice, and would die an ordained priest of the Catholic Church.) Most of his operas and other dramatic works have perished, but *Orfeo* alone would ensure his immortality. First produced in Mantua during the carnival season in 1607, it sets to music the legendary tale of Orpheus, poet and singer extraordinary. The story includes the death of his beloved bride Euridice, his successful pleading in the Underworld for her release, and her second subjection to Hades when Orpheus violates the command not to look at her until they are safely back in the world of the living. Orpheus is finally escorted to heaven by the god Apollo.

The story of *Orfeo* is often carried by monodic *recitative*—a loose form suggesting the free flow of speech, with its natural accents and emphases. A typical recitative is the Act II monologue *Tu se' morta* ("Thou art dead, my life, and I am living"), in which Orpheus laments Euridice's death and announces his determination to go to the Underworld and reclaim his bride. This monologue is basically simple in style and deliberately pathetic in effect. Often, however, the solo monody is shaped and enriched by repetition and variation—and monody is supplemented by vocal ensembles and choruses, as well as by instrumental interludes. The orchestra needed for this opera (or at least used in the early Mantuan performances) is very large for the day—nearly forty players—and is more heavily weighted toward wind instruments than most modern orchestration demands. Parts are not written for specific instruments, however; the notes are simply there, and the musical lines can be apportioned among a particular instrumental group, sometimes specified and sometimes not, in the separate pieces within the opera. Differing timbres, we should note, are not exploited within a given piece or a distinct section of a piece but only in successive pieces or sections—a practice that remained the norm in Baroque music throughout the pre-1660 period.

For an overview of *Orfeo*'s components, and its composer's structural concept, we will glance at the prologue and Act I. A *toccata* for full orchestra opens the opera—a toccata being essentially an instrumental flourish, or fanfare, based on a single chord. The monodic prologue, sung by Music herself, is preceded and interrupted by instrumental *ritornelli* (interludes). The act begins with a shepherd's monodic recitative that follows an *a b a*, repetitive pattern. A stately chorus in chordal style follows, with full orchestral accompaniment. After a nymph's monodic recitative comes a delightful polyphonic chorus, *Lasciate i monti* ("Haste from the mountains and from the fountains"), with light instrumental support appropriate for a jovial pastoral piece and twice supplemented by a second ritornello. After a shepherd's monodic statement to Orpheus, we hear the legendary singer and then his bride for the first time, in monodic recitative. The two earlier choruses, with ritornelli, now appear in reverse order. A shepherd then sings a monody of praise to heaven, and a recurring slow ritornello introduces and separates three largely polyphonic ensembles—duet, trio, and again duet. A choral celebration closes *Orfeo*'s first act.

No less heterogeneous in style, yet unified in total effect, is Monteverdi's most celebrated sacred work, his *Vespers of 1610*, also known as the *Vespers of the Blessed Virgin*. Like other composers of sacred music at the time, but with a genius especially his own, Monteverdi was capable of composing in both the "antique" style of sixteenth-century polyphony and the "modern," more progressive style. The modern manner could be monodic, as sometimes in the *Vespers*, or it could simply be a generally *concerted* (*concertato* or *concerto*) style. The latter terms did not yet in this period necessarily imply the use of solo parts against a larger group of musical forces. The essential element, rather, was the combination and cooperation of different types of performers taking independent musical lines. Thus neither the *a cappella* (unaccompanied choral) manner of the previous century nor the traditional device of doubling vocal parts by instruments would be considered concerted, whereas the alternation of vocal with instrumental parts or the simultaneous sounding of vocal and instrumental lines, with the instruments not simply doubling the voices, would fall into the concerted category. A further usual but not invariable characteristic of the concerted style is its chordal, not polyphonic, form.

The appearance of the concerted principle was no sudden historical novelty. Rather, its new popularity in the early seventeenth century was a more basic feature of the Baroque musical revolution than was even the arrival of the monodic manner. Monteverdi was no more the inventor of the concerted style than of monody, but he realized the potential of the new style and developed it with special genius.

The *1610 Vespers* is a highly varied, lengthy work—one of the monuments of Western sacred music. Investigation of a concerted but in some ways atypical section, the *Sonata sopra Sancta Maria*, is suggested because of its unusual appeal and essentially instrumental character. (At this point in history the *sonata* was simply an amorphous type of instrumental work.) A single vocal line repeats, in varying rhythms and usually after extended instrumental passages, the plainchant melody of "Holy Mary, pray for us." Eight parts are specified in the orchestra: two violins, a cello, two cornetts, and three trombones. Along the way, in the orchestra, there is immense rhythmic vitality and variety within a relatively few musical themes, and at the end a return to the opening theme rounds off the work with a classical finality.

The popularity of opera grew amazingly in the decades after 1610, first in Italy and then throughout Europe. After opera, the principal new vocal form was the *oratorio*. By mid century the oratorio had acquired its definitive characteristics: it had become a work for soloists, chorus, and instruments, in either Latin or the language of daily life, that generally treated religious subjects and that generally called for no stage performance. A key feature of the oratorio was the presence of a singing narrator to explain the action, usually in the words of biblical story.

In their music, oratorios are practically indistinguishable from operas. Thus we leave its illustration by example until the late Baroque period of the eighteenth century, when the oratorio reached its culmination in the splendid creations of Bach and Handel. Exemplary oratorios of the earlier decades include *Jephte*, by Giacomo Carissimi (1605–74), and the *Christmas Oratorio*, by Heinrich Schütz (1585–1672). Both of these works show the revolutionary fertility of an exciting age in musical history.

Recommended Reading

Arnold, Denis. *Monteverdi* (1975). Overview with illustrations and musical examples.

Baard, H. P. *Frans Hals* (1981). Good essay with plates and substantial notes.

Bacon, Sir Francis. *The New Organon and Related Writings* (1960). Bacon's writing in a readable presentation.

Brown, Jonathan. *Velázquez, Painter and Courtier* (1986). Large picture book with fine text and magnificent illustrations.

Clark, Sir George. *The Seventeenth Century* (1961). General topical history.

Friedlaender, Walter. *Nicolas Poussin, A New Approach* (1966). Picture book with notes and long essay.

Haley, K. H. D. *The Dutch in the Seventeenth Century* (1972). All facets of life, well-illustrated.

Hibbard, Howard. *Caravaggio* (1983). Life and works, well-illustrated.

Kahr, Madlyn Millner. *Dutch Painting in the Seventeenth Century* (1978). Fine introduction.

Nicolson, Benedict, and Christopher Wright, *Georges de la Tour* (1974). Long essay with many illustrations and notes.

Palisca, Claude V. *Baroque Music* (1981). Good survey.

Portoghesi, Paolo. *The Rome of Borromini* (1968). Handsome picture book with good text.

Vann, Richard T., ed. *Century of Genius: European Thought 1600–1700* (1967). Collection of primary sources in history and ideas.

Varriano, John. *Italian Baroque and Rococo Architecture* (1986). Comprehensive, well-illustrated.

Wallace, Robert, ed. *The World of Bernini 1598–1680* (1970). Fine introduction to life and times.

Wallace, Robert, ed. *The World of Rembrandt 1606–1669* (1968). Fine introduction to Rembrandt and his setting.

Warnke, Martin. *Peter Paul Rubens, Life and Work* (1980). Good introduction to Rubens.

White, Christopher. *Rembrandt* (1984). Good overview of Rembrandt's life and times.

Whitney, Charles. *Francis Bacon and Modernity* (1986). Bacon's teachings related to the modern world.

13

Baroque Classicism: 1660–1715

In the late seventeenth and early eighteenth centuries, two regimes virtually coincided—the personal rule of the French king Louis XIV (1661–1715) and the restored Stuart monarchy in England (1660–1714). France and England (the latter being absorbed within a British "United Kingdom" in 1707) were, in fact, the most vigorous European powers. Most people of the time saw France as the grander of the two, and the period has remained known to historians as the Age of Louis XIV.

France was by far the largest and most populous country in western Europe, and its dominance was increased by the problems of its potential competitors. Spain had grave economic difficulties and a feeble-minded Hapsburg monarch; it would see a partial recovery only after 1713, when his Bourbon successor's rule was no longer seriously disputed. Although Holland retained much financial and commercial prestige and even gave England a king (William III), it was simply too small to compete for long on equal terms with concentrated French or English power. The Germanies were disastrously disunited and were recovering only gradually from the Thirty Years' War. Italy was similarly divided and was politically stagnant—although the papacy made still another effort at reform and Venice went to war against the Turks (in the process managing to blow up the Parthenon).

325

In France, Louis XIV long terrorized Europe with his military might and dazzled it with his extravagant ceremonial and cultural showmanship. Some historians have seen him as an arrogant nonentity with the trappings of power and the occasional good advice of capable generals and ministers; others have seen him as a statesman of imagination and vision who truly molded his age. The truth may lie in neither view but at a point somewhere between. Louis indeed had his moments of glory, but certainly he could not always resist the extraordinary temptations of his position as Europe's grandest monarch. Always vain and often petty, the Most Christian King could stray far from the ideal of his favorite preacher Bossuet's "divine right" monarch, holder of "sacred, paternal, and absolute power." Louis did, however, maintain a high, if narrow, view of service and trusteeship to God and nation, and it is hard to explain the considerable continuity in French governmental policy across six decades except by the king's own political influence. His policy was as decisive, at least, as seventeenth-century inefficiency allowed—and compared to modern totalitarianism, his absolutism seems mild, muddled, and almost humane.

Restoration England, which returned to power the Stuart dynasty overthrown by Cromwell, was inaugurated by the reign of Charles II (1660–85), who kept his jealousy of Louis XIV's absolutism fairly well hidden and reigned within a framework of parliamentary government. James II (1685–88) was a less successful dissembler and did not hide his Catholicism as Charles had done; he was ousted in the Glorious Revolution of 1688, which established Anglican Protestantism in the land and parliamentary supremacy over the monarch. After James's flight, William III (1689–1702) was the effective ruler, although he shared the monarchy for a time with his wife, Mary, daughter of James. A firm but never very popular ruler, he was succeeded by the ineffectual Anne, Mary's sister. Independent monarchical power had declined so drastically that the last royal veto of a parliamentary measure was cast before the Stuart period was over. This does not mean that democracy was established in England at this time: for almost two more centuries landed wealth would remain the basis for political and social power, as it generally was on the Continent as well.

THE TREND TOWARD CLASSICISM

In the visual and literary art of the middle Baroque period, from 1660 to 1715, a particularly prominent strain of classicism was evident, especially in France and England. In the art of Italy, classical formalism was seldom wholly absent, but it was often overpowered by Baroque exuberance. Italian art in these decades was largely an elaboration of earlier trends.

The city of Rome remained the focus of the Baroque urge—an urge that seems to have been less creative than pedagogical. What Rome was teaching was not so much an admiration for the Baroque forms as for the city's monumental heritage from antiquity, the Renaissance, and the early seventeenth century. The preservation and restoration of antique art and architecture at last were taken seriously, with a degree of historical understanding and conscious responsibility to later generations. Not so clearly beneficial were the academies, where the principles and techniques of practical art were taught systematically, and too often mechanically. Here foreign students were much in evidence, with special prestige after 1666, when the French Academy in Rome was established to train French prize winners in painting, sculpture, and architecture. Rome and to a lesser extent all Italy became the training ground for European artists, even though Italian aesthetic authority was not always followed in the rest of Europe.

Modification and rejection of Italian tradition was nowhere more proudly flaunted than in the France that professed to revere it. More will be said about the especially classical French version of Baroque in a later section of this chapter; we will now note only one revealing instance of the love-hate feelings of the French toward Italian art. In 1665 there came to France, on invitation by the king and his chief minister, the elderly Bernini, Europe's most celebrated sculptor and architect. Bernini was praised and feted extravagantly by the French, but his highly Baroque plans for finishing the Louvre Palace—the ostensible reason for the visit—were received coolly, and ultimately they were replaced by French designs that were far more severely classical and allowed not only for ostentation but for greater royal comfort. Still later, when a giant eques-

CHRONOLOGY

HISTORY		THE ARTS	
		1622–73	Molière
		1632–75	Vermeer
		1632–87	Lully
		1632–1704	John Locke
		1632–1723	Sir Christopher Wren
		1639–99	Racine
1643–1715	Louis XIV king of France	1640–1720	Coysevox
		1642–1727	Sir Isaac Newton
		1646–1708	Jules Hardouin-Mansart
		1653–1713	Corelli
		c. 1658–62	Vermeer's *View of Delft*
		1659–95	Purcell
1660–85	Charles II king of England		
1665–1700	Charles II king of Spain		
1666	Great Fire of London	1667–70	east front of the Louvre, Paris
1667–68	Louis XIV's War of Devolution	1669–85	main construction of palace of Versailles
1672–78	Louis XIV's Dutch War	1675–1710	Saint Paul's Cathedral, London
		1676	Racine's *Phaedra* written
1682	French court moved to Versailles	1680–91	Domed Church of the Invalides, Paris
1685–88	James II king of England	c. 1685	public concerts beginning in London
		1687	Newton's *Principia*
1688	"Glorious Revolution" in England	1689	Purcell's *Dido and Aeneas*
1689–1702	William III king of England	1690	Locke's *Essay Concerning Human Understanding* and two *Treatises of Government*
1689–97	War of the League of Augsburg	1693	Locke's *Some Thoughts Concerning Education*
1700–46	Philip V first Bourbon king of Spain		
1701–14	War of the Spanish Succession: Louis XIV is defeated		
1702–14	Anne queen of England		
1707	union of England and Scotland		

trian statue of the king designed by Bernini was shipped from Rome, it was deemed too flamboyant for kingly dignity and eventually was installed in an obscure corner of the Versailles park—after being transformed discreetly from modern king to ancient Roman hero.

The only concrete product of Bernini's French excursion was a marble bust of his royal host (fig. 13-1) that deliberately sought to invest Louis with some of the traditionally accepted features of the Hellenistic conqueror Alexander the Great. The commanding appearance, the abrupt turn of the head into a gale that seemingly blows the ceremonial draperies to the king's left—all this is realized with lifelike vivacity. Upon a French courtier's objection to Bernini's stylization of the royal features, the artist is reported to have replied, "My king will last longer than yours." And, in fact, Bernini's Louis has remained more appealing than the more staid sculptured portraits by French artists. Still striking, though, is the splendid full-length painting of the king in later years by Hyacinthe Rigaud (1659–1743). Here regal majesty has a Baroque opulence that the French could not always banish from their classicism (fig. 13-2).

13-1   Gianlorenzo Bernini, *Louis XIV*, 1665. Marble, 31″ high. Palace of Versailles.

13-2   Hyacinthe Rigaud, *Louis XIV*, 1701. Oil on canvas, 9′2″ × 5′11″. Louvre, Paris.

Classicism and Authority

Louis tried valiantly to impose a decent orderliness on his age, and in doing so he became the symbol of authoritarian national monarchy in Europe, as well as of a stern cultural classicism. If Louis typified his day in his attempts to control commerce and industry, enforce religious uniformity, and inaugurate military reforms, he also set out deliberately to impose discipline and direction on the visual, literary, and musical arts. The Italian musician Lully was made virtual dictator of French theater and opera at court and in the capital city; the royal minister Colbert, by temperament a thorough classicist, prescribed priorities in the royal building program; the painter Le Brun sternly oversaw interior design for all great public projects; and the supervisor of public works, the architect Hardouin-Mansart, would leave his distinctive mark on the more Baroque architectural style of the reign's later years. All these were men of genuine gifts whose semidictatorial powers, however, did not encourage the free expression of other talents. Academies in the various arts were created and subsidized, and each academy formulated its own classicist orthodoxy that—at least

for a decade or so—would remain unchallenged. The Royal Academy of Painting and Sculpture, under Le Brun's directorship, elaborated uncompromising rules for those arts; in painting, for example, the eye must be subordinate to the intellect and color subordinate to line. Universal types and an exalted, noble beauty were to replace the particular, the common, and the indecorous. When the Academy formally ranked the artists of past ages down to its own time, it was, of course, the ancients who were most favored, and the Flemish and the Dutch who received the lowest ratings.

Such were the ideals of French art during Louis XIV's prime. Those who have condemned it as a courtly, artificial art, remote from real life, perhaps forget too quickly that other Western art too has often been courtly and artificial in origin and content. Yet there does remain a certain cold-bloodedness about the art of Louis XIV's age that may well repel us. Too often it seems deliberately manufactured for propagandistic reasons of state and tailored to an imposed schematic pattern.

The pressure of governmental authority was especially evident in Paris. The king's loyal minister Colbert had a hand in nearly all things Parisian, such as the incorporation of new craft guilds, street-lighting programs, and the organization of reputable law enforcement. Perhaps Colbert's greatest single contribution to modern Paris was the demolition of the city's ancient walls and gates, the gates sometimes being replaced by Roman-inspired triumphal arches and the walls by broad boulevards that became fashionable promenades. Well over half a million people were crowded into the city; among European cities Paris was rivaled in size only by London. Among the Parisian pastimes were going to cafés (coffee, tea, and cocoa had become very popular) and watching marionette shows and strolling musicians. All social classes frequented the theater for plays, while the opera, with its severe stylization, tended to be an acquired taste that appealed to "society" more than to ordinary Parisians.

Of all this, the splendid king saw not a great deal, and still less after his court moved to Versailles in 1682. Until then, Versailles was simply one of many royal residences. However, by the early 1680s, when Louis was at the height of his military and diplomatic prestige and French artistic classicism at its most productive, the palace and town of Versailles (fig. 13-3) had been built up sufficiently to accommodate the royal family, the largely bourgeois bureaucracy, and the court nobility. A setting of spacious yet rigid geometricism was constructed; the gardens and park of Versailles remain today a model and symbol of classical, orderly formalism. Inside the palace, spaciousness prevailed in the royal apartments and halls of state; elsewhere thousands crammed themselves into tiny living quarters for the sake of being near the king. For an aspirant to royal favor and generosity, "not to be seen" by the king was almost not to exist, and petty ceremonial functions were sought with an eagerness that can only strike us as childish. Thus, and with much routine ceremony, did the monarch tame a substantial part of the once-unruly and dangerous French nobility. Louis XIV was not the state, and (legend notwithstanding)

13-3 The palace of Versailles.

he probably never said that he was—but life at his court fostered the majestic fraud with a theatrical pomp never to be equaled in Europe.

Life and the Arts

In England the royal court set its country's social tone less rigorously than did Louis XIV's court in France. Most English aristocrats, at least, avoided such ceremonial indolence as had infiltrated Versailles. On the other hand, English high society was not notably attracted to intellectual pursuits. Still there was somewhat more intermingling of the classes—the comfortable classes anyway—than in France. But Paris as well as London saw a good deal of social mixing. Many of the French aristocrats found both the court and their own estates a deadly bore and enjoyed the attractions of Paris. Growth of a community of cultivated minds was best fostered in the large cities, as was the commonwealth of pleasure, including those greatest of social levelers, the more earthy pleasures. In all respects London had as much to offer as Paris.

By 1685 a new dimension had been added to London life—public concerts. This momentous development in the social history of music evolved out of many earlier phenomena, including domestic music making, music in church and theater, private concerts of the wealthy, and public open-air music making in the streets and at the fairs. More directly, in London's case, the first public concerts seem to have been inspired by music "meetings" or clubs, usually combining amateur and professional players, and by musical performances in public taverns. When at last indoor concerts were offered that were open to the public for an admission fee, without theatrical representation and with an emphasis on professionally performed music rather than amateur audience participation or the taking of refreshments—then and only then can it be said that public concerts in anything like the modern sense had begun. Concerts quickly caught the public fancy, multiplied, and came to be accommodated in larger facilities, sometimes built specifically for that purpose—the first true concert halls.

Public concerts were to arrive later in France. In the meantime the more traditional outlets for music flourished, both there and in England. As in the past, the royal courts were the most generous patrons of musicians and offered the most lavish musical entertainment. Louis XIV and Charles II possessed refined

musical tastes, and Charles numbered singing among his favorite amusements. Both courts hired the best of foreign and domestic performers and sometimes rewarded them well. Lully, Louis's music director, became wealthy, and Purcell—who traditionally vies with Byrd for the title of England's greatest composer—held a series of royal posts and became modestly prosperous at an early age. Few composers and performers, though, were as fortunate as these two.

Literature, Philosophy, and Science

Writing, too, provided a financially precarious living in the late seventeenth century, even for writers favored at the lavish French court and celebrated today as the brightest lights in a brilliant age of French classicism. At least they were less tightly, officially regimented than their better-paid contemporaries, the painters and other artists. Although the famous French Academy founded by Richelieu clearly favored good order and discipline in language and literature, it exerted little effective force on writers.

This is not at all to say that classical French literature was free to develop purely at will; it was, on the contrary, under formidable social and ideological pressures. By general consent, literature presumed to practice "the art of pleasing," and this meant pleasing the aristocracy and the wealthy middle class—a quite restricted group, schooled on the classics and commonly aspiring to civilized refinement and cultural "good taste." As patrons and readers they applauded the cautionary maxims of classicism's famous theorist, the poet Nicolas Boileau (1636–1711), who taught decorum, good sense, order and balance, nobility of theme and expression, and precision of language and thought. Art must imitate nature, and nature, he insisted, "is everywhere the same." To him, nature was revealed not in the disordered everyday world of transient phenomena but best of all in the refined and idealized literary expression of classical antiquity.

Moderns with far less classical, more free-ranging taste have often wondered that literature with such a narrow theoretical base has survived at all. Much of it, of course, has not. Dry formalism cannot produce greatness even in a "classical" age, as Boileau knew. Thus many modern readers have shunned the French classicists and have chosen to read, from that age, only the soul-searching meditations of Blaise Pascal (1623–62), the scientist who became one of the West's great seekers in religion and an explorer on the frontiers of religious despair. Neglect of the classicists themselves, however, is unfortunate. When wit or profundity and social or psychological insight join aptness of style in such writers as Jean Racine (1639–99) and Molière (1622–73)—writers for the tragic and comic stage, respectively—French literary classicism still can move and entertain readers today. Racine's *Phaedra*, with its ancient tale of a Greek queen's passion for her stepson, is in all senses a classic portrayal of uncontrollable impulse and tortured jealousy; it probes as deeply into the human heart as does much of the nonclassical writing of any age. Here, for example, are several lines, in translation, from Phaedra's impassioned outburst to her old nurse Enone; the queen has just learned that the stepson, object of her guilty passion, is secretly in love with another woman:

> Ah! anguish as yet untried!
> For what new tortures am I still reserved?
> All I have undergone, transports of passion,
> Longings and fears, the horrors of remorse,
> The shame of being spurned with contumely,
> Were feeble foretastes of my present torments.

Yet winds of change, away from gentility and classical antiquity, were blowing in both France and England—especially in the last three decades of Louis XIV's reign. In French literature the partial breakdown of the classical ideal was symbolized by the Quarrel of the Ancients and the Moderns, and here the tide ran in favor of the modern authors rather than the exclusive authority of the ancients. Why, wrote the defenders of the moderns, should new authors not equal and even excel the ancients? They share, after all, the human capabilities of their predecessors and have the advantages of experience, refined "good taste," and the better understanding of man and nature furnished by recent science and philosophy.

Indeed, science and philosophy were extraordinarily fruitful in these decades—and extraordinarily disruptive of the established intellectual order. Free-thinking in religion became an underground fashion, especially in Paris. Sometimes it was linked with a sort of pagan hedonism, or sometimes with the new biblical criticism that saw the Scriptures more as human documents than as inviolable holy authority. Everywhere in educated circles *deism* erupted—a religious philosophy that was based on human reason rather than Christian revelation, and that reduced religion largely to ethical precepts sanctioned by a remote and impersonal deity. Unsettling questions about all older religious, philosophical, and scientific notions were raised by the English philosopher John Locke (1632–1704) in a momentous defense of a "sensationalist" psychology that saw ideas not as innate or divinely implanted but as arising through the human senses. It was Locke, too, who most memorably presented the case for representative government; he founded his ideal on the assumption that the "natural rights" of human beings were antecedent even to the historical formation of society and political institutions. An implicit contract or agreement between the king or other ruler and the citizen body, Locke wrote, properly guarantees the natural rights of life, liberty, and property to all citizens. The people can revolt against the ruler if he violates these rights not casually or infrequently but in a long train of abuses that mock those guarantees.

Locke's writing foreshadowed the American Declaration of Independence and some modern attitudes toward toleration and education. Locke, to be sure, could not bring himself to tolerate Roman Catholics, who owed allegiance to a foreign power (the papacy), or atheists, whose sworn oaths could not, he said, be trusted. Otherwise, nearly all people could and should benefit from toleration, he said, as should the very society that was tempted to suppress religious dissent. No society or faith benefits from enforced outward conformity in religion, since "all the life and power of true religion consists in the inward and full persuasion of the mind, and faith is not faith without believing." No force applied by the state to an individual's beliefs can suppress one deeply held faith and assure triumph for another. As for the subject of education, Locke championed "a sound mind in a sound body," more equality between boys' and girls' education, avoidance of severe disciplinary measures, the reward of esteem (not material things) earned by serious study, and the replacement of Latin by modern foreign languages except for those students who aspire to higher education.

While Locke was writing on politics, education, and religious toleration, the biological and physical sciences were taking hesitant steps toward modernity, and scientific societies were being organized to facilitate scientific communication and progress. Above all, Sir Isaac Newton (1642–1727) seemed to have unveiled, in 1687, the ultimate mysteries of the physical world through his law of universal gravitation. The universe, it now appeared, operated essentially like a machine, according to fixed rules that were rationally discoverable, efficiently direct in operation, and ultimately of a gratifying simplicity. "Nature," wrote Newton, "does nothing in vain, and more is in vain when less will serve; for nature is pleased with simplicity, and affects not the pomp of superfluous causes."

Supported by convincing mathematical demonstration, the satisfying Newtonian vision was to be unchallenged for almost two centuries and would especially permeate the atmosphere of the eighteenth-century liberal movement known as the Enlightenment. However, by the end of the seventeenth century, in religion and politics as well as in science, the established worldview was under serious attack. Everywhere, especially in England and France, advanced thinkers were countering the old authorities with a rational, critical, and secular spirit that would remake the Western outlook for generations. Surrounded by his courtiers at Versailles, Louis XIV presumably knew little of all this. His descendants were to experience all too joltingly, during the French Revolution a hundred years later, some of the consequences of the general intellectual ferment of the late seventeenth century.

FRENCH ARTS IN THE AGE OF LOUIS XIV

Human reason can be put to a multitude of uses. In the France of Louis XIV these uses can be grouped conveniently under two headings—the defense and the undermining of the established order. Having noted several ways in which late-seventeenth-century critical reason was subversive of authoritarianism in government, thought, and the arts, we must now turn to reason's positive and more immediately visible contributions to the classical artistic synthesis. Here human reason represents the recurrent impulse toward the settled, the orderly, the precise—impulses commonly scorned in more exuberant or romantic ages but expressing needs that seem too deeply rooted in human nature to be permanently stifled.

French artistic development under Louis XIV fully recognized and embodied these rational, classicist needs. Yet a glance at several typical monuments of the age—in architecture, sculpture, and painting—will reveal that the frequent coolness of French classicism

could at times be tempered by Baroque warmth. Our starting point, however, must be that official governmental architecture where the scales were heavily weighted in favor of classicism. The prime exhibits of this trend are the grand palaces in Paris and Versailles that were notably enlarged under Louis XIV.

The colonnaded east front of the Louvre (fig. 13-4) represents the classical manner at its purest and most successful. Precise responsibility for this facade design (replacing the abandoned plans of Bernini) is uncertain; apparently Claude Perrault (1613–88) and Louis Le Vau (1612–70)—with the advice of Charles Le Brun (1619–90)—share credit. The most obvious elements, the columns and pediments, are classical, and the central pavilion is not unlike an ancient temple front. Behind the paired columns, though, the deep insetting of the windowed walls produces a somewhat Baroque effect of highlight and shadow. The whole possesses an elegant and forbidding grandeur appropriate to the Grand Monarchy itself. If it falls short of greatness, the main defect is typical of French classical architecture—it lacks the spontaneous and the unexpected.

Despite its grandeur, the Louvre colonnade is of proportions that the human eye can grasp. On the other hand, the whole garden front, with wings, of the palace of Versailles (see fig. 13-3) is mind-boggling in its immensity. The central section, or garden front proper (fig. 13-5), was designed by Le Vau, and the whole was completed under Louis's last famous architect, Jules Hardouin-Mansart (1646–1708), grandnephew of François Mansart. The highly visible decorative detail and the smaller relative scale of the columns make the Versailles front less austere and perhaps more Baroque than its colonnaded Louvre counterpart—but at the same time they accentuate the monotony of the whole incredible winged expanse, which probably could only have been redeemed by greater verticality and simplicity.

Still, sheer architectural size does impress and awe, as Louis XIV realized long before the skyscraper age. Versailles remains a monument to divine-right absolutism and a sobering memento of its crushing social costs. The financial burdens incurred by the French monarchy at Versailles can only be suggested by the fact that in 1685, when construction had attained gigantic proportions, over thirty-six thousand workers were employed on the project.

Much of the interior of this veritable temple to

13-4   Claude Perrault, Louis Le Vau, and others, the Louvre, Paris, 1667–70 (east front).

13-5   Louis Le Vau and Jules Hardouin-Mansart, palace of Versailles, 1669–85 (garden front).

13-6 Jules Hardouin-Mansart, Antoine Coysevox, and Charles Le Brun, Hall of War, palace of Versailles, begun 1678.

13-7 Jules Hardouin-Mansart, Domed Church of the Invalides, Paris, 1680–91.

the Sun King (as Louis was pleased to think of himself) is as imposing as the outside. Of course, the interior scale is more manageable than the exterior, even in the grandest rooms of the royal apartments. Our illustration of the Hall of War (fig. 13-6)—with a glimpse into the celebrated Hall of Mirrors—is a vision of Baroque magnificence and a prime example of artistic teamwork. The architectural framework of Hardouin-Mansart is richly filled with sculptural relief, painting, and mirrors—the latter a newly popular decorative device. Le Brun presumably was responsible for the conceptual scheme and designed at least the colorful painting; the large oval relief of Louis XIV on horseback was the work of Antoine Coysevox (1640–1720)—a piece as exuberantly Baroque as Louis's art policies permitted.

In Paris, Hardouin-Mansart undertook to build a second church for a large facility for the disabled war veterans so amply supplied by Louis's wars—the great Domed Church of the Invalides. (Louis would have been chagrined indeed if he had known that the interior would one day be altered to house the tomb of the Corsican usurper, Napoleon Bonaparte.) The facade (fig. 13-7), notably at the second level, shows the influence of the Louvre colonnade but adds planes suc-

13-8   Charles Le Brun, *Alexander the Great Entering Babylon*, c. 1666. Oil on canvas, 14′9″ × 23′. Louvre, Paris.

cessively jutting out toward the middle that suggest bursting Baroque energy. The unusually massive dome grows out of the church body in successive zones from base to cupola and spire. Despite cooler classical reminiscences, the principal effect is of Baroque magnificence.

The age of Louis XIV is not among the most important in the history of French painting. Charles Le Brun was, of course, the dominant figure, at least in the earlier years. At his most typical he was technically skilled and the most disciplined of classicists. One of his better and livelier efforts is the huge, rather crowded *Alexander the Great Entering Babylon* (fig. 13-8) painted in the 1660s when the star of Louis the conqueror was rising and when Louis was flatteringly referred to (by the French, of course) as the second Alexander. Later in the reign, painting, like architecture, assumed the more sumptuous Baroque warmth already noted as characterizing Rigaud's state portrait of Louis XIV. But this, of all paintings, is still among the most formal in tone.

Bombastic content and coolly correct style typified, by and large, the sculpture as well as the painting of Louis XIV's France; academicism reigned as triumphantly in sculpture as in painting, and even longer. Instead of choosing among the dreary thousands of stony classical deities and heroes that once cluttered the salons and gardens of the rich and powerful, let us charitably conclude our survey of French classical art by noting what was then a relative rarity—a religious work with some genuine feeling. This is the tomb of Richelieu (fig. 13-9) sculpted by François Girardon (1628–1715) in the 1670s. The scene is one of noble but human pathos: the dying cardinal offers his heart to God as a handsome draped female figure mourns at the foot of his deathbed. Frigid imitativeness is not, after all, an invariable characteristic of the French classical style.

Obviously Wren did not redesign London either dictatorially or single-handedly. In fact, the early scheme he presented for a whole new urban layout soon proved impractical in the face of surveying difficulties and the eagerness of owners to rebuild promptly on their old properties. However, as Surveyor of His Majesty's Works from 1669, and as agent of various building commissions, Wren did design a number of public secular structures and was in effective control of the enormous program of church building in the City. Above all, Old Saint Paul's Cathedral, its Gothic fabric already perilously weak before the fire and then fatally damaged in the conflagration, had to be replaced. After much discussion and several changes of plan, Wren's general design was accepted in 1675, and the foundation stone was laid in June of that year. Wren would remain in charge of the new cathedral's construction until its completion thirty-five years later. Its enormous bulk astonishingly spared during the World War II bombings, Saint Paul's remains much as Wren knew it—one of Western architecture's most impressive monuments.

13-10 Christopher Wren, Saint Paul's Cathedral, London, 1675–1710.

THE LONDON OF SIR CHRISTOPHER WREN

The most important name in late-seventeenth-century English art is that of Sir Christopher Wren (1632–1723)—who also is commonly labeled a classicist. As in the case of many early-modern architects, Wren's professional career began outside of architecture. An enlightened and creative amateur in all the major sciences, he was primarily a professor of astronomy, in London and at Oxford, before architecture became his guiding passion in the mid 1660s. When he visited Paris in 1665–66, he found the French busily embodying their classical vision and Bernini impatiently criticizing the presumed poverty of French taste. Wren admired Bernini's sketches, which the master himself showed him, but it was the more disciplined spirit of French classicism that made a greater impression, confirming his own natural bent. Wren's basic style was already formed, if not fully refined, by the time the Great Fire of London presented the magnificent opportunity of his life—the reconstruction of the City (that is, the later business and financial nucleus) of London.

13-11   Saint Paul's Cathedral (view from the southeast).

A view of the west front (fig. 13-10) reveals multiple historical influences. The dome, for example, suggests the High Renaissance of Bramante's Tempietto (see fig. 10-8); the portico and the pediment of the second level recall the Louvre colonnade; and the western towers are remarkably close to Roman Baroque. A view from the southeast (fig. 13-11) better displays the dome and also Wren's peculiar solution for the problem of the choir and nave side walls. Here the whole second level is a mere screen; the real walls and clerestory windows lie some thirty feet behind the outside wall. A classically vertical line from ground to high balustrade is thus maintained, and the Gothic flying buttresses behind the deceptive front are wholly hidden. Moreover, the additional weight of the upper front further stabilizes the lower walls upon which the buttresses are grounded. The huge dome extends over the whole width of the nave and aisles; it is, of course, massively supported, and held together in part by inner stone and iron chains. Actually the dome is triple: the curving lines seen from the outside are an aesthetic device that hides the shallow interior dome and the massive brick cone that rises between the two visible domes. It is this firm cone that actually supports the seven-hundred-ton lantern that crowns the structure.

The interior of Saint Paul's is imposing. In figure 13-12 we see mainly the nave, the aisles, and the clerestory windows, with the great dome area spreading out in the distance. At the base of the dome is an octagonal crossing: the large arches beneath the dome are not equal in semicircular completeness but are made to appear so, in the alternate arches, by simple carving upon the massive piers. Saint Paul's retains an overall majestic calm that appeals minimally to any emotional involvement and that can only be labeled classical.

Wren was seventy-seven when Saint Paul's was completed. (Saint Paul's is Europe's only great cathedral to be built under a single architect.) During his last years he was rather poorly treated and at last was ousted from the surveyorship; ambitious younger builders seem to have been frustrated by his vigorous longevity. His tomb was simple, but at least it was placed in the crypt of his own cathedral. Wren's son composed a Latin inscription for the tablet above his grave, where it may still be seen. The words, translated here

13-12   Interior of Saint Paul's Cathedral.

into English, are among the most memorable and best-justified epitaphs of famous men:

Below is laid the builder of this Church and City,
Christopher Wren,
Who lived for more than ninety years,
Not for himself alone but for the public good.
Reader, if you seek his monument,
Look around you.

DUTCH PAINTING AT THE END OF AN ERA

The 1660s and 1670s saw the end of Holland's great age of painting and perhaps the culmination of its artistic achievement. Unhappily the Dutch scarcely noticed before his early death the finest of their young artists, Vermeer, and they did not treat much better the greatest of their old. Rembrandt did some of his most impressive paintings during the decade before 1669, the year of his death, but by then he had long been rather unfashionable except among the more discerning.

Rembrandt's inwardness of vision was unique in his day, and, like most peoples, the Dutch preferred

merriment to solemnity and social activity to introspection. Thus the vogue of Jan Steen (c. 1625–79) is not surprising, especially when we consider his excellence in the craft of painting. Steen's *Merry Company* (fig. 13-13) presents his own family circle in a relaxed mood. The painter, at the right, laughingly lets his young son puff on a long-stemmed pipe as an apprentice pours wine for the mistress of the house. The grandfather chortles in the corner as the grandmother cheerfully points to the words of a song: "The young ones chirp as the old ones used to sing." Although richly and carefully painted, the canvas claims attention primarily as a jovial domestic document.

Among the most distinguished of the Dutch landscape painters was Jacob van Ruisdael (c. 1628–82), nephew of Salomon van Ruysdael but adopting a different name spelling. His works reflect two types of subject matter, untended wilds and placid farm scenes more familiar to most Dutchmen. The painting illustrated here, *The Jewish Cemetery* (fig. 13-14), clearly is in the first category. Unkempt and hauntingly romantic, the scene evokes a mood almost as vividly as do Rembrandt's searching portraits or Steen's mementos of domestic or tavern life.

Holland's last great artist of the century, by common consent today if not in his own time, was Johannes Vermeer of Delft (1632–75). Vermeer's life and personality are largely mysterious to us, beyond a few bare facts and the tentative revelations of his gentle and luminous paintings. It does seem that he was a Catholic in a land dominated by Protestants and that he was a locally respected painter who nevertheless lived mainly, and precariously, as an innkeeper and art dealer. He seems to have painted with slow deliberation. This fact, together with the world's carelessness about much of its art by little-known masters, may account for the survival of only about forty of his works.

Delft in Vermeer's time was a small city best known, as it is in our own day, for its handsome pottery and picturesque canals. One of the finest tributes ever left an artist's native town is Vermeer's extraordinary *View of Delft* (fig. 13-15), apparently painted around 1660. Perhaps no one can be convinced of the work's beauty without seeing the original in The Hague: probably the appeal of no other painting has been more elusive in photographic reproduction. In this work the town of Delft is a scene of almost eerie stillness, isolated from the viewer by the expanse of the river Schie and its sunny nearer bank. Clouds float

13-13 Jan Steen, *A Merry Company (The Young Ones Chirp as the Old Ones Used to Sing)*, c. 1663. Oil on canvas, 33″ × 37″. Mauritshuis, The Hague.

13-14 Jacob van Ruisdael, *The Jewish Cemetery*, c. 1655. Oil on canvas, 56″ × 74½″. Courtesy of The Detroit Institute of Arts (gift of Julius H. Haass in memory of his brother Dr. E. W. Haass).

13-15 Johannes Vermeer, *View of Delft*, c. 1658–62. Oil on canvas, 39″ × 47″. Mauritshuis, The Hague.

overhead against patches of clear sky. A striking effect is achieved by the brilliant sunlight that illumines the houses and the New Church in the far distance, in contrast to the deeply shadowed foreground buildings of the harbor. Tiny points of light glitter here and there with vivacious, dazzling effect.

The *View of Delft* exemplifies only one of Vermeer's approaches to light, color, and atmosphere. Nearly all the rest of his existing works are of interiors and their occupants, and in them his coloristic preoccupations most often result in softer colors and more gently diffused light than in the *Delft* landscape. But other characteristics remain constant throughout his painting, or very nearly so: the lack of visible action, the omnipresent stillness and reserve, and the keeping of the viewer at a distance behind a physical or psychological barrier. All are exemplified in Vermeer's most ambitious interior scene, *The Studio,* or more properly (following the title his widow used) *The Art of Painting* (fig. 13-16). Here a chair and massive drapery partially block the studio entrance, beyond which a painter in

archaic and elegant costume is seen at work on an allegorical figure. Amid symbols of the various arts stands the model, aglow in soft light, who perhaps was intended to impersonate Fame. Meticulous detail in the map of Holland on the wall, brilliant highlights on the burnished chandelier, and the rich rendering (with sparkling points of light) of the heavy drapery in the foreground all testify to Vermeer's skill in differentiating the tactile characteristics of materials. Yet most striking of all is the dreamlike quality of this improbable, arrested vision.

Realistic and commonplace though most of Vermeer's scenes may be, they are touched by a solemn timelessness, a spiritualized formality that may have puzzled the Dutch citizens who demanded anecdotal interest and a cozy familiarity of mood and setting in the paintings they purchased. Not until the late nineteenth century was Vermeer rediscovered and ranked among the greatest of artists. His subtlety in portraying intimate human situations exemplifies again the "formalism humanized" of classical art at its best.

13-16 Johannes Vermeer, *The Art of Painting (The Studio)*, c. 1665–70. Oil on canvas, 47″ × 39″. Kunsthistorisches Museum, Vienna.

BAROQUE MUSIC AT ITS MIDPOINT

Music flourished throughout Europe in the late seventeenth century. The exciting age of early experimental Baroque was past, with its revolutionary monodic and continuo style, and its no less revolutionary forms of opera and oratorio. The task of the new age was evolutionary—the consolidation of recent trends and the gradual introduction of modifications.

Available instrumental and orchestral resources were slowly expanding in the middle Baroque period. The most important new instrument was the oboe, a double-reed woodwind first seen shortly before 1660. At the end of the period the transverse flute was just starting to be used outside of military bands. Violin making was reaching its apex in Italy, in the workshops of Guarneri and Stradivari, and Italian violin virtuosos

were greeted everywhere as astonishing curiosities. On all instruments, *improvisation* was considered the highest of arts—that is, the spontaneous elaboration of musical lines at the moment of performance. Improvisation was encouraged by the fact that composers usually were still furnishing, for both soloists and continuo players, only skeletal notation.

As for orchestration, the modern practice of constructing idiosyncratic, independent parts according to the special effectiveness of each instrument was seldom followed. Woodwinds in Lully's time, for example, usually doubled the string parts. A bit later, as in Purcell's writing, the woodwinds acquired separate musical lines, but they were indistinguishable in style from the string parts. Occasionally in the period's later decades the woodwinds were used together in groups, as a contrast to the strings in alternating passages—a major advance toward modern orchestration, although not wholly unprecedented.

Musical Forms

The evolution in musical form sometimes led even more significantly into modernity—that is, the modernity of folk who attend concerts and hum popular tunes, rather than the modernity of nineteenth- and twentieth-century experimentalism. Full and firm tonality, above all, was finally achieved: in Corelli there was no question, as there often had been in Monteverdi, of the tonal focus of an individual piece. Also, beginning with Lully, tempo and rhythm were fully regularized—an outcropping, perhaps, of "classical" orderliness. Additional formal characteristics of the newer age included the increasing use of thematic repetition to achieve coherence in a work and the further development of the continuo and concerto devices.

As noted in the last chapter, the *continuo* was made up of a bass line and the harmonic structure above it that "continued" throughout a work. In practice the continuo generally involved at least two instruments—a keyboard instrument such as harpsichord to fill in the harmony and sometimes to add ornamentation, and a bowed instrument such as cello to reinforce the bass line. This was the reason for four instruments instead of three in the period's trio sonatas—the third part, after the two solo parts, was the continuo that required two performers. The keyboard continuo—harpsichord in chamber sonatas or organ in church sonatas—functioned primarily as a filler spanning the considerable gap between the bass and treble parts. This was a curiosity of orchestration that commonly occurred also in works for larger ensembles.

The *sonata,* by this time, had become an instrumental cycle with contrasting movements for a soloist or a very small instrumental group. At court or in a chamber its usual purpose was pure entertainment, while in the Roman Church the sonata was used to tide over any nonverbal part of the service or provide liturgical transitions and postludes. Secular sonatas were often indistinguishable from *suites,* which have contrasting movements based on dance forms and are for either a solo instrument or a larger ensemble than required for trio sonatas. As for the concerto form, its historical prime was to come later, although the basic principle of contrast between solo and orchestral parts was established before 1715.

The essential component, then, of all these forms—sonata, suite, and concerto—was the tonally and thematically unified movement, ordinarily homophonic (chordal) in style and employing the continuo. Movements were internally constructed according to regularized repetition and contrast and also followed the principle of contrast when they combined to form larger works.

Opera with its storytelling and its theatrical nature was a different matter. The poet Dryden explained the essence of late-seventeenth-century opera as follows:

> An opera is a poetical tale, or fiction, represented by vocal and instrumental music, adorned with scenes, machines, and dancing. The supposed persons of this musical drama are generally supernatural, as gods, and goddesses, and heroes, which at least are descended from them, and are in due time to be adopted into their number.

Lowlier persons, he admitted, might also be introduced if they were clearly out of the same antique past. In the music of opera, the principal trend was away from the uninteresting, rough musical lines of monody. The newer, more fluent *bel canto* ("beautiful singing") manner was replacing monody, and it often included florid vocalism for its own sake.

The first and most famous of early French operatic composers, Jean Baptiste Lully (1632–87), was actually not French but Florentine by birth. He is perhaps best known for his operatic overtures and their part in

establishing the "French overture." The overture to *Armide* (produced in 1686) is typical of that form. A gravely majestic introduction in chordal style is repeated once and then followed by a lively section with a suggestion of polyphonic imitation. This leads directly into another slow, dignified passage. A repetition of the lively section and a second slow passage brings the work to a close. The *Armide* Overture is as typical of the orderly dignity of French classicism as any piece of "Louis XIV" painting or architecture.

Alive or dead, Lully long dominated French music and still dominates the history of this musical era—with undeserved neglect too often the fate of such contemporaries as Marc Antoine Charpentier. In the meantime Italy kept its great musical reputation. Among the Italian instrumental composers, the most widely admired and imitated was Arcangelo Corelli (1653–1713). Fortunate in possessing a wealthy and loyal patron, Cardinal Pietro Ottoboni, Corelli was free from financial cares and frantic production schedules and had ample time to compose slowly and fastidiously. His total authenticated production is small: seventy-two short works, neatly packaged and published in six groups (opuses) of twelve. (The title page of Opus 3 is illustrated here, with a dedication to the duke of Modena—fig. 13-17). The first four opuses contain forty-eight sonatas, equally divided into works for church and for chamber. They are among the most delightful mementos of the Baroque period, and in their quiet serenity they remind us that Baroque music is not necessarily characterized by tension and ornate display.

The quality of these sonatas is remarkably, almost uniformly high. Suggested for study are Opus 3, no. 7, in E minor and Opus 4, no. 3, in A major. The first is a church sonata, and thus includes an unobtrusive organ in the continuo; the second is a chamber sonata, with harpsichord. The two solo instruments in both cases are violins, and the bass line is reinforced by cello. (On occasion, as in the second movement of Opus 3, no. 7, the cello part can also become ornamentive.) Both works are in four movements, in Corelli's favorite slow-fast-slow-fast pattern. Both are fully tonal and contain a good deal of polyphonic imitation. And both are quite charming.

The same graciousness, whether in slow movements or in fast, marks Corelli's Opus 6. These, however, are not trio sonatas, but *concerti grossi.* The concerto grosso would have an immense future in late

13-17 Title page to first violin part of Corelli's *Trios,* Opus 3, published in Rome, 1689. By permission of The British Library.

not the orchestra—thus foreshadowing later days when concertos were to become showcases for solo virtuosity.

A favorite extended form for keyboard music at this time was the suite. As in trio sonatas and concertos, the movements usually were alternately fast and slow. The little Harpsichord Suite no. 6, in D major, by Henry Purcell (1659–95), will serve as our introduction to that genre, and to this celebrated composer (fig. 13-18). Purcell's keyboard suites include either three or four movements, the first being a prelude in the form of a *fugue* (a polyphonic form in which the musical lines enter successively, using at first the same theme and later developing in free counterpoint), or a *fantasia* (a "flight of fancy" in indeterminate form). In the Sixth Suite the prelude is a brief but dignified fantasia embodying a single melody, free-flowing and sinuous, supported on occasion by the simplest harmony. An *almand* (or *allemande*—a "German" dance in moderate tempo) follows, and a *hornpipe* concludes the work—a lively dance in triple time, featuring a jolly,

13-18 John Closterman, *Henry Purcell,* 1695. National Portrait Gallery, London.

Baroque music; its fundamental principle was the setting off of a small group of solo instruments against a larger orchestral group. Corelli's concertos were published in 1712 but were apparently written, at least in part, long before; thus they are among the earliest examples of this form and also among the less complex. Most often the solos and *ripieno* (full orchestra) are scarcely differentiated musically: each has two violin parts and continuo, and both play virtually the same music, the soloists being heard either alone as a group or combined with the orchestra. In the First Concerto Grosso, in D major, the opening movement contrasts not only the two different bodies of sound but fast passages with slow ones. An energetic *allegro* (fairly fast) movement in polyphonic style follows. The work concludes with another fast movement, this time giving the most agile figurations to the violin soloists alone, highly ornamented melodic line and a simple chordal accompaniment.

A Small Operatic Masterpiece

Perhaps Purcell's musical genius is most striking when applied to the most unpromising texts. Many of his works were commissioned to celebrate such ceremonial occasions as royal birthdays, and their verses can be as uninspired as their music is delightful. The *libretto* (text) for the opera *Dido and Aeneas* is an example; it was written by Nahum Tate, the same author who re-wrote Shakespeare's deeply tragic *King Lear* so as to provide a happy ending.

Tate did suffer, when he wrote the libretto, from the fact that *Dido* was commissioned for performance (in 1689) at a young ladies' boarding school: there could be no love scene that would offend the young ladies and no emphasis on male roles. (Aeneas himself appears only rarely and rather insubstantially.) Primarily the story belongs to the legendary queen of Carthage, Dido, to her female companion and servants, and to the sorceress and witches who contrive her downfall. For them, as for the orchestra and the chorus whose words effectively highlight and frame so much of the operatic action, Purcell wrote music of great variety and beauty. Based on an episode in Vergil's *Aeneid*, the opera has only three short acts and is not as pompous as most tales of the classical past. In its condensation and simplicity the tragic story of Dido and Aeneas is theatrically very effective.

After the orchestra, which throughout *Dido* consists only of strings and continuo, has presented a rather pedestrian overture, the genius of Purcell becomes quickly evident. The queen's companion Belinda sings an air of good cheer to the queen; the setting of her very first word, *shake*, exemplifies the musical word-painting of which Purcell was a master. The chorus follows Belinda in attempting to encourage Dido, whose forebodings then are voiced in an aria built above a *ground*—a sequence of bass notes that is repeated again and again. A brief dialogue between Belinda and Dido reveals the sharp edges of earlier monody, never wholly abandoned by Purcell but never

used to excess; this not-very-melodic dialogue, or speech, in music is called *recitative*. After another chorus, the dialogue becomes smoother and more melodic—almost a succession of short songs. Belinda and another attendant sing a rollicking little duet to reassure Dido of Aeneas's love, and a chorus takes up the same theme before the Trojan hero makes his appearance to declare his devotion. The chorus warmly encourages (polyphonically) the new amorous alliance, as does Belinda in a jovial air. This first scene ends with Dido's implied submission to Aeneas, a chorus of rejoicing, and an orchestral "triumphing dance." The second scene features the sorceress and witches, who envy the lovers' happiness and plot Dido's tragic end by means of deception—a simulated divine intervention. The music here is mainly built around recitative and chorus and concludes with an orchestral "dance of the Furies."

Omitting Act II, in which the false deity commands Aeneas to abandon Dido and to set about founding the Latin state out of which Rome is destined to arise, we turn to Act III. It begins as Aeneas's sailors prepare a reasonably prompt departure from Carthage, although not until taking "a boozy short leave" of their "nymphs on the shore," whom they will soothe by promising to return. After this the mood becomes increasingly grim, as the witches await their imminent triumph, and Aeneas announces his departure to the shattered but still-proud Dido. The climax of the opera, and one of music's most moving moments, is Dido's final aria, "When I am laid in earth." It, too, is based on a ground, which this time is heard alone before Dido's lament begins as if to emphasize its haunting, descending-chromatic eloquence. As Dido prepares to die by her own hand, her plea is simple: "Remember me, but ah, forget my fate." Cupids appear, for a final chorus, to "scatter roses on her tomb."

So ends *Dido and Aeneas*—an opera that goes well beyond its classical subject and dramatic apparatus to achieve a truly classical spirit through directness and economy of musical style. Moreover, the formal elements of classicism in Purcell's work have been matched by variety of mood and intensity of feeling, in the sort of union that has marked much of the Western world's greatest art.

Recommended Reading

Birn, Raymond. *Crisis, Absolutism, Revolution: Europe 1648–1789/91* (1977). General history, mainly narrative.

Blankert, Albert, ed. *Vermeer of Delft* (1978). Good text, plates, and notes.

Briggs, Robin. *The Scientific Revolution of the Seventeenth Century* (1969). Good introduction.

Carr, John Laurence. *Life in France under Louis XIV* (1970). Good overview, illustrated.

Cohen, I. Bernard. *Revolution in Science* (1985). Stimulating, scholarly, massive study of science from the Renaissance to the present; good coverage of science in the seventeenth century.

Dickens, A. G., ed. *The Courts of Europe: Politics, Patronage, and Royalty, 1400–1800* (1977). Well-illustrated essays.

Dunn, John. *Locke* (1984). Brief study of life and works.

Hart, Roger. *English Life in the Seventeenth Century* (1970). Introduction to daily life, well-illustrated.

Lewis, W. H. *The Splendid Century: Life in the France of Louis XIV* (1957). Fascinating portrayal of various social groups.

Locke, John. *Locke on Politics, Religion, and Education* (1965). Large, well-chosen excerpts from his writings.

Loggins, Vernon. ed. *Three Great French Plays* (1961). Includes Racine's *Phaedra* and Molière's *The Hypochondriac.*

Maland, David. *Culture and Society in Seventeenth-Century France* (1970). Narrative and social study.

Palisca, Claude V. *Baroque Music* (1981). Good survey.

Stoye, John. *Europe Unfolding, 1648–1688* (1969). Straightforward political and economic history.

Vann, Richard T., ed. *Century of Genius: European Thought 1600–1700* (1967). Collection of primary sources in history and ideas.

Walton, Guy. *Louis XIV's Versailles* (1986). Historical study of the building of Versailles.

Whinney, Margaret. *Christopher Wren* (1971). Fine overview, well-illustrated.

Zimmerman, Franklin B. *Henry Purcell, 1659–1695: His Life and Times* (1983). The composer in his world, with documents and illustrations.

14

The Early Enlightenment, Late Baroque, and Rococo: 1715–1760

The years between the death of Louis XIV (1715) and the outbreak of the French Revolution (1789) are commonly known as the Age of Enlightenment, following the proud claim of that age itself. The *Enlightenment*—the liberal, anti-authoritarian thought of the eighteenth century—arose most obviously in England and France and bloomed most robustly in France. Only after the middle of the century would the Enlightenment make major advances in the Germanies and America and furnish topics of fashionable conversation as far afield as the court of tsarist Russia.

The political climate of Europe in the decades before 1760 was one of both permanence and change. The Low Countries had gone into eclipse not only politically but culturally, while Russia under Peter the Great (1682–1725) had become a European power. The Germanic parts of central Europe, including Austria, remained effectively disunited, despite nominal deference to the Holy Roman Emperor who nearly always was chosen from the Austrian Hapsburg dynasty. The most urgent problem of such Hapsburg rulers as Charles VI (1711–40) was simply to hold together their multinational realm when faced by the territorial ambitions of envious neighbors. Most envious and ambitious of all was the Prussian monarch Frederick II (1740–86), who seized the large province of Silesia from Austria's young Maria Theresa (1740–80); for this military exploit and others he would become known to history as Frederick the Great. (Maria Theresa had inherited the territories ruled directly by the Hapsburg family, but as a woman she could not be elected to the imperial dignity; in 1745 her husband Francis I became emperor, as their son Joseph II would become in 1765.) Fortunately Frederick possessed qualities beyond greedy ambition; at his best he was a dedicated public servant, an "enlightened despot" whose paternalistic authoritarianism sometimes paid more than lip service to the humanitarian liberalism of the French Enlightenment.

If the north-German state of Prussia was becoming increasingly powerful in European affairs before 1760, so too was Great Britain, its ally in the Seven Years' War, which raged against France and Austria at the close (1756–63) of this period. In Britain the Protestant Stuart line had died out in 1714, and the German ruler of Hanover had become Britain's George I (died 1727). George's lack of interest in things British and small acquaintance with the English language reinforced a preexisting trend toward a cabinet system of government, under which a committee of the dominant faction in the House of Commons came to rule the land. English political life was conducted by an alliance between aristocratic privilege and middle-class wealth, and the mixing of the classes frequently extended to social life as well.

France, in 1760 on the verge of military defeat and the loss of great colonial holdings in America and Asia, remained not only culturally and socially prestigious throughout Europe but basically prosperous. The greatest French problem was the vicious taxation system that barely tapped this prosperity, instead weighing heavily upon the poor, who had very little to give. The debts of Louis XIV, the demands of later wars, and the extravagance and corruption at court brought alarming government debts. None of this, however, greatly bothered the king and his courtiers. The reigns of Louis XV (1715–74) and Louis XVI would go down in French history as the *Old Regime*—the corrupt, inefficient, and seemingly directionless regime that collapsed resoundingly during the Revolution of 1789.

EUROPEAN CULTURE IN THE AGE OF ENLIGHTENMENT

France, the preeminent land of the literary Enlightenment, also saw crucial developments in the visual and musical arts between 1715 and 1760. In fact, it shared leadership with the Germanies in the lighthearted outgrowth of Baroque known as the *Rococo* style. In architecture, however, Germany quickly surpassed even French Rococo exuberance, although the German Baroque manner still existed and flourished. In music Germany produced the greatest of all Baroque composers, Bach and Handel. Handel, to be sure, had settled in England before 1715 and outshone all native English artists of the time, even the admirable painter and engraver Hogarth. Since Handel's musical inspiration, and indeed Bach's, remained so often Italian, and since the continuous Italian tradition in painting produced its last masterworks in this period, Italy, too, deserves mention in the cultural record of the age.

The German Scene

In the Germanies, Frederick the Great's Prussia saw less cultivation of the arts than did the states farther south. In architecture and interior design the lead was taken by secular and clerical Catholic leaders, ranging from petty rulers, as at Würzburg, to substantial ones, as in Bavaria. The nobility in the scores of German princedoms were extraordinarily jealous of their ceremonial and political privileges and often were ignorant, crude, and provincial—but some of the building projects they, or the Catholic Church, commissioned were lavish and tasteful. The German middle class, Catholic or Protestant, on the other hand, tended to remain culturally unambitious, preferring to congratulate themselves on their sober avoidance of aristocratic ostentation and arrogance. Above all, the burghers were suspicious and resentful of the French influences that had captivated much of the German aristocracy and that still reigned in German literature.

The Arts in England

The immediate acceptance of the German composer Handel in England reflected a widespread quest for "culture" in the land. In fact, Handel's public recognition was extraordinary. A full twenty years before his

CHRONOLOGY

HISTORY		THE ARTS	
1682–1725	Peter the Great ruler of Russia	1684–1721	Watteau
		1685–1750	Johann Sebastian Bach
		1685–1759	Handel
		1688–1744	Alexander Pope
		1694–1778	Voltaire
		1696–1770	Giambattista Tiepolo
		1697–1768	Canaletto
1700–46	Philip V first Bourbon king of Spain	1699–1779	Chardin
		1703–70	Boucher
1711–40	Charles VI Hapsburg Holy Roman Emperor	1712	Handel settles in England
1713	Treaty of Utrecht: Spanish Netherlands and Italian lands become Austrian	1712–78	Jean Jacques Rousseau
1714–27	George I king of England		
1715–74	Louis XV king of France		
1715–23	the Regency	1717	Watteau's *Pilgrimage to Cythera*
		1721	Bach's six Brandenburg Concertos dedicated to the margrave of Brandenburg
1723–74	personal reign of Louis XV	1724	Handel's *Julius Caesar* produced in London
1727–60	George II king of England	1729	Bach's *Saint Matthew Passion*
		1733–34	Pope's *Essay on Man* published
		1738–40	Boffrand's Hôtel de Soubise, Paris
1740–48	War of the Austrian Succession: Great Britain and Austria vs. France and Prussia	1741	Handel's *Messiah* written; first performed (in Dublin) in 1742
1740–63	colonial wars between France and Great Britain		
1740–80	Maria Theresa, Hapsburg archduchess of Austria, queen of Bohemia and Hungary		
1740–86	Frederick II (the Great) king of Prussia	1742	Boucher's *Bath of Diana*
		1743–72	Church of the Vierzehnheiligen
		1745	Hogarth's *Marriage-à-la-mode* paintings
		1750	Rousseau's *Discourse on the Arts and Sciences*
		1750–53	Voltaire resident at Frederick II's court
		1751	Voltaire's *Age of Louis XIV* published
		1751	first volume of Diderot's *Encyclopedia* published
		1755	Rousseau's *Discourse on Inequality*
1756–63	Seven Years' War: Great Britain and Prussia vs. France and Austria	1756	Voltaire's *Essay on the Manners and Spirit of Nations* published
		1759	Voltaire's *Candide*
		1760	Chardin's *Jar of Olives*

EUROPE IN 1715

death, he was honored by a marble statue set up prominently in one of London's popular parks, Vauxhall Gardens. Such gestures of homage to living composers have been rare in history.

Unfortunately British-born talent in the arts was in rather short supply at this time. The poet Alexander Pope (1688–1744) was the most notable English writer of the age, gaining fame as an author of satirical and philosophical verse. His *Essay on Man* was an argument in defense of providential guidance and order in the universe. Human beings, he insisted, must accept their place in the world and not presume to understand the divine scheme of things:

Know then thyself, presume not God to scan;
The proper study of Mankind is Man.

According to Pope's verse *Essay*, God created the best of possible worlds, with all creatures rising "in due degree" as He had ordained. Man, wrote Pope, has his own place in the hierarchy or chain of being, and must refrain from trying to know what God alone, designer of the big picture, can know: "'Tis but a part we see, and not a whole." We can only "hope humbly" for the future—"Hope springs eternal in the human breast"— and not judge God's actions or His own wise plans. Intellectual pride (as medieval Christianity also had insisted) is man's characteristic sin: "In Pride, in reas'ning Pride, our error lies."

Pope concluded the first section of *An Essay on Man* with a ringing exhortation to submit obediently to all that God, the great artisan of all nature, has ordained:

All Nature is but Art, unknown to thee;
All Chance, Direction, which thou canst not see;
All Discord, Harmony, not understood;
All partial Evil, universal Good:
And, spite of Pride, in erring Reason's spite,
One truth is clear, 'Whatever IS, is RIGHT.'

This acceptance of God's authorship of nature, and avoidance of complex theological speculation, would be compatible with the deist religion that became prominent in the eighteenth century. However, Pope's message of absolute submission to God's creation would soon look too much like resigned acceptance of the world's ills and thus would grate on the reformist zeal of the age. Nor would his discounting of human reason appeal to Enlightenment thinkers. Pope's immediate fate would be to become not an inspiration but a foil to the age of Enlightenment. Otherwise his main significance would be that he was the first poet to support himself by selling poems to publishers rather that appealing to aristocratic patrons for money.

Britain's hundred years of unusual distinction in painting were just beginning, with the canvases of William Hogarth (1697–1764). Hogarth was a spokesman, like such novelists as Defoe and Fielding, for middle-class habits and ideals. His best-known works are paintings and engravings on narrative, satirical subjects. In these works he was a quite unabashed moralizer, forever preaching respectability and hard work. Baroque tendencies toward theatricality and propagandistic persuasion are clearly evident in the explanation he gave for painting on "modern moral subjects." "I wished," he wrote, "to compose pictures on canvas, similar to representations on the stage; and farther hope that they will be tried and criticized by the same criterion. In these compositions, those subjects which will both entertain and improve the mind, bid fair to be of the greatest utility, and must therefore be entitled to rank in the highest class." Hogarth may have been misguided, but in any case he was forthright and, in best Enlightened form, utilitarian and humanitarian.

Hogarth delighted particularly in exposing the presumed decadence of the aristocracy. In one of the six paintings in his popular *Marriage-à-la-mode* series, *Lady Squanderfield's Dressing Room* (fig. 14-1), his obvious aim is to depict frivolous extravagance. Sumptuous classical décor and erotic paintings announce immediately the high social level and low moral tone of the scene. At the right, the noble lady is having her hair done while being entertained by her lover. The predominantly stylish guests at this informal reception are served refreshments as a pink-faced singer performs over the chatter to a flute accompaniment. Later scenes in the series make clear the inevitable sequel of such self-indulgence: sexual degradation and finally murder and suicide.

The French Enlightenment

Hogarth and many of his compatriots were convinced that vile corruption among the socially privileged was encouraged by influences from abroad—mainly from France. In truth, for good or for ill, France under Louis XV remained the social and cultural model for Europe that it had become under his predecessor. Moreover, the death of the stern Grand Monarch had led to a notorious public relaxation of French upper-class moral standards during the Regency period (1715–23) and after. Forecasting the change of tone after Louis XIV's death was the regent's moving of the court from Versailles to Paris—from an atmosphere of oppressive grandeur to the more human scale of the Palais-Royal and big-city pleasure seeking. However, the regent's tampering with the bureaucratic absolutism symbolized by Versailles, in favor of looser aristocratic control, brought dismal failure and was soon abandoned. Even the eventual return of Louis XV to Versailles could not restore the spirit of his great-grandfather's rule. Louis XV was perhaps intelligent but certainly lazy, and he let himself be ruled by advisers, official and unofficial. For two decades the most attractive among the latter group was the king's mistress and friend, Madame de Pompadour.

The physical charms and elegant grace of Madame de Pompadour are vividly evoked in François Boucher's portrait (fig. 14-2). Few royal mistresses across the centuries have sat for portraits, as Pompadour often did, in the company of books and art works. She was an amateur artist and a voracious, discriminating reader, even of those Enlightened authors who

14-1   William Hogarth, *Lady Squanderfield's Dressing Room,* from the series *Marriage-à-la-mode,* 1745. Oil on canvas, 28″ × 36″. Reproduced by Courtesy of the Trustees, The National Gallery, London.

were undermining the political and social system that had permitted her rise to power. Although her political influence was sometimes disastrous, her literate taste and her frequent protection of liberal publications were of incalculable help to the more moderate segment of the Enlightenment at mid-century. As the dean of Enlightened thinkers, Voltaire, said after her death: "She was one of us."

In its social milieu the French Enlightenment was, in fact, both bourgeois and aristocratic. Several of its celebrated leaders held titles of nobility, and the lively exchange of liberal ideas was a social activity of all educated classes. This intellectual exchange between nobles and commoners occurred most memorably in the *salons*—the drawing rooms, or regular

drawing-room gatherings—of aristocratic and bourgeois hosts and hostesses. The Enlightenment arose in a genteel environment, not in a world of ragged, revolutionary outcasts.

It was, none the less, a movement revolutionary in its implications, and in its own day it was quite as subversive as any underground conspiracy of later centuries. Of course, the harder intellectual work of the Enlightenment was done not in the salons but in the quietness of writers' studies—and when published it had to face the threat of government censorship. The sometimes flippant and witty facade of the earlier Enlightenment attracted converts among the cultivated salon audience and also served to protect it from governmental prosecution. Far more than ridicule would

14-2 François Boucher, *Madame de Pompadour,* 1758. Oil on canvas, 29″ × 23″. By Courtesy of the Board of Trustees of the Victoria and Albert Museum, London.

François Marie Arouet, known as Voltaire (1694–1778). Although Voltaire (fig. 14-3) battled unceasingly for reason and for intellectual freedom as he saw it, his fanciful philosophic tale *Candide* is a classical exposé of the world's absurdity and evil. Its witty yet sometimes bitter narrative of the successive encounters of the young, naive Candide with the imperfections, evils, and horrors of this world was a deliberate effort to refute the presumed "optimism" of Alexander Pope and his German contemporary Leibniz. The implication throughout Voltaire's tale is that if this is the best of all possible worlds, then God help us! Against the empty preachings of Candide's tutor Pangloss, a devotee of the Pope–Leibniz view, Candide can only come at last to acknowledge the harsh realities of experience—and to counsel a renunciation of philosophical theorizing and a devotion to hard work and minding our own business. The story concludes by implying that only through occupying ourselves with our daily tasks ("we must cultivate our gardens") can we survive amid meaningless catastrophes.

14-3 Jean Antoine Houdon, *Voltaire,* 1781. Marble. By Courtesy of the Board of Trustees of the Victoria and Albert Museum, London.

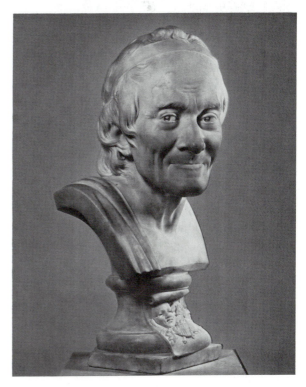

ultimately be needed to topple the Old Regime—but many a solidly established institution has been weakened by ridicule before the dead-serious wreckers have arrived.

Yet the intention of French social critics in the decades before 1760 was serious enough. Their passion for spreading the rational, antiauthoritarian spirit of Descartes, Newton, and Locke was genuine: they were dedicated enthusiasts and believers—quite as much so, in their way, as the saints and theologians of the Church they often scorned. Their way, however, was different, for they were heirs not only to the activist spirit of Christian idealism but also to the secular and scientific tradition of the Renaissance and the seventeenth century. Confronted by a religious, political, and social establishment that they considered nonsensical, corrupt, and unjust, they battled cheerfully for reform, if not yet for any ultimate earthly perfection.

Typifying this approach, and preeminent in the early generation of French Enlightened thinkers, was

In his own day Voltaire was most honored as a writer of verse tragedies in the manner of Racine; today he is remembered far more often as the author of such philosophical tales as *Candide* and as a fighter for Enlightenment causes. He was one of his century's staunchest defenders of deist rationalism, as against what he took to be the superstition of dogmatic Christianity with its mysteries and (he said) its wildly contradictory biblical foundations. He battled tirelessly for religious toleration (Roman Catholicism was the only legal faith in France until just before the Revolution) and labored vigorously to clear the names of several recent victims of intolerance. (He was not as tolerant of Jews, who were too closely linked in his mind to the origins of the Christianity he deplored; it was the German author Lessing who pleaded most strongly for toleration and humane acceptance of the Jewish people.) Voltaire wrote again and again on the madness of warfare and other instances of man's inhumanity to man, such as the vicious realities of the criminal justice of the time.

Voltaire also earned an honorable place in the history of historical writing. More than any other historian he deserves the title of father of intellectual and cultural history. His *Age of Louis XIV* set out to extol not so much the political and military exploits of that king as the "art and science and the progress of the human mind in his age." In his *Essay on the Manners and Spirit of Nations,* an ambitious attempt at world history, Voltaire went well beyond the customary approach of his day—centering on the Judaic-Christian tradition—and included substantial surveys of Arabic, Chinese, and Indian civilizations. However, his historical empathy was, by more recent standards, far from perfect; his tendency to judge other cultures by Western, Enlightened standards is usually all too obvious. Although Voltaire preached close adherence to historical fact, this ideal in practice was often subservient to his zeal for promoting Enlightenment doctrine. The "crimes, follies, and misfortunes" that Voltaire found so typical of the human past were contrasted with the goals of his own Enlightened rationalism, and too often Voltairean ideals were conveniently found among non-Western peoples that actually would have barely recognized them.

Voltaire typifies the ideals of the earlier French *philosophes*—neither profound philosophers nor pedantic scholars but publicists for a more rational, natural, and humane order on earth. "Reason" and "nature"

were words they liked to use, for they represented the most cherished concepts of the Enlightenment. *Reason* meant cool, unfettered thought, as opposed to prejudice, superstition, and all past authority. Sometimes the rational was deliberately contrasted with the emotional, and too often in practice it underrated the rich potentialities of human feeling. Usually reason's relationship with empiricism (factual observation) was left unclear, and too often reason encouraged an airy sort of abstractness that would have profited from a closer checking against the reality of hard facts.

Like "reason," *nature* was a term used in disconcertingly variable ways—but it almost never referred to the nature actually observable in the world, with all its defects and irrelevancies. "Nature" was a glowing if ambiguous ideal of how things should be rather than a description of what they actually were. Since imprecision made "nature" and "reason" all the more useful and adaptable for Enlightened propaganda, the two concepts became measuring sticks for the religious, political, economic, and social institutions of the time, most of which were found grievously defective. Further, "nature" and "reason" offered guidelines for concrete alternatives: for religious toleration and theological simplification, for civic-spirited and rational government under enlightened monarchs, for an economic life free of feudal obstructions, and for a new social order that would reward talent rather than aristocratic birth.

By mid-century these goals were being supplemented by those of more radical thinkers who stressed "utility" as a criterion for the good life, current institutions, and future reforms. Still more disruptive of the early, moderate Enlightenment were the first passionate writings of Jean Jacques Rousseau (1712–78). Rousseau's *Discourse on the Arts and Sciences* (1750) took the position that humans have become increasingly corrupted as the arts and sciences have progressed. Virtue and enlightenment, he argued, are seldom compatible: the arts and sciences have often ignored the traditional, civilizing virtues or have actually attacked them, and the consequent growth of "luxury" has further undermined wholesome virtues.

In Rousseau's second celebrated, longer essay, the *Discourse on the Origins and Foundations of Inequality among Men* (1755), he presented a still more insidious argument against traditional views and institutions: the argument that men in a rather hypothetical "state of nature" were peaceful (in contrast to Hobbes's view) but more or less equal, and that unjustified claims to "property" and their forceful defense gave rise to gross inequality and injustice. Thus the strong and rich have oppressed the weak and poor—an unhappy situation for which Rousseau only later would suggest the remedy of democracy (rule of the people). We should emphasize that this remedy emphatically did not include a simple return to the wild state of nature—a common misconstruing of Rousseau's position ever since Voltaire playfully chided Rousseau for making a person long to go again "on all fours." Rousseau was not amused.

Rousseau's earnest sentimentalism, his progressive educational theories, and his vision of a democratic society would be fully elaborated only after 1760. Few of his favorite ideas were unprecedented in the preceding decades, however. The revival of feeling and sentiment, often thought of as epitomized by Rousseau, was strikingly evident in England by the early 1740s. Already John Wesley's "Methodist" religious revival, with its fervent emotionalism, had begun, and Samuel Richardson's novel of feeling, *Pamela*, was published (1741) "in order to cultivate the principles of virtue and religion."

The Rococo Style

A revolt against rigid formalism had begun in the visual arts before Louis XIV's death—a revolt in favor of more intimate and individualistic expression. One manifestation of this revolt was the Rococo manner that bloomed from 1715 to 1760 and beyond, which offered a pleasing alternative to Baroque classicism.

The word *Rococo* was introduced by French Classicists later in the eighteenth century, in part a pun on *Baroque* in its Italian form—*barocco*. It further derived from the term for the fanciful shell-work popular in artificial grottoes built in the gardens of the aristocracy—*rocaille*. That Classicist revival was the most stern of all such revivals, and its sense of order and propriety was scandalized by what it considered the whimsical ugliness of these grottoes, encrusted with shells and irregular stones. The parallel that Classicism drew between grotto decoration and the new architectural style of the Louis XV period was forced and unkind, but it did highlight the decorative whimsy of the new manner. In still later, non-Classical periods, when decorative whimsy no longer seemed tasteless, the term *Rococo* was cheerfully applied to certain trends

not only in eighteenth-century architecture and interior design but also in such arts as painting and music.

Rococo architecture is found at its most typical in interiors and, in fact, partly originated out of rebellion against the inhuman architectural scale and drafty grandeur so much admired in the age of Louis XIV. Rococo's prototypical expression is seen in the interiors of many private *hôtels* (town houses) built in France during this period; one of the finest examples is the Oval Salon, designed by Germain Boffrand (1667–1754), of the Hôtel de Soubise in Paris (fig. 14-4). Here, rejecting Baroque monumentality, is a room of grace and intimacy, full of the fanciful, sinuous design that, near the ceiling, seeks even to conceal and deny the underlying structure. The applied *stucco* (plaster) decoration does not overwhelm, but brightens and enlivens the room. No more perfect setting can be imagined for the wit and informal elegance to which the cultivated men and women of this refined age aspired.

The Rococo style, in all the arts, sought to amuse and delight its patrons. Its greatest dangers were frivolity and excessive artifice. Europeans were to turn against it after several decades—and many had never accepted it in the first place, preferring the more formal balance of the Baroque. Outside of France and southern Germany, most of courtly and ecclesiastical Europe remained loyal to the Baroque, although in domestic interior design Rococo did make inroads. Italy, for example, favored the older, grander manner in its public structures—perhaps an assertion of native cultural dignity despite the country's political fragmentation and its domination (since 1713) by Austria.

Musical Life and Musicians

Italy remained during this time the native land of opera of the most florid sort. Fashion demanded that even most operas written outside of Italy employ Italian texts—a circumstance that doubtless contributed to opera's isolation from the populace. The main point of these lavish operatic productions was to astonish—a typically Baroque feature. The upper classes in Europe usually remained devoted to opera, even though Voltaire complained that in opera one sang what was too stupid to speak.

Many moderns have found excessive the late Baroque emphasis on mere technique in musical performance. In a period that, like preceding centuries, stressed free ornamentation by soloists and delightedly

14-4 Germain Boffrand and others, Oval Salon of the Hôtel de Soubise, Paris, 1738–40.

pushed forward the frontiers of vocal and instrumental virtuosity, the emphasis should not be surprising. Still harder for many to accept today is the small size of Baroque musical ensembles: even the grandest presentations of Handel's operas and oratorios seem to have used no more than sixty vocalists and instrumentalists, and Bach could have gathered few more than that for the first Leipzig performance of his monumental *Saint Matthew Passion.*

The institution of the public concert was gradually extended during this period, as a supplement to the opera and to conventional court, church, and domestic performances. Yet regular performances by professional musicians, open to the public for music listening alone, were still rare. In Germany, for example, professional instrumentalists and singers usually had amateur support and seldom appeared in true concert halls. Bach gave regular, secular concerts in Leipzig, but they took place at Zimmermann's Coffee House and often were marred by inadequate playing.

As always, musicians lived in varying degrees of poverty and affluence. Bach's positions brought to him and his enormous family only the most modest comfort. On the other hand, Handel became not only famous but wealthy through aristocratic patronage and as a concert and operatic impresario. By and large,

though, the unhappy truth was that the age's gradual extension of literacy and mild sophistication through the middle classes brought little increase in financial security to composers or artists. For example, the only copyright control in either area that meant anything at all was the painter's occasional right to income from engravings of his works.

Otherwise artists survived as best they could, with the highest fees going to painters in the "grand manner"—those who decorated aristocratic establishments with enormous compositions on heroic, mythological, or erotic themes. Amid the mass of hacks kept busy in this realm were a few artists of genuine accomplishment. Those who painted modest works on everyday themes received more modest compensation. Though not as independent or as visionary as Rembrandt, they, too, contributed honorably to art's long history of struggle for creative freedom.

ARCHITECTURE IN THE ROCOCO AGE

Architecture between 1715 and 1760 was as varied as was painting. National and regional traditions operated powerfully in both realms, as did the latent tension between Baroque (with varying degrees of classicism) and Rococo. In Britain and its American colonies many architects spurned Baroque altogether for a purer classicism. In the southern German-speaking lands, Austria remained more loyal to the Baroque than did the nearby Germanic states, perhaps because of its closer cultural ties to Italy. In southern Germany, though, the tide ran increasingly in favor of the new Rococo manner. The advance of Rococo can be traced in the work of Balthasar Neumann (1687–1753) in Franconia, north of the western Danube River.

Neumann collaborated with Lucas von Hildebrandt and others in designing many of the architectural interiors of the Residenz (Episcopal Palace) at Würzburg. His employers were several successive prince-bishops of that town. The Kaisersaal (Hall of the Emperor) in the Würzburg palace (fig. 14-5) is in the most magnificently Baroque style, with enormous red-marble columns accented amid the airy pastel colors, and the whites and golds, of their setting. Yet the Rococo manner is foreshadowed, not only in the general lightness of the color scheme, but in the subordination of architectural forms to the delicate sinuosity of overlaid stucco ornamentation.

Painting, sculpture, and architecture are, if possible, still more closely allied in Neumann's masterpiece of Rococo ecclesiastical architecture, the Pilgrimage Church of the Vierzehnheiligen (fig. 14-6). Here several oval units, partially defined by columns and walls, succeed each other and intersect to transform a basically rectangular area into an enchanted spatial confusion in which all sense of orderly structure is lost. Twisting, painted stucco envelops many of the vaulting ribs, deliberately negating geometry and concealing the structural elements. In the nave, within the central oval, stands a multicolored fantasy, the altar of the Vierzehnheiligen ("Fourteen Saints"); above and around it are the luminous but pale colors of stone and paint that characterize the Rococo in all lands. Ceiling frescoes seem to ooze outward and downward. Yet, in contrast to the most luxuriant Baroque manner, there are many extensive architectural areas that remain blank—the undecorated expanses that rest the eye for riotous decorative delights nearby. This decoration, moreover, is miniaturized, as in the Hôtel de Soubise; it is a happy entanglement of intimate details, not a monumental imposition of grand patterns.

Architectural Sculpture

The period from 1715 to 1760 was not one of the greatest ages for conventional sculpture. The better large-

14-5 Balthasar Neumann and Lucas von Hildebrandt, the Kaisersaal, Residenz (Episcopal Palace), Würzburg, 1719–44.

14-6 Balthasar Neumann, *Pilgrimage Church of the Vierzehnheiligen,* near Bayreuth, 1743–72.

14-7 Egid Quirin Asam, *Assumption of the Virgin,* 1718–25. Convent Church, Rohr, Germany.

scale sculpture, mainly French and German, usually appeared in close association with architecture. The *Assumption of the Virgin* (fig. 14-7)—the main altar group in the Bavarian convent church at Rohr—is a well-known example. Here Egid Quirin Asam (1692–1750) contrived a startling vision in stucco—a scene as melodramatic as Bernini's *Saint Teresa* and almost as closely integrated with its architectural setting. The Blessed Virgin, it appears, is quite as astounded at her sudden ascension as are the spectators near her empty tomb as she is bustled off to a heaven symbolized by clouds, cherubs, and a burst of sunlight. The work is on the borderline between Baroque and Rococo, with Baroque theatricality and a painted and gilded prettiness in the fluttering Virgin and angels that suggests the Rococo. Asam's *Assumption* shows us that both styles could strive for and achieve a true synthesis of all the visual arts.

PAINTING IN THE ROCOCO AGE

Despite its frequent absorption within "total" works of visual art—that is, in association with architecture and sculpture—eighteenth-century painting often is able to stand on its own. Outside its native land, German painting between 1715 and 1760 is little remembered today, but Italy and France produced painting of international stature, some of which can be ranked close to the Western world's best.

Venetian Painters

Much of the finest painting in Italy came, as it had in the sixteenth century, from Venice. By now, the famous port city had lost much of its verve and confidence. Venetians lived under an arrogant despotism, within a maze of bureaucratic restrictions, and amid a horde of government spies. Despite or perhaps because of all this, Venice had become the pleasure capital of Europe—the picturesque center of the most extravagant and cosmopolitan revelry. Countless festivities, including the famous Carnival, were held, and all Europe attended. And when "all Europe"—which, of course, meant primarily the wealthy and stylish—went home, they were likely to take with them not only a new bad habit or two but also a painted *veduta* ("archi-

14-8 Canaletto, *The Piazza San Marco*, c. 1760. National Gallery, London.

tectural view") of the city as a souvenir. Among the most fortunate were those who obtained vedute by Giovanni Antonio Canale, known as Canaletto (1697–1768). His view of the Piazza San Marco (fig. 14-8) is typical. Its dominant physical features are the ancient basilica, the buildings of the square, and the human bustle of the scene. Canaletto's paintings carefully evoke the surface of a city and are models of perspective and balanced composition.

Best typifying the grander aspirations of eighteenth-century Venetian painting was the celebrated, prolific, prosperous, and mysterious Giambattista Tiepolo (1696–1770). Few artists of such international fame and fortune in modern times have remained so little known to us as personalities; Tiepolo is understood through his art alone.

The geographical scope of Tiepolo's activity was wide—from Venice and mainland Italy, to Germany's Würzburg, and ultimately to Spain, where he ended his days. He was especially in demand for such heroic mural projects as those of the bishops of Würzburg. His subjects, above all, were mythological and historical—and he saw the whole breadth of history as a costume

pageant out of sixteenth-century Venice. This was as true of the Würzburg frescoes as of the *Banquet of Antony and Cleopatra* (fig. 14-9), which he painted for a Venetian palace. Demands of historical accuracy bothered Tiepolo not a bit; his cheerful historical anachronisms unabashedly transform and romanticize the past. The banquet scene records, in sixteenth-century dress, the legendary moment of one-upmanship when the Egyptian queen, unimpressed by the culinary extravagance of her host, prepares to dissolve a precious pearl in vinegar and drink it. Tiepolo's theatricality is Baroque, but his frequent jovial playfulness and the lightening of his color scheme to pastel shades and silvery atmosphere are typically Rococo.

Rococo and Bourgeois Painting in France

Tiepolo seems to have made little impression on eighteenth-century French viewers. Perhaps a mental association between his enormous decorative schemes and the then-discredited heroic paintings of Louis XIV's time blinded them to the fact that Tiepolo's spirit often approached that of the French Rococo. In any case, the French had already followed their own path

14-9 Giambattista Tiepolo, *Banquet of Antony and Cleopatra*, c. 1745–50. Fresco. Labia Palace, Venice.

into eighteenth-century art, usually by way of down-grading the cool and linear formality of Poussin and exalting the coloristic sensuality of Rubens. The victory of the Rubenists in their polemics against the Poussinists certainly helped prepare France for the coming of Rubens's countryman Watteau during the Regency period.

Antoine Watteau (1684–1721), who was born in Flanders only a few years after Louis XIV had annexed his native city, achieved fame and modest fortune in Paris. Study of Rubens and the Venetian painters of the past reinforced his feelings for color, nature, and amorous, pagan sensuality. Transformed by his temperament, however, these emphases were lightened by an informality and grace that are particularly associated with the Rococo. Yet Watteau's work was seldom flippant; his ill health and eventual resignation to an early death from tuberculosis may well account for the vaguely melancholic atmosphere that characterizes so many of his paintings.

One of his most celebrated paintings is the Louvre's *Pilgrimage to Cythera* (fig. 14-10), which he presented in 1717 to the Royal Academy as his "reception picture" for full membership in that august body. The subject is remotely inspired by Homer's tale of Cythera, the isle of love and enchantment, and probably by a scene from a theatrical presentation, but the mood is typically Watteau's. Pairs of lovers descend languidly to their ship at the seashore—either to embark for Cythera, according to long-standing interpretation, or more likely to take their wistful and reluctant leave of that island. The ambiguity of subject is typical of Watteau, who cherished the freedom offered by his preferred theme of the *fête galante*—an elegant, festive diversion in a parklike setting with amorous overtones. Within such a setting, many variations of pose and mood were possible, and all the more so because Watteau's informal scenes from the leisure moments of well-bred society were often deliberately indistinguishable from theatrical scenes. Although they escape the stony architectural classicism of a Poussin and enter a more natural realm, these scenes still suggest a theatrical dream world—a world far removed from everyday reality even during the French Regency.

Watteau's *Music Party* (fig. 14-11) also evokes a dream world. Delicate feminine charm and an undercurrent of flirtatiousness pervade the work, while the young man's attempt to tune a large lute suggests the elusive, fleeting nature of the moment. Music making, it should be noted, is a frequent theme of Watteau.

14-10 Antoine Watteau, *Pilgrimage to Cythera*, 1717. Oil on canvas, 50″ × 76″. Louvre, Paris.

Like his painting, music is a realm of the temporal, the shifting, and the intangible—and Rococo music, particularly, was coming to emphasize the sensitive and evocative. Very much at home in the world of music and musicians, Watteau was a careful observer and an accurate recorder of contemporary instrumental practice, such as finger positions—a reminder that his flight from everyday reality had its exceptions.

The age of Louis XV inherited Watteau's painting technique, with its harmonious and airy color schemes and his theme of the fête galante, but it rarely achieved his uncluttered pictorial composition or his psychological insight. As France came closer to revolution, the art of the privileged classes dealt more and more with isolated visual delights and hedonistic escapism. Such were the emphases of François Boucher (1703–70), a sensationally popular painter during Madame de Pompadour's heyday and one of history's most charming decorative artists.

Certainly Boucher was among the most fluent of eighteenth-century painters, and among the most Rococo. The sheer acreage of his mural and panel painting is extraordinary; it is a lifework aimed quite unabashedly at reassuring, delighting, and titillating the wealthy patrons of his day. Critics since his time have found his work shamefully frivolous. Still, from the most ambitious murals on heroic, erotic, or pastoral themes to such small panels as *The Bath of Diana* (fig. 14-12), Boucher has seldom failed to appeal to less stern-minded mortals. If much of the appeal has been that of luxuriant settings and eroticism, we are reminded that the arts have served not only to inspire and ennoble but to put human beings at ease in their world.

The tiny crescent moon amid the pearls in Diana's hair (she was goddess of the moon as well as of the hunt) and such hunting appurtenances as the hounds, arrows, and game, provide a classical aura for the *Bath's* obvious sensual appeal. The lovely pink and cream of Boucher's adolescent feminine nudes is indeed often more memorable than any connection they claim with antique narrative—as several commentators in his own day observed. But even before the change in taste that would leave Boucher outmoded, a quite different sort of art had attracted serious attention in limited circles. The greatest French practitioner of this alternative style, which has been labeled "bourgeois art," was Jean Baptiste Siméon Chardin (1699–1779).

Bourgeois art, as a current in eighteenth-century French painting, was an art of everyday life. Everyday life of the middle and lower classes had long been a

14-12   François Boucher, *The Bath of Diana,* 1742. Oil on canvas, 23″ × 28″. Louvre, Paris.

marketable if unpretentious subject for art, and at least once (in seventeenth-century Holland) it had inspired a truly national style of painting. Chardin's choice of subject matter thus was by no means an act of unprecedented rebellion. Still, if his youthful training led to this orientation, his devotion to humble subjects seems to have become increasingly a matter of pride, and a challenge to the whole Rococo complex that tended toward frivolous classicism and eroticism.

Chardin's *Morning Toilet* (fig. 14-13) meticulously portrays the dim light of early dawn as a mother makes final readjustments in the costume of her small daughter. The prayer book on the chair, the girl's muff, and the mother's cloak are intimations of the chill outside air of a wintry Sunday. This small painting appeals neither to eroticism nor to anecdotal excitement; rather, it invokes a realm of solid virtue and domestic sobriety.

Many of Chardin's paintings were copied by engravers; it is clear that they possessed popular appeal at

14-13   Jean Baptiste Siméon Chardin, *The Morning Toilet,* c. 1740. Oil on canvas, 19″ × 16″. Nationalmuseum, Stockholm.

14-14 Jean Baptiste Siméon Chardin, *The Jar of Olives*, 1760. Oil on canvas, 27″ × 37″. Louvre, Paris.

the time. Nothing in the historical record, however, suggests that this appeal was much more than that of a pleasant souvenir or a narrative. Today, on the other hand, it is the formal aesthetic qualities of Chardin that are most admired: their sturdy monumentality within miniature dimensions, their coloristic skill, and the painter's uncanny ability to give real presence to such varied materials as fur, coarse cloth, copper, and glazed pottery.

Such textural and three-dimensional qualities stand even more nobly on their own in Chardin's still lifes, such as *The Jar of Olives* (fig. 14-14). Here the formal, almost architectural pattern, the solidity of composition, and the rich depth of color bring substantiality and warmth to an ensemble of marvelous details. Years later the great novelist Marcel Proust would write: "Chardin has taught us that a pear is as much alive as a woman, and an ordinary jug can be as lovely as a jewel. This painter proclaimed the divine equality of all things before the spirit which beholds them and the light which enhances them." Chardin's work, one may add, mirrored not only the Enlightenment strain of practicality and common sense, and its growing egalitarianism of spirit, but enlarged very significantly the range of eighteenth-century creative genius.

LATE BAROQUE MUSIC

Music throughout Europe in the decades before 1760 seems to have followed its own laws of development, continuing earlier Baroque trends and working out

their implications. For example, musical thinking in terms of tonality, major or minor, was further consolidated, usually within a clearly chordal framework. However, the linear polyphonic manner was by no means wholly forgotten—and indeed Bach's massive fugal counterpoint is usually considered the culmination of polyphonic art. Bach and Handel both were masters in producing an unobtrusive collaboration between chordal writing and polyphony, all within traditional and relatively simple form-schemes such as the concerto grosso, the *da capo* (repeating in part "from the beginning") aria, and solo-instrumental forms such as the fantasia and fugue. In all these cases each unit—whether concerto movement, aria, or aria section—generally retained its individual character and feeling throughout.

Instruments and instrumentation toward the end of the Baroque era saw steady evolutionary changes. The clarinet, a single-reed instrument, entered the orchestra, as did the transverse flute and also the first "French horns" with changeable crooks for the tubing to allow a greater choice of tones. Orchestration, even if clearly specified, was likely to remain haphazard coloristically, with no great advantage usually taken of special instrumental timbres or techniques. Exceptions became more numerous during the century, although less so with Bach, or even Handel, than with the experimental French composers of mid-century and the Classicists of the final decades. In the meantime, before 1760, orchestral color contrasts between the various instrumental groups were highly valued, as were the different registrations on the more complex keyboard instruments. But these rather stark and predictable contrasts, like Baroque uniformity of mood within individual musical works or sections, would seem too mechanical and impersonal in the following century or so—and would prove refreshing to many twentieth-century musicians who were tired of the emotional expansiveness of nineteenth-century Romanticism.

Bach

Musicologists have been more reluctant than art historians to apply the *Rococo* terminology to a whole style in contrast to Baroque, perhaps because of music's

14-15 Elias Gottlieb Haussmann, *Johann Sebastian Bach*, 1748. Oil on canvas. Collection of William H. Scheide, Princeton, New Jersey.

basic continuities during a century and a half. It is preferable to speak of the Rococo in eighteenth-century music simply in terms of a mood of casual elegance. With Johann Sebastian Bach (1685–1750) we enter a very different realm—a realm of moving and impressive musical intellect. Bach is very often credited with being the greatest composer who ever lived. After a lifetime of rather provincial fame, and then a century of near-oblivion among the concert-going public, he has become a truly formidable presence in Western cultural history.

Haussmann's portrait of Bach (fig. 14-15) shows us a vigorous German burgher, crusty but by no means humorless—much the same picture we get from his surviving letters and the reports of his contemporaries. His longest period of employment was his last: he had a reliably steady job as music director and chief composer for Leipzig's Lutheran churches and as schoolmaster to the city's choir boys. Many of his Leipzig labors were

routine and frustrating, but his moments of angry impatience seem to have been balanced by a sense of his own worth and a rewarding family life. By his two wives he had twenty-one children, several of whom became talented composers.

To a large extent Bach was a traditionalist. Except in some of his daintier secular works, he was little touched by the Rococo spirit. Nor was he affected by the first attempts of younger composers to develop the "expressive" style that would contribute to the imminent Classical flowering in music. If Bach was a model of stern musical integrity, he also ended (as his municipal employers sometimes charged) by being decidedly old-fashioned.

He had not always been so, especially in the pre-Leipzig years when he held positions at secular German courts. He was an avid student of other composers of his day and copied many of their works by hand; Corelli was one of those composers. In his years as musician-in-residence at the court of Prince Leopold of Anhalt-Cöthen, Bach produced some of his lightest-hearted and most forward-looking music, including the six splendid Brandenburg Concertos. These scintillating works must have been heard not only at Cöthen but at the Zimmermann Coffee House concerts that Bach later directed in Leipzig.

The six concertos dedicated to the margrave of Brandenburg in 1721 are of varied internal structure; they constitute a collection of the concerto art up to their day, and even go beyond it. In complexity and subtlety they are among the most outstanding of all Baroque concerti grossi. The Fifth Brandenburg Concerto, in D major, employs three soloists—flute, violin, and harpsichord; the violin sometimes doubles the orchestral violin part, but the others function independently of the orchestra. In Bach's time a second, unobtrusive harpsichord may have been used in the continuo, although today one harpsichordist often functions in both roles. Certainly the harpsichordist of the solo group, or *concertino,* is a soloist, truly a virtuoso soloist—and there lies the striking novelty of this concerto grosso. Even in conjunction with the other soloists, this part is far more than a filler, as seen in the virtuoso runs in the first and last movements. Startling above all is the extended showpiece (over three minutes long) for harpsichordist alone near the end of the first movement. The last movement includes a *fugue*— a form featuring successive entrances in different musical lines, using the same theme at first and then variations on the theme. The whole concerto is a delightful work, part polyphonic and part chordal.

The Brandenburg fugues do not reach the vast proportions Bach achieved in his keyboard work and in his monumental summation, *The Art of Fugue.* To observe his fugal style at its most accessible and typical, we will look among his earlier works, such as the organ pieces that have become the backbone of the modern organist's repertoire. Here one of the clearest of fugues is the final section of his Toccata, Adagio, and Fugue in C major, BWV 564 (the number assigned to it in later times). The main theme is announced in one musical line, then taken up in succession by the three others and developed in tight counterpoint. Most consecutive entrances begin not on the same note of the scale but at an interval, usually of a fifth higher (or a fourth lower):

There are eleven entrances all together; by the eighth there has been a modulation to a different key. After another modulation, the piece returns to C major.

Bach's reputation as virtuoso organist (and composer of organ works) spread through much of Germany. He was particularly known for his skilled improvising and was much in demand as a consultant on organ construction and for the testing of new instruments. One of the many surviving German organs on which Bach played is shown in figure 14-16. Its visual magnificence, matching Bach's music, is more Baroque than Rococo.

An example of Bach's mature manner as composer for the organ is the great Fantasia and Fugue in G minor (BWV 542). The fantasia opens with a free, rhapsodic sort of melodic statement punctuated by chords and supported by long-held notes on the pedals. Four-part polyphony follows, broken by single-line passages that meander like the opening statement. In the four-part fugue, the jovial subject is developed in long, spun-out phrases, with the sort of continuous melodic expansion that is the hallmark of fugal writing, and indeed of Baroque music in general. Contrasted with

14-16 The Silbermann organ in the Frauenkirche, Dresden, 1736.

the fantasia's theatrical style, the fugue is a masterpiece of abstract structure.

Although some of Bach's work may seem more calculated than inspired, there is magnificent human warmth in much of his specifically religious music. Whether the warmth is also "religious" is quite another matter, since, like most Baroque composers, Bach sometimes transferred parts of his secular instrumental music to his sacred works. Yet Bach's personal Protestant piety doubtless did leave its mark on much of his greatest religious music—especially on the two monumental "passions" based on the Gospel narratives of Saint John and Saint Matthew. Of these, the *Saint Matthew Passion* is the more inward and reflective in mood—the more "religious," some would say—and the later in date. Its first performance, in Leipzig's Church of Saint Thomas during Holy Week, 1729, attracted little attention at the time.

The *passion*—an oratorio commemorating Jesus Christ's last days on earth, from the conspiracy and betrayal to the crucifixion and burial—had long been produced for Roman Catholic and Protestant church performance; Lassus was among Bach's most distinguished predecessors in the genre. The *Passion According to Saint Matthew* is the culmination of passion composition in scale and complexity. Serving as text are the Gospel narrative and numerous German hymns and poems that offer Christian meditations on the narrative. The music is far more diversified than the three textual divisions might imply, for the varied solos and choruses intermingle, with many changes in instrumentation. In narrative recitative and chorus Bach rises fully to the challenge of the Gospel story, while his arias and large choral settings lend immense stature to the often mediocre nonbiblical parts of the text.

Bach's style and spirit are evident in the sections near the end of the work that concern the insults to Christ just before the crucifixion and then the crucifixion itself. The Evangelist, who carries most of the narrative, tells of the indignities visited upon Jesus by the Roman soldiers (*Da nahmen die Kriegsknechte*—"Then the soldiers of the governor took Jesus into the common hall"). His tale is supplemented by the swift alternate mocking of the two choruses, on the words "Hail, King of the Jews!" The *secco* ("dry") recitative is accompanied by continuo (harpsichord and viola da gamba) alone, with the most sensitive word setting. Then comes the moving hymn O *Haupt voll Blut und*

Wunden ("O sacred head now wounded"), a solemn meditation on the outrages suffered by the Savior. The Evangelist's recitative then tells of the agonizing procession to Golgotha, with Simon of Cyrene forced to carry the cross on which Jesus would die.

As in the opera of the day, the solo passages in the *Saint Matthew Passion* include *ariosos* and *arias* as well as recitative—the arioso being a half-way point between the straightforward, continuo-accompanied recitative and the long, melodic, fully accompanied aria. The *Saint Matthew* recitative just mentioned is followed by an arioso for bass soloist: *Ja! Freilich will in uns* ("The flesh must even be crucified, if we would follow Christ"). It is typical of Bach's ariosos in its brevity, its syllabic diction (usually one note to a syllable rather than melodic elaboration of certain syllables), and its accompaniment by a small instrumental group (in this case, two flutes, solo viola da gamba, and continuo). After the subsequent long aria more recitative follows, to describe the crucifixion and the crowd's mockery ("He saved others, himself he cannot save"). Especially effective is the full-voiced unison phrase at the end of the second brief chorus, as the crowd derisively quotes Jesus' claim, "I am the Son of God."

Handel

The nineteenth-century revival of interest in Bach is usually dated from a centennial performance of the *Saint Matthew Passion* in 1829. Before then, Bach had never fallen completely out of sight; such masters as Haydn, Mozart, and Beethoven had more than an inkling of his importance. In any case, a comprehensive Bach revival did occur in the nineteenth century, however overblown the performances of his works in that Romantic age might have been. Full appreciation of his celebrated contemporary George Frideric Handel (1685–1759) would have to wait much longer; in fact, except for several much-played works such as the oratorio *Messiah*, Handel is still inadequately known and understood.

From humble beginnings in Germany, Handel gained early fame in Italy and settled permanently in England in 1712. There he wrote his most imposing works, mainly operas and oratorios. The most celebrated of his oratorios is the *Messiah* (1741), whose words are in English. It has become one of the best-loved of all musical works and certainly, in the

CHRONOLOGY

HISTORY		THE ARTS	
		1694–1778	Voltaire
		1699–1782	Ange Jacques Gabriel
		1712–78	Rousseau
		1713–84	Diderot
		1723–92	Reynolds
		1727–88	Gainsborough
		1728–92	Robert Adam
		1732–1809	Haydn
		1738–1814	Clodion
1740–80	Maria Theresa, Hapsburg archduchess of Austria, queen of Bohemia and Hungary	1741–1828	Houdon
1740–86	Frederick II (the Great) king of Prussia	1748–1825	Jacques Louis David
		1751–65	the text of Diderot's *Encyclopedia* published in 15 volumes
1756–63	Seven Years' War: Great Britain and Prussia vs. France and Austria	1755–1842	Vigée-Lebrun
		1756–91	Mozart
		1756–92	Soufflot's *Pantheon,* Paris
1760–1820	George III king of England	1759–97	Mary Wollstonecraft
1762–96	Catherine II (the Great) empress of Russia	1762	Rousseau's *Emile* (on education) and *The Social Contract* published
		1762–68	Gabriel's Petit Trianon, Versailles
		1764	Gibbon visits Rome, conceives idea of the *Decline and Fall*
1765–90	Joseph II Holy Roman Emperor (from 1780, archduke of Austria, king of Bohemia and Hungary)	1764–70	Rousseau's autobiographical *Confessions*
		1771	Fragonard's Louveciennes panels
1774–92	Louis XVI king of France		
1775–83	war of American independence	1776	Adam Smith's *The Wealth of Nations,* advocating free trade and enterprise, published
		1776–88	Gibbon's *Decline and Fall of the Roman Empire* published in installments
		1777	Gainsborough's *Mrs. Graham*
		1778	Greuze's *The Son Punished*
		1778	deaths of Voltaire and Rousseau
		1781	Haydn's "Russian" quartets
1783	independence of the American colonies recognized by Britain	1784	Beaumarchais's *Marriage of Figaro* produced
		1784–85	David's *Oath of the Horatii*
		1786	Mozart's Piano Concerto in C minor; his *Marriage of Figaro* produced
1789–99	French Revolution	1790	Burke's *Reflections on the Revolution in France*
1790–92	Leopold II Holy Roman Emperor	1791	Paris Pantheon converted from church to secular memorial
1792–1806	Francis II Holy Roman Emperor	1791–92	Paine's *Rights of Man* combatting Burke's *Reflections*
1792–1815	wars of the French Revolution and Napoleon	1792	Wollstonecraft's *Vindication of the Rights of Woman*
1793–94	"Reign of Terror" in France	1793	David's *The Dying Marat*
1799–1804	Napoleon Bonaparte first consul in France		

15-1 C. Schütz, *View of Saint Michael's Square, Vienna*, 1783. Etching, 5" × 7". Historisches Museum der Stadt Wien.

even more. Often there were impromptu concerts in the park known as the Prater and in coffee houses and taverns, although formal public concerts were still rare. Wealthy nobles and commoners had their own small orchestras or "chamber" groups, with many a footman doubling as violinist or oboist; professional orchestras became more common only late in the century.

Amateur music making in the home was a passion of the age in Vienna as in the rest of Europe, wherever a harpsichord or one of the new pianos could be found, or a few woodwinds or strings could be gathered. Wherever in Europe, and at whatever level, the music performed was almost invariably contemporary, as it had been in earlier decades; the growing "antiquarianism" of literature and the visual arts had barely begun to infiltrate the realm of music. Nor had composers yet learned the dubious imperative of later centuries—that they must write either serious or light music, not both. Haydn and Mozart, like the others, wrote for the dance hall as well as for the theater and the elegant home.

Composers still wrote largely on commission, whether from royal courts, aristocratic or ecclesiastical patrons, the wealthy bourgeoisie, or music publishers. The most fortunate musicians were employed permanently by a court. Such was the good fortune, for sev-

eral decades, of Joseph Haydn. The financial situation of other composers, such as Mozart, was usually precarious indeed. No effective copyright system had yet been devised, and music publishers pirated works shamelessly for their own profit. Late-eighteenth-century composers, like earlier ones, were almost always performers and might be paid as such (Mozart, for example, as a concert pianist and Haydn as a conductor), but proceeds for performances were erratic and uncertain, being dependent on the fickle tastes of the musical public. Even Mozart's social acceptance by the rich and the noble did not save him from genteel poverty during much of his life.

Painters and sculptors were similarly dependent on the financial favor of the eighteenth-century establishment—the aristocrats, the prosperous middle class, and, although more rarely than in the past, the Church. In distant America only a very restricted middle-class clientele existed for painters, and virtually none for sculptors. America's two most distinguished early painters, Copley and West, both abandoned America for the more promising English market. Note the splendid portrait John Singleton Copley (1738–1815) painted of Mrs. Thomas Boylston before he left the colonies (fig. 15-2). The artists Gainsborough and David were so fortunate as to marry into comfortable wealth, while Reynolds and Houdon accumulated

15-2 John Singleton Copley, *Mrs. Thomas Boylston*, 1766. Oil on canvas, 50½″ × 40¼″. Courtesy of the Harvard University Portrait Collection (Bequest of Ward Nichollas Boylston in 1828).

small fortunes of their own by catering in their portraiture to the vanity of the rich. Fragonard's experience was more varied and probably more typical. He gave lessons and painted on commission for the French government's Office of Buildings, dealers, and private collectors; he also may have received royalties on engraved prints that were made from his paintings. However, just as public concerts were starting to bring substantial assistance to composers, public exhibitions were beginning to help artists. Although in France the prestigious biennial exhibitions of the Royal Academy of Painting and Sculpture were open only to the works of its members, these and other exhibitions brought new works into active and direct competition for the attention of more buyers than before—and these buyers were increasingly from the middle class.

Literature and Thought

A parallel phenomenon, and a still more striking one, was observable in the world of literature. By the end of the century, writers had become completely emanci-

pated from private patronage and appealed more and more to the mass of middle-class buyers. Publication by subscription, as in the case of music, had sometimes been an intermediate stage, but that was a dying practice. An increasing flood of books and periodicals competed for sales in a free market. This was a free *urban* market—for it was the cities, not the courts, that possessed in quantity the consumers of culture, as well as the publishers. The critics, too, were stationed in the cities, and through their own books and journals they were becoming arbiters of taste as never before in history. Indeed, the literary community of the late eighteenth century was becoming a predominantly urban phenomenon, most notably perhaps among the writers of ideas, the *philosophes*, who found the urban concentration of intellectual life stimulating. (Rousseau, admittedly awkward and ill at ease in fashionable society, was an exception.)

One of those thinkers who, both by profession and temperament, most needed the city was Denis Diderot (1713–84), a restless, friendly, complex man excited by the interchange of new ideas. Today he is best remembered as organizer and manager of that massive project, the *Encyclopedia*—a compendium of facts and ideas and a program for the betterment of humanity. In the *Encyclopedia* the storehouse of history became an arsenal for Enlightenment—for scientific and technological as well as political, social, philosophical, and ethical Enlightenment. Scientific advance and technological achievement were proudly celebrated in the pages of the *Encyclopedia*, as it sought to bring the practical triumphs of reason and empiricism to the attention of the entire literate public.

The spirit of the *Encyclopedia*, and of the later Enlightenment as a whole, is appropriately exemplified in the article "Encyclopedia" that Diderot himself wrote for volume five:

> ENCYCLOPEDIA. . . . This word means the interconnection among all sorts of knowledge. . . . In truth, the goal of an encyclopedia is to assemble knowledge scattered over the face of the earth, to expose its general outline to those with whom we live, and to transmit this knowledge to those who will come after us . . . so that our heirs, by becoming better educated, may become at the same time more virtuous and happier, and so that we may not die without having deserved well of the human race.

The time at last is ripe, Diderot continued, for such an encyclopedic endeavor, because the age is itself truly philosophical—an age of genuine intellectual renewal and resolution.

> For this work everywhere demands intellectual courage and firmness of mind beyond what has existed in less daring centuries. Now it is necessary to examine *everything*, to discuss all things without exception and without evasion. . . . We must trample underfoot all those ancient puerilities, tear down all barriers not erected by rationality, and give back to the arts and sciences the freedom that is so precious to them.

And this we must do, he added, not just by examining books and using our rational faculties; we must examine nature and investigate the technological advances being made in the industrial crafts. He believed that trade secrets (of which there were many, zealously guarded, in Diderot's day) must not impede the diffusion of practical knowledge and technology.

In addition to the moralistic theories on art we will note later, the *Encyclopedia* represents the public Diderot known to all literate Europeans in his day. He did not publish his most startling works, however, correctly judging the time not yet ripe. Among those are *Rameau's Nephew* and *The Nun*, notable for their intimate psychological insight; *D'Alembert's Dream*, containing pioneering scientific speculations in physiology and psychology; and *Jacques the Fatalist*, which applies the innovative fictional technique of inviting the characters and the reader to help create the work itself.

In the meantime, until his death at eighty-four, Voltaire was continuing along more conventional lines with unabated vigor. This late phase of his life was characterized by unflagging *anticlericalism* (opposition to the institutional church and its representatives) and pervasive personal disillusionment that, however, never fully conquered his hopes for human progress on earth. In historical writing, however, Voltaire's place of prominence was being taken by a shining new light, the English historian Edward Gibbon (1737–94).

Gibbon's *History of the Decline and Fall of the Roman Empire* is possibly the Western world's most celebrated work of historical writing. It appeared in installments from 1776 to 1788 and immediately brought him fame and respect. The *Decline and Fall* absorbed Gibbon for more than two decades, from the time of his trip to Italy in 1764. "It was in Rome," he later wrote, "on the 15th of October 1764, as I sat musing amid the ruins of the Capitol, while the barefooted friars were singing vespers in the temple of Jupiter, that

the idea of writing the decline and fall of the city first started to my mind." In six volumes (there are modern abridgments) Gibbon traced with careful scholarship the decline and fall of the Western empire from the happy times of Augustus and the Good Emperors of the second century after Christ through the disintegration and fall of the next several centuries, and traced the Eastern empire through its glories, humiliations, and gradual diminution to its fall to the Turks in 1453. His vividly dramatic narrative of the siege and collapse of Constantinople is one of the undeservedly neglected classics of historical writing.

Gibbon concluded that the decline and fall of the Western empire were fairly simply explained. (Later historians would not be so sure of this.) The decline of Rome, he asserted,

> was the natural and inevitable effect of immoderate greatness. Prosperity ripened the principle of decay; the causes of destruction multiplied with the extent of conquest; and, as soon as time or accident had removed the artificial supports, the stupendous fabric yielded to the pressure of its own weight. The story of its ruin is simple and obvious; and, instead of inquiring *why* the Roman empire was destroyed, we should rather be surprised that it had subsisted so long.

Gibbon placed part of the blame for Rome's decline on "the introduction, or at least the abuse, of Christianity." The clergy, he said,

> successfully preached the doctrines of patience and pusillanimity; the active virtues were discouraged; and the last remains of military spirit were buried in the cloister. A large portion of public and private wealth was consecrated to the specious demands of charity and devotion, and the soldiers' pay was lavished on the useless multitudes of both sexes who could only plead the merits of abstinence and chastity.

Such words, in Gibbon's majestically measured prose, were well enough justified in historical fact. They also reflected Gibbon's own anticlerical agnosticism, well documented in his sly, or outrageous, discussion of miracles in the early Christian church and the curious phenomenon of their cessation. Gibbon was, after all, a product of the age of Enlightenment, so it is not surprising that he shared much of its outlook.

To return to general trends of Gibbon's time, we should note that the late eighteenth century saw a continuation and an expansion of that age of Enlightenment whose beginnings and basic principles were noted in the preceding chapter. "Nature" and "reason" remained the key words, still imprecise but powerful. The attack on the unnatural and the irrational now became stronger, deeper, more radical—in short, more serious. The frequent earnestness of the earlier-eighteenth-century attack had been tempered by urbanity and good humor; the witty Voltaire was its symbol. Now came the era of a fuller, more intense commitment, and it was symbolized by the dead-serious passions and far-reaching social proposals of Rousseau's later years.

The controversies of the age undoubtedly were increasing in bitterness as the Revolution approached and as the voice of Enlightened radicalism became more insistent. The forefront of religious debate was no longer a gleeful assault on the Bible and miracles and a defense of deism, but the establishment of *agnosticism* (which expresses doubt about the existence and nature of God) or even militant *atheism* (which denies outright the existence of God). In philosophy, it was argued that abstract speculation should be replaced not simply by reason and common sense but by a demanding empiricism as well. In ethics, discussion of individualistic pleasure seeking was supplemented by stern talk about the imperatives of duty to self and society; personal liberty, it was said, must be replaced by the heavy responsibilities of civic liberty.

In economics, when the Scotsman Adam Smith (1723–90) preached the virtues of free enterprise following the benevolent operation of natural economic laws, he maintained that enlightened, unfettered self-interest would further the greatest general social good.

In political theory, the rational premises of earlier writers were being pushed aside by *utilitarianism* (the theory that all institutions should be judged by their usefulness to society) and the merits of democracy were now being seriously debated. The persistence of the old ideas is seen, however, in the works of the most influential democrat of all, the Swiss-born Jean Jacques Rousseau (fig. 15-3). His major political treatise, *The Social Contract,* is less utilitarian than theoretical in its construction of a whole political and social system from such undocumented assumptions as the potential natural goodness of human beings, their corruption by wily exploiters, and the existence of a mysterious "general will" that aims at true political good even if people do not always recognize its imperatives.

For Rousseau, freedom and obedience are entwined inextricably. In his political theory the "social

15-3 Alan Ramsay, *Jean Jacques Rousseau,* 1766. National Gallery of Scotland, Edinburgh.

contract" is neither an assumption about the past nor a historical event; it is what a renovated social order *should* be based on. The contract is an agreement among the people, by which "each man, in giving himself to all, gives himself to nobody." The basic terms of the contract are these:

> Each of us puts his person and all his power in common under the supreme direction of the general will, and in our corporate capacity, we receive each member as an indivisible part of the whole. . . . This act of association creates a moral and collective body . . . or body politic.

It is this body that governs—and it governs directly, not through representatives as in Locke's political scheme of things.

Individuals would seem to have no personal rights in Rousseau's system; in fact, individual and minority rights were usually farthest from his mind. When, in some rather mysterious way (Rousseau's suggestions on this are rather incompatible), the general will is established, dissent is simply wrong and it should be isolated or abolished. Here Rousseau's most extreme statement concerns religion: once the people in some manner have established a "civil profession of faith," any dissident may be banished—and worse, "if anyone, after publicly recognizing these dogmas, behaves as if he does not believe them, let him be punished by death." The harsh authoritarian side of Rousseau is not just a myth invented by his detractors.

Despite the dictatorial implications of his system, Rousseau, like his contemporaries, professed to worship freedom. Often cited as an example of Rousseau's support for individual freedom is his support for a new approach to children's education—the forerunner of twentieth-century "progressive education." The child, he wrote, should be unshackled from classroom discipline and memorization and be free to develop out of his own spontaneous, natural impulses. Later commentators have noted that this spontaneity is "rigged" in Rousseau's scheme by a skillful instructor who presents the child with just the right stimuli and the right questions. Nature and spontaneity apparently require some outside help.

Whatever the ambiguities in Rousseau's teaching, it is clear that, in fact, the general demand for freedom was increasing mightily in the pre-Revolutionary decades—a demand for individual freedom of mind and soul, as well as for political, social, and economic freedom. One of the most frequently cited pieces of evidence of the demand for social freedom is Figaro's famous soliloquy in *The Marriage of Figaro,* a stage comedy by Pierre Augustin Caron de Beaumarchais (1732–99). The servant Figaro is being explosively indignant about the pretensions of his master the Count Almaviva—but not to the count's face:

> Because you are a great noble, you think you are a great genius! Nobility, a fortune, a rank, appointments to office: all this makes a man so proud! What did you do to earn all this? You took the trouble to be born—nothing more. Moreover, you're a pretty ordinary fellow.

Although the abolition of the nobility hardly seemed in the cards before the French Revolution broke out in 1789, other abuses were being attacked in spirited vein, and at greater length, on the printed page. Intolerance, superstition, tyranny, slavery, and warfare were the targets of the enthusiastic humanitarianism of the age—a humanitarianism that seldom called for the liberation of women, however. Humanity would advance, a growing number of thinkers argued, because human beings were perfectible. Progress, possibly even indefinite progress for the foreseeable fu-

ture, would indeed become a reality. Such was the supremely optimistic doctrine of Antoine Nicolas de Condorcet (1743–94) in his *Sketch for a Historical Picture of the Progress of the Human Mind.* During the Revolution, Condorcet and Mary Wollstonecraft (1759–97)—in her *Vindication of the Rights of Woman*—were exceptional in their insistence that freedom be extended not only to men but to women.

In the *Vindication,* Wollstonecraft (fig. 15-4) expressed her impatience with the accepted view of the time that women should be mere "gentle, domestic brutes"—that is, pliant domesticated animals. Women, she asserted, can be far more than beings "only designed by sweet attractive grace, and docile blind obedience, to gratify the senses" of men in sexual need. Misguided popular opinion has, she said, decreed women's submissive role and an education wholly inadequate to the formation of whole beings. It now is time to fashion these whole creatures, fully developed intellectually and morally, out of the ill-educated domestic ornaments that women traditionally have become. Women, like men, have minds, and their intellectual potential should be realized by a well-

15-4 John Opie, *Mary Wollstonecraft.* The Tate Gallery, London.

rounded education, if only to give a sound foundation of understanding so that women may lead an autonomous, dignified moral life.

On female education Wollstonecraft was running counter not only to the actual roles of the sexes in her time but was specifically challenging the ideas of Rousseau then in vogue. Although sometimes progressive in his notions of boys' education, Rousseau had in fact seen girls' education in a quite different light, since for him "woman is made for pleasing man." This was the old notion that Wollstonecraft sought to overcome in the last years of her relatively short life. Whether she would have moved on to stress the need for economic independence and equality cannot be known, for she died after childbirth at the age of thirty-eight. She did believe in public, democratic, remarkably comprehensive coeducation for boys and girls up to age nine, after which the less intellectually capable of both sexes would be taught mechanical trades.

Of course, not all writers, even among professed freedom-lovers, shared the optimism or the faith of Condorcet and Wollstonecraft in the rational-empirical blueprints of Enlightened social engineering. Most eminent among contemporary dissenters was the English statesman Edmund Burke (1729–97), who in 1790 published his *Reflections on the Revolution in France*, one of history's outstanding defenses of conservatism. Burke opposed the "liberal" desire to question established ideas and institutions, and he strongly upheld the "conservatism" that, in all periods of history, has emphasized conserving the best in present and past ways of doing things. Although he admitted the desirability of occasional cautious reforms, he believed that respect for long-standing tradition was the only solid foundation for the social structure. In contrast to the revolutionary radicalism then being implemented in France, British institutions were inherited, he insisted, from British forefathers; they would be passed down in turn, with only small, necessary adjustments, to future generations. Burke believed in an active, Christian God that intervenes in human affairs. He said that God's providential intervention is made manifest in "a stupendous wisdom, molding together the great mysterious incorporation of the human race"—which we can tamper with only at our peril.

Burke believed that the French, like the British, had inherited an ancient constitutional structure from their ancestors—a structure comparable to "a noble and venerable castle." The structure had become, he admitted, a bit dilapidated in the course of time, and he asserted that instead of repairing its walls, the French were wildly tearing down the whole structure, beginning everything anew from radically new, rationally devised blueprints (Enlightenment theories) unfounded in traditional wisdom and experience. He predicted that out of a revolution could only come anarchy, and out of anarchy, despotism.

As it turned out, Burke's prediction was not completely off the mark in the French case. The early, rather mild revolution that Burke knew in 1790 soon gave way to the Reign of Terror (1793–94), and this to the autocratic, if not fully despotic, rule of Napoleon Bonaparte. In the meantime Burke's *Reflections* did not lack refutations, the most famous of them coming from Thomas Paine (1737–1809). Paine's most basic argument was that the living must not be bound by earlier generations—that "government is for the living, and not for the dead." Moreover, wrote Paine, if one did pursue political theory into the realm of past precedents, Burke had stopped much too recently (at the aristocratic-bourgeois settlement of the 1688 Glorious Revolution). He should have gone back, instead, to that "state of nature" in which "all men are born equal and with equal natural right." It was an exciting age in which such arguments as Burke's and Paine's were passionately debated—and since then, for those interested in ideas and in the future of humanity, the excitement and the confrontational mood have hardly abated.

Classicism and Romanticism

Burke's distrust of rational schemes and his emphasis on the imperatives of ingrained sentiment have made him important in the study of eighteenth-century Romanticism. Most often, though, the Classical–Romantic confrontation of the age has been discussed within an artistic context—in the realms of literature, music, and the visual arts. *Classicism* has already been broadly described as formalism humanized—but for Classicism's explicit contrast with Romanticism in the eighteenth century and beyond, more specific definitions are needed. As a rough guideline for our discussion, Classicism may be defined as an approach that views respectfully the achievements of ancient Greece and Rome as models for new development and that is likely to value the qualities of rationalism and artistic discipline. *Romanticism* is an approach to the arts that emphasizes an individual's feelings and emotions, often in combination with a nostalgia for the past or the exotic, but often with an eager anticipation of future change and growth. Further, Classicism tends toward the static and the regular, whereas Romanticism tends toward the dynamic and the irregular or unexpected.

Classicism was the reigning style in music and the visual arts from 1760 through the first decade or so of the nineteenth century, but even in its heyday it was seriously challenged by those Romantic trends that would later become dominant. Certainly in England and Germany, and to a lesser degree in France, literary Romanticism flourished very healthily in the late eighteenth century. Samuel Richardson's sentimental novels had led the way; Rousseau and Goethe now followed with passionate effusions that, we are told, bathed Europe in tears. The Classical, rational restraint of earlier literature could not endure, but then neither could the manners and morals of the Rococo age. The reaction was inevitable, and thus the new literature of sentiment and feeling frequently included a strong tone of moral exhortation. The creed of Rousseau and his followers condemned the luxury and os-

tentation of the old ways and glorified the simple, the natural, and the primitive. Life in the unspoiled countryside, it now was said, was much more virtuous than life in the wicked cities—and so the queen of France had a pseudo-rustic hamlet built for her amusement in the gardens of Versailles.

Architecture and the decorative arts meanwhile had revealed another aspect of Romanticism, the twin passion for the exotic and the medieval. In Vienna, as in Paris and throughout Europe, rooms were often decorated elegantly in the "Chinese" manner, and attempts were made to decorate in "Indian" and "Turkish" styles. London's Kew Gardens boasted among other exoticisms a pagoda, a "Confucian house," and a mosque, as well as the newly inevitable Gothic ruins. The Gothic vogue was now even stronger than the exotic, especially in England; it touched even the most distinguished of architects.

The most celebrated of English neo-Gothic structures was Strawberry Hill (fig. 15-5). This country home of Horace Walpole was a strange and wonderful thing, pieced together with conscious irregularity by a largely amateur group of designers. For the Gothic

15-5 Horace Walpole, William Robinson, and others, Strawberry Hill, Twickenham, 1749–77.

novelist Walpole and his friends, and for entranced visitors from all over Europe, Strawberry Hill powerfully evoked the "charming, venerable" air of the Middle Ages, although some of its fanciful interior more accurately suggested an amiably lunatic Rococo. In any case, it was marvelously escapist and picturesque—which was precisely the point.

This was also the point of another quaint manifestation of the "picturesque" style, the building of artificial ruins. Sham ruins had first been built in English parks and gardens in mid-century, but their creation became a fad only in later decades. Moreover, ruinous Gothic arches, it was discovered, were more Romantically evocative than ever if they were surrounded by judiciously placed dead trees. All this, in fact, can be seen as part of the century's new concept of parks and gardens. No longer severe and geometrical, parks were being laid out with cunning irregularity to "look like a picture," be picturesque. Also picturesque, we should add, were rustic cottages and their well-scrubbed inhabitants—in paintings, that is, since the imitation was far preferable to the odorous original, as were sham ruins to any dingy, authentic medieval church.

However, the contemplation of true ruins could sometimes evoke delicious melancholy. The century's nostalgic admiration for ruins, and its building of artificial ruins, was as likely to involve the classical as the medieval. This is a matter of interest in any discussion of the Classical–Romantic question, for here is a surprising link between two styles that often seem so different.

Classical temples, arches, and the like had often been inserted in Renaissance and Baroque pictures, but seldom so pointedly for the purpose of suggesting melancholy as in the late eighteenth century. Resignation to death, to the passing of all things, and to decay and corruption, became a theme of immense appeal. But ancient ruins were not always pictured as ghostly shells, and most certainly they were no longer neglected by the world of art and ideas. They were, in fact, the prime inspiration of the great new Classical revival that was to dominate the visual arts for many decades. Roman remains were intensively studied and were described in numerous publications that fascinated the literate public. Moreover, Greek architecture and sculpture, which so long had been hidden behind its Roman imitators and adapters, was at last rediscovered and publicized. The German scholar Winckelmann found Greek art to be characterized by "noble simplicity and quiet grandeur"—and much of Europe agreed.

It has been argued that Classicism, as an evocation of the past, is simply a form of Romanticism. In any case it seems clear that both Classicism and Romanticism were sometimes manifestations of a remarkable eighteenth-century upsurge of historicism. *Historicism* implies not only the search for historical context but the active selection of useful features out of the past for present use. Further, it implies that a style can be chosen, that style is not imposed irrevocably by one's time. As a major feature of the creative landscape outside the realm of music, historicism was largely the invention of the eighteenth century. In the next century, the historicist idea would gain even more extensive popularity.

A CLASSICAL REVIVAL IN ARCHITECTURE

Even aside from the popularity of Oriental and Gothic exoticisms, late-eighteenth-century architectural style was very far from consistent. Especially in the first decades after 1760 the Rococo still flourished here and there, and the advent of Classicism seldom marked a clean break with the past. One of those architects whose work suggests a compromise between the Rococo and the Classical was the Scotsman Robert Adam (1728–92). Adam had spent several youthful years in Rome, but his later projects as a fashionable London architect reflect little of the bluntness or monumentality of Roman building. The front drawing room of the town house he designed for the countess of Home (fig. 15-6) features Classical pilasters and an adaptation in stucco of numerous Classical motifs, but the predominant feeling is of an airy refinement and delicacy more related to Rococo. Fluent curves, however, have already given way to the geometrical neatness and symmetry that were to be more typical of the newer age.

In France, Ange Jacques Gabriel (1699–1782) is similarly a transition figure, and all the more so for having begun his career in the Rococo tradition. In mid-century he turned from Rococo ornamentation to Classical nobility without pomposity, as seen in the Petit Trianon at Versailles (fig. 15-7). This tiny palace has a graceful charm appropriate to the Rococo heritage and to the three stylish ladies with whom it is

15-6 Robert Adam, front drawing room of Home House (now the Courtauld Institute of Art), London, 1775–77.

15-7 Ange Jacques Gabriel, the Petit Trianon, Versailles, 1767–68.

particularly associated: built at Louis XV's command for Madame de Pompadour, it later was given to his final mistress Madame du Barry, and then to Louis XVI's queen, Marie Antoinette. Although the Petit Trianon is almost square and its sides rather similar, Gabriel contrived within these limitations to produce a structure of diversity and elegance.

In the 1750s a competition had been held to plan a vast new Parisian square, and Gabriel was called on to distill the best features from the many suggestions. The resultant Place Louis XV, now known as the Place de la Concorde (fig. 15-8), was ultimately to become perhaps the most splendid of all European public squares, imposing in its vastness and symmetry. The twin buildings on the north side of the square are impressive monuments to the new Classical ideal—they are by Gabriel himself. Later construction, most of it also Classical, has completed the perspectives from the square, from the Louvre and the Tuileries Gardens to Napoleon's Arch of Triumph of the Star, and from the colonnaded National Assembly building across the Seine to the Madeleine, Napoleon's Temple of Glory.

In architecture, Gabriel's greatest French contemporary was Jacques Germain Soufflot (1714–80), whose aim was a rigorous adherence to the spirit and idiom of ancient Greece and Rome. Gabriel's training and orientation had been practical and French; Soufflot had visited Italy and was strongly affected by this direct contact with the antique past, much of it recently rediscovered. His Classical ideal thus became less French and more exacting than Gabriel's, tending at the same time to be more cold and more grandiose. Soufflot's major creation was the church of Saint Geneviève, later to become famous as the French Pantheon (fig. 15-9). The structure was unfinished at his death, but his nephew and others completed it. In 1791 the Revolutionary National Assembly decreed the building's conversion into a secular memorial to the famous men of France—TO HER GREAT MEN, FROM A GRATEFUL NATION, as the stately inscription beneath the pediment reads. The bodies of Voltaire and Rousseau were among the first to be placed there.

Originally dedicated to the patron saint of Paris, the Pantheon is appropriately impressive in scale and absolutely symmetrical (fig. 15-10). Classical discipline could nowhere be better illustrated. The Greek cross form and the presence of a dome derive mainly from the Renaissance, whereas the three-shelled dome construction is rather similar to that of Saint Paul's in London. Indeed the Pantheon's rather pompous form is derived from all the attempts, from the Roman pe-

15-8   Ange Jacques Gabriel, Place de la Concorde, Paris, from 1753. Gabriel designed the twin buildings at the top.

15-9   Jacques Germain Soufflot, the Pantheon, Paris, 1756–92.

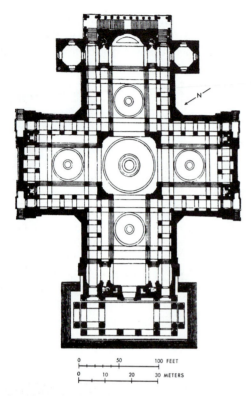

15-10   Plan of the Pantheon, Paris.

riod down to its own time, to inflate the Greek temple concept far beyond that structure's original self-contained stability.

TRENDS IN SCULPTURE

Sculpture, like architecture, saw a continuation of the Rococo manner well past 1760. In fact, the mature career of Claude Michel, called Clodion (1738–1814), the most Rococo of all sculptors, lay entirely in the period after that date. Clodion's most typical work was on a small scale and generally was executed in terracotta (baked clay). A pleasant example is his statuette called *Satyr and Bacchante* (fig. 15-11). Although the theme is ostensibly classical in its presentation of revelers from Greek mythology, the manner is Rococo. Certainly Clodion was not one to ignore sensuous appeal. It is a conception straight out of the Rococo painter Boucher, as are most of Clodion's nymphs, satyrs, and cupids.

A wholly different spirit is that of Jean Antoine

Houdon (1741–1828), the most famous of late-eighteenth-century sculptors. Yet Houdon is seldom closer to the Classical spirit than to the Rococo. More than any other sculptor of his day, he resisted classification, avoiding all doctrinaire commitments to Classicism or any other school. Above all, and especially in his immensely popular role as portraitist, Houdon was simply a realist—a realist of lively insight and tremendous skill. Although never neglecting the formal demands of the sculptural medium, he brought to his portrait busts and statues a directness and vivacity that have seldom been equaled. A prime example is the bust of Voltaire (see fig. 14-3), in which he captured the most essential traits of the man—his keen intelligence, sardonic wit, and compassionate humanity.

TRENDS IN PAINTING

England's most celebrated artist in the late eighteenth century was Sir Joshua Reynolds (1723–92), who became president of the new Royal Academy. His famous *Discourses* to the Academy present a defense of the Classicism of the day. Art, he declared, aims at beauty and virtue and, indeed, at that ideal beauty that is eternal. The artist must study diligently the great fund of antique models as well as his more immediate predecessors of the High Renaissance and the seventeenth century; natural talent must thus be supplemented by long and careful work and discipline before it can venture to trust its own powers of creative imagination.

Little of Reynolds's painting is remembered today except his portraits, which range from the mediocre to the impressive and from the informal to the pompous. Even in his less formal manner Reynolds frequently employed settings or additional figures that he felt would add interest and character to the portrait. An example is his portrait of Lord Heathfield (fig. 15-12), in which that bluff gentleman appears as governor of Gibraltar. Confidently, with sword at his side, he holds the key to the fortress he has recently defended, as the cannons in the rear cloud the sky with their smoke. The painting has the solidity and strength of its sturdy subject.

The art of Thomas Gainsborough (1727–88) avoided entirely the grander manner of Reynolds. (It is instructive to note that of the painters considered in this chapter Gainsborough alone did not study in Italy

15-11 Clodion, *Satyr and Bacchante*, c. 1775. Terracotta, 23″ high. The Metropolitan Museum of Art, New York (bequest of Benjamin Altman, 1913).

To this and other portraits Gainsborough brought considerable psychological insight and also his special brush technique. Those "odd scratches and marks" that Reynolds grudgingly admired contributed to the effect of lightness and flickering texture that marks many of Gainsborough's works. Most often his colors are subtle, his atmosphere luminous, his mood lyrical. Although seldom dipping into the gallant themes of the Rococo, Gainsborough is an honorable heir to Watteau.

So, too, was the French painter Elisabeth Louise Vigée-Lebrun (1755–1842). Like Gainsborough, she was a portrait painter and a very successful one. A beautiful woman herself, Vigée-Lebrun was an especially fine portraitist of fashionable ladies. She received prestigious commissions from Louis XVI's queen Marie Antoinette and survived the Revolution by going to Russia, Germany, Austria, and Italy. A monarchist by conviction, she lived to see the usurper Na-

and apparently never wanted to.) The classical columns in his portrait of Mrs. Graham (fig. 15-13) are for him a rare concession to the fashion of the day. Generally his portraits are straightforward and even relaxed, with no laborious attempts at pretentious effects, however elegant the sitter's style of dress. The sitters were the aristocratic and the wealthy, for Gainsborough painted portraits on commission. (Mrs. Graham's father was a peer of the realm, and eventually her husband also was.) The world reflected in Gainsborough's portraits is one of cultivated refinement, but his portraits are of individuals with recognizable human qualities. The sensuous nonchalance of Mrs. Graham, then a young bride, is one example among many.

15-12 Joshua Reynolds, *Lord Heathfield*, c. 1787. Oil on canvas, 56″ × 45″. Reproduced by Courtesy of the Trustees, The National Gallery, London.

15-13 Thomas Gainsborough, *Mrs. Graham*, 1777. Oil on canvas, 93½″ × 61″. National Gallery of Scotland, Edinburgh.

poleon Bonaparte defeated and the Bourbon dynasty restored (1814 and 1815) and then in turn expelled in 1830. Her painting had deteriorated by then, but in her prime she was a portraitist of great sensitivity and technical skill. Her early *Self-Portrait* (fig. 15-14) is sensuously appealing in its simplicity and informality. She painstakingly captured nuances in flesh tones, eyes, hair, and dress by superimposing transparent glazes on those portions of the painting. The brilliant red of sash and bow stand out in cheerful contrast to the black scarf and hat. The spirit of the work is of the Rococo in its airiness and charm.

Still more closely identified, at least in subject matter, with the Rococo ideal is Jean Honoré Fragonard (1732–1806). Fragonard's active continuation of Rococo well into the late eighteenth century in France long caused art historians to view his paintings as anachronisms in an age of newer trends. However, recent critics have found many redeeming features in his work. In any case, Fragonard's work was immensely

popular until the 1780s, despite the mutterings of philosophes who scented moral decay and social irrelevance in his work.

Most consciously influenced by the exuberant art of Tiepolo and Rubens and his own zest for life, Fragonard's themes and techniques were varied. His paintings include religious works as well as portraits and gallant subjects, allegories as well as realistic or sentimental scenes of family life—and it is not difficult to draw up a substantial list of classical influences and themes in his work. Yet Fragonard seems most typically to have been an entertainer, not a commentator on the human condition, and he was an entertainer of remarkable talent.

Splendidly illustrative of his Rococo work are four large canvas panels he painted in 1771 on commission from Madame du Barry. They were intended for a drawing room in a pavilion at Louveciennes but were never installed, perhaps because their style was thought outdated. The panels are of a politely but unmistakably erotic nature; in a word, they are "gallant." A pair of aristocratic young lovers is featured in

15-14 Elisabeth Louise Vigée-Lebrun, *Self-Portrait*, c. 1782. Oil on canvas, 25½″ × 21¼″. Kimbell Art Museum, Fort Worth, Texas.

15-15 Jean Honoré Fragonard, *The Rendezvous*, 1771. Oil on canvas, 10′6″ × 8′. Copyright, The Frick Collection, New York.

the series, proceeding from *The Pursuit* and *The Rendezvous* (fig. 15-15) to *The Love Letter* and *The Lover Crowned*. The setting, an enchanted terraced park with sculpted love goddesses and cupids, is artificial, and the ritual of desire and love is as artificial as the innocence of the players—for all of this is pure theater. Certainly the sensual message of *The Rendezvous*, known alternatively as *Storming the Citadel*, is quite obvious, despite the feigned alarm of the young woman as her lover scales the terrace wall. This is a stage set, in discreetly voluptuous colors, for a stylized script whose outcome is inevitable. It is an erotic dream world—"the dream," it has been said, "of a man asleep in a box at the opera."

Fragonard's art bore a message of enjoyment—of painting as well as of life. However, painting for the sheer joy of painting, like painting for titillation, was

coming under attack from the forces of the Enlightenment. From the philosophes to the novelists, from court officials to the educated middle class, from the new breed of art critics to the archaeologists dreaming of the revival of a classical ethic—from all Enlightened quarters, eroticism, frivolity, and disengagement from the world's problems were being bombarded with criticism. The arts, it was now generally agreed, must neither ignore nor corrupt society, but must improve society. The need seemed urgent because of widespread assertions that the arts, and indeed all types of "luxury," had already had a profoundly debilitating effect on society; Rousseau was far from alone in his yearnings for a simpler, unspoiled age. The arts thus were placed on the defensive, obliged to justify not simply their harmlessness to society but their utility in creating a better world. Art was not to be for art's sake, but for moral improvement; in short, art should be propaganda. This, of course, is a theme not peculiar to the late Enlightenment, but recurrent in Western history—from Plato to concerned moralists of today.

In the last decades before the French Revolution it was Diderot's imposing *Encyclopedia*, as mouthpiece for the progressive forces of the time, that most prominently called for ethical and social activism in the arts. According to the *Encyclopedia*, the arts, above all, must become an educational tool, appealing to sympathetic emotions in order to make better human beings. The inspirer of the *Encyclopedia*, the philosophe and art critic Diderot, has come to symbolize best the artistic ethic of the 1760s and 1770s, in his lively reports on the frequent Academic exhibitions. Diderot's favorite among the painters was neither Boucher nor Fragonard, representatives of the corrupt luxury of a decadent aristocracy, but Greuze, the preacher of domestic virtue.

Art experts today find only slight artistic merit in the anecdotal works of Jean Baptiste Greuze (1725–1805). In fact, it would be difficult to find more striking refutation of the myth that a good story makes a good picture. The uninteresting color schemes, the slickly smooth brushwork, the disorganized clutter of Greuze's typical works, repel many moderns quite as much as do his sentimentality and melodrama. Yet intelligent persons of the later Enlightenment, enchanted by Rousseau, sentiment, and honest yearnings for a nobler humanity, viewed Greuze quite differently. "Here is your painter and mine," wrote Diderot, "the first among us to bring morality to art."

In 1765 Diderot was particularly delighted by

15-16   Jean Baptiste Greuze, *The Son Punished*, 1778. Oil on canvas, 51″ × 65″. Louvre, Paris.

Greuze's sketch entitled *The Son Punished*, which later was somewhat revised as an oil painting (fig. 15-16). A preceding sketch, *The Ungrateful Son*, had depicted a young man about to desert his aged and needy parents for the army and making insolent demands on them. *The Son Punished* portrayed the sequel, as the son returns to a poverty stricken home only moments after his father has died. The young man is visibly overwhelmed with remorse as his mother gestures toward a family scene of death, consternation, and grief. Diderot was profoundly moved. "What a lesson," he exclaimed, "for fathers and for children!"

The Classicism of David

The vogue for Greuze was intense, but it barely outlasted the popularity of Fragonard. On the eve of the Revolution, France was discovering that the sentimen-

tal ideal of domestic virtue did not go far enough— that it should make way for the broader, sterner demands of civic duty. The Classical revival became the medium for this new emphasis in 1784–85, just after Diderot's death. The catalyst was David's painting *The Oath of the Horatii* (fig. 15-17); its first public showings transformed this painting into the manifesto of Classicism. Far from the first painting of the eighteenth-century Classical revival, the *Horatii* effectively divorced moral fervor from sentimental domesticity and wedded it to the civic ideals of a supposedly Classical rationalism.

An earlier visit of five years to Italy had impressed an enthusiastic Classicism on Jacques Louis David (1748–1825), and to Italy he returned in 1784 to paint the Horatian story, convinced that "only in Rome could he paint Romans." When completed, the new work caused a sensation there—even the pope requested a showing—and then in Paris. For three decades, until the fall of Napoleon, David was to be the undisputed chief of the Classical school in France and throughout Europe.

In David's painting, the three Horatii, sons of the elder Horatius, are about to depart for battle; as their women grieve, the warriors swear to their father to return victorious for Rome, or dead. The scene is one of intense patriotic drama, of the sort that soon would inspire the French Revolutionary armies; at the same time it is a stern rebuke to the supposedly indolent, hedonistic court and ruling class of France's Old Regime. Befitting so noble a story and so grim a message, David's scene is stripped to its essentials through the monumentality of the figures and the starkly geometrical background. All distractions of both detail and color are avoided. The colors are strong but certainly not voluptuous; archaeological details are remarkably correct but never obtrusive. The scene is no fleeting impression but a rigid tableau of deliberately ponderous proportions. Statuesque figures and statuesque gestures are frozen in space, immobilized for all time. The legendary moment was to be as eternal as the ideal classical beauty that David believed his work embodied.

With the coming of the Revolution, David found that his ethical and aesthetic doctrines need be confined no longer to his own brush and canvas. As leader of an unassailably triumphant Classicism, and eventually also as legislator and as member of the prestigious Committee of General Security, David became for a time the artistic ruler of France. Under the reformed monarchy and then under the republic, he led the struggle to abolish the near-monopolistic Royal Academy of Painting and Sculpture, organized the pageantry of Revolutionary festivals, planned monuments to the achievements and ideals of the Revolution, and

15-17 Jacques Louis David, *The Oath of the Horatii,* 1784–85. Oil on canvas, 10′ × 14′. Louvre, Paris.

earnestly exhorted all French artists "to help to extend the progress of the human spirit, to propagate and to transmit to posterity the striking examples of the efforts of an immense people, who, guided by reason and philosophy, are bringing forth on earth the reign of liberty, equality, and the law." No artist, it was implied, who himself was "at the height of revolutionary circumstances" could do otherwise.

If several traditional and masterful portraits at this time are ignored, David himself, as painter, set an impeccable example of Revolutionary fervor. No longer requiring the veil of antique settings, the forces of freedom and patriotism could now be portrayed at work in the contemporary world. David's special contribution would be a huge portrayal of that tennis-court oath in which the assembled representatives of the people had sworn never to disband until liberty had been firmly established in France. The painting was not completed, but a far more modest Revolutionary memento,

15-18   Jacques Louis David, *The Dying Marat*, 1793. Oil on canvas, 65″ × 51″. Musées Royaux des Beaux-Arts de Belgique, Brussels.

The Dying Marat (fig. 15-18), became David's masterpiece.

For David's contemporaries this work commemorated a shocking modern martyrdom, the death of the Jacobin journalist and "friend of the people" Jean Paul Marat. Marat had been stabbed by an enthusiast of the rival Girondist party, the young Charlotte Corday—stabbed at home in a bathtub whose cover he used as a writing desk—assassinated while performing his duties for the people of France by one of the common people he trusted. Still clutched in his hand is the deceitful message by which Charlotte Corday gained entrance to Marat's presence: "I need your kind attention simply because I am very unhappy." No essential realistic detail is omitted—from the fallen dagger to the crude wooden box holding the implements of writing. The background is vast and somber, balanced by the plain box in the foreground, inscribed FOR MARAT, DAVID. The painting is a work of stark simplicity and power, and the artist's vision and technique have matched the pathos and grandeur of the theme.

TRENDS IN MUSIC

It was in November 1781, long before the French Revolution was dreamed of, that the imperial Viennese court received a distinguished visitor, Grand Duke Paul, son of Catherine the Great and future Tsar of All the Russias. "The Grand Duke, the big noise, has arrived," commented the composer Mozart, whose informal remarks concerning the nobility often lacked reverence. During the next weeks the duke, who fancied himself something of a musical connoisseur, witnessed a contest at the piano between Mozart and a rival composer and applauded several new string quartets by Joseph Haydn (fig. 15-19). The grand duchess requested piano lessons of the famous Haydn, and in due time the duke received the formal dedication of the new quartets.

Classicism and Sonata Form in Haydn

The six string quartets of 1781, Opus 33—known as the Russian Quartets—were by no means the first or the last written by Joseph Haydn (1732–1809). Nonetheless, more than a flair for self-advertisement was involved in Haydn's public assertion that Opus 33 was "written in an entirely new and special manner."

15-19 Johann Ernst Mansfeld, *Joseph Haydn*, 1781, Mozart Museum, Salzburg.

These quartets were an evolutionary landmark in the history of this durable and flexible chamber-music form.

Haydn's previous group of quartets, completed nine years earlier, had been profoundly felt, but their form was rather tentative, sometimes including an isolated fugal movement reminiscent of the Baroque. The Opus 33 quartets are undeniably more homogeneous in their fluent chordal style, enriched only now and then by unobtrusive snatches of polyphony. However, the new quartets, deceptive in their sunny air of effortlessness, retained the same overall structure as the earlier works: four movements in contrasting yet complementary vein—the first moderate in tempo and frequently assertive in mood, the second reminiscent of a minuet or a lively peasant dance, the third slow and solemn, and the fourth quick and gay. Such, in fact, with the middle movements sometimes reversed, was to be the general form of the Classical symphony and quartet and many of their successors. The trend toward standardization of general structure in most instrumental works large and small is an outstanding trait of this late-eighteenth-century school that has come to be known as Classical.

Sonata form also characterizes music of the Classical period. The term itself is a mid-nineteenth-century invention, an attempt to explain and categorize a type of musical pattern first used by such composers as Haydn, Mozart, and Beethoven in much of their instrumental writing.

A sonata in its earlier sense had simply been a piece to be played (from the Italian *suonare*, "to play"), as distinguished from the *cantata*, which is a piece to be sung (from *cantare*, "to sing"). By the eighteenth century, the sonata had become a work for solo instrument or a small group of instruments and was organized in several movements of contrasting yet complementary natures. Soon, still more narrowly, it became a work for only one instrument or two, with at least one long section constructed in sonata form. "Sonata form," then, referred to the structure of a single movement, not to the overall pattern of a complete work. But the term came to be applied in retrospect not only to sonata movements but to certain movements in any formally patterned instrumental work. It was noted that the Classical piano trio, string quartet, concerto, or symphony had almost always included at least one movement in sonata form. Most commonly it was the first movement that took this form, although others might also.

The parts within a movement in sonata form are generally listed as exposition, development, and recapitulation. Within the *exposition,* or preliminary statement of musical themes, would appear the initial and principal "subject," or theme; a second theme in a different but related key; and a shorter, third theme in the second key, the whole then being repeated. Next would come the *development* section, elaborating at least the first theme and usually modulating into distant keys. The movement would be rounded off by a *recapitulation* of all themes, often as unadorned as in the exposition but remaining this time in the original key. A *coda* (Italian, "tail"), often reminiscent of the principal theme, might be added. Brief linking sections *(bridges)* frequently were necessary to cement the whole structure. It was a self-contained, rational, understandable, and hence humanistic structure, a fitting monument to the age of enlightened reason.

Sonata form is not as constricting as it may first seem. Not only do relatively few Classical works include the same rigid pattern outlined by the historians, but the effectiveness of this particular musical form has always depended much less on technical skill than on the musical material and the creativity of the composer. With Haydn and Mozart at their best, what seem to be mere repetition often involves much subtle variation.

The subtlety and creative imagination of Haydn are well illustrated, with the instrumental economy demanded by the string quartet genre (two violins, viola, and cello), by the Russian Quartets of 1781. In the first of the series, the Quartet in B minor, Haydn employs sonata form in three of the four movements, in each case uniting a variety of short phrases and longer thematic groups into an organic unity. The first movement (*allegro moderato*—moderately fast) has a simple opening subject that quickly turns from the graceful to the brooding. A more vigorous, contrasting second subject follows. After its development, the recapitulation surprises by its striking divergencies from the original statement, notably as the bridge to the second theme introduces new, sharply assertive chords into the otherwise dark texture. The second movement (*allegro*—fast) is constructed simply: first a theme in two parts, each repeated; then a middle section (called the *trio*) similarly constructed; and finally the theme again as first played but without repetitions. The whole is a subdued echo of those country dances so often reflected in Haydn's symphonies and chamber works. In the third movement (*andante*—rather slow) Haydn's use of a major key may lead us to expect a lightening of touch, yet the slow pace and disturbing chromaticisms hold back the sharply ascending main theme to create an uneasy ambiguity. Nor is the temper of even the brisk last movement (*presto*—fast), in its beautifully clear sonata form, wholly unambiguous. The pace is generally energetic and assertive, but there are strange variations in *dynamics* (loudness and softness), and long, mysterious chords precede the second theme in the recapitulation. Just before the ending, a surprising hold interrupts the original theme in mid course, and the last few measures are genial and strong.

Although most of Haydn's greatest quartets and symphonies were still to follow, the Quartet in B minor

embodied the main characteristics of his mature Classicism: immense creativity in both musical material and the way it is elaborated, guided by the ideals of pattern and balance. The restraints imposed by pattern and balance are gentlemanly, but Classical impulse and feeling are nonetheless dynamic. It was the nineteenth century, accustomed to more ponderous and flamboyant musical effects, and often totally deaf to Haydn's subtleties, that created the myth that Haydn's work represented mere form without emotional content, or at best an innocuous sort of naive charm.

Mozart and the Classical Synthesis

For the last decade of his short life (1756–91), Wolfgang Amadeus Mozart (fig. 15-20) and Joseph Haydn were friends in Vienna, each learning from the other. Mozart recognized the older man's preeminent position in the music world, and Haydn realized that in Mozart he had met more than his equal. Already in 1785

15-20   Josef Lange, detail from *Wolfgang Amadeus · Mozart* (unfinished), 1789. Oil on canvas, 14½" × 11½". Mozart Museum, Salzburg.

Haydn said to Mozart's proud father, "I tell you before God, and as an honest man, that your son is the greatest composer I know, either personally or by reputation." After Mozart's death the saddened Haydn phrased it more personally: "Friends often flatter me that I have some genius, but he stood far above me." Posterity has agreed with Haydn's generous assessment.

Again and again during Mozart's lifetime his music was taken to task for being too difficult, for lacking precisely in that easy grace and ready accessibility that made the work of many of his contemporaries so popular then, and so monotonous now. Yet we cannot escape the fact that Mozart was born into a Rococo world and flourished in an age of Classicism; the charm of the one is joined to the discipline of the other in his music, and melody unites the two. "Melody," he once remarked, "is the essence of music," although certainly he understood also the roles of musical elaboration and human emotion. The Classical synthesis of reason and sensitivity speaks in words he wrote to his father: "Passions, whether violent or not, must never be expressed in such a way as to excite disgust—and music, even in the most terrible situations, must never offend the ear, but must please the hearer, or in other words must never cease to be music." The result, in Mozart's case, was an art of great subtlety, in which craftsmanship and effort are never obtrusive, and the natural and the spontaneous always seem dominant.

This seemingly effortless craft is never better exemplified than in the great series of piano concertos Mozart composed for his own use as soloist. The *keyboard concerto*—a work in several movements for one or more keyboard soloists and an orchestra—was not invented by Mozart, but he was the first to dignify that relatively new instrument, the piano, with a major body of authentic concerted masterworks. Never in more than three movements, Mozart's piano concertos accommodated an unusual abundance of thematic material. His contemporary Dittersdorf, accustomed like his age to a simpler approach, expressed a typical reaction: "I have never yet met with any composer who had such an amazing wealth of ideas. I could almost wish he were not so lavish in using them. He leaves his hearer out of breath, for hardly has he grasped one beautiful thought than another of greater fascination dispels the first." In fact, it is substantially because of this richness of inspiration that Mozart's concertos live today. The richness is not one of incompatible themes indiscriminately thrown together; the themes complement each other in a unified flow of musical feeling. Even the competition between piano and orchestra seldom jolts the listener; tension, drama, and even pathos are there, but the drama hesitates just short of explosion, and coherence remains the predominant impression.

All of this is true of the Piano Concerto in C minor (finished early in 1786 and number 491 in Koechel's catalogue), although it is certainly one of the most deeply felt of the series and the largest of all in instrumental requirements. The first movement (allegro) is in sonata form expanded almost beyond recognition. A multitude of themes, shared eventually in most cases by piano and orchestra, are skillfully joined and recombined, condensed or dramatized, to constitute a masterpiece of structural balance, as well as of emotional intensity. There are quiet moments and forceful moments, both in the long orchestral introduction and in the concerted sections. Just once, toward the end of the development section, Mozart resorts to an almost physically violent passion, as the orchestra seems to challenge the piano in a series of strong, gripping figures interspersed with angry, brilliant pianistic responses. The movement's end is all the more dramatic for being subdued and hushed.

The slow movement (larghetto) is organized very simply, with frequent repetitions of the short opening theme. Whereas the initial and final moods are serene, the middle section is more disturbed in feeling, even voluptuous, in the exchanges between piano and woodwinds.

The last movement (allegretto) consists of a theme and variations, a form used often by Mozart elsewhere, as in his solo piano works, but seldom in his concertos. Appropriate for variation treatment, the theme is relatively simple, and in this case both marchlike and rather sad. Each of the eight variations, although closely joined and without major change in tempo, has its own mood—from the martial (no. 3) to the pertly gentle (no. 4) to the wistful (no. 5). The *cadenza* (a showy solo passage) is supplied by the performer, and the work concludes with a variation that is graceful and dancelike yet retrospective and rather melancholy in feeling. The ambiguities that in Haydn were only occasional have become virtually the essence of Mozart's C minor Concerto.

Of the various musical forms used by Mozart, only the opera equals and surpasses the complexities, and often the ambiguities, of his best piano concertos. *The Marriage of Figaro* exemplifies well both the complexities and the ambiguities.

Since the autumn of 1785 Mozart had devoted much time to *Le Nozze di Figaro,* in collaboration with the Italian poet Lorenzo da Ponte. The original play by Beaumarchais was already a popular success in France. On May 1, 1786, at the National Theater in Vienna, came the first official public performance of the Mozart–Da Ponte work. The general reception of *Figaro* was warm, although not as enthusiastic as that given to some other operas of the time, now forgotten, by Vicente Martín. *Figaro* was repeated several times, then not staged again in Vienna until 1789.

The direct inspiration of the opera was the second play by Beaumarchais concerning the fictional Spanish Almaviva family. In the first play, *The Barber of Seville,* Count Almaviva married the heiress Rosina, with the help of the barber Figaro and in opposition to her guardian, Doctor Bartolo, who had hoped to marry her himself. Now, several years later, a second marriage is imminent, that of the count's valet Figaro to the countess's maid Susanna. A difficulty of a most embarrassing sort has arisen: although the count, who is notable for his sexual appetites and persistence, has renounced the presumed "right of the first night" with brides in his employ, he still firmly intends to precede Figaro in the marital bed. How his scheme comes to grief, mainly through the efforts of the countess and the faithful Susanna herself, is the dramatic substance of Beaumarchais's comedy and Mozart's opera.

But what Beaumarchais wrote, on the eve of the French Revolution, as a rather open social and political satire on the heartless ambitions and social tyranny of the nobility, becomes in the opera primarily a comedy involving real human beings. And it is above all through musical expression that the characters appeal to us and are made into contradictory, complex, whole creatures.

Although it never quotes musically from the body of the opera itself, the orchestral overture to *The Marriage of Figaro* quickly summarizes the predominant moods of what Beaumarchais called a mad, mixed-up day of surprises and misadventures. Quiet conspiratorial rumbling in the strings leads to a succession of *presto* themes and dynamic surprises that suggest the fast-paced confusion of the subsequent story. As the curtain rises, Figaro and Susanna are in the half-furnished room they will occupy after their marriage. In duets and in recitative their mutual affection is made clear, and Susanna enlightens Figaro as to the count's intentions. When she leaves to answer the countess's call, Figaro bursts out into an aria, *Se vuol ballare,* challenging the count's scheme: "If you want to dance, my lord, it's my tune you'll be dancing to"— two people can play at this game. Prematurely confident, Figaro leaves the stage.

Thus the main line of development is established at the outset, although the line is shortly to take some startling turns. There are, for example, the complications made apparent immediately when the elderly Doctor Bartolo and his former mistress Marcellina plot to get Figaro married not to Susanna but to Marcellina herself, according to the terms of an old agreement. Then comes the first of a series of confusions brought about by the darting in and out of the young page Cherubino, who fancies himself desperately in love with the countess but who is captivated also by Susanna, by the gardener's daughter, and by women in general. (To capture the freshness and subtlety of this role, both Beaumarchais and Mozart prescribed a woman for the part.) At this point he sings an aria about his tremulous adolescent desires as the music alternates between fluttering agitation and soulful sighs. Somewhat later the count discovers the page on the premises, hidden and apparently eavesdropping, and decides to rid himself of the boy by sending him off to the army. Figaro brings the act to a rousing close with an ironic aria, pointing out that now Cherubino's fun and games will give way to the sterner glories of war.

Subsequent acts of *The Marriage of Figaro* bring further complexities of plot and continuing musical richness. In the concluding six minutes, the finale is a masterpiece of narrative and musical economy in which all threads of the mad day are untangled and the opera can end in universal rejoicing. The high point is the final exchange between the count and the countess, in which she begs him to forgive the steps she has taken to outwit him—to which he replies astonishingly, and apparently sincerely, by falling to his knees and asking forgiveness for himself. The scene may not carry full dramatic conviction, for we may well sense future aberrations in this curious household—but as the countess grants her forgiveness and the others sing of general reconciliation, the solemn musical transfiguration is one of the supreme moments in all opera. Yet *Figaro* is billed as a comedy, and so the curtain falls to a joyous ensemble: "To the sound of merry music we will revel all the night."

Mozart's Classicism would be followed by an age of robust Romanticism, in which emotions would be expressed more strongly and bluntly. However, we should remember that in music as in the visual arts, the least violent effects may well leave the deepest marks, especially when their emotional range is as great as Mozart's. The sureness and subtlety of his technical skill are now seldom questioned; what remains, then, for many listeners to fully appreciate is the emotional breadth and depth of his musical expression. Gaiety, vitality, pain, and repose commingle in Mozart, to-gether with grace, tenderness, and melancholy. Surely in Mozart as in Haydn there are both balance and sensitivity, both Classicism and Romanticism—and an omnipresent humanity that transcends their time. Thus ultimately it is not the visual arts but the music of the late eighteenth century that has had the broader, more lasting appeal. The age of David and Soufflot seems fated to be remembered as the age of Mozart and Haydn.

Recommended Reading

Baker, Keith Michael. *The Old Regime and the French Revolution* (1987). Collection of political and cultural sources.

Burke, Edmund, and Thomas H. D. Mahoney, eds. *Reflections on the Revolution in France* (1955). The bible of conservatism for two centuries.

Fasel, George. *Edmund Burke* (1983). Life and work quickly surveyed.

Flexner, Eleanor. *Mary Wollstonecraft: A Biography* (1973). Introduction to life and ideas.

Gagliardo, John G. *Enlightened Despotism* (1967). Concise presentation of governmental ideas and practice.

Gay, Peter, ed. *The Enlightenment: A Comprehensive Anthology* (1973). Fine selection of primary sources with commentary.

Geiringer, Karl and Irene. *Haydn: A Creative Life in Music* (1982). Life and works.

Gibbon, Edward, and Dero A. Saunders, eds. *The Decline and Fall of the Roman Empire* (1980). Abridgment of the history.

Hampson, Norman. *The French Revolution* (1975). Up-to-date introduction, heavily illustrated.

Havens, George R. *Jean-Jacques Rousseau* (1978). Introduction to life and ideas.

Hirschfeld, Charles, and Edgar E. Knoebel, eds. *The Modern World* (1980). Sizable chunks of primary sources.

Hutchings, Arthur. *Mozart—The Man, The Musician* (1976). Handsome presentation of life, times, and work.

Leonard, Jonathan Norton. *The World of Gainsborough 1727–1788* (1969). Good on life and times.

Schnepper, Antoine. *David* (1982). Fine presentation of his career and work, well-illustrated.

Starobinski, Jean. *The Invention of Liberty 1700–1789* (1964). Thoughtful study of art and ideas.

Wakefield, David. *French Eighteenth-Century Painting* (1984). Fine survey, especially from mid century.

Wangermann, Ernst. *The Austrian Achievement, 1700–1800* (1973). Illustrated political, economic, and cultural history.

Wollstonecraft, Mary. *The Rights of Woman* (1929). Original text.

16

Classicism and Romanticism: 1800–1825

I n 1799 Napoleon Bonaparte, a popular young general, seized the government of France. "The Revolution," he announced, "is ended." As First Consul, Bonaparte consolidated his power, and in 1804 a new constitution stated that "the government of the French republic is entrusted to an emperor." This First French Empire, under Napoleon I, would endure until 1814.

Napoleon had molded for himself a new authoritarian state based to some degree on Revolutionary principles, but founded more obviously on military might and his own genius as an administrator. After a chaotic decade of revolution, prosperity, self-esteem, and order, but not peace or freedom, had returned to France. Although liberty was sharply curtailed after 1799, equality was perpetuated in part by maintaining the principle of advancement according to ability, not social rank. In effect, the Revolutionary victory of the middle class was confirmed. The foundation of power, in a dawning age of industrialism, was undoubtedly the bourgeoisie, even though there existed after 1804 a new imperial nobility, based more on achievement than on breeding, and an imperial court that at times sought to surpass the splendor of even the Old Regime.

The Napoleonic structure extended far beyond the traditional French territories; the French Empire came to embrace the Low Countries, western Germany, and a large part of Italy. Beyond those borders lay such dependent areas as Spain and much of the rest of Italy and Germany. Still farther afield, at

397

the height of Napoleon's power in 1810, three great states were allied to France—Austria, Prussia, and Russia. It was these three states that eventually joined with Great Britain to bring about Napoleon's military downfall and his abdication in 1814. His brief return from exile and his resumption of control in France—the Hundred Days—were ended decisively at the Battle of Waterloo in 1815.

With the consent of the great powers at the Congress of Vienna, France entered its Restoration period under Louis XVI's brother, Louis XVIII (1814–15, 1815–24). His reign was hardly liberal but was politically moderate compared to many reactionary regimes elsewhere on the Continent; for them, "reaction" went beyond *conservatism* (the conserving of existing systems) to the revival of the still-older ways of before 1789. Of these regimes the leading symbol came to be Prince Metternich, adviser to Francis I of Austria. (Francis was the second Holy Roman Emperor of that name; the Holy Roman Empire at last had expired in 1806, after Francis had established a new Austrian empire.) Inspired by Metternich and the Russian tsar Alexander I, several reactionary interventions in European affairs were among the few international events of consequence in the first post-Napoleonic decade or so in Europe. Most Europeans, tired of Napoleonic warfare, welcomed the tranquillity imposed by their governments and an alliance of the great powers. Even in Britain the mood was reactionary—and such feeling was not unknown in the new republic across the sea, the United States of America. In western and central Europe, as in America, the powerful but undramatic trends toward industrialization and democracy would become dominant only after 1825.

THE AGE OF NAPOLEON AND BEETHOVEN

In 1810 the Spanish artist Goya began the series of etchings that are some of the most grisly reminders of human suffering in wartime. Goya was virtually unknown to the French in those heady days of Napoleon's triumphs in Europe, and French difficulties with the rebellious Spaniards were only a troublesome incident in the onward march of their empire. Cer-

tainly the difficulties with Spain were in few minds as the Column of the Grand Army was erected in the Place Vendôme in Paris (fig. 16-1). The column was dedicated on August 15 with great fanfare, and the French rejoiced with their emperor in this commemoration of French glory. It was noted with pride that twelve hundred pieces of captured enemy cannon had been melted down to furnish bronze for the column's sculpted casing and pedestal.

In that age of militant artistic Classicism, the Vendôme Column was, of course, Roman in inspiration. Originally it was to have been a "Germanic" column, evoking the grandeur of Charlemagne's wide empire as well as the recent victories of Napoleonic arms in Germany. But it was discovered that the French ruler had quietly sent back to Aachen the statue of Charlemagne that had been destined to crown the new column. Napoleon, the new Charlemagne, graciously permitted the casting of a substitute statue of himself, in Roman garb and crowned with laurel. Doubtless this was a happy inspiration, for Charlemagne himself might have been too painful a reminder to the new empress, an Austrian archduchess, of the Holy Roman Imperial title that her father had recently relinquished.

Patriotic holidays were frequent in Napoleon's day, but apparently the festive commemoration of military victories became tiresome for the Parisians, who preferred the standard urban diversions of the time. For popular amusement there were omnipresent sideshows of curiosities human and animal, and a remarkable circus. There were shops, parks, dance halls, and cafés. Among the most fashionable and elegant establishments was the Café Frascati (fig. 16-2), whose dance hall could accommodate a thousand couples. The Frascati also provided for dining and gambling and for strolling in its rustic and exotic garden. Its interior décor was classical with some unusual additions, such as Turkish and Egyptian motifs. England, too, in these decades, it might be noted, remained fond of the "Oriental" manner, as is seen in the Royal Pavilion at the resort town of Brighton (fig. 16-3). It is significant, however, that despite the supposedly "Indian" fantasy of the bulbous domes, and the hodgepodge of Gothic and Chinese detail inside, the Royal Pavilion is nonetheless classically symmetrical.

Also vitally important in the political, social, and cultural history of Napoleonic Europe was Vienna, center of the Austrian Empire. Above all, we remem-

CHRONOLOGY

HISTORY		THE ARTS	
		1724–1804	Kant
		1746–1828	Goya
		1749–1832	Goethe
1760–1820	George III king of England	1757–1822	Canova
		1770–1827	Beethoven
		1770–1850	Wordsworth
		1774	Goethe begins *Faust*
		1780–1867	Ingres
1788–1808	Charles IV king of Spain	1788–1824	Byron
1792–1806	Francis II Holy Roman Emperor	1791–1824	Géricault
1792–1802,		1795–1821	Keats
1803–15	Wars of the French Revolution and Napoleon	1797–1828	Schubert
		1798	Wordsworth's "Lines Composed a Few Miles above Tintern Abbey"
1799–1804	the Consulate in France: Napoleon Bonaparte first consul	1798–99	Goya's *Caprichos* etchings
		1800	Goya's *Family of Charles IV*
		1800	Wordsworth's preface to second edition of *Lyrical Ballads*
1801–25	Alexander I emperor of Russia		
1804	Francis II also becomes Francis I, emperor of Austria (died 1835)	1804–8	Beethoven's Fifth Symphony
		1805–8	David's *Consecration*
1804–14,		1805–8	Canova's *Pauline Borghese as Venus*
1815	First Empire in France: Napoleon I emperor	1806–8	Percier and Fontaine's Arch of Triumph of the Carousel, Paris
1806	end of Holy Roman Empire	1807–45	Vignon's Church of the Madeleine, Paris
1808–12	Joseph Bonaparte king of Spain	1808	Goethe's *Faust*, Part One, published
		1810	dedication of Vendôme Column, Paris
		1810 or later	Goya's *Disasters of War* etchings
1814–15	Congress of Vienna redraws the world map after fall of Napoleon	1814	Goya's *The Third of May*
		1814	Ingres's *Great Odalisque*
1814–15,			
1815–24	Louis XVIII king of France		
1814–48	"Age of Metternich" (Prince Metternich, adviser to Hapsburgs)		
1815	the Hundred Days: Napoleon I	1815–23	Nash's Royal Pavilion, Brighton
1815	Battle of Waterloo: Napoleon's decisive defeat, beginning of his exile on island of Saint Helena	1818–19	Géricault's *Raft of the Medusa*
		1819	Keats's "Ode on a Grecian Urn" and "To Autumn"
1820–30	George IV king of England		
1821	death of Napoleon in exile	1823–24	Schubert's *The Beautiful Maid of the Mill (Die Schöne Müllerin)*
		1826	Schubert's G major Quartet, Opus 161

EUROPE AFTER 1815

Kingdom of Prussia

Austrian Empire

Boundary of German Confederation

ber the Viennese early nineteenth century as the age of Beethoven and Schubert, rivaling the age of Haydn and Mozart for precedence at the summit of musical achievement.

The Austrian setting for this achievement, with its first adventurous steps toward full-bodied musical Romanticism, was essentially not adventurous at all. Francis I was extremely anxious to protect his land, once bullied by Napoleonic might, against new and dangerous ideas from farther west—as was his distinguished adviser Prince Metternich. Government censorship and police surveillance became facts of Aus-

trian life, and both Beethoven and Schubert seem to have been aware of the politically oppressive atmosphere. Schubert was the less politically minded, but his circle of artistic friends was often under government suspicion, and he himself was once briefly under arrest.

In general, the Viennese avoided political controversy and found their diversion elsewhere. Ever-present sources of diversion were available at the numerous coffee houses (cafés) of the city. One might sit there for hours, read newspapers, converse with friends, or play cards or billiards. At inns and garden cafés there might be musicians or conjurers or acrobats to supply enter-

16-1 *Erection of the Vendôme Column* (designed by Gondoin and Lepère), 1810. Etching. Bibliothèque Nationale, Paris.

16-2 Philibert Louis Debucourt, *The Café Frascati*. Engraving, 12¾″ × 16″. The Metropolitan Museum of Art, New York (Harris Brisbane Dick Fund, 1935).

16-3   John Nash, Royal Pavilion, Brighton, 1815–23.

tainment, and the air was highly informal. Beethoven and Schubert spent much time in public places like these, and even composed there.

After the Congress of Vienna (1814–15), which drew the major lines of the post-Napoleonic settlement, came the three decades or so of what political historians call the *Age of Metternich* and cultural historians the *Biedermeier period*. Biedermeier himself was quite fictitious—the good-natured creation of a Viennese journal—but he gave his name to an age. And, in western Europe, it was an age of bourgeois dominance.

Music was very much in evidence in Vienna; it was heard in concert halls and dance halls, in cafés and homes. The waltz had pushed aside the more formal minuet of the old aristocracy, and a dance-hall mania ensued. In aristocratic homes the servant orchestras of the previous century had disappeared or been replaced by professional musicians, and bourgeois homes with their pianos became the more significant center of domestic music making.

As to the composers' livelihoods, the cases of Beethoven and Schubert illustrate two quite different degrees of worldly success. Beethoven's reputation as a major composer was fully established in the first years of the century, and he enjoyed the patronage of aristocrats. Beethoven did not, however, fawn upon the

nobility, for it was neither in his nature to do so nor an absolute financial necessity. The late eighteenth century had seen a growing competition in the open market among writers, artists, and musicians, so that it was becoming possible to make a respectable living by selling works in such a market, especially with the beginnings of a workable copyright system.

Schubert, whom Vienna and the world never acknowledged in his own day as a truly major composer, was less fortunate than Beethoven. (One reason for his lack of recognition was that, unlike Beethoven, he did not play or conduct in public.) His several attempts to get court positions were unsuccessful, his periods of school teaching and lesson giving were brief, and his reception seldom went beyond recognition as a promising young composer. Thus he was forced into dependence on the music publishers, who generally would buy, at miserably low fees, only his songs, and keep the copyrights themselves. The publishers usually agreed that his instrumental works were far too "difficult" to be sold. Yet the world, if not Schubert himself, may have become the richer for these unsatisfactory circumstances. With only sporadic support from publishers, he often simply followed the inclination of his temperament and composed what he wanted to. Sometimes aided by the generosity of friends, Schubert undertook few works on commission and composed in relative freedom.

Literary Romanticism

With the major exception of the Romantic poetry that helped inspire Schubert's songs, there are few parallels between the predominant Classicism of the early-nineteenth-century musical and visual arts and the predominant Romanticism of the literature. The most deeply thoughtful of great artists were Goya and Beethoven, and both were more notably influenced by the eighteenth-century Enlightenment than by the thinking of their own day. It was the composers and painters of the following artistic generation who most passionately reflected the full-blown Romanticism of early-nineteenth-century writing.

Classicism in the nineteenth century, as in the eighteenth, emphasized Greek and Roman models and the importance of pattern and regularity within a static, universal framework. Romanticism stressed individual feelings and emotions and the dynamic, irregular, and unexpected. The first decades of the nineteenth century saw the full flowering of the literary Romanticism that had become a sturdy growth in earlier decades. In Great Britain this was the heyday of medieval novels by Sir Walter Scott (1771–1832); of Lord Byron's colorful life (1788–1824) and poetic fantasies; and of the rhapsodic lyricism of William Wordsworth (1770–1850), John Keats (1795–1821), and Percy Bysshe Shelley (1792–1822). Lyric poetry became a celebration of nature and beauty, and of their intermingling in the sensitive artist's soul.

Wordsworth's preface to the second edition (1800) of *Lyrical Ballads* emphasized several new trends in British poetry at the time. Wordsworth implied that he would continue to do as he had done in his first published poems—to avoid the pomposities of much past poetry, with its abstractions and heroics, and instead

> to choose incidents and situations from common life, and to relate or describe them throughout . . . in a selection of language really used by men, and, at the same time, to throw over them a certain color of imagination, whereby ordinary things would be presented to the mind in an unusual aspect; and further, and above all, to make these incidents and situations interesting by tracing in them . . . the primary laws of our nature: chiefly, as far as regards the manner in which we associate ideas in a state of excitement.

Poetry, Wordsworth continued, is in essence "the spontaneous overflow of powerful feelings." The poet is a specialist in feeling, "with more lively sensibility, more enthusiasm and tenderness" than are probably common in mankind. Most significantly, Wordsworth held that the poet "considers man and nature as essentially adapted to each other" and reflects in his own mood and thought the impulses derived from external nature.

Wordsworth had already exemplified the interconnection of external nature and human feelings in his poem "Lines Composed a Few Miles above Tintern Abbey" (1798):

> For I have learned
> To look on nature, not as in the hour
> Of thoughtless youth; but hearing oftentimes
> The still, sad music of humanity.
> Nor harsh nor grating, though of ample power
> To chasten and subdue. And I have felt
> A presence that disturbs me with the joy
> Of elevated thoughts; a sense sublime
> Of something far more deeply interfused,
> Whose dwelling is the light of setting suns,
> And the round ocean and the living air,
> And the blue sky, and in the mind of man. . . .

Perhaps the most perfect embodiment of the Romantic poetic genius in England was John Keats (fig. 16-4), who died at twenty-six of the properly Romantic, lingering disease of "consumption" (tuberculosis). Only a few years earlier he had written the long lyric-narrative poem *Endymion* based on a tale derived from Greek antiquity—Romantics could be romantic on very classical themes. Keats wrote to his young sister Fanny, explaining what he was then working on:

> Many years ago there was a handsome shepherd [Endymion] who fed his flocks on a mountain's side called Latmus . . . , little thinking that such a beautiful creature as the Moon was growing mad in love with him. However so it was—and when he was asleep on the grass, she used to come down from heaven and admire him excessively for a long time, and at last could not refrain from carrying him away in her arms to the top of that high mountain Latmus while he was dreaming.

Though classical in its inspiration, the poem was not one of heroic adventure and battle but one of love, contemplation, and beauty. Few people remember more than the first few lines:

16-4   Charles Brown, *John Keats,* 1819. Pencil drawing. National Portrait Gallery, London.

A thing of beauty is a joy forever:
Its loveliness increases; it will never
Pass into nothingness; but will keep
A bower quiet for us, and a sleep
Full of sweet dreams, and health, and quiet breathing.

We note the similarity to the familiar final lines of Keats's "Ode on a Grecian Urn":

"Beauty is truth, truth beauty"—that is all
    Ye know on earth, and all ye need to know.

Keats's themes, however, were not always as rarefied as these. Here is the last stanza of his "To Autumn," addressed to that season:

Where are the songs of Spring? Ay, where are they?
    Think not of them, thou hast thy music too—
While barred clouds bloom the soft-dying day,
    And touch the stubble-plains with rosy hue.
Then in a wailful choir the small gnats mourn
    Among the river sallows, borne aloft
    Or sinking as the light wind lives or dies;
And full-grown lambs loud bleat from hilly bourn;
    Hedge-crickets sing; and now with treble soft
    The red-breast whistles from a garden-croft;
        And gathering swallows twitter in the skies.

Individualism of feeling was especially pro-

nounced in the poetry of Lord Byron, now with an exotic and demonic cast. Although the afflicted, lonely, imperious air of Byron's heroes, as well as of the glamorous poet himself, had its precedents (for example, in the early works of Goethe), Byron's talent for self-dramatization struck the public with peculiar force. Not only his poetic gifts, but the presumed dark secrets in both his poetry and his life, and his early death while enlisted in the cause of Greek independence, were soon to inspire all of Romantic Europe—including those supremely talented Romantics we will discuss in the next chapter, the composer Berlioz and the painter Delacroix.

In Germany, one eighteenth-century predecessor of Romanticism was the philosopher Immanuel Kant (1724–1804), often considered the most important of all modern philosophers. If Kant in some ways exemplified the Enlightenment—as a rationalist, for example, or as an opponent of warfare—his thought obviously weakened that movement even more. Above all, he refuted the usual Enlightenment assertion that our minds are the product of sensory experience and declared that experience is, in a deeper way, the product of our minds. He pointed out that spontaneous organizing principles are born within human minds, not derived from experience at all; these principles may not affect daily, practical life, but they are crucial to higher thought, where they help to establish the basic unity and priority of that sort of thought. Kant's idea was not in itself Romantic—but, while attacking the usual Enlightenment belief in sense experience, it supported the importance of intuition, a prized realm of the Romantics.

An even more obvious source of German Romanticism was the early work of the poet, playwright, and scientist Johann Wolfgang von Goethe (1749–1832), who is seen in figure 16-5 contemplating the Italian countryside during his 1786–88 trip to the south. By the opening years of the nineteenth century Goethe was attaining Olympian stature among his contemporaries: his genius was admired as a thoroughly convincing demonstration of a typical Romantic theme—the superior insight of the artist. In 1808 he published Part One of the great drama *Faust*, which he had conceived and begun writing in the 1770s; ever since then it has splendidly evoked the awesome and ambiguous complexities of human existence. The venerable story of the scholar Faust, who sold his soul to the devil in return for infinite knowledge and experience, em-

16-5 Wilhelm Tischbein, *Goethe in the Campagna*. Painting. Städelsches Kunstinstitut, Frankfurt-am-Main.

bodies such Romantic concerns as yearning and striving, and became for Goethe a quest for wholeness. In contrast to the simpler insights of Goethe's earlier years, *Faust* suggests the whole convoluted destiny of humanity in its tragic grandeur.

From the complex *Faust* drama we may note first the "Prologue in Heaven" (written in 1799–1800) depicting God's agreement to allow the demon Mephistopheles to tempt the scholar Faust with the riches and pleasures of the world. God points out that ultimately

> A good man, through obscurest aspiration,
>   Has still an instinct of the one true way.

Not discouraged, Mephistopheles later appears in Faust's study to initiate the temptation and strike the bargain. Sated with scholarly knowledge, Faust eagerly embraces the opportunity to explore the "sensual deeps," declaring (in good Romantic vein) that "Restless activity proves the man!" Delightedly, after Faust leaves the stage, Mephistopheles contemplates the prospect of enslaving his victim by dragging him "through the wildest life" on to final "flat and stale indifference." In Part Two Faust does indeed become sated but is saved by his nobler qualities, as God foresaw.

A few sentences of summary and quotation can hardly represent adequately the complex richness of Goethe's drama. Certainly Goethe had progressed beyond simple Romantic attitudes. He denounced the "hospital-poetry" of Romantic morbidity and welcomed the grander vision of the great literary classics. In his search for wholeness, and for sound craftsmanship, he was both Classical and Romantic. Concentrating the deep artistic ideals of an entire age, Goethe's work matches the near-universality of spirit exemplified also in Goya and Beethoven, who similarly resist academic classification.

Obviously it is unrealistic to point to any one clear trend of early-nineteenth-century cultural life—as difficult, at least, as for the preceding decades. Probably for all ages, finding a wholly consistent style of thought and expression is a futile exercise of simplistic historians. It is so, most certainly, for the age of Goethe and Byron, of Canova and Goya, of Beethoven and Ingres and Schubert.

ARCHITECTURE AND SCULPTURE: CLASSICISM TRIUMPHANT

The architectural Classicism favored in Napoleon's day, and for some time thereafter, attempted to be

16-6 Charles Percier, Pierre François Léonard Fontaine, and others, emperor's study, Château of Compiègne, c. 1807.

16-7 Charles Percier and Pierre François Léonard Fontaine, Arch of Triumph of the Carousel, Paris, 1806–8.

more faithful to antiquity than the classicism of the preceding centuries. And it may have succeeded, especially if fidelity to Roman antiquity is specified. Decorative motifs from ancient Rome were used lavishly and indiscriminately. The strict symmetry that was the exception even in Soufflot's day became more nearly the new rule. Furthermore, an alarming trend toward systematic monotony appeared. Grand bigness was admired, whether combined with a severe manner or a pretentious richness.

Yet the demands of no Western style have completely obscured creative architectural talent. Napoleon's favorite architects, Charles Percier (1764–1838) and Pierre François Léonard Fontaine (1762–1853)—both also active in the subsequent Restoration period—showed a high level of achievement, rising well above the repetitive formulas of their pupils and imitators. The emperor's study in the Château of Compiègne (fig. 16-6) will serve as an introduction to their manner in interior design. In 1807 Napoleon had ordered the restoration of the old royal residence at Compiègne, after years of vandalism and neglect. Percier and Fontaine provided the plans, leaving the detailed realization to others. The paneling and ceiling of the study are rich, but the lines are straight and angular. Rococo reminiscences within pre-Revolutionary Classicism have been suppressed, and the result is an elegance that is more severe than graceful.

Percier and Fontaine had been friends since their student days. Both had studied first-hand such Roman monuments as Trajan's Column and the Arch of Septimius Severus. It was this arch that became their model when Napoleon decreed construction of a triumphal arch in Paris to commemorate his Austerlitz campaign. The Arch of Triumph of the Carousel (fig. 16-7) is far smaller (forty-seven feet high) and less severe than the "Arch of the Star." Relief sculpture, freestanding columns, small arches at the sides, and marbles of different colors bring a pleasing variety to the monument, which in 1808 was crowned with four antique bronze horses taken from Venice by the French and with statues of Victory, Peace, and the Emperor himself. After Napoleon's defeat at Waterloo in 1815, this statuary was dismantled, and finally replaced by a group centered on an allegorical figure of the Restoration.

Foreknowledge of these developments was, of course, absent when in 1806, on a campaign in Prus-

16-8 Pierre Vignon and others, Church of La Madeleine, Paris, 1807–45.

sia, Napoleon ordered the construction of a secular Temple of Glory as a monument to his Grand Army. It was to stand on the foundations of the Church of the Magdalene, begun four decades before but still barely rising above the ground. A competition was held to choose the architect for the temple, but the emperor disregarded the award of the judges and appointed the little-known Pierre Vignon (1763–1828), whose plan he admired for its grandiose simplicity. Work began, but after the disasters of his Russian campaign Napoleon decided that the Temple of Glory should become a church. It was as a church that it was finally completed, long after Vignon's death, under the name of La Madeleine (fig. 16-8).

From the outside the Madeleine is a classical temple on a grand scale, 333 feet in length. A rectangle lined on all sides by Corinthian columns over 60 feet high, it is surmounted by a sloping roof with pediments sculpted in high relief—with sculpture appropriate to the building's purpose of Christian worship. Since the massive walls of the *cella,* or body of the church proper, are windowless, light is admitted through circular openings in the roof, invisible from the street but the focus of shallow domes on the inside. The interior features a highly ornate conglomeration of columns and statues, with much rich gilding and painting and multicolored marble.

The Classical ideal flourished for many decades in sculpture as well as architecture. In nearly all the arts except music, a prime principle of the new Classicism was imitation of antique models. Since there were few existing examples of antique painting, however, the Classicism of eighteenth- and nineteenth-century canvases was generally limited to imitation of the subject matter rather than the manner and technique of ancient pictures. The architecture of the Greek and Roman world was far better known than its painting, but the practical demands of building usually prevented slavish imitation of the antique, except in such elements as columns. Thus it was the art of sculpture, with its many ancient models and no overwhelmingly practical limitations, that closely imitated the antique manner around 1800. Unfortunately this literal imitativeness was nearly fatal to high quality, and the story

of nineteenth-century sculptural Classicism is generally a depressing one.

Amid the sculptural gloom of the century's first decades, the brightest of several pale lights was Antonio Canova (1757–1822). It is easy to judge Canova by his bad works, since there are so many of them. Yet a few appealing and effective statues are found among his works. One of these is his portrayal in marble of Napoleon's sister, Pauline Borghese, as Venus Victorious (fig. 16-9)—a title that this lady, one of the liveliest of the Bonapartes, had done much to earn. In executing this project Canova used classical nudity and antique drapery, and the Borghese princess reclines languidly on a Roman couch. The work is characterized by Classical repose, a rather soft charm, and elegance of line. Although it was intended as a portrait, individuality has been obliged to compromise with Classical generalization.

PAINTING: CLASSICISM CHALLENGED

Jacques Louis David (1748–1825), who had reflected so clearly the patriotic Classicism of the pre-Revolution and the ardent Jacobinism of the Terror, em-

16-9 Antonio Canova, *Pauline Borghese as Venus*, 1805–8. Marble, 6′7″ long. Galleria Borghese, Rome.

braced with equal enthusiasm the imperial dreams of Napoleon Bonaparte—all of this, it should be noted, within the artistic framework of Classicism. Themes from antiquity still preoccupied him after 1799, but his least strained, most successful works were in the realms of portraiture and contemporary narrative. David, it appears, always needed a hero and a cause, while Napoleon needed a painter of David's stature to commemorate the glories of his rule. The alliance between them was inevitable and mutually satisfying. It was especially so since Napoleon, the hero risen from the Revolution, combined his professions of liberty and equality with Classical personal tastes. David was showered with Napoleonic honors, and it was of course he, as First Painter, who was commissioned to memorialize Napoleon's accession to imperial rank in 1804. The result was the great canvas of *Le Sacre,* or *The Consecration* (fig. 16-10), usually known in English, inaccurately but handily, as *The Coronation of Napoleon.*

Work on this immense canvas proceeded slowly. Most of the scores of figures had to be recognizable portraits—many, as it turned out, were splendid ones—and everything to the smallest detail had to meet the approval of the emperor and his court. The ceremonial moment portrayed had to be changed from that in David's original sketch, for it was not thought wise to show the historic gesture of Napoleon proudly placing

the crown on his own head while the pope sat helplessly by. Rather, against the Classical stage-set that had been specially installed in Gothic Notre Dame for the ceremony, the pope now was depicted with his arm raised in blessing as the emperor lifted high the crown to be placed on the head of the kneeling Josephine. The effect of the whole is remarkably naturalistic, most notably the handsomely luminous figure of the empress.

David's heir as head of the French Classical school of painting was Jean Auguste Dominique Ingres (1780–1867). Ingres lived in Italy, mainly in Rome, during most of the period discussed in this chapter. Only in 1824 did he return to France to do active battle against the rising tide of Romanticism. In the meantime he studied earnestly the traditional art that could support his Classical predilections, notably the art of Rome and of Raphael ("a god come down to earth"), but also the art of Greece, frequently falling back in his painting on exact models from the past. Decrying the influence of Rubens, who had "ruined everything," he aimed, as David had done, at "the beautiful, which is eternal and natural." Like David's, his art is usually balanced and static.

Oedipus and the Sphinx (fig. 16-11) portrays a purely classical theme, the legend of the Theban Sphinx and her riddle. (The monster's riddle—part of

16-10 Jacques Louis David, *The Consecration,* 1805–8. Oil on canvas, 20′ × 30′7″. Louvre, Paris.

16-11 Jean Auguste Dominique Ingres, *Oedipus and the Sphinx,* 1808. Oil on canvas, 75″ × 57″. Louvre, Paris.

the prehistory of Sophocles' ancient tale—demanded, on pain of death, the identity of the creature walking on four legs in the morning, two at noon, and three in the evening; only Oedipus knew that the creature was man—crawling in infancy, then walking upright, and finally in old age requiring a cane for support.) The nude figure of Ingres's Oedipus was modeled on an ancient statue of an athlete. Its antique calm is somewhat countered by the threatening landscape and the frightened man in the background. An equally exotic subject is that of the harem figure in *Reclining Odalisque* (fig. 16-12). Exoticism was more often to be a hallmark of the Romantic movement than of Classicism, but dividing lines can become very much blurred in the vexed question of stylistic schools.

The *Great Odalisque* (as it is commonly known) is modeled with the utmost subtlety, fine brushwork, and great elegance of line. The figure, however sensuous the inspiration, is simplified, aristocratic, impersonal, even rather metallic and cold. Rich color is not absent but, as in David's work, color is much less essential than is linearity.

In the brief career of Théodore Géricault (1791–1824) we encounter a spirit almost wholly foreign to that of David and Ingres. Although of necessity Géricault's training was in the Davidian tradition, he broke away early from the dogmatism of the Classical teaching, preferring a more unbridled course of his

16-12 Jean Auguste Dominique Ingres, *Reclining Odalisque (Great Odalisque)*, 1814. Oil on canvas, 36″ × 64″. Louvre, Paris.

own. This, however, did not rule out an earnest study of the masters of the past—a study facilitated in France by Napoleon's plunder of Continental art, which was placed on display in the Musée Napoléon, the old Louvre. Here, and later in Italy, it was not so much the Greek and Roman antiquities or the chaste Madonnas of Raphael that impressed themselves on Géricault's consciousness. Rather it was the more flamboyant work of Caravaggio and Rubens and the gigantic Sistine Chapel frescoes of Michelangelo that he admired. With these models, and with his personal inclination toward action and excitement, Géricault created an art that some have called Romantic and others Realist but that was distinctly his own in any case.

Géricault's most famous work, *The Raft of the Medusa* (fig. 16-13), was inspired by the shipwreck of a French frigate, the *Medusa*, while sailing to Africa in 1816. One hundred fifty men had huddled on a raft that was to be towed by lifeboats, but the ropes broke (or were deliberately cut) and the raft floated helplessly for twelve days before it was sighted by the ship *Argus*. Hunger, thirst, and fighting left only fifteen men to be rescued. In France the disaster became a public issue, with the liberals accusing the government of favoritism and shortsightedness in its choice of captain for the

Medusa and its failure to provide for adequate safety measures at sea.

Géricault, a concerned liberal and humanitarian, took up the *Medusa* story with enthusiasm. Having come already to suspect the reactionary dangers of restored Bourbonism in France, and sensing the growing social problems of an increasingly industrialized society, this young man of inherited wealth now found a humanizing mission to be embraced—a mission that might well be furthered in his chosen field of painting. Human compassion and a sense of involvement with the modern were very much a part of the background for the *Medusa* painting.

In this enormous work the raft's survivors are portrayed at the dramatic moment when they see the *Argus* on the horizon. A black sailor, magnificently drawn, dominates the scene as he waves toward the approaching ship. Whether because of their exotic appeal or because of the talk of colonial oppression at the time, black Africans were a favorite subject of Géricault. On the raft behind the black man are the dead, the dying, the mourning, and the apathetic, as well as the few who can still respond to the excitement of the moment. The scene is one of immense and varied drama, quite unlike the less equivocal, more nar-

16-13 Théodore Géricault, *The Raft of the Medusa*, 1818–19. Oil on canvas, 16′2″ × 23′6″. Louvre, Paris.

rowly focused emotion of a typical Davidian painting. Thus *The Raft of the Medusa* is an anecdotal document of social and political importance—an exercise in lively pictorial movement and a tribute to Romantic excitement and exoticism. It is also a monument to realism and to the patient industry of the artist, who had made many preliminary sketches of hospital patients, cadavers, and ocean waves before attempting the final work.

Goya

For sheer range of mature genius Géricault and most other painters in Western history must bow to the astonishing phenomenon of the Spanish artist Francisco Goya (1746–1828). Even omitting, as we must do here, nearly all of his career that falls within the eighteenth century, and omitting the two extremes of his early Rococo phase and the horrific private visions of his old age, Goya's extraordinarily comprehensive work resists all attempts at classification.

Arrogant but charming, sardonic but compassionate, endowed with a massive vitality that carried him through more than eight decades and much brutal illness, Goya was the type of gigantic personality around whom legends cluster. The truth will doubtless never be known concerning Goya's fabled exploits in tavern, bed, and brawling street, nor can it ever be determined how far his illnesses, including total deafness after his late forties, affected his creative imagination. His work does at least give evidence that his life was one of strong and profound emotions, and that he understood not only the heights of exuberance but the depths of anguish and solitude.

An intimation of Goya's fantastic imagination was revealed at the very end of the eighteenth century with the publication of a series of prints, in etching and *aquatint* (an etching technique for graduated tonal effects of light and dark), called the *Caprichos* ("caprices"). For many decades it was almost exclusively through these prints that Goya was known outside of Spain. The individual pictures, each furnished with a brief descriptive or moralizing caption by the artist, deal with a strange variety of topics, from the eternal scourges of human ignorance and folly to the tragedies of isolation, and from bitter social commentary to fantasies of witchcraft and demonology. A well-known example is *The Sleep of Reason Produces Monsters* (fig. 16-14). Of peasant stock, Goya was well acquainted with the superstitions of his day, and while at the royal Spanish court he had learned of the Enlightenment and its rational assault on such superstitions. In *The Sleep of Reason* a man, presumably Goya himself, is seen slumped at a work table as strange animals lie in wait and owls and bats flutter down upon him. At the table an owl tries to rouse him, pressing upon him a pencil with which he can resume his work. Whatever the print may tell us of Goya's state of mind, his caption states the broader message; "Imagination, deserted by reason, begets impossible monsters. United with reason, she is the mother of all arts, and the source of their wonders." This statement would have been ac-

16-14   Francisco Goya, *The Sleep of Reason Produces Monsters*, #43 from the *Caprichos* series, c. 1797–98. Etching with aquatint, 7″ × 5″. Collection of Pomona College; Gift of Norton Simon.

ceptable to broad-minded partisans of either Classicism or Romanticism.

In his paintings Goya did not always deal so directly with the problem of rationality struggling against the darker elements of human nature. Such, for example, was seldom his theme as a fashionable portraitist. Among the most celebrated of his portrait paintings is *The Family of Charles IV* (fig. 16-15), done shortly after becoming the First Painter to the Spanish king. The brilliance of painting is remarkable in this large work, most of all in the subtlety of the colors. As to the likenesses, some historians have maintained that the royal family was cannily transformed by Goya into a menagerie of horrors. In actuality most of the family seem quite ordinary and indeed agreeable persons. Even the unattractive features of the others (the king, his sister in the left background, and the queen) do not necessarily imply brutal caricature. The king, undoubtedly, was a dull creature, often hoodwinked by his unfaithful wife, Maria Luisa, and his dullness is well documented here. Maria Luisa was not beautiful—and Goya does not flatter her. But again and again she would return to Goya for new and equally unflattering portraits; she could hardly have scented cruel caricature in them.

Within a few years much had changed in Spain, and for the worse. Faced with Napoleon's successful invasion early in 1808, Charles had abdicated in favor of his still less appealing son Ferdinand, but Napoleon rejected them both, as rulers of the newly captured and soon-to-be-enlightened land. The new king was Napoleon's brother Joseph, who was supported by French force and some of Spain's native intelligentsia. The Spanish people, however, largely remained loyal to their dynasty and fiercely resentful of the French occupation. Several years later Goya recorded in two vivid paintings the bloody Madrid insurrection of May 2, 1808, against the French and the French execution of the captured insurgents the next morning. *The Third of May* (fig. 16-16) is a monument to human cruelty, as Frenchmen slaughter Spaniards who had slaughtered Frenchmen the day before.

A lantern illuminates the scene. Bloody corpses of the night's first victims sprawl in the foreground, and a third group is marched up the hill for execution after the present victims have been killed. Confronting the impersonal, faceless firing squad, the figure of one man stands out, his shirt brilliantly highlighted amid the gloom, his arms raised excitedly, perhaps in despera-

16-15 Francisco Goya, *The Family of Charles IV*, 1800. Oil on canvas, 9'3" × 11'1". Prado, Madrid.

16-16 Francisco Goya, *The Third of May*, 1814. Oil on canvas, 8'9" × 11'4". Prado, Madrid.

16-17 Francisco Goya, *They as Little as the Others,* #36 from the *Disasters of War* series, 1810 or later. Etching with aquatint, 6″ × 8″. Courtesy Museum of Fine Arts, Boston.

tion, perhaps in proud defiance. It may be that his pierced palms and his bodily posture were intended to suggest the crucified Christ. In any case we are present at the martyrdom of a man once free, of a very real and individual human being, at the hands of a robotlike firing squad who also were once free human beings.

A great series of etchings by Goya, *The Disasters of War,* may similarly be viewed as a humanitarian document as well as an instance of nationalistic protest. Here we see the wretchedness of a Spain torn by guerrilla warfare and social disruption, but symbolizing the agonies of all humanity, with brutality everywhere on the ascendant. The ghastly scene of *They as Little as the Others* (fig. 16-17) is far from the most unpleasant of the *Disasters* series. On the other hand, Goya often conveyed no moral or social message whatsoever. His language is primarily that of an artist, and we understand him only the better when, like Rembrandt, Mozart, and Beethoven, he also sees deep into the aspirations and tragedies of the human condition.

MUSIC: THE MERGING OF CLASSICISM AND ROMANTICISM

In 1787 the adolescent Beethoven visited Vienna, where he improvised at the piano for Mozart. In the early nineties, after settling down in that city, Beetho-

ven studied with Haydn. And in 1808, when Beethoven already was a celebrated composer, the younger man knelt down to kiss the hands and forehead of his aged teacher at Haydn's last public appearance, a gala performance of his oratorio *The Creation.* These facts are of more than anecdotal interest; they are useful reminders of the overlapping of Beethoven's musical career with those of the two great Classical masters. (Indeed if Mozart had survived to little more than the supposedly normal three score and ten, he would have outlived Beethoven.) Although we can exaggerate its significance, this chronological and personal conjunction of the three careers should make us suspicious of the firm distinction, once commonly accepted even by scholars, between the Classical traditionalism of the older masters and the revolutionary Romanticism of the brilliant younger composer.

Beethoven

For the last thirty years of his life, Ludwig van Beethoven (1770–1827), who came from the Rhineland, was as thoroughly Viennese as Haydn or Mozart (fig. 16-18). He scarcely left the city except for the nearby countryside. The picture of his appearance and living habits has often been sketched too broadly, by Romantic hands, to be entirely trusted. The stocky, powerful figure, the allegedly "bachelor" negligence in clothing and living quarters, the quick temper, the frequent utter absorption in musical composition that set him apart from others and gave rise to much picturesque incident—the sketch is lifelike in part, if balanced by such other features as his disciplined working habits, his frequent hearty charm, and the warmth of many of his friendships.

Possibly more significant to his creative life was the tragic deafness that was apparently evident to him by his late twenties and that became total in his last years. Moments of profound despair marked the early period of realization, but later came defiance ("I will take fate by the throat," he wrote at the end of 1801) and, ultimately, submission. How directly the whole shattering experience is reflected in his music will surely never be known. Certainly, even in months of frequent despair, Beethoven composed works of grace and brilliance, as well as those few that may be interpreted as reflecting a mood of heroic defiance.

Often categorized among the latter is his famous Fifth Symphony. Commissioned by one aristocratic

Somewhat surprisingly, the first movement (allegro con brio) is in pure sonata form of textbook clarity, compressed and disciplined to the highest degree. The slow movement (andante con moto) is a double theme with variations, and the third (allegro) presents several themes, a middle section (or trio) with fugal elements, and a return to the opening subjects. This third symphonic movement leads directly into the fourth, a rousing finale (allegro and presto) that incorporates material from the third movement.

More significant than the structural skeleton of the Fifth Symphony are its elevated spirit and the creative mastery of its elaboration. Although there are moments of great lyrical appeal, even of gentleness (such as the second theme of the first movement and the opening melody of the second), the main impression is of dogged strength, heroism, and nobility. Beethoven achieved this effect in part through intangibles of creative invention that we cannot hope to fathom, but also through some identifiable formal procedures.

The Fifth Symphony was written for a larger orchestra than used in earlier symphonic writing. There are parts for two flutes, two oboes, two clarinets, two bassoons, two horns, two trumpets, and two timpani, in addition to strings, and these are joined in the finale by piccolo, contrabassoon, and three trombones. Far more important, however, is what Beethoven does with these musical resources. In the Fifth Symphony he tends toward the sturdy and compact in his masses of sound; often they are masses of unison sound, as in the well-known opening notes of the work. Solos are rare, and the general impression is of breadth and power—in contrast to the subtle instrumental detail and characterization in, for example, Mozart's *Marriage of Figaro*. This is not to say that Beethoven necessarily denies the instruments their appropriate effects—note even in this symphony the growling good humor of the lower strings in the third movement trio, the shrill urgency of the piccolo in the finale, and the triumphant brilliance of the trombones in the same movement.

Best remembered of all the symphony's characteristics is the recurring rhythmic motif—the four notes that are ringingly sounded as the opening theme and then hammered out insistently, each time on the same tone in the third and fourth movements. This device not only helps to unify the work, but in its forthright directness it helps create the air of uncompromising urgency that pervades nearly the entire symphony. It is

16-18 Willibord Joseph Mähler, *Beethoven*, 1815. Oil on canvas. Sammlungen der Gesellschaft der Musikfreunde in Wien.

patron and ultimately dedicated to two others, the symphony may be traced to sketches from as early as 1804. It was finished in 1808 and first performed in December of that year in one of history's truly remarkable concerts. On December 22 Beethoven presented, as advertised, a program of his own compositions, "entirely new and not yet heard in public"; these included both the Fifth and Sixth Symphonies, the Fourth Piano Concerto (with Beethoven himself as soloist), and the ambitious *Choral Fantasia*. The audience was shivering with cold, and performances ranged from the insecure to the catastrophic. Yet within several decades the Fifth had become the most famous of all symphonies, a position it still maintains.

The popularity and distinction of the great Fifth, or C minor Symphony, Opus 67, derive only in part from its strictly formal elements. In this work Beethoven adopted those aspects of Classical form that served his purpose, without fearing to introduce innovations.

questionable, though, that the rhythmic motif "means" anything, in the literary or philosophical sense. Many writers have maintained that it does, and the basis for their judgment is the seemingly excellent authority of Beethoven himself. Of this motif he is reported to have said, "Thus fate knocks at the door." Whether this was a late afterthought or an actual source of inspiration, and indeed whether Beethoven even meant the remark altogether seriously, will probably never be known. Nonetheless, page after page of critical comment devoted to the challenge of fate, to suffering and heroism, all as exemplified in Beethoven's Fifth, have warmed and consoled those generations of concertgoers who have looked to music for moral uplift.

If Beethoven's specific intentions in the Fifth will never be definitely known, we can at least know something of his position on the function of music. As an earnest son of the hopeful Age of Enlightenment, he did believe that, to some extent, music can morally inspire and improve its listeners. Yet we may be permitted to suspect that he was less concerned with ethical purpose than with simple tonal creativity when he wrote most of his violin sonatas, piano trios, or even string quartets and symphonies.

At the same time, for Beethoven as for most other composers since the Baroque period, certain works surely possessed a general emotional content. However, to identify this content precisely in Beethoven's instrumental works is extremely difficult, and probably pointless. In the Fifth Symphony, for example, is defiance of fate at issue or the call to human freedom or an affirmation of life? In any case, the Fifth Symphony can be enjoyed as absolute music, springing from the Classical traditions of formal musical construction. The new degree of passion and intensity introduced by Beethoven is the musical counterpart of the rousing Napoleonic era in which he lived, but neither Beethoven nor Napoleon was a true revolutionary. Both saw value in the discipline of traditional forms and clothed the new excitement in Classical garb.

Schubert

At first sight it seems strange that the Romantics would choose Beethoven as their school's founder rather than the more likely Franz Schubert (1797–1828). Beethoven, however, was the far more familiar and prestigious of the two composers, and the human passion for finding the most distinguished possible ancestry is notorious. In his own day and several more decades, Schubert was known almost exclusively as a composer of songs and of lightweight dance music; his great G major Quartet, for example, was not published until 1851, and his *Unfinished Symphony* not until 1866. Indeed, even later ages have remained reluctant to admit Schubert to the ranks of the very great, seeing in him primarily a composer in a relatively narrow field, that of the art song. This judgment, of course, ignores two important facts: that the art song, if not flamboyant, is hardly a negligible form and that Schubert produced far more of importance than the songs and the ever-popular *Unfinished Symphony*.

This fourth great "Viennese" composer, unlike the others, was Viennese by birth; and, like the others, he possessed depths of insight that were hardly typical of that rather carefree capital. Yet superficially Schubert seemed to belong satisfactorily enough to that city, and writers have long recorded the unpretentious young man's supposedly bohemian habits, his lack of concern for the future, and the many hours of music making in private homes and convivial relaxation in coffee houses and taverns. Schubert, however, was certainly not an idler; he was a hard worker who, despite the fluency of his inspiration, practiced his musical craft with great seriousness.

In his short lifetime Schubert gave only one public concert. The most memorable of his music making took place in private homes, at "Schubertiads," with a small circle of friends and their guests (fig. 16-19). His piano music, often for four hands, was popular at these gatherings, but most in demand were the latest of his songs. Thus were middle-class Viennese homes first introduced to some of the more than six hundred songs of Franz Schubert.

These songs (*lieder*) were not wholly unprecedented in German music, but at last in the second and third decades of the nineteenth century the time had come for the full flowering of the German *lied*. The genius of Schubert was essential to this development, but aiding it significantly were several other factors, social, musical, and literary. First of all, domestic music making was popular in the homes of the growing middle class. Also a factor was the continuing development of the piano, whose rich, sustained tones could meet on more equal terms the warmth and power of the human voice than could the earlier keyboard instruments. And, finally, there was the newly available

16-19 Moritz von Schwind, *A Schubert Evening at Josef von Spaun's,* 1868. Schubert Museum, Vienna.

mass of distinguished German poetry that could lend itself to sensitive musical setting; Schubert composed music for nearly sixty poems by Goethe alone.

His songs can be very roughly divided into the strophic and the nonstrophic. *Strophic* songs employ the same melody and accompaniment for each verse; *nonstrophic* songs range from those with only slight musical differences in the verses to others that vary greatly according to the fluctuations of poetic mood or narrative. Regardless of the outward form, however, Schubert's songs nearly always achieve a masterful balance of melody and accompaniment, and of poetry and music. Although the lied is one of music's smaller forms, in Schubert's hands it is also one of the most finely chiseled and one of the most intensely concentrated.

The moods of Schubert's songs are extremely varied, from the lighthearted and naive to the grimly despairing. Most typical, though, and among the most attractive, are those songs in an intermediate realm, the songs that reflect both the beauties and the harshness, the joy and the pain of daily living. With Schubert's songs we enter that Romantic period when poet, painter, and musician reveled in feelings—often with a heart-on-sleeve pathos that today we may find embarrassing. The very romantic *Schöne Müllerin* songs are examples of this.

The Beautiful Maid of the Mill is the title of this famous group of twenty songs set by Schubert to words of Wilhelm Müller. Begun in 1823 and published the following year, they represent for Schubert a triumph over mundane circumstance: in a period of serious illness and depression he created a youthful world of genial lyricism not diminished even by the final songs of grief and death. Schubert produced some greater individual songs than any in this cycle, but its unity in variety gives *Die Schöne Müllerin* particular interest. The drama portrayed in the twenty songs is of a young miller, the narrator, who finds employment and love at another's mill and then must face rivalry, despair, and death. Throughout, with intermittent pauses, runs the flowing piano representation of the millstream that witnesses the story and subtly reflects the young miller's moods, and that finally becomes his grave.

Three songs may serve as a sampling of *Die Schöne Müllerin.* In "Whither?" ("Wohin?"), the second in the cycle, the miller follows the stream down the valley, knowing that a mill cannot be far distant. The song's apparent simplicity is deceptive: it is not strophic but involves many variations of melody, while beneath the voice the stream murmurs merrily on. "Impatience" ("Ungeduld"), however, is strictly strophic, and the flowing-stream figuration gives way to quickly repeated chords. In this well-known song the young man wants all of nature to testify to his love for the miller maid, as he happily and impatiently anticipates love's fulfillment.

In the following songs fulfillment indeed comes,

but eventually the miller maid deserts the young man for a dashing huntsman. The displaced lover's despondency deepens, and by the nineteenth song he is about to fling himself into the stream. "The Miller and the Stream" ("Der Müller und der Bach") is a dialogue between the youth and the stream, with much typically Romantic talk of the reflection of human moods and events in nature. The pathos of a minor key serves the miller as he sings of that despair that will be echoed in the drooping of the lilies and the clouding of the moon, while a serene major key accompanies the stream's assurances that with his death roses will bloom and a new star will pass to heaven. In the final stanza the miller asks the stream to sing him to rest.

Long before *Die Schöne Müllerin* Schubert had written string quartets, the earlier ones influenced obviously by the Classicists Haydn and Mozart. But by 1824, the year of the song cycle's publication, his quartet writing had become fully individual and personal. The two quartets of that year and the 1826 G major Quartet, Opus 161, are among the major monuments of quartet literature.

From the opening notes of the G major Quartet's first movement (allegro molto moderato), it is clear that much has happened in music since the quartets of the two Classical masters. A quick crescendo on the first sustained note leads to an extraordinarily forceful chord in which the violins and viola, backed by the cello, each play whole chords of their own: the effect is almost orchestral. So, too, is the breathless, fluttering bowing that follows several measures later, and that becomes characteristic of much of the movement. The loudness (*dynamics*) varies abruptly and strikingly, plucked notes follow bowed notes, the harmony is notably full and rich, and melody virtually gives way to a series of dramatic pronouncements. The fact that the long movement is based on sonata form is forgotten in its surging grandeur.

Lyricism is more prominent in the slow movement (andante un poco moto), especially in the opening cello theme. But here, too, there are daring harmonies and violent outbursts to set off the pensive character of the movement. In contrast, the following scherzo (allegro vivace) is straightforward and lively, with a melodious trio. The form is strictly Classical, but the insistent rhythm and abrupt dynamic changes are typically Schubertian. The last movement (allegro assai) again is fast and rhythmically forceful. It is an agitated *tarantella*, rushing impetuously, with alternating loud and soft passages, to its affirmative close.

Schubert, like Beethoven, combined elements of Romanticism with the Classical heritage. Certainly the Romanticism of many of his songs is evident. Still, his instrumental works were cast in Classical forms; like Beethoven he modified these forms only rarely. At the same time, Schubert went at least as far as Beethoven in introducing new content. Some of his harmonies are surprisingly daring and opulent, and the emotions frequently are effervescent and strong. With Schubert the subtleties of Haydn and Mozart had not yet given way to the heady splendors of Berlioz and Wagner, but the high tide of musical Romanticism was approaching.

Recommended Reading

Cronin, Vincent. *Napoleon* (1971). Lively biography, illustrated.

Eitner, Lorenz E. *Géricault, His Life and Work* (1982). Splendid biography.

Ford, Franklin L. *Europe 1780–1830* (1970). Straightforward history.

Goethe, Johann Wolfgang von. *Faust, a Tragedy,* trans. by Walter Arndt, ed. by Cyrus Hamlin (1976). The play, in English, with contemporary reactions and modern criticism.

Gudiol, José. *Francisco Goya y Lucientes* (1985). Long essay with color plates and substantial captions.

Halsted, John B. *Romanticism* (1969). Primary sources in literary Romanticism.

Hatfield, Henry. *Goethe, a Critical Introduction* (1963). Handy survey of life and works.

Herold, J. C., ed. *The Horizon Book of the Age of Napoleon* (1965). Splendidly illustrated evocation of an age.

Hilton, Timothy. *Keats and His World* (1971). Short, generously illustrated life and times.

Honour, Hugh. *Romanticism* (1979). History and styles of Romantic art.

Keats, John. *The Complete Poems and Selected Prose of John Keats* (1951). Comprehensive edition.

Solomon, Maynard. *Beethoven* (1977). Fine psychological biography.

Stephens, James, et al., eds. *English Romantic Poets* (1961). A comprehensive selection of the poems.

Talmon, J. L. *Romanticism and Revolt* (1967). Good, illustrated history.

Wechsberg, Joseph. *Schubert, His Life, His Works, His Times* (1977). Illustrated biography.

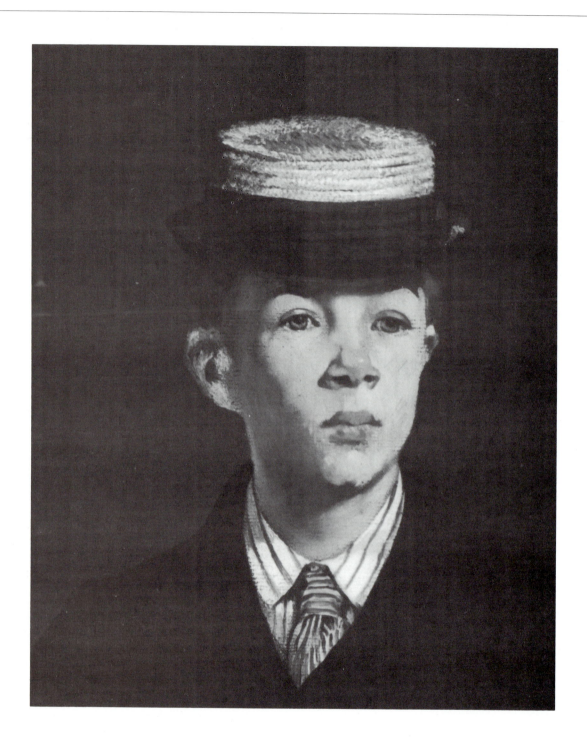

17 Romanticism and Realism: 1825–1870

he predominant themes of Western history between 1825 and 1870 were industrialization, with its political and social consequences, and the rise of nationalism. The Industrial Revolution, which had begun in England in the eighteenth century, had brought powered machinery and great factories to most of Europe, as well as political domination by wealthy industrialists and merchants. Developments in the United States were similar; the Civil War (1861–65) ended in the victory of the industrial North and the forceful solidification of national union. *Democracy*, rule of the people, was established during these decades in America, although its operations were heavily weighted in favor of the wealthier classes. In Europe there was a slow and uneven tendency toward the liberalizing of government and society—as occurred in England after the Reform Bill of 1832 somewhat extended the vote, or even in the Germanies, Austria, and tsarist Russia, in all of which serfdom was at last abolished. The first major stirrings of socialist thought and of liberal or socialist labor movements also appeared, symbolized most ominously by the *Communist Manifesto* of Marx and Engels in 1848.

Everywhere the doctrine of *nationalism* gained in potency—the doctrine that states should be established not on the basis of dynastic inheritance and exchange but according to the nationality of peoples. A consciousness of nationality arose when a people with a distinctive history, and usually a single language, came to share the same patriotic memories and aspirations. Nationalism's greatest victories

421

came at the end of the period, when the Italian states were finally united as a kingdom under the House of Savoy, and when Prussia under William I and his minister Bismarck waged successful war with France (1870) and led the Germans to national unification in a large German empire.

Great Britain was the leading industrial power between 1825 and 1870. Its gradually liberalized parliamentary regime was threatened but not toppled by the revolutions that twice disrupted the European continent, most thoroughly in the wave of internal violence that engulfed most states in 1848 and shortly thereafter. France, in many respects the culturally dominant country, was notoriously unsettled politically during these decades. The Bourbon monarchy of Charles X, brother of Louis XVI and XVIII, was overthrown in July 1830, leading to the July Monarchy of King Louis Philippe (1830–48), head of the Orleans branch of the same family. Disillusionment quickly set in among French liberals and workers when they discovered that the new government's only advice to the poor and powerless was to "get rich." Again in 1848, revolution led to disillusionment. Republican hopes were shattered by public reaction against a Parisian rising of the working class (June 1848) and by the ambitions of Louis Napoleon, nephew of Napoleon I. In due time the new Napoleon rose from the presidency of the republic to near-dictatorship, finally assuming the imperial title of Napoleon III. His Second Empire (1852–70) was characterized by continued bourgeois dominance, and by the flowering of industrialism and mass production. Materialism reigned, both in high finance and in high society, as indeed it did throughout the Western world. Napoleon III's regime collapsed during the French defeats of the Franco-Prussian War (1870).

AN AGE OF CHANGE

The combined disillusionment and promise of Restoration Europe after Napoleon I's downfall were nowhere seen more clearly than in disunited Italy. Though dominated by Metternich's autocratic Austria, Italy was stirring with the cultural and political ferment that would lead to national unification later in the century. For several decades,

though, the focus of Europe's political attention tended less toward Italy than France.

The French July Monarchy had brought prosperity, but also political unrest to the unprivileged masses and the intellectuals. Popular verse and caricature attacked the regime relentlessly, most brilliantly in the journalistic cartoons of Honoré Daumier, who satirized the passing scene even more pointedly and caustically than did the multivolume *Human Comedy* of the novelist Balzac. Many of Daumier's caricatures were good-natured enough, but no one could ignore the bitterly serious intent of his print *Rue Transnonain, April 15, 1834* (fig. 17-1). Daumier's subject was the aftermath of a rebellion of impoverished silk weavers in Lyon that had led to street rioting and the erection of barricades. Having at last removed the barricades, government troops panicked when apparently shot at, before dawn, from a working-class apartment in the Rue Transnonain. They stormed the building, bayoneting and shooting indiscriminately whomever they found there. Daumier's commemoration of the bloody event, which spared neither infants nor the elderly, sent through much of France a wave of horror that was still remembered in 1848, when the monarchy itself was destroyed by revolution.

One of the most striking outward manifestations of the age, in Europe and in America, was urban growth of truly revolutionary dimensions. Most notably in such celebrated capitals as Vienna and Paris, this

17-1 Honoré Daumier, *Rue Transnonain, April 15, 1834*, 1834. Lithograph, 12″ × 17″. Courtesy Museum of Fine Arts, Boston (William P. Babcock Fund).

CHRONOLOGY

HISTORY	THE ARTS
	1770–1831 Hegel
	1775–1851 Turner
	1798–1863 Delacroix
	1799–1886 Von Ranke
	1803–69 Berlioz
	1811–79 Bingham
	1813–83 Wagner
	1813–1901 Verdi
1820–30 George IV king of England	
1824–30 Charles X king of France	1827 Delacroix's *The Death of Sardanapalus*
1830 revolution in France	
1830–37 William IV king of England	1830–86 Emily Dickinson
1830–48 the July Monarchy in France: Louis Philippe king	
1832 First Reform Bill in England	1832–83 Manet
	1833–36 Rude's *The Marseillaise*
	1834 Berlioz's *Harold in Italy*
	1834 Delacroix's *Women of Algiers in Their Quarters*
	1835 Turner's *The Burning of the Houses of Parliament*
	1835 and 1840 de Tocqueville's *Democracy in America*
	1840–65 Barry and Pugin's Houses of Parliament
1837–1901 Victoria queen of England	1841 Emerson's *Self-Reliance*
	1844 Turner's *Rain, Steam, and Speed*
	1848 Barye's *Theseus and the Minotaur*
1848 *Communist Manifesto* by Marx and Engels	
1848–49 wave of revolutions in Europe— France, Germany, etc.	
1848–52 Second Republic in France: Louis Napoleon president	1849–50 Courbet's *Burial at Ornans*
	1850–51 Paxton's Crystal Palace
1852–70 Second Empire in France: Napoleon III emperor	c. 1856–62 Daumier's *The Third-Class Carriage*
	1857 Verdi's *Un Ballo in Maschera*
	1857–59 Wagner's *Tristan and Isolde*
	1859 Delacroix's *The Abduction of Rebecca* (Paris)
	1859 Mill's *On Liberty*
	1859 Darwin's *The Origin of Species*
1859–60 Italy largely united	1859–88 Renwick's Saint Patrick's Cathedral, New York
1861–65 Civil War in the United States	1861–74 Garnier's Paris Opera
	1862–68 Labrouste's National Library, Paris
	1863 Manet's *Le Déjeuner sur l'Herbe*
	1865 *Tristan and Isolde* produced
	1865–66 Whitman's "When Lilacs Last in the Dooryard Bloomed"
1868–74 Gladstone's first ministry in Great Britain	1869 Mill's *The Subjection of Women*
1870 Franco-Prussian War	1871 Darwin's *The Descent of Man*
1871 German Empire founded	

growth was matched by government efforts to improve the cities. Like most great European cities, Paris in 1850 was still in part medieval; the urban improvements of Napoleon I had scarcely altered its overall chaos. However picturesque, the city was unsanitary, unsafe, and congested, and its slums were a scandal even in an age not terribly sensitive to the lot of the poor. Napoleon III's main motives for his reconstruction of Paris seem to have been to improve traffic circulation while building mass political support out of gratitude for employment on public works projects—as well as to guarantee public order. Broad boulevards, after all, would presumably make it difficult for revolutionaries to erect effective barricades, and also would physically break up and isolate the disaffected working class in the slums.

Thus, under Napoleon III and his prefect of the Seine, Baron Haussmann, arose the city that is essentially preserved in the Paris of today, with its broad boulevards, monumental vistas, squares, and parks. In the process, of course, much of the past was destroyed. Yet the transformation of Paris was one of the astounding physical achievements of its century.

In Paris these were exciting decades for creative artists of all sorts. In music there were the struggles of Berlioz to turn popular taste from uninspired salon music and empty virtuosity toward a deeper seriousness, and Wagner's later controversial introduction of Germanic "music-drama" to the French capital. Although the occasional massive orchestral effects of Berlioz came to be considered more acceptable as the decades passed, the public teetered between Heine's poetic awe (Berlioz as "an antediluvian bird, a colossal nightingale or a lark the size of an eagle") and the cartoonist's amusement (Berlioz transported to heaven in a broken bass drum). As for painting and literature, creative and partisan excitement in Paris was intense. After the painter Delacroix and the poet Hugo humiliated the Classicists, Romanticism in turn was challenged by Realism, and Realism by art-for-art's-sake. One aesthetic proclamation and one avant-garde painting exhibition followed another, with the most innovative spirits in all fields banding together, at critical moments anyway, to do battle against an indignant and confused bourgeoisie.

Often the battle became playful, as the young Romantics, and later some Realists and many self-conscious aesthetes, set out to shock the bourgeoisie deliberately. Each generation had its rebels, symbol-ized by the "bohemians" with their garret living quarters, casual attitudes toward sex, flamboyant dress, and abundant hair. In 1836 the English writer Mrs. Trollope fled back home in great distress over the young bohemians' "long and matted locks that hang in heavy, ominous dirtiness." Black humor and melodramatic morbidity often characterized at least the fringes of romantic and aesthetic bohemianism, and the bourgeoisie were gleefully baited by extraordinary bohemian affectations. Human skulls and bawdy songs were much in evidence, and the writer of fantastic stories, Gérard de Nerval, promenaded through the Tuileries gardens with a leashed lobster. ("It doesn't bark," he intoned, "and knows the secrets of the deep.")

However subversive, foolish, or delightful all of this may have been, attacks on the bourgeoisie could often be a serious matter indeed. At stake, it seemed, was no less than the survival of personal and creative freedoms. The dominant middle class had arisen out of the risk-taking inventiveness of the new industrial and financial world, but inventiveness and creative modernity were the last things the bourgeoisie wanted or would tolerate in the arts or in other people's social or personal lives. To the middle class, decency often required not only personal cleanliness (modern concepts of hygiene and sanitation made great strides in this period) but also a "Victorian" morality, reflecting the sober values of England's queen (1837–1901). To the young rebels, however, the comfortable middle class represented the enemy, and especially when it averted its eyes from sexual expression and turned women into male-obeying models of self-conscious purity. Much of the women's movement of a century later would be directed against the Victorian woman-on-a-pedestal.

The rebels of the Victorian age objected to far more than the customary role of women in their day. For them the whole middle class was at fault; to them, this class was the embodiment of unimaginative tidiness and domesticity, stifling moralism, blind and self-satisfied hypocrisy, and stupid, optimistic materialism. Yet these same rebels, with all their grievances against society, usually preferred to forget that they themselves could exist only through bourgeois affluence and simultaneous bourgeois patronage and indignation. If rebellious elements were alienated from bourgeois society, they were also shaped and supported by it.

So, too, were the less rebellious, and often more productive, creative artists. Life in a rarefied dream world is not easy to sustain, and there were few mid-century artists untouched by the materialism and nationalism, the liberalism or socialism, and the science and industrialism of their century. One of the most powerful evocations of the astonishing new industrial revolution is the painting *Rain, Steam, and Speed* (see fig. 17-14) by the most Romantic of all painters, J. M. W. Turner.

Thought and the Arts

The belief in human progress, with divine sanction or not, was becoming the century's new faith. The philosopher Georg Wilhelm Friedrich Hegel (1770–1831) saw a progressive unfolding of "spirit" and human self-consciousness in history. His thinking had an immense following for many decades and encouraged an evolutionary view of the historical process. Karl Marx (1818–83), who with Friedrich Engels produced such treatises as the *Communist Manifesto*, applied the Hegelian emphasis on the *dialectic*—a synthesis out of opposites—to economic and political evolution, and thus founded the modern Communist ideology. The inherent optimism of Marx's approach was rather staggering in its presumed demonstration of the ultimate, inevitable triumph of the proletarian (working class), Communist society. *The Origin of Species* (1859) and *The Descent of Man* (1871), by Charles Darwin (1809–82), extended evolutionary doctrine to all biological species, and supported it with such scientific detail as to convince most intellectuals, aside from biblical literalists, of the reality of a biological struggle for survival across the ages and the ultimate survival of the fittest. Both Marx and Darwin contributed to the materialism and mechanistic naturalism of the century, but they also reinforced its vision of individual and social perfectibility.

Political liberalism, developed by such thinkers as Alexis de Tocqueville (1805–59) and John Stuart Mill (1806–73), had a less ruthless, essentially hopeful view of the future, although both of these writers saw dangers in the political evolution toward democracy. Both saw human freedom as an essential balance against a growing political and social *egalitarianism*—the equalizing of all adult citizens (even, for Mill, including women). De Tocqueville was fascinated by the American example (*Democracy in America*, 1835 and 1840), but alarmed by pressures there toward mediocrity, conformity, and materialism. These pressures, in Europe as in America, must be countered, he said, by such institutions as a free press and a vigilant judicial system, both in support of individual rights. Concerning the arts, de Tocqueville was less confident; he saw egalitarian democracy as inevitably leading to low-grade mass production and creative mediocrity, not the excellence demanded by the art consumers of past centuries.

John Stuart Mill (fig. 17-2) was the quintessential voice of mid-nineteenth-century, western European liberalism. We should note at the outset that this liberalism was less oriented toward social progress and the presumed social good than the liberalism of a century or more later. Because of its emphasis on the individual, Mill's liberalism is invoked today as often by libertarian conservatives as by those who call themselves liberals.

Mill's extended essay *On Liberty*, written in collaboration with his wife Harriet Mill and published in 1859 soon after her death, remains the key document in the theoretical structure of Western liberalism. It is an impassioned but closely argued defense of self-expression and individual freedom as necessities for

17-2   John Stuart Mill, c. 1865. National Portrait Gallery, London.

self-development and the advancement of the general welfare. The book's basic assumptions are utilitarian and humanistic, following the Enlightenment emphasis on human beings and the institutions and behavior patterns that foster human happiness and pleasure. Mill's chief contribution may be that he went beyond general goals for the mass of human beings and addressed the dangers inherent in majority rule—dangers to mature, competent, free individuals of both sexes. In short, he sought to remedy the problems ignored by Rousseau's theories of majority rule and the overriding, ominously autocratic "general will" of more nebulous origin. Mill directed his arguments against the "tyranny of the majority" and any authority that oppresses others in the name of some superior insight.

Mill's exposition of the role of human liberty does not claim final truth, but it does proceed systematically, indeed majestically, toward demonstrating the need for "liberty of thought and discussion," for individual expression, and for the establishment of "limits to the authority of society over the individual." A final chapter of *On Liberty* is a stimulating review of specific situations to which his principles may be applied. Some of these applications have seemed dated to some moderns, such as his defenses of absolute freedom of trade and enterprise and of extremely negative and narrow governmental functions. Other reflections by Mill, especially those concerning the role of liberty in personal behavior, remain living, contentious issues nearly a century and a half since he wrote them.

Mill's interests were wide-ranging, notably in the realms of ethics, economics, and philosophy. On women's rights he produced one of the lasting monuments of that movement, *The Subjection of Women*, in which he eloquently demonstrated that the legal subordination of women to men was totally unacceptable and should be destroyed. In his long essay "Nature" he sought to demolish the Enlightenment idea of nature as an ideal; he argued, rather, that "the spontaneous course of nature" is amoral and must be changed and mastered by human beings, not followed passively. Mill did not, however, write much formal history aside from the many historical examples that spilled from his well-stocked mind. Nineteenth-century historical writing did flourish, though, in Europe and America; one of the most voluminous historians was the influential Leopold von Ranke (1795–1886), destined apparently to be forever remembered for his confidence that

history can and must be written *wie es eigentlich gewesen*—"as it actually happened." So much for the "philosophic," ideological history writing of the Enlightenment!

One of the most striking developments in mid-nineteenth-century literature was the immense popularity of prose fiction, especially in its long form, the novel. Among the most popular of novels were adventure stories, many of them with picturesque historical settings. More serious and significant were a number of great novels that were primarily psychological studies rather than simple narratives. In France, for example, there was the work of Gustave Flaubert (1821–80), famous especially for *Madame Bovary* (1857), a carefully detailed study of a middle-class woman whose romantic fantasies led to disaster in a real world of hard facts. In Russia there were the profound psychological and spiritual observations embodied in the novels of Fyodor Dostoevsky (1821–81), whose early masterpiece was *Crime and Punishment* (1866). Characterized by the author as "a psychological account of a crime," the novel tells the story of a complex and well-educated, though impoverished, young man who committed murder without definitively incriminating himself, but who eventually gave himself up to the police after a long mental and emotional struggle.

In the United States of America, the rudiments of genuine literary and artistic creativity already were flowering, along with democratic theory and practice. Three of the most striking literary figures were Ralph Waldo Emerson, Walt Whitman, and Emily Dickinson. All were poets, but Emerson (1803–82) was also an essayist of distinction. His essay "Self-Reliance" (1841) proved a goldmine of quotations for several generations of Americans; in our own day it is cited less often—perhaps because it can rather easily become an apology for self-indulgence, willfulness, and egotism.

> To believe your own thought, to believe that what is true for you in your private heart is true for all men—that is genius.

> Society everywhere is in conspiracy against the manhood of its members. . . . Whoso would be a man, must be a nonconformist.

> The objection to conforming to usages that have become dead to you is that it scatters your force. It loses your time and blurs the impression of your character.

But why should you keep your head over your shoulder? Why drag about this corpse of your memory, lest you contradict somewhat you have stated in this or that public place? Suppose you should contradict yourself; what then? . . . A foolish consistency is the hobgoblin of little minds, adored by little statesmen and philosophers and divines. With consistency a great soul has simply nothing to do. . . . Speak what you think now in hard words and tomorrow speak what tomorrow thinks in hard words again, though it contradict everything you said today. "Ah, so you shall be sure to be misunderstood." . . . To be great is to be misunderstood.

These words of Emerson struck his age with cogent persuasiveness; they reflected not only New World assertiveness but also the Romanticism that still was strong throughout the Western world. Where had so many Romantic themes been struck at once— individualism, nonconformism, the praise of Romantic change and growth, the artist's distrust of polite society? The same chords resound in the often rough-hewn lines of Walt Whitman (1819–92) (fig. 17-3), whose verse celebrated a lively miscellany of emotional and poetic yearnings, a sturdy independence, and an openness to the surging energies of an expanding, democratic nation.

Among several of Whitman's memorials to the assassinated Abraham Lincoln, "When Lilacs Last in the Dooryard Bloomed" is also a celebration of America and self and a meditation on death.

Lo, body and soul—this land,
My own Manhattan with spires, and the sparkling and
  hurrying tides, and the ships,
The varied and ample land, the South and the North
  in the light, Ohio's shores and flashing Missouri,
And ever the far-spreading prairies covered with grass
  and corn.

Now while I sat in the day and looked forth,
In the close of the day with its light and the fields
  of spring, and the farmer preparing his crops,
In the large unconscious scenery of my land with its
  lakes and forests, . . .
And the streets, how their throbbings throbbed, and
  the cities pent—lo, then and there,
Falling upon them all and among them all, enveloping
  me with the rest,
Appeared the cloud, appeared the long black trail,
And I knew death, its thought, and the sacred
  knowledge of death.

Emily Dickinson (1830–86) was a more economical (some would say a less pretentious) poet. Virtually

17-3 Walt Whitman, Circa 1866.

unknown in her day, her verses seemed quirky, cold, and puzzling to the few who first read them. Death was even closer to the heart of her poetry than to Whitman's, and nature seemed more distant and aloof to her inner emotions. She was not a systematic thinker— few poets are—but her lines are full of insights into the world and sometimes into her own undemonstrative, elusive person. All her verses are brief and untitled; here is one of her longer poems:

There's a certain slant of light
On winter afternoons,
That oppresses, like the weight
Of cathedral tunes.

Heavenly hurt it gives us;
We can find no scar,
But internal difference
Where the meanings are.

None may teach it anything,
'Tis the seal, despair,—
An imperial affliction
Sent us of the air.

When it comes, the landscape listens,
Shadows hold their breath;
When it goes, 'tis like the distance
On the look of death.

These three American writers of the period are but a handful among many of great interest, including Poe, Hawthorne, Longfellow, and Melville. The visual arts developed more hesitantly than literature in this country. In the colonial and early national periods an architectural tradition of some significance had developed, but the rising of major talent in such fine arts as painting and music was slower. Perceptible improvement could be noted, however.

The most interesting early developments in American painting reflected a sense of spaciousness appropriate to the vast new land and a detached realism that avoided both Classicist posing and Romantic sensuousness. Portrait painting of a utilitarian sort had long flourished in America, but landscape painting now became extremely popular also and on occasion achieved real distinction, as did the best work of Thomas Cole (1801–48) and George Caleb Bingham (1811–79). In Cole's *Sunny Morning* (fig. 17-4), scrupulous realistic detail does not smother the silent gran-

deur of a hilly Hudson River valley view. On the other hand, Bingham's interest in landscape was nearly always allied with everyday scenes of the American Midwest, as in *Jolly Flatboatmen in Port* (fig. 17-5). His favorite subjects were the rivermen, the trappers, the village folk of the Mississippi and Missouri valleys, all comprising a genial view of American frontier democracy. They were subjects, he discovered, that would sell, for they appealed to both the local pride of the West and the primitivist nostalgia of the relatively sophisticated eastern seaboard. Selling of paintings in general was indeed a problem, since patronage was limited in the United States. It was not until after the Civil War that art came to be considered a social necessity in wealthier American circles, which increasingly turned for their art works to Europe and the art of the past.

European painters and composers of the mid nineteenth century relied on much the same sources of patronage as their immediate predecessors, but with a continued expansion of the bourgeois market. But even when enjoying bourgeois life styles, these artists generally viewed the new industrialism with misgivings. To many Romantics in particular, the enemy was

17-4 Thomas Cole, *Sunny Morning*, 1827. Oil on panel, 19″ × 25″. Courtesy Museum of Fine Arts, Boston (M. and M. Karolik Collection).

17-5 George Caleb Bingham, *Jolly Flatboatmen in Port* (1857). Oil on canvas, 46¼″ × 69″. The Saint Louis Art Museum (Museum purchase).

a compound of industrial filth and mass taste, of mediocrity and regimentation. Some contrived to ignore this displeasing scene, or to dismiss it with scorn—an attitude that deepened bourgeois resentment against innovative art and contributed to the modern world's growing gap between the arts and society. Other Romantics, more activist by nature, went forth in outright battle against industrial society and proclaimed in its stead the glorious mission of art. The claims of composer, painter, and poet to a superior insight into earthly problems became more and more insistent. Artists no longer were to be entertainers and craftsmen, but seers.

There was a degree of snobbishness and posturing in this, and probably a lack of appreciation for the enrichment of life that is available in an industrial society. Curiously enough, though, the Realist school of artists was not much happier with industrial society than were the Romantics. Visual and literary artists of Realist inclinations could often focus quite as narrowly on certain commonplace or sordid aspects of the present as Romanticism could upon the exotic past.

Yet the occasional kinship of the two movements is far more evident today than it was in the mid nineteenth century. Among several differences between Romanticism and Realism, one of the most obvious was the Romantics' emphasis on the interrelationship of the arts. Creative minds of Romantic bent often turned productively to more than one art. The painter Delacroix was a writer of skill and perception, and the poet Baudelaire was perhaps the best critic of the visual arts of his time. The composer Wagner wrote voluminously, and Berlioz was both entertaining and acute as a journalist. Still more significantly, the arts of the mid nineteenth century often converged in major individual creations, notably through the combination of visual or musical forms with literature. This chapter's composers all were heavily indebted to literary inspiration, even beyond the obvious domain of opera.

More and more the music of the day was written with no specific patron or scheduled performance in view, but rather "for the ages." Composers, though, could seldom remain wholly unaffected by circumstances in the concert world. An accelerating trend was the growth of urban mass audiences, with their insatiable demand for variety and excitement. Other trends in the concerts of this period were the increasing sophistication and reliability of woodwind and brass instruments, and the emergence of the independent orchestral conductor. Conductors no longer doubled at keyboard or violin, but were becoming autonomous, prestigious figures. Even without notable instrumental proficiency, composers could now, as conductors, fashion definitive performances of their works. Berlioz and Wagner both were famous conductors, and effective promoters of their own music.

Like all other periods, the mid nineteenth century saw much musical composition in the smaller, more intimate forms, but many of its best publicized innovations came in the grander orchestral and operatic realms. Here not only was sheer bigness sometimes in itself highly esteemed, but instrumental color and striking dynamic changes were more and more valued for their own sake. In large and small forms alike, the new emphasis was likely to be less on overall Classical pattern than on momentary emotional stimulation, long and casually unfolding musical themes, and increasingly complex harmonies.

Romanticism remained the dominant style in music well beyond 1870. The style is notable for its *eclecticism*—that is, its mingling of several styles in the hope of combining the best from various sources. Historical scholarship and public eagerness to investigate and revive the past were now no less evident in music than they had become in literature, architecture, and the pictorial arts. On a far vaster scale than during its eighteenth-century beginnings, cultural historicism now ruled the day, encouraged by the adventurous inclusiveness of the Romantic spirit as well as by the resourcefulness of modern historical investigative techniques. In music the Romantic era saw an immense revival of the past in scholarly research and in public performances. The luckier concertgoer now could experience, for the first time in Western history, a synthesis of the vast musical heritage of many centuries.

The simultaneous availability of several historical styles, in music as well as the other arts, also introduced possibilities for creative synthesis. Often, of course, there was no synthesis at all, but a competition among the various movements. The main choice was between coexistence, with gestures toward synthesis—most common in architecture and the concert world—and ideological battle, as exemplified especially in the several warring schools of literature and painting.

In either case, any hope for even the roughest sort of stylistic uniformity in the arts—a uniformity never fully achieved in the past but sometimes approximated in individual countries—had become absurd by mid century and has remained so ever since. Relativism of values, even when indignantly repudiated in excited ideological combat, was becoming almost a practical necessity. In fact, it was sometimes an ideal, especially among Romantics who cherished individual choice and self-expression. Relativism, eclecticism, historicism—all were related to Romanticism, and all have remained prominent threads in Western history since Romanticism's heyday. If for no other reason than this, the Romantic impact on the recent world must be judged powerful indeed.

THE MANY FACES OF ARCHITECTURE

Mid-century eclecticism and historicism ran wild in no art more than architecture and in no geographical area more than the United States. Perhaps the symptoms were exaggerated here, since America's newness largely ruled out the multitude of authentic relics of past styles that jostled each other in Europe; America's architectural "tradition" had to be created artificially. Certainly the variety and eccentricity of American architectural revivalism were astonishing throughout the 1825–70 period. In 1829, for example, the *New York Mirror* published engravings of six recent New York buildings, from sketches of Alexander Jackson Davis (fig. 17-6), with styles leaning toward Classicism but also including fanciful Gothic (a Masonic hall, lower right) and a curious Classical temple with Gothic tower (a synagogue, lower left). By 1867, after gaining much fame as an architect, Davis could impressively enumerate in his diary the following styles of domestic architecture in his repertoire: American log cabin, farmhouse, English cottage, collegiate Gothic, manor house, French suburban, Swiss cottage, Lombard Italian, Tuscan in the style of Pliny's villa at Ostia, ancient Etruscan, suburban Greek, Oriental, Moorish, and castellated (castlelike). American commercial and public architectural styles were equally varied. Architecture was, after all, supposed to be no more obviously functional than was absolutely necessary; rather, it was to be expressive—expressive in terms of the designer's tradition-bred imagination.

The European situation differed mainly in degree from the American. In Europe, however, the main surge of architectural Classicism had ended before this period, and the Gothic revival had grown from its ex-

17-6 Alexander Jackson Davis. Plate from the *New York Mirror*, 26 September 1829.

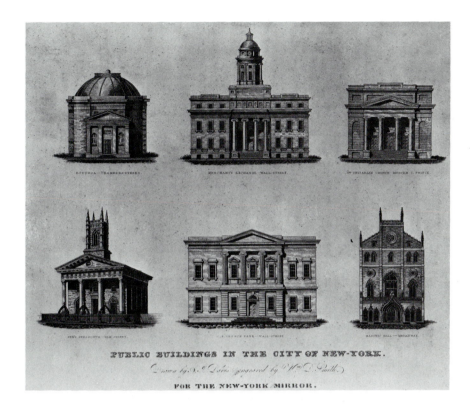

otic but tentative eighteenth-century beginnings to an exuberant bloom. Gothic was everywhere: neo-Gothic pubs and sewage disposal plants rose along with neo-Gothic churches. In all of this, to be sure, medieval building methods were being modernized by the use of iron—but the forms were strongly traditional.

Of course the new Gothic creations on the most imposing scale were the churches, and other public buildings and monuments. In England the most famous example is London's Houses of Parliament (fig. 17-7) by Sir Charles Barry (1795–1860) and Augustus Welby Pugin (1812–52). In 1836 Barry had won a competition for designing the new Parliament building (the old had burned in 1834); Pugin later worked with him and was mainly responsible for the medieval detail. The long, relatively low structure with disproportionately massive towers combined the Gothic and Elizabethan Renaissance manners. The combination, together with modern building innovations (the roof plates, notably, were of iron), proved surprisingly successful, and the Houses of Parliament are among London's most distinguished landmarks.

The century saw much scholarly archaeological study of medieval architecture and many significant restoration projects as well as neo-Gothic construction. For new churches, in Europe and America, Gothic seemed to many people almost imperative: Gothic was thought particularly Christian. The culmination of the "pointed style," as Gothic was called in America, was New York's Saint Patrick's Cathedral (fig. 17-8), designed by James Renwick (1818–95). This massive structure challenges its European ancestors in dimensions; it is 405 feet long and its spires rise to 330 feet.

However, many other revived styles disputed the mid-nineteenth-century preeminence of Gothic. From before the time of medieval Gothic came inspiration for neo-Byzantine, neo-Early Roman Christian, and neo-Romanesque building, especially for churches. From the post-Gothic heritage came Renaissance models, especially for secular buildings such as libraries, town houses, and palaces. But most popular of all in public architecture, by 1870, was a sort of neo-Baroque that was eventually identified as Second Empire style.

17-7 Charles Barry and Augustus Welby Pugin, Palace of Westminster (Houses of Parliament), London, 1840–65.

17-8 James Renwick, Saint Patrick's Cathedral, New York, 1859–88.

Sometimes recognizable by its mansard roofs (sloping, on two planes, to the summit) and always by its massive or ornate Classicism, the style was most splendidly exemplified in the Paris Opera House designed by Charles Garnier (1825–98).

The Opera House culminated with unusual magnificence one of the new Parisian vistas designed by Baron Haussmann (fig. 17-9). On the spacious, recently cleared Place de l'Opéra there arose over the years (1861–74) a grandiose pile that even Garnier's contemporaries sometimes thought a bit overdone in its colorful exuberance. The pleasure-dome facade was an array of horizontal zones arched, columned, and festooned in variegated colors and embellished with lively sculpture. The interior was equally lavish, from the grandiloquent lobby to the many-tiered auditorium and lushly golden Grand Foyer (fig. 17-10).

17-9   Charles Garnier, Paris Opera House, 1861–74.

Glass and Iron, Materials of a Revolution

Thus variously and magnificently did mid-nineteenth-century architecture adapt the styles of the past to the expressive needs of the time. What is perhaps most surprising is that this architecture broke away from past styles at all. When it did, the impetus was usually technological advances. In architecture this meant, above all, realizing the structural potentials of iron and glass. Glass was already being used on a grand scale in botanical conservatories and iron in suspension bridges, not to mention glass and iron together in railway station sheds. Several mid-century writers and architects suggested the application of new materials in less narrowly utilitarian structures also. As early as 1850, the poet and novelist Théophile Gautier wrote that "mankind must create a totally new architecture, born of today." A growing number of enthusiasts, the architectural "Realists" of their day, came to agree with him. Against all cries that strictly functional iron and glass architecture was nonhistorical and inexpressive, ugly and brutal, a number of notable experiments were carried out before 1870.

17-10   Grand Foyer of the Paris Opera House.

Of these the most famous was the Crystal Palace (fig. 17-11), built for an international industrial exhibition in London in 1851. The architect Joseph Paxton (1803–65) had designed a massive, geometrically straightforward shelter, largely of iron and glass, to house the exhibits. Nearly two thousand feet long, it had been quickly assembled from prefabricated, standardized parts—another innovation. The iron members of the long flat-roofed nave, and of aisles and arched transept, were brightly painted in blue, yellow, and red, set off in part against almost a million square feet of sunlit glass. The building proved to be a remarkably popular success and was much imitated elsewhere on more modest scales. It was dismantled in 1852 and set up again, with modifications and additions, as an amusement area and exhibition hall at Sydenham.

But even the Crystal Palace had been designed for a specialized purpose, and its popular acceptance was aided by the absence of any long-established stylistic tradition for mammoth exhibition buildings. Innovations looking toward the frankly functional use of iron and steel came far more cautiously in the standard types of public architecture; here the true revolution was postponed until the next century. For the pre-1870 period the pioneering work of one architect, though, should be noted: that of Henri Labrouste (1801–75). In his Saint Geneviève Library and his major alterations in the National Library, both in Paris, Labrouste explored the structural possibilities of iron and glass. The bookstack area of the National Library, partly visi-

17-11 Joseph Paxton and others, Crystal Palace, London, 1850–51. Lithograph. By courtesy of the Board of Trustees of the Victoria & Albert Museum, London.

ble to the public through a glass wall, is geometrically simplified, and the reading room (fig. 17-12) employs iron openly and proudly in the many slender columns and graceful arches below the large skylights centered in terracotta domes.

17-12 Henri Labrouste, reading room of the National Library, Paris, 1862–68.

PAINTING: ROMANTICISM AND ITS ABANDONMENT

J. M. W. Turner (1775–1851) was perhaps the greatest of all British painters. He was an individualist, belligerently so, and even in this he exemplified one aspect of the Romantic experience: he absolutely refused to be confined by any particular Romantic "school." His choice of subject matter was surely Romantic enough— landscape in all its metamorphoses. Indeed, his love of nature—from which he often sketched directly as the inspiration for studio painting—became the very heart of his work. What appealed to him in nature was not the pretty or the elegant, but the color, majesty, and mystery of its elemental forces. The sky, mists, and the sea—and the light that transformed them—were Turner's special realm. His later painting is notable for grandiose and luminous impressions, fixed on canvas by a powerful personality. These impressions are not fixed in photographic detail; they flee the details of reality in their struggle toward the heroic and the abstract.

Omitting the extremes among Turner's flights toward abstraction, we can see his style exemplified in two well-known works. The earliest (1835) is the Cleveland Museum's *The Burning of the Houses of Parliament* (fig. 17-13). Here is the scene Turner watched on the night of October 16, 1834, with Charles Barry, who would later design the new Parliament building.

17-13 Joseph Mallord William Turner, *The Burning of the Houses of Parliament*, 1835. Oil on canvas, 36½″ × 48½″. The Cleveland Museum of Art (bequest of John L. Severance).

The event as recorded by Turner is an awesome spectacle and a flamboyant demonstration of his skill in portraying the drama of a natural disaster.

Our second example, already mentioned, is the famous *Rain, Steam, and Speed: The Great Western Railway,* of 1844 (fig. 17-14). This painting, too, possesses uncommon drama. The vaporous, rainswept background is indicated in subdued colors, with a formlessness that approaches the abstract. Out of this setting, across a viaduct, rushes a hard-driving train; the artist contrives to propel the locomotive out of the mists with special urgency through its unusually sharp form and intensely dark color. The theme is perhaps the coming of mechanistic materialism to England, but the mood is dynamically Romantic.

Whereas Turner was a man of the people, Eugène Delacroix (1798–1863) was a man of the world. An aristocrat by taste, Delacroix projected a genteel yet forceful personality as he moved, very articulately, within the highest social and intellectual circles of his day. Nonetheless, like Turner, Delacroix startled and sometimes shocked his contemporaries. Both artists undeniably possessed what the Frenchman called "the gift of inventing powerfully, which is genius"—but powerful invention is precisely what the public is often least prepared to accept. At the same time, Delacroix possessed an intimate knowledge of past art. Most sympathetically of all he turned to the Baroque—to Rubens, whose figures' "prodigious life" excited him, and later to the profound Rembrandt, whom it was far less fashionable as yet to admire. As to his contemporaries, Delacroix was less moved by the cool Classicism of Ingres than by the intensity of Goya, Géricault, and Turner. Significantly, in his last years he found some merit even in the new Realism of Courbet. Beauty, he insisted in opposition to the Classicists, is largely subjective and can be found in all styles, even the Realist and the Classical.

Of Delacroix's artistic passions, one of the strongest was color. "Color," he wrote, "dreams, thinks, and

17-14 Joseph Mallord William Turner, *Rain, Steam, and Speed: The Great Western Railway*, 1844. Oil on canvas, 36″ × 48″. Reproduced by courtesy of the Trustees, The National Gallery, London.

speaks." Although he made some study of color theory and rejected grey as "the enemy of all painting" mainly on theoretical grounds, his approach to color remained largely instinctive. Color, he believed, should be the primary emotional reinforcement of Romantic content and dramatic action. The other side of his coloristic emphasis was his downgrading of line. Delacroix's usual broad brushstrokes were a scandal to his Classicist contemporaries, who were wedded to the ideal of clear line and precise contour. Dynamism, through color and drama and movement, is far more central in Delacroix's painting than are line and pattern.

His compositions, however, are carefully constructed. He was indeed, as Baudelaire said, "passionately in love with passion, and coldly determined to find ways of expressing passion in the most visible manner." To this, Delacroix added that, although feeling is well and good, it must be controlled, not "expressed to the point of nausea." As to subject matter, his only requirement was that it be colorful and that it have emotional, dramatic appeal. Thus Delacroix's work encompassed a vast range of human experience, well beyond the usual Romantic emphases on the medieval and the exotic. Delacroix remained a heroic painter in the grand manner, the last heroic painter of major importance during his century.

One of the earliest (1827) of Delacroix's large canvases was his *Death of Sardanapalus* (fig. 17-15). The subject is from ancient history but could hardly be

less Classical in spirit. Sardanapalus, king of Nineveh in Mesopotamia, has been besieged in his palace by attacking forces. The forces have just broken through the walls, and the king has ordered that all his slaves, concubines, and horses be destroyed as he watches, before they all are engulfed in flames. The canvas is over sixteen feet wide and the figures are life-size. Three male slaves are carrying out the carnage; the two in the foreground are fiercely dispatching a horse and a woman. Other figures struggle, lie dying, or wait their fated turn. Little if any blood flows—for this, after all, is a Romantic fantasy—but the impression is still far indeed from the steely chill of Ingres's paintings of exotic harem women. Smoke billows in from outside, depicted very broadly in contrast to the evident care with which gleaming jewelry and treasures are suggested. By and large, though, detail is subordinate to color, which sometimes is unorthodox, as in the glinting dabs of grey and blue on human flesh. Even perspective is violated, as in the disproportionately large figure of the brooding king in the background. The picture is a riot of dynamic intensity, calculated to jar the viewer into awe and pity—an extraordinary Romantic evocation of colorful, violent exoticism.

Obviously, then, Delacroix had painted exotic subjects before his 1832 trip to North Africa, and his travels of that year served mainly to confirm and reinforce existing trends in his painting. During this six-month period as artist on a French good-will mission to

17-15 Eugène Delacroix, *The Death of Sardanapalus,* 1827. Oil on canvas, 12′1½″ × 16′3″. Louvre, Paris.

17-16 Eugène Delacroix, *Women of Algiers in Their Quarters,* 1834. Oil on canvas, 71″ × 90″. Louvre, Paris.

Morocco (the day of documentary photography was well in the future), Delacroix had unusual privileges of entrance into nearly all aspects of Arab life. He sketched continually, delighting in the brilliant color and exotic appeal of the strange land. On the way home, his party stopped in Algiers, where Delacroix contrived to gain admission to a Moslem harem. The enthusiastic sketches that he made there were to refresh his memory two years later as he painted *Women of Algiers in Their Quarters* (fig. 17-16). Here the subtle nuances of color combine with feminine charm and exotic setting to create a rare evocation of delicate, perfumed sensuality.

Others among Delacroix's African and Oriental pictures replace the delicate with the dramatic and the tortured; there are countless scenes of exotic battle and animal death struggles. On other occasions his inspiration was medieval. In 1858 he completed a newer version of a subject that had occupied him years earlier, *The Abduction of Rebecca* (fig. 17-17). The inspiration is Sir Walter Scott's medieval romance *Ivanhoe;* an evil knight is carrying the unhappy maiden from the sacked and burning castle as a waiting attendant holds a spirited, saddled horse in readiness. Against a misty landscape and the massive simplicity of the castle, now

17-17 Eugène Delacroix, *The Abduction of Rebecca*, 1858. Oil on canvas, 39″ × 32″. Louvre, Paris.

emitting sulfurous smoke, the foreground is a brilliant scene of color and agitation.

The Realist School

It was precisely this sort of dramatic scene that earned Delacroix the admiration of his younger contemporary Honoré Daumier (1808–79). Daumier, however, painted fewer flights into heroic romance than Delacroix; most typically, his art was as unpretentious as his own life and habits. From the domestic calm of his rooms on the decaying Ile Saint Louis and the clutter of the upstairs workroom where he conceived the most distinguished journalistic caricatures of his day, Daumier would escape now and then to indulge the modest fancies of a modest Parisian—countryside excursions, theatrical or musical evenings in town, or drinking and smoking with the river boatmen or his artistic and literary friends. Then, in periods of unemployment or slack journalistic work, he painted. Few people were aware of the extent and worth of these paintings; decades later they were recognized as being among the century's masterworks.

Among Daumier's favorite subjects for oils and watercolors were scenes of the new railroad age, especially of station waiting rooms and passenger cars. *The Third-Class Carriage* (fig. 17-18) captures in a few

17-18 Honoré Daumier, *The Third-Class Carriage*, c. 1856–62. Oil on canvas, 25¾″ × 35½″. The Metropolitan Museum of Art (bequest of Mrs. H. O. Havemeyer, 1929; the H. O. Havemeyer Collection).

human figures a gamut of laboring-class moods and conditions—from resignation and frail old age, through seedy gentility and the sturdy, rough-hewn dignity of late middle age, to young peasant motherhood and trusting childhood. With broad brushstrokes and a limited but warm color scheme, the artist created an unsentimental scene of monumental solidity, an impression of human and aesthetic permanence akin to that of Rembrandt.

Contrasting with, yet complementing, Daumier's world of everyday nineteenth-century reality are a group of paintings based on the strange career of Cervantes's Don Quixote. The precise subject of *Don Quixote and Sancho Panza* (fig. 17-19) has been variously identified but is relatively unimportant. What matters is the contrast between the eccentric knight's wild and fevered temper and the despair of his sensible servant, who wrings his hands in anguished exasperation. Both in painting and in human significance, the contrast of the two figures is striking—frantic energy against immobility, or the Romantic and impossible dream against cautious, unimaginative Realism.

The contrast had personal significance for the painter. Daumier's dream as a crusading caricaturist had been romantic, but his robust roots had been in the everyday world of Paris—the world of lawyers and laundresses, print collectors and theatergoers, corrupt legislators and forthright children. As the most realistic of Romantics, and the most romantic of Realists, Daumier is a cautionary reminder of the frequent fusion of artistic styles.

Far more consciously limited in its tone and content was the art of Gustave Courbet (1819–77), the painter of uncompromising pictorial realism. Courbet's Realism was unsentimental, unprettified, and deliberately unaesthetic; it avoided the historical and the literary and expressed the realities of contemporary life. Thus it was an art of the people—the art of democracy itself. Courbet rejected "the trivial goal of art-for-art's-sake" and was determined to translate into painting "the customs, the ideas, the appearance" of his epoch, thus achieving a truly "living art."

It was an art emphasizing in content, above all, peasants and urban laborers, who have so often seemed more "real" to artistic and literary Realists than the middle and upper classes. Courbet's subjects, however, are surprisingly dehumanized and materialized in contrast to Daumier's delight in human personality. *Burial at Ornans* (fig. 17-20) well represents Courbet's approach; this is the huge canvas that first brought him notoriety. Over forty life-size figures crowd into the gloomy burial scene in Courbet's hometown. Although most of the figures have been identified as individual townspeople, they melt unobtrusively into the whole, leveled by the stark horizontal cliffs in the background, as if by the presence of death itself.

The murk and the rough majesty of the *Burial at Ornans* did not at first win much approval. In fact,

17-19 Honoré Daumier, *Don Quixote and Sancho Panza*, c. 1864–66. Oil on canvas, 22¼″ × 33¼″. Collection of Joan Whitney Payson, New York.

17-20   Gustave Courbet, *Burial at Ornans*, 1849–50. Oil on canvas, 10'4" × 21'10". Musée d'Orsay, Paris.

when it was exhibited at the 1850 Salon (the official exhibition by established artists) the work was greeted by indignant protest. Wrote one critic: "Probably never has the cult of ugliness been practiced more frankly." It was even said that to portray together such a multitude of common folk was politically and socially subversive.

Manet's Unintended Revolution

Courbet's failure to achieve fashionable critical acclaim was paralleled by the problems of Édouard Manet (1832–83), who unlike Courbet never aimed at artistic revolution. Yet scandal was to be Manet's recurrent fate as an artist. The worst years of all were the mid 1860s, when such works as his *Déjeuner sur l'Herbe* aroused heated accusations of indecency and outright pornography. Moreover, his early classification in the newly acceptable Realist school could not quiet the uneasy feeling that he represented something transcending and negating the Realist school—something that was frightening because it was new and indefinable.

Manet was puzzled and pained that his contemporaries found offensive his juxtaposition of fully clothed males with naked females in the *Déjeuner*. The composition and general subject matter were completely tra-

ditional; in fact, the work had been based in large part on a painting by Giorgione. And female nudity was certainly common enough—and popular enough—in the paintings of the time. What jarred viewers was the application of a frank, matter-of-fact approach to such a scene. Naked women representing goddesses or virtues were acceptable, but naked women in contemporary settings were much too close to certain Parisian realities to be hung on the wall of any self-respecting bourgeois home.

For all their similarities, Courbet and Manet represented two basically different approaches to art. Courbet tried to choose his subjects with revolutionary zeal and portray them with stonily objective naturalism; Manet took whatever subjects were at hand and made them his own through his personal vision and temperament. The modern period in art is often dated from 1863 and the *Déjeuner*. This is because Manet, an independently wealthy man who could paint what and as he chose, seems to have been the first to practice consistently what has come to be known as *art-for-art's-sake*—the belief that art, both as creative process and as finished product, is its own justification. Manet assumed, consciously or unconsciously, that painting did not exist to embody ideas or to promote morality, but had to stand on its own as a purely pictorial and formal experience. Classicism, Romanticism, Realism—

17-21   Edouard Manet, *Le Déjeuner sur l'Herbe*, 1863. Oil on canvas, 7' × 8'10". Musée d'Orsay, Paris.

all had had their messages that both transcended and cramped the sheer aesthetic appeal of their works. "Pure painting" now would stand and soar on its own.

Something of what moved and excited Manet may be seen in *Le Déjeuner sur l'Herbe* (fig. 17-21), usually translated as *Luncheon on the Grass* or, more informally, *The Picnic*. Here, as in the rest of his art, it is not the scene itself or any narrative or ideological content that is important, but mainly forms and colors. Portrayal of emotion is the least of his concerns, nor is he much interested in the subtle modeling of his forms. The outlines are clear and vigorous, and although they may be of people, the people interest us very little in themselves as individuals; they are of more importance as colored forms.

Many of Manet's contemporaries saw the matter quite differently and attacked the *Déjeuner* as an attempt to subvert morality. Others were no doubt sincerely confused by the novelty of the work and uneasy in the face of something they could not understand. Although Manet's *Luncheon in the Studio* (fig. 17-22) was greeted with no comparable scandal, its reception at the 1869 Salon was hardly warm. Above all, the subject—a studio scene with a bearded artist at table, a servant with silver coffeepot, and a boy leaning against the table in the foreground—was attacked for its in-

congruities (the juxtaposition of oysters and coffee on the table, for example) and its general pointlessness. In truth, Manet's subjects, here and elsewhere, were chosen and arranged arbitrarily as problems in painting, not as vehicles for instruction or narration or emotional elevation.

Manet's novel and revolutionary approach was to influence the rise of Impressionism (discussed in the next chapter) and the direction of a vast body of subsequent art. This influence, though under frequent attack, has survived until today, despite all cries for a more obvious relevance and involvement on the part of art. Few reorientations in the arts have even approached the lasting significance of this unintended revolution.

SCULPTURE AT MID CENTURY

Except for some interesting pieces by Daumier, and the earliest works of Rodin, the 1825–70 period is only slightly more distinguished in sculpture than were the first decades of the century. With the strongest pressures of Classicism now past, the dead weight of conformity to antique models had lightened. We will note

17-22 Edouard Manet, *Luncheon in the Studio,* 1868. Oil on canvas, 47″ × 60″. Neue Pinakothek, Munich.

17-23 François Rude, *The Departure of the Volunteers in 1792 (The Marseillaise),* 1833–36. Stone, 42′ high.

only two mid-century sculptors, and these quite briefly. Both were French.

The first of these, François Rude (1784–1855) created one work generally acknowledged to be a masterpiece, *The Departure of the Volunteers in 1792* (fig. 17-23). This huge work in stone, better known as *The Marseillaise,* is attached to one of France's most massive monuments to Napoleonic glory, the Arch of Triumph of the Star, in Paris. In more or less classical dress and undress, the figures represent the French Revolutionary troops who first surged forth to fight for liberty, equality, and fraternity in 1792. Above them, urging them on, is a magnificently forceful female figure, the spirit of Liberty herself. The onrush of dramatic movement and vitality in the work is unsurpassed in the history of sculpture.

Antoine Louis Barye (1796–1875), a friend of Daumier, is remembered especially as a sculptor of animals, in most cases animals in the throes of death struggles such as those fancied by Delacroix—hence such typical titles as *Bull Attacked by a Tiger* and *Jaguar Devouring a Hare.* The impulse, like Delacroix's, is the Romantic interest in tension and exoticism, although the anatomical studies had been made carefully from life and from the dissection of dead zoo animals. These studies also helped in his modeling of such fabulous creatures, half man, half beast, as centaurs and minotaur. *Theseus and the Minotaur* (fig. 17-24) is a small

17-24 Antoine Louis Barye, *Theseus and the Minotaur,* 1848. Bronze, 19″ high. Musée d'Orsay, Paris.

bronze of Romantic strength and vigor, combined with the Athenian hero's antique origin and impassive classical features.

THE FLOWERING OF MUSICAL ROMANTICISM

Romanticism remained a major force in music, as in sculpture, long after Romanticism in painting and literature had been supplanted by other styles. The main musical directions between 1825 and 1870 were overwhelmingly Romantic, although Classical elements were not wholly discarded. Musical Romanticism would survive as a powerful creative force well after 1870, and for concert audiences it has never lost its appeal. We have noted its beginnings—ambiguously entwined with a prominent Classicism—and now we will turn our attention to composers who were more thoroughgoing Romantics than Beethoven or even Schubert.

Berlioz

Representative of a supremely articulate generation that unabashedly proclaimed its own joys and sorrows, its yearnings and individual oddities, is Hector Berlioz (1803–69). The penetrating portrait of Berlioz by Courbet (fig. 17-25) and innumerable written anecdotes and confessions vividly portray this composer. Especially in his first decade or so as musician, music critic, and man-about-Paris, Berlioz embodied the excitability, the self-dramatization, and the occasional bitter morbidity that were so much a part of the fashionable Romantic image.

Berlioz was essentially a self-taught composer who evolved a personal idiom that to its first listeners was startling indeed. "I couldn't help saying to my colleagues yesterday," confessed an older composer to Berlioz, "that with your way of writing you must despise us from the bottom of your heart. You refuse to write like everybody else."

And so he did. He was, moreover, a conscious propagandist for the new. The greatest of earlier com-

17-25 Gustave Courbet, *Berlioz,* c. 1850. Oil on canvas, 24″ × 19″. Musée d'Orsay, Paris.

posers, however profound their originality, had seldom thought of themselves as revolutionaries; Berlioz was perhaps the first, and certainly one of the most articulate, of music's deliberate advance-guardists.

Among the characteristics of the new music of Berlioz are harmonies that are unanticipated and that violate Classical harmonic rules. His melodies, too, are unusual for their age: they are likely to be lengthy and somewhat lacking in symmetry. His rhythm, too, can be asymmetrical, embodying great freedom and variety. Above all, to the ear accustomed to Beethoven or Mozart, there are new richnesses of orchestration in Berlioz. Sometimes this implied for him an ideal immensity of orchestral (and vocal) forces, for ceremonial purposes. Far more often, though, his orchestral demands were conventional, but with an unusually sensitive attention to coloristic instrumental effects. In fact, Berlioz excelled especially in creating a spare, clear instrumental texture. All of this, and much more, is illustrated by his second symphony, entitled *Harold in Italy.*

This work for solo viola and orchestra tells no detailed story, although it was inspired, in part, by the composer's wanderings in the Abruzzi countryside near Rome and by a long poem by Lord Byron, "Childe Harold's Pilgrimage." The viola evokes the spirit of Harold as a world traveler finding himself in varied scenes but always preserving his own individuality. The principal theme of the viola, Berlioz wrote, "is reproduced throughout the work, . . . superimposed upon the other orchestral strains, with which it contrasts both in movement and character without hindering their development."

"Harold in the mountains: scenes of melancholy, happiness, and joy"—this notation on Berlioz's score informs us of the setting and the moods of the first movement of *Harold in Italy.* A slow introduction (adagio) is announced by cellos and basses; they are soon joined by solo winds and then by the full orchestra. Climaxes of massed sound punctuate the predominantly reflective mood before the entrance of the viola with its characteristic motto-theme (see below).

This motto-theme (*idée fixe,* "fixed idea") represents the poetically melancholy Harold throughout the four movements of the symphony. Later in the first movement the mood changes to one of "happiness and joy," in an allegro that sometimes is quiet but more often boisterous, with great explosions of sound in which the viola is utterly buried.

Again in the slower, second movement (allegretto) we are reminded of the basically orchestral, not soloistic, conception of the work; the viola comments on, never masters, the scene. In this "March of pilgrims singing the evening prayer," the choral song is generally entrusted to the strings, with fluttering murmured chants suggested by the winds and the repeated tolling of two bells vividly evoked by differing combinations of winds and harp. Harmonic surprises and melodic inventiveness combine with subtle instrumental coloring to form a memorable musical impression—and all, it should be noted, at a restrained dynamic level, with no orchestral heroics.

The third movement, too, is quiet. In contrast, the final movement represents a vigorous "Orgy of the brigands," labeled by the composer a "frenetic allegro." In reference to a successful German performance of the work he conducted in 1843, Berlioz described *Harold*'s finale as

> that furious orgy where wine, blood, joy, rage, all combined, parade their intoxication—where the rhythm sometimes seems to stumble along, sometimes to rush on in fury, and the brass seem to vomit forth curses and to answer prayer with blasphemies; where they laugh, drink, fight, destroy, slay, violate, and utterly run riot. In this brigand scene the orchestra became a regular pandemonium; there was something positively supernatural and terrifying in its frantic life and spirit, and violins, basses, trombones, drums, and cymbals all sang and bounded and roared with diabolical order and concord, while from the solo viola, the dreamy Harold, some trembling notes of his evening hymn were still heard in the distance as he fled in terror.

And, indeed, most of the finale is characterized by the rhythmic excitement, orchestral noisiness, and violent

contrasts of dynamics that too often have been thought to sum up the whole of Berlioz.

Verdi

The preeminent musical form of the nineteenth century in Italy was the opera. The reigning operatic monarch of the final half-century was Giuseppe Verdi (1813–1901).

Unlike the music of Berlioz, nineteenth-century Italian opera was not notably innovative, but it did change and grow with its times. Down through Verdi, and beyond, opera oriented itself more and more toward its increasingly bourgeois audience, abandoning the aristocratic heroics of antique legends and turning to the pageantry of more recent, often national, history. The passions became more flamboyant and mercurial, in approved Romantic vein, and the theatrical drama became more immediate and urgent. Verdi did his part to advance these trends, and thus his collaboration with the master-writer of the French stage, Eugène Scribe, was probably inevitable.

Verdi had already set to music Scribe's *Sicilian Vespers* when he turned to him again in the late 1850s for the story of *A Masked Ball (Un Ballo in Maschera)*. Scribe's original play, *Gustav III*, was translated and adapted by Antonio Somma, and Verdi wrote the music rapidly, in two months or so, at the end of 1857. More than a year, however, intervened before the opera's première.

The reasons for the delay were political. The contract under which the still unwritten opera was to be produced, at the Royal San Carlo Theater of Naples, had not specified the opera's subject; now the censors of the Neapolitan King Ferdinand II were shocked to find before them a work of clearly subversive implications—perhaps even of subversive intention, for Verdi's nationalistic sentiments were well known. Here, after all, was presented to the world a story of successful murderous conspiracy against a rather recent European monarch (the Swedish Gustav had been assassinated at a masked ball in 1792), and the censors knew well that many Italians would have been happy to see the highly unpopular Ferdinand suffer the same fate.

In such an atmosphere, any accommodation with the Neapolitan censors was impossible, and Verdi abandoned the idea of presenting his opera there. At last a production in Rome (1859) was arranged, with Verdi agreeing to make revisions complying with a censorship somewhat less stringent than that of Naples. Thus Verdi and Somma changed the opera's setting from Sweden to colonial Boston in the late seventeenth century. The result was an amazing, anachronistic hodgepodge. The plot revolves around an aristocratic British provincial governor, Riccardo, earl of Warwick, who inexplicably moves within a brilliant European court and vies in local popularity with the "black Indian" fortune-teller Ulrica. He loves the wife of his Creole secretary, Renato, and tolerates the irresponsible chatter of a frivolous page named Oscar. Finally he is murdered at a masked ball by two base-hearted courtiers called Samuel and Tom (fig. 17-26). Even Mozart had never had to contend with such mind-numbing absurdities for his librettos. The miraculous achievement of Verdi, like that of Mozart, is that he could clothe this strange plot, and others almost equally improbable, in effective characterization, believable drama, and musical beauty.

The opening scene of Act I, although jollier than

17-26 Death scene from *Un Ballo in Maschera*.

most of the opera, is typical of "middle-period" Verdi. The orchestral prelude (the *overture*) displays the composer's dramatic tastes and Romanticism's love of emotional contrasts by setting forth three very different themes, each of which, after the curtain rises, will reappear in its own dramatic role. The first, a quiet, hymnlike sequence, will be a chorus of "courtiers and people" praising the governor as they await an audience with him. Next comes the staccato theme of the conspirators, beginning softly on cellos and basses and developing into a fugue that suggests a convoluted conspiracy. Finally a singing, passionate melody enters; this will be associated with the governor's love for Amelia, Renato's wife. The stage action begins with chorus and conspirators together, followed by the entrance of Riccardo, as announced by the page Oscar (this part sung by a soprano). A carefree orchestral accompaniment to Riccardo's first words indicates his genial good nature, but soon a reminder of Amelia brings an outburst on the third introductory theme, entwined shortly with the words of conspirators and chorus. The group departs, thus closing a tightly, almost symphonically organized episode, Romantic mainly in its rather lush sound.

A duet follows with orchestra accompanying the recitative, between Riccardo and Renato. Renato tries to divulge a plot against the governor, who is not at all interested in hearing the details; this situation gives rise to a simple, melodious aria by Renato. A judge enters to inform Riccardo of a sentence of banishment against one Ulrica, a fortune-teller who collects about her the scum of Boston. As the scene's high point, Oscar quickly jumps in to defend Ulrica in the lilting aria "Volta la terrea" ("Her dark face turned toward the stars, how her eyes sparkle when to the pretty girls she foretells the sad or happy ending of their loves!"). The governor has a happy inspiration: he calls back the whole group and invites them to go, in disguise, to "Ulrica's place." All cheerily agree, even Samuel and Tom, although only Oscar admits any intention of getting his own fortune told. A merry chorus brings the scene to a rousing close.

It is easy to dismiss much of this as simpleminded—and many have done so. Yet Verdi's music was sincere, forthright, and concise, with instinctive dramatic sense and immense vitality. Above all, it escaped the dangers that he had described: "Art devoid of spontaneity, naturalness, and simplicity ceases to be art." He protested against excessive intellectualism in musical composition and never felt any need or desire to explain his art to the public. In both these respects he was the antithesis of his great rival for Europe's operatic affections, Richard Wagner (fig. 17-27). Moreover, in this rivalry it was undoubtedly Verdi who, in any historical sense, was the winner. He was not only the most popular operatic composer of his century but quite possibly the most popular serious composer who ever lived.

Wagner

Verdi exemplifies greatness with and of his times; the greatness of Richard Wagner (1813–83) went against the grain of his times and won understanding and recognition only slowly and painfully. The distrust of his music in his own time, moreover, was sometimes compounded by dislike for the man, for Wagner possessed an extremely difficult personality. Then there were his ideas—all expressed in voluminous writings with the

17-27 Richard Wagner, 1864.

same authority with which he composed his music—a strange mixture of elitism, socialism, and anti-Semitism, compounded with a glorification of myth and nationality that became a tiresome and dangerous Germanic chauvinism.

For the average concertgoers and operagoers of Wagner's day—those who knew only his music—there were problems enough, in just the music. The greatest barriers to an appreciation of Wagner were his novelties in tonality and harmony, impelled perhaps by the Romantic desire for freedom from old patterns of musical expression. Actually Wagner never completely abandoned the traditional tonal system, with its diatonic (major or minor) scales. His own age, however, tended to think that he had forsaken tonality altogether. Indeed, his incessant chromatic modulations confused his hearers most extraordinarily; they simply could not get their bearings amid his strange, shifting harmonies, and dissonances that lingered interminably, sometimes with no direct, relieving resolution. Decades later, his harmonies would be accepted as natural and beautiful; in their own day most music lovers initially found them baffling and perverse.

Harmony was, in fact, the very essence of Wagnerian music, for it carried forward the narrative and passion of his operas even more notably than did the vocal melody, which now was often a mere part of the harmonic structure. In Wagner's music the chords and their expressive modulations are basic. Most typically, the vocal line is not independently tuneful at all, but is extracted from the heart of the harmony. "Unending melody" was the term he himself used, mainly in reference to the abolition of the familiar contrast between operatic aria and recitative—but his more disgruntled contemporaries complained that they found no melody in Wagner at all.

The opera—or in his own terminology, the *music-drama*—was Wagner's preferred form of musical expression, and the vehicle for his most striking theories. In his later work, almost wholly without traditional arias or set-pieces of any sort and with virtually no ensemble singing, the music-drama was to be a "complete art work," disdaining superficial vocal display and combining music, poetry, and stage production in a new and powerful synthesis of the arts. Firmly in control of the whole was Wagner himself, who wrote his own librettos and directed and produced the first performances.

As to theatrical action in Wagnerian music-drama, there is usually very little. On stage his characters act far less than they narrate and discuss; they meditate and argue, they rejoice or grieve or yearn, while the stage scene itself is static. But beneath—and above—all this the music leads its own life, sometimes with passionate intensity. In much of Wagner's later work a prominent musical device contributing to this intensity is the recurrent musical theme, or *leitmotif*—a term he himself never used but that now has become standard. Each "leading motif" is associated with a particular person, object, situation, or emotion, and it can function dramatically as either a presentiment or a reminiscence.

In 1857 Wagner began writing *Tristan and Isolde,* one of the crucial art works of the century. Inspired by a medieval Celtic legend, the world of *Tristan* is simultaneously shadowy and intense. Ardent love is celebrated in words and music, intermingled with ideals of chastity, renunciation, and death. Tristan and Isolde are finally exalted through love and suffering—but still more through the gorgeously shifting patterns of Wagner's musical imagination. Wagner's chromaticism, with its lush harmonies, its incessant movement and climactic peaks, admits the listener to an unearthly realm that may well seem both bewitched and neurotic. It is a realm not for everybody, but it can be obsessively fascinating for those willing to plunge into its murky and fevered depths.

Only the opening and closing moments of the opera will be considered here. In the orchestral prelude Wagner foreshadows the mood of the opera. In his program notes for the Paris concert performances (1860) of prelude and conclusion, he summarizes both the complete story and its forecast in the prelude as a portrayal of

> . . . endless yearning, longing, the bliss and the wretchedness of love; world, power, fame, honor, chivalry, loyalty and friendship all blown away like an insubstantial dream; one thing alone left living—longing, longing unquenchable, a yearning, a hunger, a languishing forever renewing itself; one sole redemption—death, surcease, a sleep without awakening.

A series of swelling chromatic phrases opens the prelude; these lead to an intense orchestral climax, which at last subsides into quietness. Especially notable is the fate of the opening intermingled downward and upward phrases: they are not immediately varied and developed symphonically, but first are repeated, only slightly modified, at successively higher pitches and with greater intensity, until at last they expand into ever longer and richer musical ideas.

Then comes the massive body of the music-drama, three long acts that tell of the fated love, and repeated death wishes, of Tristan and Isolde, the intended bride of King Mark, Tristan's feudal lord. Their "night of love" is interrupted by the arrival of the king and the wounding of Tristan by a treacherous knight. The lovers are separated, and Tristan is left to die after a long agony, just as Isolde appears and sinks to her death by his side.

In her *Liebestod* ("love-death"), Isolde's musical line rises from the orchestra itself, escaping only now and then to soar on its own, almost in that aria form usually scorned by Wagner. The dynamics rise and fall, the instrumental parts glide and quiver ecstatically, as Isolde prepares for the ultimate union with her lover. Her final words, before the woodwind sigh of yearning and the spacious closing chords, are not of grief or resignation, but of transfigured desire. The music remains one of Romanticism's most memorable, most extraordinary monuments.

Recommended Reading

Allen, Gay Wilson. *A Reader's Guide to Walt Whitman* (1970). Interpretation and criticism of the poetry.

August, Eugene. *John Stuart Mill, A Mind at Large* (1975). Popular biography plus analysis of works.

Boudaille, Georges. *Gustave Courbet: Painter in Protest* (1969). Good picture book with biography.

Briggs, Asa. *Iron Bridge to Crystal Palace: Impact and Images of the Industrial Revolution* (1979). Splendid, fascinating introduction to the subject.

Chase, Robert. *Emily Dickinson* (1965). Her life, writing, and ideas.

Clark, Timothy J. *The Painting of Modern Life: Paris in the Age of Manet and His Followers* (1984). Manet and the Impressionists.

Clarson-Leach, Robert. *Berlioz, His Life and Times* (1983). Short biography, well-illustrated.

Emerson, Ralph Waldo. *Selected Essays* (ed. Larzer Ziff) (1982). The original essays, including *Self-Reliance*.

Goldstein, Jan, and John W. Boyer, eds. *Nineteenth Century Europe: Liberalism in an Age of Industrialization* (1987). Primary sources.

Gregor-Dellin, Martin. *Richard Wagner: His Life, His Work, His Century* (1983). Good, thorough biography.

Hirschfeld, Charles, and Edgar E. Knoebel, eds. *The Modern World* (1980). Sizable chunks of de Tocqueville, Mill, Hegel, Darwin, Marx, and Engels.

Hirsh, Diana, ed. *The World of Turner 1775–1851* (1969). Good introduction to life and times, with fine illustrations.

Mosse, W. E. *The Age of Bourgeois Realism 1848–1875* (1974). The economic, political, and social world, well-illustrated.

Passeron, Roger. *Daumier* (1981). Biography and works, well-illustrated.

Robson, John M., ed. *John Stuart Mill: A Selection of His Works* (1966). *On Liberty*, complete; large chunks of *Autobiography* and *The Subjection of Women*.

Saalman, Howard. *Haussmann: Paris Transformed* (1971). Fine short study, interesting illustrations.

Schneider, Pierre, ed. *The World of Manet 1832–1883* (1968). The artist and work in his setting, well-illustrated.

Seigel, Jerrold. *Bohemian Paris: Culture, Politics, and the Boundaries of Bourgeois Life 1830–1930* (1986). Interesting study with a few illustrations.

Trapp, Frank Anderson. *The Attainment of Delacroix* (1970). Good coverage.

Wagenknecht, Edward. *Ralph Waldo Emerson: Portrait of a Balanced Soul* (1974). His ideas—a topical summary and commentary.

Wechsberg, Joseph. *Verdi* (1974). Interesting biography, excellent illustrations.

Many critics objected that Monet's painting disintegrated all volumes and basic forms as well as lines and that effects of light, color, and atmosphere simply were not enough to give full aesthetic satisfaction. It is true that Monet's approach was far more optical than descriptive, narrative, formal, or intellectual. Few paintings, though, have been as liberating as his in terms of sheer visual delight.

Another of the original Impressionists was Edgar Degas (1834–1917). A proud and lonely man, he was more sympathetic to the artistic goals and style of Manet than to those of Monet. He was little interested in outdoor subjects except the racetrack, and he painted in the studio after sketching from life. An earnest student of the old masters in the Louvre and in the museums and churches of Italy, he practiced a high degree of calculation in his painting. "In art," he said, "nothing must be left to accident—not even move-

ment." However, his ability to capture fleeting movement may be his most Impressionist trait. Even here, though, he was different from the stricter Impressionists: whereas those painters wished to capture the passing glint of sunlight on objects, Degas was far more concerned with the movement of living figures.

Through nearly the whole of his artistic career, and in several mediums including sculpture, Degas recorded the movement of female ballet dancers. An early painting on this subject is the Metropolitan Museum's *The Dancing Class* (fig. 18-15), in which dancers are lounging, chatting, adjusting shoes, exercising, and practicing steps as an elderly violinist pauses in his accompaniment. It is a varied scene; not all of the figures are in motion, although the central, highlighted figure is indeed moving. The writer Edmond de Goncourt noted in his journal (1874) that he had just visited the studio of Degas, who had "fallen in love with the modern and, in the modern, he has cast his choice upon laundresses and dancers." De Goncourt particularly noted the filmy "white, ballooning clouds" of the dancer's tutus and the "graceful twisting of movements and gestures" of the girls. Portraying such things would fascinate Degas for decades, even after he had become virtually blind.

Sometimes Degas's subjects were still more humble. For his series of pastels of nudes bathing, the interval between sketch and final painting was probably brief, for these works embody a pleasing impression of spontaneity. *The Tub*, of 1886 (fig. 18-16), is particularly striking in its asymmetrical composition and in the daring angle of vision that foreshadows movie camera technique; the popularity of Japanese prints probably influenced Degas here. The creamy pastel flesh colors in *The Tub* are relatively voluptuous for Degas, who as a painter generally saw women simply as studies in motion.

Such a view, certainly, was not typical of Auguste Renoir (1841–1919), one of art history's most uninhibited portrayers of robust female sensuality. We see this in his *Nude in the Sunlight* (fig. 18-17) of 1875–76, but even more we see in it a study in light. Renoir had placed his model beneath tree foliage on a sunny day so

18-14 Claude Monet, *Rouen Cathedral at Sunset*, 1894. Oil on canvas, 39½″ × 25¾″. Courtesy Museum of Fine Arts, Boston (Juliana Cheney Edwards Collection; bequest of Hannah Marcy Edwards in memory of her mother).

18-15 Edgar Degas, *The Dancing Class,* c. 1871. Panel, 7¾″ × 10½″. The Metropolitan Museum of Art, New York. Bequest of Mrs. H. O. Havermeyer, 1929. The H. O. Havemeyer Collection.

that spots of sunlight would strike her body at random. The resultant dappled effect of light on the skin would scarcely have been attempted by earlier artists, who almost certainly would have regarded the effect as splotchy and unattractive. To our eyes, as to Renoir's, the play of light is scintillating, and all the more Impressionist for the bright, free brushstrokes suggesting nearby trees and flowers.

Much of Renoir's work celebrated the joys of life— not least among these, the open-air cafés of Montmartre. His *Moulin de la Galette* (fig. 18-18) is one of the period's happiest paintings, not only in the carefree

18-16 Edgar Degas, *The Tub,* 1886. Pastel, 24″ × 33″. Musée d'Orsay, Paris.

18-17 Auguste Renoir, *Nude in the Sunlight*, 1875–76. Oil on canvas, 31½″ × 25¼″. Musée d'Orsay, Paris (Caillebotte Bequest).

mood and human charms portrayed, but in the dash and vigor of the brushstrokes and the rich colors. Nor is the composition by any means haphazard, in a scene that with its multitude of figures could easily have become thoroughly chaotic. Nevertheless, it is the gay colors of Renoir's paintings and their Impressionist brilliance that make his work particularly memorable. Renoir stayed closer to Impressionism than any of that movement's leaders except Monet.

The Post-Impressionists

An artist who ventured from the Impressionist mainstream was Paul Cézanne (1839–1906). Ranked today among the world's greatest painters, in his own time he was virtually unknown to the public. The least gregarious of the original Impressionist group, he disappeared for long periods into his native southern France. His rare meetings with old friends gave rise to contradictory reports of modest affability and of terrifying arrogance and boorishness.

18-18 Auguste Renoir, *The Moulin de la Galette*, 1876. Oil on canvas, 52″ × 69″. Musée d'Orsay, Paris.

18-19 Paul Cézanne, *Still Life with Basket of Apples*, 1890–94. Oil on canvas, 24¾″ × 32″. Helen Birch Bartlett Memorial Collection. © 1987 The Art Institute of Chicago. All Rights Reserved.

A quick glance at one late still life and one very late landscape by Cézanne will show us several qualities of his art and help explain the public resistance that he encountered. The *Still Life with Basket of Apples* (fig. 18-19) has much of the rich color and the weight and solidity of a Chardin still life (see fig. 14-14)—Cézanne had long admired the work of the eighteenth-century master—but otherwise it differs fundamentally from past example. The objects seem to have been arranged with carefully perverse eccentricity; there is nothing natural about the tilted bottle, the basket propped up by a wood block, or the plate of rolls set up on a book. The angle of vision is not unitary but fractured; the rolls are seen both from a low angle and from above, and the tabletop visible to the left of the cloth is wildly askew from that at the right. Shadows are shown only inconsistently, and there is almost no conventional tonal shading of the fruit to indicate either roundness or shadow. The distortions of such paintings can today convey visual tensions, but in the 1890s they demonstrated to the average viewer an astounding ineptitude.

Cézanne's very late painting of Mont Sainte-Victoire (fig. 18-20) contains formal devices that are still further exaggerated. It is an almost wholly structural account of a visual phenomenon: the hill near Aix in southern France that Cézanne turned to, again and again, as a problem in painting. The colors are often nonnaturalistic, from the green splotches in the sky to the lavender mountain, down to the buildings and trees of the middle ground, in bright orange and green, and the intensely dark foreground. Even more startling is the reduction of natural forms to splashy brushstrokes that may seem to be chaotic planes of color. However, by the end of the century many artists and critics were coming to suspect that Cézanne knew very well what he was doing, even when he tended this far toward abstract construction—and that the result was a major revolution in painting.

What was Cézanne trying to do? He himself said that he wanted to "make of Impressionism something solid like the art of the museums." Usually painting directly from nature and using the broad brushstrokes and bright colors of the Impressionists, he nevertheless

18-20 Paul Cézanne, *Mont Sainte-Victoire*, 1904–6. Oil on canvas, 26″ × 32″. Private Collection. Partial Gift to the Philadelphia Museum of Art.

subverted the Impressionist goal by trying to capture not just visual sensations, but the substantial, underlying structure of things and their precise spatial placement in the context of other things. Cézanne's forms do not dissolve in shimmering light, and they can become palpably weighty and even monumental. They achieve these qualities both from a process of intellectual abstraction and from a way of feeling about things. Toward the end of his life Cézanne summarized his approach succinctly: "The Louvre is the book in which we learn to read. We must not, however, be satisfied with retaining our illustrious predecessors' formulas of beauty. . . . Let us try to express ourselves according to our personal temperaments."

Thus Cézanne's art derived from his study of earlier masters, and then from a way of seeing that was filtered through his temperament. He strove strenuously, even passionately, to lose himself in the structural essence of things. For him, painting was rigorously rational and passionately exploratory at the same time. What he sought was a new way of experiencing any subject, or segment of the world, and of extracting its basic components. Despite his celebrated advice to look for "the cylinder, the sphere, and the cone" in

nature, he considered other forms as well, and colors and spatial relationships also. Then came the crucial process of intellectual and emotional synthesis, while transcribing or reconstructing this synthesis on canvas.

The artist's canvas is two-dimensional, and it was in the conclusions he drew from that fact that Cézanne most sharply parted company with the mainstream of many centuries of European art. The two-dimensional canvas, he was convinced, should not be submitted to three-dimensional wrenching, at least in the manner of the old masters. Contours and spatial positions could still be indicated, but the means of doing so would be more appropriate to the canvas than the traditional techniques. Contours, as in *Still Life with Basket of Apples*, could be suggested by different colors (color "modulation," he called it), rather than "realistic" gradualized modeling and shading. Spatial depth, as in *Mont Sainte-Victoire*, need not lean on precisely linear perspective and should never be represented by any increasing haziness; atmospheric perspective was especially reprehensible to Cézanne since it denied the unity of the two-dimensional canvas, in which all parts were equal. Depth could be suggested in several ways— in the overlapping of planes, for instance, or in differing degrees of color intensity. (Note the receding effect of the lavender in Mont Sainte-Victoire itself, the pushing forward of the oranges in the middle ground, and the still more intense foreground colors.) In the *Still Life*, we see the jumbled angles of vision inducing a feeling of depth, as the point of viewing rises to permit looking down on just one part of the table, or on just one part of the rolls in the right background—instead of such techniques as blurring the focus of more distant objects.

Clearly color was immensely important to Cézanne, not as a superficial optical effect, but as a means of organizing and enlivening the canvas. Within a few years after his death this aspect of his art seemed less important to many avant-garde artists than his simplified, quasi-geometrical planes and his use of multiple angles of vision. Abstract art would owe much to Cézanne; it is not likely, however, that he ever considered nonrepresentational abstraction as a goal. Cézanne sought stability in his art, but he found this stability in nature rather than in geometry.

Although Cézanne was, in artistic terms, a great visionary and a profound thinker, he neither displayed his emotions nor advanced any message outside the realm of art. If only for that reason, he has never achieved the general popularity of two extraordinary younger contemporaries whom he survived, van Gogh and Gauguin. Neither of these painters was as much concerned about abstract balance and harmony as Cézanne; both were supremely instinctive artists and often were quite unapologetically emotional in their art. Both, but especially Gauguin, wanted to supplement new forms with a new content—and often this content was narrative or broadly symbolic, as in pre-Impressionist days. Both read and speculated widely outside the realm of painting, and Gauguin was particularly drawn to the literary Symbolist movement with its antimaterialistic esotericism. Together with Rodin in sculpture and Sullivan in architecture, they were the nineteenth century's last great Romantics in art.

Paul Gauguin (1848–1903) came to painting from an unlikely background as a stockbroker. His search for personal and artistic freedom eventually led him around the world, from Breton villages to the South Seas. The style that he evolved may seem to us primarily decorative, but it also was symbolist and expressive of the artist's feelings.

A prime example of Gauguin's painting among the peasants and fishing folk of Brittany is his *Yellow Christ* (fig. 18-21). The symbolism is less of the historical crucifixion than of myth and mysticism—the devout mysticism of simple Breton piety. The colors are strong; the forms are nearly flat and are heavily outlined to make the work understandable to even the most untutored eye. Elaborate modeling and shading, Gauguin maintained, are deceitful in their vagueness and sophisticated illusionism. Art must be simple and straightforward; it must speak to all without crafty subtlety. The whole Western tradition of illusionistic realism, from the Greeks to the present, must be reversed in favor of a vision that is naive and childlike.

This quest for childlike, primitive roots drew Gauguin to the South Seas. A typical product of this long, final period is *The Day of the God* (fig. 18-22), which reaches back for subject matter into Tahitian mythology, or to Gauguin's notions of that mythology. It is extraordinarily decorative and appealing. Colors are bright, and their outlines, usually reinforced in black, undulate in an Art Nouveau sinuosity. Natural-

18-21 Paul Gauguin, *The Yellow Christ*, 1889. Oil on canvas, 36¼″ × 28¾″. Albright-Knox Art Gallery, Buffalo New York. (General Purchase Funds, 1946.)

18-22 Paul Gauguin, *The Day of the God (Mahana No Atua)*, 1894. Oil on canvas, 27¼″ × 35½″. Helen Birch Bartlett Memorial Collection. © 1987 The Art Institute of Chicago. All Rights Reserved.

ism is almost wholly disavowed, as in the brilliant foreground patterns in the water. The painting reveals a romantic dreamland of mythical, almost childlike innocence.

A still more remarkable painter was Gauguin's friend and admirer, the Dutchman Vincent van Gogh (1853–90). No artist has lived or expressed himself with a more passionate, intense, soul-baring honesty than van Gogh. The self-portrait of 1887 (fig. 18-23) reveals much of the intensity of this essentially self-taught artist whose whole life was a quest for self and for self-expression. The painting dates from his second long stay in Paris and shows his adaptation and dramatic heightening of the color-divisionism of Monet.

Toward the end of his life, van Gogh settled in southern France. Here his painting reached torrential volume and intensity. Subject to intermittent insanity, he committed himself to an asylum in Saint Rémy but continued to paint during his lucid intervals. Out of the asylum, he moved to a village near Paris, where he committed suicide at the age of thirty-seven.

Even before he went to southern France, Paris had partly liberated van Gogh from the somber colors of his early works. The brilliant colors and sunlight of the south released whatever coloristic inhibitions remained. The new intensity of color is exemplified even

18-23 Vincent van Gogh, *Self-Portrait*, 1887. Oil on canvas, 17″ × 15″. Collection Vincent van Gogh National Museum, Amsterdam.

18-24 Vincent van Gogh, *The Night Café*, 1888. Oil on canvas, 28″ × 35″. Yale University Art Gallery, New Haven, Connecticut (Bequest of Stephen Carlton Clark, B.A. 1903.)

in indoor scenes such as *The Night Café* (fig. 18-24). Here the predominant impression is of a garish and threatening claustrophobia. Van Gogh wrote of the "Japanese gaity" of this interior, but also of "the atmosphere like the devil's furnace, of pale sulphur." The color, he freely admitted to his brother Théo, was "not locally true from the point of view of the delusive realist," but it did suggest the "emotion of an ardent temperament." "I have tried," he said, "to express the idea that the café is a place where one can ruin himself, go mad, or commit a crime."

The emphases on color, emotion, and symbolic meaning characterize all of van Gogh's typical late production. These emphases, of course, do not exclude other ingredients, such as the vigorous outlines in *Night Café*. However, van Gogh was most concerned with expressing his emotions. Although he could hardly have been indifferent to formal structure, his feelings were far more important. Both van Gogh and Gauguin helped turn many European painters away from predominantly optical or formal problems, and toward a style eventually called Expressionism.

THE SCULPTURE OF RODIN

In the meantime a less disturbing but no less original vision was being developed by the sculptor Auguste Rodin (1840–1917). Rodin did not view himself as an innovative rebel, but rather as the rediscoverer and reviver of sculpture's heroic past, before Classicism had destroyed all freedom and vigor in nineteenth-century creative expression. Above all, he idolized Donatello and Michelangelo. In addition to Michelangelo's sheer technical prowess, Rodin was deeply moved by his spirit. "If we seek the spiritual significance of Michelangelo," he wrote, "we shall find that his sculpture expressed restless energy, the will to act without the hope of success, the martyrdom of the creature tormented by unrealizable aspirations." His own sculpture would have much the same sort of spiritual content.

Two examples of Rodin's sculpture will show something of his inspiration from the past and his personal insight as well. (His work, incidentally, is remarkably accessible to direct study, since the many realizations of his most popular works are generously scattered across Europe and America. Rodin was primarily a modeler in clay, and the execution of nearly all his works in bronze or marble was left to others, sometimes with minor retouching by the master; some, indeed, were made after his death. One casting is about as much, or as little, "by" Rodin as another.) His first famous work, *The Age of Bronze* (fig. 18-25), is an especially realistic proclamation against coldly Classicist traditionalism. When it was exhibited in Brussels and Paris, Rodin was charged with imposture—with casting in bronze from plaster that had directly encased the living model. Many found the pose intolerable; nothing so unorthodox had been seen in decades, or

18-25 Auguste Rodin, *The Age of Bronze*, 1876–77. Bronze, 71″ high. Musée Rodin, Paris.

even centuries. Unhelpfully, Rodin gave the statue several different titles, including *The Man Who Awakens to Nature*. Certainly some sort of interior, spiritual drama is suggested by the strong gestures of the figure and the tentative step forward. In a day when the repertory of allowable sculptural moods and postures was restricted, and when sculptural nudes were supposed to look like Greek deities, *The Age of Bronze* was an eye-opener indeed.

The fame of this work helped get Rodin several vital commissions, and his unconventional execution of some of them aroused violent controversy and scandal. *The Burghers of Calais* (fig. 18-26), for instance, was commissioned by the municipality of Calais to commemorate a celebrated act of heroism during the

Hundred Years' War with England. In 1347 the English king had demanded that six of Calais's leading citizens be turned over to him for execution, as the price for raising a year's siege and ending hostilities. In Rodin's bronze the six volunteers proceed courageously toward the English camp, halters around their necks; they do not know that in fact their lives will be spared. The figures are firmly individualized, both bodily and spiritually, in their different ages and varying reactions to their destiny. There are gestures of deepest gloom and of proudest defiance, yet all six men advance together to meet their fate.

Unfortunately this was not at all what Calais's burghers of the 1880s had in mind. One letter to Rodin from the monument committee protested: "We did not visualize our glorious fellow citizens proceeding to the king of England's camp in this way; their dejected attitudes offend our religion." Indeed, the shock was almost as great as when the committee had learned that all six burghers were to be included, not just their wealthy and respected elder leader and perhaps a smaller allegorical figure or so, in the manner of all proper civic statuary of the time. Although Rodin's powerful group was finished, after successive battles, in 1888, it was not erected in Calais until 1895—and then was not put unfenced on a ground-level slab, as Rodin wished (to "allow the public to penetrate to the heart of the subject"), but on the traditional high pedestal surrounded by an elegant little iron railing.

Rodin expressed himself almost exclusively through the human body. Many of the more advanced twentieth-century sculptors would soon adopt other approaches. At the same time that the general public at last was catching up with Rodin, avant-garde criticism grew more and more skeptical of his worth. It took courage to admit a passion for Rodin in the 1930s, and even today many people dislike the literary, naively sentimental side of Rodin. Nonetheless, his career marked a most extraordinary renewal in the history of sculpture and influenced even those later sculptors who professed to have superseded him.

EVOLUTION AND REVOLUTION IN MUSIC

The general course taken by music in the period from 1870 to 1905 was more evolutionary than revolutionary—a situation appropriate for a realm in which

18-26 Auguste Rodin, *The Burghers of Calais*, 1886. Bronze, 82½″ × 95″ × 78″. Hirshhorn Museum and Sculpture Garden, Smithsonian Institution, Washington, D.C.

historical research was being pursued with scholarly devotion and enthusiasm. Even the most prestigious composer of the age, Johannes Brahms, was a historical musicologist who found time to prepare scholarly editions of "old" music.

In the actual practice of music—its composition and performance—most changes came only gradually, as a process of growth and refinement. Key and valve mechanisms for woodwinds and brass were perfected, but no major new instruments appeared. Symphony orchestras continued to increase in size until the turn of the century, and greater technical demands were made on the players by such composer-conductors as Strauss and Mahler. Musical interpretation, by instrumentalists and conductors as well as vocalists, was likely to be freely expressive to an extent that the next century would consider offensive. Already, however, the first symptoms of reaction were discernible: a few critics were calling for a more rigorous approach, and a few conductors, such as Mahler, made an honest effort to recreate the spirit and performance style of the ear-

lier composers whose works they played. In his own compositions Mahler went to unprecedented lengths in formulating precise verbal directions to performers, partly in the hope of circumventing undesirable interpretations of his compositions.

Only two general trends within the predominantly conservative music of the period need be noted here. The first was the conscious development of national schools of composition, paralleling the nationalism in contemporary political life. For example, a distinctive Russian school arose—although such composers as Tchaikovsky and Rachmaninoff were fully able to forswear Russian flavor when they wanted to and write in the most international manner. Secondly, there was a strengthening of the earlier Romantic trend away from conventional musical forms, such as the symphony or the sonata, toward freer forms in emotional or literarily suggestive contexts. In orchestral music the symphonic poems of Franz Liszt had most effectively shown the way; his most distinguished follower would be Richard Strauss.

Brahms and Mahler

By and large, composers between 1870 and 1905, with the exception of Claude Debussy, followed paths that had already been at least roughly mapped. Such was certainly the case with Johannes Brahms (1833–97), who was sufficiently conventional to be accepted among music's immortals during his own lifetime. In almost all musical forms except opera Brahms produced works with an air of Classic finality. Without rejecting the technical advances of his century up to Wagner, Brahms tended strongly toward Classical discipline and balance in his music. Romantic expression, to be sure, was not lacking in Brahms—it can be observed at its most succinct in many *lieder* of great beauty and at full length in much of the monumental Second Piano Concerto, in B-flat major—but it was generally kept well under control in his larger works.

Unlike Brahms, Gustav Mahler (1860–1911) was not recognized as one of the masters until many years after his death. In posthumous reputation, Mahler's destiny seems more tightly bound than most to the fate of the Romantic temper in general—for he was one of the most thorough Romantics in history. Behind the ascetic features modeled by Auguste Rodin (fig. 18-27) there burned an idealistic, passionate, anguished soul— a soul that expressed itself with complete candor in his music. The anti-Romantic mind finds Mahler's music frequently pompous, oversubjective, and downright embarrassing; his critics tire of what they consider his incessant whining. Truly Mahler's world, like Wagner's, is not for everybody.

Whatever we think of Mahler as thinker or prophet, his music possesses merits that are many and impressive. His instrumental writing is superbly crafted, and his orchestrations highly imaginative. Mahler's reputation for colossal orchestration is founded on exceptional instances; he prized his effects too highly to bury them in massive sounds. His orchestration, in fact, is usually extraordinarily clean and spare. Length is another matter; traditional formal succinctness is subordinate, in Mahler, to expressive fullness.

Among Mahler's symphonies, the Fourth, in G major, is probably the most accessible, if somewhat less lengthy and more cheerful than most. Completed in 1900, its inspiration seems to have been a setting he had made of an old German folk song from the early-nineteenth-century collection called *The Youth's Magic*

18-27 Auguste Rodin, *Gustav Mahler*, 1909. Bronze, 14″ high. Musée Rodin, Paris.

Horn. He had expected to use this as the seventh movement of his enormous Third Symphony, but instead it became the fourth and last movement of the G major Symphony and a source of thematic inspiration for the other movements. Vocal parts were often used by Mahler in his symphonic movements; their verbalizations are a prime source of our knowledge of the ideas the composer wanted to express. In the Fourth Symphony the soprano soloist presents a naive, whimsical child's-eye view of heavenly blessedness. Appropriately, then, the frequent impassioned anguish of much of Mahler's other writing is scaled down here to a gentler yearning and to a sort of ironic playfulness.

Jingling sleigh bells, flutes, and clarinets set the mood as the first movement begins. The strings enter quickly to present the jaunty first theme with *pizzicato* (plucked-string) accompaniment. Soon several other themes are introduced. Tempos and moods change markedly and in rather quick succession, although avoiding extremes. The motif of jingling sleigh bells will reappear in the last movement, and intimations of that movement's naive paradise are already heard in the first movement. The second movement is most memorable for its strange violin solo, played "as if by a street fiddle" on a violin tuned a full tone higher than normal. A notebook of Mahler's includes a reference to a legendary fiddler who draws folk on to the other world. Perhaps then this fiddler is Death himself—although the effect is more whimsical than grim.

The third, slow movement is labeled "restful," even with its several vigorous moments; the generally subdued and poignant mood is set in the flowing upper-string parts at the beginning, over a characteristic pizzicato bass line. The first two climaxes accompany a passionate melodic line in the strings, surging upward with powerful yearning—an archetypical Mahlerian theme. Then in the last movement, labeled "peaceful," comes the child's vision of paradise; the soloist, Mahler directs, must sing with "childish and serene expressiveness, without any intimation of parody." The scene described, as if by a small angel, is of merry skipping and dancing, and especially of feasting. Saint Cecilia, patroness of music, leads the heavenly musicians, whose "angelic voices," the soloist concludes, "refresh all our senses so that everything wakens in joy." The work ends not with an orchestral bang but with a mysterious stillness.

Richard Strauss

Among Mahler's symphonies, the Fourth was apparently the favorite of another celebrated conductor-composer at the turn of the century, Richard Strauss (1864–1949)—perhaps because it was the least heaven-storming of all. Strauss customarily remained very much at ease in the world, and although he and Mahler respected each other, their differences in temperament made for a certain coolness and wariness in their personal relations.

Although Strauss idolized Mozart ("the most sublime of all composers") and could on occasion recapture much of his spirit, the more obvious influences on the works of his youth were Berlioz, Liszt, and Wagner. These three had often leaned toward literary "programs," and Berlioz and Wagner had also been masters of orchestration. Strauss, of course, shared this inheritance with Mahler. However, where Mahler's sources of inspiration were spiritual, Strauss's were earthly, and where Mahler's orchestration usually preserved its clarity, Strauss's complexities could inadvertently create muddy textures or deliberately evoke a scene of extreme confusion.

Till Eulenspiegel's Merry Pranks, composed in 1895, is a compendium of marvelous orchestral effects and a thoroughly enjoyable piece of entertainment. It is one of a series of symphonic or tone poems based on Liszt's precedent. "New ideas," Strauss once wrote, "must search for new forms," and the form he used here came from an old German story. Till Eulenspiegel was a figure in a medieval legend—a prankster forever triumphant against the pomposities of his day, who was finally permitted to die in his own bed. As a dramatic touch, Strauss has Till hanged for blasphemy, but the composer's fundamental sympathies, like ours, are surely meant to be on the side of the lovable rogue.

A brief, relaxed, "once-upon-a-time" prelude in the violins leads to Till's own bouncy introductory theme, first on solo French horn and building to an orchestral climax. Immediately thereafter comes Till's second theme: an impudent, nose-thumbing gesture played by the clarinet. The themes are then developed, with no specific "pranks" indicated by the composer. This section ends with Till riding wildly on horseback through the marketplace, upsetting pots and pans to right and left, in splendid orchestral confusion. Shortly violas and bassoons introduce Till's next adventure: "Dressed as a priest," Strauss wrote, "he oozes unction and morality." When preaching, though, "he is seized with a horrid premonition as to the outcome of his mockery of religion"; muted violins and brass here play spookish triplets. Soon, however, a nonchalant theme intervenes, for Till is off to seek love. After still further adventures he finds himself in grave trouble; he is tried and learns he must go to the scaffold. Amidst threatening drum rolls are heard Till's frightened squeaks (on the clarinet)—and then, with premonition becoming reality, comes the hanging, represented by an abrupt unison descent of winds and brass, fortissimo. Till's soul escapes his body into the heavens, and a "once-upon-a-time" epilogue reminds us that it has been, after all, only a story.

A distinguished and disgruntled critic called *Till* "a veritable world's fair of sound effects." The great Debussy noted good-naturedly that it "might almost be called 'an hour of music in a lunatic asylum'" but admitted that it was a work of genius nonetheless. Undoubtedly, tone poems such as *Till* offered an option to the post-Brahmsian, post-Mahlerian age, when the old forms of symphony, concerto, and sonata seemed outmoded to many.

Debussy

With Claude Debussy (1862–1918) we enter a quite different world. According to all accounts, Debussy's physical and psychological person was a remarkably close model for his music (fig. 18-28). He had, for a Frenchman, an exotic swarthiness; after early youth he became rather plump and soft. His tastes were refined, his gestures affectedly elegant. Although he could be lively and ironically witty, his appearance and movements most typically suggested a relaxed sensuality and feline subtlety.

The main literary influence on Debussy was undoubtedly Symbolism; he absorbed much of its doctrine from Verlaine and Mallarmé themselves, at cafés and in literary "evenings." In music the most powerful influence was Wagner, even after Debussy had unfurled the banner of "French music" to lead the battle against ponderous Germanic expression. Still, Debussy kept his musical and spiritual independence to a remarkable degree, and as a musical journalist he criticized vehemently all worship of past composers. A youthful retort to an official at the Paris Conservatory, where he was studying, remained typical: when asked what rule of harmony he followed in his compositions, he replied proudly, "My own pleasure."

Debussy not only assaulted traditional harmony but then turned on tonality itself, with its built-in linear, progressional emphases. His attack on tonality was revolutionary, but his notions of harmony were part of a long liberalizing trend in music history. Since the Renaissance, the Western world's tolerance for harmonic combinations previously considered dissonant had grown, while at the same time the diatonic scales were being stretched out of shape by more and more *accidentals,* which raised or lowered single notes in the normal sequences by half-steps. As used by Wagner, these accidentals proved particularly uncomfortable to most ears—but ears did adjust, all in all, fairly rapidly. Wagner's degree of *chromaticism* (musical progression by half-tones), often involving frequent key changes, had been absorbed by Mahler and Strauss, and by most of their listeners, at century's end. But there still remained in this music, despite the initial doubts of Wagner's audiences, a feeling of tonal focus and direction, or temporal expectation, since many combinations of tones seemed unstable and destined to give way to stable combinations, or natural points of rest.

18-28 Claude Debussy *(standing)* and Igor Stravinsky in 1912.

Even though chromatic alterations might sometimes deceive one's specific momentary expectations, one always could feel assured that a musical sequence would proceed fairly promptly to a resting point.

Debussy's achievement was the partial, but very critical, loosening of this conventional *tonality* (sense of musical focus and direction). To be sure, his use of chromaticism is modest compared with that of Wagner and his followers. He did, however, accept more and more dissonances and extended considerably the available choice of harmonic resting points. Far more fundamentally, he often attacked the very notion of directional motion toward resting points in music. Sometimes he did this by abandoning the diatonic system altogether, at least momentarily—a radical approach indeed. This could mean turning to the old modes, from the time before history sorted out the diatonic scales. Or it could mean the use of the *whole-tone scale,* with its progression by equal steps, six notes to the octave—or of the *pentatonic* or *five-note scale,* most commonly construed as a scale like that playable on five consecutive black keys of a piano. In the whole-tone scale, the traditionally "restful" chords (that is, the common *triads,* with root note and the third and fifth above it) simply did not exist—and in general the effect of pentatonic and whole-tone scales was highly unsettling to traditionally oriented Western ears.

We should note, however, that Debussy used these unusual scales (inspired by Oriental and primitive music) less than he is popularly thought to have, and that even within a fairly diatonic framework he could confound the traditional directional sense of movement. Before Debussy, certain chordal transitions had come to seem logical or natural, and hence expectable. Debussy frequently employed the traditional directional logic—but he also often violated it. In effect, now, one chord could be followed by any other chord; the accepted directionality was replaced by the fleeting instinct of the composer. The harmonic, strictly aural appeal of each chord in itself was often what interested Debussy. Combining this new approach with traditional expression, he apparently believed, would prevent total chaos, while creating provocative ambiguities.

Predictably, Debussy's music opened stimulating new vistas for some of his contemporaries and left others hopelessly adrift in the musical seas. Certainly far fewer would have been converted to Debussy's new insights if he had not implemented them skillfully through rhythmic excitement and interesting variations in tone color. His skill is exemplified in his early orchestral work, *Prelude to the Afternoon of a Faun* (1892–94).

This work was inspired by Mallarmé's poem "L'Après-midi d'un Faune." The scene presented in these sensual, symbolic verses is of a faun—a mythological creature, part goat but mainly a man—awakening in the sunlit woods and recalling a vision of passionate sensuality.

Debussy's tone poem delightfully mirrors the mood and general outline of Mallarmé's poem. A solo flute immediately establishes the mood of sensuous languor in the opening passage (fig. 18-29): Harp *glissandos,* or sliding scales, and tremulous effects in the string section convey an impression of the shimmering haze through which the faun's vision is filtered. The music surges and subsides with the faun's passion, present and recollected. Traditional thematic development in the work is less crucial than are changes of orchestral color and the various impressionistic accompaniments to the themes. All of this contributes more than any harmonic or tonal ambiguities to the seemingly directionless flux of the music.

As in the paintings of Monet, Debussy's Impressionism was a matter of suggestion rather than realistic description or formal patterning. However, with his frequent literary inspiration Debussy was also a Symbolist. In fact, here in one composer we find a mingling of Impressionism and Symbolism, two of the leading schools that split the ranks of avant-garde painters in the late nineteenth century. Debussy embodied not one but two general cultural revolutions, while at the same time he revolutionized the technical language of music.

Debussy's late piano works are particularly apt illustrations not only of his general Impressionism and Symbolism but also of his formal musical revolution. A good example is *La Cathédrale Engloutie* (*The Sunken Cathedral*) from his first book of preludes (1910). The work embodies Debussy's sheer delight in isolated musical moments and a restless flux that rejects directional tonality.

The Sunken Cathedral evokes the Breton legend of the cathedral of Ys, engulfed by the sea as a punishment for the impiety of its people but briefly rising out of the waves at sunrise. There are modal and pentatonic elements and more than a suggestion of medieval plainchant. There are "gutted," or "hollow," chords (which omit the third); there are passages of medieval parallel organum, employing octaves and fourths—especially apparent in the opening measures. Tolling bells as well as medieval song are suggested, both be-

18-29 Claude Debussy, *Prelude to the Afternoon of a Faun* opening passage, for flute.

neath and above the sea; the sonorous central section, preceded and followed by rippling figures, suggests the surging of the cathedral out of the waves into the sun-light. Truly these mysterious pages, like so many others from Debussy's pen, mark the emergence of a remark-able new musical world.

Recommended Reading

Barrielle, Jean-François. *The Life and Work of Vincent van Gogh* (1984). Good coverage, brilliant illustrations.

Blunden, Maria and Godfrey, et al. *Impressionists and Impressionism* (1970). Handsome picture book and history.

Boudaille, Georges. *Gauguin* (1964). Good, well-illustrated survey of life and work.

Bullard, E. John. *Mary Cassatt, Oils and Pastels* (1972). Long essay, and illustrations with substantial notes.

Champigneulle, Bernard. *Rodin* (1967). Very good introduction, good illustrations.

Flexner, James Thomas. *The World of Winslow Homer 1836–1910* (1966). Life and times, well-illustrated.

Frenzel, Ivo. *Friedrich Nietzsche* (1967). Brief, illustrated biography.

Hendricks, Gordon. *The Life and Work of Thomas Eakins* (1974). Thorough study, well-illustrated.

Hirschfeld, Charles, and Edgar E. Knoebel, eds. *The Modern World* (1980). Sizable excerpts of the writings of Pope Leo XIII, Nietzsche, Dostoevsky, and others.

Isaacson, Joel. *Observation and Reflection: Claude Monet* (1978). Long essay with illustrations and detailed notes.

Jefferson, Alan. *Richard Strauss* (1975). A picture book and biography.

Joll, James. *Europe since 1870* (1973). General political, economic, social, and cultural history.

Jones, Howard Mumford. *The Age of Energy: Varieties of American Experience 1865–1915* (1971). Fine topical history, mainly social and intellectual.

Lockspeiser, Edward. *Debussy* (1980). Biography and analysis of his works.

Maupassant, Guy de. *Guy de Maupassant's Short Stories*, trans. by Marjorie Laurie (1934). Good selection and translation.

Murphy, Richard W. *The World of Cézanne 1839–1906* (1968). Introduction to life and times, well-illustrated.

Nietzsche, Friedrich. *The Philosophy of Nietzsche* (1954). Five major works in translation, including *Beyond Good and Evil* and *Thus Spake Zarathustra*.

Pierrot, Jean. *The Decadent Imagination 1800–1900* (1982). Good study of literature.

Rewald, John. *Post-Impressionism, from Van Gogh to Gauguin* (1978). Fine, thorough study.

Rich, Daniel Catton. *Edgar-Hilaire-Germain Degas* (1985). Handsome picture book with comments and essay.

Rouart, Denis. *Renoir* (1985). Fine introduction, handsomely illustrated.

Rudorff, Raymond. *Belle Epoque: Paris in the Nineties* (1972). Interesting social and cultural history.

Seckerson, Edward. *Mahler, His Life and Times* (1982). Fine introduction, well-illustrated.

Tannenbaum, Edward R. *1900: The Generation before the Great War* (1976). Illustrated social and economic survey.

19 Modernism: 1905–1945

In the visual arts, the period from 1905 to 1945 extends from the beginnings of Modernism, centered on Paris, to the transformations that Modernism underwent upon shifting its focus to New York after World War II. In the history of power politics, these forty years saw intensifying rivalries for world domination and ideological supremacy. About 1905 the heated struggle among the great powers for economic and political advantage led to the solidification of hostile military alliances and then, a decade later, to the terrifying First World War (1914–18). But once again, after World War I, uncontrollable national rivalries developed, and these were eventually rendered all the more urgent by the frightening economic depression that began in 1929. Only two decades after the Treaty of Versailles (1919), a second and no less tragic war erupted (1939–45). Except for a briefly hopeful period in the 1920s, and except for the humane idealism struggling for survival and effectiveness throughout these years in all nations, the four decades after 1905 were arguably the most horrifyingly brutal in Western history.

These decades were all the more brutal and tragic in contrast to the glowing promise with which the century began and the revival of hopes after Versailles. Never had such material prosperity, even for the masses, been dreamed of; never had the women's movement been so well organized and so successful in achieving voting and other political rights; never had science revealed such wonders, or the people been so well equipped by mass education to appreciate their world and to develop and govern themselves. Yet by the outbreak of World War II,

CHRONOLOGY

HISTORY		THE ARTS	
		1856–1939	Freud
		1866–1944	Kandinsky
1870–1940	Third Republic in France	1869–1954	Matisse
1871–1918	German Empire	1869–1959	Frank Lloyd Wright
		1872–1944	Mondrian
		1874–1946	Gertrude Stein
		1874–1951	Schoenberg
		1874–1954	Charles Ives
1878	Congress of Berlin: German-Austrian alliance	1876–1957	Brancusi
1880–1914	European imperialism (expansion overseas)	1881–1973	Picasso
1882	Triple Alliance (Germany, Austria, Italy)	1882–1971	Stravinsky
		1883–1955	Ortega y Gasset
		1887–1965	Duchamp and Le Corbusier
		1887–1985	Chagall
1888–1918	William II emperor of Germany	1887–1986	Georgia O'Keeffe
1894	Franco-Russian alliance	1888–1965	T. S. Eliot
		1893–1983	Miró
		1898–1937	George Gershwin
		1898–1986	Henry Moore
		1899	Freud's *The Interpretation of Dreams*
1901–10	Edward VII king of England	1900–71	Louis Armstrong
		1900–	Aaron Copland
1905	revolution in Russia: the empire accepts a Duma (legislative body)	1904–	Dalí
		1905	Matisse's *The Green Stripe*
		1905	Einstein's relativity theory
1907	Triple Entente (Great Britain, France, Russia)	1907	Picasso's *Les Demoiselles d'Avignon*
		1908–9	Matisse's *Harmony in Red*
		1909	Wright's Robie House, Chicago
1910–36	George V king of England	1909	Schoenberg's *Erwartung*
		c. 1910	maturation of Picasso and Braque's Cubist phase
		1911–12	Stravinsky's *Rite of Spring*
		1912	Kandinsky's *Concerning the Spiritual in Art*
		1913	Armory Show, New York
		1913	Gilbert's Woolworth Building, New York
		1913	Kirchner's *The Street*
1914–18	First World War (Germany, Austria-Hungary, and Turkey vs. France, Great Britain, Italy, and United States)		
		1915–23	Duchamp's *The Bride Stripped Bare by Her Bachelors, Even*

(continued)

HISTORY	
1916–22	Lloyd George prime minister of Great Britain
1917	two Russian revolutions (tsar overthrown, Bolsheviks take over)
1917–24	Lenin ruling Russia
1919	Peace of Paris, including Treaty of Versailles (Allies with Germany)
1922	official establishment of the U.S.S.R. (Soviet Union)
1922–43	Mussolini, Fascist dictator in Italy
1927–53	Stalin undisputed ruler of Soviet Union
1929	beginning of Great Depression (through 1930s)
1931	revolution in Spain, establishment of a republic
1931–40	National Government in Great Britain
1933–45	Hitler, Nazi dictator of Germany
1933–45	Franklin D. Roosevelt president of the U.S.
1936	Edward VIII king of England
1936	German-Italian alliance
1936–39	civil war in Spain
1936–52	George VI king of England
1939	Nazi-Soviet pact
1939–45	Second World War (Germany, Italy, and Japan vs. France, Great Britain, United States, and Soviet Union)
1940	fall of France
1940–45	Winston Churchill, British prime minister
1941	German invasion of U.S.S.R.; Japanese bombing of Pearl Harbor
1944	Allied invasion of Europe
1945	German surrender; first atomic bomb, Japanese surrender

THE ARTS	
1916–22	Dadaism
1917	Eliot's "The Love Song of J. Alfred Prufrock"
1918–19	Beckmann's *The Night*
1919	Léger's *The City*
1921	Mondrian's *Composition in Yellow, Red, Blue, and Black*
1922	Eliot's "The Waste Land"
1924	Breton's *Manifesto of Surrealism*
1924–25	Miró's *Harlequin's Carnival*
1925	Brancusi's *Bird in Space*
1925–26	the Dessau Bauhaus built
1926–27	Stravinsky's *Oedipus Rex*
1928	Louis Armstrong and Earl Hines's "Weather Bird"
1928	Gershwin's *An American in Paris*
1928–30	Le Corbusier's Villa Savoye
1932	Ortega y Gasset's *Revolt of the Masses* published in English
1934–36	Schoenberg's Violin Concerto
1936	Dalí's *Soft Construction with Boiled Beans*
1936	Wright's Kaufmann House ("Falling Water")
1937	Nazi exhibit of "Degenerate Art" in Munich; Picasso's *Guernica*
1942–43	Gabo's *Linear Construction, Variation*

EUROPE IN 1923

too many hopes had turned to ashes—as had, very literally, so many cities and other monuments of civilization by war's end. Even in peacetime, prosperity had led to gross materialism and the sufferings of the Great Depression. *Demagoguery*—the gaining of political influence through appeals to social discontent—gained ground almost everywhere, especially in Germany, Italy, and the Soviet Union. These three totalitarian states sought total control over their peoples, in mind as in body.

The dictatorships pressed their goals more ruthlessly than the democracies pushed their own economic and social ideals. The Soviet Union, end product of Lenin's Communist revolution of 1917 and Stalin's later consolidation, preached the brotherhood of man and the crushing of "capitalist imperialism." Nazi Germany, born of national resent-

ments and the fevered racism of Adolf Hitler, demanded the reversal of the Treaty of Versailles. Fascist Italy, under Benito Mussolini, proclaimed the advent of national pride and efficiency. Soviet ideals, however, were blackened by the killing of countless human beings and the crushing of political and spiritual freedom. Hitler's crimes equaled Stalin's and were founded on goals that often were petty and vicious. Mussolini and Hitler were ultimately defeated in the war, and their philosophies discredited. Democracy survived in such countries as the United States and Great Britain, where economic and social reforms had made it possible to avoid political extremes and where the idealism and eloquence of Franklin D. Roosevelt and Winston Churchill stirred millions and gave hope for the future.

AN AGE OF NEW CHALLENGES

At their worst, the four decades after 1905 were unspeakable in their shame and horror; at their best they were vividly, tantalizingly vibrant. The ugliness and brutality and the hope, adventure, and excitement were all mirrored in the visual arts and the music of the age as well as in its thought and literature. This period saw marvels of thought and artistry that place it among the most brilliant in the history of the Western world.

Science and the Written Word

Inevitably many writers of this period considered escapism from wars and from pressing social and economic problems to be indecent and cruel. Like their counterparts in the visual arts, they attempted to analyze their civilization and often turned to gestures of rejection and disgust. The American-born poet T. S. Eliot (1888–1965), a naturalized British citizen, wrote of the modern "waste land" (1922) of spiritual emptiness and obscene frivolity. Before that, in 1917, he had offered the public his vision of the modern individual's insignificance and lack of focus in "The Love Song of J. Alfred Prufrock." Its subject had

> . . . time yet for a hundred indecisions,
> And for a hundred visions and revisions,
> Before the taking of a toast and tea.

Prufrock admitted that he had "measured out [his] life with coffee spoons." Human existence is seen as negative, blurred, and meaningless.

A more specific, down-to-earth portrayal of modern man, mediocre and utterly swallowed up in the multitude, came from the pen of a British citizen turned American, W. H. Auden (1907–73), who in 1940 imagined ironically a monument to "The Unknown Citizen" of the day: a man with all the latest gadgets and pat opinions, and even the correct number of children for the time—five. The poem concludes:

> Was he free? Was he happy? The question is absurd:
> Had anything been wrong, we should certainly have heard.

That such views of modern life were held by more than just a smart set of Anglo-Americans was demonstrated by the Spanish philosopher José Ortega y Gas-

set (1883–1955), whose *The Revolt of the Masses* was published in English in 1932. Ortega's European "mass man" could be found amid all social classes; he was the man who drifted along yet exhibited primitiveness, violence, and an utter incomprehension of the humane, tolerant bases of Western civilization. His opposite was the "noble" man who stood for excellence and worthwhile tradition despite threats of submergence in a tide of mediocrity. Many thinking men and women of the period before 1945 shared Ortega's fears—and many were willing to accept Oswald Spengler's diagnosis of "the decline of the West" in spite of his fuzzy intuitionism and irrationalism.

The decades after 1905 indeed saw a mighty upsurge of irrationalism in virtually all types of writing. Often it was linked with opposition to political and social liberalism. From all quarters came complaints that the nineteenth-century liberal experiment was bankrupt, since it not only led to twentieth-century catastrophe but rested fundamentally on too much optimism concerning human capacities for rational thought. This view was given powerful support, however unintentionally, by the Viennese physician Sigmund Freud (1856–1939). Although he cautiously approved of a modest liberation of human instincts, Freud (fig. 19-1) was dismayed by the dark subconscious world of repressed desire and guilt. He preached the sublimation of desire into socially beneficial channels yet recognized the essentially precarious condition of a civilization based on the repression of powerful urges. What most people noted, though, was Freud's unveiling of the world of instinct, especially sexual instinct; everybody, it was often proclaimed in the 1920s, shared this instinct and might as well enjoy it.

Much of the therapeutic method of psychoanalysis Freud developed for treating psychotic disorders, as well as much of the underlying Freudian theory of unconscious instincts and repressions (including their role in dreams and "Freudian slips") has been questioned or modified since Freud's day. Continuous change and modification has become, after all, a recognized feature of scientific investigation in the last century. What is most important about Freud's work for our purposes is its impact on its own time. Above all, the ideas of Freud and such other psychoanalytic theorists as Carl Gustav Jung—with his doctrine of a myth-making but admirably creative "collective unconscious"—were used to support irrationalism in such disparate realms as politics and religion. The French

19-1 Sigmund Freud.

philosopher Henri Bergson (1859–1941) also contributed powerfully to legitimizing a romantic admiration for intuitive understanding. We must remember, however, that neither liberalism nor rationalism—nor even modest historical optimism—had died before 1945.

The prestige of science remained enormous—and most scientists advocated cautious empirical and rational investigation or, alternatively, an apolitical, coldly efficient technocratic society. A few, such as the physicist Albert Einstein, stood up unequivocally for the long-range primacy of liberal, humane goals, as opposed to the dangers of social unconcern within science and technology. Science, especially Einsteinian physics and Freudian psychology, had brought immense and terrifying complexities and ambiguities to bear on the human condition—but by no means did everybody find these to be valid excuses for a "flight from freedom" to totalitarianism, or for a flight to the comforts of religion or an escapist art and literature.

As for religion, a good number of scientists and philosophers—but by no means all—believed modern science marked the end of traditional God-oriented religion. Such a faith, according to Freud, is a childlike illusion. This was also the reaction of two British thinkers, philosopher Bertrand Russell and biologist Julian Huxley. Both Russell and Huxley wrote, rather, with passionate earnestness and presumably hardheaded optimism concerning the human potential of rational thought without religious support. Man is not yet done for, said Russell, if he can stem the tide of unreason on all fronts. The only remedy for current scientific inadequacies, said Huxley, is more science—and if reason and science never reveal all the answers, we must remind ourselves that "to become truly adult, we must learn to bear the burden of incertitude."

The traditional religions, however, were certainly not prepared to admit that their teachings were no longer true or relevant. One of the staunchest defenders of Christianity up to and beyond 1945 was the American thinker Reinhold Niebuhr (1892–1971), who was not only a Christian theologian but a writer on countless political, social, and economic issues. The brutalities of Nazism, not to mention the darker side of human experience everywhere, amply demonstrated for him that optimistic, secular rationalism hardly yielded a proper reading of the human condition. Human beings, Niebuhr asserted, need not a wishful faith in the goodness of human nature but rather a "tragic sense of life" that reveals the limits of all historical, earthly striving.

The clash and interaction of rational-liberal ideals with traditional Christianity, and also with Romantic irrationalism or various types of elitism, pervaded nearly all types of creative writing in the 1905–45 period. However, the amazing new, quasi-literary entertainment form, the motion picture, generally remained peripheral to the deepest issues of the time; film producers and directors usually avoided all but the least controversial subjects and messages and provided the public far less food for thought than escapist diversion. This generalization does not deny the frequent cinematic quest for expressive artistry, nor does it imply that the diversion offered by a Charlie Chaplin was blind to the many challenges and profound pathos of the human condition.

Art and Artists

While the movies were becoming an art form, the more conventional arts also were experimenting widely, often in conjunction with a crusading social and political awareness—a significant change of emphasis from the noninvolvement of the pre-1905 decades. Indeed, both the crusading and the experimentation only accentuated nineteenth-century trends toward public incomprehension and harassment of the arts, and the consequent isolation and alienation of artists from the mainstream of society. This situation prevailed wherever avant-garde art struggled for expression, wherever visual art and music were moving farthest from the familiar styles of the past. In totalitarian Europe the problem received a total solution of sorts: "radical" art was effectively banned. In the Soviet Union after the early twenties, art that did not conform to mass taste was held to be ridiculous and destructive. In Germany, attacks on modern art became common immediately after the 1933 National Socialist takeover and reached a climax of vicious defamation in the notorious 1937 Munich exhibition of "Degenerate Art"—an exhibition that explicitly ridiculed all the advanced German art of the time. Under the Nazis, artists were driven into exile, and thousands of modern museum works were confiscated for later sale abroad or for destruction.

The liberal West at least would allow time and a free market to dispose as they would of the new art. Of all cities, Paris still seemed most congenial to the tolerant philosophy of live-and-let-live. When its relative prewar cordiality toward artists of all persuasions was revived and broadened in the twenties and thirties, the French capital became even more of a magnet for artists and ideological refugees of the Western world. The sculptor Brancusi and the painter Picasso had arrived from Rumania and Spain, respectively, long before World War I; after the war there came the Dutch painter Mondrian and massive waves of Russian and German exiles. Musicians also came to Paris. The Russian composer Stravinsky had lived there before the war and settled in France, for two decades, in 1920; his fellow countryman Prokofiev, too, was there, until he finally returned to the Soviet Union in the thirties.

Many Americans also came to Paris after 1918 and more or less settled in that city. The two young composers Aaron Copland and Virgil Thomson studied in Paris in the twenties, and Thomson was an expatriate for many years. One of his most stimulating older friends was the American author Gertrude Stein (1874–1946), who would eventually furnish librettos for two of his operas, and who had long before become one of the earliest patrons of those two patriarchs-to-be of twentieth-century art, Henri Matisse and Pablo Pi-

casso (fig. 19-2). Stein's eccentric yet insightful prose was often compared to the fractured dislocations of the Cubist art that caused an immense stir in Paris before World War I.

The Arts in America

Whereas Gertrude Stein had settled permanently in France, most of her literary compatriots there eventually went home. The enormous, continuous party that was Paris—for a few fortunate and lively expatriates and exiles—at last was over, or simply fizzled out, in the 1930s. The Depression had reached Europe, and the world was changing. For many sensitive and creative souls, the social imperatives of the 1930s were replacing the search of the 1920s for freedom and individualism. Black American authors, for example, were being read by other blacks and by a few members of the white community. Among these authors was Langston Hughes (1902–67), who wrote bitterly of the deferred dreams of blacks and of the stirrings of black conscious-

19-2   Pablo Picasso, *Gertrude Stein*, 1906. Oil on canvas. 39¼" × 32". The Metropolitan Museum of Art, New York (bequest of Gertrude Stein, 1946).

ness. Here is Hughes's brief poem of the 1920s, "The Negro Speaks of Rivers":

I've known rivers:
I've known rivers ancient as the world and older than the flow of human blood in human veins.

My soul has grown deep like the rivers.

I bathed in the Euphrates when dawns were young.
I built my hut near the Congo and it lulled me to sleep.
I looked upon the Nile and raised the pyramids above it.
I heard the singing of the Mississippi when Abe Lincoln went down to New Orleans, and I've seen its muddy bosom turn all golden in the sunset.

I've known rivers:
Ancient, dusky rivers.

My soul has grown deep like the rivers.

In various types of writing, other social sores were being exposed in this country, such as the deficiencies of urban life and the lack of humane care for the poor and the neglected. In the arts it seemed that America might be ready to move again, after the artistically conservative 1920s. The market for "culture" was mushrooming in the United States, even though the culture most admired was not very modern.

Indeed, the contrast was startling between American advances in technology and industry and American aesthetic conservatism. At least until the Great Depression the period was one of tremendous economic vitality—an age of great business empires, coal and petroleum, automobiles and railroads, and an immense growth of cities. Economically fortunate United States citizens could live most pleasantly and even absorb a good part of the European cultural heritage. Downtown areas of American cities were "beautified," if not made more efficient. Many of the Classical civic structures that survive today as post offices, libraries, museums, and concert halls were built in this period; although they were tasteful and imposing, they owed almost nothing stylistically to their own century. And the skyscrapers grew bigger, if not better. Although it is easy to deride the applied Gothicism of New York's 1913 Woolworth Building (fig. 19-3), the structure possesses at least as much dignity as the more streamlined skyscraper that surpassed it in height in 1930–32, the Empire State Building.

But Modern art had also come to America—most notably in the "Armory Show" of 1913, first held at the National Guard armory in New York. (Part of the show was later seen in Chicago and Boston.) Reactions of critics and the public to the more adventurous art in the show ranged from rage to condescending joviality. Yet for America the Armory Show awakened a lively public interest in Modern art and, for the sophisticated few, an appreciation for some of its trends. Many American artists started trying to catch up with the new movements from abroad. Until after World War II, however, Europeans were more successful creators in the visual arts.

Predictably, then, the United States in the decades before 1945 saw widely varied trends in painting and sculpture. In the Depression and New Deal years, under conditions of real national crisis and reformist zeal, the trend again was toward social realism. There were even some mutterings about the degeneracy of "radical" European art—a rather disconcerting associ-

19-3 Cass Gilbert, Woolworth Building, New York, 1913.

ation with the Nazi mood of the time. Most artists, however, avoided blatant ideologies. Among these artists were Georgia O'Keeffe (1887–1986) and Edward Hopper (1882–1967). Both of these artists were committed to portraying the American scene—Hopper the Northeast, and O'Keeffe the Southwest. While O'Keeffe emphasized the forms of nature, human beings and their works often entered Hopper's paintings.

Despite its modest dimensions, O'Keeffe's *Black Cross, New Mexico* (fig. 19-4) breathes a spirit of grandeur and monumentality. In the very near foreground looms the massive wooden cross of the Penetenti Indian sect, outlined against stylized rolling hills, a pale sky, and a brilliant sunset between the horizon and the arm of the cross. Forms are predominantly hard-edged, though with smoothly molded gradations of color; they suggest eternal stability and immobility. Hopper's *Freight Cars, Gloucester* (fig. 19-5) is less grand and forbidding. Its forms, however, are sturdy, and its air is of unpeopled quietness. Compared with the art of O'Keeffe and the innovators abroad, it was a conservative work. For the most exciting revolutionary painting of this period we must turn to Europe.

PAINTING: TWO MASTERS

In the decade immediately preceding World War I, two broadly divergent tendencies became clear within Modernist painting and sculpture, the tendencies com-

19-4 Georgia O'Keeffe, *Black Cross, New Mexico*, 1929. Oil on canvas, 39″ × 30″. The Art Institute Purchase Fund. © 1987 The Art Institute of Chicago. All Rights Reserved.

19-5 Edward Hopper, *Freight Cars, Gloucester*, 1928. Oil on canvas, 29″ × 40″. Addison Gallery of American Art, Phillips Academy, Andover, Massachusetts.

monly called Expressionism and Formalism—although in many ways they simply up-dated the older Romantic and Classicist trends. Expressionism, by and large, stressed emotional involvement on the part of artist and viewer; its immediate ancestry included Gauguin and van Gogh. Formalism, on the other hand, represented emotional detachment, with a quest for order and discipline; its most vital inspiration from the recent past was Cézanne. Each movement had its own living standard-bearer; Expressionism looked particularly to Henri Matisse, and Formalism to Pablo Picasso. But neither of these masters could be neatly contained within one category, since each possessed a genius that went beyond conventional boundaries.

Matisse

Henri Matisse (1869–1954) first gained wide recognition in 1905 as one of a group of painters called, by a none-too-friendly critic, the *fauves* ("wild animals"). Fauvism above all was characterized by the free, subjective use of pure and violent colors for emotional and formal expression; the colors were to be wholly liberated from any need for naturalistic representation. Matisse's 1905 portrait of his wife, *The Green Stripe* (fig. 19-6), exemplifies the movement's goals. The vivid colors range from the vermilion, violet, and green of the three separate background areas to the dark blue of the hair and the yellow-green of the stripe that divides the face vertically from hairline to dress. Yet the color areas are not haphazardly placed; they achieve a balance that acknowledges formal as well as subjective and emotional qualities. Neither Matisse nor his Expressionist followers were slaves of uncontrolled impulse. Like his followers, Matisse was determined, however, to cast off the sophisticated complexities of academic painting and to resume contact with the wellsprings of direct and honest feeling. The prototypes of honest aesthetic perception, he believed, were the creations of children, folk artists, and primitive peoples. The latter source had already been stressed by Gauguin and had been encouraged by the nineteenth-century interest in history. The other sources would coincide nicely with the new century's sociological and psychological sympathies, including Freud's theories on the importance of childhood and the subconscious.

Several years after 1905, Matisse had carried his reduction of painting to its simplest expressive and formal elements still farther, as in *Harmony in Red*, or *The*

19-6 Henri Matisse, *The Green Stripe*, 1905. Oil on canvas, 16″ × 13″. Statens Museum for Kunst, Copenhagen (J. Rump Collection).

Red Room (fig. 19-7). Here the whole interior space is unified by a flat red that includes tablecloth as well as wall, and by the blue arabesque pattern imposed on both areas. Through the window appears another flat, stylized pattern, with a red house uniting the most distant part of the view to the foreground of the picture. Formal linear perspective is almost abandoned, and atmospheric perspective, with its dimming of distant objects, wholly ignored.

In 1908 Matisse summarized the aesthetic doctrine to which he would adhere for the next half-century. "What I dream of," he wrote, "is an art of balance, of purity and serenity devoid of troubling or depressing subject matter . . . , something like a good armchair in which to rest from physical fatigue." He characterized his artistic purpose bluntly: "What I am after, above all, is expression. The whole arrangement of my picture is expressive." Certainly the brilliantly decorative and expressive art of Matisse is a reminder that expression and Expressionism need not be violent

19-7 Henri Matisse, *Harmony in Red (The Red Room)*, 1908–9. Oil on canvas, 71″ × 97″. Hermitage, Leningrad.

or bitter, and that the calm celebration of pleasure is never wholly outdated.

Picasso

In fact, violence and bitterness could at times be powerfully conveyed by the master of anti-Expressionist Formalism in twentieth-century art, Pablo Picasso (1881–1973). Over an extraordinarily long creative span, and through a succession of striking styles, Picasso was one of the most energetically prolific painters of all time. Moreover, in addition to painting, his creativity encompassed major careers in sculpture, ceramics, drawing, and print making.

In 1900 Picasso left his native Spain to visit Paris; in 1904 this city became his permanent residence until after World War II. His earliest mature works were of a coloristic brilliance that prefigured Fauvism; these were followed by a series of sentimental but moving studies of life's underdogs, all bathed in a melancholy blue tonality. By 1905 he had moved from this "Blue Period" to his "Rose Period"; sentimentality still prevailed, but it was a bit subdued. Typical of this style is the *Family of Saltimbanques* (fig. 19-8), which portrays an emotionally ambivalent world of carnival acrobats, jugglers, and clowns. The style is basically naturalistic, lyrical, and elegant.

By 1906, as seen in the facial features of the Gertrude Stein portrait (see fig. 19-2), a harsher, more angular manner was emerging in his work. Increasingly Cézanne's formal constructions impressed Picasso at this time, as did prehistoric art and black African art. Soon, under their influence, he abandoned both naturalism and sentimentality for more strictly formal preoccupations. By 1907 his new approach was embodied in one of the century's most important paintings, *Les Demoiselles d'Avignon* (fig. 19-9), often called the first Cubist picture. Clearly Picasso had devoted much thought to the work; he had made many preliminary sketches, worked on the unusually large canvas for months, and apparently revised significantly. (The two masklike faces at the right seem to be a later addition, influenced by African art rather than by prehistoric sculpture as were the other faces.) When he showed the canvas to other artists and friends, many of them outstanding devotees and promoters of avant-garde art, it was greeted almost universally with shock and bewilderment. Embittered by such reactions, Picasso rolled up the canvas and for many years refused to sell it. The dealer Kahnweiler, however, was perceptive enough to buy the early sketches. Through them, and some private showings of the painting, the *Demoiselles* quickly became a legend and a powerful influence on Modern art.

19-8 Pablo Picasso, *Family of Saltimbanques,* 1905. Oil on canvas, 83¾″ × 90½″. National Gallery of Art, Washington, D.C. (Chester Dale Collection, 1962).

19-9 Pablo Picasso, *Les Demoiselles d'Avignon,* 1907. Oil on canvas, 8′ × 7′8″. Collection, The Museum of Modern Art, New York (acquired through the Lillie B. Bliss bequest).

The title, *The Young Ladies of Avignon,* was an afterthought of a friend of the painter's: the somewhat playful reference was to a house of prostitution on Barcelona's Avignon Street. Much of the work's rude shock appeal can be felt even today, especially in the contrasting gaunt and spiritually disembodied faces. More significantly, the figures are denied all spatial context and are themselves fragmented into rough and angular planes and wedges, assembled jaggedly without regard for realism. Cézanne, who could simultaneously depict objects from different angles of vision, is surpassed in the right foreground figure, whose face and back we see at the same time.

It was this breaking up of objects into planes or geometrical components and reassembling them unnaturally that came to be called *Cubism.* Sometimes it is explained that, since the components of a Cubist picture are reassembled from various sides of an object, it offers "complete vision"—a more comprehensive grasp of reality than is possible for a viewer at a given time and vantage point. (Picasso himself said, "In Cubism you paint not what you see, but what you know is there.") Other commentators have emphasized the time differential implicit in Cubist vision; that is, the successive viewings of an object that are reported on canvas imply a movement in time around the object.

Cubism obviously marked a radical new step away from the naturalistic assumption that any object has a stable form of its own that can be recorded by the artist. Like Monet and Cézanne, Cubists demonstrated that artists interpret nature and impose form on objects, and that objects are not isolated but take on qualities from other objects. Cubism, in fact, entangled objects and spaces more radically than its predecessors had done. Moreover, it confounded the externality and internality of objects; ultimately it revealed not only the front and back of an object but what was inside as well.

19-10   Georges Braque, *Violin and Pitcher*, 1910. Oil on canvas, 46″ × 29″. Oeffentliche Kunstsammlung Basel, Kunstmuseum.

19-11   Pablo Picasso, *Daniel Henry Kahnweiler*, 1910. Oil on canvas, 39½″ × 28½″. Gift of Mrs. Gilbert W. Chapman in memory of Charles B. Goodspeed, 1948. © 1987 The Art Institute of Chicago. All Rights Reserved.

All of this occurred not in one innovative step but in several. Picasso's early experiments were paralleled by those of Georges Braque (1882–1963), and for several years the two artists worked closely together. By 1910 they had evolved the style seen in Braque's *Violin and Pitcher* (fig. 19-10) and in Picasso's portrait of the art dealer Henry Kahnweiler (fig. 19-11). Both works exemplify a much more systematic stage of Cubism than that seen in the *Demoiselles* painting. The trend toward abstraction has intensified in the two 1910 paintings, and the violin, the pitcher, and Kahnweiler melt into their surroundings. In the Kahnweiler portrait there are some clearly identifiable features—most of the face, for example, and the watch-chain and clasped hands. (The Braque still life includes a curious, perhaps humorous, bit of naturalistic illusionism: the nail painted, complete with shadow, at the top.) Cub-

19-12 Pablo Picasso, *The Pipes of Pan*, 1923. Oil on canvas, 80½″ × 68½″. Musée Picasso, Paris.

ism, critics agree, must have at least some recognizable representational basis. Cubism, as an art of dislocation, reconstitution, and somewhat arbitrary creation of forms, had immense, revolutionary impact on its century.

In the decade or so after 1910, Picasso's art underwent further surprising changes. *The Pipes of Pan* (fig. 19-12) is in his neo-Classicist manner of the early 1920s—a manner to which he would occasionally revert in later years. In this painting the human figure is presented with no extreme distortions; in fact, the figures are reminiscent of the rather coarse, squatty sculpture of late imperial Rome. The primitive musical instrument suggests classical Greece and introduces a certain lyricism into the work's predominant sturdy monumentality.

In Picasso's famous *Guernica* of 1937 (fig. 19-13) Expressionism is united with Formalism. Here expressive effect attains its most memorable peak of intensity in the whole Cubist-derived movement—a peak quite as high as in any product of the strictly Expressionist school. The mural was inspired by the extermination-bombing of the Spanish town of Guernica on 26 April, 1937 by German war planes in the service of Franco's Nationalist rebels against the Spanish Republic. Despite the desperate civil war that had begun in 1936, the Spanish Republic was planning a pavilion for the

19-13 Pablo Picasso, *Guernica*, 1937. Oil on canvas, 11′5½″ × 25′5¾″. Prado, Madrid.

1937 world's fair in Paris, and a mural for it had been commissioned from Picasso. Picasso's strong pro-Republican, anti-Fascist passions were aroused by news of the Guernica tragedy and they spilled forth on the immense canvas. The whole is painted in black, white, and greys, and is a powerful grouping of starkly simplified forms portraying suffering, terror, and violent grief. With such violently distorted figures as the wounded, terrified horse, to the woman burning alive (at the right) and the mother bewailing her dead child (at the left), Picasso created an overpowering, devastating vision—a vision appropriate to the inhuman brutalities of its age.

DIRECTIONS IN PAINTING AND SCULPTURE

Picasso's *Guernica*, like the vast production of his previous and subsequent decades, demonstrates the impossibility of neatly categorizing his work. By and large, however, it seems to have been Picasso's more calculated, Formalist approach, especially his Cubist constructions, that most impressed his contemporaries and successors in painting and sculpture. In Picasso the Formalist movement in twentieth-century art found its most prestigious exemplar—the movement that, as we have noted, embodied emotional detachment and a quest for order and discipline. Since most artists could not match Picasso's chameleon moods and enthusiasms, the period through World War II saw the rise of countless more specialized talents.

Formalist Trends

Just after the First World War there came the flowering of several Formalist art trends in Europe. In France, for example, the painting of Fernand Léger (1881–1955) emphasized the impersonality of the industrial machine age. Dynamism was not Léger's concern, but rather the monumental, geometrical solidity of forms. Even the human figure became for him, as he phrased it, "purposely inexpressive"; most often he portrayed human beings as integral, mechanized components of a mechanized world. In *The City* (fig. 19-14) the human figures are as nearly abstract and impersonal as the various physical features of their urban environment. The prominent foreground pole is shaded and modeled real-

19-14 Fernand Léger, *The City*, 1919. Oil on canvas, 7′7″ × 9′9″. Philadelphia Museum of Art (A. E. Gellatin Collection).

istically enough to impart a sense of depth to the rest, but conventional perspective is wholly denied. The canvas is an abstraction of modern industrial life—bold, powerful, and still recognizably representational.

Abstraction, its proponents have typically held, is a matter of summation from within reality: it extracts presumably essential geometrical or spiritual characteristics. An abstract work may then show stylized traces of realistic representation, as in Léger's *City,* or it may be "totally" abstract—that is, representing nothing recognizable in external nature. This totally abstract art is therefore properly called *nonrepresentational.* Such is the mature art of another postwar painter, the Dutch Piet Mondrian (1872–1944).

Mondrian's *Composition in Yellow, Red, Blue, and Black* (fig. 19-15), like most of his other mature work, employs only the primary colors, distributed among blacks and greys; other canvases commonly include white also. The design is geometrically nonrepresentational—a product of the careful balancing of squares, rectangles, and straight lines, as well as of color. In Mondrian's words, "the straight cannot be made more abstract: it is the most extreme possibility of the purely plastic." And *plasticism* was his artistic goal—the creation of form without (in his case) any reference to external nature. His nonrepresentational art, he asserted, was real because it existed, and indeed more real than

19-15 Piet Mondrian, *Composition in Yellow, Red, Blue, and Black,* 1921. Oil on canvas, 23" × 23". Collection Haags Gemeentemuseum, The Hague.

the formlessness of nature. Out of form alone could come the transcendent harmony that must quench spiritual restlessness and bring clarity and truth and order to the human soul. If Mondrian's art was mathematical and unsentimental, it was thus also mystical and optimistic; he was convinced that purity of art would induce purity in individual souls and in human institutions. Mondrian's paintings were regarded by many people as handsomely decorative, and his style inspired many types of popular design. Mondrian would have thought these interpretations and adaptations of his work trivial and frivolous; he hoped to remake people, not to divert and amuse them.

The mainstream of European Formalism emphasized art's formal function as a revelation of the essence of things. Such was the philosophy of a group of Russian artists that, before and after the Revolution and inside and outside Russia, explored various routes to abstraction. Among the most talented sculptors in the group was Naum Gabo (1890–1977). He may be labeled a *Constructivist,* since his work was ordinarily not carved from a central mass of material or molded into a central mass, but constructed in space out of various materials and intermingled with space rather than formed into a compact object.

Gabo's *Linear Construction, Variation* (fig. 19-16) is spectacularly yet delicately balanced in space—a thorough denial of traditional sculptural mass. It is made of a plastic frame and taut nylon thread, indicating Gabo's imaginative use of the new synthetic materials that were becoming available. The *Linear Construction* and also his later, more curvilinear creations are remarkably elegant and graceful. "I am trying," he said, "to tell the world that there is beauty in spite of ugliness and horror. I am trying to call attention to the balanced, not the chaotic, side of life—to be constructive, not destructive."

The career of the British sculptor Henry Moore (1898–1986) ran a gamut of styles. A few of his works are Expressionist in feeling—especially some of his more realistic versions of two favorite themes, the reclining female figure and the mother-with-child. Even these themes, though, were embodied with increasing abstraction and Formalism, leading to such works as the ponderously monumental *Reclining Figure* shown in figure 19-17. Moore's earlier attempts to metamorphose woman into a primitive earth goddess of fertility gave way in this 1939 work to a formal study in solids and voids. The great holes around which this figure

19-16 Naum Gabo, *Linear Construction, Variation,* 1942–43. Plastic and nylon thread construction, 24½" × 24½". The Phillips Collection, Washington, D.C.

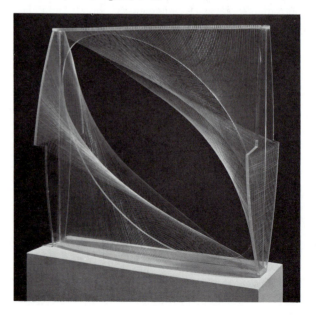

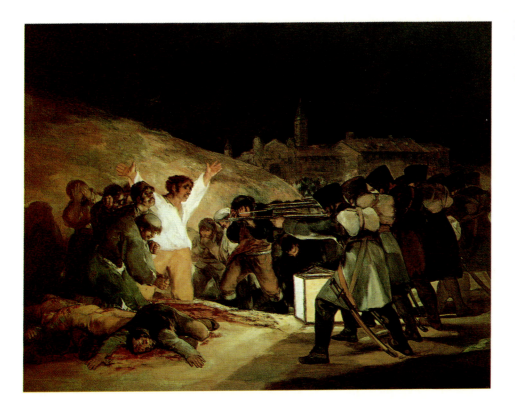

Plate 37 Francisco Goya, *The Third of May*, 1814. Oil on canvas, 8'9" × 11'4". Prado, Madrid.

Plate 38 Joseph Mallord William Turner, *Rain, Steam, and Speed: The Great Western Railway*, 1844. Oil on canvas, 36" × 48". Reproduced by courtesy of the Trustees, The National Gallery, London.

Plate 39 Edouard Manet, *Le Déjeuner sur l'Herbe*, 1863. Oil on canvas, 7′ × 8′10″. Musée d'Orsay, Paris.

Plate 40 Claude Monet, *Rouen Cathedral at Sunset*, 1894. Oil on canvas, 39½″ × 25¾″. Courtesy, Museum of Fine Arts, Boston (Juliana Cheney Edwards Collection; bequest of Hannah Marcy Edwards in memory of her mother).

Plate 41 Paul Cézanne, *Mont Sainte-Victoire*, 1904–1906. Oil on canvas, 26″ × 32″. Private Collection. Partial Gift to the Philadelphia Museum of Art.

Plate 42 Vincent van Gogh, *The Night Café*, 1888. Oil on canvas, 28″ × 35″. Yale University Art Gallery, New Haven, Connecticut (bequest of Stephen Carlton Clark, B.A. 1903).

Plate 43   Henri Matisse, *Harmony in Red (The Red Room)*, 1908–1909. Oil on canvas, 71″ × 97″. Hermitage, Leningrad.

Plate 44 Pablo Picasso, *Les Demoiselles d'Avignon,* 1907. Oil on canvas, 8′ × 7′8″. Collection, The Museum of Modern Art, New York (acquired through the Lillie B. Bliss bequest).

Plate 45 *(above)* Jackson Pollock, *Convergence (Number 10, 1952)*. Oil on canvas, 7¾′ × 12½′. Albright–Knox Art Gallery, Buffalo, New York (gift of Seymour H. Knox, 1956).

Plate 46 Mark Rothko, *Orange and Yellow*, 1956. Oil on canvas, 91″ × 71″. Albright–Knox Art Gallery, Buffalo, New York (gift of Seymour H. Knox, 1956).

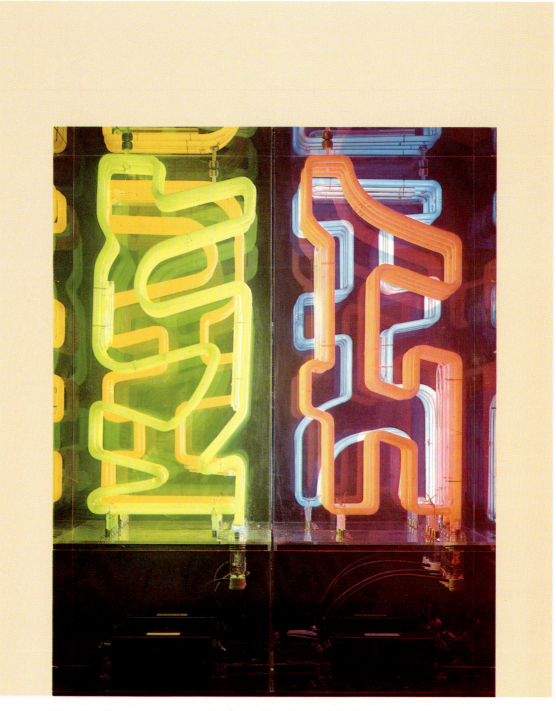

Plate 47 Chryssa, *Fragments for the Gates to Times Square II*, 1966. Programmed neon and Plexiglas, 43″ high. Collection, Whitney Museum of American Art (Purchase, with funds from Howard and Jean Lipman).

19-17 Henry Moore, *Reclining Figure*, 1939. Elmwood, 37″ × 79″ × 30″. © 1987 The Detroit Institute of Arts. Gift of the Dexter M. Ferry, Jr., Trustee Corporation.

grows serve not only to lighten and open that form, but to underline mass and depth.

The most typical works of the Rumanian sculptor Constantin Brancusi (1876–1957), like Gabo's, fall within a style of ease and grace—but within the older sculptural tradition of central mass rather than spatial construction. Most of Brancusi's works tend toward the outer limits of abstraction. He did over thirty versions— with minor modifications in size, materials, and litheness—of *Bird in Space;* like the others, the highly polished bronze version in figure 19-18 is traceable representationally to a bird's feather. From this humble origin it was refined to evoke the soaring of a bird, the very "essence of flight," as Brancusi himself said. He would always maintain that of all art his was "the most realistic, because what is real is not the outer form, but the idea, the essence of things." This statement captures the heart of most modern abstract art.

Expressionist Trends

Perhaps the United States Customs officials deserve more sympathy than generally accorded them in reports of the long litigation over the import duty to be assessed on *Bird in Space*—which was, said the offi-

cials, not a work of art but an object of manufacture. (Brancusi finally won.) The "object" had a glistening, machinelike polish, it was quite nonrepresentational, and it hardly brought the patriotic or sentimental uplift that Customs officials had associated with "sculpture." Most assuredly, it was not conventionally recognizable and "expressive."

Samples from the large wave of Western art that can be broadly called the Expressionist movement, and that flourished concurrently with the Formalist trend, would not have presented such a dilemma for the Customs officials. As a movement stressing emotional involvement on the part of artist and viewer, Expressionism usually contained recognizable references to natural phenomena—more so than most Formalist art.

Expressionism within the figurative tradition had its practitioners among both painters and sculptors, but it was at its liveliest in painting. Many of the liveliest paintings came from the brush of Marc Chagall (1887–1985), a Russian Jew who spent most of his career in France. His earliest work there, from 1910, reveals

19-18 Constantin Brancusi, *Bird in Space*, 1925. Polished bronze, 50″ high. Philadelphia Museum of Art (Louise and Walter Arensberg Collection).

19-19 Marc Chagall, *Birthday,*
1915–23. Oil on canvas, 32″ × 39½″.
Collection, The Solomon R.
Guggenheim Museum, New York.

occasionally Cubist devices, but a much stronger Fauvist feeling. Some of his paintings earnestly explore human destiny; more of them are celebrations of light-hearted joys. *Birthday* (fig. 19-19) is a whimsical souvenir of Chagall's love for his young wife, Bella. In a somewhat flattened, Matisse-like room Chagall soars ecstatically in the air, conquering anatomy to swoop down with a backward kiss for his bride. It is a happy, festive image with which even the least sophisticated viewer can empathize, despite its distortions. Chagall would become one of the century's most popular artists.

German Expressionism turned toward lurid and even melodramatic emotional expression—toward a violent new romanticism. The most prestigious theorist of this Expressionism was not German but Russian—Vasily Kandinsky (1866–1944); his career, however, centered in Germany both before World War I and again from late 1921 until the Nazi assumption of power. In 1910 he wrote, and in 1912 saw published, a slim theoretical treatise, *Concerning the Spiritual in Art,* which came to possess almost scriptural authority for many of the German Expressionists. In it he insisted on the spiritual basis of art—the spiritual uniqueness of each age, and hence its distinctive artistic forms. "Every work of art," he asserted, "is the child of its time." The essential function of art is to express and impart the emotional states that arise in a given age, without any verbal or associative aids. Form, line, and especially color work directly on the soul, and all the more so as the art is more abstract—as, in effect, it is more like music. When any contemporary painting becomes emancipated from nature it also emancipates itself from descriptive or rational meaning and analysis and makes possible a revelation of its "internal feeling."

Kandinsky practiced what he preached. He proceeded all the way to total, nonrepresentational abstraction, while avoiding the disciplined quasi-mathematical order of the Formalists. Although he allowed varying degrees of spontaneity in his paintings, he maintained that his art was all feeling, not calculation. The *Painting with White Form* (fig. 19-20) is a colorful abstract canvas presumably expressing Kandinsky's spiritual "inner necessity" in an instinctive way.

Kandinsky, however, moved much faster toward nonrepresentational art than his friends and admirers were willing to follow. The paintings of Ernst Ludwig Kirchner (1880–1938) depicted urban life. *The Street* (fig. 19-21) was inspired by the big-city bustle, with its isolation of individuals, in 1913 Berlin. Against a generalized urban setting a furred and plumed woman of the streets eyes the bemused gentleman at the right—but all other figures seem depersonalized and isolated.

19-20 Vasily Kandinsky, *Painting with White Form*, 1913. Oil on canvas, 47¼″ × 55″. Collection, The Solomon R. Guggenheim Museum, New York.

19-21 Ernst Ludwig Kirchner, *The Street*, 1913. Oil on canvas, 47½″ × 36″. Collection, The Museum of Modern Art, New York (purchase).

Spiky, jagged forms and garish colors contribute to the impression of nervous dynamism and blatant production-line sensuality.

Max Beckmann (1884–1950), a German painter who rebelled at being categorized in any way, even as an Expressionist, also turned in his art to the lurid horrors and vulgarities of the outside world. The precise action of *The Night* (fig. 19-22) is unclear; apparently the innocent are being tortured and murdered by sadistic thugs, and some erotic depravity is thrown in for good measure. The vicious nightmare is intensified by the compression of tangled persons and objects into a claustrophobically shallow picture space. Whether the scene was intended to evoke the criminality of a postwar world or the obscenity of inhuman vice and violence in general, it is a gruesome memento of its century.

A brief survey can barely hint at the fascinating scope of German Expressionism in painting, a movement labeled "degenerate" by the Nazis. Nor can we

19-22 Max Beckmann, *The Night*, 1918–19. Oil on canvas, 52″ × 60″. Kunstsammlung Nordrhein-Westfalen, Düsseldorf.

linger over the remarkable Expressionist experiments in realms outside painting—such as the pathfinding silent film of 1919, *The Cabinet of Dr. Caligari,* which suggested mental illness by sets, lighting, makeup, costumes, and even lettering that reflected the most jagged, melodramatic Expressionism. We must return now to the more traditional mediums.

Dada, Duchamp, and Surrealism

At many points Expressionism touches the Surrealist movement of the 1920s and later. Surrealism drew in part on the inventive creations of the Dadaists and of Marcel Duchamp. The Dada–Duchamp–Surrealism stream in Modern art could take on, seemingly at will, the superficial characteristics of both Expressionism and Formalism. The new stream, however, was sufficiently distinctive, and its influence sufficiently powerful, to merit a separate discussion here.

Dada was invented by a group of refugee artists and writers in Switzerland during World War I as a revolt against the values of the age. The terrors of the war, the inhumanities of industrialism, the presumed delusions of rationalism and liberalism, and the pomposities of fashionable art were among many targets. Sometimes these artists' reactions were bitter indeed.

The Dadaists mocked both the machine age and emotionalism; they emphasized provocative unintelligibility, and sometimes engaged in fantasy, buffoonery, and whimsical irony.

The realm of whimsy was often inhabited by Marcel Duchamp (1887–1968). By the time of his first New York trip in 1915, Duchamp had given up conventional painting. After 1923, when he was living alternately in New York and Paris, he even discontinued most of his artistic activities and settled down to being a legend and oracle.

Art, Duchamp declared, is made by its time, and for its time alone; it is more a part of sociology than of aesthetics. Against the overwhelming trend of advanced art since Manet toward the ideological and social autonomy of art, Duchamp set up the "antiretinal" principle: that all art that addresses itself simply to the eye, and thus to formal aesthetic feelings, is simply on the wrong track. The only true value of art is as an outlet and a stimulant of ideas. Often, initially anyway, it is the mere choice of the artist that counts: the artist need not make the art object at all, but merely designate any existing item as art. Thus arose the first of Duchamp's "readymades" in 1913. The handiest definition of readymades would come from the founder of Surrealism, André Breton. They are, he said, "manufactured objects promoted to the dignity of objects of art through the choice of the artist." Thus Duchamp created *Fountain* by so designating a detached urinal, which he signed "R. Mutt," and displayed a snow shovel entitled *In Advance of the Broken Arm*. All of this, of course, was a radical attack on art of all periods. These concepts of Breton and Duchamp would break down age-old ideas of the nature of creativity and beauty and would eliminate all distinctions between art and everyday life. Predictably, Duchamp's antiaesthetic antiart made a lively impression—but for many decades only in very restricted circles. As we will see in the next chapter, after World War II Duchamp's principles would be absorbed into the important movement known as Conceptual art.

19-23 Marcel Duchamp, *The Bride Stripped Bare by Her Bachelors, Even (The Large Glass)*, 1915–23. Mixed media, 8'11" × 5'7". Philadelphia Museum of Art (bequest of Katherine S. Dreier).

The most complex of Duchamp's creations was not a readymade, but a long-pondered construction. *The Bride Stripped Bare by Her Bachelors, Even*, known also as *The Large Glass* (fig. 19-23), occupied Duchamp for many years, although intermittently so because of his travels and the "laziness" that he always genially acknowledged. Done directly on one sheet of glass and covered with another, the construction employs such materials as wire, foil, dust, and varnish to create, rather obscurely, what is generally held to be a sexual concept, or indeed a sort of sex machine. (When the glass was later found to have been shattered, Duchamp is reported to have pronounced, "Now it is complete.") Commentators have laboriously sought out the precise symbolism of the work, although Duchamp himself asserted in the 1960s that it had no interpretation and was simply a "sum of experiments" toward the "renunciation of all aesthetics."

Many of the ideas of Dada were taken up by a group of young artists and writers of the 1920s who called themselves the Surrealists. Their approach was based, as Breton wrote in his first *Manifesto of Surrealism* (1924), "on the belief in the superior reality of certain forms of previously neglected associations, in the omnipotence of dream, in the disinterested play of thought." Surrealism, he cheerfully admitted, is completely irrational and illogical, and indeed sets out to destroy ordinary reason and logic. "Complete nonconformism," with full freedom from conventional thought mechanisms, is both the method and the goal. Ideas and feelings must express themselves by absolutely unpremeditated freedom of association, as in the therapeutic practice of Freud, but with Freud's rational ideals utterly repudiated.

Breton made much of "psychic automatism," by which the mind would act "in the absence of any control exercised by reason, exempt from any aesthetic or moral concern." The unfettered, freely roaming Surrealist mind is often reflected in the work of the Spanish painter Joan Miró (1893–1983). In Paris after World War I, Miró responded enthusiastically to several of the new art styles that made that city preeminent in creative excitement; but then he developed a Surrealist vision of originality and charm. Although his *Harlequin's Carnival* of 1924–25 (fig. 19-24) is painted with meticulous detail, it is thoroughly unrealistic and virtually two-dimensional (unless we believe that the stylized view through the window at the upper right introduces an element of depth). Above all, the painting

19-24 Joan Miró, *The Harlequin's Carnival*, 1924–25. Oil on canvas, 26″ × 36¾″. The Albright–Knox Art Gallery, Buffalo, New York. (Room of Contemporary Art Fund, 1940.)

offers an exuberant conglomeration of many of Miró's favored motifs—such as the ladder, eye, and ear—and a most extraordinary picture of confusion and good humor. The one human figure (toward the left, with pipe, extravagant mustaches, and round blue and red face) stares gloomily at the viewer, but all the strange little creatures or organisms around him are obviously having a splendid, jolly time.

However, most artists who joined the Surrealist movement, especially so traditional a draftsman as the Spaniard Salvador Dalí (born 1904), went about their painting with a good measure of careful realism. This realism, nonetheless, was ordinarily of isolated pictorial elements that were weirdly developed or placed in strange contexts. And, despite Breton's teachings, the Surrealists occasionally displayed a moralism that was very earnest indeed. Dalí's *Soft Construction with Boiled Beans: Premonition of Civil War* (fig. 19-25), with its frightening anatomical originality and its figure's repellently decaying head, foot, and hands, foreshadows most unpleasantly the horrors of the Spanish civil war. Still, the work illustrates Dalí's pronouncement that the time had come "to systematize confusion and to contribute to discrediting completely the world of reality."

TRENDS IN ARCHITECTURE

Public taste, even in the most dynamic and democratic ages, ordinarily changes very slowly in the more serious arts, if not in "pop" culture. Of the major arts, architecture is traditionally the most public. Modern Westerners can refuse to buy avant-garde painting or sculpture and can keep their distance from the more adventuresome art galleries and concert halls, but only hermits can avoid seeing and perhaps using the larger buildings of their civilization. Dependent, then, on some degree of public approval, architecture has ordinarily clung to past forms more strongly than have the other arts. This was almost as true in the decades just after 1905 as in those just before; in both cases the popular mood favored eclectic architectural revivalism. Yet in less popular, more restricted circles after 1905, radical architecture finally was welcomed in almost all types of building, not simply in commercial structures or engineering projects such as bridges and towers. Although the average person remained largely unreceptive, the period before 1945 did see a great deal of extremely important architectural pioneering.

By the 1920s compromise with older architectural

19-25 Salvador Dalí, *Soft Construction with Boiled Beans: Premonition of Civil War*, 1936. Oil on canvas, 39″ × 39″. Philadelphia Museum of Art (Louise and Walter Arensberg Collection).

forms was being rejected by such architects as Walter Gropius, Le Corbusier, and Mies van der Rohe—the founders and leaders of what came to be called the International style of architecture. (Mies will be considered in chapter 20.) The machine shop wing of the Dessau Bauhaus (fig. 19-26), by Walter Gropius (1883–1969), was built in 1925–26; with its inner supports and outward sheath of plate glass, it displays the clean lines, clarity, and impersonality for which the International style would be known.

The state Bauhaus, of which Gropius was director for a decade, was literally a "house for constructing things"—a school for training artists and designers to collaborate with architects in building practical environments for people. (Its overtones were too radical for the Nazis, under whose pressure it dissolved in 1933.) Mondrian and Kandinsky taught there; both of them

were self-conscious prophets of spiritual uplift through art, with Mondrian particularly emphasizing art as a force for moral betterment, as we have seen. Something of this approach would remain with architects of the International style: clean architectural lines, it was hoped, would make clean human lives.

In stylistic qualities the International style reflected the Formalist trend in Modern art, especially the Constructivist movement. Its usual characteristics included the unconcealed use of basic materials; the centering of support inward, leaving only a light covering of glass or other material on the outside; the elimination of extraneous decoration; the free, functional arrangement of interior space and the removal of many traditionally walled enclosures; and the determination of external appearance by interior organization. In addition, the teaching and example of Gropius (at the

19-26 Walter Gropius, machine shop wing of the Bauhaus, Dessau, Germany, 1925–26.

Bauhaus and eventually at Harvard) served to help establish a collaborative spirit among International style architects and designers.

Wright and Le Corbusier

Painting had its Matisse and Picasso, one a crucial figure in Expressionism and the other in Formalism; architecture had its Frank Lloyd Wright (1869–1959) and Charles Édouard Jeanneret, known as Le Corbusier (1887–1965). Again, however, lines between schools are hard to draw when genius is comprehensive. Although Wright tended strongly toward Expressionism and Le Corbusier toward Formalism, neither man's work can be adequately categorized so simply.

Wright's career began in the office of Adler and Sullivan, which was among the most progressive Chicago firms, and his inclinations were immensely strengthened by Sullivan's example. Wright held the romantic view of the architect as a loner against the world, as an isolated creative force. Being of a younger, more daring architectural generation than Sullivan, Wright moved well beyond his master into Modernity.

Wright's favorite term, *organic architecture,* im-

plied the oneness of an evolving universe, and hence a necessary relationship between architecture, life, and environment. In practical terms this meant an adaptation of the building to the site and to the owner's needs and personality—as interpreted and encouraged by the architect. This approach is well illustrated in Wright's series of "prairie houses," exemplified in 1909 by the Robie House (fig. 19-27) in Chicago. In these structures Wright rebelled against the "typical American house" as it existed in 1893 when he set out on his own as an architect. "It lied about everything," he later wrote. "It had no sense of unity at all nor any such sense of space as should belong to a free people. It was stuck up in thoughtless fashion. It had no more sense of earth than a 'modernistic' house" (the latter comment a rebuke to the International style and its derivatives). The house of the 1890s, he wrote, was "a bedeviled box with a fussy lid—a complex box that had to be cut up by all kinds of holes made in it to let in light and air, with an especially ugly hole to go in and come out of. The holes were all 'trimmed'—the doors and windows themselves trimmed, the roofs trimmed, the walls trimmed." For such insensitive fussiness, Wright substituted a simple, nobler, more organic style

19-27 Frank Lloyd Wright, Robie House, Chicago, 1909.

suitable to the flatness of the Midwestern prairie regions. "Shelter," he said, "should be the essential look of any dwelling." The Robie House—with its large, open interior spaces, its deep-set windows, and its flat, sheltering slabs *cantilevered* into space (that is, supported at only one end)—embodies Wright's ideal of domestic building on an ambitious scale.

A fine example of Wright's later domestic architecture is the Kaufmann House, called "Falling Water," of 1936 (fig. 19-28). The site is rugged country terrain, and the house, in fact, is built over a waterfall. Steel framework supplements concrete rather than brick; the cantilevered planes jut into space to echo the shallow waterfall ledge below. "Organic architecture," Wright insisted, "includes all materials, accepts all forms so they be natural to purpose, considerate of ways and means, and respectful to environment."

Architects in the International style considered Wright old-fashioned; he in turn condemned the rival school for its "use of man by the machine." Le Corbusier, the Swiss-born, French-based embodiment of International style ideals, of course professed quite the contrary. Architecture, he maintained, was not for show but for service. The house, to be sure, was a

"machine for living"—but the point was precisely its human function. Le Corbusier admitted that many of his houses were starkly simplified and impersonal—but this, he pointed out, made mass production possible, benefiting those of modest income. Much of his effort also was directed toward urban planning of the "garden-city" sort—apartment houses, shops, and recreation areas set amid broad boulevards and spacious parks. Although his plans generally remained hypothetical, they were extremely influential later.

The Villa Savoye (fig. 19-29) at Poissy, near Paris, is one of Le Corbusier's larger-scale homes. The ground floor combines a garage, service area, and entrance hall with stairs and ramp to the living area above. The main floor contains extensive uninterrupted spaces, as in a terrace–living room complex. All is airy, sunlit, and rather antiseptic. Aside from the omnipresent glass, the basic structure is of reinforced concrete, inside and out; like the walls, the *pilotis* ("pilework," or series of freestanding piers), which so prominently supports much of the main floor, is of this material. The whole, like many of Le Corbusier's public buildings, is reminiscent of Mondrian's geometrical abstractions.

19-28 Frank Lloyd Wright, Kaufmann House ("Falling Water"), near Bear Run, Pennsylvania, 1936.

19-29 Le Corbusier, Villa Savoye, Poissy, 1928–30.

MUSIC: INNOVATION AND TRADITION

Like painting and architecture, music between 1905 and 1945 could claim two symbolic master figures, each receiving excited and even fanatical homage from his devoted followers. Polarization between devotees of Schoenberg and Stravinsky could be so exclusivist and bitter that it is rather surprising to find any common threads at all in the concert music of the period.

Diverse musical trends, however, shared certain characteristics. Perhaps most important, after the generalized revolt against musical Romanticism, was a fuller knowledge of music's past than ever before. The musicological investigations of the nineteenth century were now greatly extended, and led not only to the rediscovery of vast quantities of long-neglected music but to more authentic performances. Musical instruments that had become archaic were given new life through restoration and reproduction; the harpsichord and the Baroque organ, most notably, came back into use. The crisp and clean sound of those instruments corresponded nicely with the ideal of clarity and sharp definition in musical performance of works from the recent, generally Romantic, past as well as for revivals of Classical and "old" music. The conductor Arturo Toscanini became an international symbol of perfectionist accuracy in the literal reading of the written score—as contrasted with the liberties commonly taken by earlier interpreters.

Gradually the musical public came to know the work of Toscanini, and of precisionists in all mediums of musical performance, through the magic of radio and phonograph records. But Toscanini did not achieve his greatest popularity until the very end of the 1905–45 period (and then usually for the wrong, hero-worshipping reasons)—nor did the general public necessarily prefer sensitive vocalism and interpretation to flashy technique or heroic sounds by singers. Similarly, popular favor came only slowly, if at all, to the relatively dry, precise effects of such avant-garde composers as Schoenberg and Stravinsky. The disconcerting truth was at least as clear as the parallel situations in contemporary architecture, painting, and sculpture: the musical audience's tastes and understanding had not developed sufficiently to keep up with the advances in composition.

19-30 Arnold Schoenberg in the late 1920s. Österreichische Nationalbibliothek, Bildarchiv, Vienna.

Schoenberg

Few clearer instances of the gap between public and composer can be found than in the career of Arnold Schoenberg (1874–1951, fig. 19-30). Seldom has an object of such intense cult worship within a small but influential circle been so blithely ignored or so indignantly repudiated by most listeners. Even in his native Vienna, and in Berlin, where he also composed and taught, only the traditionalist Romanticism of his earliest, neo-Wagnerian period made a wide impression. Except for a small circle of refugees and academics, Los Angeles barely recognized his existence, although he lived there the last seventeen years of his life.

"I venture," wrote Schoenberg in 1931, "to credit myself with having written truly new music, which, being based on tradition, is destined to become tradition." His radical innovations evolved in two stages. The first, achieved before 1910, was the vast extension of atonality, to become the pervasive element of a composition rather than an occasional piquant flavoring as in Debussy's music. The second innovation, involving a thoroughgoing, serial systematization of atonality, came later, by about 1921.

As seen in the previous chapter, atonality implies an increasing tolerance for harmonies considered dissonant in the eighteenth century and most of the nineteenth—and above all it rejects the directional emphases (progressional logic) of tonal music. Implicit in atonality is the possibility of literally all combinations and sequences of tones.

In most writers' opinion, Schoenberg had reached an advanced atonal stage by the time he wrote *Erwartung (Expectation)* in 1909. If we may loosely compare music's traditional tonal system with painting's traditional naturalistic perspective, *Erwartung's* style is comparable to the Cubism of Picasso's Kahnweiler portrait (see fig. 19-11): there are recognizable bits of the traditional language in each, but the balance has swung decisively toward a revolutionary new manner.

The mood of *Erwartung* can be considered Expressionist, since this "monodrama," as Schoenberg called it, details a horrendous event in the life of the human soul. A woman—the single vocal soloist—seeks her lover in a dark wood, although he has apparently deserted her for another. Finally she finds his murdered body. A monologue of passion, jealousy, and resignation follows, concluded by a plaintive *Ich suchte* ("I was looking for . . .") as the orchestra eerily trails off into stillness. The drama, however, is more psychic than real; it reflects an emotional state, or an anguished stream of consciousness spilling out as if under psychoanalytic encouragement. The work is less memorable for any emotional highlights than for its diffusely hypnotic mood.

The trend of Schoenberg's later work, after his invention of the twelve-tone, or *dodecaphonic*, method, was more unequivocally Formalist, less Expressionist than the style of *Erwartung*. It was for this second revolutionary innovation that Schoenberg would be revered by composers and theorists of a later generation called "serialists" (see chapter 20). The attractions of twelve-tone composition were diverse. Many musicians thought that by Schoenberg's day the resources of conventional tonality had been exhausted. Some undoubtedly found technique more fascinating than traditional creative inspiration, or impersonality more comfortable than emotional expression. Others

professed quite the contrary approach and indignantly maintained that the twelve-tone system was simply a new and powerfully expressive technique, no more mechanical or confining than traditional tonality—which, after all, had its own rules and limitations.

The twelve-tone system went well beyond its name; it meant more than accepting the traditional Western convention of twelve half-tones to an octave, or even the atonalist assumption of the essential equality of all twelve tones (as opposed to the tonal emphasis on certain focal notes). What the twelve-tone system offered was no less than a whole new method of composition, by which atonality could be systematized within a consistent pattern. First the composer would establish a specific arrangement of the twelve tones: this became the *tone row*, or series (hence the later term *serial composition*), upon which a whole piece would be based. In sequence the row might be played forward, backward, upside down, or upside-down backward—but in any case an unalterable order would be followed. Exceptions and refinements, however, quickly appeared in Schoenberg's writing: above all, notes might be played in harmonic clusters, not just in sequence.

Schoenberg's Violin Concerto of 1934–36 is a work much admired for its intellectual discipline, its rigorous yet inventive dodecaphony. (The basic tone row is heard in the first two phrases, in the solo violin and its harmonic cello accompaniment.) The instrumental writing is very complex, especially for the soloist. The concerto has the three traditional movements—moderate tempo, slow, and fast—and demonstrates a skill in manipulating varied orchestral color, dynamics, and rhythm that would have delighted such a nineteenth-century master as Berlioz. What Berlioz, who sometimes thought even Wagner rather mad, would have made of a work that so aggressively obliterated every vestige of nineteenth-century tonality is another matter. More relevant was what most of Schoenberg's contemporaries thought of his music—and, emphatically, most of them did not like it.

Stravinsky

Many listeners in the 1930s found only slightly more palatable the neo-Classicist production of Schoenberg's rival, Igor Stravinsky (1882–1971, fig. 19-31). Only Stravinsky's first ballets, written two decades earlier, were entering the standard concert repertoire, al-

19-31 Pablo Picasso, *Igor Stravinsky*, 1920. Drawing. Private collection.

though his influence on other composers was already profound.

Stravinsky's first international fame came in 1910, when his ballet *The Firebird* was produced in Paris. It was a fairly conservative work, brilliantly orchestrated and dramatically powerful. But already Stravinsky had sighted a more radical vision. "I saw in imagination," he later wrote, "a solemn pagan rite: wise elders, seated in a circle, watching a young girl dance herself to death. They were sacrificing her to win the favor of the god of spring." Inspired by thoughts of this vision, and by boyhood memories of "the violent Russian spring . . . that seemed to begin in an hour and was like the whole earth cracking," Stravinsky composed *The Rite of Spring* in 1911–12 while living in Switzerland and Russia. The 1913 première, in Paris, gave rise to a violent demonstration and a small counter-demonstration. This historic evening was a symbolic event in twentieth-century avant-gardism comparable to the Armory Show in New York that same year.

Stravinsky's innovations at this point in his career

were, at least in tonal matters, less striking than Schoenberg's—but far better publicized. (Schoenberg's *Erwartung* was not even performed in public until 1924.) Stravinsky was by no means as doggedly atonal as Schoenberg, although sometimes he employed *bitonality* or *polytonality*—that is, the concurrent use of two or more keys. He did, however, employ dissonance (by prevalent standards) to an unprecedented degree and elevate jolting rhythmic irregularities to an ideal. Both practices particularly characterized *The Rite of Spring,* as in the notorious, irregularly stressed chords at the beginning of the "Auguries of Spring" section, immediately after the introduction to Part I.

The *Rite* presents a rhapsodic vision from primitive, pagan Russia. The themes are repeated, altered, and reconstituted without attention to traditional notions of thematic development, and early hearers found the work to be a jungle of sounds. The program is in two parts—the first an "adoration of the earth," the second a "sacrifice" culminating in the sacrificial dance of the Chosen Victim. With the immense orchestra, the careful attention to contrasts in instrumental tone color, and the effective presentation of a dramatically exotic scene, the *Rite* is rather close, spiritually, to romantic Expressionism.

Nor is the music of Stravinsky's so-called neo-Classical phase (the three decades or so after World War I) as coldly and impersonally forbidding as some have described it. Nonetheless there is a leanness and restraint in Stravinsky's neo-Classicism that is reminiscent of the Classicism of Mozart and Haydn, who also were capable of deep feeling.

In 1926–27 Stravinsky joined with Picasso and the French writer Jean Cocteau to produce a monument of modern neo-Classicism, *Oedipus Rex. Oedipus*—inspired by the play of Sophocles—was first publicly performed in Paris in 1927, as a tribute to Diaghilev on his twentieth anniversary as a ballet impresario. Audiences, critics, and Diaghilev were puzzled and even hostile: nearly everybody wondered why Stravinsky could not simply churn out more and more Firebirds. The new work for vocal soloists, chorus, and orchestra was first performed in concert version as a secular oratorio; later attempts to present it on stage as an opera were only moderately successful, since it was exceptionally static—a succession of long, rhetorical set pieces, as in Baroque opera or oratorio. Stravinsky had searched, he said, for "some universally familiar subject," so that he could "concentrate the whole attention of the audience, undistracted by the story, on the music itself." He also had decided that, "for subjects touching on the sublime," the vernacular tongue should be avoided; thus he chose Latin. Cocteau's French thus was put into Latin, except for brief insertions for a narrator, who would forecast upcoming developments and comment on their dramatic significance.

The second and final act of *Oedipus Rex* is particularly recommended for study. Here Oedipus, king of Thebes, comes to realize that he has unwittingly killed his father and married his own mother, Jocasta; the queen commits suicide, and Oedipus blinds himself and prepares for exile. Musically there is immense variety—from the lyrical passion of Jocasta in her first aria, as she pours scorn on oracles, to her later panic as she pleads with Oedipus to inquire no further into the mystery of the late king's murder, and from the jubilant choral *glorias* at the beginning of the act to the hushed choral farewells to Oedipus at the end. There is much that is genuinely moving here, but all is within a framework of truly classic dignity. In this work, music and drama undeniably become ritual.

Other Directions in Music

Stravinsky and Schoenberg symbolize stylistic extremes in serious music of the first half of the twentieth century. Other composers usually fell somewhere between and below those extremes. Many, however, gained greater popular acceptance for their music than did these masters.

Among the early-twentieth-century composers of authentic genius were certainly Alban Berg (1885–1935) and Béla Bartók (1881–1945), who leaned toward the styles of Schoenberg and Stravinsky, respectively. Four relatively conservative European composers of great ability were Paul Hindemith (1895–1963), Francis Poulenc (1899–1963), Sergei Prokofiev (1891–1953), and Dmitri Shostakovich (1906–75). In the United States many a disgruntled concertgoer wished that his own compatriots were writing music as pleasing and comprehensible as theirs. Of course a great many Americans were doing exactly that. Much of this music was very handsomely crafted, as in the cases of Roy Harris (1898–1979), Walter Piston (1894–1976), and Roger Sessions (1896–1985). Still more conservative was Virgil Thomson (born 1896),

who wrote spare-textured music of sophisticated artlessness—such as the opera *Four Saints in Three Acts*, composed to a rather unfathomable though charming libretto (with "Pigeons on the grass alas") by Gertrude Stein.

America also had its avant-garde composers. In later decades, the patriarch came to be Charles Ives (1874–1954), who had scarcely been known before 1945. Ives was a composer of astounding originality who anticipated atonality, polytonality, and virtually all the technical novelties of music up to mid-century. His mystical conception of the wholeness of humanity, especially of the American people, led him to employ all available musical resources, with special emphasis on American folk, religious, and other popular tunes. Frequently these tunes intermingle polyphonically. This effect so characteristic of Ives may be observed within an intimate, almost Classical setting in the first movement of his Second Sonata for Violin and Piano or, on the grandest scale, throughout the massive, complex Fourth Symphony.

Perhaps the most stylistically versatile of American composers in the years before (and after) 1945 was Aaron Copland (born 1900), who turned his hand to atonal and twelve-tone composition, as well as to a folkish conservatism and nearly everything in between. His most popular manner is exemplified by his ballet music for *Appalachian Spring*, which is alternately solemn, lively, lyrical, and passionate—and accessible to virtually any audience.

The musical scene in Europe and America was incredibly fragmented in the early twentieth century. In addition to the various warring styles of art music, popular music had readily accepted the status of a lower, less dignified form. This great divide between popular and so-called "classical" composition, which would have puzzled and probably appalled such jovial older composers as Mozart and Haydn, had been encouraged by the air of high seriousness that entered Western music in the nineteenth century. The creation of concert music had come to be seen as something holy, and its performance a solemn rite. Then in the twentieth century there came those immense complexities and ear-wrenching novelties that put almost insurmountable barriers between art music and "the people."

Throughout history, music of the people has continually tended to move upward from the humbler strata of society to become the music of all classes.

Often scorned at first by the world of higher "art," it has also sometimes been adapted for incidental use in art music. An extraordinary example of this is the jazz of the early twentieth century.

The most distinctive qualities of early jazz are usually traceable to the west-African origins of black Americans. The continuous, propulsive rhythm of early jazz and its immediate ancestors seems mainly African, as do various subtle rhythmic complexities. In melody and harmony the European influence grew significantly stronger, and the European influence was strongest of all in the adoption of specific musical instruments, although not necessarily in playing technique. Instrumental imitation of uninhibited vocal expression, for instance, frequently has characterized jazz.

Jazz appeared as a distinct musical form during the first quarter of the twentieth century. Born among the blacks of New Orleans and the American Midwest, and at first known only among blacks, it soon spread to whites in this country and eventually to all races and peoples. In fact, the French were the first to take jazz seriously enough to write reasonably scholarly books on the subject.

Among authentic types of early jazz were the *blues*—primarily a vocal form. Slow and plaintive, the blues had simple melodies and a very limited range of chords based on a scale that lowers the intervals of third and seventh. Blues singing is well exemplified in the recordings of Bessie Smith (1898–1937)—in such numbers as "Cold in Hand Blues" (1925), in historic collaboration with Louis Armstrong on the cornet, and two 1928 cuts, "Put It Right Here" and "I'd Rather Be Dead and Buried in My Grave."

One of the most obvious characteristics of jazz as it had developed by the mid twenties is apparent in the three listed recordings by Bessie Smith. Jazz was not primarily a composer's art, but a performer's art; what mattered most of all was the unique magic of a particular performance—which on records meant roughly a particular three minutes, the playing time of a ten-inch, 78-r.p.m. record. Sometimes performance included extensive improvisation by a soloist. More often it meant overall freedom to render a tune and its accompaniment in different ways at different times, and broad expressive freedom for soloists and ensemble in such matters as slides, breathing, note values, wideness of vibrato, and variations of tone color—freedoms vastly exceeding those in the performance of

art music. On the other hand, jazz musicians were little interested in achieving the slow build-ups, the complex technical development, or the kaleidoscopic changes that characterized much art music.

Probably the greatest jazz master of the later twenties, when jazz had achieved its maturity, was the trumpeter and singer Louis Armstrong (1900–71, fig. 19-32). Recommended as an introduction to his art are two 1928 recordings that feature Earl Hines on piano. "Weather Bird" is a complex duet in which the two players alternate in rival improvisations. In "West End Blues," also improvised, the trumpet shares solo rights with several other instruments and Armstrong's own *scat singing* (wordless vocalizing); it is a gem of inventive compression.

Jazz took many further turns before 1945 and after. But before 1945, jazz and art music remained worlds apart, with only rare exceptions. Duke Ellington experimented with composed jazz in longer forms, and such composers as Debussy, Stravinsky, and Copland incorporated occasional jazz influences in their work. One of the most successful instances of European adaptation of jazz characteristics to concert music was *The Creation of the World* (1923) by Darius Milhaud (1892–1974). As music to accompany a dance version

19-32 Louis Armstrong and His Hot Five, 1926.

of an African creation myth, this pleasant work is evocative of jazz qualities rather than literally imitative of jazz techniques. At the very outset the listener notices the blues mood, the *syncopation* (off-beat stresses), and the use of the saxophone, which had finally come into its own as a jazz instrument.

The most remarkable infusion of popular music elements into art music occurred in the concert writing of the American composer George Gershwin (1898–1937, fig. 19-33), although he is still better known for the splendid melodies and sophisticated craftsmanship of his popular songs, most of them written for Broadway musicals. The composer of such songs as "Embraceable You," "But Not for Me," and "Someone to Watch over Me," he deserves an honored place in musical history for this reason alone. In the context of the intermingling of popular and serious musical elements, Gershwin is especially remembered for three orchestral works—*Rhapsody in Blue* (1924, with the most familiar orchestration, by Ferdé Grofé, dating from 1942), the Concerto in F for piano and orchestra (1925), and *An American in Paris* (1928).

An American in Paris is a tone poem, or "program music," in the tradition of Liszt and Strauss but with strong popular elements that would have astounded those masters. A jaunty "walking theme" introduces the work, representing an American visitor exploring the French capital. The music proceeds through many metamorphoses evoking the city and even reflecting some momentary homesickness of the visitor; many listeners are charmed by the integration of authentic Parisian taxicab horns into the thematic material. The work, in very traditional tonal language, is a bravura

19-33   George Gershwin composing at the piano.

production that has become solidly established in the orchestral repertoire. However, *An American in Paris,* Gershwin's other orchestral pieces, and his dramatic and touching opera, *Porgy and Bess,* were relatively isolated phenomena in the serious-music world before 1945, and they were long regarded by most concert musicians and critics as amusing curiosities. Not until later decades would musicians consider at all searchingly the question of bringing together the powerful traditions of popular music and art music.

Recommended Reading

Boyer, John W., and Jan Goldstein. *Twentieth-Century Europe* (1987). Primary sources.

Clark, Ronald W. *Freud, The Man and the Cause* (1980). Thorough biography, very readable.

Daix, Pierre. *Cubists and Cubism* (1982). Comprehensive, beautifully illustrated.

Daval, Jean-Luc. *Avant-Garde Art 1914–1939* (1980). Comprehensive survey of painting and sculpture.

Descharnes, Robert. *Salvador Dali* (1985). Handsome picture book, with comments and essay.

Dube, Wolf-Dieter. *Expressionism* (1972). Fine overview of German Expressionism.

Ewen, David. *George Gershwin, His Journey to Greatness* (1970). Informative biography with some musical analysis.

Freud, Sigmund. *The Origin and Development of Psychoanalysis* (1955). Five 1910 lectures; good introduction to Freudianism.

Geist, Sidney. *Brancusi: The Sculpture and Drawings* (1975). Picture book with good introduction.

Haftmann, Werner. *Marc Chagall* (1984). Long essay plus color plates with long notes.

Huxley, Julian. *Religion without Revelation* (1967). Huxley's evolutionary humanistic religion, written from 1920s to 1964.

Jones, Max, and John Chilton. *Louis: The Louis Armstrong Story, 1900–1971* (1971). Good introduction to his career.

Lichtheim, George. *Europe in the Twentieth Century* (1972). Good scholarly history; narrative and topical.

Lynton, Norbert. *The Story of Modern Art* (1980). Fine introduction, c. 1905–1980.

Lyttleton, Humphrey. *The Best of Jazz: Basin Street to Harlem* (1978). The important musicians and their recordings, to 1930.

Martin, William R., and Julius Drossin. *Music of the Twentieth Century* (1980). Concise history, by composer, with musical examples.

Melville, Robert. *Henry Moore, Sculpture and Drawings 1921–1969* (1969). Fine survey.

Niebuhr, Reinhold. *The Essential Reinhold Niebuhr* (1986). Selection of typical essays 1934–60.

Ortega y Gasset, José. *The Revolt of the Masses*, ed. by Kenneth Moore (1985). The original work with commentary.

Reich, Willi. *Schoenberg, A Critical Biography* (1971). Good biography.

Rossiter, Frank R. *Charles Ives and His America* (1975). Thorough biography.

Rubin, William S. *Dada and Surrealist Art* (1968). Thorough coverage, well-illustrated.

Russell, John. *The World of Matisse 1869–1954* (1969). Fine life and times, well-illustrated.

Tomkins, Calvin. *The World of Marcel Duchamp, 1887–* (1966). Duchamp, Dadaism, and Surrealism; well-illustrated.

Twombly, Robert C. *Frank Lloyd Wright, His Life and His Architecture* (1979). Thorough survey.

Vlad, Roman. *Stravinsky* (1978). Life and music.

Wertenbaker, Lael. *The World of Picasso 1881–* (1967). Good introduction to life, work, and setting.

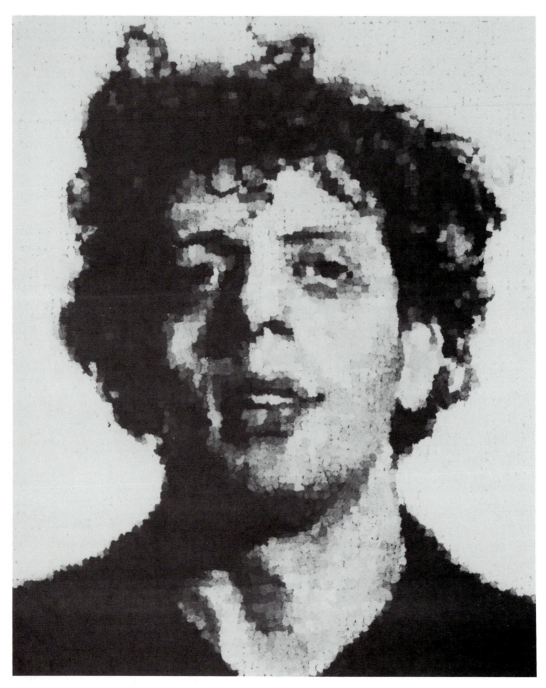

Chuck Close, *Phil*, 1983. Pulp paper on canvas,
98⅛″ × 72⅛″. Courtesy of the Pace Gallery, New York.

20

The Contemporary World: Since 1945

orld War II ended in 1945 with the exhaustion of Nazi Germany and the suicide of its leader Adolf Hitler, and then with the collapse of an enfeebled Japan presumably faced with massive devastation by United States nuclear bombs. The wartime alliance of Communist and capitalist nations against their common enemies broke up in disputes over territory and in fear of each other's intentions. Both sides maneuvered for power—sometimes recklessly—and nuclear destruction remained, and still remains, a grim threat.

Meanwhile most of the colonies of the West, especially in Asia and Africa, sought and obtained independence. When the British and French empires, among others, crumbled, the new superpowers of the Soviet Union, China, and the United States tried to move into the vacuum. When this happened in Vietnam, freed of French colonialism but at war within itself, the United States entered a struggle that drained its strength for more than a decade.

American intervention in Vietnam collided head-on not only with the Third World independence movement but also with a strong domestic movement in the sixties and later that sought political, social, and economic justice for such groups as women, students, blacks, and ethnic minorities. Domestic as well as international opinion concerning the goals and strategies of the United States was

CHRONOLOGY

HISTORY		THE ARTS	
		1900–	Louise Nevelson
		1901–66	Alberto Giacometti
		1901–74	Louis I. Kahn
		1901–85	Jean Dubuffet
		1906–65	David Smith
		1908–80	Jean Paul Sartre
		1908–	Elliott Carter
		1910–61	Eero Saarinen
		1910–	Wright Morris
1914–18	First World War	1910–	Francis Bacon
		1923–	James Dickey
		1924–87	James Baldwin
		1924–	Philip Pearlstein
		1927–	John Ashbery
		1929–	Claes Oldenburg
		1930–87	Andy Warhol
		1931–	Robert Morris
		1931–	Alice Munro
1933–45	F. D. Roosevelt president of the U.S.	1933–	Robert Birmelin
		1933–	Sam Gilliam
1939–45	World War II	1940s	Bop (jazz style)
1940–45	Winston Churchill prime minister of Great Britain	1940s–60s	"rhythm and blues"
1941	entry of U.S. into World War II	1941–	Jennifer Bartlett
1945	beginning of the nuclear age; end of World War II in Europe and the Pacific; founding of the U.N.	1941–	Jan Dibbets
		1941–	Bob Dylan
1945–48	establishment of East European communist satellites		
1945–51	Clement Attlee prime minister of Great Britain		
1945–53	Harry Truman president of the U.S.		
1947	independence of India and Pakistan	1947–	Laurie Anderson
1948	state of Israel established		
1949	Chinese People's Republic, German Federal Republic (W. Ger.), and German Democratic Republic (E. Ger.) established	1949	Miller's *Death of a Salesman*
1949–63	Konrad Adenauer chancellor of West Germany	1950s	first long-playing records
		1950s–60s	Abstract Expressionism at its height
1950–53	Korean War	1951	Mies van der Rohe's 860–880 Lake Shore Drive Apartments
1951–55	Winston Churchill prime minister of Great Britain	1952	de Beauvoir's *The Second Sex*
1952–	Elizabeth II queen of Great Britain	1952	Pollock's *Convergence (Number 10, 1952)*
1953	death of Stalin, leader of U.S.S.R.	1952–53	Stockhausen's *Kontra-Punkte*
		1953	de Kooning's *Woman VI*
1953–61	Dwight Eisenhower president of U.S.	1955–59	Rauschenberg's *Monogram*
1957	U.S.S.R.'s first space probe	1956	Rothko's *Orange and Yellow*
1957–63	Harold Macmillan prime minister of Great Britain	1957	Bernstein's *West Side Story*
1958	U.S.'s first space probe	1958	Cage's *Aria with Fontana Mix*

(continued)

HISTORY

1958–	Fifth French Republic
1958–64	Nikita Khrushchev leader of U.S.S.R.
1958–69	Charles de Gaulle president of France
1960s–70s	civil rights movement in U.S.
1960s–80s	women's movement in U.S.
1961–63	John Kennedy president of U.S.
1963–69	Lyndon Johnson president of U.S.
1964–70	Harold Wilson prime minister of Great Britain
1964–82	Leonid Brezhnev leader of U.S.S.R.
1968	student riots in U.S., France, etc.
1968–73	height of U.S. counterculture and protest movement
1969	first moon landing
1969–74	Richard Nixon president of U.S.
1969–74	Georges Pompidou president of France; Willy Brandt chancellor of West Germany
1970–74	Edward Heath prime minister of Great Britain
1973–74	"Watergate" crisis in the U.S.
1974–76	Harold Wilson prime minister of Great Britain
1974–77	Gerald Ford president of the U.S.
1974–81	Valéry Giscard d'Estaing president of France
1974–82	Helmut Schmidt chancellor of West Germany
1976–79	James Callaghan prime minister of Great Britain
1977–81	Jimmy Carter president of the U.S.
1979–	Margaret Thatcher prime minister of Great Britain
1981–	Ronald Reagan president of the U.S.
1981–	François Mitterand president of France
1982–	Helmut Kohl chancellor of West Germany
1985–	Mikhail Gorbachev leader of the U.S.S.R.

THE ARTS

1959	C. P. Snow's *The Two Cultures*
1960	Tingueley's *Homage to New York*
1960s	Pop art
1960s	height of the Beatles' popularity
1960s–	"music with repetitive structures"
1960s–	rock; soul
1961	Brown's *Available Forms 1*
1962	Britten's *War Requiem*
1966–67	Stockhausen's *Hymnen*
1967	García Márquez's *One Hundred Years of Solitude*
1967	R. Buckminster Fuller's American Pavilion, EXPO 67, Montreal
1970	Smithson's *Spiral Jetty*
1970	Crumb's *Ancient Voices of Children*
1970–71	Close's *Kent*
1971	Shostakovich's Symphony #15
1971–77	Pompidou National Center, Paris
1974	Heller's *Something Happened*
1976	Christo's *Running Fence*
1979	Sondheim's *Sweeney Todd*
1979	Styron's *Sophie's Choice*
1980	Glass's *Satyagraha*
1980s	Compact discs introduced
1981	Lloyd Webber's *Cats*
1982	Graves's Public Service Building, Portland, Oregon
1983	Christo's *Surrounded Islands*
1983	Kiefer's *Shulamite*
1983	Leslie's *The Thirteen Americans;* Bartlett's *Pool*
1983	Zwilich's *Chamber Symphony*
1984	Rabe's *Hurlyburly*
1984	Johnson and Burgee's Republic Bank Center, Houston
1984	Reich's *The Desert Music*
1984	Metheny's *First Circle*
1984	Lloyd Webber's *Requiem*
1984–85	Adams's *Harmonielehre*
1985	Salle's *The Farewell Painting*
1985	Wonder's *In Square Circle;* Sting's *Dream of the Blue Turtles*
1986	Pfaff's *Superette*
1986	Byrne's *True Stories*
1987	U2's *The Joshua Tree*

bitterly divided. Only with the ending of the war in Vietnam and the resolving of serious political scandals did the American nightmare come to an end. In the 1980s most Americans found the ebullient optimism of Ronald Reagan bracing and reassuring, although a significant minority expressed dismay over the persistence of underlying human and environmental problems and the catastrophic potential of the continuing nuclear rivalry with the Soviet Union.

Outside the United States, the non-Communist world displayed many encouraging signs of strength in the 1960s. Western Europe completed its recovery from the ravages of World War II and experimented in economic and political collaboration across national borders. Germany and Japan, although they had lost the war, gained economic positions even stronger than those they had held before. International cooperation has been increasingly recognized as the only viable alternative to devastating warfare. Following other Western precedents, the United States finally opened up relations with the People's Republic of China, a nation whose partial isolation had made it seem especially dangerous.

The extraordinary ferment of the postwar period in the West both built on and defied its vast economic and technological achievements. The technological possibilities offered by computers have increased daily but have not been able to lift ultimate world responsibilities from human shoulders. The exploration of outer space and the landing of men on the moon were other startling symbols of the new technology, but even these achievements were often ignored by a public that had seen so much in so little time. In any event, earthbound needs were becoming more pressing. Above all, industrialization, affluence, and an explosion of world population have induced an environmental crisis of staggering dimensions. Cities and countryside alike have been increasingly blighted. The existence of a world energy crisis of ominous proportions was finally recognized, then sometimes discounted or simply forgotten. The peoples of the world clearly have faced immense problems as well as exhilarating opportunities.

Daily crises, of course, have involved deeper issues, spiritual and moral. One of the deepest has concerned the fate of human freedom, so long the essence of the Western experience.

AN UNSETTLED HALF-CENTURY

Everywhere amid the pervasive change and confusion of the years after World War II there was an uneasy or desperate search for values. The lesson of past religion and philosophy and modern psychological science seems to be that human beings require both consolation and a firm sense of direction. The search for values has been extraordinarily earnest. Predictably, many people after the war sought refuge in human relationships or in religion, or both. Some theologians, such as the German Paul Tillich and the American Reinhold Niebuhr, found hope in a return to a judgmental Christian God not unlike the stern God of Luther and Calvin. Other theologians emphasized religious directions that were experimental or exotic. Although rational approaches continued to offer alternatives, the broad cultural pendulum continued its swing away from intellectualism. To be sure, philosophy—the traditional forum for debating the large issues of human existence—sometimes renounced any quest for ultimate answers and limited itself to mathematics and logic.

Existentialism—probably the most widespread and certainly the best publicized of postwar philosophies—did not limit its subject matter so strictly and dealt with many of the broad and profound issues of traditional philosophy. The French novelist, playwright, and philosopher Jean Paul Sartre (1908–80) elaborated a godless but not militantly atheistic brand of Existentialism. He did not accept God's existence, as some Existentialists did, but he regarded the question of deity as relatively unimportant, since the existence of the individual person was what truly mattered. Man first exists, said Sartre, and then must deliberately define his nature. "Man is nothing else but what he makes of himself." Man is a thing "that propels itself toward a future and is aware of doing so." Existentialism, he continued, makes man fully responsible for his own existence. Thus Sartre's Existentialism assumed an essentially romantic, even heroic stance, rejecting values that are externally imposed on individuals. He insisted on the urgent importance of personal, often anguished, choice in a lonely world dominated by the image of death.

The Existentialist stance was too heroic for most people, or the choice too empty, and so the search for alternatives continued. Outside the religious route, the most promising road for many intellectuals seemed for a time to be *Structuralism,* which was only peripherally a philosophy at all. Unlike Existentialism, Structuralism focused not on the individual but on composites and groups. It was a general tendency of thought, most notably in linguistics and anthropology, that sought to identify and study basic aspects of human culture as systems or "structures" of linguistic signs or other cultural phenomena. Elaborated by such French thinkers as Claude Lévi-Strauss and Jean Piaget, the Structuralist method would be applied also to such realms as history, mythology, psychology, and philosophy. Indeed it seemed that all social manifestations of human life could perhaps be analyzed in terms of a basic language of some sort—not of isolated words or ideas, but in terms of integrated networks of relationships. These relationships (like Freudian urges in earlier decades) appeared to exist not on the surface of empirical reality but beneath it. By the late 1970s, however, after much initial enthusiasm for ferreting out these structures, many thinkers were coming to question the ultimate significance of such structures as useful human guideposts. Moreover, outside of intellectual circles Structuralism had never aroused much interest or exerted much real charm, in contrast to the more accessible and dramatic teachings of Existentialism.

Thus, by the 1980s, many articulate men and women have found themselves adrift in dubious philosophical seas. For many people the solution has involved not only a return to traditional ideas—whether in religion or outside it—but also personal absorption in specific restricted areas of interest. The modern explosion of knowledge—of information and disinformation—seems to require highly specialized training and thinking, and even those persons with extensive intellectual curiosity often are frustrated by the sheer bulk of material to be comprehended and mastered. As late as the age of Diderot and Goethe (the decades somewhat before and after 1800) an inquisitive mind could become knowledgeable about most important things outside of technological detail—but the growth of knowledge since then has made this impossible for even the best minds in the late twentieth century. In 1959 the British scientist and novelist C. P. Snow, in his essay *The Two Cultures,* particularly deplored the prevailing ignorance of humanists concerning science, and of scientists concerning the humanities. Other commentators have noted that even within each of these two realms there are other frontiers seemingly just as impassable. This growth, fragmentation, and specialization of knowledge and the consequent limitations on human potentialities have appalled a good number of civilized souls but are only dimly recognized, if at all, by most of the Western world as a real human loss.

The Western Experience and Literature

Along with the failure of many Westerners to think and to experience widely, there often has come a sense of human mechanization and depersonalization. The American novelist Joseph Heller (born 1923)—who had already memorably epitomized the self-defeating absurdity that could characterize the military life in *Catch 22* (1961)—turned in his 1974 novel *Something Happened* to the malaise of an un-rooted middle class. The second novel's first-person protagonist is chronically uneasy and insecure; his responses to life's demands are often empty and pointless. Much of the novel's spirit comes through in section headings such as "I get the willies," "My wife is unhappy," "My daughter's unhappy," "My little boy is having difficulties," and "My boy has stopped talking to me." The section "The office in which I work" is a devastating portrayal of the American workplace at its comfortable worst, with its institutional fears, shallowness, and pretense.

By no means *all* of mid- and late-twentieth-century life has appeared so disaffected and meaningless, in either the Americas or Europe. In the world of higher culture there has been an incredible succession of lively and excited movements and causes to be battled over, as we will see. In the realm of historical writing, not only has the debate continued on whether history is an art or a science; there also have been heated arguments over whether Freud's insights can be absorbed into history as "psychohistory," and there has been much inquiry into the history of past "mentalities." In countries with substantial black or other nonwhite racial minorities there have been strong movements, some of them at least partially successful, to establish political, social, and economic equality. In nearly all Western nations there have been renewed efforts toward the equality of women with men. In the 1950s the movement was sparked most notably by *The Second Sex,* a powerful book by Simone de Beauvoir (1908–86). In figure 20-1 we see de Beauvoir and her friend Sartre in a photograph taken at the height of

20-1   Simone de Beauvoir and Jean Paul Sartre, 1956.

their influence in 1956; here the ordinarily very earnest twosome are sharing an atypically jovial moment.

The Second Sex is closer to philosophical abstraction than to pragmatic politics, and it strikes few readers today as being very radical. In the early fifties, however, it offered a broad foundation for upcoming battles, with memorable thumbnail characterizations of the tradition of sexual inequality. "Thus humanity," she wrote, "is male, and man defines woman not in herself but as relative to him; she is not regarded as an autonomous being." "If woman seems to be the inessential which never becomes the essential, it is because she herself fails to bring about this change." Of women, de Beauvoir declared that "they have gained only what men have been willing to grant; they have taken nothing, they have only received"—and she went on to urge cooperative organizing for women's unity. The new woman, she concluded, must shed her passivity and seize her equal and independent role in human society.

As for poetry and fiction—novels, plays, and short stories—contemporary literary expression has been extraordinarily diverse. In the recent Western world no single voice like that of Plato or Dante or Shakespeare, no handful of exemplars recognized by the age itself as its spokesmen, like Voltaire and Rous-

seau for the Enlightenment, has as yet emerged—and, of course, judgment from the perspective of later decades and centuries is still unavailable to us. Here we can only sample the contrasting and complementary literary textures of our age, hoping to get some sense of the creative richness of recent literature. To narrow the focus a bit, only authors from the Americas are noted here.

In poetry there have been many voices of popular culture, especially in the lively youth movement or "counterculture" of the sixties; we will glance at Bob Dylan, Joan Baez, and Paul Simon later, in reference to their music. Taken several degrees more seriously by the literary establishment than these three writers was the 1960s poetry of James Dickey (born 1923). The theme of "Cherrylog Road" is a sexual encounter in an automobile junkyard. The passion is heightened by the summer heat, the junked cars, and the cars' lively small wildlife inhabitants, as well as by the danger threatened by Doris Holbrook's wrathful father. At the end the young narrator roars away on his motorcycle, drunk with speed, power, and sexual release, "wild to be wreckage forever." If the poem is comic, as some readers maintain, it is certainly also as exhilarating and rebellious as the excitable youth and the surging student movement of the sixties. In the same 1965 volume of poetry, *Helmets,* is found Dickey's "Drinking from a Helmet"—an anguished reflection of the speaker's experience as a seventeen-year-old infantryman in the Second World War. As for echoes of war, the next decade would give birth to other authors' memoirs and fictional reflections of the unfortunate Vietnamese experience—an experience that would haunt and fascinate the subsequent generation.

Still higher than Dickey in the usual critical pantheon of contemporary poets has been John Ashbery (born 1927). Ashbery's artful, private, often difficult verse offers challenges to its readers, and occasional shocks of recognition, as well as a salutory reminder that there is more than one way to read and interpret a poem. As a poet preferring thoughtfulness and rumination to narrative excitement, Ashbery has frequently pondered the human soul, as in "Self-Portrait in a Convex Mirror" (1975) and "Otherwise" (1981). In both poems the soul appears fixed and confined—in the second to be "fussed over," and in the first to be imprisoned by art, which reduces it to only "our moment of attention."

The American theater has had its ups and downs since 1945, as always. Three strong plays may be mentioned, from 1949 and from three or four decades later. *Death of a Salesman* by Arthur Miller (born 1915) has come as close to classic status as any post-World War II literary work. Its story is commonplace yet poignant, and its style unadorned and realistic—in stark contrast to centuries-old classics such as *Oedipus the King* and *Hamlet*. In its simplest terms, the plot tells of a salesman in his sixties, Willy Loman, who is fired from his job for lacking productive vitality. Despite a certain genuine sense of personal dignity, Willy kills himself in a moment of distraction. Almost as important to the plot as Willy's fate are the failed dreams of his son Biff, and at least three other personalities also are well delineated. Out of a very ordinary subject and several less than heroic characters, Miller devised a drama of real power and pathos.

Two interesting playwrights of more recent years are David Rabe (born 1940) and Beth Henley (born 1952). Rabe's *Hurlyburly*, first produced in 1984, reflects a scene of what most readers and viewers would consider sordid realism, complete with omnipresent sex, profanity, and drugs. Its underlying theme is individual human isolation from the lives of others, as well as intractable interpersonal involvements. The basic tone of *Hurlyburly* is serious, even grim, despite the intrusion of lighter moments of a sort banned in Miller's *Death of a Salesman*.

The mood of Henley's *Crimes of the Heart,* produced on Broadway in 1981, is ambiguous: the director and actors in a given production can vary the proportions of comedy and tragedy. Here, as in much recent theater, the long history of progressive breakdown of the distinctions between comedy and tragedy in Western drama has led to the abandonment of all rigid distinctions and a thorough amalgamation of the serious and the frivolous. The plot reveals the tenuous grasp of reality on the part of each of three sisters in small-town Mississippi: the eldest is at best neurotic; the youngest, intermittently psychotic. All of the characters are delineated with both clarity and affectionate sympathy as the older sisters react to the murder perpetrated by the youngest. In the course of three acts the delinquencies and secrets of all three sisters are revealed as their self-protective defenses are peeled away. At the end no solution to the desperate situation of the youngest sister is suggested; centuries of neatly resolved theater plots seem irrelevant as the curtain falls on a scene of apparent lighthearted sisterly solidarity.

Certainly we leave neither *Crimes of the Heart* nor *Hurlyburly* with any sense of a world made right. The same can be said of most of the better novels and short stories of the contemporary age. *Sophie's Choice* (1979), a much-praised novel by William Styron (born 1925), proceeds from cheeriness and even buffoonery to dark anguish, as successive layers of experience are stripped from the life of Sophie Zawistoski, a strikingly beautiful Polish survivor of one of Hitler's wartime concentration camps. The backward and forward movements of fictional time that Styron employed were far from experimental anymore in the 1970s. In comparison with Diderot's *Jacques the Fatalist* or Gertrude Stein's fractured writings, *Sophie's Choice* is positively, solidly old-fashioned, even in its insight into the dark places of the human soul.

One modest approach to novelistic originality in this period was the flourishing of Magical Realism, most notably in Hispanic American literature. Elena Garro, born in Mexico in 1920, made *Recollections of Things to Come* (1963) an experiment in the feeling and the transformations of time as well as a revelation of human passion. The widely translated novel by the Colombian-born author Gabriel García Márquez (born 1928), *One Hundred Years of Solitude* (1967), demonstrated Magical Realism very strikingly. Despite many leaps in time, it is a relatively straightforward, traditionally realistic narrative that often interjects the fantastic without interrupting the narrative or the tone. Appearing randomly in the novel are a town-wide plague of insomnia, several returns to life because the solitude of death is unbearable, the repeated levitations of a priest, a rain of yellow flowers, and precise memories that are hereditary as well as personal. Yet the novel goes far beyond the cleverness and excitement of exotic or science fiction in its depth of character portrayal and its serious, indeed tragic intent. This is a mythic creation of an imaginary Colombian town that can represent nearly all of humanity. Sometimes, however, the town seems made up of very real individuals, many of them imprisoned in their own solitude.

The short stories of the period that seem likely to survive are still more conservative in style than the novels. "Sonny's Blues" (1957) by James Baldwin (1924–87, fig. 20-2)—a distinguished novelist and commentator on the condition of blacks in the modern world—explores the world of the New York ghetto with its painful problems. The narrator, a school teacher who has nearly pulled himself out of the ghetto world, gradually becomes aware not only of the pain but of the tragic dignity and uplifting emotional intensity that exist in the black culture of Manhattan. At

20-2 James Baldwin, 1963.

last when he enters the jazz world of his younger brother Sonny, a pianist, he finds comprehensible not only one young man's personal struggle but the spirit of the black experience everywhere.

> Sonny's fingers filled the air with life, his life. But that life contained so many others. And Sonny went all the way back, he really began with the spare, flat statement of the opening phrase of the song. Then he began to make it his. It was very beautiful because it wasn't hurried and it was no longer a lament. I seemed to hear with what burning he had made it his, with what burning we had yet to make it ours, how we could cease lamenting. Freedom lurked around us and I understood, at last, that he could help us to be free if we would listen, that he would never be free until we did.

Many other contemporary short stories were less committed to social causes, and often their meanings were ambiguous despite their straightforward realism. Among the skilled writers of short stories in the seventies and eighties were the Canadian writer Alice Munro (born 1931) and Wright Morris (born in Nebraska in 1910). Morris was fascinated by themes of discomfort and disorientation in unfamiliar territory, as shown by two of his stories: "In Another Country"

(1972) reflects a tourist's awkwardness in Spain, and "Glimpses into Another Country" (1983) portrays an elderly Californian calmly facing unreality and victimization in New York. Munro wrote with unsentimental, seemingly effortless precision of Canadian life, as exemplified by two stories published in 1983. "Hard-Luck Stories" focuses on the feminine experience in Toronto and the everyday emotions of men and women, and "The Moons of Jupiter" relates a woman's reactions to her father's terminal illness. The father is sketched deftly, in short sentences: "He worked in a factory, he worked in his garden, he read history books. He could tell you about the Roman emperors or the Balkan wars. He never made a fuss."

Innovation in the Arts

Although fictional writing in the postwar Western world operated most memorably within traditional modes of expression, music and the visual arts saw a faster pace and a greater variety of innovations than in any previous age. However, even in these arts some continuity was maintained, if only because many artists and composers of the prewar period continued a fairly unadventurous creative activity for several postwar decades. Stravinsky, to be sure, confounded his listeners by adopting the serialism of the twelve-tone school in the early 1950s—but the serialism of the twenties was by no means innovative in the fifties. In the visual arts, any survey of creative activity in the decades after 1945 must acknowledge not only the occasional inspirational example but also the sustained productive presence of such respected artists as Miró, Chagall, and Picasso, even though they were no longer in the vanguard of artistic innovation.

The intense experimentation in the visual art of the forties and fifties was almost entirely in the hands of younger artists—and it was no longer centered in Paris but in New York. The political upheavals of the sixties brought still another wave of talent in the visual arts and music, this time widely diffused in America and Europe. This new art raised many fundamental questions concerning the structure of the art world and the nature of art itself. The art world recognized, far more fully than before, the contributions of women and minority artists. With rare exceptions, women artists had been almost invisible before the later sixties.

In the United States, politically conscious art sometimes merged with the art of women and of blacks, which raised urgent issues concerning the function of art. To many of the artists who confronted political and social issues, much of the struggle of the past for art-for-art's-sake seemed misguided. In the view of activist artists, art should serve specific causes in the righting of existing social and political wrongs.

For most artists, however, the age-long struggle for artistic autonomy retained its relevance and urgency. But what, in fact, was the nature of art? What was art seeking to become? One very crucial trend had been receiving increasing emphasis in the practice and thinking of artists beginning with the Impressionists: an increasing "reductionism." More and more the arts seemed to involve less and less—less and less, for example, of photographic realism, of technical virtuosity in illusionistic effects, or of emotional involvement. Forms were being reduced to their most elementary state. Although there were a number of important exceptions, art in the sixties seemed to be moving toward minimalism. In extreme cases, paintings were little more than brushwork, and music was reduced to simple rhythm or even to absolute silence on the part of the performer. The significance of this evolution has been hotly debated in this age of heated and exciting debate. To many people, the process of reduction has seemed to herald the end of art; to others it promises to be a starting point for a new and infinitely more complex art.

In the meantime, serious visual and musical art tended to move in directions that left the average culture consumer unmoved. For the most advanced experimental new music—probably the most extreme example—few outlets and patrons remained except the universities, the moneyed foundations, and the buyers of records. In other areas of music, however, long-playing records and tapes (and to a lesser degree, compact discs in the 1980s) accomplished a veritable revolution in music consumership, achieving far more for musical education and the pervasiveness of music in contemporary life than the many well-intentioned and sometimes effective and imposing cultural centers erected in the cities of Europe and America (see fig. 20-9). Handsome physical facilities, it was discovered, offered new opportunities but hardly guaranteed excellence, whether in music, theater, the visual arts, or their vigorously blooming experimental combinations.

Aside from such synthetic explorations as we will note later, the most promising newer mediums seemed to be films and television. With some encouraging ex-

ceptions, television failed in its first decades to live up to its promise; happily the film medium produced enough masterpieces to be tentatively judged the most successful art form of the post-1945 years. In almost every part of the world, films of truly exceptional quality were produced—films that won international acclaim and, perhaps, furthered understanding between peoples. We will now review a few representative developments in the historic artistic disciplines of architecture, sculpture, painting, and music, and their mixed-medium offshoots.

A NEW ARCHITECTURE

In architecture, the post-1945 period saw extensions of the geometric, cool International style and the more personalized expression of Frank Lloyd Wright—with the two schools gradually coming to share ideas. Almost wholly in the International tradition was the work of the distinguished German architect Ludwig Mies van der Rohe (1886–1969), whose main impact on the architecture of his adopted United States came in the 1950s and later. The International style offered new options to skyscraper builders, and Mies brought designs of great refinement and visual simplicity to the style. The 860–880 Lake Shore Drive Apartments in Chicago (fig. 20-3), with their glass shells and black steel plating over fireproofed columns, were perhaps the most cleanly vertical in appearance of all skyscrapers at mid-century. A similar spare sleekness is seen in his S. R. Crown Hall of the Illinois Institute of Technology (fig. 20-4)—a horizontal rectangular slab, glassed in, whose main floor is a large open space that permits changeable divisions. Mies always vigorously denied the inevitable charges of cold architectural impersonality, insisting that the indeterminacy of his spacious interiors offered the greatest of all opportunities for individualized and flexible décors and uses.

The Miesian style, with its emphasis on jewel like precision and elegance, was much cheapened in its countless imitations in America and Europe. Still other new buildings embodied a massive and forbidding air; this manner that originated in the fifties was often known as *Brutalism*; a modest example is Rochester's First Unitarian Church (fig. 20-5) by the American architect Louis I. Kahn (1901–74). Very high window placement eliminates direct glare inside—

20-3 Ludwig Mies van der Rohe, 860–880 Lake Shore Drive Apartments, Chicago, 1951.

perhaps an adequate rationale for the fortresslike gloom of the walls (later enlivened, inside, by iridescent wall hangings designed by Kahn). Although Brutalism may well have derived its name from the *béton brut* (rough, unfinished, concrete) of Le Corbusier, the general stylistic emphasis sometimes tended less toward frank acceptance of materials than toward a deliberately crude, indeed brutal severity for its own sake.

Most architecture after mid century was less grim. Eero Saarinen (1910–61) won extraordinary popularity with the public for his sometimes whimsical, always graceful architectural forms. The David S. Ingalls Hockey Rink at Yale University (fig. 20-6) is a product of the fertile Saarinen imagination and embodies multiple stylistic influences. Built largely of reinforced concrete, the structure is topped by a roof in the form of a parabolic arch, rather resembling a boat turned upside down. The arch is continued in reverse at both ends by cantilevered finlike forms, in which floodlights are mounted. The elegant curves of the rink recall both the airy concrete structures of Le Corbusier's Formalist period and the freedom of Wright's Expressionism—not to mention the influence of modern sculptural abstraction.

Architecture later in the century would often return to the spirit of Saarinen's amiable eclecticism. Other architects ventured into new paths, especially under the influence of engineering and social plan-

20-4 Ludwig Mies van der Rohe, S. R. Crown Hall, Illinois Institute of Technology, Chicago, 1952–56.

20-5 Louis I. Kahn, First Unitarian Church, Rochester, New York, 1963–64.

20-6 Eero Saarinen, David Ingalls Hockey Rink, Yale University, New Haven, Connecticut, 1956–59.

ning. As an especially practical art, architecture has always been combined with engineering and social concerns, but the decisive power of one or the other has sometimes been exceptionally obvious. Both defined the work of the American designer and seer R. Buckminster Fuller (1895–1983). Fuller contributed strikingly to the architectural application of engineering principles. Above all, he introduced and popularized the *geodesic dome*—a structure whose structural strength and stability is based on the equilibrium resulting from an efficient domelike grid of intersecting straight bars. The geodesic principle could theoretically be applied on any scale (even for total living areas several miles across) and with a great variety of materi-

als. Fuller's American Pavilion at EXPO 67 (fig. 20-7), an international exposition in Montreal, illustrates the geodesic idea on a large scale. This principle—which combines stability, maximum interior volume, minimum surface area, and ease of construction at minimal cost—gained substantial popularity in domestic architecture in the 1970s. Fuller's vision, in fact, included both engineering and concern for such critical environmental and social problems as pollution and energy conservation.

Other builders in the later twentieth century experimented in directions less obviously determined by any single engineering principle. Varied experiments in engineering continued to satisfy specific aesthetic

20-7 R. Buckminster Fuller, American Pavilion, EXPO 67, Montreal, 1967.

and social requirements. Often these new projects sought to solve urgent needs in urban and suburban planning, or envisaged immense, sprawling structural units with attached, perhaps disposable, mass-produced elements. Architects most often now were working not as independent designers but within large architectural firms. Two of these—Caudill, Rowland, Scott of Houston, and Dalton, van Dijk, Johnson and Partners of Cleveland—were largely responsible for a striking building in Akron, Ohio, the Edwin J. Thomas Performing Arts Hall of the University of Akron. The hall was intended to serve for concerts, theater, dance, and opera; the size of the auditorium is adjustable through the lowering of portions of its ceiling to cut off successive seating areas. Hanging in the main lobby (fig. 20-8) are chrome-plated steel cylinders that appear to be immense chimes but that actually are counterweights connected by partly visible pulleys and wires to the movable auditorium ceiling.

In the late eighties there has been no fuller agreement on ideal architectural forms for the future than there was in previous decades. Dissatisfaction and im-

patience with the International style, and with Brutalism, were common, but there was certainly no consensus on an alternative style. One widespread trend was the exuberant use of color in new buildings, regardless of the basic architectural forms. Sometimes this color was applied not to traditional architectural elements such as walls and piers, but to air ducts, girders, and other utilitarian devices that were being

20-8 Caudill, Rowlett, Scott; Dalton, van Dijk, Johnson, and Partners; and others, main lobby of the Edwin J. Thomas Performing Arts Hall, The University of Akron, Akron, Ohio, 1973.

20-9 Renzo Piano
and Richard Rogers,
Georges Pompidou
National Center for
Art and Culture
(Beaubourg Center),
Paris, 1971–77.

exposed quite frankly to view in the interior of new buildings, as in the case of the Thomas Hall counterweights.

A more drastic innovation was embodied in the Georges Pompidou National Center for Art and Culture in Paris (fig. 20-9). This ambitious cultural center was built to the winning design (in an international competition) of Renzo Piano and Richard Rogers—Italian and English, respectively. French President Pompidou had conceived the idea of this center for all the contemporary arts, and it came to house a museum of modern art, a public library, and centers for art documentation, industrial design, and research in musical sound. Its most novel architectural feature was the externalization of its service devices. The brightly painted air ducts, escalators, and the like are on the exterior of the structure, which preserves the interior space for the building's purposes. This gave the structure the novel appearance of having been turned inside out. The opinions of Parisians and visitors differed markedly on the merits of the center's design, but no one could deny its demonstration that there was excitement in contemporary architecture.

Even as the Pompidou Center was eliciting wonder and controversy, a different sort of excitement was brewing in the architectural world. New theories and structures generally termed post-Modern have been challenging much of the Modernist concept of building. The ultimate target for destruction by post-Modernism in architecture is the International style, still dominant at least in skyscrapers, together with such offshoots as Brutalism and the more graceful styles such as we have seen at Yale and in Montreal. All this building, say the post-Modernists, is too self-consciously, rootlessly innovative; it also is far too austere. Now cold precisionism can be replaced by more variety and detail, more color, and even sometimes more intimacy than the rigorous Modernist movement offers. Above all, some sense of history will be given to architecture. This will entail a rejection of Modernism's revolt against the chains of the past—a revolt that the post-Modernists say goes counter to the public's yearning for a sense of architectural propriety and familiarity. If post-Modernism means an echoing of Egyptian pyramids, Gothic cathedrals, classical temples, and neo-Classical churches, so much the better. Architecture, the post-Modernists assert, will again make the people feel at home in their world by appealing to a sense of nostalgia.

Post-Modern architecture has retained, however, technological advances of Modern building, and usually a substantial degree of the older style's clarity and precision. Sometimes the merging of styles has made classification difficult, as in much of the late work of the veteran architect Philip Johnson (born 1906). The radical historical eclecticism of Johnson's style, in collaboration with John Burgee and others, is handsomely embodied in the Republic Bank Center in Houston that was completed in 1984 (fig. 20-10). The main part of the building is a tower 780 feet high, faced in red Swedish granite with ample window space. A lower structure echoes the enormous, steep, stepped-back gables of the tower. Small obelisks reminiscent of Egyptian monuments surmount each jutting corner of the gables, which themselves recall the steep gables of much domestic and civic building of medieval and early modern Germany and the Netherlands. An interior view of the lower structure (fig. 20-11) shows the interior treatment of the stepped gables, together with a starkly perforated wall that may suggest elegantly ruinous remains from the past.

Except for the ruddiness of its exterior, the colors used in the Republic Bank Center are rather muted, although they go well beyond the black–grey–white

20-10   John Burgee Architects, with Philip Johnson, Architect, Republic Bank Center, Houston, 1981–84.

20-11   John Burgee Architects, with Philip Johnson, Architect, hall in Republic Bank Center, Houston, 1981–84.

range of most Modernist architecture. Much of the architecture of the post-Modernist Michael Graves (born 1934) uses a still greater range of color, and indeed of texture. Graves's Public Service Building in Portland, Oregon (fig. 20-12), was completed in 1982 and was immediately perceived as a scandal to the Modernist establishment. A later building in rather similar style, the headquarters of Humana Corporation in Louisville, Kentucky, has aroused less controversy, although it is even more eclectically inventive. Both structures make exuberant use of color and (especially in the second building) of forms that seem more sculptural than Modernistically functional. The basic form of the Portland building is a box, with insets and protuberances; over this framework are presented a mixture of contrasting colors and stylistic elements. Critics have said that the building's decorative elements seem loud and cheap and its eclecticism debased. In any case its blue-green tiles at street level, and the brown, beige, and yellow superstructure with stylized blue garlands and a

20-12 Michael Graves, Public Service Building, Portland, Oregon, 1982.

blue topping are a world away—in appearance if not in basic structure—from the stern steel and glass of Modernism and the monochrome concrete of Brutalism. The long-term viability of this rather extreme post-Modernist manner is doubtful; certainly it will fade in time, as have all styles architectural or otherwise.

NEW CURRENTS IN PAINTING

Excitement in the art world in the decades after 1945 was not confined to architectural design. Among the traditional disciplines, painting perhaps saw the most exciting and far-reaching changes of all. Yet even the most innovative painting often had discernible links with the past, as well as with the political, social, and philosophic currents of its own age.

Figure Painting after World War II

Experiments in figure painting after World War II continued to be largely Expressionist, distorting or abstracting the human form. The visions of the figure painters were frequently fantastic and frightening, like fragments of a nightmare. Prominent among these painters was Francis Bacon (born 1910) of Britain, whose work reflected "an obsession with life"—and especially with life's lonely agonies at or beyond the frontiers of the bearable. In his *Portrait of Isobel Rawsthorne* (fig. 20-13), the woman's face is cruelly twisted and slashed by the broad, curving brushstrokes of which it is composed. Ironically, the tragic frenzy of Bacon's image is heightened by the gracefulness of the forms and the refinement of his technique. In his own unorthodox way, he has brought expressive beauty to human misery and despair.

For many of Bacon's contemporaries, distortion and pain in the human figure were in large part inspired by the ravages of World War II. The same sense of meaninglessness and the squalor of the human con-

20-13 Francis Bacon, *Portrait of Isobel Rawsthorne*, 1966. Oil on canvas. Tate Gallery, London.

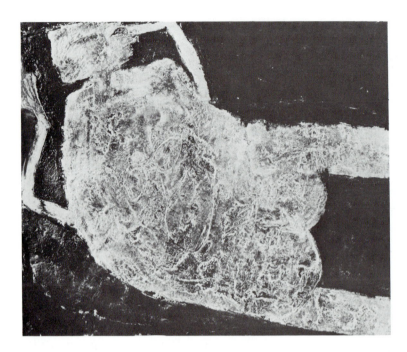

20-14 Jean Dubuffet, *Olympia (Corps de Dame)*, 1950. Mixed media on canvas, 35″ × 45¾″. Courtesy of Pierre Matisse Gallery, New York.

dition that moved Sartre and other writers to the sometimes bleak vistas of Existentialism brought many painters to attack not only the figure but the canvas itself. One of the most important artists of the postwar period was the Frenchman Jean Dubuffet (1901–85), whose early attempts to break with tradition often veered toward the realm of sculpture in their building up of thick, richly tactile surfaces of paint, sand, glue, and even asphalt. Art, said Dubuffet, must not serve only "the pleasure of the eyes," but is an intellectual language that tells us about the world. For one period, Dubuffet sought to capture the spontaneity of children and madmen and of primitive and savage peoples, with their "instinct, passion, mood, violence, madness." As an exercise in the "rehabilitation of scorned values" he portrayed and interpreted the female figure as repulsively as possible—to replace what he regarded as the degrading "fine arts" ideal of the feminine nude with a new honesty. One of the *Bodies of Ladies* series, *Olympia* (fig. 20-14), shows us a hideously bloated torso with gross legs and vestigial arms—a caricature of Manet's picture of a reclining courtesan, painted this time with lumpy pigments mixed with foreign objects, then scratched and daubed to form a messily eroded human landscape.

Willem de Kooning (born 1904) came to the United States from Holland as a twenty-two-year-old stowaway in 1926 and remained here to become a painter of great power and an important influence on postwar American art. He became a champion of the absolute autonomy of the individual artist and denounced the attempts of painters and critics to establish distinct schools and doctrines of art. "In art," he stated bluntly, "one idea is as good as another." He argued that "style is a fraud," since it demands conformity to standards imposed on the artist either by the art world or by contemporary society.

Usually, although by no means invariably, de Kooning retained natural forms as the basis of his paintings. Woman remained a recurrent theme in his work, although his female figures are sometimes barely recognizable as such. *Woman VI* (fig. 20-15) is one of a series done in the 1950s. His broad brushstrokes—red, pink, green, and black are predominant—evoke a female figure merging with an indeterminate background. Slashing distortions in facial features suggest an unstable compound of sensuality, schizophrenia, mystery, and terror, all portrayed as if in a passing flash of recognition. Antecedents of this sort of insight would seem to include the simultaneous vision of Cubism and the psychological ambiguities and distorted creations of Surrealism.

20-15 Willem de Kooning, *Woman VI*, 1953. Oil on canvas, 69″ × 59″. The Carnegie Museum of Art, Pittsburgh. Gift of G. David Thompson, 1955.

in New York came the most important art movement of the immediate postwar period.

Abstract Expressionism consisted of two rather different branches: the Action Painting branch, which concentrated on gesture, and the Chromatic Abstraction branch, which stressed atmosphere. Vasily Kandinsky's pathfinding work and theory had foreshadowed the development of Action Painting, as had the Surrealist concept of psychic automatism, but both branches stressed the unpremeditated—at least in the final canvas, if not necessarily (for the Chromatic branch) throughout the painting process. Where the Surrealists had flocked to the banner of Freud and tried to release their own personal demons on the canvas, the Abstract Expressionists were attracted to the ideas of Carl Jung—in particular to his theory of the collective unconscious. Personal as their work appears, it was nevertheless directed at discovering forms and emotions that were universal.

At the center of the Action Painting branch—and often thought of as the most typical of it—was Jackson Pollock (1912–56). It was Pollock who, in 1947, made the daring and astonishing break with the tradition of brush painting. Working with the canvas spread out on the floor, he poured, dripped, and splattered paint from cans and brushes, seldom physically touching the surface of the painting himself. His gestures, movements, and rhythms were recorded by the loops and threads of paint that fell. Concerning his method, he wrote:

> When I am in my painting, I'm not aware of what I'm doing. It is only after a sort of "get acquainted" period that I see what I have been about. I have no fears about making changes, destroying the image, etc., because the painting has a life of its own. I try to let it come through. It is only when I lose contact with the painting that the result is a mess. Otherwise there is pure harmony, an easy give and take, and the painting comes out well.

As for occasional unintentioned smears or puddlings of paint, these could be retained, covered over, or used as jumping-off points for further improvisation.

In addition to the new freedom of gesture and thought, this way of working offered two other major

Abstract Expressionism and Its Offshoots

Recognition as a painter of note came no faster to de Kooning than to his New York friends who (with his own intermittent participation) were establishing Abstract Expressionism. The New York School, as it came to be called, emerged as a group of artists struggling for survival in the years of World War II and immediately thereafter. Not all of them consistently produced thoroughly abstract art, and hardly any were native New Yorkers; Mark Rothko's origins, for example, were Russian, and Jackson Pollock had grown up in California and Arizona. The reception of these artists paralleled that of the Impressionists in the late nineteenth century. Both groups moved slowly from being objects of indifference, amusement, and scorn in their early years to eventual enthusiastic acceptance within the cultural establishment. In each case the first years were difficult. The Greenwich Village section of New York became the equivalent of the Impressionists' Montmartre in Paris, and heated discussions and mutual encouragement aided the rise of the new movement as it had the earlier one. Out of these humble beginnings

20-16 Jackson Pollock, *Convergence (Number 10, 1952)*. Oil on canvas, 7¾' × 12½'. Albright–Knox Art Gallery, Buffalo, New York. Gift of Seymour H. Knox, 1956.

opportunities for the artist. One was that equal emphasis could be given each part of the work, resulting especially from the freedom to move around the canvas. *Convergence (Number 10, 1952)* (fig. 20-16) is typical of the drip paintings both in technique and in the "all-over" approach to structure. It is of consistent texture throughout, the similarity of the lines and their complex, interweaving patterns making it impossible to discern structural elements smaller than the whole. Such a composition can seem to stretch out beyond the edges of the painting. The other major opportunity, closely related to the first, developed from the fact that Pollock was concentrating on the surface of the work, laying his networks of paint directly on the canvas with no attempt to create the illusion of space. In this way, what came to be known as *optical* (flat) *space* was created—as compared to the pictorial space of earlier art. This was the first significant change in the artist's treatment of space since the Cubists had begun to fracture and fragment pictorial space some forty years earlier.

The artists of the Chromatic Abstraction branch had goals that were similar to those of the Action Painters. They, too, sought spontaneity, depth of feeling, and simplified all-over structures, and they, too, created nonrepresentational works. However, they differed from the Action Painters in their means and techniques. Rather than attempting to capture the intensity of a moment through gesture, they stalked a more contemplative image, one that would affect the viewer more subtly. Where the Action Painter used line to capture a dynamic emotion, the Chromatic Abstractionist used color to suggest a quiet and more mysterious feeling.

Mark Rothko (1903–70) was perhaps not the most typical of these painters; his large and luminous canvases seem softer and less flat than those of the others. Nearly all his typical works (as opposed to a relatively few but celebrated ones by Pollock) are extremely large; with such artists as Rothko and Pollock the postwar cultivation of the truly big canvas begins. And Rothko's surprisingly simple treatment of color and form was as innovative in its way as Pollock's violent break with past techniques. In Rothko's combining of stained canvas with forms painted on in more opaque pigments, in his tall, open compositions and the landscape-like quality of the color and space, we catch a glimpse of new, refreshing vistas. These vistas are not, however, of real or Surrealist images, but of an atmosphere or an abstract event on which to meditate. "I think of my pictures as dramas," Rothko said; "the shapes in the pictures are the performers. . . . They begin as an unknown adventure in an unknown space. It is at the moment of completion that, in a flash of recognition, they are seen to have the quantity and function which was intended." The "performers" in

20-17 Mark Rothko, *Orange and Yellow*, 1956. Oil on canvas, 91″ × 71″. Albright–Knox Art Gallery, Buffalo, New York. Gift of Seymour H. Knox, 1956.

Orange and Yellow (fig. 20-17) are two colored, roughly rectangular areas that seem to float nebulously in front of a space of yet another color; the brushwork at the edges of these forms is especially loose, thinning out almost imperceptibly so that the division between color areas is extremely vague.

The abstract art of the generation that followed was more influenced by the Chromatic Abstractionists than by the Action Painters, but it was more formal and impersonal in its effects. From both branches the new generation took the idea of all-over painting and the concept of optical space. In the end they favored a "color field" approach, preoccupied with the power of color but adopting a far less personal attitude than the Abstract Expressionists had displayed. Reacting against the rhetoric of the Abstract Expressionists and their attempts to create an art of universal, mythic power, the new group swung away from Expressionism toward a more objective art and sometimes a geometri-

cal precision. Where Abstract Expressionism had broken with traditional beliefs about subject matter and space, these painters wished to go a step (or more) beyond. They tried to carry the process of elimination and reduction as far as it could go, to free painting of all preconceptions so that they might work only with what is basic to the art. Their work has been called *postpainterly* or *nonpainterly*, since they deliberately avoided the "painterly" effects of modeling and contour that had dominated traditional painting since the Renaissance.

The earlier work of the Postpainterly Abstractionists, artists like Morris Louis (1912–62) and Kenneth Noland (born 1924), tended to be simple and almost geometric. Contrasting color schemes and strong structures were often balanced, though, by a gentle lyricism. One technique that was developed to soften and flatten forms was staining the raw (unprimed) canvas with water-soluble acrylic paints. The Postpainterly movement has since broken up into many different approaches to dealing with color and shape. The untitled work by Sam Gilliam (born 1933) shown in figure 20-18 is a good example of some of the newer ideas. He has not only stained but knotted the canvas, then hung it from four nails and added a witty reference to traditional picture shape by suggesting a "corner" with a piece of cord.

While much of the avant-garde art of the postwar period was initiated by Americans, not all of it was. In Europe a milder Abstract Expressionism had grown out of the work of Dubuffet and others, an art that stressed surface textures and introduced unusual materials. However, the strongest, and ultimately more influential, movement was that of the latter-day geometric artists of Paris that has come to be known as Op art (from *optical*, shortened to resemble the name Pop art). This movement was a direct outgrowth of the Formalist art of Mondrian and the Constructivists but was marked by an almost scientific concern with the application of optical effects. At the center of this movement was the Hungarian-born French artist Victor Vasarely (born 1908), who proclaimed in his 1955 "Notes for a Manifesto" that "form and color are one." Vasarely was interested above all in theories of perception, especially in total visual contexts, not simply painting; thus he became a pioneer of both the optical art and the mixed-medium techniques of the 1960s. His *Eridan II* (fig. 20-19), of 1956, demonstrates the retinal illusions of change and shifting movement that

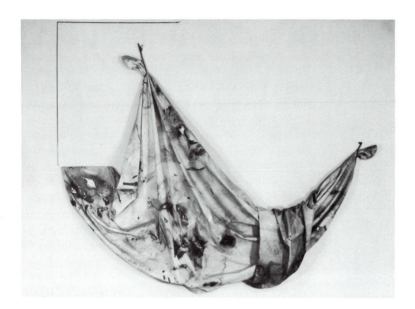

20-18 Sam Gilliam, *Untitled*, 1969. Acrylic on canvas, 74″ × 76″. Collection of Dr. and Mrs. Leon O. Banks, Los Angeles.

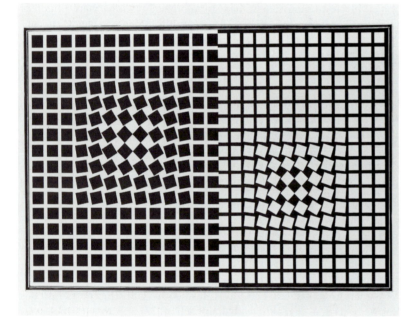

20-19 Victor Vasarely, *Eridan II*, 1956. Oil on canvas, 51″ × 76¾″. © 1987 The Detroit Institute of Arts, Founders Society Purchase, W. Hawkins Ferry Fund.

were exploited successfully by the Op artists of the middle and late sixties.

SCULPTURE AFTER WORLD WAR II

The development of sculpture after World War II followed paths parallel to those taken by painting, in both figurative and abstract forms. Figurative sculpture, like painting, tended to reflect the horrors of the war, and abstract sculpture underwent a process of reductionism, or a peeling away of the inessential.

Well before 1945, the sculpted human figure had often become almost unrecognizable by naturalistic standards; after 1945, ugliness, violence, agony, and protest came to be emphasized. In his last decades Alberto Giacometti (1901–66), a Swiss who spent most of his life in Paris, specialized for a time in gaunt figures

20-20 Alberto Giacometti, *Man Pointing*, 1947. Bronze, 70″ high. Tate Gallery, London.

irregularly matched compartments of these works are reminiscent of Cubist planes, although they do not serve to form any representational pattern. *Royal Tide IV* (fig. 20-21) exemplifies her skill and the oddly imposing and mysterious effect achieved by her handsome constructions.

Much post-1945 sculpture has been wholly nonfigurative. Of particular interest are the facts that most of these works have been constructed rather than carved or molded—a heritage of the years before 1945—and that significant use has been made of industrial components.

David Smith (1906–65) was a much admired American sculptor whose training was less in art than in welding and mechanics. After the war he settled on a farm in upstate New York, where his *Cubi XVII* (fig. 20-22) first stood with a series of similar works in the open fields. This piece, like the others, is constructed of gleaming stainless steel. The metal cubes have been polished, scraped in all-over patterns, and assembled on a cylindrical base. The work is in the Formalist tradition of such artists as Mondrian and emphasizes balance and (since it is sculpture, not linear painting) weight. Smith's late works achieved a monumental simplicity.

These qualities were carried still further by the sculptural manner of the sixties and seventies known as Minimal art. Robert Morris (born 1931) has worked intermittently in this manner, although objecting to both "minimal" and "reductive" as descriptions of his style. A leading theorist in the sixties, Morris believed that such terms placed an incorrect emphasis on the individual elements instead of on the impact of the work as a whole. In any case, a reductive tendency had made the elements of many of his works indeed minimal—as, for example, the untitled sculpture in figure 20-23. The elements are twelve identical steel boxes that can be variously arranged; in our illustration they are shown leaning on each other in a row like fallen dominoes. Morris used many different materials (including metal, wood, fiberglass, and heavy felt strips) and declined to disguise their surfaces by painting or any other treatment: he wanted them to be quite frankly what they are. A work like *Untitled*, he said, means a return to the cubic form that is "a kind of unit in a syntax that has been in culture since the Stone

such as the *Man Pointing* (fig. 20-20). Pitted and ravaged, these figures are ghostly presences that stand starkly isolated from the everyday world. They are monumentally alone, isolated even when sculpted in groups. The vision is Existentialist, a product of the Parisian scene in the age of Sartre. And just as Existentialism emphasized the heroic integrity of the individual alienated from a menacing or uncaring world, the slender figures of Giacometti stand not pleading or pitiful, but self-contained and aloof.

A popular post-1945 sculptural form that is sometimes figurative in whole or in part is the art of *assemblage*. This is a three-dimensional art that combines all types of found objects, often the most ordinary junk. Sometimes interpreted as commentaries on the swift obsolescence of things in modern life, few assemblages have been explicitly ideological—unlike many Dadaist efforts of earlier years. Some assemblage artists have raised craftsmanship to levels of true elegance, as exemplified in the work of Louise Nevelson (born 1900). This exceptional American artist specialized for many years in assembling neatly crafted parts of old furniture into tiers of boxlike wooden enclosures and then spraying the whole with black, white, or gold paint. The

20-21 Louise Nevelson, *Royal Tide IV*, 1960. Painted panel, 11′ × 14′. Museum Ludwig, Cologne.

20-22 David Smith, *Cubi XVII*, 1963. Polished stainless steel, 9′ × 5′4½″. Dallas Museum of Art, The Eugene and Margaret McDermott Fund.

Age." Also, he continued, such works reflect modern industrial production with its standardization of parts that can be multiplied indefinitely. Thus, we might add, old and new are symbolically united.

The modern machine age was reflected still more obviously in *kinetic sculpture*—sculpture that moves. The concept, of course, was not new in the postwar period. The mobiles of Alexander Calder (1898–1976) had moved in the thirties, and a few other works still earlier. Even machine-activated sculpture antedated World War II. The postwar years, however, saw a real flowering of kinetic art. It was seen that this art, like other art, could awe, inspire, delight, amuse, or satisfy the feeling for form. Some works of kinetic sculpture produced during this period were complex mechanisms of fascinating whimsy, such as most of those created by the Swiss sculptor Jean Tinguely (born 1925). Tinguely's works, such as M. K. III (fig. 20-24), jiggle and wheeze furiously, and typically accomplish nothing at all. Their forms are undisciplined and asymmetrical, and their construction is often casual enough to leave a bit to chance; this unpredictability only adds to the

20-23 Robert Morris, *Untitled,* 1969. Steel, twelve pieces, each 6″ × 18″ × 24″. Norton Simon Museum of Art, Pasadena, California (gift of the artist, 1969).

machines' charm. Certainly they are among the most accessible, most popular successes of postwar art.

POP ART

The major type of figurative art in the sixties, Pop art, was embodied in both painting and sculpture, and sometimes in a combination of the two. Pop art pre-

sented itself as an art of popular life, not an elitist art for connoisseurs. Its practitioners and fans saw it striking out boldly and joyously as an art of a democratic age and a celebration of common taste, even when it satirized that age and taste.

Undoubtedly the rise of Pop owed much to the abstract art of the postwar period, for which it professed to offer an antidote. Abstract Expressionism—and above all Action Painting, which the public still

20-24 Jean Tinguely, *M. K. III,* 1964. Iron, 36¼″ × 82½″. The Museum of Fine Arts, Houston (purchased with funds donated by Dominique and John de Menil).

tended to regard as pretentious or impossible to understand—seemed to the Pop artists and their enthusiasts to be an art of too much seriousness. Pop portrayed a less solemn view of life and brought a refreshing sense of humor to the art world. The image-breaking spirit of Dada was often present in Pop, but not its bitterness. Certainly Pop was one of the most exuberant phenomena in recent art history.

The freewheeling spirit of the late fifties and early sixties was further aided by the opening up of new possibilities in art materials. A far greater variety of objects was used than before, and new industrial materials were available. At other times, paradoxically, the very unavailability of expensive art materials to struggling artists led to unusual inventiveness in the use of discarded objects and materials from the urban environment. Such was the case with Robert Rauschenberg (born 1925), a young painter from Texas (by way of Paris and North Carolina) who in the fifties found himself in New York with very little money but a great deal of curiosity and few inhibitions about the limits of art. Eventually there would be few aspects of recent art uninfluenced by Rauschenberg—and his first admirers included the New York leaders of Pop.

Rauschenberg ultimately employed many techniques, but he was best known for some time as the creator of loose assemblages that he called "combines." Much less formally organized than Nevelson's assemblages, Rauschenberg's works contained an unusual variety of found objects including street rubbish, clothing, bedding, and stuffed animals. His well-known *Monogram* (fig. 20-25) features a stuffed Angora goat standing on a wheeled platform with an automobile tire around its belly. Various smaller objects are attached to the platform, and paint is daubed on it and on the goat's muzzle. Rauschenberg maintained that such combines arose not from any idea but from a spontaneous collaboration with materials.

The fully developed Pop art of the sixties used even more complex assemblages—a whole bedroom, for example—but far more typically its individual pieces took the form of either painting (sometimes combined with mechanical reproduction) or sculpture. Soup cans, comic strips, the humblest domestic objects, the most blatant manifestations of American advertising—all these and many more were their subject matter. The spirit was often of ironical good nature, with implied commentary on the modern consumer society. Pop art claimed to be an art of the real world, not (like Abstract Expressionism) of the artist's emotions. In fact, many artists remained as aloof as possible from their imagery, and this aloofness could be furthered by semimechanical copying of images, as in silkscreen printing. (In this process pigments are forced through those areas of a silkscreen that are not blocked by a stencil or by varnish.) Series of images produced

20-25 Robert Rauschenberg, *Monogram*, 1955–59. Mixed media, 4′ × 6′ × 6′. Moderna Museet, Stockholm.

20-26 Andy Warhol, *Elvis,* 1964. Acrylic and silkscreen enamel on canvas, 82″ × 60″. Private collection, Milan.

this way were a specialty of Andy Warhol (1930–87), a former commercial artist who combined tantalizing personal reticence with skillful self-promotion. Warhol confessed a yearning for impersonal, machinelike monotony and achieved great success in this specialty. His *Elvis,* of 1964 (fig. 20-26), is a triple image, mechanically reproduced, of Elvis Presley, the popular singer and movie star.

A Pop sculptor of the sixties, Claes Oldenburg (born 1929), produced surprising versions (often on an immense scale) of such familiar objects as hamburgers, pastries, and bathroom fixtures. *Soft Toilet* (fig. 20-27) exemplifies the Pop preoccupation with the familiar and the utilization of new industrial materials (in this case kapok, vinyl, and Plexiglas)—but it startles and amuses by its floppy malleability. A deadpan sense of humor enabled Oldenburg to transcend, in his own way, the banality of scores of other Pop artists.

NEW VISTAS IN THE ARTS

By the late 1960s the definition of art had become extraordinarily flexible. Art, said Robert Morris, is "anything that's used as art." However, most artists sought to be more specific—and they could hardly avoid being so, when each new experiment became part of the new definition. One of the broader, looser, and more important categories of the new art came to be known as Conceptual art.

Conceptual Art and Earthworks

Conceptual art is an art in which visual and formal considerations are seen as subordinate to ideas. Essentially it was the culmination of the broad twentieth-century experimental trend toward an art of ideas rather than an art of objects. Among its most firmly established roots were the art and theories of Dada and Marcel

20-27 Claes Oldenburg, *Soft Toilet,* 1966. Vinyl filled with kapok, painted with liquitex, and wood. 52″ × 32″ × 30″. Collection Whitney Museum of American Art, 50th Anniversary Gift of Mr. and Mrs. Victor W. Ganz.

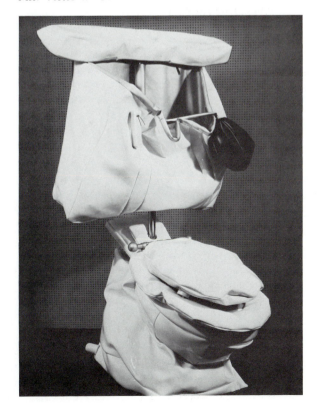

Duchamp, but it was also linked to the reductionist tendencies of more recent art. As art objects became more and more simplified, the role of the artist as the creator of ideas increased. For the Conceptualists, art had become primarily a means of presenting ideas or providing information. In fact, it may be difficult to distinguish a work of Conceptual art from a treatise on linguistics or a demonstration of a scientific principle.

Two other roots of Conceptual art were problems of the art world in the sixties and later. One was the gallery system—the tremendous financial and aesthetic power that was concentrated in the hands of commercial and public art galleries. Many Conceptual artists dreamed of bypassing the galleries, since the types of works they produced could not be displayed or sold there. This hope soon proved rather delusive, mainly because the artists needed to earn a living. So they devised means of documenting their works (which often were ephemeral)—usually photographs, letters, written accounts, and video tapes—and this brought them income from sponsors or (very much as in the past) the galleries.

Another significant problem that Conceptual art sought to solve was partly self-generated within the movement—that is, the physical or legal impossibility of carrying out their grander and more whimsical ideas

now that art was virtually limitless in its conceptual range. For example, Oldenburg's proposals for colossal monuments—among the most famous and appealing of the early pieces of Conceptual art—were almost always theoretically possible but not feasible or likely to find financial backing. One of his ideas was a giant upside-down Good Humor bar to be built on New York's Park Avenue on such a scale that it "could be constructed as a sheath over the existing Pan Am building." Don Celender (born 1931), a Conceptual artist in Minnesota, specialized in concepts for projects that are usually downright impossible, and then exhibiting the written proposal and the response from the person or organization he proposed it to. For example, he wrote to Sherman E. Lee, Director of the Cleveland Institute of Art, requesting that he put a thousand of the institute's best Far Eastern pieces into a weather balloon and release them over the state of Alabama. Lee sent a letter replying that he had "mentally performed" the proposal and congratulated both Celender and Alabama on the project.

Not all of the works designed on a monumental scale were meant to be amusing comments. At the same time that Conceptual art developed, a related movement grew up that used the landscape itself as an art material. As some Conceptual artists have done

20-28 Robert Smithson, *Spiral Jetty*, 1970. Black rock, slate crystals, earth, red water (algae), 1500′ long by approximately 15′ wide. Great Salt Lake, Utah. Later submerged.

20-29 Jan Dibbets, *Perspective Correction: My Studio I/2*, 1969. Photograph. Courtesy of the artist, Amsterdam.

mentation process itself. A simple example of this approach is to be found among the early pieces of Jan Dibbets (born 1941), of Holland, a work from his *Perspective Corrections* series (fig. 20-29). The neat square shown on the left seems at first to have been superimposed on the photograph but actually was drawn on the wall in trapezoidal shape before the photograph was taken. The Conceptual aspect of the piece lies in its comment on the way the camera affects what and how we see; the appeal lies in the contradiction between what we see to be true and what we know to be true. A different kind of comment was made by Robert Morris in an untitled piece done for an exhibition at Finch College in 1969. Morris hung a photo mural and a mirror in a room and filmed the room with a motion-picture camera that revolved in the room's center. For the show he removed the mural and mirror and projected the film against the bare walls of the room, the projector rotating at the same speed and in the same position as the camera had. As in the case of the Dibbets piece, the primary feature of the work was the concept in the creator's mind, and the secondary feature was the mental effort required of the viewer to appreciate the artist's conception.

Mixing Mediums

Among the striking phenomena of the late-twentieth-century art world is the lively experimentation in the mixing of artistic mediums. This is by no means without historical precedent, however. The long but scattered record of multimedia expression in Western art extends back to the combination of painting, sculpture, and architecture in Greek temples, to the synthesis of music, drama, and visual art in the operas of the Baroque age and Richard Wagner, and to such avantgarde experiments of the earlier twentieth century as the constructions of Duchamp.

In the 1950s a new and much more drastic round of medium mixing began. Early works ranged from the relatively tame mixing of painting and sculpture in Rauschenberg's "combines" to the often jarring amalgamations of theater, music, painting, and sculpture of the "Happening," invented by Allan Kaprow (born 1927). By the late sixties the traditional boundaries of art had often completely disappeared and new, hybrid forms with names like Performance, Event, and Environment had been devised. The visual arts were no longer limited to wall pieces but were now as likely to

works that involved altering the natural world, the line between Conceptual art and Earth art is sometimes difficult to draw. As a general rule, Earthworks are closer in origin and spirit to the art, architecture, and landscaping of past ages than the Conceptual pieces, which tend to use the landscape to illustrate an idea. Echoes of distant ages are often evoked by Earth art, from primitive monuments such as Stonehenge to Egyptian pyramids and Mayan temples.

One of the most accomplished creators of Earthworks was Robert Smithson (1938–73), who died in an airplane crash while completing a project in the Texas desert. His best-known work is the *Spiral Jetty*— 6,650 tons of earth and rock constructed at the edge of the north shore of the Great Salt Lake in Utah (fig. 20-28). This very substantial creation was built under Smithson's direction by construction workers using loaders and dumptrucks. Serving no utilitarian purpose and leading nowhere, it was nevertheless an impressive work. Smithson also made a film documenting the jetty's construction and linking its conception to a rather mystic philosophy of earth, energy, and time.

At the other end of the Conceptual scale are works that examine, use, or comment on the docu-

20-30 Chryssa, *Fragments for the Gates to Times Square II,* 1966. Programmed neon and Plexiglas, 43″ high. Collection Whitney Museum of American Art. Purchase, with funds from Howard and Jean Lipman.

fill a room or—in the case of Earthworks—even a landscape.

In the narrow sense, *Environments* were a type of art for the viewer's contemplation or manipulation; they were spaces, often set up in galleries, that invited spectators into unusual settings—a hut of yarn, a tunnel of light, a balloon, a waterfall, and so forth. Colors, sounds, odors, and tactile sensations as well as action planned and unplanned might be part of such an experience. The spectator might even be invited to modify the environment with various materials.

Some of the earliest Environments were created with light—an outgrowth, at least in part, of the neon sculptures of artists such as Chryssa (born 1933). Her *Fragments for the Gates to Times Square II* (fig. 20-30) features computer-programmed neon lights and a Pop feeling. Chryssa wrote that, when she arrived in New York after a gloomy wartime childhood in Greece, she "became fascinated with the lights and signs of Broadway and Times Square. It appeared to me like a garden

of light and I was unable to capture what I felt or saw in the medium of paint"—hence the animated dazzle of this later neon tribute to her adopted city.

Happenings extended Environments of the participatory sort to rather elaborate group productions. Virtually any publicly, consciously staged event, whether or not employing traditional artistic materials and concepts, could be a Happening—if the stagers called themselves artists and their effort a work of art. (An element of fantasy helped but was not absolutely essential.) Involvement and improvisation by the spectator-participants in specially contrived settings was ordinarily required, as contrasted with the physical and psychological separation between stage and audience in traditional theaters. Participants might exchange clothes, join in painting the ground silver, or be bombarded with strange sights and sounds (live or on film). The possibilities were endless, but usually they implied a combination of planning and spontaneity. In any case, "art" and "life" were thoroughly confused.

Performances, in recent terminology, are productions that are put on in a gallery or in the street. They are often multimedia presentations, and the spectator does not actively participate. Perhaps the best known Performance was the one produced by Jean Tinguely on 17 March 1960—the self-destruction of his *Homage to New York.* This Performance was somewhat atypical, since the main performer was not human but a quaint and complex kinetic sculpture similar to Tinguely's other kinetic works. It actually bungled its own destruction—before a fashionable audience in the garden of New York's Museum of Modern Art—and required the services of axe-wielding firemen in its final agony.

The public immolation of *Homage to New York* was a mixture of several arts and various materials; even the sense of smell was assaulted by several stink bombs. Enthusiasm grew in the sixties and seventies for Performances that combined several different mediums of artistic expression. They might include, for example, speaking, singing, and dancing, generally in the most advanced or experimental forms and often with deliberate lack of traditional synchronizing of activities. Improvisation and the role of chance predominated. Involved in these Performances were such innovators as Morris and Rauschenberg, the composer John Cage, and the dancer-choreographer Merce Cunningham.

Events are harder to define, and they have often overlapped with Performances, Happenings, and Envi-

20-31 Christo, *Running Fence,* 1972–76. Nylon, fabric, steel, cables, and hooks; 18′ high, 24½ miles long. Sonoma and Marin Counties, California. Removed after two weeks.

ronments. An Event usually involves a production on an extraordinary scale in which the artist supervises large numbers of helpers. Many Events modify the natural environment (a temporary modification, instead of the relative permanence of Smithson's Earthworks) and involve grand scenic effects. Such were several ambitious and long-prepared projects by the Bulgarian-born artist Christo (born 1935). His *Running Fence* (fig. 20-31) was a twenty-four-and-a-half-mile-long, eighteen-foot-high construction of white nylon fabric supported by steel posts. For two weeks in 1976 it wandered across the hills and valleys of northern California and into the sea. Drawings and models were sold, mainly in Europe, to cover the expenses of more than three million dollars, much of which went for legal costs. The on-going struggle with environmentalist groups and other objectors became an actual part of the project, which also included Christo's original concept and direction, the help of local people, and the admiration of most observers. *Running Fence,* rippling in the wind and subtly changing color under different conditions of light and atmosphere, was not only an Event but an object of remarkable beauty, even by the most conventional standards. Christo's *Surrounded Islands* (1983) was perhaps even more spectacular than *Running Fence,* if not as elegant. Eleven islands in Bis-

cayne Bay, Florida, were surrounded, atop the water, by more than six million square feet of bright pink fabric.

Realism Reconsidered

Some but not all of the traditional aesthetic standards in painting seemed to be revived by the resurgence of realism in the late sixties. Most basically the New Realism meant a return to portraying completely recognizable human beings and their environments. In doing so, it brought to the surface an undercurrent of twentieth-century art that had never wholly succumbed to more innovative and better publicized movements. At the same time it could also be seen as an option available in the permissive avant-garde aesthetics. In either case, it went beyond simple realistic representation of things and people. Thus several types of realism emerged, differing in aim, spirit, and technique.

Alfred Leslie (born 1927), for example, has sometimes gone so far in his traditionalism as to paint historical and allegorical themes similar to those of the old masters. However, his large canvas of *The Thirteen Americans* (1982, fig. 20-32), painted for the Lyndon B. Johnson Library in Austin, Texas, is not

20-32   Alfred Leslie, *The Thirteen Americans*, 1982. Oil on canvas, 9′ × 11′. Lyndon B. Johnson Library, Austin, Texas. Copyright © Alfred Leslie.

specifically historical; its subject is simply thirteen family members and friends, and they are portrayed with insight and sympathy. Allegorical overtones, but no more, may be read into these figures that run a gamut of American experience—perhaps intended to exemplify the comprehensive social goals of President Johnson's "Great Society." The lighting is sharp and dramatic, as it is in the works of Leslie's most obvious inspiration from the past, Caravaggio. Social commentary is most directly apparent in the stenographer's T-shirt worn by the young black man at the right; the shorthand printed on the shirt states, "I am tired of being dictated to." There are only two major non-human, but very American, intrusions in the picture—a shopping cart and the small girl's stuffed dog, whose string across the foreground seems to pull the work together. Leslie has been accused of sentimentality, but few can deny his consummate craftsmanship.

The subject matter in the work of Alice Neel (1900–84) is only a bit more restricted than that of Leslie. Neel, too, was a figure painter in fairly traditional vein. Her 1973 canvas of *The Soyer Brothers* (fig. 20-33) portrays two other American figure painters of distinction, Raphael and Moses Soyer. The poses typify Neel's general approach to portrait composition—letting the subject or subjects simply talk and relax at

first, falling into a natural, characteristic pose instead of conforming to the artist's psychological assumptions or formal preferences. Her compositions, she insisted, were intuitive, not thought out carefully or in any sense strained. Neel painted subjects of all ages but was particularly drawn in her later years to the aged, whose faces and bodies she found unusually expressive—poignant or resigned at times but often determined and dignified. The psychological insight shown in the Soyer double portrait is heightened by predominantly subdued colors, which contrast with the parchmentlike brittleness of the two elderly faces.

Philip Pearlstein (born 1924) usually has organized his figure compositions much more self-consciously than Neel did. In works such as *Two Models in Bamboo Chairs, with Mirror* (fig. 20-34), Pearlstein focuses on a basic concern of traditional art, the portrayal of the naked human body. The people in these paintings are of no personal interest to him or to his viewers. Their bodies are merely compositional elements, painted with cool, unflattering naturalism. The arbitrary cropping of faces and other parts of bodies at the edges of the canvas repeats an effect common in photography, as do the steep floor angles that push the figures forward in a shallow space. However, Pearlstein has rejected working from photographs and paints from

20-33 Alice Neel, *The Soyer Brothers*, 1973. Oil on canvas, 60″ × 46″. Collection Whitney Museum of American Art. Purchase, with funds from Arthur H. Bullowa, Sydney Duffy, Stewart R. Mott, and Edward Rosenthal.

20-34 Philip Pearlstein, *Two Female Models in Bamboo Chairs with Mirror*, 1981. Oil on canvas, 72″ × 72″. The Toledo Museum of Art. Gift of Edward Drummond Libbey. © Toledo Museum of Art 1982.

20-35 Chuck Close, *Kent*, 1970–71. Acrylic on canvas, 8′4″ × 7′6″. Collection, Art Gallery of Ontario, Toronto.

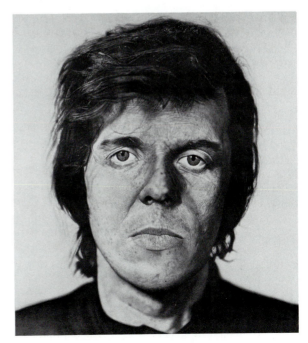

live models. The typical Pearlstein canvas avoids both sensual exploitation and Expressionist or Formalist distortion of the figure; it is a study of the human object.

Photo Realism is a precise realism that may employ photographs quite unabashedly to attain effects that the photograph largely monopolized in the past. More than the looser and more traditional realism exemplified by Leslie, Neel, and Pearlstein, it tends to restrict itself to extremely individualized subjects, generally persons or urban scenes. In *Kent* (fig. 20-35), Chuck Close (born 1940) depicts a face in immense magnification (most of his paintings are nine feet high), every pore and blemish visible. For each of his magnified portraits, Close photographs the subject very close up, focusing so tightly on the eyes that even the end of the nose is blurred. This blurring, reproduced in the painting, is essentially a photographic effect not characteristic of human vision. Close has said that his main concern in these paintings has not been realism as such, but the photographic image—if only because that image is so pervasive in modern life. Like other contemporary realists, he attempts to keep the content of his paintings as minimal and unemotional as possible. Even though he paints the human face— potentially the most emotional image of all—he manages to keep his models' expressions relatively neutral. And by working up close to the canvas, where the forms are abstract rather than human, and giving equal attention to every part of the canvas, he manages to keep his concerns painterly rather than humanistic. It can be argued that this work, which at first glance seems very much in the traditional vein of figurative painting, is in fact close to the spirit of abstract art.

In the 1970s such American painters as Richard Estes (born 1936) and Ralph Goings (born 1928) made names for themselves as painters of the urban scene, generally proceeding from photographs. They painted such things as storefronts, figures in the street, and buildings seen from inside the plate-glass windows of other buildings, thus displaying a complex confusion of reflections. In the eighties have come a burst of works that focus more intimately on human beings and their interactions. Eric Fischl (born 1948) has often made frank sexual references in his meticulous canvases, which has led some viewers to interpret them as essays on moral decadence. Robert Birmelin (born 1933) has painted fractured street scenes—vignettes of urban life usually from skewed angles, as in Pearlstein's otherwise quite different, deliberately posed portrayals of nudes. Birmelin's titles indicate the paintings' subject matter and something of their frequent street-smart stance: *The Street—A Gesture from a Stranger, Fire on Seventh Avenue, On the Street—An Event with Two Cops. Noticing Separate Things*, from 1985 (fig. 20-36), is an intimate but ambiguous close-up of a street scene. A hand at the left grasps a pole, implying a threatening blocking of the viewer's passage. A woman's legs and high-heeled shoes dominate at the right, but the most striking focus is upon a more distant figure, a street person sleeping on a sidewalk grate. The figures are isolated and some of them seem vaguely dangerous, but the painter's composition is so well thought out, or chosen, that the "separate things" constitute a formal whole.

20-36   Robert Birmelin, *Noticing Separate Things*, 1985. Acrylic on canvas, 48″ × 96″. Courtesy of Sherry French Gallery, New York.

20-37 Judy Pfaff, *Superette*, 1986. Mixed-media installation, 12′ × 33′ × 10′. Courtesy of Holly Solomon Gallery, New York.

Other Trends of the Eighties

Beginning in the 1970s the pace of change in the visual arts decreased significantly, and often—but not always—the arts turned toward more conservative styles and traditional subject matter. Financial support for both new and established artists came more and more from business corporations and private foundations—a situation that may not have been wholly irrelevant to the increasingly conservative-traditionalist trend in the visual arts. Among other social aspects of the new art was the increasing recognition of the achievement of women artists. Of course, the achievement itself was no novelty in the history of art, as demonstrated by the work of Gentileschi, Vigée-Lebrun, Cassatt, O'Keeffe, and Nevelson. However, after 1945 there were proportionally greater numbers of serious women artists, and few if any critics were left to argue any inherent lack of talent among these artists. Women artists of the past began to receive new recognition in the histories, and the talent of several older contemporary artists such as the Franco-American sculptor Louise Bourgeois (born 1911) was at last accepted as top-flight. Among the contemporary younger women artists, we will note two, the painter Jennifer Bartlett and the sculptor and "installation" artist Judy Pfaff.

Judy Pfaff (born 1946) is, at least in her simpler works, a descendant of the pre-World War II Constructivist sculptors such as Gabo; that is, she has tended to construct her works in space rather than mold them out of solid material. Other works, on such a scale as to be called "installations," show the influence of Nevelson and Rauschenberg. In figure 20-37 we see one of her sizable installations entitled *Superette*, one of her series of "wall works." This wall work uses three white gallery columns to divide it into three increasingly exuberant zones. At the left there is a grid somewhat resembling a musical staff with notes on it. In the center we see striped formica strips and discs of Plexiglas, attached by metal rods to the background. At the right is a joyous collage of such objects as spheres and advertising signs. The mix of media is broad and inventive, and all parts are painted brilliantly in a carnival of colors, culminating in a bright yellow, drumlike halfsphere and a large purple sphere at the top.

The works of the American artist Jennifer Bartlett (born 1941) are colorful, like Pfaff's *Superette*, but typically they are in the traditional painting medium. Bartlett's painting is impressionistic but basically realistic. *Pool* (1983, fig. 20-38) is one of several works inspired by the garden of a house near Nice in southern France. The three canvases of the work show, from varying perspectives, the empty tiled pool, a statue of a small boy, and the grass, gravel, and trees beyond. Splashes of bright color on the pool tiles and broad brush strokes for the background give an extemporized feeling, as do the differing angles derived from photographing the scene repeatedly with deliberate carelessness. The spontaneity becomes dramatic when set against the precise linear perspective of the pool tiles. Bartlett has often been moved to present her painting segmented on a grid of actual tiles, as in her enormous, sprawling *Rhapsody* of the mid-seventies, which first brought her to prominence in the art world.

Despite the relative conventionality and the frequent attraction to art traditions seen in the art of the eighties, a broad pluralism in artistic expression has not been stifled. Certainly the experimental forms of the sixties have continued to have their very vocal advocates and practitioners, although with decreased levels of creativity at times. Reductionism or Minimalism, for example, has stubbornly refused to die—and indeed this movement has gathered some strength from its highly successful parallel in music, as we will

20-38 Jennifer Bartlett, *Pool*, 1983. Oil on three canvases, 84″ × 180″. Collection of Mr. and Mrs. Aron B. Katz, Boulder, Colorado. Courtesy Paula Cooper Gallery, New York.

see later in this chapter. A broad range of Conceptual art—in which the idea is thought to be more basic than the vision—has remained. Photography and film as well as television—the resounding pop-cultural phenomenon of the post-1945 era—are largely excluded, reluctantly, from our study here, since they would require far more than the available space. They have continued, of course, to flourish during the eighties, sometimes at high artistic levels. From them have come several outgrowths straining toward older art media, *Video art* being the most obvious example. In Video art, television and/or videotapes are used in ways that are inventive if sometimes unsatisfying and self-indulgent; sometimes they have been combined effectively with sculptural installations.

In the traditional artistic realms, the new Expressionism in painting was getting the lion's share of attention and attracting the most controversy in the late eighties. Some found in this Expressionism only spineless, and sometimes violent, derivations from the past, while others saw it as a genuine renewal in art, ultimately more meaningful than what they considered the pointless floundering in many mediums during the sixties. Moreover, if both trends were recognized

within the new Expressionist movement, there was no consensus whatsoever as to which artists would fit best into each category. Here was a genuine, lively issue in the art world, and one that even nonartists might find significant, since it was occurring in a traditional medium.

Many artists, European and American, were involved in the new Expressionism. Those who drew the most attention were generally the painters who had imposed some individuality on their works—or, less kindly expressed, who were characterized by certain trademarks or gimmicks. Thus Julian Schnabel became best known for strong globs of paint, some of them painted over broken pieces of pottery, others suggesting a mottled collage of fish scales or seashells. The young artist Jean Michel Basquiat, of Haitian and Puerto Rican ancestry, painted stark, often skull-like faces amid menacing or childlike surroundings. Susan Rothenberg painted visionary apparitions, pale and wraithlike. The Italian Sandro Chia produced enormous, bloated human bodies on canvases that seemed to parody the forced "heroic" art of the Mussolini era between the two World Wars. The German Georg Baselitz produced unreal figures usually positioned upside down and thus presumably the more dramatic to the viewer. Much of all this striking art has been violent and aggressive, reflecting the rough and dangerous realities, international and social, of the late twentieth century.

Let us glance at the work of two of the new Expressionist painters of the eighties whose manners (and probably significance) stand in sharp contrast to one another: the American David Salle and the German Anselm Kiefer. Salle (born 1952) became a "hot" artist in the mid eighties by quoting widely from existing art in photography, paint, or some other medium, and then commenting enigmatically on these quotations. Most of his paintings are enormous (like most Expressionist canvases of the time), the imagery sometimes sexually raw or titillating, and the colors lurid. A mild example from 1985 is *The Farewell Painting* (fig. 20-39). Like nearly all of Salle's paintings at this time, the work is sectioned abruptly—the actual farewell of a couple at bottom right, the ambiguous comments elsewhere (although in other works they may also be superimposed on the more realistic section). Salle has insisted that his work is not Pop art but represents serious

structure and form for their own sake, even when appropriating or referring to older images. He declines to assign specific meanings or ideas to his paintings, and possibly none exist.

Anselm Kiefer (born 1945) is a far more sober artist than the sometimes flip Salle, and his images are less personalized and more broadly symbolic than Salle's. Among Kiefer's obsessive themes have been the German soil and landscape and the heavy burden of the German—especially the Nazi—past. His painting is of mood and idea, not of anecdote and narrative. Buildings in his paintings are always of literally weighty significance; usually he begins with photographs of the ponderous, pretentious civic buildings of the Nazi era and constructs the heavy surface of each work not only with oil paint but with such other materials as shellac and straw, his favorite. Both of these materials, and others, are used in *Shulamite* (fig. 20-40), one of a series of large stone spaces that he has evoked on canvas. The original of this crypt was destined by Hitler's government to be a monument to Germany's great men; Kiefer's painting has become a stern, elegiac monument to national loss. Torches for German heroes have been blacked out (most obviously near the left foreground), and seven flames rise from the hearth at the end of the hall, symbolizing Hitler's legacy of murdered Jews. The work is Expressionist indeed—a deeply felt and somber experience.

20-39 David Salle, *The Farewell Painting*, 1985. Oil and acrylic on canvas, 125″ × 120″. Elaine/ Werner Dannheisser Collection, New York. Courtesy of Mary Boone Gallery, New York.

NEW CHALLENGES IN MUSIC

Music experienced a series of challenges and crises rather similar to those that faced the other arts after 1945. In serious music, as in the visual arts, appeals to the unity of art and life frequently led to an impassioned rejection of traditional musical "beauty," stability, and internal unity. This rejection had no great impact on the masses who, if they were aware of the situation, resented the threatened denial of traditional values or found music simply a source of pleasure and enjoyment. A related trend appeared in the performance of older concert music, where some erosion occurred in the precisionist tradition of musical interpretation: it was increasingly realized that few past eras had advocated playing the notes and only the notes as written, and performers (especially of Baroque and Romantic music) began to return to old traditions of

20-40 Anselm Kiefer, *Shulamite*, 1983. Oil, acrylic, straw, and other materials, 9½' × 12'. Doris and Charles Saatchi Collection, London.

embellishment and general interpretive freedom, although sometimes now on more authentic instruments and in orchestras of more authentic size than in previous decades. Of course, by no means all of the new freedom was intended to provide authenticity; a great deal derived from a generalized romantic impatience with the supposedly spiritless academicism of the recent past. More and more freedom also marked the adaptation of older music to new forms (especially pop) and new instruments (especially electronic). All of this, despite much purist indignation, was in the long-established, flexible tradition of Western music from Renaissance parody masses to Stravinsky.

One of the more striking characteristics of the musical scene after 1945 followed and accentuated still another centuries-old tradition: a clash between avant-garde and conservative composition. Post-1945 experimentalism sought justification in the historical precedent of society's intolerance for musical novelty, pointed to modest gains in audience acceptance of the advanced music, and insisted that only another decade or so was required to accomplish its victory. The conservative opposition maintained that the scope and depth of general resistance to Modernism far surpassed any historical precedent, that the solid core of experimentalist enthusiasm was infinitesimal compared to the support for older serious music, and that quite

enough decades had already passed to demonstrate the incompatibility of avant-garde music and basic musical instincts.

In any case, conservative as well as innovative works were produced in great quantity in the decades after 1945. Musical conservatism flourished especially in popular songs and in the musical theater. Indeed, the world of pop music barely recognized the innovations that Schoenberg, Stravinsky, or even Debussy had introduced long before into serious music.

Composers of concert music often followed traditionalist paths also. The Russian composer Dmitri Shostakovich (1906–75) continued until his death to write straightforward music-for-the-people spiced by mild dissonances. This style can be sampled in the first movement (allegretto) of his Fifteenth Symphony (1971). The movement is a sunny introduction to an otherwise predominantly solemn and majestic work. Although scored for full orchestra, the orchestral texture is generally light and transparent. The first movement evokes the scene of toys coming to life in a toy shop at night. A toy soldier plays several times the one tune he knows, the fanfare motif from Rossini's overture to *William Tell* (early nineteenth century). The repeated quick rhythm (two short notes and a long) of this motif is typical of the Shostakovich movement: it is integrated within the movement's formal structure rather than seeming a foreign intrusion. Shostakovich was quite as willing as Stravinsky to borrow from the past when it served his purposes.

Shostakovich and such other composers as Benjamin Britten (1913–76) were happy to work within the traditional framework of Western music, both in compositional techniques and in performance resources. But many striking innovations were under way elsewhere in the musical world. The most widespread development in musical performance after 1945 was the application of electronics to sound sources. Electronic amplification systems for conventional instruments in serious music remained uncommon for many years but became standard in much popular music, initiating a new cult of loudness, most notably in rock. Adaptable equally to serious or pop music were various electronic developments in basic sounds. Early experiments in tape recording showed that musical or nonmusical sounds could be manipulated extensively to produce new effects. Sounds, moreover, could be electronically produced from electronic wave-generators—and soon fascinating new sonorities were being produced by a variety of techniques. These sounds were not limited to those that imitated or approximated the sound of traditional instruments; indeed, the possibilities seemed infinite both for electronic devices alone and for combined electronic and conventional sources.

Nor were new sounds the only outcome of electronic music making. For the electronics-trained, serious composer, the most challenging opportunity of all was that of working directly on the performing medium. This could be done in the studio directly before an audience. At last the composer could dispense with an interpreter. The development of computerized electronic synthesizers in the late sixties was especially encouraging to composers who had earlier been frustrated by limitations in technical capacity and human adaptability.

Chance and Indeterminacy

In the meantime, experimentalism in musical composition had been rampant—for the more radical Modern composers had long been busily undermining nearly all the traditional aesthetic foundations of Western music, sometimes in alliance with their counterparts in the visual arts, drama, and dance. Experimentalism in music, as in the visual arts, not only was related to the gestural aspect of Abstract Expressionism

but owed much to the earlier innovations of Dada and Surrealism. Like those movements, avant-garde music after 1945 found traditional aesthetic concepts painfully limited. Among the most extreme of the new experimentalists, and a major influence on the musical avant-garde here and abroad, was the American John Cage (born 1912). Cage has remained for decades in the vanguard of musical practice and has made the most thoroughgoing of all attacks on the older musical aesthetics.

"Everything we do is music," said Cage. Cage believed that music is part of nature and that nature is a continuum, interrelated in all its parts. (Here he was influenced by Zen Buddhism and other Oriental thought.) He cheerfully declined to accept the traditional distinction between noise and music, since all sounds are natural. Similarly, music should shun the patterns of the past, since nature is a random process and all attempts to deny nature are deceitful and ultimately self-defeating. Atonality, Cage believed, had been a step in the right direction but had become largely irrelevant in a world of random sounds, noises, silences, and processes. However, he thought the subsequent strict patterning and systematizing of atonality (in the serial school of composition, which we have noted in chapter 19 and will soon discuss again) was wholly unnatural.

With such principles, and in the spirit of the random effects often achieved by Dada, Cage inaugurated the "music of chance." Curiously enough, Cage found that it is not easy to compose by chance—that is, simply at random. For a time he used a painstaking compositional method of coin tossing and applied it to elaborate charts indicating by number all possibilities in such aspects of composition as pitch, tempo, dynamics, and silences.

The title 4′ 33″ of one of Cage's most famous works refers to the length of the piece in minutes and seconds. At its first presentation (1952) the performer sat silently before a grand piano, simply closing and reopening the keyboard lid to divide the work into three parts; other instruments and types of division into parts were also possible. Cage's concern was not, of course, the instrumentation but the natural sounds heard by the audience and generated by it during the four minutes and thirty-three seconds. It might be aware of sounds from outside the auditorium (wind and rain during the first performance), and eventually would add its own whisperings, chair creakings, foot shufflings, or even indignant exits from the room. Indeed, those who reacted most indignantly were those who contributed most richly to the performance. The point of the work was the unity and continuity of the situation, in which the audience was actively participating. As in other types of contemporary art, the audience became involved; it acted as well as being acted upon.

One might recommend as a more accessible example of Cage's special talents his *Aria with Fontana Mix* (1958). This is a simultaneous performance of two separate pieces: the "Fontana Mix," named after Cage's landlady, comprises a random imposition of several tapes of electronic sounds one upon the other; the vocal "Aria" is a work for a single performer who produces a hodgepodge of pitches, sounds, words, and phrases (in five different languages), unrelated to each other or to the "Mix." Simultaneous presentation of unrelated processes also characterized Cage's many complex collaborations with dancers, readers, and actors. In these joint efforts the stage action, poetry reading, dancing, and musical efforts proceeded quite independently, again with a degree of contrivance in the spontaneity.

Cage also was a pioneer in notational devices—which the new music clearly required for guiding the performers. This was especially true whenever the composer left significant choices to the performers. For example, the score of Cage's "Aria" dispenses altogether with conventional notation and consists of sketchy diagrammatic indications plus one page of general instructions. The twenty pages of sketches include wriggling lines to indicate the general range and direction of vocal pitches, the words to be sung or spoken, and black squares to indicate noises to be made by the performer (fig. 20-41). The soloist chooses his or her own noises, such as bird call, "hoot of disdain," and "ha, ha (laughter)." Next to nearly every black-ink wriggling line roughly indicating vocal pitch is a parallel, colored line. The soloist chooses any code for the eight colors; for example, the original singer in 1958 equated green with folk-singer style and brown with a nasal quality. Cage's instructions end by indicating that dynamics and any other unnotated matters are left to the discretion of the performer.

Compared to Cage's work, most other contemporary serious music has seemed a bit tame. Since its roots have ordinarily been grounded in the pre-1945

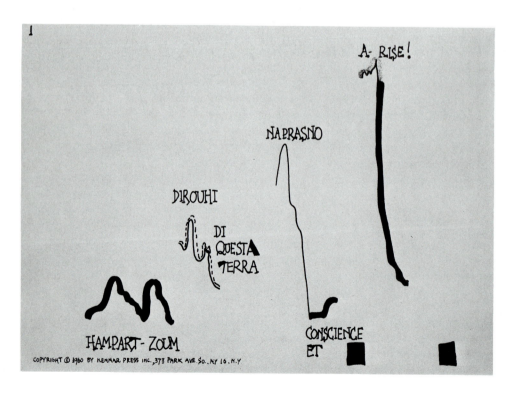

20-41 John Cage, first page of score of "Aria," 1958. Copyright © 1960 by Henmar Press, Inc., 373 Park Avenue South, New York, NY 10016. Reprinted by permission of the publisher.

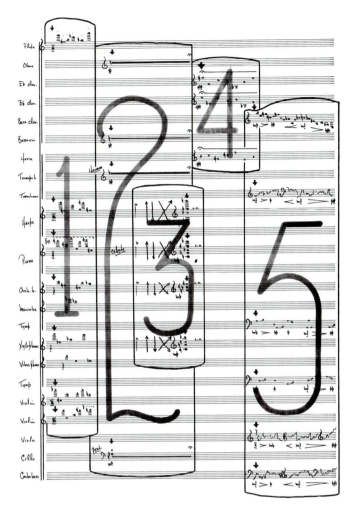

20-42 Earle Brown, fourth page of score of *Available Forms 1,* 1961. Copyright © 1962 by Associated Music Publishers, Inc. Used by permission.

given material." In *Available Forms 1* (1961), for eighteen performers, Brown's material is on six large, separate pages of score, with each divided into four or five events (fig. 20-42). In his own words, "The conductor may begin a performance with any event on any page and may proceed from any page to any other page at any time, with or without repetitions or omissions of pages or events, remaining on any page or event as long as he wishes." The conductor would adjust at will a movable arrow on a placard visible to all the performers—an arrow that indicated the event to be played. Thus the music became, for the conductor, extraordinarily flexible. In various compositions by other composers, the freedom to improvise was further extended to individual performers.

If we may hazard generalizations about the characteristics of the diverse products of the school of musical indeterminacy or chance, we may cite the virtual abandonment of traditional melody, harmony, and rhythm in favor of exploiting sounds of all sorts. When the sounds were recognizable musical tones, and especially when they were produced on conventional instruments, they tended to be brilliant, harsh, or shrill, as befitted their predominantly percussive function. Since tonality was ignored, the jagged outlines of the music deliberately avoided the sense of direction, progression, and climax emphasized in traditional, tonal composition. These characteristics of the school of indeterminacy or chance, however, can also be found in most music of the school that is its exact theoretical opposite, the school of total serialism.

Total Serialism and New Sounds

Total serialism was an expansion of the serial (twelve-tone) system of Schoenberg, who had been concerned primarily with tone rows, or series, of pitches following prescribed sequences and sequential transformations. After World War II the total serialists addressed their rigid patterning not only to the notes but to such other aspects of composition as timbre, duration, and harmonic density. Theoretically every element in a work could be serialized, then balanced against the others—but in practice, in the first experiments of precomputer days, this was a huge, almost futile task. An early move (1952–53) toward total serialism was the ten-minute *Kontra-Punkte* ("Counterpoints") for ten instruments, based on infinitely careful calculation, by the young German composer Karlheinz Stockhausen (born

decades, most of its bases have already been noted in these pages. Our survey can serve to indicate a few survivals and extensions of earlier theory and practice.

First of all, not uninfluenced by Cage have been further denials of musical cause-and-effect patterning—an outgrowth of atonality, the original denial of tonal patterning. Most extreme, after Cage himself, have been offshoots of his music of chance. Some composers, however, disliked that name or its popular synonym, *aleatoric music.* Earle Brown (born 1926), for example, spoke in terms of "open form," or a limited indeterminacy "through varying realizations of the

1928). The outcome is predictably and intentionally as rigidly impersonal as any work of improvisatory freedom.

Stockhausen composed *Kontra-Punkte* when he was a student in Paris, and it was first performed shortly after his return to Cologne in 1953. The various elements of the work (for example, six different instrumental timbres and six different degrees of volume) are organized into serial patterns. These patterns fall within given limits set by the composer, and the effect of their superposition and combination, Stockhausen maintained, is one of mediation between extremes. Unity is brought to *Kontra-Punkte* by using the same general pattern of limitations for all elements in the work rather than completely separate guidelines for pitch, timbre, and the like. Stockhausen's search for unity would become one of the most constant concerns in his subsequent extension of musical horizons.

Kontra-Punkte employs traditional musical instruments. In the month of its first public hearing, Stockhausen became associated with the electronic music studio of West German Radio in Cologne, and in 1962 he became the studio's director. In those decades he did not abandon music on traditional instruments but stressed electronic music and contributed significantly to its development (fig. 20-43).

In 1966–67 Stockhausen composed one of his most ambitious electronic works, *Hymnen (National Anthems)*. This work—or at least its first four parts, since he expected to return to it at a later date—was a synthesis of his electronic experimentation and a culmination of his philosophical development.

The full title of *Hymnen,* literally translated, is *Anthems for Electronic and Concrete Sounds.* Concrete sounds are sounds, musical or otherwise, that are external to the electronic equipment and that may be incorporated unaltered but are more often transformed electronically into sounds different from the original. *Electronic sounds,* as the term is used by Stockhausen, are those generated electrically without any basis in external sounds. Often it is difficult for the ear to distinguish the two, although *Hymnen* offers many natural sounds that are still recognizable despite their electronic distortion, fracturing, or combination. Heard in *Hymnen* are, for example, aural mementos of schoolrooms, gambling sessions, ship launchings, military parades, shopping scenes, bird calls, and (since the period was the politically activist sixties) student demonstrations. Above all, there are excerpts and transformations of innumerable national anthems "of all peoples." The composer is seeking to evoke a vision of global human unity, transcending all national distinctions, and finally suggesting an eternal, very physical humanity through the amplified sound of breathing

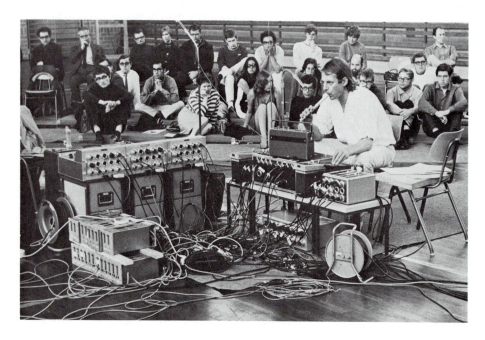

20-43 Karlheinz Stockhausen performing *From the Seven Days* in 1969.

(the composer's own) in the last of the four "regions" covered in the 1966–67 production and recording.

The first region of *Hymnen* lasts nearly a half-hour as recorded by the composer and has as its two focal points the Communist hymn (the "International") and the French anthem (the "Marseillaise"). Sizable chunks of the West German anthem (to the melody of "Deutschland über Alles") are included, as are snippets of other anthems. The section begins with a confusion of short-wave radio broadcasts from various nations. Bits of anthems are heard separately or simultaneously, together with sounds from a gambling casino. Male speaking voices in several languages play on many meanings and contexts of the word *rouge* ("red") and gradually transform themselves into an approximation of plainchant lines combining polyphonically. Throughout, the "International" has sporadically dominated the proceedings. Eighteen minutes after the beginning, a roaring upward glissando of electronic sound heralds a new orientation—toward the "Marseillaise." Fragments of the rousing French anthem are combined with those of other anthems but give way in a few minutes to recognizable sequences from the French hymn. The "Marseillaise," however, has been decomposed into its note-by-note or chord-by-chord elements and recomposed after electronic alterations in pitch and in quality. (The process is a rather striking musical parallel to Cubism in the visual arts.) Whining and swooping electronic sounds give way to imposing, deep gonglike eruptions derived from the "Marseillaise" played at extremely slow tempos. Finally, high-pitched hovering sounds, as of innumerable Indian bells, serve as a bridge to the second region of *Hymnen*.

The confusion of sounds that may at first seem to characterize *Hymnen* is actually, in Stockhausen's view, not confusion but a synthesis of modern life on an international scale. He hoped the work would heighten people's awareness of the totality and unity of the human condition. Ideally the listening experience should not occur in isolation but with a group that not only responds to outward sounds but experiences a true spiritual communion. Stockhausen pioneered ideas for total immersion in sound in specially designed environments—a parallel with developments in the visual arts during the 1960s.

Stockhausen has insisted that his work represents far more than an amusing or ironic combination of sound effects. Not only do his compositions claim deep spiritual significance, they also embody careful formal craftsmanship. Stockhausen can retain, when he wants to, as rigid a control over the progression of electronic sounds as he has done in his works for conventional instruments.

The American composer George Crumb (born 1929) has become best known for his attractive sounds in works both large and small. His immense *Star-Child* (1977) requires a chorus, soprano soloist, and no less than four conductors to supervise its complexities. Other works by Crumb are more modest in their requirements, such as *Music for a Summer Evening (Makrokosmos III)*, completed in 1974. This work for two electronically amplified pianos and percussion is, like most of Crumb's composition, partly tonal and partly atonal; Crumb has not followed the serialist path since the 1950s. His main concerns throughout his mature career have been the evocation of mystery and awe, the exploration of sonorities, and the creation of scores of great notational and calligraphic elegance. (See fig. 20-44 for the opening of *Star-Child*, in which the circular staffs indicate repetitions continuing quietly throughout the work.)

For a closer glance at Crumb's production we turn to the first two parts (with instrumental interlude) of *Ancient Voices of Children* (1970). Midway in complexity between *Music for a Summer Evening* and *Star-Child*, it is a song cycle for soprano, boy soprano, oboe, mandolin, harp, amplified piano, percussion, and miscellaneous instruments, including a musical saw and a toy piano; special effects involve the pressing and sliding of a "⅝-inch chisel with smooth cutting edge" against the piano strings and the moving of the oboist to various points on and off stage. The five songs employ texts by the Spanish poet Federico García Lorca (1898–1936) on themes of death, childish innocence, and the moods and essence of nature.

In formal terms, Part I—"El niño busca su voz" ("The little boy is looking for his voice")—may be viewed as a technical exercise for the soprano soloist, who sings virtuosic chromatic melodies interspersed with unusual vocal effects (flutter-tonguing, imitating a muted trumpet, and the like) to evoke a rather primitive, exotic mood. The soloist is occasionally supported by amplified piano, harp, and percussion. This largely vocal piece is followed by a dance interlude, "Dances of the Ancient Earth," quite literally an accompaniment, if so desired, to a solo dance performance. A somewhat Oriental atmosphere is created primarily by the chromatic oboe line, but also by the

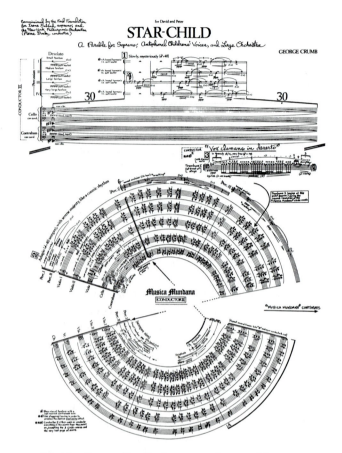

20-44 George Crumb, first page of score of *Star-Child*, 1977. Copyright © 1977 by C. F. Peters Corporation, New York.

percussionists' shouts, the slight "bending" of oboe and mandolin tones, and unusual effects derived from Asian instruments and a harp with paper threaded through its strings. This interlude is followed by "Me he perdido muchas veces por el mar" ("I have lost myself in the sea many times . . . as I lose myself in the heart of certain children"). This, like the first vocal solo, is instrumented very sparely. Only at the end does the soprano actually sing, with wordless vocalizing; the earlier verses are whispered through a speaking tube. The whispering, together with harp-string scraping and the sounds of musical saw and "chisel-piano" (as Crumb calls it), creates a meditative air that is eerie and haunting.

ART MUSIC IN THE EIGHTIES

Art music in the eighties continued the trends of earlier decades, but with several shifts of emphasis. For fifty years or so, *serialism* had been the most prestigious method of composition among many serious composers; serialism organized music not according to scales and tonal progression and direction, but around a specific twelve-note tone row selected for the particular work and then transformed in various ways. The most obvious shift in the seventies and eighties was the virtual abandonment of the serial style of composition, at least by younger composers. Perhaps three-quarters of a century of estrangement from the vast majority of even relatively enlightened concertgoers was enough. Still, the abandonment was not total, and a few survivors of serialism doggedly maintained their ways. Some other composers who were not serialists or even atonalists also held the gates against public accessibility by adhering to highly intellectualized composition and refusing to compromise with human preferences for recognizable melodies, agreeable harmonies, and rhythmic excitement.

Chief among these tonal-but-difficult composers was still the veteran American craftsman Elliott Carter (born 1908). Along with a generation of enthusiastic music critics, knowledgeable audiences in this country and Britain would probably be agreeable to Carter's nomination as the most distinguished contemporary composer of art music, but they have been much less willing to listen seriously to his work. Carter has been a very private composer and a master of precise, not flashy, rhythmic complexity. His work demands extreme attention from performers and audience alike, and many have found the reward worth the effort. Individual parts in his scores retain extraordinary independence in rhythm and general character (including characteristic note intervals), as seen most clearly in a work with modest instrumentation like his Second String Quartet (1959). Even here, however, many hearings or a study of the score are required for full appreciation; without it, listeners are likely to be dismayed by the austerity, dissonance, and almost unrelieved tension of the work. There are not even any full breaks in the music; the four movements are linked by complex solo cadenzas.

Carter would remain an active composer in the

1980s and an omnipresent ideal for a number of serious composers. One of his students, though for only a brief period, was Ellen Taaffe Zwilich (born 1939), whose works have been almost as concentrated as Carter's but more immediately appealing. Her Chamber Symphony (1979) is scored for solo instruments, primarily flute, clarinet, violin, viola, cello, and piano. As in Carter's work, there are long musical lines and precise effects; there also is a genuine emotional warmth, predominantly elegiac in tone. Her First Symphony (1983) for full orchestra is bolder, brassier, and more insistently rhythmical, while also displaying real melodic appeal.

Several degrees farther toward accessibility are the compositions of two other Americans, John Corigliano (born 1938) and David Del Tredici (born 1937). Corigliano's several concertos for different wind instruments and the *Alice in Wonderland*–inspired vocal and orchestral works by Del Tredici, such as *In Memory of a Summer Day* (1980), are recommended for new listeners. Stern-minded critics of this music have muttered of sell-outs to public taste—but at least the music demonstrates that contemporary art music can be comprehensible and enjoyable for general concert audiences in our day.

Repetitive Structures in Music

Such composers as Corigliano and Del Tredici, in fact, caused much talk in the early eighties of a possible new Romanticism in music—and indeed much of this composition suggests the lush harmonies and melodic attractiveness of nineteenth-century music. Whatever the ultimate fate of this trend, a still more remarkable movement, in part a countertrend, was emerging at the same time—a trend that was causing even more of a stir than composers like Corigliano and Del Tredici aroused. This trend was often labeled *reductionism* or *minimalism* because of its affinity with trends in the visual arts. More accurately—and more to the taste of most of its composers—it is called a "music with repetitive structures." Its most notable practitioners have been three Americans: Steve Reich, Philip Glass, and John Adams.

Reich and Glass were among the pioneers of this music, which at first (in the sixties and seventies) did indeed seem "minimal"; it was spare in instrumentation, brief in its musical lines, and (said its critics) short in musical substance. Above all, a single musical movement of several minutes' duration would unfold slowly and gradually out of a single musical line or theme, a single rhythmic pattern, or a single chord progression. Since transformations were slow, much repetition was inevitable—so much so that the disgruntled among early hearers sometimes spoke of "trance music." The music was accused of being appallingly simple and static, of going nowhere, of sounding like a "stuck record." (These were pre–compact-disc days when needles could in fact get stuck in record grooves.) However, even mildly close attention would have revealed that the music was constantly changing degree by degree, in accentuation, rhythm, and instrumentation at the very least—a continuing musical "process," as Reich put it. But the critics had their points: the themes were indeed quite minimal—and, above all, the many modulations, sudden events, build-ups, and relaxations of tension that had marked Western music for some centuries were disconcertingly absent. The music seemed ritualistic, and capable of going on forever into infinity. The ritualistic aspect of the music would later be exploited successfully in theater music with repetitive structures, whenever a ritualistic feeling was appropriate.

Within some fifteen years after the first self-conscious musical minimalism, the repetitive structures had become more complex and more ambitious. Large orchestras were now available for its performance, as were many operatic stages. Moreover, with the basic technical language now firmly established, experiments were being made toward loosening the structures, and even toward compromising with more customary musical elements such as long-spun-out melodies. Certainly in the eighties much territory still remained open to exploration by these musicians, since the music did not rigidly demand any particular degree of tonality or atonality, or necessarily even rule out all improvisation in performance. In actuality, however, most repetitive structures in the late eighties were carefully calculated and thoroughly composed, not improvised; they also were typically tonal. This latter fact was a built-in advantage as this music vied for popular and "middlebrow" favor.

Let us look at three examples of the mature repetitive-structure manner as it developed in the eighties. By the time Steve Reich (born 1936) approached the poems of William Carlos Williams (1883–1963) as inspiration for *The Desert Music* (1984), he was ready for a full-fledged work for chorus (twenty-seven amplified voices) and orchestra (eighty-nine pieces). In this work the chorus intones fragments of the Williams verses in chordal declamation, as the orchestra supplies the constant, throbbing pulse and the droning background chords typical of most repetitive-structure music. The "desert" of the title is not a picturesque sandy landscape impressionistically rendered, but an infinitely expanding setting for a vision of pulsating light. The texts are snippets ranging from a portion of Williams's version of an idyll of Theocritus to an urgent exhortation in the nuclear age for a change in human priorities (third movement, part three):

> Man has survived hitherto because he was too ignorant to know how to realize his wishes. Now that he can realize
> them, he must either change them or perish.

Reich's paramount message here seems to have changed from experimental musical technique, as in his modest efforts of the sixties, to urgent pronouncement on a cosmic scale.

Philip Glass (born 1937), like Reich, began his minimalist experiments on a small scale in the mid sixties. He reached his first peak a decade later with the opera *Einstein on the Beach,* in collaboration with the innovative producer Robert Wilson. If some of this production was a trifle whimsical, Glass was dead serious by the time of his next opera *Satyagraha* in 1980 and in his later opera of visionary religious implications, *Akhnaten.* "Satyagraha" is the name of the philosophy and living spirit of nonviolent resistance practiced by the Indian leader Mohandas K. Gandhi. Gandhi was assassinated in 1948 after his nonviolent resistance approach had become a powerful political weapon of the movement for Indian independence from Great Britain.

Glass's *Satyagraha* focuses on the early phase of Gandhi's career, in South Africa, when he was developing Satyagraha as a tool of emancipation for the numerous Indians in South Africa. The story is told in three acts. The words sung by Gandhi and his South African friends and enemies are not of that era at all, but are texts, in the original Sanskrit language, from ancient sacred Hindu writings; they are appropriate only in tone and sentiment to the specific events of the South African struggle. Above and to the back of this hybrid stage action, in each act there appears one of three embodiments of the Satyagraha spirit—Count Leo Tolstoy (the Russian novelist and social visionary) in Act One and the Indian sage Rabindranath Tagore and Martin Luther King, Jr., in the subsequent acts. These figures serve as (nonsinging) witnesses to the continuing power of Satyagraha.

Glass's music for the opera is in his usual repetitive-structure form but has become rich and sometimes emotionally compelling. There are few attempts to indicate conversational emphases or to convey momentary excitement or calm, but the intensity of the first scene of Act One, overall, does swell and subside dramatically. Finally, the solitary spiritual authority of Gandhi is movingly portrayed in the quiet music that closes the scene—in surprisingly melodic lines (by the tenor singing Gandhi's role, and by instruments) and in the final incantatory words of Gandhi, all of which are superimposed on a repetitive phrase in the lower strings.

The work of the younger composer John Adams (born 1947) has moved still farther toward emotional expression and commitment through a compromise between repetitive structures and Romantic sensibility. *Harmonielehre* ("Theory of Harmony") of 1984–85 takes its name, somewhat oddly, from a pre–First World War treatise by Schoenberg. Adams was attracted less to the specific teaching of Schoenberg than by his Expressionist vigor. Adams's *Harmonielehre* is an orchestral suite in three parts (movements), the titles of the last two conveying explicit historical or personal references. Part Two, "The Anfortas Wound" is named for the legendary wounded knight, here symbolizing anguish and impotence yet ultimate spiritual transcendence; and Part Three, "Meister Eckhardt and Quackie," portrays the old German mystic gliding through the starry heavens carrying on his shoulders Adams's baby daughter Emily ("Quackie"), who is whispering to him the secret of God's grace. The first movement (untitled) is particularly interesting to the student of the repetitive-structure genre: sometimes pulsing repetitive phrases are forgotten (as they are throughout Part Two), most strikingly in the pounding, grinding chords that open the movement. More often the repetitive phrases are supplemented by dramatic statements or by arching melodies of amplitude and grace. If there would truly be a new Romanticism in music after the mid eighties, this would be a possible route for its arrival.

POP, JAZZ, ROCK, AND MUSICAL SYNTHESIS

In music of lesser pretensions—pop, rock, the musical theater, and jazz—there was immense vitality in the decades after 1945. More and more observers of contemporary music were becoming convinced that complexity and solemnity did not guarantee musical respectibility, and that the "music of the people" also deserved serious attention. Even a few published critics and writers became reasonably adept in reporting and judging both "'serious" and popular music—a development that scandalized many keepers of the "classical" (art music) flame. Undeniably, competence in music criticism, through the whole range of musical expression, was difficult to attain due to the great variety and specialization within contemporary music.

Popular song writing has continued to flourish here and there during recent decades. Sometimes melody is the prime message, as in the songs of Paul Simon, and other times melody is subordinate to the words, as when Bob Dylan or Joan Baez (fig. 20-45) wrote and sang as spokespersons for youth in the rebellious sixties. Baez began as a singer of traditional folk music but later sang many songs for which she had written both lyrics and music. (Attractive examples are the wistful title song and the reflective "Winds of the Old Days" from her *Diamonds and Rust* album of 1975.) Simon and Dylan have often been categorized as singers of "folk-rock." In France the Belgian Jacques Brel was one of a handful of postwar composer-writer-performers who achieved a satisfying balance of melody and verbal message.

In jazz, as the postwar decades began, there occurred a rather unexpected development in depopularization—the fate of a very substantial segment of jazz in the decades after World War II. In effect, most so-called Modern jazz seemed to have been transformed from pop music into art, and from mass entertainment into an enthusiasm mainly for connoisseurs. The change was associated above all with the advent of *bop* in the war years and its flowering in the later forties, with the talented saxophonist Charlie Parker as its earliest symbolic hero. Bop retained the insistent beat and harmonic sequences of earlier jazz, but embellished them and added new melodic runs and harmonic surprises. Bop sometimes shaded off into the "cool" version of Modern jazz that developed in the fifties and

20-45   Joan Baez and Bob Dylan.

sixties with such players as Miles Davis, Gerry Mulligan, Chet Baker, and Dave Brubeck as leaders, perhaps epitomized by the smoothly sophisticated style of John Lewis's Modern Jazz Quartet.

By the seventies, all these and other jazz styles disputed the jazz terrain. Still, although the beat went on, most jazz had strayed far from its initial direct appeal. Although there remained infinitely more melody in jazz than in experimental serious music, the melody could get bewilderingly lost; novelty was introduced in harmonies also, which alienated many jazz fans. Symptomatic, above all, of the new orientation was the fact that Baker, Brubeck, and Lewis expected their music to be listened to: jazz was not background for dancing or chattering or anything else, but an art deserving the respectful silence of concert audiences. At its best, jazz deserved this attention—but while getting it, it lost some of its early excitement.

In the fifties and sixties, with jazz becoming relatively esoteric, a new groundswell of truly popular music arose, the music commonly known as *rock*. It is difficult to describe a music so eclectic as rock in all its manifestations, exceptions, and quirky offshoots.

However, its predominating tendencies include loud electronic amplification, rhythmic insistency, rather obvious harmonizations, no great emphasis on flowing melody, and verbal messages of urgent significance to much of the youth culture, from the informally personal to the social and political. The lyrics seldom reached poetic heights, but they dealt with many youthful enthusiasms of the day. What mainly mattered in the sixties was the appeal to group awareness and solidarity. In the seventies and later this message was generally absorbed within the context of sheer entertainment.

Such were the predominant trends of rock, even in such divergent British groups as the relatively mild Beatles and the hard-driving Rolling Stones, with their aura of social and sexual aggressiveness. Before their disbanding, the Beatles had become gloriously, eclectically inventive, as is evident in their *Sgt. Pepper* album and their subsequent *White Album.* The Stones drifted fitfully toward complexity but maintained a more consistent image for decades. Other groups experimented more widely and often far less appealingly; one effective exception was The Who's innovative rock opera *Tommy.* Most other rock operas (such as *Jesus Christ Superstar*) and rock musicals (such as *Hair*) owed less to rock than they professed and more to the traditional musical stage.

By the 1970s, individual rock numbers as well as large stage works showed some sign of a trend toward emphasis on melody. A new wave of balladry by individual singers and composers was apparent. One contributory current toward melody was black popular music, whose broader contribution, right along, to white rock and pop was almost as great as it had been to jazz. The blues of the twenties (see chapter 19) had largely given way by the fifties to the more heavily accented, hard-edged "rhythm and blues," which had influenced the phenomenally popular white singer Elvis Presley as well as the Beatles and Rolling Stones. In the late sixties and after, black pop often was known as "soul" (or as "gospel" when specifically Christian-oriented). Soul ballads relied not only on rhythm and the black experience in its search for identity; it had melodic and personal emotional appeal as well. Among its best performing artists were Ray Charles and Aretha Franklin. In its grittier, more "low-down," less melodic phase, some black music had come to be known as "funk"; this, too, contributed to the soul phenomenon.

Newer Jazz and Rock: The Eighties

The 1970s saw the emergence of a remarkable phenomenon in his own right—the pop-soul artist Stevie Wonder (born 1951, fig. 20-46). Wonder began as a singer and became composer-lyricist, arranger, producer, and multi-instrumentalist as well. Sometimes he created all or nearly all of the "tracks" for a recording himself and then superimposed and "mixed" them, following the usual pop-recording practice. After his juvenile-star phase the themes of his songs turned from love and youthful emotional turmoil to a very substantial array of ethical, social, and spiritual issues, many of them of urgent importance to the black community. This charismatic performer would be one of pop's compelling forces in the late seventies and the eighties. In his album of 1976, *Songs in the Key of Life,* his themes ranged from the breadth and intensity of love ("As") to paternal affection ("Isn't She Lovely") and on to the hopelessness of much black life ("Village Ghetto Land"). *In Square Circle* (1985) included such pleasant ballads as "Whereabouts" and "Overjoyed" but also an anthem against South African racial segregation, "Its Wrong."

20-46 Stevie Wonder.

Rock continued its development in the seventies and eighties, and often it rose well above youth-cult status. Bruce Springsteen, for example, became virtually a national American hero for the intensity and integrity of his musical and social vision. Much rock remained musical junk-food (there was junk in Mozart's day, too), while some tried to be serious art. Art-rock was never very precisely defined, except that it represented a "fusion" between rock and more serious music, whether art music or jazz. "Fusion," too, was a nebulous term: it could apply as well to the cross-fertilization of jazz and art music. To stay for the moment with rock-based music, we may note the successful collaboration of the British rock artist Sting (born 1951) with a jazz group for the 1985 album *Dream of the Blue Turtles*. A conglomeration of styles and subject matter mark the album; the jazz element is particularly strong in "Consider Me Gone" and "We Work the Black Seam," the first also containing elements of repetitive structures, the second with an urgent antinuclear message. "Moon over Bourbon Street" was a somewhat less daring departure for a rock star in 1985 than it would have been a decade or so earlier—it is a straightforward ballad of forthright melodic appeal. In 1987, another appealing, stylistically complex album was released in the United States—*The Joshua Tree*, performed by U2, an insightful Irish group.

A more far-reaching expansion of rock horizons is embodied in the 1980s career of the American composer-performer David Byrne (born 1952), whose group Talking Heads became a source of what was sometimes called thinking man's rock. This music is almost incredibly diverse in style from song to song, but the individual songs are often less interesting. Byrne has experimented in areas usually considered outside of pop, including repetitive structures. He contributed songs using repetitive structures for *The Catherine Wheel* (1981), a dance production on Broadway, and *The Knee Plays* (1984), a section of Robert Wilson's enormous opera *the CIVIL warS*. The ambitious scope of Byrne's own work was demonstrated well in a film of 1986, *True Stories*, and an accompanying book of the same name, the whole forming an eccentric view of American life at its most "American"—that is, in Texas. Byrne wrote the varied songs and lyrics for the project and also served as actor, director, designer, and occasional photographer.

Jazz, too, followed multiple paths in the eighties. A style that flourished in the sixties and seventies,

"free" jazz, survived into the following decade, although it had generated only sparse enthusiasm among jazz fans. Free jazz employed "collective improvisation," as opposed to improvisation by individual soloists against a predetermined accompaniment, normally of chord progressions. It was great fun for the performers but a trial for the listeners, many of whom found in it nothing but a bedlam of sounds freed from all constraints of key, melody, rhythm, and chord progressions. Free jazz, in short, was a further step in the depopularization of jazz that we have noted earlier.

In its more broadly acceptable postwar forms jazz incorporated some "free" moments for musical spice, but the main trend of jazz by the seventies and eighties was toward greater, not less, accessibility and popular appeal. This does not imply that jazz became easy and unchallenging to listen to. There were genuine subtleties in, for example, the work of composer and arranger Carla Bley (as in her witty, inventive jazz opera of 1971, *Escalator over the Hill*), in the diverse flights of Chick Corea on piano and electronic keyboards, and in the work of Weather Report (Joe Zawinul and others), one of the most innovative and free-ranging jazz groups. Jazz and jazz-rock at their skillful but accessible best can be sampled in the several styles of the Pat

20-47 Laurie Anderson, 1981.

20-48   Andrew Lloyd Webber.

Metheny Group in their 1984 album *First Circle*. Metheny (born 1954), a guitarist, combines acoustic with electric instruments (the latter including most notably the keyboards of Lyle Mays), and ranges in *First Circle* from a jokey off-key march to a hymn of sorts, by way of straight jazz, ballads, and suggestions of Latin American rhythms.

A a final example of pop-jazz-rock styles we might note the work of the Performance artist Laurie Anderson (born 1947, fig. 20-47). Anderson is one of several artists who have placed music squarely at the center of their Performances or "live art," combining it with such other mediums as photography, video, and mime. Her whimsical Performances can be ambiguous or even surreal, and many of them have been preserved in books, on video, and in recordings. She often plays a violin and/or other instruments and gives recitations and sings in her Performances, one of which can be sampled in her 1984 record *Mister Heartbreak*.

Such performances are by no means completely foreign to traditional *musical theater*—a genre in which the theatrical element is a powerful component of the production, at times compensating for an insubstantial musical score. It was impossible, however, to dismiss as insubstantial the music of many musicals of the early postwar period, among them *South Pacific*, *Kiss Me Kate*, and *My Fair Lady*. Many composers displayed much real craftsmanship in these works of great immediate appeal.

A Musical Synthesis?

Fine musicals were still being produced in the seventies and eighties, some of them turning toward synthesis with traditional art music. In general, popular musicians seemed to be more interested in this synthesis than did the serious concert world. However, the theater music of Leonard Bernstein (born 1918), a celebrated orchestral conductor and conservative concert-composer, was an exception. Although many critics found his self-conscious forays in the seventies into art–pop fusion unsatisfying (for example, his *Mass* and the song cycle *Songfest*), few denied the magic of his earlier *West Side Story* (1957)—a fresh, inspired stage collaboration of talented, conservative art music and the best of popular styles. The story, too, although at least as old as Shakespeare, was certainly up-to-date—youth-gang warfare in New York and the ill-fated love of two young people from opposing groups. Bernstein's music ranged from the spiky, complex "Rumble" music to moving ballads such as "Maria" and "Tonight."

West Side Story became the prototype for much serious music theater of the seventies and eighties. The young lyricist for *West Side Story*, Stephen Sondheim (born 1930), developed into a skilled composer as well; in the seventies and eighties he was tackling subjects far beyond the time-honored frivolities of the Broadway musical stage, as in *A Little Night Music* and the melodramatic but authentically powerful *Sweeney Todd, the Demon Barber of Fleet Street* (1979). In these works there was substantial use of music not only for set pieces, whether songs or ensembles, but also to enhance the dialogue. Many argued that *Sweeney Todd* was true opera—and in fact it has been performed by traditional opera companies.

The biggest name in music theater in the 1980s, and an exemplar of art–pop synthesis, was the Britisher Andrew Lloyd Webber (born 1948), seen in figure 20-48 in front of advertising posters for three of his hit shows. The lyrics of his immensely successful musical show *Cats* (1981) come from T. S. Eliot at his most atypical, the light-hearted *Old Possum's Book of Practical Cats* (1939). The stage and almost the whole theater become an urban alley-playground for cats. With convincing choreography, costumes, and makeup, and with music that is tuneful but by no means simpleminded, *Cats* is a lively celebration indeed, though with its touching moments.

At least as much artistry is seen in *Cats* as in much art music. Lloyd Webber also entered the art music realm effectively, as in the "dance" section of *Song and Dance* (1985); the "song" section, incidentally, is unusual in that it tells the story by songs alone, without dialogue. In 1984 Lloyd Webber wrote *Requiem*—not theater at all but a concert work set to the traditional Latin text of the Roman Catholic Church. The commemoration and supplication for the souls of the dead is set to music only fleetingly pop in style; more often it is serious and conservative—sometimes sharp and angular but at other times gentle and truly affecting. Only time will tell if it is eventually accepted by the mainstream art-music establishment. Nonetheless, it is one of the more successful efforts of the 1980s toward a true musical synthesis.

Thus the quest for stylistic synthesis has continued in music as in the other arts, and some people have hoped that, in due time, all styles will finally coalesce into one. Others have hoped that a single, specialized style will emerge as victor over the others—an outcome that seems extremely unlikely given the stylistic complexities of most past ages. Our Western heritage has provided us with a rich variety of traditions, as well as a growing awareness of our non-Western heritages. However, traditions must develop out of individual creations before they can be inherited. Throughout history, every major creation in the realms of visual art, music, literature, and thought has brought something new to its own age. Today this long-established practice of pushing forward the frontiers of the humanities remains alive and flourishing.

Recommended Reading

Ashton, Dore. *American Art since 1945* (1982). Solid survey.

Baldwin, James. *Going to Meet the Man* (1965). Collection of stories.

Berendt, Joachim-Ernst, ed. *The Story of Jazz* (1978). Essays on historical styles, with informal photographs.

Bowman, Russell. *Philip Pearlstein, the Complete Paintings* (1983). Picture book with long essay.

Cott, Jonathan. *Stockhausen: Conversations with the Composer* (1973). Understandable, mainly in the composer's own words.

Crease, Robert P., and Charles C. Mann. *The Second Creation: Makers of the Revolution in Twentieth-Century Physics* (1986). Interesting, anecdotal, explanatory.

Diamondstein, Barbaralee. *American Architecture Now II* (1986). Interviews with architects.

Feather, Leonard. *The Passion for Jazz* (1980). Lively essays on artists, events, and styles.

Frank, Elizabeth. *Jackson Pollock* (1983). Systematic coverage.

García Márquez, Gabriel. *One Hundred Years of Solitude* (1970). A novel of Magical Realism.

Gochberg, Donald S., ed. *The Twentieth Century* (1980). Good selection of stimulating writings.

Goldman, Albert. *Freakshow: The Rocksoulbluesjazzsickjewblackhumorsexpoppsych Gig and Other Scenes from the Counter-Culture* (1971). Interesting glimpses of 1960s pop culture, mainly on music.

Goldwater, Marge, Roberta Smith, and Calvin Tomkins. *Jennifer Bartlett* (1985). Beautifully illustrated survey.

Hills, Patricia. *Alice Neel* (1983). Commentary and artist's words on works illustrated.

Johnson, Philip, and John Burgee. *Architecture 1979–1985* (1985). A picture book with essays.

Lane, Peter. *Europe since 1945: An Introduction* (1985).

Straightforward narrative, with excerpts from documents.

Laporte, Dominique. *Christo* (1985). Summary of his projects.

Lipman, Jean. *Nevelson's World* (1983). Comprehensive, well-illustrated.

Lucie-Smith, Edward. *Art Today: From Abstract Expressionism to Superrealism* (1983). Comprehensive.

Lynton, Norbert. *The Story of Modern Art* (1980). Fine introduction, c. 1905–80.

McIntire, C. T., ed. *God, History, and Historians* (1977). Christian thinkers on history and modern crises.

Martin, William R., and Julius Drossin. *Music of the Twentieth Century* (1980). Systematic and concise on serious music, by composer, with musical examples.

Miller, Arthur. *Death of a Salesman* (1967). The play, plus criticism.

Rockwell, John. *All-American Music: Composition in the Late Twentieth Century* (1983). Fine introduction to leading composers and trends, both serious and pop.

Roseberry, Eric. *Shostakovich* (1982). Life and times, illustrated.

Russell, John, and Suzi Gablik. *Pop Art Redefined* (1969). Survey of 1960s Pop art.

Sartre, Jean-Paul. *Existentialism and Humanism* (1948). Good introduction to Sartre's work, plus commentary.

Schulze, Franz. *Mies van der Rohe: A Critical Biography* (1985). Life and works.

Seitz, William C. *Abstract Expressionist Painting in America* (1983). Survey of principal artists.

Siegel, Frederick F. *Troubled Journey: From Pearl Harbor to Ronald Reagan* (1984). Good U.S. history 1939–81.

Ward, Ed, Geoffrey Stokes, and Ken Tucker. *Rock of Ages: The Rolling Stone History of Rock and Roll* (1987). Comprehensive.

Glossary

Italics in the definitions indicate terms that are themselves glossary entries. Boldface type is used in the definitions simply for emphasis.

a b a pattern   A musical pattern with two main sections, each with its theme (*a* and *b*), the first of these being repeated. The simplest type of **rondo** form, in which further sections (*c, d,* and so on) may be introduced, but with recurrences of *a*—hence *a b a c a d a . . . .*

absolute music   Music with no implications or direct associations outside of itself—as against *program music* or vocally verbalized music.

Abstract Expressionism   A twentieth-century art style, flourishing especially in the 1950s, that combines *abstraction* with *expressionism*. The two branches of this movement are *Chromatic Abstraction* and *Action Painting.*

abstraction   By the process of abstraction, the depiction of real objects in nature is de-emphasized or done away with, generally on the assumption that a truer, more inward and essential reality is being reached. When it does away completely with representation of real objects, it may be called *nonrepresentational* or *nonobjective* art.

academicism   In the arts, an approach emphasizing tradition and conventionality, especially through adherence to long-standing rules.

a cappella   Italian for "in the church style." Designating choral music without instrumental accompaniment.

accidental   A sign in musical notation used to raise or lower a note one-half step or to cancel such a raising or lowering. The most common accidentals are sharps (raising a note) and flats (lowering a note).

accompaniment   In music, a subordinate part or parts.

acrylic paint   Modern plastic-based, water-soluble paint, more versatile than and becoming more popular than oil paint.

Action Painting   A branch of *Abstract Expressionism.* A way of painting that emphasizes spontaneous gesture.

adagio   Musical tempo indication: slow. A piece in that tempo.

advance-guard   See *avant-garde.*

aesthetic   Concerning the beautiful, often as against the useful or the moral.

aestheticism   Attachment or devotion to aesthetic values or the sense of the beautiful.

aesthetics   In philosophy, the study and theory of the beautiful, especially as it applies to the fine arts, music, and literary expression.

aisle   In architecture, a long, relatively narrow open space, especially that which parallels the nave in basilican construction, and which is set off from the *nave* by rows of *columns* or *piers.*

aleatoric music   Also called music of chance, music of indeterminacy, and open-form music. The composition and/or performance of such works is to some degree determined by methods of random selection or by requiring the performers to make some of the decisions. These techniques first began to be used on a large scale in the 1950s.

allegretto   Musical tempo indication: a bit faster than *moderato,* not quite as fast as *allegro.* A piece in that tempo.

allegro   Musical tempo indication: fast. A piece in that tempo.

allegro assai   Musical tempo indication: rather fast. A piece in that tempo.

allegro con brio   Musical tempo indication: fast, with spirit and vigor. A piece in that tempo.

allegro moderato   Musical tempo indication: moderately fast. A piece in that tempo.

allegro molto moderato   Musical tempo indication: very moderately fast. A piece in that tempo.

allegro vivace   Musical tempo indication: fast and lively. A piece in that tempo.

all-over   Having consistent texture or no focal point of visual interest over the whole surface of a work of abstract painting or sculpture.

altarpiece   A picture or carving behind and above an altar in a Christian church.

alto (contralto)   A low-range female voice.

ambulatory   A covered passage. In a church, it is usually the aisle around the east end, between the enclosed *choir* area reserved for the clergy and the radiating chapels.

amphitheater   A theater, usually oval, with rising tiers of seats.

andante   Musical tempo indication: a very moderate, deliberate "walking" speed, between *adagio* and *allegretto.* A piece in that tempo.

andante con moto   Musical tempo indication: andante "with motion"—faster than andante. A piece in that tempo.

andante un poco moto   Musical tempo indication: andante "with a little motion"—a bit faster than andante. A piece in that tempo.

apse   A projecting section of a building, especially of a church in basilican form, usually semicircular in shape, and vaulted or partially domed.

aquatint   An etching technique for graduated tonal effects of light and dark, often combined with regular (linear) *etching.* An acid bath of the plate finely dotted with resin produces a gradation of printed grey tones depending on the fineness of the granulated resin and the time the plate is exposed to the acid.

arabesque   In the visual arts, an interlacing of plantlike forms, generally stylized.

arcade   A series of arches supported by columns or piers.

arch   In architecture, a structural member of wedge-shaped pieces built over an opening in a wall so as to span space and to be self-supporting and weight-bearing. A structure, such as a **triumphal arch,** that is mainly characterized by an arched opening.

archaeology   The study of material remains from the human past.

archaic   Old. (The implication of being old-fashioned or obsolete should usually not be drawn.) In ancient Greek art, the word refers to the period of the seventh century to about 480 B.C.

architecture   The art and science of building, and the product of building. It is a visual art as well as a field of engineering.

aria   A solo song, usually substantial and rather complex, with orchestral accompaniment. Ordinarily it is a self-contained piece in a larger work such as an *opera* or *oratorio.*

ars nova   In music, the "new art" of the fourteenth century. It delighted in structural subtleties and complexities for their own sake, most notably in rhythmic construction.

art   The process or the product of creative endeavor, as in painting, sculpture, music, dance, literature, and so on. Traditionally refers especially to making or doing things that appeal to a sense of beauty.

art-for-art's-sake   The doctrine that art requires no justification, social or moral or practical, outside itself. The emphasis on form rather than message in art.

art music   One of several terms, all unsatisfactory (including concert music, serious music, and classical music), for music of self-conscious aesthetic appeal—as opposed to popular music.

assemblage   The construction of three-dimensional works of art (as opposed to *collage*) that employs various materials and objects other than traditional art materials. The product of such construction.

asymmetry   Lack or conscious avoidance of *symmetry.*

atonality   In music, partial or total avoidance of *tonality*

with its urge toward restful harmonies and thus its sense of musical focus and direction. Atonality assumes the essential equality of all twelve tones in the *octave;* there is no *tonic,* or pitch indicating a particular key.

automatism or **psychic automatism**   Terms used by practitioners of Surrealism to describe the process of free mental and pictorial association with no concern for reason, morality, or traditional aesthetics.

avant-garde   French for "advance-guard." Those artists who are involved in experiments and innovations that go beyond the generally accepted art of a time.

axis   In the visual arts, such as architecture and painting, an imaginary central line around which the parts of a mass are symmetrically arranged.

ballad   In art music, usually a narrative song. Almost any sort of popular song today.

ballade   A musical form suggestive of a ballad, used for certain piano works with contrasting heroic and lyrical sections.

ballet   Stylized theatrical, staged dancing, ordinarily accompanied by instrumental music. The musical work designed to accompany such dancing.

balustrade   A row of balusters—that is, of upright supports of a railing. Often a railing simply for decorative purposes.

baptistery   An ecclesiastical building, or section of a larger structure, designed to accommodate the rite of baptism.

Baroque   An artistic style that flourished especially in the seventeenth and early eighteenth centuries. At its most typical it involved exuberant, rather theatrical expression and an appeal for viewer involvement, although it often employed classical forms and subjects and embodied a greater or lesser degree of controlled tension. The word is sometimes applied also to music, literature, and so on.

basilica   A pagan Roman structure, basically rectangular in shape, used for judicial and other public functions. Adapted to Christian uses, it became a rectangular church with a long central hall (*nave*) and an *apse,* often with lower side aisles beside the nave. Must not be confused with the nonarchitectural term **basilica,** which is a title of special honor given to certain churches by the pope. Such churches may or may not be in basilica form.

bass   A low-range adult male voice. The double bass, or any instrument or part maintaining the *bass line,* such as an electric guitar in many rock groups.

bass line   The lowest line in a musical work.

bassoon   A double-reed woodwind instrument of the *oboe* family with a long, conical tube twice bent back on itself. The **contrabassoon,** with a lower range, has a still longer tube, four times doubled on itself.

bay   In ecclesiastical architecture, a compartment with *columns* or *piers* at its corners, and *vaulting* above.

Beasts of the Apocalypse   The four creatures envisioned by Saint John in the Book of Revelation (New Testament) and equated with the four Evangelists. Man or angel is equated with Matthew, winged lion with Mark, winged ox with Luke, and eagle with John.

beat The unit of musical measurement. In simple music, successive measures (bars) generally have a fixed number of beats. In recent popular music, beat may imply a regular succession of heavy accents.

bel canto Italian for "beautiful song." The ideal vocal qualities of Italian singing in the seventeenth and eighteenth centuries (and sometimes later), emphasizing beauty of tone and brilliance of technique rather than emotion and drama.

binder The ingredient used to hold pigments together to make paint.

bitonality The simultaneous use of two different *keys* in the *melodies* or *chord* sequences of a composition.

blues A type or precursor of early jazz. Primarily but not necessarily vocal, the blues were generally slow and plaintive and incorporated **blue notes** (usually the third and seventh) with unstable intonation between major and minor keys.

book of hours A book, especially a medieval manuscript, used for private devotions. Some of these medieval books were decorated (illuminated) lavishly.

brass instrument A *wind instrument* with metal body and a cup- or funnel-shaped mouthpiece, such as the French horn, trumpet, cornet, trombone, and tuba.

Brutalism A twentieth-century architectural style embodying a massive, severe air, and often displaying rough, unfinished concrete.

bust In sculpture or painting, a portrait including head, neck, shoulders, and part of the chest.

buttress An architectural support built against and projecting from a wall to counteract the thrusts from within, such as the weight and sidewise pressure of the vaulting. A **flying buttress** is arched away from the wall, and consists essentially of an inclined bar connected to an upper wall and grounded in a masonry mass some distance away from the wall.

cadence A melodic phrase or harmonic formula that suggests the conclusion of a musical work or a portion thereof.

cadenza A showy solo passage near the end of a musical piece, as in an operatic aria or a concerto movement.

campanile A bell tower.

canon In the visual arts, a formal rule of proportions—as of parts of the human body in classical Greek sculpture, or of parts of a column in classical Greek architecture. In music, a type of polyphonic composition in which a musical line is imitated strictly by one or more other lines that enter one after the other, proceeding from the same or different initial pitches.

cantilever To extend a beam beyond its supports. A projecting beam.

cantus firmus In medieval polyphonic music, usually an existing *plainsong* melody borrowed as the basis of the work; it generally employed long notes and appeared in the *tenor* part. Later it could come from other sources, such as Protestant hymn tunes.

canvas A heavy fabric, usually linen, that is stretched over a wooden framework and painted on. A painting on a mounted canvas.

capital The topping of a column, pilaster, or pier, forming a transition to the arch or the horizontal member (*entablature*) above the column.

cartoon In *fresco* painting, a full-sized preparatory drawing or painting used to guide the painting of the mural.

caryatid A sculptured figure of a woman, serving as a column.

casting In sculpture, a process of reproducing a work by using a mold. The material (such as bronze) is introduced in liquid form; after it solidifies, the mold is removed.

cathedral The church of a bishop, where his **cathedra** (official throne) is located.

cella The windowless area of a classical temple, enclosed on three sides, ordinarily designed to contain a large statue of a deity.

cello or **violoncello** A bowed-string instrument of the violin family, between the viola and double bass in size and range.

centralized church A church structurally organized around a central point. It is usually round or octagonal, as opposed to the typical long, rectangular form of a basilican church.

ceramics The art of making clay objects, such as pottery and sculpture, and firing them in a kiln (heated chamber) for permanency. The objects produced by this process.

chamber music Music for a small group of instrumentalists, with one player to a part. A chamber trio has three players, a quartet four, a quintet five, and so on. When one part of a string group is replaced by another instrument, the group or work is known by that instrument's name—piano trio, for example.

chance, music of See *aleatoric music*.

chanson French for "song." A secular song with French text. In the fourteenth through sixteenth centuries it was usually *polyphonic*.

chant *Monophonic* liturgical music in free rhythm. **Gregorian chant** is a term used for all *plainsong*.

chapel A small church, a separate section of a church, or a room in a substantial home that contains an altar and is designed for liturgical and devotional use. A **radiating chapel** is one of the several chapels projecting from the choir of a church.

chiaroscuro   In painting, the shadow-formed contrast of light and dark in the rendition of forms.

choir   In architecture, the section (usually the east end) of a church beyond the *crossing*, for the use of the clergy; usually contains an *apse*, an *ambulatory*, and radiating *chapels*.

chord   The sounding of several different notes simultaneously.

chordal   Of chords. Often used as a synonym for *homophonic*.

chorus   A sizable group of singers (more than one singer to a part), or the work that they sing.

Chromatic Abstraction   A branch of *Abstract Expressionism* distinguished by a particularly expressive use of color.

chromatic scale   A scale with twelve notes, all half-tones, to the octave.

chromaticism   In music, a succession of half-tone intervals, or the use of half-tone intervals where whole tones would be normal in a *diatonic scale*, especially.

clarinet   A woodwind instrument with a beak-shaped mouthpiece with a single reed fixed to its back, a straight cylindrical bore, and a small bell-shaped opening at the other end.

classical   In music, loosely used to refer to serious, concert, or art music, as opposed to popular forms. More properly, referring to the musical style of the later eighteenth century, especially as tending toward the standardization of musical form.

classical or **classic**   Referring to a high point of development in any of the arts—the best in a particular class. Often used to describe the art and civilization of ancient Greece, especially from c. 480 B.C. to the late fourth century B.C. Sometimes applied to the art and civilization of the ancient European and Near Eastern world, both Greek and Roman. See also *Classicism*.

Classicism   A style in the visual arts, music, and literature that emphasizes formal pattern, proportion, and discipline, without (at its best) sacrificing human feeling. It tends toward the rational and the static, rather than exuberant self-expression. Its heyday was the late eighteenth and early nineteenth centuries, when it coexisted with *Romanticism*, with which it is often contrasted. (See also *neo-Classicism*.)

clerestory   In ecclesiastical architecture, the area, with windows, that is the upper zone of an inner wall (of nave, transept, or choir). It stands clear of any projecting roof and vaulting above the side aisles.

coda   Italian for "tail." The fourth section of a movement in *sonata form*.

coffer   A recessed panel in a ceiling or a dome. It may be formed of successively indented squares.

collage   The method or product of sticking together various materials, such as paper, on a panel to create an art work in two dimensions or very low relief—as opposed to a three-dimensional *assemblage*.

colonnade   A series of *columns*.

color   A quality perceived in and through light. In painting, color derives from the pigments employed and is usually more crucially characteristic of the work than is line, which predominates in drawing. The **primary colors,** out of which all other colors may be formed, are red, yellow, and blue.

color-field painting   A type of twentieth-century abstract art, mainly in the 1960s, emphasizing color and often executed with geometrical precision.

column   In architecture, an upright support, tall and usually round. Classical columns usually have three main parts: base, shaft, and capital. Columns may be freestanding or attached—that is, not in the round, but projecting somewhat from a wall and often flattened. A column may also be nonarchitectural, as a freestanding monument in a form similar to architectural columns.

complete art work or (in German) **Gesamtkunstwerk**   A nineteenth-century term popularized by Richard Wagner to define his *music-drama* as a union of several arts—musical, visual, theatrical, and literary. Loosely, any art work involving several mediums.

composer   A writer of music—that is, of musical compositions.

composition   In the visual arts, the structure or arrangement of forms in a work. In music, the process or science of writing music, or a musical work itself.

Conceptual art   Ideational art, especially of the 1960s and later. Visual and formal considerations are seen as subordinate to ideas; verbalization is sometimes employed.

concert music   See *art music*.

concerted style   In the early Baroque period, a musical style involving the combination of different types of performers taking independent musical lines—as opposed to, for example, *a cappella* singing or doubling vocal parts by instruments. The concerted style may mean, for example, the alternation of vocal with instrumental parts, or the simultaneous sounding of vocal and instrumental lines, with the latter not simply doubling the former. After about 1660, the concerted style started to imply an instrumental work setting off a small group of solo instruments against a larger orchestral group. See also *concerto grosso*.

concertino   See *concerto grosso*.

concerto   A musical work in *concerted style*. Since the beginning of the Classical period, about 1750, it dropped the *continuo* device of the Baroque era and was likely to feature one solo instrument. In general, it became a work in several (usually three) movements for one or more prominently featured solo instruments and orchestra.

concerto grosso   A musical work in *concerted style*, after about 1660, setting off a small group of solo instruments (the **concertino**) against a larger orchestral group (the **ripieno**); the two groups sometimes played separately and sometimes (in concerted sections) together. In the Baroque era the work employed the *continuo,* had several unified movements, and usually was *homophonic* in style.

concrete   A building material made of cement, sand, water, and such other substances as gravel or crushed stone. **Reinforced concrete** (also known as **ferroconcrete**) is a building material consisting of concrete reinforced within by iron, steel bars, or mesh arranged to reinforce the major points of tension or compression. In twentieth-century music, descriptive of sounds transformed electronically from sounds outside the electronic equipment.

conductor   The leader of a performing musical group. The conductor generally beats time, indicates expressive effects, and otherwise coordinates the performance.

consonance   In music, a pleasing or restful effect produced by certain intervals or chords.

consort   An instrumental chamber group—term used in the late Renaissance and early Baroque periods.

construction   The process or product of building up a form by assembling and joining, as in sculpture or (less literally) in painting.

Constructivism   A method of sculpture in which the work is not carved from a central mass of material, or molded into a central mass, but constructed in space out of various possible materials and intermingling with space.

continuo   In music of the Baroque era, the bass line and the harmonic fabric above it that "continue" throughout the work. Generally played by both a bowed and a keyboard instrument, with the bowed instrument (such as cello) providing or reinforcing the bass line.

contrapposto   A bodily pose in pictorial art in which a part of the human body is turned in a direction opposite to that of another.

Corinthian   An order of classical architecture resembling the *Ionic,* but with *capitals* of stylized sculptured leaves of the acanthus plant—the most ornate of the three Greek orders.

cornet   A brass instrument rather similar to the trumpet, but with a shorter tube.

cornett   A wind instrument, mainly of the Middle Ages and Renaissance, that was long and straight, or somewhat curved; usually made of wood and having a cup-shaped mouthpiece. Not to be confused with the modern cornet.

cornice   In classical architecture, the top of the entablature—that is, a projecting molding. Any projecting, horizontal molding that serves as a decorative feature.

counterpoint   Commonly, *polyphony*—especially its compositional technique. Counterpoint emphasizes multimelodic structure rather than chordal structure. (The adjective is **contrapuntal.**)

crescendo   A term in musical dynamics: increasing loudness.

crossing   In a cross-shaped church, the space where the transept intersects the long nave–choir or nave–apse area.

crucifix   In the visual arts, a representation of Christ suffering or dead on the cross.

Cubism   A twentieth-century movement in painting and sculpture that portrayed objects by breaking them up into planes or geometrical components and reassembling the components unnaturalistically.

cupola   A dome. Usually a small structure topping a large dome, tower, or roof.

da capo   Italian for "from the beginning." To be repeated, in part, from the beginning. In seventeenth- and eighteenth-century opera and oratorio, the da capo aria was common—an aria in two sections, with a repetition of the first.

Dada or **Dadaism**   A literary and artistic movement that developed partly as a reaction to World War I. It mocked both the machine age and emotional effusiveness, and emphasized whimsy and provocative unintelligibility.

decorative   Ornamental. Decorative art is a term often used for art embellishing a useful object.

development   In music, the second section of a movement in *sonata form.*

diatonic scale   See *scale.*

diptych   A pair of paintings on hinged panels.

dissonance   A displeasing or tense effect produced by certain musical intervals or chords.

dodecaphony   See *twelve-tone method of composition.*

dome   A concave covering for space that can be thought of as a continuous revolving succession of arches with the same center.

donor   The commissioner and giver of a work of art. Donor portraits are especially common in religious works of the late Middle Ages and the Renaissance.

Doric   In classical architecture, the *order* characterized especially by sturdiness of appearance, unadorned square capitals, and usually a sculptured frieze with panels alternately geometrical (*triglyphs*) and pictorial (*metopes*).

double bass   A bowed-string instrument, the lowest in range of the violin family. In orchestras its strings are most often bowed, in jazz groups they are most often plucked.

drawing   The process or product of delineating forms on a surface such as paper or canvas by using an implement such as a pen or pencil. The linear element ordinarily predominates, rather than color or mass.

duet   A musical work for two performers, or their performance, with or without accompaniment.

dynamics   Relationships, degrees, and changes of loudness in music.

Earth art   Since the 1960s, a large-scale art, done in natural settings, that alters landforms.

easel   A supportive frame for holding a painter's panel or canvas upright during the painting process or for exhibition.

ecclesiastical   Of the clergy or the church as an institution.

eclecticism   The mingling of several styles, methods, or approaches in thought or the arts, in the hope of combining the best from various sources. Often implies a mixture of incompatible or ill-matched ingredients.

electronic music   Music made by electronic generators or instruments, with or without any external sound source. See also *concrete* and *synthesizer*.

embellishment   Musical ornamentation written out by the composer or improvised by the performer.

enamel   To glaze a surface (as of terracotta or bronze) so as to produce a very hard, durable finish. The finish itself.

encaustic   A painting medium in which color pigments are mixed with wax, and the mixture is driven into the backing by applying heat with irons or similar implements.

engraving   The process or product of printing from a gouged, inked metal plate; the ink is wiped from the surface but remains in the grooves, against and into which the paper is pressed. See also *etching*.

ensemble   A group of musical performers or a group performance. In opera, a section for several soloists, or for soloists and chorus, in addition to orchestra.

entablature   In architecture, the structural parts supported by columns, sometimes supporting a *pediment*. In a classical building, the entablature may include an **architrave** (the horizontal lintel—see *post-and-lintel*), a *frieze*, and a *cornice*. In describing a nonclassical building, the word may be used loosely for any element somewhat resembling a classical entablature.

Environmental art   Art in which the natural or artificial setting around the artist or observer is modified, manipulated, or contemplated.

equestrian monument   A large work of sculpture portraying a rider on horseback.

estampie   An instrumental dance form of the thirteenth and fourteenth centuries, with a series of sections, each repeated with a new ending.

etching   The process or product of printing from an inked metal plate into which the design has been eaten by acid in the areas that have been scratched clear of a protective coating. See also *engraving*.

euphonious   Having a smooth, pleasing sound.

Event   A type of twentieth-century multimedia art that features the activity of the artist. Events often involve a production on a very large scale, in which the artist supervises many helpers, as in the case of Christo's 24½-mile-long *Running Fence*. See also *Happening* and *Performance*.

exposition   In music, the first section of a movement in *sonata form*.

expressionism   Emphasis on expression in the various arts.

Expressionism   The broad trend in twentieth-century visual art that represents or emphasizes emotional involvement on the part of the artist and viewer, as against detachment, order, and discipline. Sometimes the term is more specifically applied to the work of the German Expressionists of the early part of this century.

facade   The face or front of a building.

fantasia   An instrumental piece implying a "flight of fancy," not following conventional form.

fantasy   A whimsical or fantastic element embodied in a work of art.

Fauvism   The approach of several French painters (the **Fauves,** or "wild animals") early in the twentieth century, characterized usually by the free, subjective use of pure and violent colors as a means of emotional and formal expression.

fête galante   As a subject for painting (mainly eighteenth century), an elegant, festive diversion in a quasinatural or parklike setting, usually with gallant, or fashionably amorous, overtones.

fifth   See *interval*.

figurative   Of human figures.

figure painting   The representation of the human figure in painting.

fine arts   Traditionally, the more "noble" arts—often limited to painting, sculpture, and music. The term has fallen into disfavor, since it appears to slight the dignity and worth of other forms of artistic expression, and as boundary lines between arts have grown increasingly hazy.

flat   See *accidental*.

flute   A keyed woodwind instrument with a mouth-hole and a straight cylindrical bore, generally now made of silver.

fluting   A series of grooves (**flutes**) in an architectural member, for decorative purposes. Used especially on *columns* and *triglyphs*.

flying buttress   See *buttress*.

folk music   A community's or people's music, in contrast to music written by trained composers.

foreshortening   A *perspective* device applied to an object or mass, so as to suggest the receding of bulk in space.

form   In the visual or musical arts, the type or kind of a work, such as etching or concerto. In the visual arts, a shape or group of shapes in a work, or the work's basic structure. In music, the ways in which a work is organized and structured.

formal   Of form or forms. Concerning structure in the arts. **Formal values** are the essential structural values of an art work, as opposed to those that are primarily representational, narrative, or moral.

formalism   Emphasis on form in the arts.

Formalism   The broad trend in twentieth-century art that represents or emphasizes emotional detachment and structural order.

forte   A term in musical dynamics: loud.

fortissimo   A term in musical dynamics: very loud.

found object   An object chosen by an artist for exhibition, either by itself or as part of an art work.

fourth   See *interval*.

foyer   In architecture, a promenade or lobby.

French horn   A brass instrument with a funnel-shaped mouthpiece; a spiral, mainly conical bore; and a broadly flaring bell.

fresco   Italian for "fresh." The process and product of wall (mural) painting on fresh plaster, which easily absorbs and stabilizes the pigments.

frieze   In classical architecture, the intermediate part of the *entablature* surmounting the columns. It is a horizontal band, either with alternating *triglyphs* and *metopes* (in Doric building) or sometimes with continuous relief sculpture (in the other classical *orders*). Loosely, any horizontal band of figurative relief sculpture or other ornament.

fugue   Polyphonic composition in which the musical lines enter successively, using at first the same theme (subject) and later developing in free *counterpoint*, although the counterpoint often incorporates recurrent *motifs*.

gable   In architecture, a peaked exterior section under slanted roof lines.

gallery   In architecture, a long passage—for example, above and behind the arcaded *nave* wall of a church.

genre   A type or category of art.

genre painting   Realistic painting of a modest everyday scene.

geodesic dome   A light-weight domelike structure with a grid of intersecting straight bars. Its structurally strong surface derives from principles of physical equilibrium.

glissando   A rapid *scale* executed on an instrument by using a sliding movement.

Gothic   A style of European art and architecture that grew out of Romanesque in the twelfth century and flowered in the thirteenth through fifteenth centuries. In architecture it gave a greater impression of airy lightness than did Romanesque; this was made possible through the combined application of the flying *buttress*, the pointed arch, and the

ribbed vault. **High Gothic** is a term usually applied to the thirteenth century, with **late Gothic** coming thereafter. **Flamboyant Gothic,** a type of late Gothic, is characterized by exuberant elaboration and a suggestion of flamelike, restless movement.

Gregorian chant   See *chant*.

ground   In music, especially of the Baroque era, a melodic line (usually short) repeated again and again in the bass.

half-tone (semitone)   An interval of a minor second—the smallest interval normally employed in Western music.

hall church   A type of church (usually late Gothic) essentially modeled as a unified hall covered by a single roof. The side aisles are the same height as the nave, or only slightly lower.

Happening   From the late 1950s, a multimedia event consciously staged as a work of art, sometimes employing traditional artistic materials and concepts and often involving spectator participation. See also *Event*.

harmony   The chord structure of music—that is, the way different tones sound together.

harp   A stringed instrument, generally plucked, with strings perpendicular to the soundboard.

harpsichord   A stringed keyboard instrument with plucked strings.

hold   In music, a pause.

homophony   Music consisting of a single melodic line, supported by chords. (The adjective is **homophonic**.)

horn   In orchestras and for other concert music uses, generally the French horn, a brass instrument not to be confused with the woodwind **English horn,** which is related to the oboe.

hornpipe   An English dance; musical dance form in lively triple time.

humanism   An emphasis on human beings on earth and their potentialities. Often used, especially in the Renaissance, to refer to the study of ancient Greek and Roman literature and art, which were seen as embodying human emphases.

icon   A holy image, usually painted on a wooden panel. In Eastern Orthodox churches icons are to be venerated by believers, not worshipped as idols.

iconography   In the pictorial arts, the representational scheme, or the study of subject matter, in individual works.

idealism   In the arts, representation according to stylized, perfected forms or types, in contrast to *realism*.

ideational   Of ideas. In the visual arts, the primacy of ideas (concepts) over visual or formal considerations. See *Conceptual art*.

illuminated manuscript   A book written by hand, and decorated with ornaments and often pictures (*miniatures*).

image   A pictorial or evocative representation of a person, thing, event, or emotional state.

imitation   A procedure in polyphonic composition (in canons, fugues, and so on) in which a melody or theme is closely followed by successive restatements in other parts.

Impressionism   A school of painting of the late nineteenth century that emphasized visual fact and atmosphere. Especially by breaking up light and color, it sought to record lively, fleeting visual impressions.

improvisation   Spontaneous musical performance, without aid of memorization or written music.

indeterminacy, music of   See *aleatoric music.*

individualism   In the arts, realistic representation of specific forms, as opposed to idealized forms or types. Creation emphasizing the artist's individuality.

instrument, musical   With the exception of the human voice, any mechanism that produces musical sounds. See also *keyboard, string(ed) instrument, woodwind, brass, percussion,* and *synthesizer.*

intermezzo   Musical interlude. In the seventeenth century it was a short, light musical play performed between acts of a more serious play or opera.

International style   In painting, a broadly European style of around 1400, characterized by delicately swirling outlines and an air of courtly luxury and elegance. In architecture, a Formalist style of the twentieth century, characterized most obviously by plainness, clarity, and unconcealed structural materials.

interval   The distance in pitch between two tones of a musical *scale,* as expressed in the number of tones comprised in that distance. In the *diatonic scale,* the distance from C to E, and from E to G, on the musical *staff* is a **third;** from C to E is a **major third** (with two whole tones), and from E to G is a **minor third** (with a whole tone and a half-tone).

Ionic   In classical architecture, the *order* characterized by a somewhat more decorative quality and greater delicacy than the *Doric,* by its relatively slender columns topped by scroll-like *capitals,* and often by a continuous sculptured *frieze.*

jazz   Popular music that arose around 1900 among black Americans and eventually spread to other peoples throughout the world. Originally and most typically it had a powerfully propulsive rhythm, allowed soloists to improvise on the basic harmonic structure, and involved overall freedom in performance.

jazz-rock   A popular, sometimes highly sophisticated, combination of jazz and rock that achieved popularity in the 1970s.

key   On a keyboard or woodwind instrument, the device pressed by a player's finger to determine the *tone* sounded. The key of a piece or section of tonal music is its precise *tonality* (C major, A minor, and so on) as determined by its predominant *scale* and *chords.*

keyboard   A set of keys on a piano, organ, harpsichord, and so on, that activate a sound-producing mechanism (vibrating string or column of air, for example). Keyboard instruments include, among others, the virginal, harpsichord, piano, organ, piano accordion, and synthesizer.

kinetic art   A type of modern sculptural art that incorporates motion.

lancet   A narrow, pointed window or arch.

lantern   A small ornamental structure on a dome or roof that admits light to the interior.

larghetto   Musical tempo indication: somewhat faster than *largo.* A piece in that tempo.

largo   Musical tempo indication: very slow. A piece in that tempo.

leitmotif   German for "leading motif." Term used for any one of the many motifs in Wagner's *music-dramas;* each motif can be associated with a particular person, object, situation, or emotion.

libretto   The verbal text of an opera, oratorio, or other substantial work for voices and orchestra.

lied   A song in German. (The plural is **lieder.**)

lute   A plucked-string instrument with a halved-pear-shaped body, popular especially in the sixteenth and seventeenth centuries.

Madonna   (Italian, "My Lady") The Virgin Mary, or a pictorial representation of her, usually with the Christ Child.

madrigal   In sixteenth- and early-seventeenth-century music, a relatively brief composition with words in the vernacular, usually secular and for unaccompanied voices, one voice to a part. A madrigal might be *polyphonic* or *homophonic,* or a mixture of both.

major mode or **major scale**   See *scale.*

mandolin   A plucked-string instrument with metal strings that are usually paired for each tuning pitch.

Mannerism   Affectation. The word has been most often applied in the visual arts to certain trends in the mid and late sixteenth century, ranging from rigid adherence to past styles to a tortured striving for novelty. Perhaps it is best restricted to the enthusiastic application of recent technical advances in the arts—as a search for visual effects rather than naturalism or emotional exaltation, and a taste for the elegant and the consciously artificial.

mansard roof   A roof that slopes in two stages to the summit, the lower slope being steeper than the upper.

masonry   Stone or brick, or sometimes stone and brick, construction.

Mass   The central rite of the Roman Catholic Church, commemorating and re-enacting the change of bread and wine into the substance of the body and blood of Jesus Christ (the Eucharistic sacrament).

mass   A musical setting of most of the unchanging verbal portions of the Mass.

measure   In music, a "bar," or group of beats, the first of which is usually accented. In musical notation, measures are separated by **bar lines** (vertical lines crossing the *staff*).

medieval   Of the Middle Ages.

medium   (**Mediums** and **media** are plural forms.) In the arts, a material used (such as paint or stone) or a type of communication (such as dance, song, or drama).

melody   A succession of single musical tones, with its own rhythmic and modal (scale) arrangement.

meter   In music, a pattern of regular, recurring accents. It is indicated by a **time signature**. For example, 6/4 meter (**time**) indicates that the basic values are quarter notes, and that every sixth quarter note is most heavily accented. In this case, bar lines separate each metric group of six quarter-note units into a measure. **Duple meter** refers to there being two units in the measure, **triple meter** refers to three, and so on.

metope   In classical architecture, a sculptured figurative or pictorial relief panel in a Doric *frieze*.

microtone   In music, an *interval* smaller than a *half-tone*.

Middle Ages   A term for the thousand years in Europe between the fall of the Roman Empire and the Renaissance—that is, roughly, the fifth through the fourteenth centuries. See also *Romanesque* and *Gothic*.

miniature   A manuscript miniature is a small picture in a book written and painted by hand. It may appear in the text or border of a page, or may occupy a whole page.

Minimal art   A movement of the 1960s, principally in sculpture, characterized by very elementary forms and use of industrial materials.

minor mode or **minor scale**   See *scale*.

minuet   A dance or musical dance form in moderate triple time. It flourished in the seventeenth and eighteenth centuries, and in the latter it became a movement in many sonata-type works (symphonies, for example).

mixed media   A combination of two or more traditional or new materials, as in the case of abstract paintings that make use of a combination of latex paint and marble dust to produce a stonelike surface.

mobile   A twentieth-century form of sculpture (invented and named by Alexander Calder) consisting of rods or stiff wires with objects suspended and balanced, set in motion by air currents.

modal   Of modes in music. (See *mode*.) Often today the term is applied only to the modes traditionally accepted by the Roman Catholic Church, apart from the major and minor modes of the diatonic scale; the latter are called tonal (see *tonality*), with the term *modal* often being applied just to the Church modes.

mode   The arrangement of pitches into a scale pattern, as in the major and minor modes of the modern diatonic scale. (See *scale*.) Half-tones (semitones) appear at different points in scales proceeding predominantly by whole tones; the different arrangements (as of the medieval Church modes) are most easily thought of as sequences of the piano's white-key notes, beginning on different tones. See also *modal*.

modeling   The shaping of three-dimensional, sculptural form. In painting and other two-dimensional mediums, the representation of three dimensions, usually through light and shadow.

moderato   Musical tempo indication: moderate. A piece in that tempo.

Modernism   An approach to art, beginning around 1905, that consciously rejected the past. It broke with traditional Realism and decorative design.

modulation   A change of *key* in a musical composition, most often effected by interposing a *chord* containing notes that are common to both keys.

monody   Solo song with *continuo* accompaniment, especially in seventeenth-century Italian composition. It was designed for dramatic expression rather than flowing lyricism.

monophony   Music consisting of a single melodic line, without accompaniment. (The adjective is **monophonic**.)

monumentality   In the arts, the quality of simplicity and breadth of style, rather than minute detail, whether in large or small works.

mosaic   The process or product of creating pictures or designs by the juxtaposition of small pieces of hard, colored material such as stone or glass stuck against a flat or nearly flat surface.

motet   A type of polyphonic church music that flourished from the thirteenth century through the Renaissance and later. In the Middle Ages it generally added two parts above the basic tenor, which was taken from *plainsong*. By the sixteenth century, original melodies were usual throughout the varying number of parts, and the motet had become, in general, an unaccompanied vocal setting of any sacred Latin text aside from the mass.

motif   In the arts, a leading feature or theme. In music, a short figure or design, often fragmentary.

movement   A major, self-contained division of a suite or sonata-type work.

multimedia   A combination of mediums and types of art work—such as music, theater, and sculpture—often involving the participation of the spectator.

mural   Of a wall. Wall painting. See also *fresco*.

music   In early Greece, the creative arts represented by the nine Muses, or goddesses of the arts. More specifically (and today almost exclusively), the tonal art—the art and science of deliberately arranging and combining vocal and/or instrumental sounds in an expressive or effective way. These sounds or arrangements themselves.

musical saw   A handsaw held between the player's knees, bent (to produce different pitches) by the player's left hand and bowed (with a violin bow) by the right.

music-drama   The type of opera devised and composed by Richard Wagner in his later decades—a complete art work disdaining vocal display and combining music, poetry, and stage production in a synthesis of the arts.

musicology   The scholarly study of music, especially through its historical development—although it may include all other aspects of music except composition and performance.

narthex   The vestibule of a church, leading to the *nave*.

naturalism   Realism in the visual and literary arts—that is, an approach that strives for resemblance to natural conditions and appearances. As a conscious school of writing in the later nineteenth century, **Naturalism** strove to be a scientific, objective systematization of Realism.

nave   In architecture, the long (usually western) section of a church normally used by the congregation of worshippers. When there are side aisles, nave refers just to the central section.

neo-Classicism   Any "new" classicism—that is, since classical antiquity. A twentieth-century art movement emphasizing Classical elements. Twentieth-century musical neo-Classicism involved a leanness and restraint reminiscent of the Classicism of Mozart and Haydn.

nonobjective or **nonrepresentational**   In the visual arts, representing no recognizable object. Totally abstract.

notation   The system used for writing down music so that it may be read or performed.

note   A musical sound with a given pitch and duration, or the written sign for the sound.

note value   In music, the relative length of a note.

oboe   A double-reed woodwind instrument with a straight conical bore.

octave   The interval of an eighth in the diatonic scale or twelve half-tones. Notes an octave apart are given the same letter name and give the impression of duplicating each other.

off-beat   In music (especially jazz and other popular forms), accenting, for example, not the first and third but the second and fourth beats in 4/4 time.

ogee arch   A curved, pointed arch, shaped with the curve reversed near the point, thus making the point sharper.

oil painting   Painting done with pigments mixed with linseed or other vegetable oil. This has been the most popular medium for easel (canvas or panel) painting since its development in the fifteenth and sixteenth centuries.

Op art   An art style of the 1950s and later, aiming at optical illusions of change and shifting movement.

opera   A dramatic work for voices and orchestra, designed to be enacted on stage.

opera seria   An eighteenth-century opera sung in Italian, written on a "serious" historical and heroic theme.

optical space   See *picture plane*.

opus   A musical work. (The plural is **opuses** or **opera.**) Term (abbreviated as op.) indicating the chronological position of a work (a single piece or a group of pieces) among publications by a composer—thus indicating order of publication, not composition.

oratorio   A substantial work for voices and orchestra, generally with a religious subject, that does not in principle call for stage performance, but has a narrator to explain the implied action.

orchestra   In music, a large group of instruments or performing instrumentalists—as opposed to a *chamber music* group, with one player to a part, or a group playing specialized instruments (such as a band of wind instrumentalists). The main instrumental sections of a **symphony orchestra** today are strings, woodwinds, brass, and percussion.

orchestration   The art of composing for an orchestra, using instruments in ways appropriate to their capabilities and tonal properties, according to the composer's desired effects.

order   A characteristic style of classical architecture, pertaining to the organization, parts, and proportions of the columns and the entablature surmounting the columns. See *Doric, Ionic,* and *Corinthian,* referring to the Greek orders. Rome added to these three the **Tuscan** (a simplified Doric) and the **Composite** (combined Ionic and Corinthian) orders.

organ   A keyboard instrument in which traditionally the sound is produced by columns of air vibrating in vertical pipes. A pedalboard, played by the organist's feet, is generally included.

organum   Early medieval polyphonic composition built on a plainsong melody. In **parallel organum** the added part or parts follow the *plainsong* at a fixed interval, ordinarily parallel fifths or fourths.

ornamentation   In the arts, decorative embellishment. In music, it may be written out by the composer or improvised by the performer.

overture   An instrumental work that serves to introduce a vocal and instrumental work such as an opera. Sometimes it is an independent work, such as the Baroque French overture or the nineteenth-century concert overture.

painting   The process or product of applying paint to a surface, most often two-dimensional, for aesthetic effect.

panel   A flat, rigid support, such as wood, on which easel painting may be done. In painting or relief sculpture, any self-contained picture, such as an altar or door panel.

part   A single musical line or the music for a particular instrument in a group.

part-song   A vocal work in several parts. The term is most often used for *homophonic* writing but is sometimes applied to *polyphonic* composition.

Passion music   A musical setting of the biblical story of Jesus Christ's last days on earth, through his death and burial. After about 1700 it became an *oratorio*, abandoning the biblical text or supplementing it with paraphrases and poetic commentaries.

pastel   A pictorial medium, or the artwork made with it; powdered pigment is mixed with a gum and molded into sticks, which are used like pieces of chalk. The results resemble drawings or paintings.

pediment   In classical architecture, a shallowly triangular area above the horizontal *cornice*, topped by slanting cornices. It often contains sculpture. Pediments (without inner sculpture) may also appear above doors or windows.

pentatonic scale   A scale with five tones to the octave, most commonly like that playable on five consecutive black keys of a piano.

percussion instrument   An instrument on which sound is produced by striking or shaking, including cymbals, celesta, various drums, and so on. The piano may be classified as either a percussion or a stringed instrument.

Performance   A type of twentieth-century multimedia production that is presented on a stage or in a less formal viewing area, without active participation by the spectator. See also *Event* and *Happening*.

perspective   In pictorial art, the many illusionistic ways of suggesting spatial depth when the form used is flat or shallower than in the natural scene portrayed. **Linear perspective** refers to most systems of decreasing sizes for increasingly distant objects, especially by the convergence of lines at vanishing points on the horizon. **Atmospheric (aerial) perspective** is based on color rather than line, and generally fades colors and blurs outlines of objects portrayed as being in the distance.

Photo-Realism   A form of Realist painting of the 1960s and later that emphasizes precision and, usually, employs techniques associated with photography, such as limited focus or snapshot composition.

pianissimo   A term in musical dynamics: very soft.

piano   A term in musical dynamics: soft. A stringed keyboard instrument with strings struck by hammers; also called **pianoforte**.

piano trio   An *ensemble* comprised of a piano and two stringed instruments, ordinarily violin and cello, or a work in several movements for such a group. See *chamber music.*

piccolo   A small, high-pitched flute.

pictorial space   See *picture plane.*

picture plane   The plane that corresponds to the physical surface of a painting. Before the twentieth century, painting was thought of as being like a window through which one views an imaginary space; in much of the art of this century, however, a painting is seen as a flat, two-dimensional surface. The flat space achieved by many painters since *Abstract Expressionism* is sometimes called **optical space**—as opposed to the **pictorial space** of window-on-the-world painting.

pier   In architecture, a substantial vertical support of solid masonry, usually square or rectangular. When visible it is often decorated, as with pilasters, attached or half columns, and so on. See also *column.*

Pietà   A representation of the dead Christ held in the Virgin's arms.

pilaster   A flattened attached column. Ordinarily decorative but may also serve for support. See also *column.*

pitch   The high or low placement of a musical tone, as determined by the tone's frequency, or number of vibrations per second.

plainsong   In the Western medieval Church, monophonic vocal music in free rhythm.

plane   In the visual arts, a flat surface or a solid section that suggests flatness.

plastic   Giving or receiving form, as in the visual (or sometimes musical) arts. Capable of being modeled.

polyphony   Music emphasizing the melodic function of each part—not just melody accompanied by chords (*homophony*). Musical lines in a polyphonic work may or may not be imitative of one another, but in any case they proceed as independent entities, each making musical sense in itself. (The adjective is **polyphonic**.)

polyptych   A hinged piece of art in more than three panels, especially for forming an altarpiece.

polytextual   Employing two or more texts simultaneously in a musical composition.

polytonality   The simultaneous use of several different *keys* in different musical parts (melodies or chord sequences) of a composition.

Pop art   An art style, especially of the 1960s, that aimed at celebrating or commenting on everyday life by adapting the most commonplace, popular themes and visual experiences to representational art, often with the least possible personal intervention by the artist.

porphyry   A very hard rock with crystals embedded in a dark red or purplish mass.

portal   A door. An imposing doorway or group of doorways, as at the west front or on a transept arm of a cathedral.

portico A porch, or covered entrance to a building, with a colonnade.

post-and-lintel In architecture, a simple structural system using upright posts and a horizontal beam (lintel) that spans the space between posts.

Postpainterly Abstraction A twentieth-century painting movement that evolved from *Abstract Expressionism*. It was characterized by an interest in color. See also *color-field painting*.

prelude A musical introduction. A short work suggesting a mood or *program*.

presto Musical tempo indication: very fast. A piece in that tempo.

print An impression made on paper from a figured original such as a block, plate, or stone. See also *engraving, etching,* and *woodcut*.

program music Music with a **program**—that is, a nonmusical or literary idea—as opposed to *absolute music*. Ordinarily it also has a descriptive, programmatic title.

psalter A book of psalms, especially a medieval manuscript, for clerical or private religious use.

psaltery A medieval instrument with plucked strings.

psychic automatism See *automatism*.

quartet A musical work for four similarly important performers; it may or may not have accompaniment. Often, a group of four instrumental performers or the work they perform. A string quartet includes four stringed instruments—usually two violins, viola, and cello. See also *chamber music*.

quintet A musical work for five similarly important performers; it may or may not have accompaniment. Often, a group of five instrumental performers or the work they perform.

readymade A manufactured *found object* chosen for exhibition as a work of art.

realism In the pictorial and literary arts, an approach that strives for resemblance to natural conditions and appearances. As a conscious school of art in the nineteenth century, Realism strove to be an unsentimental and unprettified expression of the realities of contemporary life, especially among the nonprivileged classes.

recapitulation In music, the third section of a movement in *sonata form*.

recitative A style of composition for voice with accompaniment, in which the vocal line comes close to dramatic speech. It is often narrative in function, and may be used in any storytelling work, such as opera or oratorio. When sung in quick, free rhythm with *continuo* accompaniment,

mainly in eighteenth-century works, it is called *secco,* or recitativo secco.

reed instrument See *woodwind instrument*.

relief A type of sculpture in which figures project from a background. In low relief, figures project only slightly; in high relief, they project substantially and may in part be detached from the background.

reliquary A container, generally richly decorated, for sacred **relics** (physical remains or objects closely associated with holy persons).

Renaissance French for "rebirth." A much disputed term often applied to the early phase of postmedieval European civilization, and more specifically to the self-conscious turning to the literary and artistic ideals and forms of ancient Greece and Rome, especially in the fifteenth and sixteenth centuries. In the arts, **early Renaissance** may refer to the period before 1470 or a decade or so later; **High Renaissance** to the period from 1470 or 1490 to about 1530; and **late Renaissance** to the period from about 1530 to about 1600. See *Mannerism* for one artistic style of the late Renaissance.

repetitive structures, music from Music from the 1960s to date involving lengthy repetition and gradual transformation of a short theme, rhythmic pattern, and chord progression. Often called "reductionism" or "minimalism."

representational Depicting natural or visible forms or images.

resolve In music, to follow a dissonant interval by one that is consonant or less dissonant.

rhythm In music, organization in terms of time. Rhythm may be either flexible (free) or organized according to a special scheme, but in modern Western music it is generally thought of as being accentual—that is, with recurring accents.

rhythm and blues The predominant black popular music in the United States from the 1940s into the 1960s. A heavily accented *blues,* it greatly influenced later *soul* and *rock*.

rib In architecture, a long, continuous structural member projecting somewhat from a *vault*. It may be used to hide the uneven juncture of vaults and sometimes has a supportive function, helping to concentrate and ground the weight of the vault on piers or columns below.

ripieno See *concerto grosso*.

ritornello In seventeenth-century opera, an instrumental interlude.

rock A broad category of popular music that developed by the 1960s. It is usually electronically amplified.

Rococo In the arts, an outgrowth of Baroque, especially in the eighteenth century up to about 1760. It tended toward grace, intimacy, and decorative whimsy.

Romanesque A style of European art and architecture that flowered in the eleventh century and remained predominant through the twelfth century. In architecture, despite many variations and its gradual merging with Gothic, it may be said to have stressed heaviness, relatively small window areas, and rounded arches (in windows, vaulting, and arcades).

romanticism   A style in the visual arts, music, and literature that emphasizes individual feelings and emotions, and the dynamic, irregular, and unexpected. The earlier nineteenth century is generally called the **Romantic period,** but romanticism has been a recurrent cultural phenomenon in the Western world. Usually contrasted with *classicism.*

rose window   A large circular window, with tracery suggesting a rose in full bloom, usually in the *facade* or *transept* wall of a Gothic church.

rotunda   A round building, or large round room, ordinarily covered by a dome.

sacristy   A room in a church where clerical vestments and sacred utensils are kept.

sarcophagus   A stone coffin that is not buried underground but exposed to view.

saxophone   A single-reed woodwind instrument of conical bore, made of metal, of various shapes depending on range.

scale   The basic melodic building material of music, with tones arranged in consecutive order of pitch. The most common scale in modern Western music is the **diatonic scale,** which in its major mode, proceeds by whole tones except between the third and fourth tones and the seventh and eighth tones, which are half-tone (semitone) *intervals.* The minor mode of the diatonic scale takes several forms, each having a semitone between the second and third tones.

scherzando   Musical indication: playful.

scherzo   Italian for "joke." A *movement* (most often the third) in symphonies, quartets, and so on, after about 1800. It is in fast triple time and is generally vigorous or whimsical rather than graceful or soulful. Sometimes an independent keyboard piece with similar characteristics.

score   The written or printed form of music. If the work is for more than one performer, the parts for individual performers generally appear one above the other on different staffs.

sculpture   Art created in three dimensions—that is, in depth as well as in height and width—by constructing, carving, or modeling. It is either in the round (freestanding) or in relief.

secco   Italian for "dry." Musical *recitative* (in opera, oratorio, and so on) in quick, free rhythm with *continuo* accompaniment—mainly used in eighteenth-century works.

serialism   See also *twelve-tone method of composition.*

Serialism may, however, go beyond the organization of tones into **total serialism**—that is, the patterning not only of the notes (the *tone row* and its transformations) but (theoretically) of all other aspects of composition, such as timbre, duration, harmonic density, and so on.

series   In the *twelve-tone method of composition,* a *tone row.*

serious music   See *art music.*

set piece   Within a larger musical work, a self-contained piece, such as an operatic aria, designed to make an impressive effect.

seventh   See *interval.*

78 r.p.m.   The speed (78 revolutions per minute) at which phonograph discs were played on a turntable until the long-playing (33⅓ r.p.m.) record was introduced in mid twentieth century.

sfumato   In painting, a smoky or mistlike tone that results from subtle color gradations and the defining of areas not by precise outline but by blurring the boundaries between objects.

shaft   The main part of an architectural **column,** between base and capital.

sharp   See *accidental.*

silkscreen print   A print produced by forcing color through those areas of a silk screen where it is not stopped by a stencil or by varnish on the screen.

sixth   See *interval.*

Social Realism   In the pictorial arts, an approach of the post-World War I era that strove to express the realities of contemporary life, especially among the nonprivileged classes. In Soviet art it professed also to embody political and economic truth.

solo   Italian for "alone." In music, a work played or sung by one person, with or without accompaniment.

sonata   Before the mid seventeenth century, a sonata could be any piece to be "played," as opposed to a piece with voices. In the next hundred years or so it became an instrumental work with contrasting movements for a soloist or a very small instrumental group (see *trio sonata*). By the late eighteenth century it became a work for only one or two instruments (such as piano, or violin and piano), with at least one movement constructed in *sonata form.*

sonata form   A form followed (to varying degrees), since the Classical period of music, in individual movements of formally patterned instrumental works, such as the sonata, symphony, or string quartet. It is very common in first movements but may appear in others as well. The main sections within a movement in sonata form are generally called exposition, development, and recapitulation; the latter is usually followed by a coda. The **exposition** contains the main musical ideas, ordinarily expressed in two or three themes, the second in a key different from the first. The **development** elaborates at least the first theme and sometimes incorporates new themes. The **recapitulation** repeats the material of the exposition but with the second theme in the same key as the first. The **coda** is a closing statement, usually of modest length.

song   A short musical composition for single (*solo*) voice. Generally it is less a vocal showpiece than a fairly simple textual setting. In serious musical composition it is sometimes called an **art song.**

sonority   In music, a characteristic quality of sound.

soprano   A high-range female voice.

soul   The predominant black popular music in America from the 1960s and later, which grew out of such forms as *rhythm and blues.* Its messages arose from the black experience—its mood ranging from challenging to elegiac, and its style from smooth to "funky" or "gritty."

spire   A slender, tapered structure, topping a tower or any high construction.

staff   A notational device in music. It is a series of horizontal lines on and between which notes are written so as to designate their *pitch.*

steeple   A church tower, usually topped with a spire.

still life   A picture of an arrangement of inanimate objects.

string(ed) instrument   An instrument on which sound is produced by stretched strings, including violin, viola, cello, double bass, viols, harp, piano, harpsichord, lute, guitar, and so on. The piano is also a *percussion instrument.*

strophic   Designating songs using the same music (melody and accompaniment) for each verse. **Nonstrophic** songs range from those with only slight changes in the different verses to others (through-composed) with new music for each verse, according to the fluctuations of mood or narrative.

stucco   A plaster material used to cover walls, or modeled decoratively.

style   In the arts, a characteristic mode of expression, construction, or execution. The characteristics may not conform absolutely to any given listing but are likely combinations of tendencies. Thus we speak of Gothic, Rococo, Classical, and so on, styles, and also of styles of individual artists.

stylize   In the pictorial arts, to represent natural forms only approximately, through simplification or generalization.

subject   In music, a basic *theme* or *melody* in a composition.

suite   An instrumental musical form that groups together several movements, most commonly dancelike, of contrasting character. It was especially popular in the Baroque period.

Surrealism   A literary and artistic movement in the decades after World War I. It emphasized the irrational, the realm of dream, and the unpremeditated free association of ideas. See *automatism.*

symbol   A sign or form that suggests or stands for something else. Often a visible sign for something invisible.

symbolism   The use of symbols. A style that emphasized this use. The Symbolist schools of poetry and painting were especially active in the late nineteenth century.

symmetry   Balance or similarity of forms, especially on both sides of a dividing line.

symphony   A musical composition that, in its modern form, dates from the early Classical period of music. It is written for orchestra and involves a sequence of sections (movements), one or more of which is usually in *sonata form.*

syncopation   A deliberate violation of a regular, expected rhythm, or regular succession of strong and weak beats—especially by stressing the weak beat, having rests on the strong beats, or holding a note over a strong beat. This often occurs in only one part, while others continue the regular beat.

synthesizer   An electronic instrument that generates, modifies, and combines sounds produced by electronic wave forms. In theory, a synthesizer can produce any imaginable sound. Often employed in rock music as well as much avant-garde art music.

tapestry   A heavy textile embodying pictures or designs woven into the cloth and used especially as a wall hanging.

tarantella   A lively Italian dance in 6/8 time.

tempera   A painting technique employing colors made from pigments in a water-miscible medium, usually including egg yolk. Tempera on panels was the main type of easel painting before oil painting was developed and popularized in the fifteenth and sixteenth centuries.

tempo   Italian for "time." The pace of a musical work, following the speed of the basic beat. Italian tempo indications have been generally used since the seventeenth century, ranging from largo (very slow) to prestissimo (extremely fast).

tenebroso or **tenebrism**   In painting, the predominance of deep shadow out of which rise several striking highlights.

tenor   The highest natural voice of the adult male. In medieval polyphonic music, a slowly moving part (commonly the lowest) that was borrowed from plainsong and was usually carried only on a single syllable, word, or brief phrase, and that served as the *cantus firmus.* When four-part writing developed in the fifteenth century, the tenor became the second-lowest part, with bass being the lowest.

terracotta   Baked clay, used in pottery, sculpture, and architectural decoration.

text   The wording (structure of words) of a poem, novel, song, and so on. See also *libretto.*

theme   A melody that is basic in a musical composition, as in sonata form or theme and variations.

third   See *interval.*

timbre   Tone quality or *tone color.*

time   See *meter.*

time signature   See *meter.*

timpani or **kettledrums**   A set of basin-shaped copper or brass drums with a calfskin head adjustable for tension and hence for pitch.

toccata   Around 1600, an instrumental flourish or fanfare. Also then, and later, a keyboard work including chords and quick runs of notes.

tonal   In the visual arts, refers to qualities of vividness in color. In music, refers to qualities of tones or musical sounds, or to *tonality.*

tonality   In the visual arts, the predominance of a color quality or the interrelation of color qualities. In most modern Western music, the quality of adhering to one key at a time. Tonality implies an urge toward the tonal center or *tonic,* and to other relatively restful harmonies; tonal music thus has a sense of musical focus and direction. Tonality is sometimes contrasted with *modality*: tonality involves major or minor modes or keys, and modality uses (or is influenced by) the traditional Church modes.

tone   A musical note. A whole tone, or interval of a major second.

tone color   The characteristic quality of a given instrument or voice.

tone poem   In the nineteenth century and later, a piece of *program music* for orchestra.

tone row   The basic building block of the *twelve-tone method of composition.*

tonic   The first and most important note (key note) of a scale or key. A **tonic chord** is a *triad* based on this note.

tracery   A system of lines, generally curved, in ornamental stonework, as in Gothic windows.

transept   In ecclesiastical architecture (or in secular architecture based on church models), the area that crosses the longer nave–choir or nave–apse section. Loosely, either arm or projecting end of a transept.

tremolo   Italian for "trembling." Tremolo bowing refers to quick repetitions of the same note by up and down movements of the bow on a stringed instrument.

triad   A three-tone chord, with a root (basic note) plus the third and fifth above it.

triforium   In ecclesiastical architecture, the horizontal zone, usually arcaded, below the clerestory and above the nave, choir, or transept arcades. Ordinarily it has no windows.

triglyph   In classical architecture, a *frieze* panel of geometrical sculpted design, with vertical *fluting.*

trio   A musical work for three similarly important performers, with or without accompaniment. (See *chamber music.*) Also, in a sonata-type work (a symphony, for example), the middle section between a first section (with its theme) and its repetition.

trio sonata   A musical composition of the Baroque era, in several movements, employing two soloists and continuo, the latter requiring two performers (keyboard and a bowed instrument such as viola da gamba or cello). The harpsichord was the usual keyboard instrument in the chamber sonata, and the organ in the church sonata.

triple time or **triple meter**   Musical meter with three units (beats) to a measure.

trombone   A brass instrument with a cup-shaped mouthpiece, a mainly cylindrical bore, and a medium-sized bell. Pitch is determined partly by a manipulated U-shaped slide in its bore, instead of by valves as with other brass instruments.

trumpet   A brass instrument with a cup-shaped mouthpiece, a mainly cylindrical bore, and a medium-sized bell.

twelve-tone method of composition   An extension of atonality (which denies tonality and its traditional compositional techniques but establishes no rigid system). The twelve-tone method, as introduced by Arnold Schoenberg, proceeds in a given work from a tone row, or series of the twelve notes in the chromatic scale, arranged in a particular way. The row may be played in four, usually unalterable orders—forward, backward, upside down, or upside down and backward—with occasional exceptions and refinements.

tympanum   In medieval architecture, masonry (usually carved stone) over a doorway, enclosed by a *lintel* and *arch.*

unison   In music, the simultaneous sounding of notes that are at the same pitch or precisely one octave or multiple octaves apart.

vanishing point   In perspective, the point at which receding parallel lines seem to converge and vanish.

vault   An arched masonry covering for space; an arch extended in depth. A **barrel vault** is a simple rounded vault— a long, continuous, rounded arch. A **groin vault** or **cross vault** is the intersection or crossing of a vault by another vault, or a series of such crossings. A vault may or may not be ribbed. (See also *rib.*)

vibrato   Italian for "shaken." In instrumental or vocal performance, a quick, slight wavering or fluctuation of pitch on sustained notes, for expressive effect.

viol   Any one of a family of bowed-string instruments, producing a lighter, more delicate sound than the parallel, later-developed violin family. The **viola da gamba,** for example, is roughly equivalent to the cello. Viols are held on or between the knees, unlike the smaller instruments of the violin family (violin and viola).

viola A bowed-string instrument of the violin family, next-highest in range to the violin. See also *viol*.

violin A bowed-string instrument, the highest in range of the violin family (violin, viola, cello, and double bass).

virginal A stringed keyboard instrument with plucked strings—a predecessor of the harpsichord.

virtuoso Exhibiting, or a person who exhibits, great technical facility, as in musical performance or the visual arts.

visual arts Types of art (such as painting, sculpture, or architecture) that depend for their perception and comprehension primarily on human sight. Traditionally the verbal or literary arts have been excluded from this category.

votive statue A sculptured work dedicated or offered to a deity, usually in fulfillment of a promise.

waltz A dance or musical dance form, mainly of the nineteenth century, in moderate triple time.

watercolor A painting technique employing colors made from pigments in a gum arabic solution in water. (Gum arabic comes from acacia trees.) Also the paint used, or the work produced in this way. Modern watercolor is generally done on paper, but watercolor has also been common on parchment (in medieval manuscripts), ivory, and silk.

whole-tone scale A scale proceeding solely by intervals of whole tones (as between the tones of A and B).

wind instrument An instrument in which sound is produced by an enclosed column of vibrating air. The main, broad types of wind instruments are brass and woodwind instruments. The *timbre* of the instrument is largely determined by its general shape and its mouthpiece (single or double reed, mouth-hole, cup or funnel-shaped mouthpiece, and so on).

woodcut A print made from a flat, carved, inked block of wood; the ink adheres to the parts of the surface that have not been cut away with knives and gouges.

woodwind instrument A wind instrument with an air column activated (in modern instruments) through a mouth-hole, as in the flute and piccolo, or by reed(s), as in the bassoon, saxophone, clarinet, and oboe. The body of a woodwind is not necessarily made of wood: modern flutes and piccolos, as well as saxophones, are made mainly of metal.

Illustration Credits

Fig. 4-7, Adapted from Frank Sear, *Roman Architecture*. Copyright © Frank Sear 1982. Used by permission of the publisher, Cornell University Press. Fig. 4-19, Adapted from Carl Roebuck, 1966, *The World of Ancient Times* (New York: Scribner Book Co., Inc.), p. 650 bottom. Fig. 5-6, Adapted from G. Dehio and G. von Bezold, 1901, *Die Kirchliche Baukunst des Abendlandes* (Stuttgart: J. G. Cotta). Fig. 5-9, Adapted from M. Mazzotti, 1954, *Rivista di Archeologia Cristiana*, Vol. 30 (Rome: Pontifica Commissione di Archeologia Sacra). 5-16, Adapted from Hugh Honour and John Fleming, 1982, *A World History of Art* (London: Macmillan), p. 235A, top. Fig. 5-18, Adapted from Richard Krautheimer, *Early Christian and Byzantine Architecture*, (Pelican History of Art , 1965, 1975, 1987), copyright © Richard Krautheimer, 1965, 1975, 1987. Reproduced by permission of Penguin Books, Ltd., p. 362A. Fig. 6-8, Adapted from John Harvey, 1956, *The English Cathedrals*, 2nd edition (New York: Hastings House), Fig. 27, p. 61. Fig. 7-5, Adapted from Florens Deuchler, 1970, *The Year 1200: A Background Survey* (New York: New York Graphic Society and the Metropolitan Museum of Art), p. 8 (top). Fig. 9-19, Adapted from H. W. Janson, 1959, *Key Monuments of the History of Art* (Englewood Cliffs, N.J.: Prentice–Hall). Fig. 15-10, Adapted from Henry A. Millon, 1965, *Key Monuments of the History of Architecture* (Englewood Cliffs, N.J.: Prentice–Hall).

Map Credits

Page 6, Adapted from Chester G. Starr, 1965, *A History of the Ancient World* (New York: Oxford University Press), pp. 84–85. Page 32, Adapted from Marvin Perry, et al., 1985, *Western Civilization: Ideas, Politics, and Society*, 2nd edition (Boston: Houghton Mifflin Co.), p. 57. Page 62, Adapted from *The Heritage of Hellenism*, by John Ferguson. Copyright © 1973 by Harcourt Brace Jovanovich, Inc. Reproduced by permission of the publisher. Page 88, Adapted from Brendan D. Nagle, 1978, *The Ancient World* (Englewood Cliffs, N.J.: Prentice–Hall), p. 351. Page 114, Adapted from Arthur E. R. Boak and William G. Sinnigen, 1965, *A History of Rome to* A.D. 565, 5th edition (New York: Macmillan), p. 494. Page 134, Adapted from Otto Demus, 1970, *Romanesque Mural Painting* (London: Thames & Hudson), p. 157. Page 184, Adapted from Malcolm Vale, 1981, *War and Chivalry: Warfare and Aristocratic Culture in England, France, and Burgundy at the End of the Middle Ages* (Atlanta: University of Georgia Press), facing p. 1. Page 212, Adapted from Marvin Perry, et al., 1985, *Western Civilization: Ideas, Politics, and Society*, 2nd edition (Boston: Houghton Mifflin), p. 271. Page 242, From *A History of the Modern World*, 4th edition, by R. R. Palmer and Joel Colton. Copyright © by Alfred A. Knopf, Inc. (pp. 72–73). Pages 302, 350, and 400, Adapted from Marvin Perry, et al., 1985, *Western Civilization: Ideas, Politics, and Society*, 2nd edition (Boston: Houghton Mifflin), pp. 353, 405, and 531. Pages 454 and 486, From *A History of the Modern World*, 4th edition, by R. R. Palmer and Joel Colton. Copyright © by Alfred A. Knopf, Inc. (pp. 576–77 and 760–61).

Photo Credits

Sources not included in the captions are listed below.
Abbreviations: AR for Art Resource, New York
ARS for Artists Rights Society, Inc., New York
CNNHS for Caisse nationale des Monuments et des Sites, Paris
Chapter Opening Photographs
Page 2, Coffin of Tutankhamen (detail), mid 14th century B.C. Gold with precious stones; coffin is 6'11" long. Egyptian Museum, Cairo. Photo, © F. L. Kennett. Page 24, *Apollo* (detail), 460 B.C. From the marble sculpture on the west pediment of the Temple of Zeus, Olympia, Museum, Olympia. Photo, Deutsches Archaeologisches Institut, Rome. Page 58, Agasias of Ephesus?, c. 100 B.C. Bronze portrait head from Delos, 12¼" high. National Museum, Athens. Photo, Hirmer Fotoarchiv München. Page 84, *Roman Lady*, A.D. 80–100. Marble portrait, 3'3¾" high. Museo Capitolino, Rome. Photo, Deutsches Archaeologisches Institut, Rome. Page 110, *Empress Theodora and Her Retinue* (detail), c. 547–548. San Vitale, Ravenna. Photo, Alinari/AR. Page 130, *Saint John the Evangelist*, c. 1146. Manuscript miniature from the *Gospel Book of Liessies*, 13½" high. Société Archéologique, Avesnes, France. Photo, Bibliothèque Nationale, Paris. Page 156, *Melchizedek and Abraham*, after 1251. Stone. Interior west wall, Reims Cathedral. Photo, Foto Marburg/AR. Page 180, Hubert and Jan van Eyck, *Angel Musicians* (detail), c. 1425–32. *The Ghent Altarpiece*, 65" × 29". Cathedral of Saint Bavon, Ghent. Photo, A.C.L. Brussels. Page 208, Luca della Robbia, *Singing Boys* (detail), from the *Cantoria* (reconstruction, with panels in replica), original 1431–38. Marble, 17' long. Cathedral Museum, Florence. Photo, Alinari/AR. Page 238, Raphael, *Baldassare Castiglione*, c. 1515. Oil on canvas, 32" × 27". Louvre, Paris. Cliché des Musées Nationaux, Paris. Page 270, Jacopo Carucci da Pontormo, *The Descent from the Cross (The Entombment)* (detail), 1525–28. Panel, 10'3" × 6'4". Santa Felicità, Florence. Photo, Alinari/AR. Page 299, Frans Hals, *The Merry Drinker*, c. 1627–30. Oil on canvas, 32" × 26". Rijksmuseum, Amsterdam. Page 324,

Aerofilm, Ltd., London. Fig. 13-4, © A. F. Kersting, London. Figs. 13-5, 13-6, Giraudon/AR. Fig. 13-7, Foto Marburg/AR. Fig. 13-8, Cliché des Musées Nationaux, Paris. Fig. 13-9, Giraudon/AR. Figs. 13-10, 13-11, © A. F. Kersting, London. Fig. 13-12, © Edwin Smith, Essex. Fig. 13-13, Foto A. Dingjan, The Hague.

Chapter 14
Fig. 14-4, © CNNHS/ARS NY/SPADEM, 1988. Fig. 14-5, © Helga Schmidt-Glassner, Stuttgart. Fig. 14-6, Foto Marburg/AR. Fig. 14-7, © CNNHS/ARS NY/SPADEM, 1988. Fig. 14-9, © Helga Schmidt-Glassner, Stuttgart. Fig. 14-10, Cliché des Musées Nationaux, Paris. Fig. 14-11, Alinari/AR. Fig. 14-12, Cliché des Musées Nationaux, Paris. Fig. 14-14, Scala/AR. Fig. 14-16, Deutsche Fotothek, Dresden.

Chapter 15
Fig. 15-5, © A. F. Kersting, London. Fig. 15-6, Royal Commission of the Historical Monuments of England. Fig. 15-7, © CNNHS/ARS NY/SPADEM, 1988. Fig. 15-8, © Charles Rotkin, PFI, New York. Fig. 15-9, © A. F. Kersting, London. Figs. 15-16, 15-17, Cliché des Musées Nationaux, Paris.

Chapter 16
Fig. 16-3, © A. F. Kersting, London. Fig. 16-5, © Ursula Edelmann. Figs. 16-6, 16-7, 16-8, © CNNHS/ARS NY/SPADEM, 1988. Fig. 16-9, Alinari/AR. Fig. 16-10, Cliché des Musées Nationaux, Paris. Figs. 16-11, 16-12, Alinari/AR. Fig. 16-13, Giraudon/AR. Fig. 16-16, Alinari/AR. Fig. 16-19, The Bettmann Archive, Inc.

Chapter 17
Fig. 17-3, The Bettmann Archive, Inc. Fig. 17-6, The Library of Congress. Fig. 17-7, © A. F. Kersting, London. Fig. 17-8, © Louis Goldman/Photo Researchers, Inc. Fig. 17-9, © Herbert Jaras, Paris. Fig. 17-10, Photographie Bulloz, Paris. Fig. 17-12, © CNNHS/ARS NY/SPADEM, 1988. Figs. 17-15, 17-16, 17-17, 17-20, Cliché des Musées Nationaux, Paris. Fig. 17-21, Alinari/AR. Fig. 17-23, Photographie Bulloz, Paris. Figs. 17-24, 17-25, Cliché des Musées Nationaux, Paris. Fig. 17-26, The Bettmann Archive, Inc. Fig. 17-27, Culver Pictures.

Chapter 18
Fig. 18-1, Giraudon/AR. Fig. 18-2, © CNNHS/ARS NY/SPADEM, 1988. Fig. 18-4, The Bettmann Archive, Inc. Fig. 18-5, Giraudon/AR. Fig. 18-6, Photograph courtesy of The Museum of Modern Art, New York. Fig. 18-7, © Hedrich–Blessing, Chicago. Fig. 18-8, Chicago Historical Society. Fig. 18-9, Property of Thomas Jefferson University, Philadelphia, Pa. Figs. 18-12, 18-16, 18-17, 18-18, Cliché des Musées Nationaux, Paris. Fig. 18-26, Scala/AR. Fig. 18-27, © Bruno Jarret, Paris. Fig. 18-28, The Bettmann Archive, Inc.

Chapter 19
Fig. 19-1, National Library of Medicine, Bethesda, Md. Figs. 19-2, 19-6, © ARS NY/SPADEM, 1988. Fig. 19-7, © ARS NY/SPADEM, 1988; photo from Giraudon/AR. Figs. 19-8, 19-9, © ARS NY/SPADEM, 1988. Fig. 19-10, © ARS NY/ADAGP, 1988. Figs. 19-11, 19-12, 19-13, 19-14, © ARS NY/SPADEM, 1988. Figs. 19-18, 19-19, 19-20, © ARS NY/ADAGP, 1988. Figs. 19-23, 19-24, © ARS NY/ADAGP, 1988. Fig. 19-26, Photograph courtesy of The Museum of Modern Art, New York. Figs. 19-27, 19-28, © Hedrich–Blessing, Chicago. Fig. 19-29, © ARS NY/SPADEM, 1988; photo © Lucien Herve, Paris. Fig. 19-31, © ARS NY/SPADEM, 1988; photo from Giraudon/AR. Fig. 19-32, Institute of Jazz Studies/Rutgers University. Fig. 19-33, The Bettmann Archive, Inc.

Chapter 20
Fig. 20-1, AP/Wide World. Fig. 20-2, UPI/Bettmann Newsphotos. Figs. 20-3, 20-4, © Hedrich–Blessing, Chicago. Fig. 20-5, © John Ebstel, New York. Fig. 20-6, © William Dyckes, New York. Fig. 20-7, Courtesy of the Buckminster Fuller Institute, Los Angeles/© Else Frieson. Fig. 20-8, The University of Akron News Service. Fig. 20-9, © Lionel Delevingne/Stock, Boston. Figs. 20-10, 20-11, © Richard Payne. Fig. 20-12, Courtesy of Michael Graves, Architect; photo © Paschall/Taylor. Fig. 20-14, © ARS NY/ADAGP, 1988. Fig. 20-16, © ARS NY–POLLOCK/KRASNER FOUNDATION, 1988. Fig. 20-19, © ARS NY/SPADEM, 1988. Fig. 20-20, © ARS NY/ADAGP, 1988. Fig. 20-21, Rheinisches Bildarchiv, Köln. Fig. 20-26, Leo Castelli Gallery, New York. Fig. 20-27, © Geoffrey Clements, New York. Fig. 20-28, © Gianfranco Gorgoni, New York. Fig. 20-31, Photo by Wolfgang Volz; copyright Christo 1976. Fig. 20-38, © Geoffrey Clements, New York. Fig. 20-39, © Zindman/Fremont. Fig. 20-40, © J. Littkemann, Berlin. Fig. 20-43, © Werner Scholz, Mechenheim. Fig. 20-45, AP/Wide World. Fig. 20-46, UPI/Bettmann Newsphotos. Fig. 20-47, AP/Wide World. Fig. 20-48, UPI/Bettmann Newsphotos.

Colorplates

Plate 2, SEF/AR. Plate 3, Scala/AR. Plate 5, Hirmer Fotoarchiv München. Plate 7, Nimatallah/AR. Plates 8, 9, 10, 11, 12, Scala/AR. Plate 14, SEF/AR. Plate 15, © Murray Davison. Plates 17, 18, Giraudon/AR. Plates 19, 20, 21, Scala/AR. Plate 22, Josse/AR. Plates 23, 24, 25, 26, 28, 29, 30, Scala/AR. Plate 31, Cliché des Musées Nationaux, Paris. Plate 32, © A. F. Kersting, London. Plate 33, Scala/AR. Plate 34, Bridgeman/AR. Plates 35, 36, 37, Scala/AR. Plate 39, Giraudon/AR. Plate 43, © ARS NY/SPADEM, 1988; photo from G. Roos/AR. Plate 44, © ARS NY/SPADEM, 1988. Plate 45, © ARS NY–POLLOCK/KRASNER FOUNDATION, 1988.

Index

Black-and-white illustrations are indicated by italic page numbers; color plates, by the abbreviation *pl.*